India in a Globalising World

Published by Academic Foundation
in collaboration with

CENTRE FOR ECONOMIC AND SOCIAL STUDIES,
(CESS), HYDERABAD

The Editors:

R. Radhakrishna
Director, Indira Gandhi Institute of Development Research
(IGIDR), Mumbai

S.K. Rao
Director General, Administrative Staff College of India
(ASCI), Hyderabad

S. Mahendra Dev
Director, Centre for Economic and Social Studies
(CESS), Hyderabad

K. Subbarao
Consultant, World Bank, Washington D.C.,
and former professor at Institute of Economic Growth, Delhi

For detailed information about the contributors to this volume, kindly refer pages 19-28.

India in a Globalising World

SOME ASPECTS OF MACROECONOMY, AGRICULTURE AND POVERTY

Essays in Honour of C.H. Hanumantha Rao

EDITED BY

R. Radhakrishna
S.K. Rao
S. Mahendra Dev
K. Subbarao

Academic Foundation

NEW DELHI

First published in 2006
by :

ACADEMIC FOUNDATION
4772-73 / 23 Bharat Ram Road, (23 Ansari Road),
Darya Ganj, New Delhi - 110 002 (India).
Phones : 23245001 / 02 / 03 / 04.
Fax : +91-11-23245005.
E-mail : academic@vsnl.com
www : academicfoundation.com

in association with :

Centre for Economic and Social Studies
(CESS), Hyderabad
www.cess.ac.in

India in a Globalising World :
Some Aspects of Macroeconomy, Agriculture and Poverty
Editors : R. Radhakrishna, S.K. Rao, S. Mahendra Dev and K. Subbarao

ISBN 81-7188-516-0

Typeset by Italics India, New Delhi.
Printed and bound in India.

CONTENTS

List of Figures, Tables, Boxes and Annexures 9

Preface 17

Contributors to the Volume 19

Prof. C.H. Hanumantha Rao: A Tribute 29

Prof. C.H. Hanumantha Rao's Publications,
Awards and Other Accomplishments 35

Introduction and Overview 53

Section I
Macro Issues in Development

1. Economic Reforms and Changing Role
   of the Reserve Bank of India
   Y.V. REDDY 81

2. Fiscal Federalism: Some Current Concerns
   C. RANGARAJAN 115

3. Economics, Politics and Governance
   BIMAL JALAN 125

4. Perspectives on Macroeconomertric Models for India
   K. KRISHNAMURTY 135

5. Shocks and Long Run Growth in Agriculture:
   A Macroeconomic Analysis
   B.B. BHATTACHARYA • SABYASACHI KAR 165

6. Globalisation, Liberalisation and Performance of Firms:
    Emerging Trends from Literature
    N.S. Siddharthan 187

Section II
Issues in Agricultural Development

7. Indian Economic Strategies After Doha
    Yoginder K. Alagh 205

8. Pro-Poor Growth—The Relation between Agricultural
    Growth and Poverty Reduction
    John W. Mellor 233

9. Some Aspects of Total Factor Productivity
    in Indian Agriculture
    K.L. Krishna 277

Section III
Equity and Emerging Institutions
in Agricultural Development

10. Agrarian Communities Across Asia:
    A Provisional Framework for Comparison
    Yujiro Hayami 299

11. Agricultural Growth and Regional Variations
    G.S. Bhalla 309

12. Trade Policies, Incentives, Investments
    and Institutions in Indian Agriculture
    Ashok Gulati 347

13. Withdrawal of Subsidies from Irrigation and Fertiliser:
Impact on Small and Marginal Farmers
KANCHAN CHOPRA 373

14. Globalisation: Neo-Liberal Economic Policies
and Small Farmer Development
Y.V. KRISHNA RAO 391

15. Changes in Agrarian Structure and Agricultural
Technology: Is Peasant Farming Sustainable
under Institutional Retrogression
D. NARASIMHA REDDY 409

16. Insuring Against Bad Weather: Recent Thinking
PETER HAZELL • JERRY SKEES 429

Section IV

Poverty and Environment

17. The Elusive Goal of Empowerment: A Review
of the Emerging Phase in Poverty Reduction
V.M. RAO 453

18. Environment, Employment and
Sustainable Development:
Understanding the Linkages in India
INDIRA HIRWAY • PIET TERHAL 477

19. Climate Change and Its Abatement:
Towards a Better Project Design
GOPAL K. KADEKODI 503

List of Figures, Tables, Boxes and Annexures

FIGURES

5.1 The Association between Rainfall and Growth of Agricultural GDP 169

5.2 The Association between Rainfall and Growth of Aggregate GDP 169

5.3 Agricultural GDP Growth Rate (%) with HP Trend 176

5.4 Share (%) of Public Investment in GDP at Market Prices
in Agriculture (SIGA), for Agriculture (SFIGA) 177

5.5 Share (%) in GDP at Market Prices Subsidy (SSUB)
Public Investment in Agricultural (SIGA) for Agricultural (SFIGA) 178

5.6 Share (%) in GDP at Market Prices Subsidy (SSUB)
Total Investment in Agriculture (SIA) for Agriculture (SFIA) 179

5.7 Share (%) of Private Investment in GDP at Market Prices
in Agriculture (SIPA) for Agriculture (SFIPA) 179

5.8 Share (%) of Private Investment in GDP at Market Prices
in Agriculture (SIA) for Agriculture (SFIA) 180

5.9 Share (%) of Private Investment in GDP at Market Prices
in Agriculture (CORA) for Agriculture (CORFA) 181

7.1 Yield versus Cost of Machinery and Land 224

11.1(a) Growth Rates of Yield 315

11.1(b) Growth Rates of Output 315

11.2 Agricultural Exports and Imports in $ million 321

11.3 Terms of Trade Prices Received and Paid, DES 324

11.4 Terms of Trade–GDP Deflators 324

11.5(a) GDP Growth 1983-84 to 1993-94 and Poverty 1993-94 333

11.5(b) GDP Growth 1993-94 to 1999-00 and Poverty 1999-00 333

11.6(a) Agricultural GDP Growth 1983-84 to 1993-94
and Rural Poverty 1993-94 335

11.6(b) Agricultural GDP Growth 1993-94 to 1999-00
and Rural Poverty 1999-00 335

11.7(a) Per Worker Agricultural GDP 1993-94 (Rs. 000)
and Rural Poverty 1993-94 337

11.7(b) Per Worker Agricultural GDP 1999-00 (Rs. 000)
and Rural Poverty 1999-00 337

11.8 Per Worker Productivity in Agriculture in Rupees 1998-99 338

11.9 Per Worker Agricultural GDP and Per cent Share Secondary Workers
1993-94 and 1999-00 341

11.9(a) Per Worker GDP in Agriculture and Share of
Secondary Workers: 1993-94 341

11.9(b) Per Worker GDP in Agriculture and Share of
Secondary Workers: 1999-00 341

11.10 Per Worker Agricultural GDP and Per cent Share Non-Agriculture
Workers, 1993-94 and 1999-00 342

11.10(a) Per Worker GDP in Agriculture and
Share of Non-Agriculture Workers, 1993-94 342

11.10(b) Per Worker GDP in Agriculture and
Share of Non-Agriculture Workers, 1999-00 342

12.1 Getting Prices Right: Reducing Anti-Agriculture Bias 349

12.2 NPCs of Selected Commodities in India – 1965-2002 350

12.2(a) Nominal Protection Coefficients for Wheat
in India 1965-2002 350

12.2(b) Nominal Protection Coefficients for Rice
in India 1965-2002 350

12.2(c) Nominal Protection Coefficients for Maize
in India 1965-2002 351

12.2(d) Nominal Protection Coefficients for Jowar
in India 1965-2002 351

12.2(e) Nominal Protection Coefficients for Gram
in India 1965-2002 352

12.2(f) Nominal Protection Coefficients for Soyabeans
in India 1974-2002 352

12.2(g) Nominal Protection Coefficients for Mustard
in India 1965-2002 353

12.2(h) Nominal Protection Coefficients for Copra
in India 1965-2002 353

12.2(i) Nominal Protection Coefficients for Groundnut
in India 1965-2002 354

12.2(j) Nominal Protection Coefficients for Sunflower
in India 1976-2002 354

12.2(k) Nominal Protection Coefficients for Sugar
in India 1965-2002 355

12.2(l) Nominal Protection Coefficients for Rubber
in India 1965-2002 355

12.2(m) Nominal Protection Coefficients for Cotton
in India 1965-2002 356

12.3 Relative Prices of Agricultural and GFCF 358

12.4 Agricultural Tariffs and Trade Flows 359

12.5 Public Investments and Subsidies in Indian Agriculture 361

12.6 Farmer Heterogeneity and Market Access and Efficiency Gaps 363

19.1 Trend in the Total Malaria Cases and P. Falciparum in India 506

19.2 Trend in Number of Deaths Due to Malaria in India 507

19.3 Average Yearly Mean Temperature
in Karnataka (Various Districts), India 507

19.4 Highest Temperatures at Select Places of Karnataka 508

19.5 Lowest Temperatures at Select Places of Karnataka 508

19.6 Total Yearly Precipitaton in Karnataka (Various Districts) 509

19.7   Percentage Deviation in Annual Rainfall from Normal 511

19.8   Trend in Malaria Cases in Dakshina Kannada District 515

19.9   Trend in Malaria in Mangalore City 516

19.10 Estimates of Time Preference Rate 522

19.11 Time Dependent Climate Discount Rate 523

TABLES

5.1   Effect of Rainfall Shock 174

5.2   Effect of Rainfall Shock with Policy Response 175

5.3   Base-Run and Alternative Scenarios for the Tenth Plan Period 184

7.1   Growth of Agricultural Trade in the Nineties 207

7.2   Incremental Net Exports in Agriculture 208

7.3   Growth Rate in Macro Parameters during 1960-61 to
      1995-96 (per cent compound annual in 1980-81 prices) 210

7.4   Production of Agriculture and Allied Products in the Nineties
      (mn. Tonnes/bales for Cotton) 210

7.5   Fluctuations in Sugar Production 211

7.6   Tariff Rates on Sugar 212

7.7   Domestic Availability and Import of Edible Oils
      (Quantity: Million Tonnes) 213

7.8   Wholesale Price Index (Average of Weekly Base –1993-94) 213

7.9   Per cent Change in the Prices Paid for Intermediates
      and Output Prices in Nineties 216

7.10 Gross Fixed Capital Formation in Public and Private Sectors 216

7.11 Protection Rate for Agriculture (in Per cent) 217

7.12 Agriculture Public Expenditure Expressed as a Share
      of Agricultural GDP 218

7.13 Desirable Economic Profiles for Paddy Under Two Assumptions 224

8.1   Annual Increments to Employment, by Sector, 1980-81–2005-06 261

9.1   Estimates of Growth of GDP and TFP in Agriculture and
      Non-agriculture Sectors of Indian Economy: 1900-47, 1950-2000 283

9.2   Estimates of Growth of GDP and TFP in Agricultural and
      Non-agricultural Sectors of the Indian Economy
      During Pre-liberalisation and Post-liberalisation Periods 284

9.3   TFP Growth in Agriculture and Manufacturing
      in Selected Countries: 1967-92 285

9.4   Estimates of TFP Growth (Tornquist Index) in Crop Sector,
      Livestock Sector in Four South Asian Countries: 1961-80, 1981-2001 286

9.5   Mean Technical Efficiency (TE) Change, Technical Change
      and TFP Change in Agriculture - Selected Countries – 1980 to 1995 287

9.6   Starting Level and Annual Growth Rate of the Malmquist Index of
      Agricultural TFP and its Components (per cent per annum) 1965-96 289

9.7   Growth Rates of Partial and Total Factor Productivities
      for the Three Phases of Technical Change:
      Indian and Pakistan Punjabs: 1966-94 290

9.8   Growth Rates of Output, Input and TFP by Cropping System
      in Indian and Pakistan Punjabs: 1966-94 291

9.9   Crop-wise Determinants of TFPG in India, 1971-95 292

10.1 Agrarian Structures in India and Japan Before
      and After Land Reforms 306

11.1(a) Growth Rates of GDP and Per Capita Income 1993-94 Prices 312

11.1(b) Growth Rates of GDP and Per Capita Income 1980-81 Prices 312

11.2 All India Compound Growth Rates of Area, Production
      and Yield of Major Crops 314

11.3 Use of Major Inputs and Increase in Yields
      of Major Crops During 1970-71 to 1999-00 316

11.4 Percentage of People Below Poverty Line 1983-2000 318

11.5 Agricultural Exports and Imports and Their Share
      in Total Exports and Imports 321

11.6(a) Growth of Workers UPSS — 1972-73 to 1999-00: Rural plus Urban 322

11.6(b) Per cent Distribution of Usually Working (UPSS)
        by Broad Group of Industry: Rural India 322

11.7 Number Unemployed and the Incidence of Unemployment,
     1973-74 to 1999-00 323

11.8 Index of Terms of Trade Between Agriculture and Non-agriculture 324

11.9 Capital Formation in Agriculture (Rs. Crore) 325

11.10 Percentage Annual Compound Growth 328

11.11 State-wise Growth of Agricultural Output, 1962-65 to 1996-99 330

11.12 Hypotheses Test: Results of Linear Regression 331

11.13 Growth of GDP and Incidence of Poverty 332

11.14 Agricultural Growth and Rural Poverty 334

11.15 Per Worker Productivity and Incidence of Poverty 336

11.16 Share of Agriculture in GDP (at 1993-94 prices) and Employment 338

11.17 Per Worker (UPSS) GSDP by Sectors in Rupees per year 1999-00
      at Constant 1993-94 Prices 339

11.18 Results of Linear Regression 340

13.1 Groundwater Irrigation: Dependent Variable:
     Gross Irrigated Area/Gross Cropped Area: 1997-98 380

13.2 Canal Irrigation Dependent Variable: GIA/GCA: 1997-98 381

13.3 All Irrigation Dependent Variable: GIA/GCA 382

13.4 3SLS Estimates of Simultaneous Equations Model: 1991-92 386

13.5 3SLS Estimates of Simultaneous Equations Model: 1997-98 386

14.1 Share of Agricultural and Allied Sectors in Gross Capital Formation 402

14.2 Declining Plan Allocations to Agriculture and Allied Activities
     and Development Programmes 403

15.1 Changes in the Distribution of Operational Holdings in India
     (Per cent share of each size group) 412

15.2 Gross Capital Formation (GCF) in Agriculture in India 418

15.3 Trends in Public Expenditure on Agriculture
and Allied Activities in Andhra Pradesh (As Percentage of GSDP) 419

15.4 Source-Wise Net Area Irrigated in Andhra Pradesh
(Area in '000 hectares) 420

15.5 Short-Term and Long-Term Loans for Agriculture
and Allied Activities by Formal Financial Institutions
(Amount in Rs. Crore) 421

15.6 Trends in Number and Amount Outstanding of Small Borrowal
Accounts (SBAs) in All the Rural Financial Institutions 422

15.7 Source-wise Interest Changes on Agricultural Loans
in Select Villages of Andhra Pradesh 423

15.8 Land-Holding Structure in Select Villages of Andhra Pradesh 424

15.9 Peasant Migration According to Labour Use Classification
of Households in 10 Villages of Andhra Pradesh 425

15.10 Agricultural Power Tariff in Andhra Pradesh (Rs./H.P) 426

15.11 Water Cess in Andhra Pradesh (Rs. per acre) 426

17.1 Estimates of Incidence of Poverty in India 453

17.2 UNDP Indices of Human Development 461

17.3 States in India with Very Low HDI Values 462

17.4 Rural Landless Households 467

17.5 Distribution of Owned Holdings 467

17.6 Occupations of Young Males (15 to 35) 470

17.7 Occupations of Young Males (Age 15 to 20) 472

19.1 Changes in Cropping Pattern (per cent Net Sown Area (NSA)) 512

19.2 Incidence of Malaria in Karnataka State
and Dakshina Kannada District 515

19.3 Cost of Various Carbon Dioxide Mitigation Options for India 517

19.4 Estimates of Discount Rates 522

BOXES

7.1 Correcting for India's Large Size Reduces
Significantly the Apparent Policy Bias Against Agriculture 218

19.1 Extracts on Long-term Climate Change Effects
on Indian Sub-Continent 505

ANNEXURES

A-19.1 Some Glimpses on the International Climate Change Scene 527

A-19.2 Incidence of Malaria in India 527

A-19.3 Activities Implemented Jointly (AIJ)
Projects Endorsed by the Government of India 528

Preface

Prof. C.H. Hanumantha Rao is one of India's most distinguished economists. He has contributed immensely to both research and policy-making in India. In his student days, as an activist of the All Hyderabad Students Union, he participated actively in the freedom struggle. His meticulously prepared research papers have enlightened students, researchers and policymakers alike. In addition to a distinguished academic career, Professor Rao has been at the forefront of several high level policymaking bodies under Government of India. He has received many awards during his illustrious career including 'Padma Bhushan.' He has also contributed immensely to the growth of two ICSSR research institutes *viz.*, Institute of Economic Growth (IEG), University of Delhi and Centre for Economic and Social Studies (CESS), Hyderabad. As a token of gratitude, we decided to pay a tribute on his 75th birth anniversary by bringing out a volume containing research papers relating to few important themes on India in the context of globalising world.

The papers in the volume were prepared by eminent academicians and policymakers. We are grateful to them for their contributions. The papers were first presented in a seminar organised by the CESS and Administrative Staff College of India (ASCI) held at ASCI during November 16-17, 2004. All the papers have been revised in the light of the discussions following each presentation. Thanks are due to the discussants, chairpersons and participants of the seminar.

The themes covered in the volume include areas on which Prof. Rao has worked and also the emerging topics where he wishes others to get involved in research. The themes included in this volume are presented in four sections. The volume begins with *Macro Issues in Development* covering issues such as changing role of Reserve Bank of India, fiscal federalism, performance of firms, macro modelling and governance. The next two themes are *Macro-Issues in Agricultural Development* and *Equity and Emerging Institutions in Agricultural Development*. These sections cover important issues relating to agriculture ranging from WTO and trade to small farmer development. It is known that Prof. Rao has extensively worked on agriculture and rural development in India. The last section is on *Poverty and Environment*. The papers included in this section cover issues on poverty reduction, sustainable development and employment and climate change.

We are grateful to Dr. N. Chandrasekhara Rao for his help in organising the seminar, persuading the authors to revise the papers and getting the manuscript ready for publication. Thanks are also due to Dr. C. Ramachandraiah, Dr. Sarvanan, Dr. Deepita Chakravarty, Dr. Jeena, ASCI and CESS staff for their help in various activities relating to seminar and in preparing the manuscript.

We hope that this volume comprising several analytical and empirical aspects of the Indian economy in a globalising world will be invaluable for researchers, policymakers and students of Indian economic development.

R. Radhakrishna, S.K. Rao
S. Mahendra Dev and K. Subbarao

Contributors to the Volume

Yoginder K. Alagh	K. Krishnamurty
G.S. Bhalla	John W. Mellor
B.B. Bhattacharya	R. Radhakrishna
Kanchan Chopra	C. Rangarajan
S. Mahendra Dev	S.K. Rao
Ashok Gulati	V.M. Rao
Yujiro Hayami	Y.V. Krishna Rao
Peter Hazell	D. Narasimha Reddy
Indira Hirway	Y.V. Reddy
Bimal Jalan	N.S. Siddharthan
Gopal K. Kadekodi	Jerry Skees
Sabyasachi Kar	K. Subbarao
K.L. Krishna	Piet Terhal

Brief profile of the contributors follows...

Yoginder K. Alagh

Prof. Yoginder K. Alagh is currently Chancellor, Nagaland University and Vice-Chairman of Sardar Patel Institute of Economic and Social Research, Ahmedabad. He is a Trustee of the Rajiv Gandhi Foundation. He was earlier Minister of Power and for Planning & Programme Implementation with additional charge of the Ministry of Science & Technology. He has been Member, Planning Commission (in the rank of Minister of State); Chairman, Bureau of Industrial Costs and Prices, Ministry of Industry and Secretary to the Government of India. He holds a Doctoral Degree and a Master's Degree in Economics from the University of Pennsylvania. He also holds a Masters Degree in the same subject from the University of Rajasthan. He has taught Economics at the University of Rajasthan, Indian Institute of Management (Calcutta), University of Jodhpur, Swarthmore College and the University of Pennsylvania. He has been Chairman, Agricultural Prices Commission of India; Director, Sardar Patel Institute of Economic and Social Research, Ahmedabad; Adviser to the Planning Commission of India and Chairman of the Economic Group of Indian Institute of Management, Calcutta. He has been awarded the VKRV Rao Award in Economics in 1981. He was Vice-Chancellor, Jawaharlal Nehru University and Senior Fellow, World Institute of Development Economic Research, United Nations University, Helsinki.

G.S. Bhalla

Currently Professor Emeritus, Centre for the Study of Regional Development, Jawaharlal Nehru University, New Delhi. He is a former Member of the Planning Commission, Government of India and former Chairman, Commission for Agricultural Costs and Prices, Ministry of Agriculture.

Prof. Bhalla who holds Masters Degrees in Mathematics and Economics and has done his Ph.D. in Economics from the London University has had a rich and distinguished academic career. He was a Professor of Economics and Dean, School of Social Sciences at the Jawaharlal Nehru University, New Delhi and Professor at Punjab University Chandigarh. He has also taught at Carleton University, Ottawa, Canada and the University of Rajasthan, Jaipur. Professor Bhalla was President of the Indian Association of Agricultural Economics and of Indian Economic Association.

Professor Bhalla has written, edited and co-authored a large number of books and articles.

B.B. Bhattacharya

Prof. B.B. Bhattacharya has joined as the Vice-Chancellor of Jawaharlal Nehru University, New Delhi, in June 2005. Before that he was a Professor of Economics and Director of the Institute of Economic Growth, Delhi, a premier social science research and training institute in India. He passed

M.A. in Economics (first position in order of merit) from the University of Allahabad in 1966, and Ph.D. in Economics from Delhi School of Economics, University of Delhi in 1971. He was a UNESCO fellow in Polish Academy of Sciences, Warsaw, in 1974 and was a Ford Foundation Post-Doctoral Scholar in the University of California, Berkeley in 1980-81. He specialises in macroeconomics, monetary economics, development economics, public finance and international finance. He has published 9 books and has written more than 100 technical papers in national and international journals. He is one of the leading experts in econometric modelling and forecasting, and his forecasts and analysis are frequently quoted by both print and electronic media and are used by governments and national and international agencies, such as the Planning Commission, Reserve Bank of India and the World Bank.

Kanchan Chopra

Kanchan Chopra is Director, Institute of Economic Growth, Delhi. She also heads the Environmental and Resource Unit. In the last two decades, she has published extensively on issues at the interface of environment and development, in particular water and forest resource management and common property resources. She is Associate Editor, *Environment and Development Economics* and member, Editorial Advisory Board, *Ecological Economics*. Prof. Chopra is an Associate of the lately initiated Ecological and Environmental Economics Programme of the Beijer Institute of Ecological Economics hosted by the ICTP, Trieste. She was one of the Founder members of the Indian Society for Ecological Economics and its First President. She was President for the 64th Conference of the Indian Society of Agricultural Economics (December 2004).

S. Mahendra Dev

Prof. S. Mahendra Dev is currently Director, Centre for Economic and Social Studies, Hyderabad. He did his Ph.D from the Delhi School of Economics and his Post-doctoral research at the Economic Growth Centre, Yale University and was faculty member at the Indira Gandhi Institute of Development Research, Mumbai for 11 years. He was Senior Fellow at Rajiv Gandhi Foundation during 1996-97 and Visiting Professor at University of Bonn, Germany in 1999. He has written extensively on agricultural development, poverty and public policy, food security, employment guarantee schemes, social security, farm and non-farm employment. He has more than 70 research publications in national and international journals. He has been a consultant and advisor to many international organisations like the UNDP, UNICEF, World Bank, International Food Policy Research Institute and ESCAP. He has been a member of several government Committees including Prime Minister's Task Force on Employment.

Ashok Gulati

Dr. Ashok Gulati, earlier Head of the NABARD Chair Unit at the Institute of Economic Growth, is presently the Director of International Food Policy Research Institute (IFPRI) in Washington, D.C., USA. Prof. Gulati's research has been on agriculture and rural development, and he has published several books and a large number of papers in professional journals. He has served a number of international organisations and has worked as a member for several committees of the Government of India.

Yujiro Hayami

Yujiro Hayami is Chairman, FASID Graduate Program, Foundation for Advanced Studies in International Development, Tokyo, Japan. Professor Hayami received his B.A. in Liberal Arts from University of Tokyo, Japan (1956) and Ph.D. in Economics from Iowa State University, USA (1960). He served as professor of economics at the Tokyo Metropolitan University (1966-86) and at the Aoyama Gakuin University (1986-2000). His primary interest is in agricultural and economic development in developing economies. His publications include *Agricultural Development: an International Perspective* (John Hopkins University, first ed. 1971, second ed. 1985) and *Development Economics: From the Poverty to the Wealth of Nations* (Oxford University Press, first ed. 1997, second ed. 2001, third ed. 2005). He is the fellow of the American Agricultural Economics Association and the honourable life-time member of the International Society of Agricultural Economists. He has received the Purple Ribbon Medal (1999) and was designated as the Person of Cultural Merit by the Government of Japan (2004).

Peter Hazell

Hazell is Director of Development Strategy and Governance at the International Food Policy Research Institute (IFPRI), Washington, D.C., USA. He has devoted most of his career to research and advisory work on policy issues related to agricultural development. Initially trained as an agriculturalist in England, he completed his Ph.D. in agricultural economics at Cornell University. He joined the World Bank as a young professional in 1972 and has since held various positions at World Bank and the International Food Policy Research Institute (IFPRI), Washington, D.C., USA. He is currently Director of the Development Strategy and Governance Division at IFPRI, Washington, D.C., USA. Peter's extensive and widely cited publications include works on new methods of using mathematical programming to solve farm and agricultural sector planning problems under risk; the impact of technological change on growth and poverty reduction; the appropriate role of agricultural insurance in developing countries; and farm-nonfarm growth linkages. One of his earliest *AJAE* papers on risk programming became an ISI "citation classic."

Indira Hirway

Prof. Indira Hirway has been the Director of Centre for Development Alternatives, An Academic Research Centre at Ahmedabad. Her research studies have appeared in several research journals in India and abroad. She has to her credit a number of books published by reputed publishing houses. She served as member of many important committees and commissions of the Government of India. She was the Chairperson for Technical Committee of Time Use Study of Department of Statistics of Government of India and Study Group of Anti-Poverty Programmes of National Commission on Women of Government of India. She has been a member of the Board of Directors of Gujarat Institute of Development Research, Ahmedabad; Centre for Social Studies, Surat; Development Support Centre, Ahmedabad and Water Resources Centre. She was Visiting Faculty/Fellow at the Queen Elizabeth House, Oxford University, Oxford; International Institute of Asian Studies, University of Amsterdam and Erasmus University, Rotterdam, Netherlands.

Bimal Jalan

Bimal Jalan, educated at Presidency College, Calcutta, and Cambridge and Oxford Universities, was nominated as a Member of Parliament (Rajya Sabha) by the President of India in August 2003 for distinguished public service. He was Governor of the Reserve Bank of India from 1997-2003. Earlier, he served as Finance Secretary, Member Secretary, Planning Commission, and Chief Economic Adviser to the Government. He was also Chairman of the Economic Advisory Council to the Prime Minister and represented India on the boards of the IMF and the World Bank.

His books on India include *India's Economic Crisis; The Way Ahead, 1991; India's Economic Policy: Preparing for the Twenty-First Century, 1996; India's Economy in the New Millennium, 2002; The Future of India: Politics, Economics and Governance, 2005* and, as editor, *The Indian Economy: Problems and Prospects* (Revised edition, 2004).

Gopal K. Kadekodi

Currently Director of the Institute for Social and Economic Change, Bangalore. He has been Research Professor at the Centre for Multi-Disciplinary Development Research, Dharwad and a Professor at the Institute of Economic Growth, New Delhi. He was Visiting Professor at Erasmus University, Rotterdam and Technical University, Twente. His areas of research include Common Property Resources Valuation, Energy, Natural Resource Accounting and Economic Development. He has been the President of the Indian Society for Ecological Economics. He is Editor, *Journal of Social and Economic Development*, and is on the Editorial Boards of *Environment and Resource Economics, The Pacific and Asian Journal of Energy* and *Journal of Quantitative Economics*. He has published over 12 books and more than 100 articles in national and international journals.

Sabyasachi Kar

Sabyasachi Kar is a faculty at the Institute of Economic Growth, Delhi. His interests are in macroeconomics and development economics with particular focus on the Indian economy. In the last few years, he has been working on the Indian macro-economy and presented forecasts and policy analysis of the economy on a regular basis. He also studies regional issues within the Indian economy and has a number of publications from his research. Dr. Kar teaches growth economics, regional economics and macro-modelling techniques at the Institute. He is a consultant to the Global Development Network (GDN) and a Member of the Advisory Committee to the ASSOCHAM.

K.L. Krishna

Prof. K.L. Krishna got his Ph.D. from the University of Chicago in 1967. He was at the Delhi School of Economics for 42 years, 1958-2000, teaching and researching. His fields of specialisation have been Econometrics and Industrial Economics. He was President of the Indian Econometric Society for one year in the 1990s.

K. Krishnamurty

K. Krishnamurty had a long tenure as Professor, and for some years as Director, at the Institute of Economic Growth. Having held NLC Chair Professor, he is currently honorary Professor at the Administrative Staff College of India. He had been on the research staff of the World Bank and the IMF. He was President of the Indian Econometric Society and also of the Andhra Pradesh Economic Association. Krishnamurty's research is largely focused on India. His contributions lie in the areas of macro econometric modeling, consumption, savings, investment and external trade behaviour and international trade in primary commodities. He has several research publications to his credit. He served on the Editorial Committees of Indian and International academic journals. He was associated with several committees of government and academic institutions.

John W. Mellor

John W. Mellor is Vice-President of Abt Associates, a policy-consulting firm. Previously he was President of John Mellor Associates. He was the founding Director of the International Food Policy Research Institute; Chief Economist of USAID and Professor at Cornell University in Economics, Agricultural Economics, and Asian Studies. He has been a Visiting Professor at Balwant Rajput College, the Indian Agricultural Research Institute and the American University, Beirut.

He was awarded the Presidential Hunger Award (the White House USA) and the Wihuri Prize (Finland) for his work in reducing hunger in the world. He has won numerous prizes from professional associations for the quality of his research work on development. These include prizes for best research and for research of continuing importance for his seminal book on the economics of agricultural development. He is author of eight other books and numerous journal articles.

He is an elected fellow of the American Academy of Arts and Sciences, the American Association for the Advancement of Science and the American Agricultural Economics Association.

R. Radhakrishna

Prof. R. Radhakrishna is the Director, Indira Gandhi Institute of Development Research (IGIDR) in Mumbai since March 2001. From April 1998 to March 2001, he was the Vice-Chancellor of Andhra University. After his doctorate from Gokhale Institute of Economics and Politics, Pune, Prof. Radhakrishna had about three decades of career in research, teaching and administration of academic institutions.

He was the Member Secretary, ICSSR and was the Director, Centre for Economic and Social Studies, Hyderabad. He was the recipient of VKRV Rao prize in Social Science Research for his significant contribution in the field of Economics.

He was President of the Agricultural Marketing Society and of the Indian Society of Labour Economics for the year 2001. He was a consultant to international organisations like ADB, FAO, The World Bank and UNDP and UNESCO.

He was a member of several Government Committees including the Expert Group on Estimation of Proportion and Number of Poor (Lakdawala Committee), Planning Commission, Government of India (1989-93) and High Power Committee for Long term Grain Policy (Abhijit Sen Committee), Government of India, 2000-02.

C. Rangarajan

Dr. C. Rangarajan is a leading economist of the country, who has played a key role both as an academician and a policymaker. He is currently Chairman, Economic Advisory Council to the Prime Minister. Prior to this, he was Chairman of the Twelfth Finance Commission. He was Governor of Andhra Pradesh between 1997 and 2003. He was Governor, Reserve Bank of India during 1992-97. During this period, he gave a major thrust to financial sector reforms and effected the transition to a market-based exchange rate regime. He was a Member of the Planning Commission in 1992. He was, for well over a decade and half, Professor at the Indian Institute of Management, Ahmedabad. He was President of the Indian Economic Association in 1988 and President of the Indian Econometrics Society in 1994.

He was awarded Padma Vibhushan in 2002.

S.K. Rao

Dr. Rao was educated at Andhra and Cambridge Universities and taught Economics at the University of Cambridge and Jawaharlal Nehru University. Dr. Rao also worked at the Commonwealth Secretariat at London for 18 years between 1978 and 2001 in various diplomatic capacities. He was Economic Adviser to the Ministry of Commerce, Government of India during 1986-87. Dr Rao is currently Director General of Administrative Staff College of India, Hyderabad.

V.M. Rao

V.M. Rao is Honorary Visiting Fellow, Institute for Social and Economic Change, Bangalore. He is also associated with Indian School of Political Economy, Pune, and Public Affairs Foundation, Bangalore. He was earlier a faculty member in Department of Economics, University of Bombay and Institute for Social and Economic Change. He was Member, Commission for Agricultural Costs and Prices, Government of India from 1991 to 1995, Devaraj Urs Professor of Development Economics, Institute of Development Studies, University of Mysore in 1995-96 and National Fellow, Indian Council of Social Science Research from 1998 to 2000. He has had a long Association with Indian Society of Agricultural Economics, Mumbai. He was elected as President of 51st Annual Conference of Indian Society of Agricultural Economics held in Hyderabad in December 1991. His writings have been published in many academic journals including Indian *Journal of Agricultural Economics* and *Economic and Political Weekly*.

Y.V. Krishna Rao

Presently, he is the Director, Neelam Rajasekhara Reddy Research Centre, Hyderabad. Joined the National Movement for freedom in 1929. Joined the Communist Party of India in 1937. Working among the peasantry since more than 60 years. Elected as a member of the Secretariat of the Andhra Pradesh Committee, CPI in 1951 and continued in that post till 1987.

He was elected to the Andhra Pradesh Legislative Council and worked as its member during 1966-78. He authored/edited 19 books in English, 46 books in Telugu, 1 in Kannada and 1 in Hindi. He has contributed more than 2000 articles since 1945 in Telugu and English dailies, weeklies and monthlies. Served as Non-official member of the Commission for Agricultural Costs and Prices (CACP), Ministry of Agriculture, Government of India, New Delhi, for 3 years from 1997-2000.

D. Narasimha Reddy

D. Narasimha Reddy retired recently as Professor of Economics and Dean, School of Social Sciences, University of Hyderabad. His areas of interest include Political Economy of Development and Labour Economics. Besides a number of research papers, the books edited by him include Political

Economy of Globalisation (2000) and Crime, Corruption and Development (2001). He was also Conference President of the Indian Society of Labour Economics (2004) and Andhra Pradesh Economic Association (2002). Presently he is Visiting Professor, Institute of Human Development, New Delhi.

Y.V. Reddy

Dr. Yaga V. Reddy is Governor, Reserve Bank of India since September 2003. He is also Alternate Governor of the International Monetary Fund. He earned his M.A. from Madras University and Ph.D from Osmania University. He holds a Diploma in Economic Planning from I.S.S., Netherlands. He was awarded Doctor of Letters (Honoris Causa) by Sri Ventakeswara University, Tirupati.

Prior to this, he was the Executive Director for India, Sri Lanka, Bangladesh and Bhutan at the International Monetary Fund. He has held several positions in the Government of Andhra Pradesh including Principal Secretary/Secretary, Finance, Planning and Public Enterprise Departments, Collector and District Magistrate and Deputy Secretary. He was Secretary, Ministry of Finance and Additional Secretary in the Ministry of Commerce with the Government of India. Dr. Reddy also was the Adviser to Executive Director at the World Bank. He joined the Reserve Bank of India as Deputy Governor in September 1996 where his responsibilities included Monetary Policy Public Debt, Exchange Rate and External Investments, Economic Analysis and Policy and Government Accounts.

Emerging Markets, a publication of the Euromoney Institutional Investor PLC has named Dr. Reddy as "Best Central Bank Governor of the Year for Asia." The issues considered for nominations to the award include "strong track record, ability to turn around world situations and the ability to make a mark on their country."

N.S. Siddharthan

N.S. Siddharthan, Ph.D., is Head, V.K.R.V. Rao Centre for Studies in Globalisation, Institute of Economic Growth, Delhi. He works in the areas of technology, multinationals, and globalisation. His research studies have appeared in journals such as, *The Economic Journal, Oxford Bulletin of Economics and Statistics, The Journal of Development Studies, Economics of Innovation and New Technology, Applied Economics, Development and Change, Journal of Economic Behaviour and Organisation, Journal of Business Venturing, Japan and the World Economy, International Business Review, Developing Economics, Weltwirtschaftliches Archive, Transnational Corporations, The Indian Economic Review,* and *Economic and Political Weekly.* He also has to his credit a number of books published by reputed publishing houses in India and abroad. Dr. Siddharthan has ongoing and past collaborations in research with several institutions that include Hitotsubashi University, Tokyo; Institute of Developing Economies, Tokyo; Erasmus University, Rotterdam;

United Nations University INTECH, Maastricht, The Netherlands; University of Toronto, Canada; Georgetown University, Washington DC, USA; University of Oxford UK and University of Antwerp, Belgium.

Jerry Skees

Skees is the H.B. Price Professor of Agricultural Policy and Risk at the University of Kentucky. He is also president and founder of GlobalAgRisk, Inc.

K. Subbarao

Dr. K. Subbarao was until recently a lead economist in the Africa Region of the World Bank, responsible for research and operations in social protection, poverty and vulnerability. He is currently a consultant on safety nets and social protection for the South Region of the Bank. Prior to joining the Bank, he was a professor of economics at the Institute of Economic Growth, Delhi, and a visiting research fellow at the University of California at Berkeley.

At the Bank, Dr. Subbarao played a major role in analytical and policy work on poverty, particularly in the domain of safety nets. He has published extensively on the subject, and is the lead author of *Safety Net Programs and Poverty Reduction: Lessons from Cross Country Experience* and *Reaching Out to Africa's Orphans: A Framework for Public Action*. Dr. Subbarao's past research spanned a variety of issues bearing on India's agricultural price policy and income distribution equity and efficiency of farm price and input subsidies, public distribution system and other anti-poverty programmes. He has authored or co-authored 8 books and over 50 research papers in various professional economic journals.

Piet Terhal

Dr. Piet Terhal (1935) worked closely with the late Prof. Jan Tinbergen, among other subjects on the economics of conflict and peace. He taught development planning and was Director of the Centre for Development Planning at Erasmus University Rotterdam. His PhD thesis (1988) reflected on humanity's evolutionary past and prospect on the basis of theories of Simon Kuznets, Immanuel Wallerstein and Pierre Teilhard de Chardin, and was titled *World Inequality and Evolutionary Convergence*. Piet Terhal has also studied several aspects of the Indian economy, among others dairy development (Operation Flood) and the impact of military expenditures on Indian economic growth. Together with Indira Hirway he did research and published on employment guarantee in India.

PROF. C.H. HANUMANTHA RAO

Prof. C.H. Hanumantha Rao

A Tribute

Prof. Chennamaneni Hanumantha Rao is one of India's foremost thinker, economic administrator, policymaker and above all, a social equity conscious and highly distinguished development economist. The qualities that distinguish Prof. Rao are his intellectual integrity, resilience and humility. He is open to argument and always tries to help students, scholars and institutions. His services to the profession of economic policy making in India are evident in the manner in which he steered the course of several institutions in India, and continues to do so despite his other heavy commitments. Currently, he is the Chairman, Board of Governors, Centre for Economic and Social Studies (CESS), Hyderabad, and Institute of Economic Growth (IEG), University of Delhi, Delhi, and a member of the National Advisory Council, Government of India. His achievements in academic research and contributions to policymaking are well known. Less well known are perhaps his early association with political movements in the years prior to India's Independence, and immediately after Independence. A summary of his activities in the early years as a student are given below, followed by other contributions as an academician, policy adviser and administrator.

Participation in Freedom Struggle as a Student

He was actively involved in the student movement for 12 years from 1945-1957. While at high school, he joined the Communist Party of India and was an activist of the students' movement at Karimnagar in Andhra Pradesh. In 1945, he was secretary of Hyderabad Students Federation in Karimnagar. When he was in the 9th grade, his results were withheld in 1946 because of his participation in political activities opposing the Nizam rule. The authorities wanted him to apologise to the Nizam government. His family and relatives also had put pressure on him to agree to the demands of the Government. But he refused to resign from the All Hyderabad Students Union and to tender apology to the Nizam

Government for participating in political activities. Afterwards, he shifted to Hyderabad and completed Matriculation privately from Aligarh University. He joined the City College in 1948-49. During that time, the Telangana Armed Struggle was at its peak. He was arrested in 1949 and while in jail he, along with other prisoners, was beaten by the police. When his health condition was deteriorating, the police left him at Jalna railway station. During that difficult situation, one young railway gangman took him to his house and later Prof. Rao was sent back to Hyderabad. He became general secretary of All Hyderabad Students Union. During the 12 long years up to 1957, the shared goal was to bring about social transformation through the political movement. For various reasons, 1957 was a watershed year in his career. It suddenly dawned on him that given his personal circumstances, he could pursue the same goals more effectively through research in economics and economic policy. Prof. A.M. Khusro and Prof. V.K.R.V. Rao encouraged him to do Ph.D. at the Delhi School of Economics. It was remarkable that he moved from activist politics to academic pursuits so very quickly and with ease. After doing post-graduation from Osmania University, he moved to Delhi for pursuing research towards his Ph.D. degree.

Contributions to Research

Prof. Rao worked on several areas including agriculture, rural development, food security, poverty, technology, environment, sustainable development, experience of East Asian economies, regional disparities, Centre-State financial relations etc. He has published 15 books (including edited books) and over 100 research papers. His publications include two well known books: *Technological Change and Distribution of Gains in Indian Agriculture*, 1975 and *Agricultural Growth, Rural Poverty and Environmental Degradation in India*, 1994. His style of writing is unique, balanced and clear. We all benefited from his writings on these topics. In preparing research papers, he spends much time in search of new material, and talks to different people in that area. His empiricism is not casual but causal and his policy conclusions are based on solid empirical foundations and the prevailing institutional setting.

On research, particularly on economic reforms and development, he has balanced views. According to him reforms and globalisation are needed but with a human face. His recent book entitled *Agriculture, Food Security, Poverty, and Environment: Essays on Post-Reform India* examines economic performance and policies in interrelated areas including the agricultural sector, food security, rural poverty, and sustainable development in India and suggests an agenda for further reform. Throughout this book, Prof. Rao suggests policies for achieving growth with equity. Thus, policies that reduce disparities across regions, classes, and social groups would improve both growth and equity. According to him, the success of economic reforms in a democratic polity depends on the support from wider sections of population.

He is also influenced by the East Asian experience. This experience shows that reforms need not increase poverty. In fact poverty declined faster in many of the East Asian countries during periods of outward oriented growth. In a recent conference on China and India held at Beijing, his inaugural address was appreciated by many people. He said that China was a 'mobilising society' while India was a 'debating society.' When a policy is introduced in India, we debate so much that valuable time that can be better utilised in implementing it is lost, while in China it is implemented instantly. In drawing out a comparative perspective between post-reform India and East Asia, Prof. Rao attributes the extraordinarily high GDP growth rate in agriculture, speedier demographic transition and the rapid pace of poverty reduction achieved by East and Southeast Asia to not just an open and market driven economy, but to the ability of the state to implement radical land reforms, infrastructure and human resource development in the pre-reform period.

Contributions to Policy

In addition to a distinguished academic career, Prof. Rao has been at the forefront of several high level policymaking bodies under Government of India. As Planning Commission member, along with persons of distinction such as Sukhamoy Chakravarty and Manmohan Singh, he made significant contributions to the formulation of policy. He argued for more allocations for rural development. He was a member of the Seventh and Eighth Finance Commissions. Prof. Rao was also Chairman of several Government committees and commissions. Three committees are well known—one committee gave important guidelines for watershed development, second is the National Commission on Rural Labour, which discussed important problems of the rural labour in the country, and third is the High Powered Committee on Fertilisers. All the three Committees gave important policy recommendations. When he was Chairman of these Committees, he spent almost full time on them to ensure quality of the reports. His other positions include: Member, Economic Advisory Council to the Prime Minister; Chairman, Technical Advisory Committee on DPAP & DDP, Ministry of Rural Development; Member, Technical Advisory Committee (TAC) of the Consultative Group on International Agricultural Research and Member, Board of Directors, Reserve Bank of India.

Perhaps he is one of the few economists who have had great impact on agricultural policy over the last three decades. His stature in the economics profession and his integrity enabled him to arrive at consensus on controversial issues. It is this reputation that prompts the Government of India to look to him for his advice and views. However, he is very selective in accepting invitations to serve on Committees. The Committees that he chaired have received his full attention and their recommendations have had significant influence on policy.

Contributions as an Administrator and Institution Builder

Both the Institute of Economic Growth (IEG) and the Centre for Economic and Social Studies (CESS), with which he has been associated since their inception, grew under his leadership. He was the Director of IEG in the late '70s. It was considered a golden age during that time. His administrative skills are admirable. He was rule oriented in letter and spirit, and kind to every category of staff. His office door was open to all. He is a man who believes that academicians should enjoy full freedom in their academic endeavour.

On administration and other activities he advises that we should take personal interest. According to him, we should go and check personally whether things are working. On selecting people for academic positions, he gave importance to merit than any other consideration. Even in personal life, he always says caste and religion are private. One should not bring them to public life.

His involvement with the academic programme of CESS has been very intensive since he moved to Hyderabad in the early 1990s. His recent joint work on Andhra Pradesh Development with one of the editors of this book and the faculty members of CESS has initiated debates on the critical issues confronting Andhra Pradesh.

Professor Rao received many offers of coveted positions abroad but he shunned them. Perhaps, he believed that he could do the same good work being on the Indian soil itself. He is very philanthropic. Many institutions benefited from his generous donations from his academic awards, own earnings and savings.

Professor Hanumantha Rao has received several awards in recognition of his professional excellence. The award of Padma Bhushan by the Government of India is for his overall contribution to public life. However, we feel, he deserves much more. Here is the man from whom the aspiring young social scientists will have to learn a lot. He has been a source of inspiration to all of us in our work and personal lives.

**R. Radhakrishna, S.K. Rao,
S. Mahendra Dev and K. Subbarao**

Prof. C.H. Hanumantha Rao's Publications, Awards and Other Accomplishments

A Listing

Articles

1. 1962, "The Optimum Firm and the Optimum Farm - A Comment," *The Economic Weekly*, November 10.

2. 1963, "Wage-Profit Relations in Agriculture: A Study in Andhra Pradesh," *The Economic Weekly*, September 21.

3. 1963, "Farm Size and the Economies of Scale," *The Economic Weekly*, December 14.

4. 1964, "Growth of Agriculture in India (1951-61): Problems and Prospects," *Bharat Krishak Samaj Year Book*, New Delhi.

5. 1964, "Intensive Agricultural District Programme: An Appraisal," *The Economic Weekly*, November 28.

6. 1965, "Agricultural Growth and Stagnation in India," *The Economic Weekly*, Vol.XVII, No.9, February 27.

7. 1965, "The Marketable Surplus Function for a Subsistence Crop– Comment," *The Economic Weekly*, April 17.

8. 1965, "Growth of Agriculture in the Punjab during the Decade 1952-62," *Indian Journal of Agricultural Economics*, Vol. XX, No.3, July-September.

9. 1965, "Problems of Agricultural Production in Kerala," Seminar on Agricultural Production in Kerala, Trivandrum; reproduced in, C.H.H. Rao, *Agricultural Growth, Farm Size and Rural Poverty Alleviation in India*, Academic Foundation, New Delhi, 2005.

10. 1966, "The Zonal System: Increasing Disparities," *The Times of India*, February 18.

11. 1966, "What is Wrong with Indian Agriculture?" *CONSPECTUS*, Vol.2, No.2, Quarterly Journal of the India International Centre, Second Quarter.

12. 1966, "Alternative Explanations of the Inverse Relationship between Farm Size and Output Per Acre in India," *Indian Economic Review,* October.

13. 1967, "Incentive Prices for Farm Produce," *The Economic Times,* November 14.

14. 1968, "Fluctuations in Agricultural Growth: An Analysis of Unstable Increase in Productivity," *Economic and Political Weekly,* Annual Number, January.

15. 1968, "Farm Size and Yield Per Acre: A Comment," *Economic and Political Weekly,* September 14.

16. 1969, "Agricultural Policy under the Three Plans," in N. Srinivasan (Ed.), *Agricultural Administration in India,* Indian Institute of Public Administration (IIPA), New Delhi, March.

17. 1969, "Resource Prospects from the Rural Sector–The Case of Indirect Taxes," *Economic and Political Weekly,* Review of Agriculture, March 1969, pp. A-53-58; "Reply," *Economic and Political Weekly,* Vol.4, No. 26, Review of Agriculture, June.

18. 1969, "Budgetary Surpluses of Telangana," *Economic and Political Weekly,* October 18.

19. 1969, "India's 'Surplus' Cattle: Some Empirical Results," *Economic and Political Weekly,* Vol. IV, No. 52, Review of Agriculture, December.

20. 1970, "India's 'Surplus' Cattle: Reply," *Economic and Political Weekly,* Vol. V, No. 40, October 3.

21. 1970, "Prospects for Crop Insurance in India," published in C.H.H. Rao, *Agricultural Growth, Farm Size and Rural Poverty Alleviation in India,* Academic Foundation, New Delhi, 2005.

22. 1970, "Farm Size and Credit Policy," *Economic and Political Weekly,* Vol. V, No. 52, Review of Agriculture, 26 December.

23. 1971, "Uncertainty, Entrepreneurship and Sharecropping in India," *Journal of Political Economy,* Vol. 79, No. 3, May/June.

24. 1971, "Sectoral Planning for Telangana: Some Issues for Consideration," Paper prepared for the Expert Group for the preparation of the Perspective Plan for Telangana, Government of Andhra Pradesh, July 31; published in C.H.H. Rao, *Essays on Development Strategy, Regional Disparities and Centre-State Financial Relations in India,* Academic Foundation, New Delhi, 2005.

25. 1972, "Farm Mechanisation in a Labour-Abundant Economy," *Economic and Political Weekly*, Annual Number, February.

26. 1972, "Ceiling on Agricultural Land-Holding: Its Economic Rationale," *Economic and Political Weekly*, Review of Agriculture, June 24.

27. 1972, "Differential Rates of Interest: A Comment," *Economic and Political Weekly*, Vol. VII, No. 37, September 9.

28. 1972, "Agricultural Taxation: Raj Committee's Report," *Economic and Political Weekly*, November 25.

29. 1973, "Rationale for Smaller States: The New Imperatives," *Seminar*, April.

30. 1973, "Strategy for Removal of Poverty: Lopsidedness of the Fifth Plan Approach," *Economic and Political Weekly*, Vol. VIII, Nos. 31-33, Special Number, August.

31. 1974, "Factors Underlying Technological Change in Agriculture: Experiences of India and other Asian Countries," published in *Studies in Asian Social Development*, No. 2, Institute of Economic Growth, Vikas Publishing House, Pvt. Ltd.

32. 1974, "Employment Implications of the Green Revolution and Mechanisation: Case Study of the Punjab," presented at a Conference held by the International Economic Association at Bad Godesberg, West Germany; published in Nurul Islam (Ed.), *Agricultural Policy in Developing Countries*, Macmillan.

33. 1974, "Socio-Political Factors and Agricultural Policies," *Economic and Political Weekly*, Vol. IX, Nos. 32-34, Special Number, August.

34. 1976, "Marketing of Rice in India: An Analysis of the Impact of Producers' Prices on Small Farmers" (Jointly with K. Subbarao), *Indian Journal of Agricultural Economics*, Vol. XXXI, No. 2, April-June; also in *Teaching & Research Forum*, The Agricultural Development Council, Regional Research and Training Programme, Bangkok, Thailand.

35. 1976, "Agricultural Policy," Paper presented at the *Regional Programme of Management of Agriculture*, 6-24 September 1976, under the joint auspices of ESCAP (United Nations), Asian Centre for Development Administration and the Indian Institute of Public Administration; published in, J.N. Mongia (Ed.), *India's Economic Policies, 1947-77*, Allied Publishers.

36. 1976, "Factor Endowments, Technology and Farm Employment: Comparison of East Uttar Pradesh with West Uttar Pradesh," *Economic and Political Weekly*, Review of Agriculture, 25 September.

37. 1977, "Agricultural Growth and Rural Poverty: Some Lessons from Past Experience," *Economic and Political Weekly*, Vol. XII, Nos. 33-34, Special Number, August.

38. 1977, "Criteria for the Distribution of Financial Resources Among States," published in C.H.H. Rao, *Essays on Development Strategy, Regional Disparities and Centre-State Financial Relations in India,* Academic Foundation, New Delhi, 2005.

39. 1978, "General Comments on Policy," in *Economic Consequences of the New Rice Technology*, International Rice Research Institute, Los Banos, Philippines; also in C.H.H. Rao, *Agricultural Growth, Farm Size and Rural Poverty Alleviation in India*, Academic Foundation, New Delhi, 2005.

40. 1978, "Urban *vs.* Rural or Rich *vs.* Poor?," (Review Article on the book: *Why Poor People Stay Poor – Urban Bias in World Development*, by Michael Lipton), *Economic and Political Weekly*, Vol. XIII, No. 40, October 7.

41. 1979, "Farm Mechanisation," in C.H. Shah and C.N. Vakil (Ed.), *Agricultural Development in India: Policy and Problems*, R.P. Nivatia Felicitation Volume, Orient Longman.

42. 1979, "Poverty and Development: Characteristics of Less-Developed Regions in India," *Economic and Political Weekly*, Vol. XIV, Nos. 30, 31 & 32, Special Number, August.

43. 1980, "Fluctuations in Foodgrains Output, 1950-51–1979-80: Implications for Policy," *The Economic Times*, February 8; also in C.H.H. Rao, *Agricultural Growth, Farm Size and Rural Poverty Alleviation in India*, Academic Foundation, New Delhi, 2005.

44. 1979, "Growth, Poverty and Tax Effort: An Inter-State Comparison with Special Reference to Bihar," Lecture Delivered at the Annual Day Function of the A.N. Sinha Institute of Social Studies, Patna, March 2; published in *Journal of Social and Economic Studies*, Vol. VIII, Part I, March 1980.

45. 1981, "On Indian Agrarian Scene," *Link*, January 26; also in, C.H.H. Rao, *Agricultural Growth, Farm Size and Rural Poverty Alleviation in India*, Academic Foundation, New Delhi, 2005.

46. 1981, "A New Look at Agriculture in the North-West: How to Overcome Limits to Growth," *Times of India*, July 22; reproduced in C.H.H. Rao, *Agricultural Growth, Farm Size and Rural Poverty Alleviation in India*, Academic Foundation, New Delhi, 2005.

47. 1982, "Planning for Development and Removal of Regional Imbalances with Special Reference to Bihar," Keynote Address at the National Seminar on *Planning for Development and Removal of Regional Disparities with Special Reference to Bihar* held at L.N. Mishra Institute of Economic Development and Social Change, Patna, September 29-30; in C.H.H. Rao, *Essays on Development Strategy, Regional Disparities and Centre-State Financial Relations in India*, Academic Foundation, New Delhi, 2005.

48. 1982, "Development of Tribal Areas: The Case of Bastar," Planning Commission, December 31; in C.H.H. Rao, *Essays on Development Strategy, Regional Disparities and Centre-State Financial Relations in India*, Academic Foundation, New Delhi, 2005.

49. 1983, "Appraisal of Urban Development Projects: Concepts, Techniques and Practice," Inaugural Address at the Workshop on *Appraisal of Urban Development Projects: Concepts, Techniques and Practice* at the School of Planning and Architecture, New Delhi, January 17; published in C.H.H. Rao, *Essays on Development Strategy, Regional Disparities and Centre-State Financial Relations in India*, Academic Foundation, New Delhi, 2005.

50. 1983, "Consumption of Fertilisers in Indian Agriculture: Emerging Trends and Policy Issues," *Fifteenth Lal Bahadur Shastri Memorial Lecture*, Indian Agricultural Research Institute, New Delhi, February.

51. 1983, "Pricing Policy and Strategy for Surplus Generation," presentation at the Seminar on *Prices, Profits and Pattern of Investment in Public Enterprises* in New Delhi on August 19, 1983, published in *Prices, Profits and Pattern of Investment in Public Enterprises*, Centre for Public Sector Studies, New Delhi; also in C.H.H. Rao, *Essays on Development Strategy, Regional Disparities and Centre-State Financial Relations in India*, Academic Foundation, New Delhi, 2005.

52. 1983, "Pricing Policy and Generation of Resources," Paper presented at the Seminar on *Prices, Profits and Pattern of Investment in Public Enterprises* in New Delhi on August 17-19, 1983, published

in *Prices, Profits and Pattern of Investment in Public Enterprises*, Centre for Public Sector Studies, New Delhi; also in C.H.H. Rao, *Essays on Development Strategy, Regional Disparities and Centre-State Financial Relations in India*, Academic Foundation, New Delhi, 2005.

53. 1983, "Quality of Life, not the Contraceptive–A Key to Success of the Family Welfare Programme," Inaugural Address at the Seminar on *Significance of Family Welfare Programme for the Scheduled Castes and Scheduled Tribes*, Dr. B.R. Ambedker Research Institute, New Delhi, September.

54. 1984, "Planning for Removal of Poverty: Some Issues Concerning Approach and Strategy," Presidential Address at the *Second Conference of the Andhra Pradesh Economic Association*, Warangal, 10 March; also in C.H.H. Rao, *Agricultural Growth, Farm Size and Rural Poverty Alleviation in India*, Academic Foundation, New Delhi, 2005.

55. 1984, "Approach to the Seventh Plan: A Note," in C.H.H. Rao, *Essays on Development Strategy, Regional Disparities and Centre-State Financial Relations in India*, Academic Foundation, New Delhi, 2005.

56. 1984, "A Special Programme for Breakthrough in Rice Output in Eastern States," July 1984, Planning Commission; in C.H.H. Rao, *Essays on Development Strategy, Regional Disparities and Centre-State Financial Relations in India*, Academic Foundation, New Delhi, 2005.

57. 1984, "Observations on Planning and Implementation of the Special Programme for Rice Production," based on the field visits in Orissa, Madhya Pradesh, Assam, Bihar, West Bengal and Uttar Pradesh following the Introduction of the Special Programme for Rice Output; published in *Essays on Development Strategy, Regional Disparities and Centre-State Financial Relations in India*, Academic Foundation, New Delhi, 2005.

58. 1984, "Indira Gandhi's Contribution to Economic Planning in India," Memorial Talk at the All India Radio, November 5, published in C.H.H. Rao, *Essays on Development Strategy, Regional Disparities and Centre-State Financial Relations in India*, Academic Foundation, New Delhi, 2005.

59. 1985, "Changes in Rural Poverty in India: Implications for Agricultural Growth," *Dr. Rajendra Prasad Memorial Lecture*, 39th Annual Conference of the Indian Society of Agricultural Statistics, Punjabrao Krishi Vidyapeeth, Akola, December.

60. 1985, "Poverty Eradication in India by the Year 2000: Some Macro-Economic Implications," (Jointly with S.P. Gupta and K.L. Dutta), *Man and Development*, December.

61. 1985, "Fertiliser in the Seventh Plan," (Jointly with Padam Singh), *The Economic Times*, December 16.

62. 1986, "Infrastructural Development and Rural Poverty in India: A Cross-Sectional Analysis," (Jointly with Devendra B. Gupta and P.S. Sharma), in Mellor, John W. and Gunvant M. Desai (eds.), *Agricultural Change and Rural Poverty – Variations on a Theme by Dharm Narain*, Oxford University Press, New Delhi.

63. 1986, "Science and Technology Policy: An Overall View of Broader Implications," *Indian Journal of Agricultural Economics*, Vol.41, No. 3, July-September.

64. 1986, "Agriculture-Industry Interrelationships: Issues of Relative Prices and Growth in the Context of Public Investment," (jointly with B.B. Bhattacharya), presented at the *Eighth World Economic Congress*, 1-5 December, New Delhi.

65. 1986, "Agriculture in India and China," in C.H.H. Rao, *Agricultural Growth, Farm Size and Rural Poverty Alleviation in India*, Academic Foundation, New Delhi, 2005.

66. 1987, "Instability in Agricultural Performance: Lessons from the Current Drought," *Economic Journalist*, September; also in *Economic Times*, October 19, 1987, and in C.H.H. Rao, *Agricultural Growth, Farm Size and Rural Poverty Alleviation in India*, Academic Foundation, New Delhi, 2005.

67. 1988, "Centre-State Financial Relations: A Perspective for National Economic Integration," *Dr. Zakir Hussain Memorial Lecture*, 8 February, New Delhi, Dr. Zakir Hussain Educational and Cultural Foundation; published in C.H.H. Rao, *Essays in Development Strategy, Regional Disparities and Centre-State Financial Relations in India*, Academic Foundation, New Delhi, 2005.

68. 1988, "Current Agrarian Scene: Policy Alternatives," *Kambhampati Satyanarayana (Senior) Memorial Lecture*, Visalandhra Vignana Samiti, Vjayawada, January, Published in *Economic and Political Weekly*, Review of Agriculture, 26 March 1988.

69. 1988, "Efficiency of Investments in IRDP: A Study of Uttar Pradedh," (jointly with P. Rangaswamy), *Economic and Political Weekly*, Review of Agriculture, 25 June.

70. 1988, "Eighth Plan: Major Issues of Concern," *Mainstream*, Annual, October 8. Also in C.H.H. Rao, *Essays in Development Strategy, Regional Disparities and Centre-State Financial Relations in India*, Academic Foundation, New Delhi, 2005.

71. 1988, "Agricultural Development and Ecological Degradation: An Analytical Framework," *Economic and Political Weekly*, December 24-31.

72. 1989, "Planning in India: An Overview of Experience," in *India: Forty Years of Independence*, Publications Division, Ministry of Information and Broadcasting, GoI, New Delhi; also in, C.H.H. Rao, *Essays in Development Strategy, Regional Disparities and Centre-State Financial Relations in India*, Academic Foundation, New Delhi, 2005.

73. 1989, "Decentralised Planning: An Overview of Experience and Prospects," *Economic and Political Weekly*, Vol. 24, No. 8, February 25.

74. 1989, "Implications of Modern Biotechnology for the Structure of Agriculture in the Less Developed Countries," invited paper presented at the *Conference of the International Association of Agricultural Economists*, Tokyo, August 22-9; published in the Proceedings Volume of the IAAE, 1989.

75. 1989, "Technological Change in Indian Agriculture: Emerging Trends and Perspectives," Presidential Address delivered at the 49th Annual (Golden Jubilee) Conference of the Indian Society of Agricultural Economics, IGIDR, Bombay, December, published in the *Indian Journal of Agricultural Economics*, Vol. 44, No. 4, October-December, 1989.

76. 1989, "Impact of Farm Size and Tenure on Agricultural Productivity, Income and Income Distribution: The Indian Experience," Paper presented at the *Seminar on Improvement of Agricultural Structure*, Asian Productivity Organisation, Tokyo, August; published in *Improving Agricultural Structure in Asia and the Pacific*, Asian Productivity Organisation, Tokyo, 1990.

77. 1990, "Some Interrelationships between Agricultural Technology, Livestock Economy, Rural Poverty and Environment: An Interstate Analysis for India," in *Agricultural Development Policy: Adjustment and Reorientation*, Indian Society of Agricultural Economics, Oxford and IBH, New Delh.

78. 1990, "Central Assistance to State Plans: Improving Equity of Gadgil Formula," *The Times of India*, July 16; also in C.H.H. Rao,

Essays in Development Strategy, Regional Disparities and Centre-State Financial Relations in India, Academic Foundation, New Delhi, 2005.

79. 1990, "Job Reservations for Backward Classes," *Mainstream,* September 8.

80. 1991, "Technological Change and Development of Capitalist Relations in Indian Agriculture," Inaugural Presentation at the *Seminar on Technological Revolution and Changes in Social Relations in Agriculture,* All India Kisan Sabha, at Ajoy Bhawan, New Delhi, January 19-20.

81. 1991, "The Role of Public Sector in Indian Economy," *The Economic Times,* February 27; also in C.H.H. Rao, *Development Strategy, Regional Disparities and Centre-State Financial Relations in India,* Academic Foundation, New Delhi, 2005.

82. 1991, "Rural Society and Agricultural Development in Course of Industrialisation–Case of India," Paper presented at the Institute of Developing Economies (IDE) *Thirtieth Anniversary Symposium on Development Strategies for the Twenty-First Century,* Tokyo, December 1990; published in *Economic and Political Weekly,* Annual Number, March 1991.

83. 1991, "Implications of Modern Biotechnology for the Structure of Agriculture in the Less Developed Countries," Invited paper on the Plenary Address: *Key Elements of Modern Biotechnology and Relevance to Agriculture* by W. James Peacock, CSIRO Division of Plant Industry, Canberra, Australia, presented at the *Conference of the International Association of Agricultural Economists,* August 22-29, Tokyo, Japan. Published in the Proceedings Volume of the IAAE.

84. 1991, "World Development Report, 1991: An Appraisal," *Indian Economic Review,* Vol. XXVI, No. 2.

85. 1992, "Agriculture: Policy and Performance," in Bimal Jalan (Ed.), *The Indian Economy: Problems and Prospects,* Viking, Penguin Books India (P) Ltd.

86. 1992, "The Links between Sustainable Agricultural Growth and Poverty," (Jointly with Kanchan Chopra), *Quarterly Journal of International Agriculture,* Vol. 31, No. 4, October-December, Frankfurt (Main).

87. 1992, "Integrating Poverty Alleviation Programmes with Development Strategies: Indian Experience," Keynote Address at the *Commonwealth Consultation on Rural Poverty Alleviation,* Colombo,

Sri Lanka, October 5-9; published in *Economic and Political Weekly*, Vol. XXVII, No. 48, November 28, 1992.

88. 1992, "Chakravarty on Development Strategy in India," *Indian Economic Review*, Special Number.

89. 1993, "Tasks Before the Tenth Finance Commission," in C.H.H. Rao, *Essays in Development Strategy, Regional Disparities and Centre-State Financial Relations in India*, Academic Foundation, New Delhi, 2005.

90. 1994, "Policy Issues Relating to Irrigation and Rural Credit in India," in G.S. Bhalla (Ed.), *Economic Liberalisation and Indian Agriculture*, Institute for Studies in Industrial Development, New Delhi.

91. 1994, "Agricultural Growth, and Rural Poverty in India: Emerging Trends and Perspectives," *Dharm Narain Memorial Lecture*, Institute of Economic Growth, Delhi, published in *Indian Economic Review*, Vol. XXVIII, No. 2, 1994.

92. 1994, "Economic Reforms and the Prospects for Rural Labour," *V.V. Giri Memorial Lecture*, 35th Conference of the Indian Society of Labour Economics, Ahmedabad, 22 January, published in the *Indian Journal of Labour Economics*, Conference Number, 1994.

93. 1994, "Reforming Agriculture in the New Context," *Economic and Political Weekly*, Vol. XXIX, Nos. 16 and 17, April 16-23.

94. 1994, "Economic Liberalisation and Agriculture: Requirements of Agricultural Research and Technology," Keynote Address at the *Mid-Term Meeting of the Consultative Group on International Agricultural Research (CGIAR)*, 23 May, New Delhi, Published in *Yojana*, Annual Number, August, 1994.

95. 1994, "Indian Agriculture: Emerging Perspectives and Policy Issues," (jointly with Ashok Gulati), *Economic and Political Weekly*, Vol. 29, No. 53, 31 December.

96. 1994, "Price Policy Reforms for Water and Fertilisers in India," (jointly with Ashok Gulati), (mimeo), International Food Policy Research Institute, Washington, D.C.

97. 1994, "Changing Roles of Planning and Markets in Development: The Emerging Pattern in India," *Ravi Narayan Reddy Memorial Lecture*, Ravi Narayan Reddy National Foundation, Hyderabad, 7 September, published in *Mainstream*, Annual 1994, November 26; also published as "Changing Role of the State in Relation to

Markets' and 'Social Welfare: When the Market Fails" in C.H.H. Rao, *Essays in Development Strategy, Regional Disparities and Centre-State Financial Relations in India*, Academic Foundation, New Delhi, 2005.

98. 1995, "Attack on Poverty and Deprivation: Role of Structural Change and Structural Adjustment," Presidential Address at the 36th Annual Conference of the Indian Society of Labour Economics, *The Indian Journal of Labour Economics*, Vol. 38, No. 1, January-March, 1995.

99. 1995, "The Burden of Reforms," *The Hindu*, May 1; in C.H.H. Rao, *Essays in Development Strategy, Regional Disparities and Centre-State Financial Relations in India*, Academic Foundation, New Delhi, 2005.

100. 1995, "Liberalisation of Agriculture in India: Some Major Issues," Keynote Paper, *Indian Journal of Agricultural Economics*, July-September.

101. 1996, "Economic Reforms, Agricultural Growth and Rural Poverty: Some Reflections on the Relevance of East and South-East Asian Experience for India," *Sukhamoy Chakravarty Memorial Lecture* at the 78th Conference of the Indian Economic Association at Chandigarh, *The Indian Economic Journal*, Vol. 43, No. 4, April-June, 1996.

102. 1997, "Economic Reforms and Rural Development," address at the *Sixteenth Convocation of the Institute of Rural Management*, Anand, April 10, Published in *Mainstream*, July 5, 1997; Also in, C.H.H. Rao, *Agricultural Growth, Farm Size and Rural Poverty Alleviatioin in India*, Academic Foundation, New Delhi, 2005.

103. 1997, "Inaugural Presentation at the Seminar on Liberalisation and the Small Farmer," in Y.V. Krishna Rao (Ed.) *Liberalisation and the Small Farmer*, All India Kisan Sabha and International Labour Organisation, New Delhi, September.

104. 1997, "Uttarakhand: Case for a Separate State," *Mainstream*, Annual Number, December 20.

105. 1997, "National Food Security: A Policy Perspective for India," (jointly with R. Radhakrishna), presented at the *XXIIIrd International Conference of Agricultural Economists*, 10-16 August, Sacramento, California, U.S.A.

106. 1997, "Agriculture in the Ninth Plan," in Bhupat M. Desai (Ed.), *Agricultural Development Paradigm for the Ninth Plan Under New*

Economic Environment, Indian Institute of Management, Ahmedabad, Oxford and IBH.

107. 1998, "Agricultural Growth, Sustainability, and Poverty Alleviation in India: Recent Trends and Major Issues of Reform," *IFPRI Lecture Series 5,* December 1997, International Food Policy Research Institute, Washington DC, published in *Economic and Political Weekly,* Vol. 33, No. 29, July 18.

108. 1997, "Sustainable Development with Special Reference to India: An Economist's Perspective," Keynote Address, in *The Challenge of the Balance-Environmental Economics in India;* proceedings of a National Environment and Economics Meeting (Anil Agarwal, Ed.) *Centre for Science and Environment,* New Delhi.

109. 1999, "Amartya Sen and the Empowerment of the Poor," *Economic Times,* 1 January; also in C.H.H. Rao, *Agricultural Growth, Farm Size and Rural Poverty Alleviation in India,* Academic Foundation, New Delhi, 2005.

110. 1999, "Sustainable Agricultural Development in India: An Economist's View on Performance and Perspectives," Keynote Speech at the *First Asia-Pacific High Level Conference on Sustainable Agriculture,* Beijing, China, October 4-8,1998, in Suteera Nagavajara (Ed.), *Agricultural and Ecological Resilience – Striking a Balance in the Pacific Rim,* American Association for the Advancement of Science, 1999.

111. 1999, "Sustainable Development of Agriculture," presentation at a Plenary Session of the *First Biennial Conference of the Indian Society of Ecological Economics,* Bangalore, December 20-22; published in *Ecological Economics for Sustainable Development,* Indian Society for Ecological Economics, Academic Foundation, New Delhi, 2001.

112. 1999, "Declining Demand for Foodgrains in Rural India: Causes and Implications," Presidential Address at the 13th National Conference on Agricultural Marketing, NIRD, Hyderabad, October 12, published in *Economic and Political Weekly,* January 22, 2000.

113. 2000, "Watershed Development in India–Recent Experience and Emerging Issues," *Lovraj Kumar Memorial Lecture,* (SPWD), *Economic and Political Weekly,* Vol.35, No.45, November 4.

114. 2001, "Changing Economic Structure of the Rural Economy in Asia and the Pacific," in *Rural Transformation in Asia and the Pacific 1,* Asian Productivity Organisation, Tokyo.

115. 2001, "WTO and Viability of Indian Agriculture," *6th Foundation Day Lecture* at the National Academy of Agricultural Sciences, IARI, New Delhi, June 5, published in *Economic and Political Weekly*, Vol. XXXVI, No. 36, September 8, 2001.

116. 2002, "Sustainable Use of Water for Irrigation in Indian Agriculture," Presidential Address at the *Second Biennial Conference of the Indian Society of Ecological Economics*, Bhopal, December 19-21, published in *Economic and Political Weekly*, Vol. XXXVII, No. 18, May 4, 2002.

117. 2002, "Foodgrain Surpluses: Causes and Policy Implications," *C.D. Deshmukh Memorial Lecture*, Council for Social Development, Hyderabad, March, published in *Mainstream*, May 11, 2002.

118. 2003, "Reform Agenda for Agriculture," Rajiv Gandhi Foundation, published in *Economic and Political Weekly*, February 15, 2003.

119. 2003, "Andhra Pradesh: Economic Reforms and Challenges Ahead– An Overview," (jointly with S. Mahendra Dev), *Economic and Political Weekly*, Vol. XXXVIII Nos. 12 and 13, March 22-28/29- April 4, 2003.

120. 2003, "Rural Non-Farm Sector and Lessons from Asian Experience," in Nayyar, Rohini and Alakh N. Sharma (ed.) *Rural Transformation in India: The Role of Non-Farm Sector*, Institute for Human Development, New Delhi.

121. 2004, Preface to *State of the Indian Farmer: A Millennium Study* (27 volumes + CD ROM), Department of Agriculture and Cooperation, Ministry of Agriculture, Government of India; published by Academic Foundation, New Delhi.

122. 2005, "Rural Transformation in China and India: Comparative Experience in the Post-Reform Period," Keynote presentation at the Conference of the Chinese Academy of Agricultural Sciences (CAAS) and the International Food Policy Research Institute (IFPRI) on *Dragon and the Elephant: Agricultural and Rural Reforms in China and India*, Beijing, November 10-11, 2003; published in *Economic and Political Weekly*, Vol. XL, No.33, August 13-19, 2005.

123. 2005, "Crisis in Indian Agriculture," Inaugural presentation at a Seminar under the auspices of the Sundaraiah Vigyana Kendra, Hyderabad, July 24, 2004; published in *Mainstream*, Independence Day Special, Vol.XLII, No.34, August 13, 2005.

124. "Economic Reforms with Human Face," Inaugural Address at the Conference on "Economic Reforms with Human Face," held at the India Council of Social Science Research (ICSSR), New Delhi, 13-14 August, 2004, published in *Mainstream*, Vol.XLIII, No.36, August 27, 2005.

125. 2005, "Rural Job Scheme and Tasks Ahead," *Economic Times*, September 5, 2005.

126. 2005, "Growing Regional Disparities in Development: Post-Reform Experience and Challenges Ahead," *Professor A.M. Khusro Memorial Lecture*, 88th Annual Conference of the Indian Economic Association, Visakhapatnam, 27-29 December, 2005.

Books

1. 1965, *Agricultural Production Functions, Costs and Returns in India*, Asia Publishing House.

2. 1966, *Taxation of Agricultural Land in Andhra Pradesh*, Asia Publishing House.

3. 1973, *Inflation and India's Economic Crisis*, Vikas Publishing House, New Delhi (Jointly with V.K.R.V. Rao, A.M. Khusro, P.C. Joshi, K. Krishnamurty and Ajit K. Dasgupta, Institute of Economic Growth, Delhi.

4. 1975, *Technological Change and Distribution of Gains in Indian Agriculture*, The Macmillan Company of India Limited, New Delhi.

5. 1988, *Unstable Agriculture and Droughts: Implications for Policy* (Jointly with Susanta K. Ray and K. Subbarao), Vikas Publishing House, New Delhi.

6. 1994, *Agricultural Growth, Rural Poverty and Environmental Degradation in India*, Oxford University Press, New Delhi.

7. 2005, *Essays on Development Strategy, Regional Disparities and Centre-State Financial Relations in India*, Academic Foundation, New Delhi.

8. 2005, *Agriculture, Food Security, Poverty and Environment – Essays on Post-Reform India*, Oxford University Press, New Delhi.

9. 2005, *Agricultural Growth, Farm Size and Rural Poverty Alleviation in India*, Academic Foundation, New Delhi.

Edited Books:

1. 1979, *Reflections on Economic Development and Social Change: Essays in Honour of Prof. V.K.R.V. Rao* (Jointly with P.C. Joshi), Allied Publishers Private Limited, New Delhi.

2. 1988, *Dharm Narain: Studies on Indian Agriculture* (Jointly with K.N. Raj and Amartya Sen), Oxford University Press, New Delhi.

3. 1996, *Economic Reforms and Poverty Alleviation in India* (Jointly with Hans Linnemann), Indo-Dutch Studies on Development Alternatives–17, IDPAD, Sage Publications India, New Delhi.

4. 2003, *Water Resources, Sustainable Livelihoods and Eco-System Services* (Jointly with Kanchan Chopra and Ramprasad Sengupta), Indian Society of Ecological Economics, Concept Publishing Company New Delhi.

5. 2003, *Andhra Pradesh Development: Economic Reforms and Challenges Ahead* (Jointly with S. Mahendra Dev), Centre for Economic and Social Studies (CESS), Begumpet, Hyderabad, 2003, Distributed by Manohar Publishers and Distributors, New Delhi.

6. 2004, *Indian Economy and Society in the Era of Liberalisation and Globalisation: Essays in Honour of Professor A.M. Khusro* (Jointly with B.B. Bhattacharya and N.S. Siddharthan), Academic Foundation, New Delhi.

Ph.D. Supervision

Supervised, individually or jointly, the following six scholars for their Ph.D. theses submitted to the University of Delhi:

1. K. Subbarao, formerly Professor, Institute of Economic Growth, Delhi; presently with the World Bank, Washington, DC; subject of the thesis: *Market Structure in Indian Agriculture*; completed in 1973.

2. P. Rangaswamy, formerly Reader, Agricultural Economic Research Centre, University of Delhi; subject of the thesis: *Economics of Dry Farming in Selected Areas*; completed in 1980.

3. Uma Kapila, formerly Reader, Department of Economics, Miranda House, University of Delhi; presently Senior Editor, Academic Foundation, New Delhi; subject of the thesis: *Stagnating Oilseeds Economy of India—A Case Study of Groundnut*; completed in 1980 (Joint Supervisor: R. Thamarajakshi).

4.   A.K. Bandopadhyay, presently Chief General Manager, NABARD; subject of the thesis: *An Analysis of Agricultural Credit with Special Reference to Small Farms in West Bengal*; completed in 1982.

5.   Kailas Sarap, presently Professor of Economics, Sambalpur University, Orissa; subject of the thesis: *Interlinked Agrarian Markets in Rural India*; completed in 1986 (Joint Supervisor: K. Subbarao).

6.   T. Palanivel, formerly at the United Nations University, Tokyo; presently with the UNDP, Asia-Pacific Regional Centre, Colombo; Subject of the thesis: *Inter-Sectoral Terms of Trade and Resource Flows: Some Implications for Agricultural Output*, Income and Poverty in India; completed in 1992 (Joint Supervisor: K. Subbarao).

Membership of Expert Bodies

1.   Member, National Advisory Council, Government of India.

2.   Member, Central Board of Directors, Reserve Bank of India, 1994-2000.

3.   Chairman, High Powered Fertilisers Pricing Policy Review Committee, Government of India, 1997-98.

4.   Chairman, Expert Committee on Rehabilitation & Environmental Aspects of Tehri Hydro-Electric Project, Government of India, 1996-97.

5.   Member, Technical Advisory Committee (TAC), of the Consultative Group on International Agricultural Research (CGIAR), 1981-82 & 1995-97.

6.   Chairman, Advisory Committee, National Accounts Statistics, Government of India, 1992-95.

7.   Chairman, Technical Committee on Drought Prone Area Programme and Desert Development Programme (DPAP & DDP), Ministry of Rural Development, Government of India, 1993-94.

8.   Chairman, Working Group on Major and Medium Irrigation Projects for the Ninth Five Year Plan, Ministry of Water Resources, Government of India.

9.   Chairman, National Commission on Rural Labour, Government of India, 1990-91.

10.   Chairman, Expert Committee for Review of Methodology of Cost of Production of Crops, Ministry of Agriculture, Government of India, 1990.

11. Chairman, Advisory Council on the Implementation of the 20-Point Programme, Government of India, 1987-89.

12. Chairman, Task Force to Evaluate the Impact of Sheep & Goat Rearing in Ecologically Fragile Zone, Ministry of Agriculture, Government of India, 1987.

13. Chairman, Expert Group on Cropping Pattern, Ministry of Agriculture, Government of India, 1987.

14. Chairman, Study Group on Agricultural Price Policy for Balanced Development of Agriculture, Planning Commission, Government of India, 1985-86.

15. Member, Planning Commission, Government of India, 1982-86.

16. Member, Economic Advisory Council to the Prime Minister, 1983-85, (Chairman: Sukhamoy Chakravarty).

17. Chairman, Working Group on District Planning, Planning Commission, Government of India, 1984.

18. Member, Eighth Finance Commission, Government of India, 1982-84.

19. Member, Economic Administration Reforms Commission, Government of India, 1981-82, (Chairman: L.K. Jha).

Distinction/Awards

1. Awarded Rafi Ahmed Kidwai Memorial Prize for 1974-75, by the Indian Council of Agricultural Research, for Outstanding Contribution in the field of Agricultural Economics.

2. Fellow, National Academy of Agricultural Sciences, New Delhi.

3. Received Sri Kambhampati Satyanarayana (Senior) Memorial Award, Visalandhra Vignana Samiti, Vijayawada, in January 1988.

4. Received the honorary degree of Doctor of Philosophy from the S.K. University, A.P. in 1991.

5. Received Sri Ravi Narayan Reddy Memorial Award, Ravi Narayan Reddy National Foundation, Hyderabad, in September 1994.

6. Received K.H. Batheja Award for the Best Book published in Economics during 1993-94 (*Agricultural Growth, Rural Poverty and Environmental Degradation in India*, Oxford University Press, 1994).

7. Received the Financial Express Award for Lifetime Work in Economics, in 1995.

8.   National Fellow, Indian Council of Social Science Research, 1994-1996.

9.   Received the honorary degree of Doctor of Philosophy from the Kakatiya University, Andhra Pradesh in 1998.

10. Received 'Telugu Atma Gaurava Puraskaram' from the Government of Andhra Pradesh in 2000.

11. Conference President: Indian Society of Agricultural Economics, 1989; Indian Society of Labour Economics, 1995; and Indian Society of Ecological Economics, 2001.

12. Awarded 'Padma Bhushan' by the President of India in 2004.

Introduction and Overview

R. RADHAKRISHNA, S.K. RAO,
S. MAHENDRA DEV, K. SUBBARAO

1. The Context

At the time of independence, there was deep distrust of market forces and international trade due to the strong feeling among the nationalists that the *laissez faire* policy of the British had drained India's wealth and capital. The initial success of Soviet Planning and the intellectual appeal of Fabian socialism had influenced the policy-making in favour of import substitution industrialisation strategies. Under Rajiv Gandhi in the 1980s, there was some relaxation of controls, including selective deregulation of control on private investment and on transactions on trade, mostly on non-competing imports. It was not until the 1991 balance of payments crisis in 1991, when India was close to default in repayment of debt, that she began to deregulate and adopt market- and outward-oriented reforms. It was a shift from import substitution to one oriented towards the international market. The 1990s witnessed wide ranging reforms in industrial, financial, monetary, fiscal and trade sectors.

With the opening up of the economy since the early 1990s, issues relating to open economy have become more relevant for macroeconomic policy than in the past. The trade regime has been significantly liberalised with the abolition of quantitative restrictions and reduction in tariff rates. In brief, economic policy in the recent past has been oriented towards India taking advantage of the forces of globalisation.

Globalisation, however, offers both opportunities and challenges. As moves towards integration in a globalising world gather strength, a careful monitoring of many macro variables including capital account transactions is called for, with a view to maintain sustainability of the balance of payments and overall macroeconomic stability. Establishment of WTO provides for a stronger rule-based and liberal trade regime and needs careful monitoring of fairness of trade practices. Globalisation impacts on rural livelihoods as all sectors are affected, *viz.*, agriculture, industry and services. Of course, the impact on agriculture is much more important for rural areas as the livelihoods of majority of people depend on this sector.

Post-reform period has seen some achievements and some adverse consequences for the economy and society. There have been improvements in some indicators such as balance of payments, resilience to external shocks, significant accumulation of foreign exchange reserves especially since 2002, spread of the use of information technology, improvement in telecommunications, etc.

Economic growth in the 1990s, however, is not significantly different from the 1980s, except that it was characterised by a higher growth in services. GDP growth, which stood at 6.7 per cent per annum during 1992-97 (Eighth Plan), declined to 5.5 per cent during 1997-2002 (Ninth Plan). During the Tenth Plan period, GDP growth is likely to be around 7 per cent as compared to the target of 8 per cent. Industrial growth also decelerated in the later part of 1990s. Similarly, investment rate has fallen in the Ninth Plan period. Public investment as proportion of GDP fell from 8 per cent in Eighth Plan to 6.6 per cent in the Ninth Plan. Private corporate investment as a proportion of GDP declined from 7.3 per cent to 6.1 per cent during the same period. The combined fiscal deficit is still around 10 per cent. There was a decline in inflation in terms of wholesale price index. However, the growth rates in the consumer price index numbers for agricultural labourers and industrial workers were higher in the 1990s as compared to 1980s.

According to official estimates, poverty declined by 10 percentage points during the period 1993-94 to 1999-00. Studies by independent researchers show that rates of decline were lower than the official estimates suggest. It is now common knowledge that employment growth in the post-reform period was much lower than in the pre-reform period. Particularly, there was stagnation in employment in agriculture. The growth rate of employment decelerated even in industry and services. Another feature of this period of economic reforms is that inequalities have increased over time. First, regional inequalities have increased. State Domestic Product and private expenditures grew faster in Southern and Western states as compared to poor states. Second, inequalities in consumption between different classes have risen. Third, rural-urban disparities have also increased. Inequality within urban areas increased in many states.

One of the concerns in the post-reform period, particularly since the mid-1990s, relates to the performance of agriculture. It is known that better performance of agriculture is crucial for a reduction in poverty. However, agricultural growth declined from 4.7 per cent in the Eighth Plan to 1.8 per cent during Ninth Plan. During the Tenth Plan agriculture growth is likely to be around 2.2 per cent per annum.

Thus, the period of reforms was marked by some achievements, but also some deep concerns. There have been gains in external sector due to better integration with world markets. Now there is widespread optimism that India is catapulted onto a higher growth path of 7 per cent or more per annum. In the last two decades, India was among the ten to twelve highest growing economies in the world. A report by Goldman Sachs suggests that India may continue to realise the growth rate witnessed in the past two decades. The report pointed out that Brazil, Russia, India, and China—the BRICs economies—could become a large force in the world economy by 2050. On the other hand, there are concerns regarding social sector achievements, agricultural growth, employment generation and equity. Globalisation is inevitable and the challenge is to achieve higher growth with equity in a globalising world.

The rationale for the ongoing economic reforms in India, their consequences and prospects has generally been discussed in the parlance of economics. However, these economic phenomena represent largely a superstructure, which is profoundly influenced by the underlying socio-political factors. The economic reforms may not be sustainable if the burden falls disproportionately on the poorer sections of the population. Therefore, there may be a need for meaningful economic reforms that are in line with socio-political realities in India.

Prof. Hanumantha Rao's work on agriculture and rural development is well known. His academic and policy interests and contributions, however, are wide ranging and covered macro issues relating to economic reforms and globalisation. His writings also stress the importance of achieving higher growth with social justice in the post-reform period. Keeping in view his interests, this volume of papers presented at a seminar in his honour examines some aspects of macro economy, agriculture and poverty in the context of economic reforms and globalisation. The 19 papers in the volume are organised into four sections: macro issues in development; issues in agricultural development; equity and emerging institutions in agricultural development; and poverty and environment. Given below is a summary of the chapters in each section.

2. Macro Issues in Development

Six papers in this section examine various macro issues in the context of economic reforms. Some of the issues discussed in this section are: the role of Reserve Bank of India (RBI) in the post-reform period, some issues in fiscal federalism, the interrelationships among the three elements of our national life *viz.*, economics, politics and governance. In addition, some papers address specific questions such as: How to make the macro econometric models relevant to the current times? How do we model the short run and long run growth prospects of the agriculture sector? What are the effects of rainfall shocks and increase in public investment on the performance of the agriculture sector and the Indian economy? What is the impact of globalisation and liberalisation on Indian firms?

All over the world, there have been changes in the role of Central Bank in the era of globalisation. **Y.V. Reddy (Ch.1)** examines the evolutionary trends in the functioning of Reserve Bank of India (RBI) in the context of economic reforms. If we look at the history of RBI, it has four phases: (a) initial phase (1934-1948), (b) the maturing phase (1948 till bank nationalisation in 1969); (c) the phase of Government dominance (1969-91), and (d) economic reform phase (1991- till date). In the last phase, there have been significant changes in the role of RBI in terms of its various functions, such as, monetary authority, public debt manager, bank regulator, lender of last resort etc. The legal and institutional changes acted as catalysts for these changes.

RBI's function as a monetary authority has undergone significant transformation from a repressed regime to a deregulated, decentralised, competitive and open financial system. Some of these measures are: deregulation of interest rates, rationalisation of Cash Reserve Ratio (CRR) and Statutory Liquidity Ratio, phasing out of *ad hoc* Treasury Bills, activation of the Bank rate as a policy instrument and reduction in the reliance on refinance. For example, the changes in interest rate in the 1990s reflect the reform in RBI. While the bank rate was changed only once in the 1980s it was changed 10 times in the 1990s. Thus, the "shift from the direct to the indirect instruments, adoption of multiple indicators, increasing emphasis on financial stability, and opening up of the 'erstwhile' postulate of closed economy—all constitute the evolving contours of the changing face of monetary policy" in the era of gradual opening of a closed economy. However, attaining price stability and ensuring credit to productive sectors still continue to be important objectives.

Unlike the absence of active debt market in the 1980s, the 1990s witnessed development of an active government security market. In the context of financial sector reform, there have been substantial changes in RBI's role as a debt manager of both Central Government and State governments. Although, these changes led to market determined auction based system, the fiscal situation of governments has not improved. In the case of external sector, the recommendations of Rangarajan Committee (RBI, 1993) were implemented in a phased manner. The exchange of rupee became market determined in 1993. Foreign exchange policy is now on management rather than control. It was realised that apart from accumulating foreign reserves, the quality of reserves was also important.

In the role of regulation and supervision, there has been change in both organisation as well as form. In terms of regulation, RBI has adopted a three-pronged strategy: "a) strengthening the regulatory and supervisory norms, b) ensuring diverse ownership through listing and partial divestiture of the public sector banks, and c) ensuring competition through entry of private banks." The reforms also include changes in the developmental functions of RBI. This role has focused on development of markets through promoting institutions in order to make the markets function in a more efficient and transparent manner. Steps were also taken by RBI to improve the flow of institutional credit to agriculture in recent years.

Finally, chapter 1 also provides outlook and issues on the changing role of RBI for short and medium terms. The experience so far in the post-reform period indicates that RBI has been able to meet most of the challenges of changing requirements due to globalisation.

What are the concerns of fiscal federalism in recent years? **C. Rangarajan (Ch.2)** examines the concerns of fiscal federalism in the light of new developments. First one is the impact of globalisation on federal structures. They will have to undergo a change in order to respond to the forces of globalisation and international competition. Private sector and markets are being given larger space in the new paradigm. It may be noted, however, that 'more market does not mean less government but only different government.' Increasing role of markets change the rules of the game for the government at various levels. Second development is the importance being given to decentralisation in the form of greater role of sub-national governments and local bodies in a democracy. In India, 73rd and 74th Amendments to the Indian Constitution reflect this democratic process.

The traditional functions of fiscal federalism such as the assignment of taxes and correction of vertical and horizontal imbalances continue to remain important even now. Revenues collected by the Federal or Central Government differ from country to country. For example, Central or Federal Government collects 65 per cent of the total revenue in India, 69 per cent in Australia and 48 per cent in Canada. In a multi-tiered system of government, inter-governmental transfers are important to correct the imbalances. Inter-governmental transfers as a percentage of provincial or state revenues have been 41 per cent in Australia, 40 per cent in India and 20 per cent in Canada in recent years.

In India, the Constitution provides for a Finance Commission to determine the distribution between the Union and the States of the net proceeds of taxes and the grants-in-aid to states. With the 73rd and 74th Amendments to the Constitution, which mandates states to have decentralisation, the Finance Commissions also have to suggest measures for increasing the resources for *panchayats* and municipalities. One important issue that is debated regarding fiscal transfers is whether vertical imbalance has increased or declined in the post-reform period. A good transfer system should serve "the objectives of equity and efficiency and should be characterised by predictability and stability." In the post-reform period, the experience has shown that the developed states with better infrastructure, market institutions and broad industrial base have attracted private investment and have grown faster than others. The transfer system has to take into account these disparities in a competitive environment. On the other hand, we should take into account 'efficiency' considerations. The states that perform efficiently in delivering services or collecting revenues should not be penalised. Thus, a sound transfer system has to maintain balance between equity and efficiency.

The economic policies in India have undergone fundamental changes since the early 1990s. Shift to market based development and facing global competition need policy changes, formation of market institutions and decentralised governance. A spirit of cooperative federalism is needed to implement reform agenda at both the Centre and States. At the same time, a healthy competition is also important across States for efficiency considerations. The improvement in efficiency should be reflected not only in the services provided but also ensuring improvements in resource efficiency for all economic agents. Thus, both competitive and cooperative federalism are needed to face the new challenges.

Economic strategies have seldom reflected our political and social realities. In this context, **Bimal Jalan**'s paper **(Ch.3)** deals with an interesting theme entitled 'economics, politics and governance.' We have good economists, functioning democracy and operational governing structure. Inspite of this, the achievements in economic and social development in the last 50 years have been far from satisfactory. At the beginning of the Second Plan in 1956, it was outlined that we would have poverty-free India with full employment in 25 years *i.e.* by 1981. We have not achieved that goal even now. "An important question which needs to be debated is why this combination of economics, politics, and civil service did not lead to the kind of results that the people of our country could have legitimately expected." There has been substantial gap between economically sound and politically feasible policies. In other words, economic strategies have not taken into account political aspects. Also, administrative implications of economic policies are not considered particularly at the ground level.

On the issue of disjuncture between economics and politics, Jalan cites Prof. Hanumantha Rao's work on agricultural subsidies. The growing subsidies, which largely benefit large farmers, have reduced the public investments in agriculture. This is not economic but political which is due to the influence of large farmers in the decisionmaking process. Even the continuation of Mahalnobis-Nehru development strategy for more than 40 years could be attributed to political factors.

The political decision-making on economic issues is often driven by special interests rather than the common interests of the general public. The so-called majority is divided by several factors such as caste, religion, location or occupation. These special interest groups try to protect their share of the national economic output. Here the issue is not market *versus* state. The problem of the Indian economy is not that market is less or more free but the freedom is in the wrong hands.

The economic reforms launched in 1991 have yielded positive results. However, the gains can disappear unless we improve our economic decision-making processes, remove scope for political discretion, reduce unproductive expenditure and improve the quality of governance. The whole system must be made to work in the interests of public in general rather than few interest groups. In order to achieve this objective several measures are needed. Some of them are: adopt pragmatic and flexible approaches in making economic policies by avoiding policies based on 'ideological certainty;' avoid political interferences in implementation by having clear distinction between decisions on policy and their implementation; fiscal policy should be responsive to changing requirements *i.e.* reducing subsidies and increasing investments; need for legal reforms by focusing on public interests and for improving accountability of administration; review the working of the public institutions—including academic institutions and NGOs—and improve their accountability and; reduce administrative discretion as they have become serious sources of corruption.

There is a renewed interest on macro econometric models in the new policy regime. **K. Krishnamurty (Ch.4)** provides a review of five generations of macro econometric models for India and offers suggestions to make the models relevant to the current times. Several conclusions have emerged from, 'what if' policy simulations on recent models. Public investment crowds-out private investment in some sectors and crowds-in for some sectors, increases in fiscal deficit tend to widen the balance of payments gap, there are trade-offs between growth and inflation, etc. There has been substantial progress in model construction but there are two caveats: one, policymaking in the real world is complex because political economy rules the roost; second, more quantitative detail is required as there are lags in release of data, and changes in policy regimes results in changes in the parametric structures of the models.

The introduction of economic reforms in the early 1990s has given rise to a number of questions relating to modelling that need to be addressed. One important issue is whether the models which cover pre-reform years are relevant in the new policy regime. The rates of change for some sectors are much higher in the post-reform period as compared to pre-reform years. For example, one can visualise that financial and capital markets and, foreign trade, balance of payments and exchange rate may experience faster change compared to say productivity, saving and investment behaviour. There has also been a change in the role of state. In the new policy regime, the role of state is important in creating critical physical and social infrastructure and for strategic and coordinated intervention to provide the right market signals to the private agents. In this context, macroeconometric models may have a useful role to play. It is desirable to have a main frame model with several sectoral models, which can be operational in 'stand alone' mode and/or within the fold of main frame model. Several satellite sub-models for important, fast changing and growing sectors are needed to capture structural changes in the post-reform period.

Agriculture is still the crucial sector in the Indian economy for both output and more importantly for employment. It is important to know the factors that influence agricultural growth in the short and long run for framing better policies. The study of **B.B. Bhattacharya and S. Kar (Ch.5)** makes a macro analysis of short and long run growth prospects of agricultural GDP. It examines the effect of rainfall shocks and increase in public investment on the performance of the agriculture sector and the Indian economy.

The primary focus of the rainfall shocks is to study their impact on aggregate growth rates. The results on rainfall shock (20 per cent below the normal in two consecutive years) shows that it has a strong growth retarding effect both in the short- as well as the long-run. However, the long-run effects are moderate possibly due to resilience of the economy to the rainfall shock. Another issue from the policy point of view is whether the shock leads to inflationary situation or not. The study finds that the rainfall shock leads to inflation. Another point of interest is to examine whether shock leads to instability in the growth process by disturbing equilibrium in the fiscal and external sectors. The study shows that the rainfall shock does not have any significant negative impact on both fiscal deficit and external sectors.

The impact of government intervention in the face of rainfall shocks is also examined in the study. The results indicate that the government intervention in the form of higher food imports, government consumption and government transfers can somewhat moderate the inflationary impact of the shock and provide marginal push to the growth rates. Finally, the study examines the effect of public investment on the long run growth of agriculture and overall GDP. The results reveal that increased public investment enhances the long run growth rate of all the sectors as well as aggregate output. In particular, higher public investment in agriculture leads to higher growth in that sector as well as higher growth in other sectors because of interlinkages with agriculture.

The studies on impact of globalisation and liberalisation on industry sector focus, in general, on inter-country samples or inter-industry samples in a given country. However, it may be noted that the impact of liberalisation differs even across firms in an industry. **N.S. Siddharthan (Ch.6)**, therefore, concentrates on the findings from inter-firm studies rather than inter-country or inter-industry studies. His study discusses the impact of liberalisation and FDI inflows on the growth of firms, exports and productivity spillovers in India and other developing countries. The review indicates that there are some discerning trends in the case of the influence of FDI and liberalisation on growth of firms. On the other hand, clear-cut trends are not to be seen for exports and productivity spillovers and generalisations could not be made.

The determinants of a firm's growth drastically change when the economic regime change from a controlled to a liberal one. Liberalisation did not have uniform impact on all firms. Firms with superior technological base and firms that networked with other firms through strategic alliances performed better. There has been no consensus on the role of multinational enterprises (MNEs) and FDI in influencing exports. Most studies did not find any significant relationship between MNE presence and exports. However, China is an exception. More than 55 per cent of exports in China come from fully owned foreign ventures or joint-ventures. The share of foreign firms in the exports of high tech industries is even higher. But for most of the other developing countries, the evidence is mixed and ambiguous. In the case of India, MNEs have not emerged as important exporters. It seems MNEs have come to India to seek the host market and not exploit opportunities for exports. Studies on Sri Lanka and Brazil also did not find any significant relationship between MNE presence and exports.

On the contrary, several studies show the crucial role of small and medium enterprises (SMEs) in promoting exports in both developed and developing countries and in particular the vital role of internet in promoting business to business (B2B) commerce. Studies show that technology and productivity spillovers from MNEs to local firms are not automatic. Spillovers will depend on the nature of the investing MNE and the technological base, ownership and managerial practices of the domestic firms. The firms that already enjoyed a good technological base, had a smaller productivity gap with regard to MNEs, and spent on in-house R&D captured spillovers. The rest did not. Furthermore, in several industries local firms also enjoyed high productivity levels than the MNEs. In the regulated regimes, the quality of FDI in terms of spillovers and domestic sourcing of components was higher while in the liberalised regimes the quantity of FDIs could be more. If we accept this finding, the plan of elimination of regulations under WTO regime could lead to decline in the spillovers from FDI. In order to meet the challenge of competing successfully with MNEs under WTO regime, developing countries should develop positive strategies like non-equity strategic alliances and net working with other firms rather than passively wait for spillovers to occur.

3. Issues in Agricultural Development

Agricultural development is crucial for higher overall growth and poverty reduction. Three papers in this section look at some selected issues in agricultural development. The issues discussed in this section are: what should be India's strategies on agriculture in the light of Doha Round negotiations and open economy? What is the mechanism through which agricultural growth reduces poverty? What are the trends in total factor productivity in agriculture?

Indian agriculture has to face new challenges in the light of WTO negotiations in particular and globalisation in general. **Y.K. Alagh (Ch.7)** discusses global economic strategies to be followed by India after the Doha WTO meetings. His paper examines the following: (a) the impact of the global economy on the macro performance of the Indian economy in the 1990s, the fluctuations in it, and the evolution of trade responses; (b) the interesting issues of a conceptual and applied nature raised in the negotiations. For example, the controversy on the definition of subsidies and domestic support has a long history in earlier Indian debates. These are discussed since the issues are bound to persist in the future and understanding them is central to resolving them; (c) the approaches, India is developing to adjust her trade and fiscal policies in the agriculture sector; and (d) the nature of the coalitions emerging in the agricultural negotiations and India's role in them, seen from the angle of the coalition building around interest groups in the context of global paradigms.

According to the study, Indian economy has been opened to the forces of international trade without adequate policy preparedness and institutional back up for effective market support to producers facing a highly distorted global market. Growth of output and employment has gone down particularly in the second half of the 1990s. Diversification of the agricultural and rural economy and structural change have either got reversed or stagnated. Profitability of agriculture has fallen. Investment is stagnating. This is the time for preparing for a more vigorous agricultural economy. Globally, India must continue to play a leading role in a coalition of developing countries. India should rely more on non-quantitative tools of intervention, particularly tariff, monetary and tax instruments and use quantitative mechanisms as a last resort for achieving policy objectives. The study works out a framework of illustrative policies for paddy crop. The interesting point now is that farmers are demanding sensible trade policies and not procurement prices, which do not work. India has played a leading role in the WTO negotiations. In the global reform, India should represent the developing world and earn its place in the top since it is the fourth largest economy in the world.

In recent decades, there has been remarkable reduction in poverty and food insecurity in Asian countries. On the other hand, poverty and famines have increased in Africa. However, the pace of poverty reduction has slowed down in Asia in the last decade. Rapid poverty reduction is yet to take place in large areas of India. In this context, **John Mellor (Ch.8)** discusses about the importance of agricultural growth in poverty reduction. Particularly, its effect on employment in the small-scale rural non-agricultural sector is important. The study then shows the importance of public expenditure on agricultural growth and in turn poverty reduction and draws conclusions regarding development expenditure in particular for foreign aid.

The evidence shows that although economic growth reduces poverty, there are substantial variations in the magnitude of poverty reduction. In other words, structure of growth matters. It is agricultural growth that brings down poverty in low-income countries with the presence of substantial agricultural sector. A study on India, for example, shows that 84.5 per cent of the substantial poverty reduction in India during 1950 to 1993-94 was due to agricultural growth. Similarly, the impact of rural growth on poverty reduction is nearly three times as great as urban growth.

How do we explain the association between agricultural growth and reduction in poverty? It depends very much on multipliers of agricultural growth on the employment intensive rural non-farm sector. High agricultural growth is generally accompanied by growth in rural non-farm sector. Because of the immense increase in employment in the local non-farm sector, the poor benefit as employment increases and then again as real wages rise, which is due to tightening of labour market. That is why poverty declines so rapidly with high agricultural growth rates.

The conclusions of the study are: (a) growth does not always bring down poverty levels because of the wrong structure; (b) right structure takes time as the system has to work through indirect effects; (c) poverty declined faster in Asia because of its focus on agriculture; (d) in the last decade, the pace of poverty reduction declined in Asia because of less focus to agriculture; (e) Africa has not been successful in reducing poverty because of urban bias and orientation as compared to Asia; and (f) In Africa, foreign aid has given little attention to agricultural growth. If pro-poor growth is to occur, foreign aid must return its attention to agriculture.

Productivity and total factor productivity in agriculture continues to be an important research area in view of the important role of productivity in the growth process. **K.L. Krishna's** study **(Ch.9)** based on a critical review of studies on total factor productivity in agriculture, deals with three aspects of total factor productivity (TFP) growth in Indian agriculture: the performance of agriculture relative to non-agriculture and relative to manufacturing; the performance of agriculture in India relative to China and other countries in South Asia; and the determinants of TFP in agriculture.

The evidence is that agriculture performed better than manufacturing in India as elsewhere. Over the 50-year period, 1950-2000, there was no difference in average TFPG between agriculture and non-agriculture, the rate of TFPG being 1.13 per cent per annum according to one recent study. During the first 15 years, 1950-51 to 1964-65, agriculture (1.47 per cent) scored better than non-agriculture (1.2 per cent). In the 1980s, agriculture (1.89 per cent) was slightly behind non-agriculture (1.98 per cent). During the 1990s when agricultural output growth decelerated, non-agriculture (2.04 per cent) went far ahead of agriculture (1.69 per cent). Another study, however, shows that the divergence between the two sectors was very sharp in the post-liberalisation period. This study shows that TFPG in agriculture improved from 0.36 per cent in the pre-liberalisation period to 1.34 per cent in the post-liberalisation period while for non-agriculture it improved quite phenomenally from 0.62 per cent to 3.39 per cent during the same period. Thus, the evidence on the relative productivity performance of Indian agriculture is not unambiguous.

In an inter-country perspective, the productivity performance of Indian agriculture during 1980 to 1995 was superior to that of other South Asian countries, but much inferior to that of China. However, the evidence from different studies does not reveal the expected convergence (across studies).

A review of comparative agricultural productivity performance in Indian Punjab and Pakistan Punjab shows that Indian Punjab fared better in terms of output growth and TFP growth. In both Punjabs, growth in the post-Green Revolution phase showed signs of unsustainability especially in the wheat-rice cropping system because of resource degradation.

One attractive and important feature of research studies on agricultural productivity is that several of them examined the determinants of TFP growth. The available evidence shows that agriculture research is an important determinant of TFP growth for each of the four important crops *viz.*, rice, wheat, sorghum and maize. Next in importance are agricultural extension and infrastructure.

4. Equity and Emerging Institutions in Agricultural Development

Seven papers in this section examine issues relating to equity and emerging institutions, which have become important for raising agriculture growth and poverty reduction. Some of the issues discussed in this section are: (a) framework for comparing agrarian communities in different regions of Asia; (b) agricultural growth and regional variations in India; (c) changes in trade and exchange rate policies in the reform period and their impact on incentives, investments and growth in agriculture; (d) effects of withdrawal of subsidies from irrigation and fertilisers on small and marginal farmers; (e) impact of liberalisation policies on small farmer development; (f) changes in agrarian structure and technology and sustainability of peasant farming; and (g) recent thinking on insurance against bad weather.

Relationships and structures in communities such as tribes and villages are the basic determinants of production and resource use in agrarian economies. In this context, **Yujiro Hayami (Ch.10)** attempts to build a conceptual framework for comparing the community characteristics across major regions in Asia. Platteau and Hayami advanced a hypothesis to explain the differences in community relationships and structures between Africa and Asia in terms of differences in agricultural production modes corresponding to different resource endowments. In this chapter, Hayami tries to examine the applicability of the Platteau-Hayami hypothesis to explain differences and similarities among the agrarian communities of three major regions in Asia, namely, South, South-East, and North-East Asia.

The agrarian communities in South-East Asia lie in the midst of a continuous spectrum ranging from Africa to Noth-East Asia. Differences in the community characteristics across those three regions could be largely explainable in terms of differences in the endowment of natural resources relative to population. The population density is the lowest in Africa and the highest in North-East Asia while South-East Asia lies in-between.

Correspondingly, different modes of agricultural production prevailed traditionally. Africa was based predominantly on mobile agriculture including hunting-gathering, nomadic grazing and shifting cultivation with little investment in land infrastructure while North-East Asia had sedentary agriculture with heavy investment in land infrastructure, particularly irrigation, represented by irrigated rice cultivation. In the case of South-East Asia, dominant traditional mode of production was rainfed rice cultivation in low land plains/valleys and shifting cultivation in mountain areas, although, irrigated agriculture was prevalent in some areas. Community norms were developed in North-East Asia to take care of local commons especially irrigation systems. Villages in South-East Asia have their own mechanism of guaranteeing subsistence to poor members in the same community. A system of sharing income through sharing work as a guarantee of subsistence to the poor seems to have been established as a basic norm in the peasant communities in South-East Asia.

The communities in South Asia, particularly India, are not located on the same spectrum as those of Africa, South-East and North-East Asia. India's land endowment relative to population and labour force has traditionally been in-between South-East and North-East Asia. There seems to be major differences in the social organisations between East Asia and South Asia. In East Asia, interclass differences are economic but not social. On the other hand, the situation in India seems to be sharply different as its class differentiation is based on castes rather than land asset holdings (though these two are generally correlated). Corresponding to such a difference in community structure, there is a major difference in agrarian structure in terms of size distribution of farms. East Asia is dominated by small farms while in South Asia we have coexistence of small farms based on hired labour even in the food crop sector excluding plantations. Apart from intensive data collection on community relationships and structures, a major research agenda is to examine how the differences in community structures is related with differences in market and state government structures.

Understanding factors responsible for regional variations in agriculture is important for framing better policies to achieve equity. **G.S. Bhalla (Ch.11)** reviews the pattern of agricultural growth at the national and regional level and examines the main reasons for regional variations in levels and rates of agricultural growth. His study starts by giving a brief review of agricultural growth in India since 1950 at the national level. It comes out that agricultural growth recorded a significant deceleration during the 1990s thereby belying the hopes of policymakers who had expected growth to accelerate as a result of economic reforms initiated after 1991. The deceleration was sharp after 1997-98. It had many adverse consequences. First, the income levels of peasants and of agricultural labourers deteriorated. Second, export buoyancy could not be sustained. Third, crop diversification slowed down. Fourth, employment growth decelerated. The main cause of deceleration was very sharp deceleration in public investment since the mid-eighties.

India has witnessed a significant decline in both rural and urban poverty during the recent period especially since the mid-1980. The growth rate of GDP has also recorded visible acceleration since 1980. Consequently, it is generally inferred that rapid growth rate has made a significant dent on poverty in India.

Currently, a theory has been put forward that the reduction in poverty is because of introduction of economic reforms and structural adjustment policies in 1991. In this context some scholars have looked at regional performance and have come to the conclusion that the states that have reformed the most have achieved maximum growth and that the laggard states are the ones that have failed to reform. The entire emphasis on these exercises is to look at aggregate growth rate of the economy and growth of GDP at the state level. There is no reference to sectoral patterns of development. Nor has any reference been made to the structure of employment and incidence of rural and urban poverty. Again, no account is taken for the relationship between agricultural growth and its impact on rural poverty reduction at the state level. This is a reversal of the earlier position taken by some of the scholars like Montek Ahluwalia who had demonstrated the existence of negative relationship between agricultural growth and rural poverty.

An attempt is made in the study to look at Poverty and Agricultural Development in a regional perspective and see if agricultural growth has played a significant role in the context of poverty reduction in India since 1983-84. Bhalla's study puts forward the argument that it is labour productivity in agriculture which plays an important role not only in poverty reduction but also promotes diversification of the labour force from agriculture to non-agricultural occupations. The argument is that increased labour productivity in agriculture results in higher wages and incomes for agricultural workers. Since agricultural workers constitute a very high proportion of work force, the increased income is very widely spread among a large number of workers. This leads to reduction in rural poverty. Furthermore, higher incomes of this mass of workers result in rapid growth of manufacturing and service sectors because of very strong input, output and consumption linkages. The overall result is both a decline in rural poverty as well as in diversification of the economy.

Combination of three I's – incentives, investments, and institutions are important for higher agricultural growth and to reduce hunger and poverty. **Ashok Gulati's** study **(Ch.12)** looks at the broad changes in trade and exchange rate policies during the reform period and how they have impacted upon the incentives, investments and growth in agriculture. While there is evidence that trade policy reforms have had favourable effect on the incentives for agriculture, which also contributed to increasing private sector investment in agriculture, its impact on growth is not very clearly discernible. During the initial period of reforms characterising major changes in trade and exchange rate policies, the average annual rate of growth in agriculture accelerated dramatically: from about 3 per cent during the pre-reform period of 1980-81–91-92 to 4.7 per cent during the early post-reform period of 1992-93–96-97. But thereafter, it experienced an equally dramatic fall during the period 1997-98 through 2003-04 to about 2 per cent per annum.

Gulati's study proposes several hypotheses that may help explain this decline. Broadly, these hypotheses indicate emerging demand constraints on the one hand and supply bottlenecks on the other. The demand constraints for some commodities resulted from the crash in their world prices as well as hikes in domestic prices, while supply bottlenecks emerged from falling public sector investments and lack of any major institutional reforms pertaining to power, water, credit and research and development, targeted to agriculture. Regarding institutions, the study discusses three types that are needed for improving agricultural growth. These are: (a) marketing institutions that help promote vertical integration, especially in high value agriculture, mitigate market risk and lower transaction costs; (b) land and credit institutions that can help small and marginal farmers to move up on high value agriculture; and (c) institutions that can promote a fundamental reform in the management of state dominated agricultural research, power and water supplies for rural areas.

The study finally looks at the emerging structure of agriculture that is fast moving towards high value agriculture (HVA) comprising fruit and vegetables, livestock (dairy and meat, including poultry), and fishery, and suggests institutional changes that are essential for promoting vertical integration between farms, firms and forks, with a view to mitigate market risk and cut down transaction costs, especially of small holders. This would help Indian agriculture emerge globally competitive and small holders to share in that prosperity. The share of HVA in gross value of output in agriculture is going to increase in future. However, the policy environment is still hung up with the priorities of 1960s and 1970s. HVA is largely driven by the initiatives of the private sector and is demand led. Public policy has to ensure that there is level playing field for private sector in HVA. This also needs a different type of infrastructure and institutions than what was created for cereals.

The distributive impact of subsidies remains a major question in the minds of policymakers. Will the small and marginal farmer be affected more adversely than the large farmer by the withdrawal of subsidies? **Kanchan Chopra's** study **(Ch.13)** attempts to respond to this question. It examines subsidies given to fertilisers and irrigation water (both surface and ground water irrigation) with the explicit objective of determining whether their phased withdrawal will impact the small and marginal farmers more than that for large farmers. This study uses data sets from the 1990s to investigate into the likely effects of a withdrawal of irrigation and fertiliser subsidies on small and marginal farmers. Both single equation and simultaneous equation models are used to analyse data for 1991-92 and 1997-98.

It is found that, among the factors determining farmers' demand for fertiliser the statistically significant ones are: Irrigated area per hectare of gross cropped area (representing technological requirement of the crop mix) and access to credit. The results show that increasing area irrigated will raise area fertilised by 4.6 per cent for small farmers and by 4.2 per cent for large farmers. On the other hand, increase in fertiliser prices by 10 per cent will lead to negligible reduction in area fertilised by small and marginal farmers while that of larger farmers will decrease by 0.7 per cent. It implies that investment in irrigation infrastructure is preferable to subsidising irrigation water from the viewpoint of the small and marginal farmers. Their demand for fertiliser would increase more by increased investment in irrigation infrastructure than from a continuation of the subsidy regime. When looked at in conjunction with the finding (from NSS 1997-98) that small and marginal holdings have a smaller proportion of their area located within canal commands, this finding points towards the need to improve physical access to water through more infrastructure investment.

It is also found that a withdrawal of subsidy and a consequent rise in power tariff will have an adverse effect on spread of ground water irrigation. However, the adverse effect will be felt more or less uniformly by holdings of different size groups.

For surface water too, adoption of better technology as exemplified by improved seeds and location in canal command are the important factors determining proportion of area irrigated by a holding. Irrigation water charges and size of the holding are insignificant. This is uniformly true for the set of small, large, and all holdings.

There are three policy conclusions from the study. These are: (a) increases in canal irrigation charges shall not reduce use of irrigation by smaller farmers, provided they are located in canal commands. Policy must, therefore, concentrate on providing equitable access for smaller farmers to location within canal commands; (b) a gradual withdrawal of fertiliser subsidy shall not have an adverse impact on fertiliser use by smaller farmers if infrastructure by way of access to irrigation and credit is created; and (c) power price increases shall result in a decreased access to groundwater irrigation by all farmers but here again smaller farmers are not more adversely affected than large farmers.

The worst sufferers of the agrarian crisis in the 1990s are the small and marginal farmers and tenants. **Y.V. Krishna Rao (Ch.14)** attempts to analyse the root causes of the present agrarian distress and also the importance of small farmer economy in the agriculture sector and offers some policy prescriptions in the end. Presently Indian agriculture faces an acute, unprecedented and multi-dimensional crisis. The manifestations of this crisis are not restricted to a single region or sub-sector but are visible throughout the country affecting the entire farm sector with varying degrees of severity. The most tragic indicator of the deep and growing agrarian crisis is the alarming increase in the numbers of farmers committing suicides.

It is very necessary as well as important to realise that India will continue to be a small farm dominated economy and the planners and the rulers have to plan for viability and sustainability of these small farms. A development model for agriculture, giving a central place for all round development of small farms, is very much needed.

The study provides several policy prescriptions for raising agricultural growth to 4.0 or 4.5 per cent. These are: (a) public investment in agriculture and allied sectors should be stepped-up at least to the level of 10.0 per cent of the GDP from agriculture, so that this can attract more private sector investments; (b) while doubling the flow of rural credit, steps should be taken to see that 50 per cent of the credit in the public sector should go to the small and marginal farmers. Restructuring and democratisation of cooperative sector is needed; (c) 100 days Rural Employment Guarantee Scheme should be made a legally enforceable right and the scheme should be orientated to create permanent assets in agricultural and rural development sectors; (d) restructuring of agrarian relations by strictly implementing the land reform Acts and also by unearthing *benami* transactions. Distribution of all cultivable government waste lands as well as the reclaimed waste lands should be taken up without further loss of time; (e) a different model of development taking into consideration country's specifics should be worked out and implemented by mobilising our abundant land and labour resources; (f) States and Central Government should encourage and establish small-scale agro-based and skill-based rural industries on a big scale to provide employment to all the unemployed in the rural side. (g) to find financial resources for all such developmental schemes, the present low Tax-GDP ratio should be raised; and (h) Fiscal Responsibility and Budget Management Act should be scraped, so that it gives government elbowroom to take some monetary measures to raise funds for productive purposes. In addition government should take steps to un-earth the black money and end corruption.

The needs of the peasants have been growing over time while the regulatory institutional structures are crumbling. In this context, **D. Narasimha Reddy's** study **(Ch.15)** brings out the hiatus between the peasantry's growing need and willingness to switch to high productivity agriculture on the one hand, and the failure of the support systems, including public investment in infrastructure, research, extension, insurance, institutional credit, marketing and regulatory systems on the other.

The discussion on changes in agrarian structure shows that land reforms, in spite of inadequacies, along with demographic change led to a change in the landholding structure predominantly in favour of small and marginal holdings. There are many emerging challenges for small farmers. First, there has been technological shift from crops based on traditional variety to high-yielding varieties to hybrids to Genetically Modified (GM) crops. Second, there has been growing pressure on the agricultural resource base leading to land degradation, excessive use of chemical fertilisers and pesticides and soil erosion. Third, the institutional sources of credit, and other input supplies like fertilisers, pesticides and seeds have been on the decline over the years. Fourth, non-farm sector has not developed. Fifth is the challenge of facing WTO agreements.

The evidence at both macro and micro level presented in the study shows that there has been a rapid retrogression in the agricultural support systems, which have been at the root of the present crisis in the agricultural sector in general, and the vast majority of the poor peasantry in particular. Decline in public investment in agriculture, poor performance or collapse of public institutions relating to extension, credit, seeds, marketing etc. are responsible for this crisis. One of the worst set backs to agriculture in general and small farmers in particular relates to the diminishing share of institutional credit. There was a decline in the share of both short-term and long-term loans as share of total commercial bank credit to agriculture. The small borrowers are worst affected. Even if we ignore cooperatives, the special institutions like Regional Rural Banks (RRBs) have been completely disoriented towards profits without priority under the reforms. A micro survey in Andhra Pradesh shows that the institutional loans account only for about 20 per cent of the total loans and about the same proportion of the amount borrowed. The modal interest rate on the private credit is 36 per cent and over 83 per cent of private lending is at 24 per cent or more. This is one of the main reasons for farmers' suicides. Similarly, farmers face many problems in marketing as the trader and other middlemen exploit the farmers.

With no immediate prospect of any substantial shift of workforce to non-agricultural sector, the prospects of improving the condition of the peasantry is linked to switch towards higher productivity on-farm and off-farm activities. This requires improved capabilities of farm households and improvements in infrastructure. There is a need for higher levels of public investment in education, health and housing facilities and improved institutional support systems for the small farm agriculture in order to come out of the crisis and face global competition.

Natural disasters can be extremely disruptive to farmers and to others whose incomes depend on a successful crop. Society can gain from more efficient sharing of crop and natural disaster risks. However, the costs associated with traditional agricultural risk programmes have historically exceeded the gains from improved risk sharing. Against this background, the study of **Peter Hazell and Jerry Skees (Ch.16)** explores government intervention in agricultural risk markets and discusses new approaches to risk sharing with limited government involvement. In particular, the paper builds a case for introducing negotiable state-contingent contracts settled on area crop yield estimates or locally appropriate weather indices. These instruments could replace traditional crop insurance at a lower cost to government while meeting the risk management needs of a wider clientele.

Area-based index contracts, such as regional rainfall insurance, could meet all the requirements of creating an effective insurance mechanism. The essential principle of area-based index insurance is that contracts are written against specific perils or events (e.g., yield loss, drought, or flood) defined and recorded at a regional level (at a district level or block level in the case of yields, or at a local weather station in the case of insured weather events). In its simplest form, insurance is sold based on the value of protection desired. The insured should be able to select any value of insurance. The premium rate can be quoted as rupees per one hundred rupees of protection. Buyers in the same region would pay the same premium rate. Likewise, once an event has triggered a payment, all buyers in the region would receive the same rate of payment. That rate would be multiplied by the value insured. Area-based yield insurance requires long and reliable series of area-yield data, and this kind of data is not available in most developing countries. Hence, alternative weather indices may be more attractive, such as area rainfall or temperature, for which there are available time-series data collected on a regular basis.

Area based index insurance has some attractive features such as less adverse selection, less administrative costs, potential for a secondary market, can be sold to non-farmers, can be linked to microfinance and can clear the way for innovation in mutual insurance. However, despite the promise of area-based index insurance, there are significant issues that must be resolved before it could be widely adopted. These include a) the need for secure weather event measurements; b) the actuarial challenges that are present due to oscillations in sea surface temperatures; c) the covariate risk problem for the insurer; and d) the high frequency of some catastrophic events.

Significant developments have emerged in India in recent years to offer rainfall insurance contracts. ICICI Lombard General Insurance Company began a pilot insurance programme that will pay farmers when there are rain shortfalls in one area, and pay others in case of excess rain. In the first year, ICICI Lombard offered drought policies *via* a small microfinance bank in southern India (BASIX) and the excess rain covers through the ICICI Bank. BASIX used ICICI Lombard and technical assistance from the Commodity Risk Management Group of the World Bank to develop and launch the new rainfall insurance products. BASIX began operations in March 2001, in the districts of Mahbubnagar in Andhra Pradesh and Raichur and Gulbarga in Karnataka. In 2003, the new rainfall insurance was targeted at individual farmers for three categories of groundnut and castor farmers: small, medium, and large.

Given the apparent attractiveness of area-based index insurance, private sector should have entered this field quickly. But, this has not happened on any widespread scale. One reason for this is that there are several setup problems that might require public intervention to jumpstart activity, particularly in developing countries. Setting up basic infrastructure to get started may be an important role for government.

5. Poverty and Environment

Three papers in this section look at selected issues relating to poverty and environment. The issues discussed in this section are: How to achieve empowerment of the poor? What are the linkages among environment, employment and sustainable development? How to develop a model to have better project design for climate change effect and its abatement?

The anti-poverty strategy in India is in the process of shifting its focus from poverty ratios to human development and empowerment of the poor. In this context, **V.M. Rao (Ch.17)** looks at the transition of anti-poverty strategy in India from its somewhat simplistic beginning with the poverty ratio to the current phase marked by far more sophisticated conceptualisation of poverty in terms of multiple deprivations including dimensions like power, dignity and justice. The purpose is to point out the weaknesses in the strategy and the blocks impeding its progress.

To demonstrate the weak foundations for empowerment of the poor, the study selected three critical policy areas: employment, food and land security; human development and access to resources and decision-making related to resources. Without an adequate measure of security in relation to availability of employment (including access to land) and basic needs like food, the poor would not be able to look and plan beyond the day-to-day struggle for subsistence. The next step is to provide them with opportunities to invest in their own health, education, skills and assets to strengthen their capabilities to participate in and benefit from mainstream growth and development processes. There are by now several examples of developing countries achieving dramatic reduction in poverty by promoting human development. In a democratic polity like India, improvement in human development needs to be complemented by building up institutions enabling the poor to play a role in the formulation of development strategies and priorities affecting their lives and welfare.

The mainstream economy presents a far more formidable barrier to empowerment of the poor than those noted above. These are the poverty generation process operating in the economy. Two illustrations for the marginalisation process are given in the study. The first illustration is the marginalisation process in agriculture. The second illustration is in a sense complementary to the first. There are clear indications that even after acquiring education beyond the school level the rural poor are unable to have access to urban growth activities and stagnate in informal sector with wages and working conditions no better than those in agriculture.

The shift needs a strong foundation in the form of improving the security of the poor and meeting their basic needs. The indications are that the achievements made so far fall far short of this requirement. The weakness lies in the very basics of the policymaking to help the poor. The emphasis has remained on giving relief to the poor rather than confronting the powerful poverty generating processes operating in the society. However, momentous changes are occurring among the rural poor and in village communities in the course of their opening up to the wider world. A careful consideration of these changes could lead poverty researches towards issues and themes helping these researches to gain in relevance and usefulness. We have spent far too much time in measuring poverty and in settling the statistical quarrels. The need is to move towards understanding the poor and investigating how developing societies generate and mitigate poverty.

Understanding the prospects and conditions for sustainable development is necessary for framing better policies on development. Keeping this in view, the study of **Indira Hirway and Piet Terhal (Ch.18)** examines the linkages among environment, employment and sustainable development. The study aims at integrating various dimensions of sustainability in a capital-theoretic context. It also discusses the prospects of and conditions for sustainable development with reference to empirical studies in three Indian states.

The disruptive capital accumulations of the established growth model and the prevalence of the present unequal global system can be challenged through initiating virtuous circles, to start with at a local level, that strengthen the links between natural capital and man-made capital through the use of human agency, *i.e.* massive employment generation. The virtuous circles at the local level can collectively impact on the macro level under an enabling macro environment.

The three environmental problems addressed in the study are (1) degradation of coastal regions in Gujarat, (2) depletion and degradation of forests in Orissa, and (3) environmental degradation in dry regions in Andhra Pradesh. One common feature of all the three regions is that economic growth has put tremendous pressure on environmental resources, and as a result, the environment is severely depleted and degraded in these regions. It seems that the development strategies adopted by the state governments have not viewed natural capital as an important component of the total capital stock. The process of man-made capital accumulation, therefore, has neglected natural capital, leading to its destruction.

Instead of mainstreaming natural capital by integrating it with the development strategy, all the three governments have designed programmes for environmental regeneration at the micro level to address the micro level problems emerging from the environmental degradation. NGOs also have taken up such programmes on their own or under government programmes. The major programmes are watershed development programmes, joint forest management programmes, soil and water conservation programmes, wasteland development programmes, water-harvesting structures etc. These programmes primarily address the sufferings of the local people including the poor. They attempt to meet their basic needs like fuel wood, fodder and water; to protect their livelihood in agriculture, forestry, fishery, animal husbandry etc. and to protect them from natural calamities (caused by environmental depletion and degradation) like droughts, floods, cyclones and even tsunamis. In short, the programmes aim at promoting virtuous circles of poverty reduction and environmental regeneration.

One major observation of the different successful case studies is that strong community organisation, identification of the right technology, equitable ownership of assets, equal distribution of benefits and inclusion of the poor are some of the essential conditions for virtuous circles to operate successfully.

Efforts to turn the vicious circles between environmental degradation and poverty in to virtuous circles between poverty reduction and environmental regeneration at the micro level are not only welcome, but also essential for reversing the impact of disruptive capital accumulation. The case studies have given enough evidence to indicate that such efforts are feasible and desirable. The virtuous circles at the local level do contribute to poverty reduction and can contribute more in the long run. However, they can collectively impact on the macro level under an enabling macro environment.

Climate change effects are being talked as a global common problem. **Gopal Kadekodi (Ch.19)** takes up the issue of designing a specific economic problem of accounting for the costs and benefits of abating and developing adaptation strategies. More specifically, it examines the question of appropriate discount rate for an abatement project.

Climate change effects are visible only slowly, but very remarkably and irreversibly over long periods of time. The net effects are permanent losses of soil, soil fertility, forest cover, changes in water resources and surface hydrology and increasing human health problems. These invariably lead to a cycle of human misery and migration due to threats to food and livelihood security and increased risks. Policy interventions, therefore, need to be woven into other sectoral, social and economic measures.

Both national economies, multi-lateral agencies such as UNEP and World Bank and major civic society groups such as CITIES, WWF, Greenpeace and IUCN and several others are posing one common economic question: How to develop models of climate change impact, and strategies (scientific, economic and political) to abate their growing adverse effects? Climate change being such a slow process that generation-by-generation one can afford to ignore it or develop short run strategies.

While introducing any economic and investment oriented projects and strategies, one has to deal with the long term costs and benefits from abating and arresting climate change effects and development of adaptive strategies. That begs a major question on discounting the costs and benefits on such activities.

An attempt is made in this study to deduce the path of long term social discount rate to be more appropriate for assessing investments and climate change abatements strategies and to provide some indicative estimates based on very limited data from India. The estimates using Indian National Accounts data show that the average discount rate is 10.73 per cent during 1990-98. Using the mean and variance during this period, the study derives time dependent declining discount rate for three phases. In the first phase of ten years the discount rate be maintained at 10.75 per cent, in the next leg of ten years it can be kept at 6.75 per cent, subsequently, the discount rate be kept a low of 1.5 per cent. This analysis indicates that in the climate change related negotiations on compensations for the effects of ocean rise, temperature rise and shifts in the maximum and minimum temperatures, shifting of rainfall cycles, or green house gas emissions, countries such as India should make a case for compensations and investment strategies against long run health and other adverse impacts on land, water and forests. This is possible with models of possible impacts in the long run only. Thus, a case can be made for having declining discount rates in the relevant economic models.

Section I

Macro Issues in Development

1

Economic Reforms and Changing Role of the Reserve Bank of India

Y.V. REDDY

1. Introduction

Professor Lance Taylor of MIT once commented that an economist is one who teaches the students in the morning, writes academic papers in the evening, and advises the authorities on policy matters in the afternoon. Spanning a career from teaching at the Institute of Economic Growth (among others), to an author of innumerable articles on agricultural economy, food security, rural poverty and environmental issues, as well as a member of the Union Planning Commission, the Seventh and the Eighth Finance Commissions, and the Economic Advisory Council to the Prime Minister, Professor C. H. Hanumantha Rao is a living example of this principle. Professor Rao's contribution in the field of agricultural economics, amongst others, is particularly seminal, both in academic as well as in policy sphere.

Amongst his various positions in the public policy arena, it may not be well known that he was also a member of the Board of Directors of the Reserve Bank of India (RBI) for six years during 1994-2000. This period witnessed momentous changes in Indian financial sector in general and the RBI in particular with a migration from the direct to indirect instruments of monetary policy, reduction of the extent of statutory pre-emptions, introduction of prudential regulations, development of the government debt and foreign exchange markets, effective management of large external capital flows, and a number of innovations in the payment and settlement system. An account of the evolutionary trends in the functioning of the RBI would, therefore, be a fitting tribute to Professor Rao.

The aim of this paper is not to narrate the financial sector reforms in India; instead, it tries to capture the evolution of the functioning of the

RBI in the context of the economic reforms.[1] The discussion is both temporal as well as functional. Thus, the paper begins with an identification of the different phases of the changing role of the RBI in Section 2. Section 3 probes into the changing role of the RBI in terms of its various functions, such as, monetary authority, public debt manager, bank regulator, lender of last resort, and others. The legal and institutional changes that acted as catalysts for the changes in the role of the RBI are discussed in Section 4. Finally, Section 5 presents various issues and the outlook in this regard.

2. Evolution

The changing role of the RBI can be reviewed in four broad phases. These are: (a) the initial phase (1934-1948), (b) the maturing phase (1948 till bank nationalisation in 1969), (c) the phase of Government dominance (1969-1991), and (d) the economic reform phase (1991-till date).[2]

The RBI was inaugurated as a shareholders' bank on April 1, 1935 in accordance with the provisions of the Reserve Bank of India Act, 1934, as the central bank of the erstwhile British India. The objective of the Bank, as set out in the Preamble to the Act is to focus on monetary stability and operations of currency and credit system in India. Even after the separation of Burma (now Myanmar) in April 1937, the Bank functioned as the currency authority of that country till June 5, 1942 and as banker to the Government of Burma till March 31, 1947. On partition of the country in August 1947, the Bank continued to render central banking services to the Dominion of Pakistan until June 30, 1948. In view of the need for close integration between policies of the RBI and those of the Government, the question of State ownership of the RBI was raised from time to time even during the pre-Independence days. With the cessation of the Bank's role as the central banker to India as well as Pakistan after September 30, 1948, the intention of State ownership of the RBI fructified in the form of the Reserve Bank of India (Transfer to Public Ownership) Act, 1948 which nationalised the RBI and it became a State-owned institution on January 1, 1949. During this initial phase (since inception of the RBI till its nationalisation in 1949), the RBI, even as a private institution, was made to function under the dictates of the Government. During this period, measures were, in fact, taken to curb its capacity for independent actions and even threats were issued to supersede the Bank's

---

1. For an account of the contours of financial sector reforms in India, see Reddy (1998) and Mohan (2004).

2. See RBI (1970) and Balachandran (1998) for a discussion of the first two phases.

Board should it recommend monetary and exchange rate policies incompatible with the Government's scheme of actions.

After the country's Independence from the British rule in 1947 and the nationalisation of the RBI in 1949, the RBI was required to perform, besides the traditional central banking role, a wide range of promotional functions to accelerate the pace of economic development with social justice through the process of planning. Thus, one of the major tasks of the RBI was building up of a modern, sound and adequate banking and credit infrastructure. The RBI was vigorously involved in promoting the institutionalisation of credit delivery to agriculture and industry, and promotion and mobilisation of overall savings in the economy. This required active involvement of the RBI in institution building and expansion of its activities, as observed up to the nationalisation of 14 major banks in 1969. Through necessary legal changes, the functions of debt management, banking regulation, deposit insurance, and exchange control were conferred on the RBI. Thus, under the provisions of the RBI Act, 1934, the Public Debt Act, 1944 and the Public Debt Rules, the RBI was conferred the power to manage and administer the public debt of the Central and State Governments. The Bank was empowered under the Banking Regulation Act, 1949, to curb undesirable banking practices and protect the interests of depositors. Deposit Insurance Corporation of India was set up in 1962 (renamed as Deposit Insurance and Credit Guarantee Corporation in 1978) as a wholly owned subsidiary of the RBI to provide insurance cover to the bank depositors. The co-operative banking system was partially brought within the statutory ambit of the Bank in 1966. The majority ownership of the country's largest commercial bank, namely the State Bank of India, set up in 1955 as the successor to the Imperial Bank of India, was vested with the RBI. The RBI also had a role in setting up of several specialised financial institutions at the national and regional levels, which, *inter alia*, include the erstwhile Industrial Finance Corporation of India, the erstwhile Industrial Development Bank of India, State Financial Corporations and the erstwhile Unit Trust of India. In the interest of making the most prudent use of the foreign exchange resources, the Foreign Exchange Regulation Act was enacted in 1947 and provided the statutory basis for placing the subject under the RBI's control. This Act remained in force for little over half-a-century though with substantial modifications in 1973. The RBI's responsibilities and functions were significantly redefined through various statutory amendments, to enable it to function as an important agency in building post-independent India.

The period during 1969 to 1991, *i.e.*, up to the initiation of economic reforms, may be called the phase of Government dominance. With the nationalisation of 14 major banks in 1969 and another six banks in 1980, the RBI became an important instrument for planned development. During the period from the nationalisation of the RBI in 1949 until nationalisation of 14 major commercial banks in 1969, the RBI matured into a full-fledged professionally managed central bank, perhaps one of the foremost in the developing countries. However, it was during this phase of institution building and ascendancy of planned economic development that the system of *ad hoc* Treasury Bills and automatic monetisation of government deficit got institutionalised. It was agreed between the Government and the RBI that the RBI would replenish the Government's cash balances by creation of *ad hoc* Treasury Bills in favour of the RBI. The *ad hoc* Treasury Bills, which were meant to be temporary, gained, over the years, a permanent as well as a cumulative character. Indeed, it became an attractive source of financing government expenditures since it was available at an interest rate pegged at 4.6 per cent per annum since 1974, *i.e.*, actually at a negative real interest rate!

The nationalisation of major banks brought about a situation where the Government became the owner of a number of banks, but the supervision of these banks was, in turn, conducted by the RBI, which was also owned by the Government. The development financial institutions (DFIs), on the other hand, were not only under the control of the Government but were also not subjected to prudential regulation or supervision. Though the situation was not unique to India and was somewhat similar to that in some European countries, in India, persistence of high fiscal deficits posed serious problems for prudent monetary management. For cost-effective and easy access to market borrowings, the interest rates were administered and the Statutory Liquidity Ratio (SLR) requirements of the banking sector were periodically hiked. With the government ownership of banks, there was a captive market for Government securities. At the same time, recourse of the Government to RBI credit led to high levels of monetisation. To neutralise the effect of monetisation on the price level, the RBI had to intermittently increase the Cash Reserve Ratio (CRR) requirements for the scheduled commercial banks. Besides, the above pre-emption of funds, banks were required to extend a large share of their credit to priority sectors at pre-determined interest rates. Thus, only a small proportion of banks' funds was left for credit to non-priority sectors at much higher rates of interest. There was, thus, a significant cross subsidisation of interest rates across sectors within the administered interest rate structure, wherein there was little scope for banks to assess or price the risks of borrowing entities.

The period since 1991 till date, which marks the phase of economic reforms, has seen ongoing efforts by the Government in designing and implementing various reform measures, especially in the external and the financial sectors. The crisis of 1991 was essentially a balance of payments crisis triggered by the Gulf-crisis, which caused huge increase in the price of oil. In view of India's heavy dependence on imported oil, the import bill surged and foreign exchange reserves fell steeply from US $ 3.11 billion in August 1990 to US $ 845 million in January 1991, amounting to less than two weeks' imports. There was a sharp downgrading of India's credit rating and foreign private lending dried up. Though the immediate task at hand was that of stabilisation, these developments led to the realisation that behind the crisis lay the deep structural imbalances in the form of structural rigidities, lack of effective competition, poor performance of public enterprises, lack of fiscal prudence and an incentive framework inconsistent with productivity gains. The stabilisation programme was thus accompanied by measures of structural reforms to remove the structural rigidities afflicting the various sectors of the economy, of which the reforms of the financial and external sector are the important constituents. The reforms in the financial sector were guided by the Report of the Committee on Financial System (Narasimham Committee I, Government of India, 1991) and the Report of the Committee on the Banking Sector Reforms (Narasimham Committee II, Government of India, 1998) while that of reform in the external sector, accompanied by other changes, was guided by the Report of High Level Committee on Balance of Payments (Chairman: Dr. C. Rangarajan; RBI, 1993).

It is essential to recognise that reforms in the financial and external sectors are, in a large measure, part of the overall economic reforms and necessarily involve redefining the role of the public institutions as well as the market participants. Since financial sector reforms in India were taken up in the early part of the reform cycle, the changing role of the RBI acquired prominence in the reform process as a whole. Further, perhaps unlike some reforms in a few countries where policies were driven by compulsions of crises or sudden structural shifts from a socialist to market oriented economies, India adopted public policies largely designed domestically to suit the country context. In this, the RBI could play a significant role in both advising other public institutions of policy and transforming itself to enhance efficiency coupled with stability. There is a wide spread recognition of the achievements of the reform process in both financial and external sectors.

It would be useful to explore the changing role of the RBI in this success and seek the emerging challenges to meet the national aspirations for higher growth accompanied by stability, while emphasising equity. The RBI performs several functions and it may be appropriate to trace the changes in regard to each of the major functions, namely, as monetary authority, debt-manager, manager of external sector, regulator and supervisor, lender of last resort, and other functions relating to currency and payments system.[3] It is useful to trace this evolution since 1990s in terms of the functional features of the RBI.

3. Changing Contours of Functional Roles of the RBI

It can be argued that in several countries the text-book description of functions of central banks has undergone changes in the context of the economic reform programme; these changes are significant in Indian case. There is, however, no single model of the changing functionalities of a central bank as an economy undergoes a process of economic liberalisation. On the contrary, the contours of a specific function would crucially depend upon the phase of development and the objective conditions of the economy. Hence, the discussion of the changing role of the RBI, since the initiation of reforms in the Indian economy, will essentially be in terms of a "before-after" analysis.

3.1 Monetary Authority

How had the RBI's function as a monetary authority changed in recent years? In order to appreciate the context, a mention must be made of the basic traits of the scenario in the pre-1990s era. The scenario was essentially one of 'financial repression', *a la* Mckinnon and Shaw. The regime was characterised by: a) high level of automatic monetisation of the fiscal deficits; b) Government's market borrowings at rates of interest unrelated to market conditions; c) a plethora of other administered interest rates; and d) a high level of statutory pre-emption of resources from the banking sector. Besides, with various forex-related regulations, the quantum of cross-border capital flows was limited and the monetary policy was conducted essentially in a closed economy framework. As a

---

3. See Capie (1997), Siklos (2002), and Crockett (2002) for a discussion on evolution of central banking; see Chandavarkar (1996), Vasudevan (2003), and Udeshi (2004) on central banking in developing countries.

result, the RBI had to rely on the use of the direct instruments of monetary control, such as Cash Reserve Ratio (CRR) and Statutory Liquidity Ratio (SLR) along with various interest rate and credit controls to regulate the monetary system. The reform process initiated since the early 1990s changed all these in a phased manner. With deregulation of interest rates, rationalisation of CRR and SLR, structural reforms in the real economy, phasing out of *ad hoc* Treasury Bills, activation of the Bank Rate as a policy instrument and reduction in the reliance on refinance, the scenario was gradually transformed from a repressed regime to a deregulated, decentralised, competitive and open financial system. What were the consequent changes in RBI's conduct of monetary policy?

For policy analysis, the assumption of a 'closed' economy was increasingly changed to an 'open economy' – this is perhaps the first basic trait of the changing facets of monetary policy. Illustratively, whereas in 1989-90, 'net RBI credit to the Central Government' accounted for 95 per cent of Reserve Money (RM) and 'net foreign exchange assets of RBI' accounted for eight per cent of RM, with stoppage of automatic monetisation and liberal capital inflows, these figures as on February 18, 2005 were (-)1.0 per cent and 125 per cent, respectively.[4] Such changes in the composition of reserve money had profound implications for operation of monetary policy. From the vantage point of 2005, it seems surprising that the finite amount of government paper at the disposal of RBI posed a constraint for monetary policy operations.

Since 1985-86, in line with Chakravarty Committee's recommendations, the operating framework of monetary policy was, what may be loosely called "monetary targeting with feedback" (RBI, 1985). Questions were raised about the appropriateness of such a framework in the face of financial innovation and the resulting perceived instability in the money demand function. The Working Group on Money Supply (1998) had sought to address some of these issues (RBI, 1998). The Group redefined the monetary aggregates and recommended compilation and analysis of credit and liquidity measures as also flow of funds for a better appreciation of the evolving financial structure. The most significant observation of the Group was on the changing nature of transmission mechanism as it highlighted that the interest rate channel is gaining in importance. In line with this thinking, the scenario changed in 1998-99

---

4. On account of presence of RBI's net non-monetary liabilities (an offsetting term in RM), sources of RM like 'net RBI credit to the Central Government' or 'net foreign exchange assets of the RBI' can account for more than 100 per cent of RM.

with the pronounced adoption of a "multiple indicator approach." In fact, the Monetary and Credit Policy for the First Half of 1998-99, noted categorically that:

> "It is not easy to evolve, in the present circumstances, a monetary conditions index or a clear–cut interest rate channel of transmission of effects of monetary policy. The information base required for such an exercise is substantial. In the absence of frequent data on output developments with minimal lags, and on turnovers in different markets, the information on rate movements alone would not give a full picture of the monetary conditions, and therefore, such information should be interpreted with circumspection. It can, however, be utilised in conjunction with other more reliable indicators for purposes of policy-making. As a first step to move in this direction, it is necessary to adopt a multiple indicator approach wherein interest rates or rates of return in different markets (money, capital and government securities markets) along with such data as on currency, credit extended by banks and financial institutions, fiscal position, trade, capital flows, inflation rate, exchange rate, refinancing and transactions in foreign exchange available on high frequency basis are juxtaposed with output data for drawing policy perspectives."

As far as objectives of monetary policy are concerned, attaining price stability and ensuring availability of adequate credit to the productive sectors of the economy still continue to be the over-riding concerns. The relative emphasis on either of these objectives, however, depends on the prevailing circumstances in the economy. The recent period has seen the increasing emphasis on another aspect, *viz.*, financial stability. In the Indian context, financial stability could be interpreted to embrace: (a) ensuring uninterrupted financial transactions; (b) maintenance of a level of confidence in the financial system amongst all the participants and stakeholders; and (c) absence of excess volatility that unduly and adversely affects real economic activity.[5] In fact, a look at the recent monetary policy statements allows one to discern a distinct effort towards increasing the operational effectiveness of monetary policy by broadening and deepening various segments of financial markets and strengthening prudential and supervisory norms. The emphasis of financial stability is not confined to banking sector alone. As avoiding volatility in financial markets can be seen as a public good, the basic philosophy of RBI's intervention in money, forex and government securities markets had been dictated by the concern to ensure the uninterrupted availability of this public good.

Along with the changes in the monetary framework, the operating procedure of monetary policy also underwent significant transformation with an increasing emphasis on the indirect instruments. The interest rate regulations have been almost completely dismantled barring a few

---

5. See Reddy (2004a) for details on the Indian experience on financial stability.

exceptions. The liquidity management in the system is carried out through reverse repo/repo operations under a Liquidity Adjustment Facility (LAF), open market operations (OMO) in the form of outright sales/purchases of government securities and the Market Stabilisation Scheme (MSS). The OMO are supplemented by strategic private placement of government securities, access to the RBI's standing facilities and direct interest rate signals through changes in the Bank Rate/LAF rates. The LAF enables the RBI to modulate short-term liquidity under varied financial market conditions in order to ensure stable conditions in the overnight (call) money market. LAF is well placed to emerge as the principal operating instrument, with fixed overnight reverse repo and repo interest rates providing the corridor to stabilise overnight interest rates, as the interest rate channel of monetary transmission continues to strengthen. Further, in order to address the issue of sterilisation in view of the declining stock of marketable government securities with RBI, MSS was introduced in April 2004 to absorb liquidity of a more enduring nature by way of sterilisation through issuances of Treasury Bills/government dated securities. The reliance on reserve requirements, particularly CRR, has been reduced as an instrument of monetary control.

Another change in the functioning of monetary policy is with regard to the refinancing facilities available to the commercial banks. Till the early 1990s, scheduled commercial banks were provided refinance under various facilities, such as Food Credit Refinance, Stand-by Refinance, Export Credit Refinance, 182-day Treasury Bill Refinance. A major change in this context occurred in October 1991 when all sector-specific refinance facilities (excepting Export Credit Refinance) were withdrawn. Subsequently, refinance against government securities was introduced in October 1992 but withdrawn in July 1996 due to its poor utilisation. Presently, liquidity support is provided under two schemes, *viz.*, collateralised lending facility to PDs and export credit refinance facility to scheduled banks. The new arrangement has implications for the effectiveness of the monetary policy. The collateralised standing facilities available at the discretion of banks/PDs provide a limited automatic liquidity cushion to stabilise short-term interest rates. In the process, it complements the main operating instrument of LAF which is available at the discretion of the Reserve Bank.

A major step towards market-based monetary policy was reactivation of the Bank Rate as a policy instrument in April 1997, which had become dormant since the 1980s. In fact, a comparison of the decade-wise number of changes in the use of Bank Rate reveals an interesting fact—while during the 1980s, the Bank Rate was changed only once, during the 1990s, it was changed as many as 10 times. Of late, with market-determined price of primary money essentially at rates emerging out of LAF auctions, the Bank Rate is used essentially as a signalling instrument of the monetary policy.

In order to obviate the problem of lack of government paper for monetary operations, a memorandum of understanding detailing the rationale and operational modalities of the Market Stabilisation Scheme (MSS) was signed between the Government of India and the RBI on March 25, 2004. The intention of the MSS is essentially to differentiate liquidity absorptions by way of sterilisation from the day to day normal liquidity management operations. Thus, at the current juncture, while not ruling out outright transactions in government securities through OMO, the RBI seeks to manage the liquidity mainly through two instruments, *viz.*, MSS and LAF. With the introduction of MSS, as the volumes under MSS rose, the visible liquidity under LAF declined. The active use of LAF supplemented with MSS has minimised the volatility in the short-term interest rates and exchange rate. Further, it has been bringing about a progressive convergence of the market repo rates, call rates and collateralised borrowing and lending obligations (CBLO) rates with the LAF reverse repo rate thereby imparting stronger inter-linkages amongst these funding markets.

This shift from the direct to the indirect instruments, adoption of multiple indicators, increasing emphasis on financial stability, and opening up of the "erstwhile" postulate of closed economy—all constitute the evolving contours of the changing face of monetary policy in recent years in the context of a gradual opening of a closed economy.

3.2. Debt Manager

What was the nature of the government debt market in the 1980s? With the administered interest rate structure and higher statutory pre-emptions, there was little scope for development of an active debt market. The Government was borrowing at the pre-announced coupon rates almost wholly from a captive group of investors, particularly banks.[6] In a significant departure from this scenario, the 1990s saw the development of an active government security market.

---

6. For a discussion on the development of debt markets in India, see Chapter 18 on "Development of Debt Markets in India" in Reddy (2000) and Chapter 6 on "Issues and Challenges in the Development of Debt Market in India" in Reddy (2002).

But why was the RBI interested in development of debt market? The primary interest of the RBI in debt market is premised on its criticality in the transmission mechanism of monetary policy especially with a move towards reliance on the indirect instruments of policy. Currently, the Government securities market is the overwhelming part of the entire debt market and the interest rates in this market provide benchmarks for the system as a whole.

The reforms have encompassed the market practices in both primary and secondary markets, strengthening the institutional structure, developing new and innovative instruments, widening the participant base, establishing a regulatory framework, initiating changes in legal framework and imparting transparency in operations. Since 1992, through the introduction of the auction system, the government borrowings have been at market-related interest rates. The abolition of automatic monetisation, in the mid-1990s, has further enhanced the market orientation of government securities. Furthermore, the pre-emption of their funds, especially of banks, has been reduced through the progressive reduction of the SLR.[7]

Many new instruments across the maturity spectrum have been introduced and experimented with. Apart from the traditional fixed coupon bonds, instruments such as zero coupon bonds, floating rate bonds and capital indexed bonds were also introduced, of which the floating rate bonds have proved to be more attractive. Treasury Bills of various maturities too ranging from 14-day to 364-day were introduced from time to time in different combinations to offer a wider choice to investors. The maturities of most of the new dated securities were initially compressed below 10 years as it coincided with the period of high interest rate cycle. Moreover, the initial years of introduction of the auction system also required shortening of the maturity structure. In the last two to three years, to bring a balance in the maturity structure and to mitigate the roll-over risk, longer maturities have been preferred, and consequently, the tenor has been elongated up to 30 years.

Is there a conflict between the RBI's role as a debt manager and authority for implementing monetary policy? It is often argued that being the debt manager for the Government creates problems for the central

---

7. Despite lowering the SLR to the statutory minimum of 25 per cent, banks continue to hold a much higher level of government securities. This could be attributed more to portfolio choice rather than regulatory fiat as evident from the recent reduction in excess SLR holdings by banks. The excess holding of SLR securities was accompanied by higher credit growth.

bank as the timing and amounts of government securities issuance may not always coincide with the imperatives of its monetary stance. The stated intention is to remove the friction by separating the debt management function from the central bank when certain pre-conditions relating to institutional framework are fulfilled especially since in a situation of high fiscal deficit, separation of the two functions could increase the risk. Thus, the separation of debt and monetary management functions is a medium-term process contingent upon the development of financial markets, reasonable control over the fisc and the establishment of necessary institutional arrangements and legislative changes. In this context, the Fiscal Responsibility and Budget Management (FRBM) Act, 2003 promises to instil fiscal discipline and to bring down the fiscal and revenue deficits within an identified time span.[8]

As part of the debt market reforms, the borrowings by the States, which were virtually managed by RBI as a tranche for all States with a standard maturity, are now differentiated through a combination of a tranche route and an auction route from 1998-99. Through the auction route the State Governments enter the market on their own to the extent of 5 to 35 per cent of their gross borrowings of the year, which is decided by the Government of India and the Planning Commission. The timing and volume of issues for auction, however, is decided by the RBI in consultation with the State Governments, taking into account the market and liquidity conditions. Some of the State Governments are able to borrow under the auction route at a rate lower than the tranche rate – the latter being broadly fixed with a 25 to 50 basis points mark-up over the yield of corresponding stock of the Central Government. Further, as part of overall financial sector reforms, the RBI and the State Governments have strived to cap the guarantees given by the latter and also ensure that banks and other financial institutions invest in projects on commercial considerations rather than depend on government guarantees for this purpose. The States have also been emphasising fiscal rectitude through measures for revenue augmentation, expenditure containment and institutional reforms to strengthen the process of fiscal consolidation. Some of the states have also initiated measures to provide statutory backing to fiscal reforms through an enabling legislation. The objective is to eliminate the revenue deficit and contain the fiscal deficit in the medium-term.

---

8. Embedded in the Act is the provision that the RBI will not participate in the primary market of government securities from 2006. However, it could continue to have the freedom to operate in the secondary market.

Thus, in the context of financial sector reform, there have been substantial changes in RBI's role as a debt manager—of both the Central Government and the State Governments. While these changes have led to a market-determined auction based system, they have not necessarily led to an improved position of the fisc. Nevertheless, with the enactment of the FRBM Act, 2003 by the Union Government and several State Governments, one would expect the situation to improve.

3.3 Managing the External Sector

As already mentioned, a basic feature of the changes in monetary policy was a switch away from the assumption of 'closed economy' for policy purpose. Thus, managing the external sector is expectedly a major aspect of the changing face of the RBI in recent years.

It is well-known that in view of the colonial past, the Indian public opinion was punctuated by caution and conservatism about the external sector. Thus, the pre-reform management of external sector was marked by export pessimism, pegged exchange rate regime (initially to pound sterling till 1975 and later to an undisclosed currency basket till 1992), and large-scale capital controls. The initiation of reforms changed all these. The broad approach to reform in the external sector, as guided by the Report of the High Level Committee of Balance Payments chaired by Dr. C. Rangarajan (RBI, 1993), was marked by its recommendations for: a) improvement in exports (both merchandise and invisibles); b) modulation of import demand on the basis of the availability of current receipts; c) enhancement of non-debt creating flows to limit the debt service burden; d) adoption of market-determined exchange rate; e) building up the foreign exchange reserves to avoid liquidity crises; and f) elimination of the dependence on short-term debt.[9]

Almost all these recommendations were implemented in a phased manner. After a year's experience with a dual exchange rate system, exchange rate of the rupee became market-determined in March 1993. With the main objective being to ensure that economic fundamentals are reflected in the external value of the rupee, market intervention is primarily aimed at countering excess volatility and speculation. Payment restrictions on all current account transactions were removed with the acceptance of the obligations of Article VIII of the IMF's Articles of Agreement in August 1994. Non-debt creating flows in the form of foreign

---

9. These measures are discussed in detail in Chapter 8 in Reddy (2002); see also Rangarajan (2000), Jalan (2002), and RBI (2004).

direct and portfolio investment, and long maturity commercial borrowings were encouraged. Short-term debt, banking capital, and non-resident deposits were modulated. Furthermore, significant relaxations have been allowed for capital outflows in the form of direct and portfolio investments, non-resident deposits, repatriation of assets and funds held abroad. Indian residents can now open foreign currency accounts with banks in India. What had been the change in the functioning of the RBI as a result of these measures?

It needs to be recognised that one of the basic functions of the RBI up to the early 1990s was related to administration of various kinds of controls on foreign exchange transactions. A major departure from that regime is that the focus of the foreign exchange policy now is on management, rather than control.[10] The Foreign Exchange Regulation Act (FERA), 1973 has been replaced by the Foreign Exchange Management Act (FEMA), 2000 with effect from June 1, 2000. FERA sought to control and to regulate foreign exchange transactions with the express intent of conserving foreign exchange and it contained various prohibitions and administered regulations by 'grant of permission.' With the replacement of FERA by FEMA, the focus of foreign exchange management has shifted from conservation of foreign exchange to facilitating trade and payments as well as developing the financial markets.[11] Furthermore, as already mentioned, pursuant to assumption of the obligations under Article VIII of the Articles of Agreement of the International Monetary Fund, the current account was made convertible in August 1994. Although the capital account is yet to be made fully convertible, there has been gradual policy liberalisation.

India's approach to reserve management until 1991 was essentially based on the traditional approach, *i.e.*, to maintain an appropriate level of import cover in terms of number of months. The Indian economy, when it faced the crisis in 1991, had reserves worth less than US dollar one billion, capable of handling only two weeks of imports. We have come a long way to a level of reserves close to US $ 130 billion in February 2005

---

10. It is interesting to note that the name of the concerned Department of the RBI too has been changed from "Exchange Control Department" to "Foreign Exchange Department." Semantics apart, the dropping of the word "control" is noteworthy.

11. FEMA does not require seeking general or specific permission for most of the transactions, though the RBI (in consultation with the Government) has retained the right to regulate/prohibit certain payments by issuing notifications/circulars. The enforcement provisions have been considerably systematised to prevent arbitrary use of powers. The legal reforms are discussed in more details in the next section.

and the period from 1992 to 2005 so far has really been a journey from agony to comfort.[12] The reserve accretion has been accompanied by some redemption of past debt, part prepayment of high cost debt and lending of foreign currency resources to the IMF under Financial Transactions Plan. The need for augmenting foreign exchange reserves has been strongly felt with increased globalisation and large and volatile cross border capital flows. With the introduction of market determined exchange rate, there was a change in the approach to reserves management and the emphasis on import cover was supplemented with the objective of smoothing out the volatility in the exchange rate. Furthermore, in the backdrop of currency crisis in the East Asian countries, it was realised that besides the size of reserves, the quality of reserves was also important. Accordingly, ensuring high quality reserves assets, net of encumbrances such as forward commitment, guarantees and other contingent liabilities, had been the mainstay of the policy. Within the broader framework of exchange rate policy, the reserves became an outcome of portfolio management by the RBI, which was guided by the objectives of ensuring safety, liquidity and optimisation of return, with the level of reserves in consonance with key factors like the size of the economy, current account vulnerability, capital account vulnerability, exchange rate flexibility and opportunity cost (Jalan, 2003).

In the recent times, gold, besides having important policy implications for fiscal policy and exchange rate management, has attracted attention in regard to its use as a financial instrument. Indian gold market has always been linked to international gold market in view of large domestic requirements of imported gold. Given the inevitable integration between the global and local markets, there is considerable merit in following the global trend of integration of gold markets with financial markets synchronised with progress in capital account convertibility. Accordingly, though the RBI has not been an active participant in the gold market, it has been taking active role in promoting gold markets. A Standing Committee on Gold and Other Precious Metals was established within the RBI in 1992, which was enlarged and activated in 1997. In July 1997, the RBI authorised the commercial banks to import gold for sale and loan to jewellers and exporters, which has succeeded, to a large extent, in curbing illegal operations in gold and in foreign exchange markets. The RBI has also been actively pursuing the issue of upgrading the quality of trade and

---

12. The issues relating to India's foreign exchange reserves are discussed in detail in Reddy (2002a).

products through a system of assaying and hallmarking of gold jewellery with the Government of India and Bureau of Indian Standards (BIS).

3.4. Regulation and Supervision

In India, as in many other countries, there are several agencies entrusted with the task of regulation and supervision of different institutions and market participants in the financial sector.[13] While the RBI continues to regulate and supervise the major part of the credit system, there has been a change in its approach to regulation in post-reform years; this change is both in terms of organisation as well as form.

There is a literature advocating separation of regulation and supervision from the monetary authority (Goodhart and Shoenmaker, 1995). The main argument for divorcing the monetary policy role from the regulatory authority is that the combination of these functions might lead to a conflict of interest. This conflict can arise in different ways. First, the most important instance is that for the sake of health of the banking system, interest rates could be maintained at a low level, even when monetary policy considerations warrant higher rates. Secondly, substantial intra-day credit exposures in large value payment systems could give rise to settlement problems which could potentially generate a systemic crisis. The resolution of the crisis could require conflicting solution from monetary policy as against the supervisory perspectives. Settlement risk is, therefore, increasingly an area of supervisory concern for central banks. Arguments exist on the other side as well. Illustratively, it has been argued that supervision provides central banks with the information base that could be extremely helpful for conducting monetary policy and creates information-related synergies between supervision and core central banking functions (Peek, Rosengren and Tootell, 1999). Besides, there is the systemic risk argument which emphasises the close relationship between prudential controls of individual intermediaries and the assessment of risks for the financial system as a whole.[14]

As a pragmatic measure, banking supervision in India is under an independent Board for Financial Supervision (under the aegis of RBI)

---

13. At a recent count, it was found that the Indian Financial Sector had at least nine regulators, *viz.*, RBI, SEBI, NABARD, IRDA, Pension Funds Regulatory Development Authority, SIDBI, NHB, Department of Company Affairs of the Government of India, and Registrar of Cooperative Societies.

14. It is instructive to turn to Goodhart (2001) in this context, who said, "I doubt whether the pressures to establish a unified, specialist, supervisory agency are quite as strong in most developing countries ... I do not believe that the case for separation, which has become stronger in the developed countries, should be transposed also to the developing countries."

while policy co-ordination is sought to be achieved through a High Level Co-ordination Committee on Financial and Capital Markets, consisting of three financial regulators (*viz.*, IRDA, SEBI and RBI) and the Ministry of Finance, and presided over by the Governor, RBI (Reddy, 2002).

In terms of organisation, there are a number of major aspects of the changing face of the RBI. First, the Board for Financial Supervision (BFS) has been established within the RBI for an integrated oversight over the banks, non-banking financial companies, select all-India financial institutions and the Primary Dealers. The BFS had adopted a four-pronged approach, consisting of restructuring the system of supervision (consolidated supervision of parent and subsidiary banks), setting up of off-site surveillance capability, enhancing the role of external auditors, and strengthening corporate governance, internal controls and audit procedures. The on-site and off-site supervisory oversight has been supplemented with risk-based supervision. More recently, systemically important financial institutions have been brought under closer monitoring by the RBI. Second, the regulation of money, government securities and forex markets has been formalised. In terms of notification issued under Section 16 of the Securities Contracts (Regulation) Act (SCRA), 1956 and under the amended Section 29A of the Act, in March 2000, the Government of India delegated powers to the RBI to regulate dealings in government securities, money market securities, gold related securities and securities derived from these securities as also ready forward contracts in debt securities.[15] Third, a consultative process between the RBI, the market participants and the experts was initiated and placed on a permanent footing through advisory committees. Illustratively, the Technical Advisory Committee on Money, Foreign Exchange and Government Securities Markets reviews, examines and recommends various practices relating to these markets. All these constitute major changes in the organisation of regulation and supervision on the part of the RBI.

In terms of the changes in the form of regulation, the RBI has adopted a three-pronged strategy, *viz.*, a) strengthening the regulatory and supervisory norms, b) ensuring diverse ownership through listing and partial divestiture of the public sector banks, and c) ensuring competition through entry of private banks.

---

15. By the same notification, Securities and Exchange Board of India (SEBI) will have regulatory jurisdiction over the corporate debt markets.

Among the three, the first one is directly related to the changing face of the RBI. The regulatory and supervisory norms were strengthened so as to induce greater efficiency and market discipline amongst the participants, adoption of international benchmarks as appropriate to Indian conditions, improvement in management practices and corporate governance. The response of the financial sector to the RBI's initiatives has been encouraging. These efforts have enabled the banking system to emerge as a stronger, efficient and resilient system to meet global competition. There has been substantial progress in the implementation of asset-liability management and risk management systems in banks leading to efficient internal control system, improved treasury management and higher profitability. There were improvements in prudential parameters of the system, such as higher capital adequacy and declining net NPA ratios, reinforcing its stability. This has also been endorsed by the international rating agencies with an upgradation in their country rating for India. While certain changes in the legal infrastructure are yet to be effected, the developments so far have brought the Indian financial system closer to global standards.

Furthermore, in the Indian banking system, diversified ownership of public sector banks has been promoted over the years and the performance of their listed stocks in the face of intense competition indicates improvements in the system. They co-exist with several old and new private sector banks, and some of the new private sector banks have proved to be of global standards. In February 2004, transparent guidelines were issued by the RBI in regard to the prior acknowledgement from the RBI for any acquisition/transfer of shares of a private sector bank which would take the aggregate shareholding of an individual or a group to equivalent of five per cent or more of the paid up capital of the bank. While this requirement already existed, transparency was imparted by the guidelines. In July 2004, a comprehensive draft of the policy framework for ownership and governance in private sector banks was placed in the public domain, by the RBI, for wider public debate. These developments have been changed the face of regulation in India.

Further, with a view to strengthening the forces of competition within the Indian banking sector, the bank licensing policy was liberalised in the early 1990s, permitting the entry of private sector banks. Pursuant to this policy, a number of new generation private sector banks became operational in the system and now account for more than 12 per cent of aggregate assets of the scheduled commercial banks. Some of the new private sector banks have achieved global standards in their operations.

Incidentally, the second largest bank in the Indian banking system at present is a private sector bank.

3.5 Developmental Role

Central banking in a developing country is perceived to have a large developmental role. In India too, as an instrument of planned development, many financial institutions were nationalised or created to subserve the need for mobilisation of savings, and allocation of investible resources mainly through public sector and/or administered prices of financial products. Even during the post-reform period, financial institutions were created to help develop financial markets. In this process of institution building, the RBI played an active role, and many of the financial institutions were either owned by the RBI or RBI was the major shareholder of these institutions.[16] Following the Narasimham Committee II recommendations that the RBI should not own the institutions it regulates, the RBI gradually divested its holdings in some of these financial institutions. While the ownership in DFHI, STCI and IDFC has been divested, similar divestment has also been proposed for SBI, NABARD and NHB.

As part of the reforms, many of the developmental functions of the RBI have been redefined. The critical difference in the developmental role of the RBI between the pre-reform and the reform periods is that in the former, the role was primarily in the nature of institutional development and support through funding of the institutions by way of refinance for their lending activities. In the reform era, however, the developmental role has focussed on market development through promoting institutions that make the markets function in a more efficient and transparent manner. What were the major changes in the developmental role of the RBI?

First, in consultation with the Government of India, the traditional support provided to the developmental institutions by RBI through what is known as Long Term Operations (LTO) Funds has been discontinued and the surplus is transferred to the Government, which would be the best arbiter of fund allocation for development. The RBI has also transferred the debt portfolio (the outstanding loans and advances) granted to DFIs out of its National Industrial Credit (LTO) Fund to the

---

16. These financial institutions, *inter alia*, included Discount and Finance House of India Ltd. (DFHI), Securities Trading Corporation of India Ltd. (STCI), State Bank of India (SBI), National Bank for Agriculture and Rural Development (NABARD), Infrastructure Development Finance Company Ltd. (IDFC) and National Housing Bank (NHB) and Deposit Insurance and Credit Guarantee Corporation of India (DICGC).

Government of India.[17] Thus, the RBI had shed its direct developmental role in the sense of direct financing, by ceasing to operate the relevant provision of the RBI Act while simultaneously transferring its surplus to the Government of India.

Second, sectoral refinancing is being phased out and instead of financing development activities directly, emphasis has been placed on ensuring availability of credit for all productive purposes by promoting efficiency and maintaining stability in the financial system.

Third, the developmental role has been refocused on the development of self-regulatory organisations and institutions, improvement in technology and market efficiency. Self-regulatory bodies like the Fixed Income Money Market and Derivatives Association of India (FIMMDA) and the Primary Dealers Association of India (PDAI) have been encouraged by the RBI as part of the reform process to give an impetus to the development of bond and money markets in India. Clearing Corporation of India Limited (CCIL) is now facilitating clearing and settlement of transactions in money, government securities and foreign exchange markets, through novation, thereby minimising credit risk. An electronic Negotiated Dealing System (NDS), at the Public Debt Offices (PDOs) has been operationalised since February 2002 to facilitate transparent electronic bidding in auctions and secondary market transactions in government securities. As a result of the move towards reliance on indirect instruments of monetary policy and the increasing use of technology, development of financial markets and the linkages amongst them have assumed critical importance for effective transmission of monetary policy.

Fourth, the reforms have accorded greater flexibility to banks to determine both the volume and terms of lending with the RBI having moved away from micro-regulation of credit to macro management. Statutory pre-emptions have been lowered substantially, leading to more lendable resources at the disposal of banks. The movement towards competitive and deregulated interest rate regime on the lending side has been completed with the conversion of multiple prime lending rates (PLRs) into a benchmark prime lending rate (BPLR) with full freedom to banks in pricing their loan products both on fixed or floating basis in a transparent manner. As a result of all these, borrowers are able to get credit at lower interest rates. The average lending rate between 1991-92

---

17. These included the erstwhile Industrial Development Bank of India (IDBI), EXIM Bank, Industrial Investment Bank of India Ltd. (IIBI) and Small Industries Development Bank of India (SIDBI).

and 2004-05 has declined from about 19.0 per cent to current levels of 10.25 – 11.00 per cent.[18] Thus, because of the overall flexibility in interest rate structure, it has been possible for the banks to reduce their lending rates and still improve their spreads. In terms of priority sector credit also, the element of cross-subsidisation has been brought down although an element of credit allocations to agriculture, small-scale industry (SSI), weaker sections and export sector has been retained. Except for small loans up to Rs. 200,000 for which BPLR is the ceiling interest rate, banks have the freedom to determine interest rate even within the priority sector. Recognising the emerging priorities in certain sectors of the economy, the definition of priority sector has been gradually expanded to help the banks extend loans to these sectors on commercially viable terms though the credit pick up was not up to the mark till recently. Also, while in general, the rates of interest have come down, the lower rates are available more to the highly rated borrowers than to the small and medium enterprises. There is, thus, considerable concern about the inadequate flow of resources to rural areas, and in particular agriculture, for which interest rates have not been reduced to the extent they were for the corporate sector (Reddy, 2004b). In view of the foregoing, the Indian Banks' Association had advised the public sector banks to charge a rate of interest not exceeding nine per cent on crop loans up to Rs. 50,000.

The steps taken by the RBI to improve institutional finance to agriculture include extension of Special Agricultural Credit Plan scheme to private sector banks from the year 2005-06 and revision of the Kisan Credit Card Scheme to also cover term credit to agriculture. Several recommendations of the Advisory Committee on Flow of Credit to Agriculture and Related Activities from the Banking System under the chairmanship of Prof. V.S. Vyas have been communicated to banks for implementation. In view of the importance of the housing sector, the ceiling for direct housing loans under the priority sector has been enhanced to Rs.15 lakh. To encourage securitisation of assets in the SSI and housing finance sectors, investment by banks in securitised SSI loans and in Mortgage Backed Securities have been allowed to be treated as part of their priority sector lending. In order to encourage banks to lend directly to the priority sector, the facility of treating investments by banks in special bonds issued by specified institutions as part of their priority

---

18. The actual lending rates for top rated borrowers can be even lower since banks are permitted to lend below Benchmark Prime Lending Rate (BPLR). Further, since banks invest in Commercial Paper (CP), which is more directly related to money market rates, many top rated borrowers are able to tap bank funds at highly competitive rates.

sector lending is being phased out. In order to enable banks to freely extend rural credit and to enable the rural borrowers to choose their bank, the restrictive provisions of the Service Area Approach have been dispensed with.

3.6 Lender of Last Resort

The concept of the lender of last resort (LOLR) is somewhat ambiguous and may have different connotations. The LOLR function is traditionally interpreted as provision of emergency liquidity (i.e., not risk capital) at the discretion of the central bank to individual banks or to the market as a whole. The main problem associated with the function of LOLR is that of moral hazard. The proponents of this view argue that as a generality, the central banks should not lend to individual banks. In their view, the market is better informed about the relative solvency or otherwise of the institution and the central bank should only infuse liquidity through open market operations. Thus, given enough liquidity in the system, illiquid but solvent banks will be able to borrow in the inter-bank market whereas insolvent banks will be driven out of the system (Goodhart and Huang, 1999).[19] The key issue here is whether the market will be able to distinguish between illiquid and insolvent institutions during a crisis. It was evident during the crisis related to the Long Term Capital Management (LTCM)[20] that the market exhibits no such discipline in a crisis and the general tendency is for all participants to exit the market. Reverting to the open market operations argument, infusion of liquidity in the market for further reallocation to solvent but illiquid institutions can happen if there are only a few institutions facing a crisis. Where there is a large number of institutions involved in a crisis or if liquidity injection is institution-specific, direct intervention by the central bank might be required.

The function of LOLR in India is currently closely related to the concept of Emergency Liquidity Assistance (ELA).[21] In the recent past, there have been several instances where RBI provided liquidity support to

---

19. Non-discretionary LOLR, however, could be a possible source of conflict between the supervisory and monetary policy making functions of the central bank.

20. It may be recalled that in September 1998, the Fed organised a rescue of Long-Term Capital Management, a very large and prominent hedge fund in the U.S, on the brink of failure, so as to avoid possible dire consequences for world financial markets.

21. The ELA could be provided under two provisions of the Reserve Bank of India Act, 1934, *viz.*, (a) under Section 17(4)(a) against the collateral of excess holding of Government of India securities/Treasury Bills over their SLR holding, and (b) Section 18 empowering RBI to provide support against any security for a period not exceeding 90 days under very extreme conditions.

various financial institutions and banks to enable them overcome their short- to medium-term liquidity problems. During the decade of 1990s, the erstwhile Unit Trust of India (UTI) approached RBI on a few occasions for liquidity support to tide over their difficult fund positions. While such liquidity support was initially extended by RBI by way of outright purchase of government securities, the repo facility at the Bank Rate became a commonly employed tool for extending the liquidity support to UTI during late 1990s. In 1999, RBI provided liquidity support to Deposit Insurance and Credit Guarantee Corporation (DICGC) to enable it to tide over difficulties arising from an unanticipated large cash outflow mainly for making advance tax payments to the Government specially since DICGC is not a notified institution for undertaking repo transactions with the market participants whereas a distress sale of government securities could distort the secondary market prices. More recently, the RBI provided liquidity support to a commercial bank to overcome its liquidity problems.

Thus, the notion of LOLR is traditionally linked to institution-specific liquidity support. The question arises to whom should the support be given? In this context, distinction is often made between two basic features of such institution, *viz.*, insolvency and illiquidity. It may, however, be noted that in reality it is extremely difficult to distinguish between the two and there are elements of judgment in discerning the nature of the liquidity crisis. Interestingly, during the period between bank nationalisation and early 1990s with predominance of government holding in public sector banks, the issue of insolvency generally did not arise. However, in a few cases where necessity arose, after the commencement of the reform, two factors had to be kept in view. First, in all such cases where the RBI had to provide liquidity, it was consciously decided not to take a hit on its balance sheet. It was ensured that such support is backed by securities with appropriate margin. Second, it may be noted that LOLR may not be the solution in case of insolvency. After all, the cost of not bailing out an insolvent bank could be weighed in terms of the amount of potential outflow from deposit insurance - hence, the option of adopting strategic merger of such banks with viable ones becomes extremely relevant.

With increasing liberalisation, the LOLR took a new dimension. As against liquidity of a particular bank, there are instances of what may be called general liquidity problems. Over the past five years there had been some cases of support or assurance of support to general liquidity problems. The experience of May 17, 2004 is a case in point. It may be recalled that on May 17, 2004, the BSE Sensex recorded a fall of 17 per cent within a day, triggering the index-based circuit-breaker twice during the day. In such a situation the RBI assured liquidity to the financial system—after which there were indications of stability in the stock market. Interestingly, this episode of possible liquidity support to clearing banks was not related to what in popular parlance is called a "bank-run". On the contrary, this was related purely to systemic illiquidity. Acting as some sort of LOLR to maintain the integrity of the payment system in such situations is indeed another aspect of the changing face of the RBI in recent years.

3.7 Other Functions: Currency and Payment Systems

There are also a number of other functions, both traditional as well as offshoots of its developmental role, which are being redefined as part of the financial sector reforms.

First, as banker to the Government, the objective is to help governments to get better and efficient service with safety of funds. More recently, private banks promoted by the AIFIs, which meet the pre-defined criteria, have been inducted as agency banks for conduct of government business.

Second, as banker to banks, it is perceived that since banks are the eventual payment service providers to the rest of the non-banking community, various RBI facilities such as SGL facilities, current account and, access to call market should be confined to banks. With the technological upgradation taken up in the area of payment system through mechanisms such as Clearing Corporation of India Ltd. (CCIL), Negotiated Dealing System (NDS), and Real Time Gross Settlement (RTGS), the access of non-bank entities to the RBI facilities is being gradually eliminated.

Third, in view of the interlinkages among payment systems that are being introduced and the role they are going to play, the intention is to have a designated body/entity assigned with the work of regulating and supervising the payment systems. This body would be responsible for formulation of payment systems policies, regulation of the payment systems, implementation of Core Principles relating to the payment systems (as enunciated by the Bank for International Settlements) and other international standards. The RBI is, therefore, in the process of setting up a Board for Regulation and Supervision of Payment and Settlement Systems (BPSS), on the lines of the Board for Financial Supervision, which would function as a Committee of the Central Board, chaired by the Governor. The BPSS would lay down the policies for the regulation and supervision of payment and settlement systems, both paper-based and electronic, encompassing domestic and cross-border systems.

Fourth, in the process of improving the overall efficiency of the payment and settlement systems in the country, RBI, apart from performing the regulatory and oversight functions, has also undertaken promotional and institutional activities. These activities include developing and implementing magnetic ink character recognition (MICR) based cheque processing system, Indian financial network (INFINET), electronic funds transfer (EFT) system, national electronic funds transfer (NEFT) system, electronic (debit and credit) clearing system (ECS), negotiated dealing system (NDS), securities settlement system (SSS), centralised fund management system (CFMS) and real time gross settlement (RTGS) system. Further, the Institute for Development and Research in Banking Technology (IDRBT) established by RBI has set up a National Financial Switch to facilitate apex level connectivity of other switches established by banks for electronic transfer of funds, and to act as an e-commerce payment gateway. The switch was inaugurated in August 2004 and 15 banks have already become its members.

Fifth, the demand for currency has gone up with the growth in population and economic activity. Due to insufficient currency production from the Note Presses at Nashik and Dewas, owned by the Government of India to meet this increase in demand, the Bank had set up a wholly owned subsidiary, the *Bharatiya Reserve Bank Note Mudran Ltd.* (BRBNML) to meet the currency requirements. The BRBNML commissioned two new presses with the state-of-the-art printing facilities at Mysore and Salboni in 1996 which were made fully operational during 1999-2000. With the augmentation of the printing capacity, the Bank has initiated various measures to ensure clean currency notes in circulation.

3.8 External Relations Environment

Financial sector reforms have also necessitated changes in the relationship between the RBI and various other entities ranging from the Government to other regulatory bodies and international agencies.

First, there has been a better appreciation of the need for coordination between the monetary and fiscal policies. The coordination with the Government is moving from some kind of joint-family system to that of a system with checks and balances between the monetary authority, the

RBI, the fiscal authorities, and the various levels of government. Examples are: delegation of powers to regulate dealings in government securities to the RBI through issue of notification under SCRA; abolition of the system of automatic monetisation of deficit through the creation of *ad hoc* Treasury Bills and replacing it by WMA; introduction of auction system for market related interest rates in government borrowing; regular conference of State Finance Secretaries and the MOF with the RBI to deliberate on the common problems and developing best practices in regard to government finances; changes in the guarantee policy of the Governments in terms of selectivity in giving guarantees, institution of limits/ceilings on guarantees by the State governments and setting up of Guarantees Redemption Fund; and regulation and supervision of government-owned entities.

Second, relations with other regulators such as the Securities and Exchange Board of India (SEBI), the regulator of equity and corporate debt markets and, Insurance Regulatory and Development Authority of India (IRDA), the regulator of insurance sector are maintained through High-Level Committees and Working Groups as a means of effective regulatory co-operation by sharing specified market information on a routine and automatic basis.

Third, India has been gaining in importance in the global financial community and RBI has been playing its relevant role. In 1996, India gained membership in the Bank for International Settlements and has been active in utilising the facilities and contributing to its deliberations. India has also been a member of the Core Principles Liaison Group (CPLG) constituted by the Basle Committee on Banking Supervision as also of the Core Principles Working Group on Capital (CPWC). India has been a founding member of the G-20 since September 1999 and is represented by the Ministry of Finance and the RBI (comprising G-7 countries, 11 other countries and two institutional representatives). India has been involved in almost all the discussions of G-20 where developing countries have been represented.

Fourth, with deregulation and increasing cross-border flows, central banks of most of the countries have gained some degree of autonomy and with it a sense of accountability. Hence, central banks do see some advantage in communicating in as transparent a manner as appropriate, their policy intentions and operations. Well-informed market participants enable, though not assure, improved functioning of markets. The RBI, thus, endeavours to provide credible statistics for dissemination through the media and various other ways with updating of data on its website, daily press releases, policy statements, speeches, and its weekly, monthly, quarterly and annual publications. Besides, RBI has also subscribed to the Special Data Dissemination Standard (SDDS) of the International Monetary Fund (IMF) since January 1999 and is now fully compliant in furnishing the stipulated data series periodically to the IMF for wider publication and use. More recently, in line with the recommendation of an Expert Group on Central Database Management System (CDBMS) (Chairman: Professor A. Vaidyanathan), the RBI has placed a substantial part of CDBMS in the public domain for the convenience of researchers, analysts and other users.

Fifth, attempts have been made on an on-going basis to improve customer service by simplifying procedures and reducing paper work. In this regard, the Regulations Review Authority (RRA) was constituted in April 1999 to review the Reserve Bank's rules, regulations and reporting systems based on the suggestions received from general public at large, market participants and other users of services of the RBI.[22] With the setting up of the RRA and Grievances Redressal Cells at the Regional Offices of the RBI, there has been considerable rationalisation of the regulatory canvass. The RBI has set up a Committee with functions to undertake procedure and performance audit on public services and regulatory clearances in the RBI and advise and co-ordinate with the *ad hoc* Committees on Customer Services set up by banks for rationalisation of instructions on procedures prescribed by RBI that impinge on the customer services of banks. The objective is to benchmark the current level of service, review the progress periodically, enhance the timeliness and quality, rationalise the processes taking account of technological developments, and suggest appropriate incentives to facilitate change on an on-going basis. Many of the recommendations of the Committee have already been implemented by the RBI and commercial banks.

4. Legal and Institutional Changes

A number of changes in the legislative and institutional framework was brought about commensurate with the evolving role of the RBI. Some discussion on these aspects already appears in the preceding section;

---

22. During two years of its operation, till the expiry of term in March 2001, RRA implemented number of suggestions received, which helped in removal of redundancies in the reporting system, simplification of rules and internal procedures in various functional areas within RBI and also brought about some improvement in operational efficiency in commercial banks, which enabled better customer service.

nevertheless, for the sake of completeness, it is useful to give an account of these legal and institutional changes.

First, as already indicated, several legislative changes have been brought about. Effective from June 2000, Foreign Exchange Act was replaced by Foreign Exchange Management Act. Relevant sections of the Securities Contracts (Regulation) Act (SCRA), 1956 were amended in March 2000, to delegate powers to RBI to regulate dealings in government securities, money market securities, gold related securities and securities derived from these securities. With the passage of the Recovery of Debts due to Banks and Financial Institutions Act, 1993, special Tribunals have been set up since 1993 to speed up the process of recovery by specific legislation. In order to make the Tribunals an effective machinery for recovery of debts expeditiously, and in the light of experience gained, the Government amended the Recovery of Debts due to Banks and Financial Institutions Act in March 2000 vesting Debt Recovery Tribunals (DRTs) with new powers as also incorporating new provisions, which focus on improving the infrastructure facilities of DRTs by way of posting of additional Recovery Officers, etc. Legal regime for recourse to assets in cases of sticky loan portfolios has been strengthened through the Securitisation and Reconstruction of Financial Assets and Enforcement of Security Interest (SARFAESI) Act. A Corporate Debt Restructuring (CDR) mechanism was stated in 2001 and the mechanism was strengthened in February 2003. It seeks to provide a timely and transparent mechanism for restructuring corporate debt outside the purview of legal proceedings, including those under DRT.

Second, many more legislative changes are being proposed. The draft legislative bills suggesting amendments to the Reserve Bank of India Act, 1934; comprehensive amendment to the Banking Regulation Act, 1949; and an outline for a new Bill for Amendment of Deposit Insurance and Credit Guarantee Corporation Act have been forwarded to the Government. The Financial Companies Regulation Bill, 2000, Banking Companies (Acquisition and Transfer of Undertaking) and Financial Institutions Laws (Amendment) Bill, 2000, Negotiable Instruments (Amendment) Bill 2001, Companies (Amendment) Bill, 2001 and Companies (Second Amendment), 2001 have all been introduced in the Parliament. The proposals for replacement of Public Debt Act, 1944 by Government Security Act, amendments to the Special Court (TORTS) Act, 1992 and legislative amendments relating to Urban Co-operative Banks are also under consideration of the Government.

Third, though the RBI has been articulating the need for appropriate changes in law and assisting the Government in the process, it has also been bringing about changes in the financial sector without necessarily waiting for changes in the law. For instance, the RBI's regulatory jurisdiction has been invoked in commercial paper and certificate of deposit markets. Current account convertibility in external sector was implemented even before a new law was introduced by recourse to large scale relaxations. Regulations of clearing houses, operating payment systems and functioning of electronic trading came even before the regulations under the Information Technology Act came into force.

Fourth, the directions of gold policy have been and will continue to be decided by the Government and the RBI would continue to play its advisory role in this regard. Similarly, the RBI will continue to play the advisory role to the Government in the areas of external debt management, administered interest rates and other fiscal issues.

Fifth, a number of institutions have been developed in order to manage change in the financial sector brought about by reforms. In this change, self-regulatory organisations (SROs) serve as a crucial layer between the regulator and market. Over the years, the SROs have emerged as an effective and efficient form of supplementing the regulatory framework for the complex and dynamic financial services industry.[23] The activities of the SROs are closely co-ordinated with the policies of RBI, while the RBI also carefully and constantly observes their functioning.

As already discussed, internal consensus within the RBI is developed through Financial Markets Committee, Monetary Policy Strategy meetings and Inter-Departmental Groups. Formal consultative mechanisms with market participants have been established through two Technical Advisory Groups—(a) one on Money, Government Securities and Forex Markets, and (b) another on Financial Regulation—where important policy and operational changes proposed to be implemented are discussed. These Advisory Groups have representation from banks, mutual funds, financial institutions, credit rating agencies, SROs, independent economists, apart from representation from the Government. To advise on the design and development of the payment systems, National Payment Council (NPC)

---

23. In addition to the two existing SROs *viz.*, Indian Banks Association (IBA) and Foreign Exchange Dealers Association of India (FEDAI), two more entities *i.e.*, the Fixed Income and Money Market Derivatives Association (FIMMDA) and Primary Dealers' Association of India (PDAI) have also been established as SRO during the 1990s as self-regulator of the money and bond markets with active encouragement from the RBI.

has been set up at the apex level with members drawn from banks, financial institutions and the Government apart from the RBI. NPC is supported by a Payment Systems Advisory Committee (PSAC) consisting of Heads of departments concerned within the RBI. There are also *ad hoc* internal, external and joint groups.

Sixth, the RBI has been taking an active role in the evolving process on the international financial architecture after the Asian crisis. RBI is one of the select few to be represented in the consultation process on new norms being considered for banks' supervision. RBI was associated with a working group constituted by the newly setup Financial Stability Forum. RBI was also associated with an international group on Settlements. A Standing Committee on International Financial Standards and Codes was constituted in India with joint membership of the Government and the RBI. The main task of this Committee was to identify and monitor developments in global standards and codes and consider its applicability to the Indian financial system. On the initiative of the Standing Committee and its Advisory Groups, considerable progress has been made in implementation of various recommendations and furthering national position in this regard. The same has been documented recently in a staff review that has been placed in public domain by the RBI. The RBI is also actively involved in G-20 meetings that discuss international financial issues of contemporary importance.

Seventh, the process of managing change can be characterised in terms of caution, move towards international practices with appropriate sequencing and pacing for the regulators, building consensus, committee approach, flexibility, transparency and managing exceptional circumstances. The reform process has been calibrated with circumspection with a tilt towards preserving stability. Reforms have progressed towards the international best practices, which are constantly reviewed in inter-departmental Working Groups within RBI before designing and operationalising changes. There has been careful sequencing of the reforms with a clear agenda. It has been ensured that the pace of reforms remains consistent with the overall framework, global developments, state of the market participants and infrastructure developments. Building consensus is another important facet of the reform process, which involves gaining acceptability from within the RBI and other stakeholders, and at the operating level, the committee approach adopted has facilitated the coordination. Transparency has been the hallmark of the reform process, achieved by generating public debate through announcement of intentions and proposals well in advance through Policy Statements, speeches of senior officials and disclosure of information. The market intervention under exceptional circumstances has been credible.

5. Outlook and Issues

The role of RBI in the economy in general and financial sector in particular would continue to evolve to suit the changing requirements. While it is difficult to speculate on the trajectory of evolution over a longer period, it is possible to explore some of the issues in the near to medium term, which are presented here merely to illustrate, while not being exhaustive.

First, as a monetary authority, it will be necessary for the RBI to enhance timeliness and quality of data and information relevant for policy-making. Some of the relevant areas may be on inflation-expectations, capacity-utilisation, housing-startups, retail sales, inventory-build up, and employment-trends, etc. The analytical underpinning may also need to be simultaneously strengthened. These would encompass, for example, external sector, inflation and financial stability. Operationally, the prohibition on RBI's participation in the primary-market with effect from April 1, 2006 would need a greater emphasis on open market operations— warranting technological, institutional and skill upgradation, both in RBI and among the market-participants. These operations have to take account of several factors, and in particular, the level of fiscal deficit and the capital flows at this juncture.

Second, as the debt-manager of the Government, there may be a need to recognise the demarcation between the role of the manager and that of the regulator, in both policy and operational dimensions. The role of the RBI as a debt-manager in regard to States could pose major challenges in view of the differences among the States' fiscal strength coupled with the need for maintaining sovereign nature of all state-government paper.

Third, as a regulator of banks, a comprehensive banking policy may get evolved focussing on constant rebalancing between market-discipline, corporate governance and regulation. Irrespective of whether a single regulator emerges or multiple regulators persist in the financial sector, coordination and harmonisation of regulatory regimes will gain in importance.

Fourth, the focus of the RBI's developmental role in future may be on enabling credit culture, appropriate credit pricing and adequate but timely credit delivery through the banking system, recognising that it becomes only one of the several financing options for economic-activity, the other but growing avenues being domestic capital markets and external sources apart from internal accruals of the borrowers. Close coordination with governmental agencies will continue to be critical in this regard.

Fifth, the 'lender of last resort' function should normally be confined to provision of systemic liquidity rather than specific banking entities due to expanding private financial instruments in the market for liquidity for any solvent institution. However, the principle of constructive ambiguity may still be of relevance.

Sixth, in the currency and payments areas, it is a moot point whether scope for seignorage will come down dramatically due to emergence of e-money in the near term. In any case while currency management will continue to dominate the concerns of the common person for transaction purposes, even accounting for growing use of credit or debit cards, the regulation of payments systems will gain in significance. The functioning of the proposed Board for Payments will be path breaking.

Seventh, external relations will be dominated by concerns relating to communications—in substance, especially in regard to monetary policy and in processes and effectiveness. It may be necessary to have more frequent structured communication with markets on developments and policies.

Finally, the greatest challenges would be in the area of human resources. Existing personnel, no doubt highly skilled, need to be continuously exposed to enhancement of their skills. There is need to ensure that working conditions are conducive in the RBI. There is also a need to attract talent for initial recruitment and obtaining of highly specialised and skilled professional services to supplement in-house expertise, where appropriate and inevitable. Indeed, it is the people in RBI who have built the outstanding reputation and they would be a key factor in RBI continuing to evolve as a valuable and respected public institution.

References

Balachandran, G. (1998). *The Reserve Bank of India: 1951-1967*, New Delhi: Oxford University Press.

Capie, Forrest (1997). *The Evolution of Central Banking in Reforming the Financial System: Some Lessons from History*, Cambridge: Cambridge University Press.

Chandavarkar, Anand (1996). *Central Banking in Developing Countries*, London: Macmillan Press.

Crocket, Andrew (2002). "Central Banking in the New Millennium," in M.S. Ahluwalia, Y.V. Reddy, and S.S. Tarapore (eds.) *Macroeconomics and Monetary Policy: Issues for a Reforming Economy*, Delhi: Oxford University Press.

Goodhart, Charles (2001). "Whither Central Banking?," Eleventh C.D. Deshmukh Memorial Lecture, *RBI Bulletin*, January.

Goodhart Charles and Shoenmaker D. (1995). "Should the Functions of Monetary Policy and Banking Supervision be Separated?," *Oxford Economic Papers*, (pp. 539-560).

Goodhart, Charles and Haizhou Huang (1999). "A Model of the Lender of Last Resort," *IMF Working Paper*, WP/99/39, March 1999.

Government of India (1991). *Report of the Committee on the Financial System* (Chairman: Shri M. Narasimham), Mumbai: Reserve Bank of India.

———. (1998). *Report of the Committee on Banking Sector Reforms* (Chairman: Shri M. Narasimham), New Delhi: Government of India.

Jalan, Bimal (2002). *India's Economy in the New Millennium*, New Delhi: UBPSD.

———. (2003). "Exchange Rate Management: An Emerging Consensus" *RBI Bulletin*, September 2003.

Mohan, Rakesh (2004). "Financial Sector Reforms in India: Policies and Performance Analysis," *RBI Bulletin*, October.

Peek, J., Rosengren, E. and G. Tootell (1999). "Is Bank Supervision Central to Central Banking," *Quarterly Journal of Economics*, Vol. No. 114,(pp.629–53).

Rangarajan, C. (2000). *Perspectives on Indian Economy: A Collection of Essays*, Delhi: UBSPD.

Reddy Y.V. (1998). "Financial Sector Reform: Review and Prospects," *RBI Bulletin*, December.

———. (2000). *Monetary and Financial Sector Reforms in India: A Central Bankers' Perspective*, Delhi: UBS Publishers' Distributors.

———. (2002). *Lectures on Economic and Financial Sector Reforms in India*, Delhi: Oxford University Press.

———. (2002a). "India's Foreign Exchange Reserves: Policy, Status and Issues," *RBI Bulletin*, June.

———. (2003). *Economic Policy in India: Managing Change*, Delhi: UBS Publishers Distributors.

———. (2004a). "Financial Stability: Indian Experience," *RBI Bulletin*, July.

———. (2004b). "Monetary and Financial/Sector Reforms in India: A Practitioner's Perspective," in Kaushik Basu (ed.) *India's Emerging Economy*, Cambridge Massachusetts: MIT Press.

Reserve Bank of India (1970). *History of the Reserve Bank of India, 1935-1951*, Mumbai: Reserve Bank of India.

———. (1993). *Report of the High Level Committee on Balance of Payments* (Chairman: C. Rangarajan), *RBI Bulletin*, August.

———. (1985). *Report of the Committee to Review the Working of the Monetary System* (Chairman: S. Chakravarty), Mumbai: RBI.

———. (1998). *Report of the Working Group on Money Supply: Analytics and Methodology of Compilation* (Chairman: Y.V. Reddy), Mumbai: RBI.

———. (2004). *Report on Currency and Finance, 2002-03*, Mumbai: RBI.

———. (2005). *Review of the Recommendations of the Advisory Group Constituted by the Standing Committee on International Financial Standards and Codes: Report on the Progress and Agenda Ahead.*

Schinasi, Gary J., (2003). "Responsibility of Central Banks for Stability in Financial Markets," *IMF Working Paper* WP/03/121.

Siklos, P.L. (2002). *The Changing Face of Central Banking: Evolutionary Trends since World War II,* Cambridge: Cambridge University Press.

Thornton, Henry (1802). *An Enquiry into the Nature and Effects of the Paper Credit of Great Britain,* Reprinted: 1939, New York: Rinehart and Co.

Udeshi, Kishori (2004). "Role of Central Bankers in an Emerging Country Like India," *BIS Review* No.17.

Vasudevan A. (2003). *Central Banking for Emerging Market Economies,* New Delhi: Academic Foundation.

2

Fiscal Federalism: Some Current Concerns

C. RANGARAJAN

Professor C.H. Hanumantha Rao has been a distinguished economist who has made outstanding contributions to both academic thinking and policy-making. His main interest has been in the area of agricultural and rural development. However, his contributions have not been confined only to these areas. He was twice Member of the Finance Commission and had dealt with problems of fiscal federalism. In paying tribute to Professor C.H. Hanumantha Rao, I have chosen to write on the theme of Fiscal Federalism.

Two sets of factors have pushed to the fore discussions on federalism. First is the impact of globalisation and the growing integration of countries on the way federal structures function. If we are moving towards a borderless world, how much boundaries within a country matter or should matter? Federal structures will have to undergo a change in order to be able to respond to the forces of globalisation and international competition that emerges as a consequence. Globalisation is also occurring at a time when the respective roles of government and markets are being re-written. Private sector and markets are being given a larger space to operate, even in countries, which have been traditionally state-centered. The role of State as a producer of marketable goods and services is being de-emphasised. However, this has not diminished the role of the government. As is being somewhat paradoxically remarked: 'More market does not mean less government but only different government.' The critical question is in what way this government is different. Obviously the increasing role of market does alter the rules of the game for the government as a whole and for different levels of government. The second set of factors relates to another trend where the advantages of de-centralisation are being emphasised. There has always been a school of thought, which has emphasised the importance of sub-national governments and local bodies as an essential part of the democratic process. The Seventy Third and Seventy Fourth Amendments to the Indian

Constitution in 1988 giving explicit recognition to the roles of local bodies in the governance process are reflective of this trend. Similarly, in the United Kingdom, both Scotland and Wales have their own regional parliaments.

Federalism—As a Form of Government

Federalism is an old concept. Its origin is mainly political. It is well-known that the efficiency of government depends, among other factors, on the structure of government. Federalism as a form of government has, therefore, been concerned with functions and instruments that are best centralised and those that are best placed in the sphere of de-centralised levels of government. Particularly, in large countries, it has been felt that sub-national governments are required and that only a federal structure can efficiently meet the requirements of people from different regions. Underlying this proposition is the premise that preferences vary from region to region. Thus, the rationale of federalism lies in promoting welfare through decentralisation and sub-national autonomy in combination with the benefits of a large market and size.

In our country during the Independence struggle, provincial autonomy was regarded as an integral part of the Freedom Movement. However, after Independence, several compulsions including defence and internal security led to a scheme of federalism in which the Centre assumed greater importance. Also in the immediate post-Independence period when the Centre and all States were ruled by the same party and when many of the powerful provincial leaders migrated to the Centre, the process of centralisation gathered further momentum. Economic planning at a nation-wide level and the allocation of resources by a central authority also helped this centralising process. The size of the States in India is largely determined by language. After the formation of linguistic States, the size and population of a State is determined by the number of people speaking the same language. However, more recently in large States where people are speaking the same language, demands have been made for dividing them on grounds of regional neglect. Some of these demands have also been met. A similar evolutionary process has been noted elsewhere. Even in the American case, there has been a transition from the earlier era of 'dualism' where the two tiers had comparable responsibilities to growing centralisation, which according to some writers has passed through successive phases of 'centralising federalism' to 'cooperative federalism,' and more recently, to 'creative federalism' where the Central Government continues to take an active part in the State and local problems.

Fiscal Federalism

Fiscal federalism is the economic counterpart to political federalism. Fiscal federalism is concerned with the assignment, on the one hand, of functions to different levels of government and on the other with appropriate fiscal instruments for carrying out these functions. It is generally believed that the Central Government must provide national public goods that render services to the entire population of the country. A typical example cited is defence. Local governments are expected to provide goods and services whose consumption is limited to their own jurisdictions. The argument here is that output of such goods and services can be tailored to meet the preferences and circumstances of the people in that jurisdiction. Such a process of de-centralisation enhances the economic welfare above what could result from the more uniform levels of such services that are likely under a centralised regime. Apart from the provision of national public goods, the Central Government is to be vested with the responsibilities for economic stabilisation and for income re-distribution. While income re-distribution to some extent is possible even within sub-national government jurisdictions, a truly re-distribution effort is possible only at the national level. An equally important question in fiscal federalism is the determination of the specific fiscal instruments that would enable the different levels of government to carry out their functions. This is the 'tax-assignment problem,' which is discussed very much in the literature. In determining the taxes that are best suited for use at different levels of government, one basic assumption made is in relation to the mobility of economic agents, goods and resources. Very often it is assumed that while there is no mobility across national barriers, there is a much greater mobility at de-centralised levels. This proposition holds good only partly in an era of globalisation. Once again, it is generally argued that the de-centralised levels of government should avoid non-benefit taxes on mobile units. This has the implication that Central Government should have the responsibility to levy non-benefit taxes and taxes on mobile units or resources. Building these principles into an actual scheme of assignment of taxes to different levels of government in a Constitution is indeed very difficult. Different Constitutions interpret differently what is mobile and what is purely a benefit tax. For example, in the United States and Canada, both Federal and State Governments have concurrent powers to levy income-tax. On the contrary, in India,

income-tax is levied only by the Central Government though shared with
the States. It is interesting to note that the revenues collected by the
Federal or Central Government vary sharply among different countries. For
example, the Federal Government collects 69 per cent of the total revenue
in Australia, 65 per cent in India and 48 per cent in Canada. Thus, the
traditional issues in fiscal federalism have been how to determine the
assignment of taxes and responsibilities to different levels of government.
Recognising, the possibility of imbalance between resources and
responsibilities, many countries have a system of intergovernmental
transfers. In fact, intergovernmental transfers constitute a distinctive
economic policy instrument in fiscal federalism. For example,
intergovernmental transfers as a percentage of provincial or State revenues
have been 41 per cent in Australia, 40 per cent in India and 20 per cent
in Canada in recent years. Correcting vertical and horizontal imbalances
has been a major concern with which fiscal federalism has wrestled. While
actual designs of fiscal transfer systems differ across federations, these
constitute experiments in search of satisfying the twin objectives of equity
and efficiency in a multi-tiered system of government. Conceptually, the
emphasis has been on providing enough resources at the sub-national level
to ensure provision of a set of services at comparable or minimum
acceptable levels in all jurisdictions. This attempt at 'equalisation' impedes
the search for efficiency through relocation of households and firms, but
is justified on the grounds of congestibility of service provision and on
ethical grounds such as those related to equity. There has also been a
consideration of rigidities in the mobility of households, which may itself
be a function of education, which is one of the services considered for
equalisation.

Fiscal Transfers

The roots of fiscal federalism in India go back to the Government of
India Acts of 1919 and 1935. While the Act of 1919 provided for a
separation of revenue heads between the Centre and the Provinces, the
1935 Act allowed for the sharing of Centre's revenues and for the
provision of grants-in-aid to Provinces. The Indian Constitution carried
these provisions a step forward by providing for a Finance Commission to
determine the distribution between the Union and the States of the net
proceeds of taxes and the grants-in-aid to be provided to the States, which
are in need of assistance. While the Constitutional provisions relating to
the functions of the Finance Commissions have remained unchanged, one
notable change in the framework of federal fiscal arrangements was

brought out by the 80th Amendment, which broadened the ambit of the sharable Central taxes. The enlargement of the sharable pool to cover all Central taxes except those listed in Articles 268 and 269 and earmarked cesses and surcharges, has enabled States to share in the overall buoyancy of taxes. It has also provided greater stability to resource transfers as fluctuations in individual taxes are evened out. With the 73rd and 74th Amendments to the Constitution, which have provided Constitutional support to the process of decentralisation, the Finance Commissions are also required to suggest measures to augment the resources for the *panchayats* and municipalities.

The Indian Constitution lays down the functions as well as taxing powers of the Centre and States. It is against this background that the issues relating to the correction of vertical and horizontal imbalances have been addressed by every Finance Commission, taking into account the prevailing set of circumstances. Central transfers to States are not, however, confined to the recommendations of the Finance Commissions. There are other channels such as those through the Planning Commission as well the discretionary grants of the Central Government. The Eleventh Finance Commission recommended that 29.5 per cent of the net proceed of the sharable taxes should go to the States. It suggested that in the overall scheme of transfer, 37.5 per cent of the gross revenue receipts of the Centre should be transferred to the States. One important issue that has been raised in this regard in the light of the recent changes of the economic policy aimed at liberalisation is whether the vertical imbalance has increased or decreased. At least one State Government has argued before the Twelfth Finance Commission that assigning a greater role to the market has diminished the function of the Central Government as compared with State Governments. The shift in economic policy has altered the functions of the both Central and State Governments. While the constitutionally mandated functions have remained the same, the emphasis has changed. It is not clear whether the shift in economic policy has necessarily increased vertical imbalance. However, this is an aspect, which needs a fuller consideration.

Fiscal transfers require to be guided by certain definitive principles. Most analysts agree that a good transfer system should serve the objectives of equity and efficiency and should be characterised by predictability and stability. Equity can be conceptualised and understood in a number of ways both with respect to its vertical and horizontal dimensions. The considerations that should go in determining the distribution of transferred resources among States have been examined in great length by the various Finance Commissions. Equity issues have dominated such discussions, as they should be. The effort has been to identify variables, which reflect the equity concerns. Equity factors have had a maximum weight in resource transfer formulae. In designing a suitable scheme of fiscal transfers, three considerations seem relevant—needs, cost disability and fiscal efficiency. Needs refer to expenditures required to be made but not met by own resources. Cost disabilities refer to such characteristics of a State that necessitate more than average per capita cost in service provision due to factors that are largely beyond its control like large areas with low density of population, hilly terrains, poor infrastructure, proneness to floods and droughts. Fiscal efficiency encompasses parameters like maintaining revenue account balance, robust revenue effort, economies of expenditure linked to efficient provision of services and the quality of governance. Equity considerations must in effect aim for ensuring the provision of selected services at minimum acceptable standards across the country. It can be seen that on average, the low income States spend only half of the average per capita expenditure of high income States in social services. In a competitive environment, States that are able to access the market better are likely to grow faster than others. The growth experience of the 1990s shows that developed States with broad industrial base and developed market institutions and infrastructure has performed much better than those without them. The transfer system has also to take this factor into account. At the same time, 'efficiency' in the use of resource should be ensured and promoted. States that perform more efficiently in the delivery of services or raise more revenues relative to their tax bases should not be penalised. The task of formulating a sound transfer system has to establish a fine balance between equity and efficiency, a system where fiscal disadvantage is taken care of but fiscal imprudence is effectively discouraged.

Competitive and Cooperative Federalism

Much of the mainstream literature on federalism assumes that (i) governments are run by altruistic agents and are essentially benevolent, and (ii) different units of the government have essentially a co-operative relationship. Thus, federalism and its corollary—decentralisation is supposed to bring in welfare gains. One school of thought has argued that ideas of co-operative federalism founded on these premises do not always function efficiently and Coasian bargains do not always work.

Existence of competitive relationship between governmental units is a key feature of the literature on competitive federalism. Existence of competition brings in the importance of transaction costs of coordinating policies and their implementation vertically between different levels of government and horizontally between different units within each of the levels. It looks at the system of checks and balances and in such a system, explores the pre-conditions for achieving efficient intergovernmental competition. The efficiency is not merely in terms of providing public services but also in creating a favourable environment in which the markets can function. It is also argued that governments tend to emulate policies of other governments, and the voters and opposition parties benchmark performances of other governments and pressurise their own governments to emulate them. The American tradition is focused more on inducing efficiency by the process of 'voting by feet' where households or firms locate themselves in those jurisdictions where the mix of the publicly provided goods is closer to their preferences. In the original Tiebout formulation, jurisdictional competition leads to increase in efficiency through 'sorting and matching.' Others have suggested that such inter-jurisdictional competition may also serve as a disciplinary device to punish inappropriate market intervention by lower governmental officials.

There is a parallel development in the federalism literature from the political science perspective and that is called the 'market preserving federalism.' This approach, however, assumes that the various levels of government have a common philosophical approach to the importance of the market. Obviously, if there is a convergence of opinion on the role of the markets, it follows, that the structure must reflect this philosophy and try to act in a way in which the markets are allowed to function effectively. You may recall the famous book in management literature entitled 'Strategy and Structure.' An essential message of this book is that the structure of any corporate unit must flow from the strategy it has adopted to fulfill its objectives. Government interventions can be market-distorting or market-complementary. For example, administered prices are market-distorting, while a good legal system with enforceable contracts is market-complementary.

The extent and areas in which various levels of government in a country functions in a competitive manner are to be determined partly empirically and partly by the nature of the government structures. Sub-national governments such as State Governments in India do compete for capital, both domestic and foreign. That is why the policy framework and infrastructural availability are key elements in this competitive process. However, this competition should not result in a 'race to the bottom' when the States taken as a whole suffer. In fact competition in tax concession leads to serious erosion of revenues. With this realisation, State Governments in India have come together to fix floor levels with respect to taxation and to reduce tax concessions. It is, no doubt true, not only capital but also people will move to jurisdictions where the provision of services is better. However, one must recognize that there are areas in which such competition may have a limited role. With mobility of people constrained by various considerations, primary health and primary education are some areas in which competition is not possible. However, benchmarking and rating sub-national governments, whether it be in terms of human development or fiscal performance or infrastructural facilities has had a beneficial effect. In some ways, competition and coordination have to co-exist.

In meeting the challenges of globalisation, the Indian federal structure must respond in such a way as to create in the first place a large common market within the country. Restrictions on movement of goods and various other impediments have to go. Reform of the tax system has become essential. Introduction of a nation-wide Value Added Tax (VAT) will require a cooperative agreement among the States. While some States have expressed difficulties in introducing VAT, there is at least an agreement in principle to introduce VAT. Our country will have to move faster in this direction.

The economic policy environment in India has undergone a fundamental change. Transition to an increasingly market based development and opening up of the economy to face global competition will require policy changes, creation of market institutions and a responsive de-centralised system of governance. The reform agenda of both the Centre and States should be calibrated in a coordinated manner in the spirit of cooperative federalism. At the same time, it is necessary to recognise that governmental units in the federation have also a competitive relationship. It is important to nurture this competition to secure efficiency gains. Thus, both coordination and competition are needed and this makes the challenge formidable.

The traditional concerns of fiscal federalism such as the assignment of taxes and responsibilities as well as the correction of vertical and horizontal imbalances continue to remain important. However, it is necessary to take note of the changes in the environment in which Governments operate. Fiscal federalism must enable national and sub-national governments to operate in such a way that it lead to efficiency in the use of resources. This improvement in efficiency must be reflected not only in the services provided by the various levels of government but also in creating an environment in which all economic agents use resources efficiently.

3

Economics, Politics and Governance*

BIMAL JALAN

The subject of this paper is "Economic, Politics and Governance." On the face of it, the inter-relationship among these three elements of our national life is self-evident and does not require much discussion. After all, the country's economic policies and programmes are decided by the government and institutions created by it. These policies and programmes are generally approved by the elected representatives of the people in Parliament. Political leadership in framing these policies and programmes also has access to technical and economic advice.

Among developing countries, India is reputed to have one of the better governance structures at the centre, states and districts. The so-called "steel frame" was the envy of the post-colonial world. Even after allowing for some weakening of the frame, our civil services still remain a viable instrument of administration. Ever since independence, India has also been fortunate in having a string of top economists to advise the government in the process of planning and economic policy formulation—among them are well known names like Prof. Mahalanobis, Prof. K.N. Raj, Dr. Pitambar Pant, Professor Lakdawala, Prof. Sukhamoy Chakravarty, Dr. I.G. Patel, Prof. Raj Krishna, Dr. Manmohan Singh, Prof. Hanumantha Rao and several others. On the political side, we can rightfully take pride in our vibrant and functioning democracy. India was ruled by a single party with repeated mandates from the people for nearly 50 years after independence with some brief interruptions. During this period, there were a number of short-lived governments with varying mandates, but which nevertheless did their best to serve the country under difficult circumstances. In respect of governance, the administrative structure of India, with the so-called "steel-frame" of a permanent bureaucracy, has been the envy of the post-colonial developing world. Even after allowing

---

* The subject of this paper was also the theme of the Convocation Address delivered at the Indian Institute of Management on 3rd April 2004 and draws heavily on that address.

for a considerable rusting and weakening of the frame, the governance structure at the Centre, states, districts, and *panchayats* still remains largely intact.

Thus, we have had a fine combination of good economists, an operational governance structure, and functioning democracy—all working together. Yet, the results on the ground in terms of social or economic development over the long period since independence—leaving aside the most recent period—were rather disappointing. For the first fifty years after Independence, India lurched from one crisis to another. We also had low growth, low literacy, and an abundance of poverty. The vision outlined in 1956, at the beginning of the Second Plan, of a poverty-free India with full employment in 25 years, *i.e.* by 1981, still eludes us. An important question which needs to be debated is why this combination of economics, politics, and civil service did not lead to the kind of results that the people of our country could have legitimately expected.

Despite appearances to the contrary, since the very beginning of the planning process in India, the reality is that there has been a substantial gap between what was considered to be economically sound and what has been found to be politically feasible in different sectors of the economy. Economic strategy has seldom reflected our political or social realities or real political considerations. Similarly, the administrative implications of policies, launched with great conviction, have been seldom considered or, when considered, these implications did not affect, the actual evolution of economic policies or programmes on the ground.

Incidentally, the issue of a disjuncture between economics and politics was also posed by Prof. Hanumantha Rao while examining the reasons for India's slow progress in bringing about reforms in the agricultural sector. In an essay that he had contributed to the volume on Indian Economy edited by me more than a decade ago, his observations on the interface of economics with politics in agriculture are illuminating.[24] According to him, part of the problem in agriculture has been the monumental increase in subsidies—open as well as hidden—which benefit only a relatively small proportion of surplus farmers. Growing subsidies have undermined the capacity of the government to make productive investments in agriculture. The reason for this outcome is not economic but political and represents the dominant influence of larger farmers in the decision-making process, which is inevitable in a democratic polity.

---

24. Bimal Jalan (Ed.), "India's Economy: Problems and Prospects," Viking-Penguin, New Delhi, 1992.

To further illustrate the point, let me refer to the Mahalanobis-Nehru development strategy, which dominated our post-independence economic policies for close to 40 years. It is striking that despite many problems and tribulations, the basic framework of economic policies introduced soon after independence remained intact for as long as four decades and more because of its political appeal.

The basic elements of the post-independence economic strategy are too well known to need repetition. The Indian nationalist movement during the colonial period had given very high priority to making India economically independent—in addition to political independence—through aggressive import substitution and reduction in India's dependence on foreign trade and foreign investment. Also, based on the Soviet experience, it was believed that economic independence and high domestic savings could be achieved only if the "commanding heights" of the economy were in the hands of the public sector. It was assumed that if the means of production were owned by the State, all the value-added in production will flow to the people. Further, if consumption was discouraged, public savings would automatically increase. These savings could then be used for further investment and growth, and India could soon catch up with the developed world.

This was a most heart-warming economic vision, supported by leading economists of the day and widely respected academic models of savings, investment, and growth. Unfortunately, it paid scant regard to the political and administrative implications of the favoured strategy. The political assumption was that the representatives of the people, freely elected to power, will selflessly promote the greatest good of the greatest number. In public enterprises, in the absence of private capitalists, labour and management were expected to work together in harmony without political interference, in line with national priorities as laid down by the planners. Another important assumption was that India was one, and as was the case during the struggle for political independence, all Indian citizens will work selflessly without sectional interests to achieve the country's economic objectives.

The reality has proved to be vastly different. The political decision-making on economic issues in our country, as indeed in most democracies, is often driven by special interests rather than the common interests of the general public. These special interests are also more diverse in India than in other more developed and mature economies. Thus, there are special regional interests, not only among states, but also within states, depending on the electoral strength of the party in power in different parts of the state. Economic policy-making at the political level is further affected by occupational divide (*e.g.* farm *vs.* non-farm), the size of enterprise (*e.g.* large *vs.* small), caste, religion, political affiliations of trade unions, or asset class of power-wielders, and a host of other divisive factors. As a result, most of the economic benefits of specific government decisions are likely to flow to a special interest group or, in Mancur Olson's famous phrase, to "distributional coalitions." These coalitions are always more interested in influencing the distribution of wealth and income in their favour, rather than in the generation of additional output which has to be shared with the rest of society.

Also, the delivery of government benefits to special groups has given rise to a whole process of bargaining and conflict resolution among various interests. As a result, a large number of middlemen have emerged across the political spectrum. Further, as elections have become more expensive and more frequent with uncertain time period during which funds can be collected in different states, there is a greater tolerance of political corruption as an unavoidable feature of the electoral process.

Thus, contrary to what was envisaged by the founding fathers of our republic, and contrary to the vision of our planners, the political-economic balance, in actual practice, has turned out to be self-centric, narrow, and wasteful. An interesting question is: how did the stranglehold of special interests last so long? Where were the majority of the people who did not gain sufficiently from the economic bargaining process? The answer is not difficult to find. The simple fact is that the so-called majority is fractured into a large number of sub-groups of individuals who are divided among themselves by several factors (such as caste, religion, location or occupation), while special interests are united in protecting their share of the economic output. This is really why the so-called "haves" are so much more powerful than the "have-nots" in our society. It is, for example, the trade union of employed persons (or, the "haves") which is likely to go on strike when their economic interests are threatened, rather than the vast majority of the unemployed (or, the "have-nots") across the country.

At this point, I must make it clear that what I have said so far about the power of special interests in determining political economy outcomes is not an argument in favour of unfettered free markets, or the need for an economy without government regulations and laws. The issue here is not "markets *vs.* government." It is that the political priorities are distinct from priorities laid down by economists and experts. Thus, the problem with the Indian economy is not that its market is less or more free, but that its freedom is in the wrong domains. It is common knowledge that in most parts of India, government permissions, regulatory approvals, or licences can be purchased at a price. In these domains, the problem is that of excessive marketisation. On the other hand, in other areas where the market ought to be more free (for example, the labour market or international trade), India is strapped in bureaucratic red tape.

Two more caveats are necessary in considering the power of dominant coalitions in determining economic policy outcomes in our country. The point is not that these coalitions always emerge as winners in determining the direction of public policy, or that all politicians pander only to special interests. There are honourable exceptions, and there certainly are leaders who give primacy to the general public interests. But they are likely to be exceptions rather than the rule. They are also likely to face considerable hurdles in successfully pursuing economic policies that adversely affect the special interests of the organised groups. Similarly, there are situations (such as war, a natural catastrophe, or religious conflict) when a unity of purpose emerges among all sections of the people to promote the common good.

Another important assumption in the choice of post-independence development strategy was that public sector enterprises would generate public savings, which could be used for higher and higher levels of investment. However, instead of generating savings, the public sector soon became a drain on public savings. Despite commanding the *"commanding heights,"* public sector savings are now negative by as much as 4 per cent of GDP. These negative savings have led to fast accumulation of internal public debt and lower investment than would have been the case otherwise. In the annals of development history, it is hard to find another example of a perfectly sensible idea—the need for higher public investment for greater public good—leading to exactly the opposite result, i.e. higher public consumption with diminishing returns for the public!

Let me now move to the third aspect, namely, the governance structure for the delivery of public services to the people. As mentioned above, eminent economists have advised us, from time to time, on what should ideally be the country's development priorities, and elected political leaders have taken their own policy decisions on various economic issues according to their political perceptions. These policy and other decisions, once taken, have to be implemented through the multi-level administrative structure at the Centre, states, districts, and villages. The basic premise of India's plans, as well as the early development literature, was that the required administrative response would be forthcoming in abundant measure. The system of administration at different levels was expected to work in complete harmony, delivering savings and investments as postulated, and implementing programmes as scheduled.

It must be said to the credit of our planners that the Second Plan did ask itself the question whether the civil service would prove equal to the tasks assigned to it by the Plan. The Third Plan, too, explicitly recognised that the administrative machinery had become strained and the available personnel to implement the Plan were not adequate in quality and number. The subsequent Plans, particularly the Seventh Plan, sounded a note of desperation about widespread administrative inefficiencies and bottlenecks that were slowing down the economy. However, this desperation was not reflected in actual planning. We went on adding newer, larger and more comprehensive schemes to tackle national problems in virtually every walk of life, calling for greater and greater administrative involvement.

In fact, as perceived needs and requirements of the economy became greater and resources shrank, the administrative process became even more complex, requiring more people to perform the same task. As a result, there are more people employed by government in what statisticians euphemistically call "community and personal services" than in the public sector manufacturing enterprises or the private organised sector! To bring about this sort of result, some kind of an "invisible" dominant coalition has certainly been at work. One has to recall the functioning of the exchange control system in the past to appreciate how far removed policy planning was from administrative realities. Or, take the urban ceiling laws, which were supposed to free excess or surplus land for public housing and other uses. Even after 30 years, hardly anything has been acquired and these laws, instead of increasing the supply of affordable housing, have simply frozen the availability.

It is not that the problems were not understood or that people who ran the system were ill-motivated. It is an unfortunate fact of administrative and political life that systems and programmes, once introduced, acquire a momentum of their own because of the benefits and patronage that they provide to some sections of the people, including those who administer the programmes. When implementation problems occur, inefficiencies are identified, or misuses are detected, the response normally is to add one more step or one more level to the administrative chain.

More than 40 years ago, a well-known economist A.H. Hanson, a sympathetic observer of the Indian scene, felt compelled to ask this question: "Men are able, the organisation is adequate, the procedures are intelligently devised. Why then have the Plans since 1956 so persistently run into crisis?" This question was asked in 1963. Many of us are probably asking still the same question. Hanson's answer to his own question is also of some interest. In his view, the real problem was not with the theory of planning or the people who were making the plans, but with the unrealistic assumptions about the way people and societies were likely to respond. Too many of the government's assumptions about economic behaviour were simply unrealistic and differed from the way in which people acted in their own or in their groups' interests.

The recent controversy over the decision of the former Minister of Human Resource Development in the previous government regarding the level of fees charged by the Indian Institutes of Management (IIMs) issue also vividly illustrates the interplay of these three elements—economics, politics and governance. From a purely economic point of view, the critical issue is not the fees that the IIM charges, but the entry policy and the cost per student. If the entry is competitive and a particular level of cost, after due scrutiny, is found to be justified, then any teaching institution— through pricing, endowment, subsidy or a combination of these—has to recover the cost. Otherwise, it will either go out of business or the quality of its output will deteriorate. Now, let us assume that the government, in its wisdom, decides to further subsidise and reduce the fees that a particular institution charges to cover its costs. Then the economic issue from the public policy point of view is: why this larger subsidy from public funds, and for whose benefit?

This is where political considerations come in. It is always a popular move to say that no one, irrespective of income, should have to pay for use of water, electricity, food, education, including higher education. However, no government in the world has the ability to subsidise everyone and everything. Therefore, the political leadership has to choose among various kinds of subsidies and target groups. If the government decides to subsidise specialised technical or management education by more than what is necessary, from the public interest point of view, it is legitimate for the public to ask: why should the government increase subsidy even for those who can pay? In the parlance of public choice theory, an across-the-board subsidy of this kind, irrespective of the need for it, leads to "perverse equity." Instead of making government expenditure more equitable for society as a whole, an across-the-board subsidy of this type makes the system more inequitable and less progressive. The economics and politics of the ministerial decision on the fee issue was also linked to the governance aspects. Who should govern the IIMs—their own managements or the government of the day?

Looking at our past development experiences, it is established—beyond reasonable doubt—that our past economic strategy seldom reflected political realities. Similarly, governance or administrative implications of development or public expenditure policies were seldom taken into account in framing those policies. This is about the past. What about the present and the future? The process of liberalisation and economic reforms, launched in 1991, and pursued actively in recent years, has yielded positive results, removed some of the structural rigidities, and created potential for higher growth. At the same time, it will be a mistake to be complacent about our recent successes. These gains can disappear very quickly unless a stronger programme is launched to further improve our economic decision-making processes, remove scope for political discretion, reduce unproductive expenditure, and improve the quality of governance at all levels. The system must be made to work in the interests of the public in general, rather than the few, including those who are supposed to serve the public, namely, government servants and elected representatives.

To achieve the above objective, we need to move on a number of fronts. Let me mention some of them. In the area of economic policy, we need to avoid "ideological certainty." As pointed out by Albert Hirschman in a highly perceptive essay on the experiences of Latin American countries, the blame for economic disasters in several of these countries lay *not* in the use of policies considered by economic theorists to be wrong but in the blind pursuit of policies considered by theorists to be right— of the structuralist variety in the 1960s and of the neo-classical persuasion in the 1970s and 1980s.[25] Development economists tended to take ideological positions (both left and the right) on such matters as planning, the market mechanism, foreign investment, inflation, the rule of the State, and so on. Although, in India, in view of our democratic tradition, public policymakers may not have gone to the same extremes as in Latin America, there is little doubt that, as mentioned above, for a very long time after independence there was a strong tendency among our economic

---

25. Hirschman, A.O. (1987). "The Political Economy of Latin American Development: Seven Exercises in Retrospection," in *Latin American Research Review*, Vol. 22, No. 3, 1987.

thinkers to ignore political and administrative realities. Of late, fortunately, there has been a shift from ideological certainty to a more questioning and pragmatic attitude. This has yielded favourable results, for example, in India's external sector management. For the first time, after more than a half-century of independence, the balance of payments constraint or fear of periodic crises is no longer a factor in determining our economic policy. In the making of economic policy in other areas also, we must adopt similar pragmatic and flexible approaches, which take into account contemporary realities.

Final decisions on policy matters must continue to be made by political authorities, who are accountable to the people through Parliament and legislatures. However, there should be a clear distinction between decisions on policy and their implementation. Once policy decisions have been made, the latter has to be left to professional administrators without political interference but with due accountability. To make such a division of responsibility work, it is essential to avoid governmental micro-management, and remove procedural bottlenecks and case-by-case considerations of applications by individuals and organisations. Simplifying policies and procedures is an absolute priority. The scope for political or administrative discretion must be eliminated for all, but the very few large cases, which have economy-wide implications. The detailed case-by-case approach to policy implementation is an important hurdle in the country's economic life. In the last decade, some progress has been made in simplifying procedures, but not enough. Similarly, in the interest of transparency, there should be full disclosures of financial decisions made by multifarious agencies on a daily basis rather than annually in aggregate form. There is no reason why, except in matters of national security, all decisions made at the ministerial or secretary level cannot be put on a notice board in the ministry concerned on daily basis.

As pointed out by Prof. Hanumantha Rao regarding the impact of subsidies in agriculture, it is ironical that higher and higher fiscal deficits on this account over time have not resulted in increasing the government's ability to spend where higher expenditure is required, for example, for productive investments in irrigation or in the maintenance or expansion of public services. Most of the government expenditure is now committed to servicing past debt or meeting salary and other past commitments. We now have a high fiscal deficit without fiscal empowerment. A wholesale change in the government's fiscal policy and making it more responsive to changing requirements are now essential. This is a most difficult task in view of the dead weight of the past, but it can no longer be avoided.

For the administration to work with accountability, we urgently need legal reforms to focus sharply on the interests of the public, and not only those of the public servant in the functioning of the governmental and public delivery systems. Clear mechanisms for establishing accountability for performance are essential, and all forms of special protection for persons working in government or public sector agencies (except for the armed forces or agencies engaged in the maintenance of law and order) deserve to be eliminated.

Many of our public institutions—including academic institutions and non-governmental organisations (NGOs)—have to necessarily depend on the government for annual grants to meet part of their essential expenditure. As they use public funds, their accountability for performance is essential. However, it has to be ensured that there is arm's length relationship between government and autonomous public institutions of national importance. Damage inflicted by unwarranted political or bureaucratic interference can cause permanent damage to an institution within a very short period, and has to be avoided in public interest. The best way of enforcing accountability for performance is to set up appropriate annual audit mechanisms by outside professionals and periodic reviews, of academic performance, say, every five years, by a review committee of experts or peer groups.

In taxation and other financial areas, administrative discretion or reliance on inspectors and searches has to be eliminated except under well-defined circumstances involving high crimes such as treason, terrorism, and smuggling or money laundering on a scale which affects national security or economic stability. There is clear and irrefutable evidence from our past experience that administrative discretion has not led to an improvement in fiscal receipts or better compliance with laws. On the other hand, such powers, and the impunity with which they can be used, have become serious sources of corruption in society.

Let me conclude on a somewhat more cheerful note. Notwithstanding our past performance, I am sanguine about India's economic potential and our ability to achieve high growth with financial stability. The reason for this confidence is that, despite problems in governance, the innate ability of our people is immense and has been demonstrated beyond reasonable doubt. The open, participative and democratic system ensures that a change, where necessary, can be delayed, but it cannot be avoided altogether. If we act now, and if we are able to realise our full potential in the next 20 years, India's poverty would become a distant memory.

4

Perspectives on Macroeconometric Models for India

K. KRISHNAMURTY

1. Introduction

This paper presents a birds eye view of perspectives on macro-econometric models for India and offers suggestions to make the models relevant to the current times. Computable general equilibrium, input-output and programming models are outside the purview of the essay.

Macro econometric modelling research has been a long march ever since its start in mid-fifties but in an environment not so encouraging for research on Tinbergen - Klein type macroeconometric models for India in the earlier decades. But it was not a lonely trail. Several researchers joined the march despite heavy odds and low returns. There are several reasons for poor encouragement for such research. Foremost among them was that they were the hey-days of Input-Output techniques and planning models. The attitude towards macro econometric models has now turned favourable under the new policy regime.

We now turn *first*, to an outline of evolution of econometric models for India, *second*, to some theoretical and empirical issues relevant to macro modelling, *third*, to use of models in forecasting, policy analysis and planning,[26] *fourth*, to future agenda of research with some suggestions and finally, concluding observations.

2. Evolution of Econometric Models

India has perhaps been among the first few developing countries for which economy-wide econometric models were estimated. The earliest work dates back to the mid-fifties when macro modelling as a professional academic activity even in many developed countries was still in its infancy.

---

26. For a more detailed discussion on some of the issues, see for instance Bhaduri (1982), Krishnamurty (1992, 2002) and Pandit (1995, 1999).

The earliest model for India was estimated by Narasimham under the guidance of Nobel Laureate Professor Jan Tinbergen. The hazards in attempting to model an underdeveloped economy at that time are self evident. Problems arising from the absence of comprehensive and empirically feasible theoretical framework relevant to developing countries, weak and inadequate database, and lack of perspective as regards the role of such models in less developed countries (LDC) are quite evident from the early models. Since then there has been considerable progress.

Broadly speaking, models for India can be grouped into five generations. Fifth Generation models are now on line.[27] A good number of models belong to the earliest generation. These were obviously the most severely constrained by a variety of data problems on top of the usual hurdles and disadvantages associated with new explorations. Most of the First Generation models were Ph.D. dissertations many of which were prepared under the supervision of Nobel Laureate Professor Lawrence R Klein. Time and resources, apart from data availability, were severe constraints on the researchers. Unlike their counterparts working on developed countries, researchers on Indian models have had very little to draw upon in term of sectoral econometric studies. Therefore, it is not surprising that they had to be small, simple and often rather close to the text book macroeconomic theory.

Nevertheless, these models served well as explorations in an important branch of economic analysis. They uncovered the weaknesses of the available database—many of which have been reduced since then and also prompted further quantitative research at the sectoral level. Eventhough, models belonging to the First Generation were simple, they were by no means routine. Despite considerable odds, each model had a specific focus and innovated wherever it dealt with problems common with other models. To be specific, the major focus in different models belonging to this generation (early sixties to mid-seventies) includes issues such as price behaviour (Choudhry, 1963; Marwah, 1963 and 1972; Chakrabarty, 1977), investment behaviour and endogenous population expansion in a two sector model focussed on growth (Krishnamurty, 1964), integration of real, monetary and foreign trade sectors with endogeneous capacity utilisation (Choudhry and Krishnamurty, 1968), role of foodgrain output in growth and price stability (Pandit, 1973), interaction between monetary

---

27. Paradigm shift in economic regime and major revisions in the database in the nineties have necessitated overhaul of even the latest models. They are in the process of being reformulated, re-estimated and being put to test in forecasting, scenario and policy analysis; see Pandit *et al.*, (2002) and Nachane *et al.*, (2004).

and real variables in the monetised component of the economy (Bhattacharya, 1975), the structure of monetary and financial markets (Gupta, 1973; Mammen, 1973) , external trade (Choudhary, 1963; Dutta 1964), and growth in a dualistic economy (Agarwala, 1971).

Among the Second Generation models (mid-seventies to early eighties) we have the ones by Pani (1977), Ahluwalia (1979), Bhattacharya (1982), Pandit (1982), Srivastava (1981), and Rangarajan (1982). The most important feature that distinguishes these models from the earlier ones is their emphasis on policy analysis.

Most of the other features flow from this objective. They are more disaggregated and, therefore, much larger. There is an explicit recognition of the mixed nature and some other institutional characteristics of the Indian economy.

They also went one step ahead of their predecessors by allowing for lagged, more varied and somewhat more complex adjustment processes. Unlike their predecessors, the Second Generation models had the advantage of a considerably improved database, a large variety of rigorous micro and sectoral empirical studies that have emerged since the sixties, and an increased professional interest in applied econometric research. Notwithstanding, until about the mid-seventies, progress had been in fits and starts.

Progress of macro econometric research has been considerable in the eighties. Several models were estimated. They are labelled as belonging to the Third Generation. These include (a) Ghose, Lahiri, Madhur, and Roy (1983), (b) Pani (1984), (c) Bhattacharya (1984), (d) Krishnamurty (1984), (e) Pandit (1984, 1985, 1985a, 1986, 1986a and 1989), (f) Bhattacharya and Rao (1986), (g) Ahluwalia and Rangarajan (1986), (h) Narain Sinha (1986), (i) Pandit and Bhattacharya (1987), (j) Bhattacharya (1987), (k) Madhur (1987), (l) Chakrabarty (1987), (m) Krishnamurty, Pandit, and Sharma (1988), (n) Kannan (1989), (o) Panchamukhi and Mehta (1991), and (p) Bhattacharya and Guha (1992). Unlike the work in the earlier decades, econometric modelling in the eighties had the benefit of many in depth sectoral econometric studies.[28] The Third Generation models cited are in many ways similar to those belonging to the Second Generation. But they are larger in size, better disaggregated and seek to carry forward the analysis of policy issues initiated by the Second Generation model builders. The distinguishing features of the Third

---

28. For select studies, see the section on references at the end.

Generation models are that they explicitly deal with the problems of macroeconomic adjustment and venture to address issues that have not been discussed earlier in formal quantitative terms. Many of these models were put to a variety of policy simulations more rigorously than those belonging to the Second Generation.

The special focus of each of the Third Generation models is briefly presented in the following Table:

Broad Features of Third Generation Models

	Author	Period	Special Focus
1.	Ghose, Lahiri, Madhur, and Roy (1983)	1960-78	General purpose model covering agriculture, industry, government, money and trade with high level of disaggregation.
2.	Pani (1984)	1970-82	Output, demand and prices, and their interaction.
3.	Bhattacharya (1984)	1952-76	Public expenditures, inflation and growth.
4.	Krishnamurty (1984)	1962-80	Inflation and growth; supply side, infrastructure, money and prices public investment and its interrelationship with private investment and fiscal operations and growth - inflation trade-off.
5.	Pandit (1984)	1951-78	Medium term analysis of outputs and prices.
6.	Pandit (1985)	1951-75	Macroeconomic structure, stabilisation policies and growth.
7.	Pandit (1985a)	1955-80	Supply, demand and monetary policy.
8.	Pandit (1986)	1951-80	Growth performance and relative roles of supply and demand; tests made to detect structural break in mid-sixties.
9.	Pandit (1986a)	1954-81	External trade in detail and price formation; varying periods for different equations; used in the Global LINK model.
10.	Bhattacharya and Rao (1986)	1967-84	Agriculture-industry interrelationship and public investment.
11.	Ahluwalia and Rangarajan (1986)	1961-80	Agriculture-industry linkages
12.	Pandit and Bhattacharya (1987)	1961-80	Resource mobilisation, growth and inflation.

Contd...

...Contd...

Author	Period	Special Focus
13. Bhattacharya (1987)	1951-85	Effectiveness of monetary policy and inflation.
14. Madhur (1987)	1952-85	Macro impacts of monetary and fiscal policy changes; *ex ante* forcasts.
15. Chakrabarty (1987)	1963-84	Linkages among sectors: real (domestic and foreign), fiscal and monetary sectors.
16. Krishnamurty, Pandit and Sharma (1988)	1962-83	Parameters of growth, productivity, infrastructure, imports, exports, public investment and its Interrelationship with private investment, and relative prices.
17. Kannan (1989)	1968-85	Monetary approach to balance of payments: includes trade, invisibles and capital account.
18. Panchamukhi and Mehta (1991)	1970-84	Emphasis on trade flows.
19. Mehta and Sinha (1991)	1952-85	External trade and public sector
20. Rastogi (1991)	1951-87	Two sector rational expectations model with government budget, external trade and debt, and labour market.
21. Bhattacharya and Guha (1992)	1970-89	Public sector resource gap, external trade and public debt—domestic and external.

The Fourth Generation models were developed in the nineties. These models to name a few, are (1) Anjaneyulu (1993), (2) Chakravarty and Joshi (1994), (3) Bhattacharya, Barman, and Nag (1994), (4) Rangarajan and Mohanty (1997), (5) Mammen (1999), and (6) Klein and Palanivel (1999). They all address issues relevant to new policy regime and carry out many 'what if' policy scenario simulations. These models are large in size, provide emphasis on sectoral details and inter-links and trade-offs between sectors.

Each successive generations of models, needless to add, have benefited from the earlier generation models by avoiding pitfalls of the earlier ones and gaining from the advances made earlier even if such advances were only incremental in character.

It is to be emphasised that most of the modelling exercises in India have been the result of efforts of individual researchers. They were constructed, put to validation tests and useful policy simulations were carried out. However, none of them were maintained and serviced on a sustained basis for policy analysis and forecasting. The trend elsewhere in the world has been towards collective efforts of several scholars working in teams complimenting each other and maintaining the models on a continuous basis. Large size models were the need of the day. The need to comprehend complexities of the functioning of the economy, build comprehensive models incorporating complexities and maintain them are beyond the scope and efforts of one or two individuals.

In tune with the times and the needs, a group of researchers—N K Choudhary, Meghnad Desai, D B Gupta, K Krishnamurty, K L Krishna—under the leadership of A L Nagar with a modest support from the Indian Council of Social Science Research (ICSSR) made an effort to build and maintain a model for India in the early seventies (1974). The team received substantial academic support from Professor A M Khusro in this venture. Considerable time and effort went into building the database and constructing insightful sectoral models but for locational disadvantages in times not so well endowed with communication network as of today, a complete model could not be put together and analysed.

As the foremost institutional effort, the National Council of Applied Economic Research (NCAER) in mid-eighties built a Computable General Equilibrium (CGE) model. NCAER improved it over the years by updating, supplementing it with behavioural sub-systems and also with anticipatory survey data. They make forecasts and policy simulations regularly. By the very nature of the CGE models, the forecasts are for a year at a time and over time sequential forecasts do not generally imbibe dynamic interlinks. Notwithstanding these factors, this continuing effort is a laudable example of collective attempt with institutional backing.

Professor Klein was a close observer of model building efforts in India. Some of us were his students and he kept abreast of developments in the field. In his Institute of Economic Growth (IEG) Silver Jubilee Lecture (1984), he said:

> that Indian research on model building for the nation should proceed. The many world class econometricians in India should persevere and keep on trying. Many fine examples of econometric model building, some of a pioneering nature, have been completed for India but none has, up to this point, been regularly maintained........Models go out of date fast. Databases get revised, new kinds of economic problems come to the fore; and sometimes behaviour changes. A model must be continually administered and kept up to date in order to remain useful ... . India appears to be in need of a serious model building effort, drawing on the best econometric talent, and designed to function as an ongoing effort, over many years, turning out rolling forecasts

every month or two on the most refined time period possible—probably annually at the present time. Such a project should have the form and appearance of the best efforts in western industrial countries, and I hope that in this academic enclave such a research effort will be launched.

The clarion call from their teacher led Krishnamurty, Pandit and their associates (IEG-DSE Team) to launch macroeconometric modelling for India in early nineties on a sustained basis with support from the National Science Foundation (NSF, USA), Industrial Development Bank of India (IDBI) and the ICSSR. The Model research was carried out in the Reserve Bank of India (RBI) Endowment Unit at the IEG. They were greatly helped by Klein in his role as US Cooperating Scientist for the project. The model has been extensively used for forecasting and policy simulations. It underwent several revisions with updated data. The project moved to the Centre for Development Economics (CDE) at the Delhi School of Economics (DSE) in 1999. It is a live project and is now referred to as CDE-DSE model. Several papers were put out in the public domain on the system (IEG-DSE Research Team, 1996, 1997 and 1999).

About the same time as the launch of IEG-DSE model, the Planning Commission set up the Development Planning Centre at the IEG. The faculty of the Centre, in collaboration with Central Planning Bureau of the Netherlands and the Planning Commission, completed a preliminary version of the model in 1998 (IEG-CPB-IPC, 1997-98). Subsequently, the model seems to have undergone substantial revisions and is being used for forecasting and policy analysis.

With these models *viz.*, NCAER, IEG-DSE/CDE-DSE, and IEG, the macro modelling in India came of age. We have entered what may be called the phase of Fifth Generation models. These models are large, dynamic, incorporate better inter-dependence of sectors compared to many of the earlier models and attempt to incorporate change in policy regime.

From mid-fifties until now about fifty macroeconometric models have been built for India. Tinbergen helped to initiate the process and Klein evinced continued interest and provided intellectual support. The two pioneers and their contributions have signally helped to promote research in this area and assisted in attaining the current status.

Forecasting, which was not taken seriously in the early days of macroeconometric modelling is now respectable. Apart from the three established research institutions, various private agencies are in the field but the database and structure of their models on which the forecasts are based are not transparent to the academia as the models are not in the public domain. The pendulum has swung to the other end but the academic profession has to ensure that forecasting and model based policy analysis retain hard earned respectability.

The IEG-DSE Research Team and its members individually and collectively developed several dynamic macroeconometric models of Tinbergen-Klein type since the eighties, which have been put to several simulation exercises. They have also been used to provide biannual forecasts of major macroeconomic variables and medium-term economic scenarios under alternative assumptions with appropriate adjustment factors to account for recent changes in the economy. The IEG-DSE/CDE-DSE model is a part of the Global LINK Model.[29] The results are regularly presented at the Fall and Spring meetings of Project LINK and subsequently published.

The main characteristics of the latest published version of the model are[30]:

(1)   It is the largest of its kind for India with close to 350 equations,

(2)   It is disaggregated into five sectors, namely, agriculture, manufacturing, infrastructure, economic services and public administration. Agriculture is further sub-divided into food and non-food agriculture,

(3)   The sectoral price levels and capital formation are determined in the system with public sector nominal capital formation being exogenous,

(4)   There is a large output sector, a price system and an investment block,

(5)   The trade flows are disaggregated into edible products, raw materials, POL products and manufactures,

(6)   The quantity of imports and exports is determined with exogenous import prices and endogeneous exchange rate. The export prices are not fixed, so giving rise to an upward sloping supply curve. This implies that an increase in external demand on account of devaluation will not yield the full benefits since the supply curve is not horizontal. Pass-through effects dampen the increase in export revenues in foreign exchange terms,

---

29. The LINK Model was initiated by Professor Klein in the late sixties and initially comprised of largely developed OECD Countries. Progressively over time many more countries were brought into the system including a large number of developing countries. The model is now operating under UN auspices and includes about 80 countries (Klein *et al.*, 1999).

30. See IEG-DSE Team (1999) and also, Pandit and Krishnamurty (2004).

(7)   In agriculture, prices are determined by flex price system while other prices follow mark-up mechanism with monetary factor and administered prices having their role in both the sectors,

(8)   It has a comprehensive sub-model dealing with public finances and resource gap,

(9)   It has also a fairly well disaggregated monetary sector model dealing with financial flows and structure of interest rates,

(10) A comprehensive treatment of saving behaviour of households and corporate sectors is built in,

(11) Crowding-in and crowding-out effects of public investment on private investment are incorporated,

(12) Prices play an important role in domestic resource allocation and foreign trade,

(13) Interest rates and inflation expectations have an important role in determining financial flows and savings, and their composition,

(14) The model provides more emphasis on demand side compared to its earlier versions of the model but supply side continues to be dominant,

(15) The system is driven by weather, public sector nominal investment and its composition, and global trade and external prices, among others, and

(16) All parameters are estimated on the basis of historical data and no benchmark estimates are used.

3. Some Theoretical and Empirical Issues

The theoretical framework for macroeconometric models appropriate for developing countries remains hazy even today. One proposition that held sway for long is the inappropriateness of Keynesian economics to LDCs. Notwithstanding; two points need to be noted in this context. *First*, the debate failed to maintain a distinction between the Keynesian methodology and the Keynesian policy conclusions. Second, while there might have been a case against the applicability of the Keynesian theory, no need was felt to explain why classical theory was more relevant to less developed countries and that LDCs suffer more from supply than demand constraints. The belief that demand deficiency is not a problem may be an exaggeration. For instance, India has experienced several episodes of demand constrained growth, including the recent one.

Importance of the distinction between the Keynesian methodology and the policy recommendations following from this methodology when combined with specific empirical assumptions has been quite effectively brought out by Chakravarty (1979a, 1979b and 1983) in late seventies and early eighties. The upshot is that one may accept the methodology and, not necessarily the empirical assumptions and the consequences that flow from it. It has also been argued by Pandit and Rakshit that the various assertions rightly made about the nature of markets, and the scarcity of information in LDCs strengthen the case of Keynesian *albeit* quantity adjustments rather than that for classical price adjustments.

Even though these distinctions are well known, it is pertinent to identify the basic features of developing economies, which appear to be relevant to macroeconomic modelling. Most of these were in fact highlighted by Klein nearly four decades ago and again recently in mid-eighties. These features are as follows:

First, governments in most LDCs besides formulating and executing economic policies, also predominate in many markets as producer, investor and consumer. Consequently, government behaviour is neither fully exogenous nor market oriented.

Second, partly because of the predominance of government intervention by way of investment and output controls, administered prices and procurements that prevailed earlier, prices may cease to be flexible in a large segment of the economy. This implies a larger role for quantity adjustment than is usually allowed for.

Third, since interest rates were, by and large, policy determined in the organised money markets, equilibrium would partly be attained through price level changes. However, with near abolition of controls on private investment, liberalisation in the financial sector and a significant departure from administered price regime in India, the relative role of quantity and price adjustments may gradually tend to shift in favour of the latter compared to the situation under the earlier policy regime.

Fourth, credit, as distinct from money may play an important role in production as well as in investment. Thus, credit availability will tend to affect output *via* supply as well as demand. The interdependence between monetary and fiscal policies in LDCs is also very pertinent in this context.

Fifth, the process of liberalisation along with macroeconomic adjustment policies pursued in India since early nineties has led to fiscal restraint. These measures have a serious actual and potential impact on the role of the state in the development process and in particular on its investment activities. In this context, it is necessary to understand and evaluate the extent to which public and private investments are competitive or complementary and the nature of changes in the relationship that may have taken place and is taking place under the present economic regime. This has been particularly emphasised recently by Desai (1997).

The effect of public investment on private investment has two aspects. First is related to whether the ultimate effect of the former on the latter is one of displacement. The second is concerned about the channels through which the impact is transmitted. According to the classical theory and its modern versions, public investment must displace private investment or, more generally, expenditure. The impact works through the rate of interest. It may also work through movements in the price level depending on how such investment is financed and the extent of capacity utilisation in the economy. On the other hand, the effect of increase in public investment on private investment will be positive in a Keynesian world, *via* the multiplier if the economy is operating below capacity. However, in so far as public investment is targeted in nominal terms and financed by money creation, price effects may erode real public investment and, consequently, have a dampening effect on private investment.

In most LDCs—and this is certainly true of India—public investment has typically taken the form of infrastructure facilities like irrigation, power generation, transport, communications, and manufacture of critical intermediates like steel, manufacture of heavy machinery, electricals, etc. To the extent this is so, public investment should stimulate and facilitate private investment. Moreover, extension of activities like transport and power helps create new capacities. With regard to financing, the important point to note is that credit in the formal capital market made available at administered low interest rates is usually rationed. Government used its pre-emptive power that it had enjoyed in the past, to exercise the first claim on resources. This may have driven up the cost of credit to investors. Also, if public investment is financed by borrowing from the central bank there will be some rise in prices, eroding the real value of outlays which are usually set in nominal terms. Some recent studies reveal the following: (i) a generally crowding-in phenomenon, (ii) weakening of this phenomena in the last decade or so, presumably because of the reduced infrastructure-creating role of such investment and, (iii) crowding-out through financial markets and due to price effects.

Finally, it does not appear justifiable to assume away either supply bottlenecks nor demand constraints. Supply constraints may arise from inadequate infrastructure, shortage of imported inputs, poor harvests due to natural factors and capital shortages. All the same, the supply inflexibility should not be exaggerated as has often been done. This constraint is unlikely to be binding in all sectors and at all times. Equally, demand constraints also cannot be ignored. Restraint on public expenditure, as for instance, in the recent years of macro economic adjustment seems to have led to demand induced economic slow down. Shifts between demand and supply constrained regimes have not been an uncommon feature.

A dispassionate and balanced evaluation of the different analytical issues and empirical considerations suggest that the approach for macromodelling of LDCs would be eclectic in character drawing on various theories relevant to specific structure and changing conditions of the economy under study. In the Indian context, the earlier models laid relatively more emphasis on demand compared to supply while latter models concentrated more on supply constraints and consequently, what is needed is a model that properly emphasises relative importance of supply as well as demand factors and can distinguish regime shifts.

Despite various conceptual and data problems, the issues that need to be addressed in modelling LDCs have been highlighted by Klein in his IEG Silver Jubilee Lecture as under:

(1) the need to emphasise conditions of supply,

(2) demand factors and, enhanced roles of income/wealth distributions and the influence of inequality,

(3) population, its growth and structure,

(4) the extreme importance of trade and its strategic significance, in many cases, of key commodities that are closely tied to world market conditions, especially world prices,

(5) detailed treatment of capital flows, reserves and foreign debt,

(6) exchange rate and its determination,

(7) money supply sensitivity to interrelated twin balances—the internal budget balance of government and the external balance of trade and payments, and its impact on prices,

(8) the necessity of imports, especially of capital equipment, technologies and basic raw materials, making import multipliers positive with respect to these particular type of imports, and

(9) the large size and importance of public sector, responsible for the economy's infrastructure and public goods that meet the basic needs of the poor, such as, wage goods.

Addressing the above issues should throw considerable light on the following important features of the economy:

(a) The role of well identified supply and demand factors in determining sectoral and overall growth performance,

(b) Interdependence of sectors for growth and price stability,

(c) Trade, balance of payments and short run as well as long run problems arising there from,

(d) The growth-inflation trade-off and the fine tuning of monetary and fiscal policies including administered pricing and subsidies,

(e) The saving-investment process and its relationship with factors such as inflation, budget deficits, balance of payments and, internal and external debt and their structure,

(f) The place of the public sector and government's regulatory policies in influencing growth and stability, and

(g) Importance of wage goods defined in a broader way to include not only food but also clothing, shelter and other manufactured goods particularly certain type of consumer durables.

It needs to be noted that though several issues raised by Klein have been addressed in the Indian models in varying degrees, no single model so far has focused on all the issues in a comprehensive and well articulated manner.

The introduction of new policy regime in early nineties has given rise to a number of questions which need to be addressed. In brief, one needs to consider whether macroeconomic models which cover several pre-reform years and few years of post-reform period are of any relevance in dealing with the contemporary policy issues and forecasting as the processes of adjustment are bound to undergo changes. All sectors do not respond to policy changes with the same speed. At best one can visualise that financial and capital markets and, foreign trade, BOP and exchange rate may experience faster change compared to say productivity, saving and investment behaviour.[31] If this view is correct, then it would follow that some of the segments of the on-going models will have to be checked for possible slow changes while others with faster change may need to be overhauled substantially. The use of econometric models for scenario analysis or for forecasting is not a mechanical job. It is an art requiring judicious judgements about the functioning of the economy. Also, some

---

31. For a comprehensive analysis, see Pandit (1995).

of the critical relationships need to be put to frequent re-estimation with new information even if they are preliminary in nature to capture changing responses, if any. Many factors of socio-economic and political nature cannot be captured in any mathematical or quantitative models and, thus, cannot be properly dealt with.

To meet the objectives of macroeconometric modelling highlighted earlier, we should be broadly concerned with disaggregating the economy into sectors, which are more or less homogeneous as regards price and output adjustments keeping in view availability and reliability of data. This will depend partly on whether activities are publicly or privately controlled.

Following these considerations, it appears advisable to disaggregate the real side of the economy into five sectors, namely

(a) 'Agriculture' and related activities and within it, food and non-food sectors,

(b) 'Manufacturing',

(c) 'Infrastructure' consisting of construction, power generation, transport, communications, mining, water supply, etc.,

(d) 'Economic Services' including real estate, banking, insurance, trade, hotels, etc., and,

(e) 'Public Administration and Defence.'

This extent of disaggregation is, on the one hand, meaningful and manageable and, on the other, reliable in terms of data. Moreover, this disaggregation permits incorporating interdependence between sectors, say for example, the role of infrastructure in determining level of activity in other sectors such as manufacturing or traditional interdependence between agriculture and manufacturing.

Further, it is now widely agreed that for 'Agricultural' sector, output is largely fixed in the short run but relatively flexible in the medium and the long run. Also, prices in this sector are market clearing subject to rachet effects of procurement and support prices determined by government. For 'Manufacturing' there is general consensus that output may possibly be demand-constrained and that prices are mostly subject to the Kaleckian mark-up on unit costs. For 'Infrastructure' sector output is likely to be resource constrained and prices administered subject to unit production costs. In the case of 'Economic Services' output can safely be assumed to be capable of adjusting to demand and, therefore, related to the level of economic activity in the commodity-producing sectors including infrastructure. Modelling of price behaviour is difficult but not impossible. For 'Public Administration and Defence' both output and price are hard to disentangle. The nominal value added in this sector is merely determined by expenditure. Any unscrambling of this value into prices and quantities is quite arbitrary. Finally, it is necessary to note that whereas 'Agriculture' is overwhelmingly privately controlled, 'Manufacturing' and 'Economic' services are mixed, and 'Infrastructure' is predominantly in the public sector and likely to remain so even in the wake of economic reforms for some more years to come. The last one, 'Public Administration and Defence' is entirely constituted of government activities. As mentioned earlier, the public sector should preferably not be combined with private sector activities but data availability poses problems in this context.

In addition, there would be differences within each sector so that inaccuracy arising from ignoring these differences is a cost one has to bear to ensure manageability of the model. However, it is believed that as a result of the scheme followed in Krishnamurty and Pandit's models, the inaccuracy would not be too large. The foregoing discussion, thus, suggests that in modelling both outputs as well as prices, one need to adopt a differential approach across sectors because of differences in (i) the extent to which the resource constraints may or may not be binding, (ii) nature of the market structure, (iii) the extent to which activities are publicly or privately managed, (iv) nature of public intervention in price determination, and (v) nature of the product, associated technology and organisation of production. Clearly, disaggregation of the economy into only agriculture and non-agriculture as was done in early studies is not at all adequate.

Further, it may be postulated that unlike other sectors 'Manufacturing' may be either demand-constrained or resource-constrained in the sense that demand may either exceed or fall short of the capacity output. Clearly, the actual output *ex post* must be equal to the smaller of the two. Thus, the level of activity in this sector and the rest of the economy might switch between two regimes, generating a pattern of cyclical growth. An approach which allows for this would be better than those from the methodologies of 'only aggregate demand' or 'only aggregate supply.' Capacity output needs to be constrained by the stock of capital, raw material supply, and availability of infrastructural facilities.

4. Forecasting and Policy Use of Models

Despite the early start that macro modelling has had for India, we have not gone as far as many other LDCs have in developing, maintaining and using such models for planning, policy analysis and forecasting. In the past, the attitude of planners and policymakers as well as of the academic profession at large, has generally been one of scepticism and at best, lukewarm. A few points need to be highlighted in this context.

First, a large segment of policy formulation and evaluation in India, as in other LDCs, is concerned with institutional and structural changes which are rather difficult to deal with in terms of econometric models. For the methodology adopted in econometric models does not permit the freedom in choosing either the values of parameters or the types of relationships required for such changes. Moreover, many of the policy instruments designed to achieve structural changes cannot be quantified nor viewed in isolation of a variety of socio-political considerations. Consequently, the use of formal modelling, of whatever kind, is considerably restricted.

Second, planning concerns have largely been with long run rather than with short run problems. The long run policy has predominantly taken the form of inter-temporal and inter-sectoral allocation of investment and has been handled in the framework of input-output models. The behavioural segment of the complete model has usually been taken care of by means of simple and isolated relationships. However, this situation has changed in recent years.

Third, as mentioned earlier, early generation models, which were available till the eighties, were largely exploratory. They brought out important features of the functioning and inter-linkages between different segments of the economy. But they were not well suited nor intended to be used for practical policy analysis or forecasting. The models that emerged in later eighties and early nineties were serious and large scale attempts meant for policy analysis and forecasting. However, they were only used for policy analysis through 'what if' simulations but the modellers generally shied away from using them for forecasting. This may be because there was no serious dialogue among the model builders themselves and between them and others in the profession on the one hand. And on the other, there was also no interaction with planners and policymakers to instil the required confidence. The situation has, however, changed in the nineties with the ushering of new economic regimes. Policymakers have begun to show serious interest by interacting, promoting and collaborating in macroeconometric model building activity with a view to use them as an aid in planning, policy-making and forecasting. Thus, the recent models have come to assume importance in planning and forecasting and to a limited extent in policy-making. Quantification helps in calibrating policy responses. However, a lot more needs to be achieved before the models could be used with some confidence in policy-making in practise.

The macro modellers can now say with some confidence that to a variety of questions, econometric models can provide answers which are not only plausible and internally consistent but also much better than what the other available techniques can offer. They may relate to planning, policy formulation, policy evaluation, scenario analysis or merely to a description of the structure of the economy. For instance, a number of questions relating to the dynamics of price behaviour, consequences of the alternative patterns of public finance on savings and capital formation, choice of an appropriate exchange rate policy and, intersectoral linkages and trade-offs can be handled better with the help of econometric models. However, one needs to note that the macro models are ill-equipped to provide answers to micro issues that policymakers often pose.

We have referred to planning and policy analysis based on econometric models. First, IEG-DSE/CDE-DSE and IEG models were used to make *ex ante* macro-projections for recent Five Year Plans. In the very early years of macroeconometric modelling, Krishnamurty and Marwah made *ex ante* projections for the Third Five Year Plan period. Desai in his survey notes that the estimates were in the same ball-park as the realisation compared to Plan projections, which were way away. Another important point to note is that the recent models are regularly used for forecasting and outcomes analysed *ex post*.

The implications of various policies—direction of effects and trade-offs—revealed in different studies are broadly in the same ball-park but differ in some specific details. The broad conclusions that emerged from 'what if' policy simulations on recent models[32] are:

(1) Monetary expansion is an important factor in influencing inflation apart from increases in the costs of critical imports and other domestic inputs; administered prices have a role in inflation

32. These broad conclusions are drawn from the studies of (a) Krishnamurty (1984); (b) Krishnamurty, Pandit and Shrma (1989); (c) Bhattacharya, Barman and Nag (1994); (d) Krishnamurty, and Pandit (1996); (e) Rangarajan and Mohanty (1997); (f) IEG-DSE Team, (Krishnamurty, Pandit *et al.*, 1999) and (f) Reserve Bank of India (2002), among others.

management. Relative prices play an important role in the functioning of the economy as several activities are sensitive to price structure;

(2) Monetary expansion is catalysed, given monetary policy stance, largely by Reserve Bank net credit to government and accretion to foreign exchange reserves; in recent years the increase in foreign exchange reserves has assumed importance;

(3) Increase in public investment though crowds out private investment in some sectors and for some years, investment particularly in agriculture and infrastructure crowds in private investment. Increase in public investment favours output growth and tones up activity all around, leaving aside efficiency aspect. Higher efficiency in public sector infrastructure in particular and in general, other sectors provides a strong push to over all growth;

(4) Increase in fiscal deficit tends to widen balance of payments gap although the extent critically depends how deficit is financed *viz.*, barrowing and deficit financing;

(5) There are trade-offs between growth and inflation on the one hand and, growth and balance of payments on the other;

(6) Liberal monetary policy may not be necessarily desirable. This is due to the fact that higher growth of money supply tends to raise inflation rate. This in turn erodes the real value of public investment, which is set in nominal terms in government budgets. Consequently, any increase in private investment due to easy monetary policy—lower interest rates and larger flow of credit, is out-stepped by reduction in real public investment. The net outcome of complimentarity and crowding out effects of slow down in real public investment tends to over shadow any favourable effects of easy monetary policy on real private fixed investment. Monetary policy combined with fiscal policy is more effective in promoting growth with moderate inflation. Further, trade policy needs to be supplemented by monetary policy and monetary policy by fiscal policy if benefits in one direction are not at the cost of those in the other direction. Also, down sizing fiscal deficit through public investment has often been a soft instrument. Public investment, as noted earlier, has externalities, which can be repeated by private investment, particularly public investment in infrastructure. Discretionary fiscal stabilisers say government current expenditures tend to provide only temporary stimulus to

growth. This again emphasises the need for compositional shifts in fiscal expenditures in favour of public infrastructural investment while trying to achieve fiscal consolidation to attain growth with stability; and

(7) Regarding external sector, general tendencies noted are: (a) accelerated growth of the economy is not sustainable unless accompanied by policies to promote larger export earnings, (b) exchange rate depreciation by itself does not considerably change export earnings in dollars—though it promotes an expansion of volume of exports as well as export earnings in rupees, (c) exchange rate adjustments are quite effective in dealing with imports in terms of volume, as well as value (in rupees and in dollars). Hence, exchange rate instrument is quite effective if the objective is a reduction in trade imbalance as such and finally, results indicate that reduced import duties and export subsidies are not likely to play havoc with trade deficit if a proper exchange rate adjustment is used. It may be noted that exchange rate depreciation has pass-through effects implying higher domestic prices and this tends to raise export price. Whether exchange rate depreciation and appreciation effects are symmetrical is a question mark and needs investigation.

The above consensus is inspite of the fact that size, structural details and time period of models differ and the studies from which above tendencies are drawn are from both academic and policy-making arena. Substantive progress has been achieved in using models for planning and policy analysis. Yet, there is a long way to go before they could be used in actual policy-making. Policy-making in real world is complex. Firstly, because policy-making is in the realm of political economy and secondly, because even in a pure model framework much more quantitative detail is required for use as a back-drop for policy-making and evaluation. Consequently in many countries official agencies have in-house models built by their own in-house experts and some times in collaboration with outside academics and institutions. Official agencies have lot more access to detailed information even leaving aside confidential information. Collaboration between official agencies and outside researchers can bring sharp focus, detail, necessary relevance and latest methodologies to macro modelling, apart from resources needed to finance such an effort. It is indeed an arduous task for researchers in academic institutions/ universities to build and maintain large models for many years at a stretch and raise adequate resources to finance such an effort. Collaborative effort with autonomy and independence is needed to establish credibility and public confidence that such an effort should command. We in India have already made a beginning and should move forward.

There are further limitations in the use of models. Even the latest models get dated, as there are lags in release of data sets by official agencies. Changes in policy regime could result in changes in parametric structure embedded in the models. Even updating the models, would not capture structural changes induced by change in policy regime. Sufficient time has to lapse under the changed policy regime for the impact of new policies to fully percolate into the system to enable researchers to capture their impacts, and to identify parametric changes or structural breaks. Even updated models would require, as suggested earlier, recalibration of the parametric structure of the models to assess the implications of change in policy regime and for forecasting.

The role of planning and planning models assumed importance in the new policy regime and substantive debates have taken place on the subject. It is tempting to infer that the new economic policies will necessarily lead to a dilution of the role of the state. However, in our view, in some ways it also enhanced that role. In respect of creating critical physical infrastructure, at least in the medium term, public sector investments will continue to have an important role. Its vital role in social infrastructure, needless to add, remains. Also, its role in influencing private sectors decisions-both investors and consumers-through appropriate policies including creating and defining the role of regulatory agencies will become more critical than before. Strategic and coordinated intervention will be required to provide the right market signals to the private agents. In this context, macroeconometric models have a useful role to play. They can also help to check for behavioural consistency between various plan targets and instruments (Tinbergen, 1956). In order to achieve this effectively, macroeconomic model specification should be reconsidered and structured to explain realisations as deviations from plan targets as recently suggested by Desai (1997).

5. Future Agenda: Some Suggestions

We can now venture to make some suggestions for future work. We have made considerable progress in recent years yet much more needs to be accomplished to move forward and gain sufficient creditability for macroeconometric modelling. Models have to be made more relevant to the context and times to make them useful in planning, policy-making and forecasting.

Foremost task on the agenda is to search for structural changes in the nineties that may have taken place due to the effect of macroeconomic and structural adjustment policies. Considerable work seems to be currently underway. On broad comparable assumptions on exogenous variables consistent with observed data, the models should be mapped over each other through simulation techniques in backward and forward mode. A comparison of the trajectories of the two models for important variables for the common period 1980 to 1990 and for 1991 to 2002 should help in uncovering parametric drifts or structural changes during the period and in particular, in the nineties. If they do exist in noticeable degree and spread, the latter version of the model *viz.*, based on 1980–2002 data is obviously more suited for planning, policy analysis and forecasting for the coming years. However, if long time series, covering the period say 1970-2002, is needed to provide more degrees of freedom to accommodate use of advanced estimation techniques, appropriate parametric shifts should be accommodated in the model structure and in estimation it would be preferable to shed the decade of seventies. In the past, most of the researchers have dropped the decades of fifties and sixties from the purview of their recent models with a view to have a near comparable data and homogeneous economic environment for model estimation and avoid structural breaks. Until the experiments on new data base come to fruition, the existing models need to be used with care. Fine tuning the models in simulation is needed whether it be for policy analysis or forecasting by suitable parametric recalibration and/or by adding adjustment factors to the equation wherever needed. Such fine-tuning by adjustment factors is an age-old practice. Second, to extract segments of best track record of each of the recent models, comparative evaluation of them needs to be attempted. Third, macroeconometric modeling has been 'learning by doing.' We, in India, have over the years moved from small sized textbook type models to large models. This has helped to capture to some extent complexities of the economy. However, there are diseconomies associated with large size models though modern computing power permits such a venture. Larger the size, the more difficult it is to build comparable and reliable database for various segments of the economy and to unearth the complexities of the inter-linkages. Modern computing power is too fast to comprehend and coherently interpret quickly the result of policy simulations and forecasts. Large models require assumptions on a large number and variety of exogenous variables. To make appropriate and consistent assumptions in forward mode is difficult and time consuming. When forecasts have to be made available quickly atleast on major economic indicators, large models need more time and effort to operate and understand.

At this stage it must be admitted that we are not making a case against large models but only pointing to the need to have moderate sized main frame model with several satellite sub-models for each of the important sectors. This helps to build macromodels with sufficient details to map complex structure of the economy, to enable in-depth understanding of its functioning and to track economy-wide responses to various policy induced or exogenous shocks. Even with moderate sized IEG-DSE/CDE-DSE model with about 450 equations, but large by our standards, it has not been possible to cover within its fold many important elements of the agenda outlined earlier. Specific issues have been dealt in one or the other model in some depth, but they need to be pulled under one umbrella.

Therefore, we advocate fairly large but not too large a main frame model with several sectoral models, which can be operational in 'stand alone' mode and/or within the fold of main frame model. This helps to answer some specific sectoral issues in more detail than the main frame model in its stand 'alone mode.'

At the present time, one would suggest construction of sub-models for the following sectors, to name a few, they are:

a) agriculture to bring out changing cropping pattern and difference in price determination;

b) sub-model for manufacturing to distinguish differential behaviour of important segments with in it say capital, intermediate, and consumer durable and non-durable goods, and, also between private and public sectors within each category; similarly between registered and unregistered sectors;

c) detailed treatment of infrastructure to enable identification of impacts arising from deregulation and privatisation which are currently underway;

d) separate module for service sector to account for heterogeneity and to accord separate treatment for fast growing segments say, as for instance, software industry;

e) On the demand side, a sub-model to enable disaggregation with emphasis on the income/wealth distributions to capture the effect of inequalities. This would help to identify overall and sectoral excess/deficient demand in the system;

f) sub-model for foreign trade, BOP and exchange rate to enable more disaggregation on the goods side of trade with destination-wise focus than has been accomplished so far; to accord more incisive treatment to invisibles particularly software exports which have grown in importance and to permit specific treatment in BOP to private capital flows—direct and portfolio[33]; to allow for more exhaustive analysis of exchange rate determination particularly, the role of private foreign inflows, foreign exchange reserves and RBI intervention in the market;[34]

g) detailed sub-models for fiscal, financial and monetary sectors; analysis of capital markets in the financial sector, and the role of the operations of the Reserve Bank of India in influencing interest rates and flows in money-capital markets; and

h) sub-models to understand in depth investment, savings and financing patterns; flow of funds at some stage needs to be integrated in the modelling exercise. Data is not a constraint. RBI has been regularly releasing annual data over the past several years.

The shopping list is large. Scanning the literature, one finds that a lot of very interesting research work has gone-on on several aspects mentioned here and such work is growing.[35]

There is a need for an intensive interaction among model builders, specialists, planners and policymakers to sort out issues, priorities, data availability- reliability-sustainability, and work out contours of main frame and sub-sectors models. Such an interaction should lead to coordinated and collective effort to bring out well articulated comprehensive model for India.

Fourth, it is time to utilise high frequency data that is now available for many important economic indicators. Most important, NAS data on quarterly basis for the recent years is there now to draw upon. Atleast a modest attempt to construct a quarterly model should be made. This will supplement annual models and will go long way in improving forecasts.

---

33. For a recent study on capital account of BOP, see Ranjan and Nachane (2004).

34. Deregulation of money – capital markets has catalysed work on integration of financial markets, interest determination and its nexus with foreign exchange rate. See for example Bhoi and Dhal (1998), Dua and Pandit (2002) and Dua et al., (2003).

35. See a very interesting recent study by Kalirajan and Bhide (2003); a novelty of the study is specific introduction of regional dimension with regard to agriculture in a disequlibrium macroeconometric model framework. Also a modest beginning has been made at regional modelling with emphasis on agricultue, see for instance Bhattacharya et al., (2004).

Fifth, considerable and commendable research work is now happening in India in utilising modern time series techniques. Attempt should be made to strengthen and enrich macromodels with latest methodologies and techniques.

Sixth, an observation relating to macro model estimation is in order. Almost all the models have been estimated by ordinary least squares (OLS). OLS seems to be the order of the day due to degrees of freedom and other constraints. A move towards block recursive models should enable use of appropriate systems method of estimation to obtain more robust parameter estimates. In large systems there is need to explore this.

6. Concluding Observations

It has been a long and stressful march over many years. Thanks to the efforts of many researchers, macromodelling has come of age in India. The march has to continue. The goal is a shifting one. Databases get revised, policy regimes change, new problems emerge and there are many advances in economic and econometric methodologies. The model builders must keep pace with these changes and advances.

At the present stage, attempts to construct new models with several satellite sub-models for important, fast changing and growing sectors to capture structural change is needed. An all round effort of this type calls for a co-operative and well coordinated collective effort of several researchers and, intensive interaction with and active co-operation of policy making agencies to make models relevant and useful in practice.

References

Agarwala, R. (1971). *An Econometric Model of India*, Frank Cass.

Ahluwalia, I.J. (1979). *Behaviour of Prices and Outputs in India: A Macroeconomic Approach*, Delhi: Macmillan.

―――. (1985). *Industrial Growth in India*, Delhi: Oxford.

Ahluwalia, I.J. and C. Rangarajan (1986). *Agriculture and Industry : A Study of Linkages, the Indian Experience*, VIII, World Economic Congress of International Association, December.

Anjaneyulu, D. (1993). "Macroeconomic Linkages in the Indian Economy: Inter-links Between Imports, Output, Exchange Rate and External Debt," *Reserve Bank of India Occasional Papers*, December 1993.

Balakrishnanan, P. (1991). *Pricing and Inflation in India*, Delhi: Oxford.

Bhaduri, A. (1982). *Existing State of Macroeconometric Modelling in India*. (Mimeo.), Bangkok: ESCAP.

Bhattacharya, B.B. (1975). *Short-Term Income Determination*, Delhi.: Macmillan.

―――. (1982). *The Government Budget, Inflation and Growth in India* (Mimeo.), Delhi: Institute of Economic Growth.

―――. (1984). *Public Expenditure, Inflation and Growth: A Macroeconomic Analysis for India*, New Delhi: Oxford University Press.

―――. (1987). "The Effectiveness of Monetary Policy in Controlling Inflation: The Indian Experience, 1951-85," *Prajnan*, Vol. XVI, (4).

Bhattacharya, B.B., R.B. Barman and A.K. Nag (1994). *Stabilisation Policy Options*, Development Research Group, Department of Economic Analysis and Policy, Reserve Bank of India.

Bhattacharya, B.B. and C.H. Hanumantha Rao (1986). *Agriculture-Industry Interrelations: Issues of Relative Growth in the Context of Public Investment*, (Mimeo.), Delhi: Institute of Economic Growth.

Bhattacharya, B.B. and Srabani Guha (1992). "The Behaviour of Public Debt in India: A Macroeconometric Analysis," *Journal of Quantitative Economics*, January.

Bhattacharya, B.B., N.R. Bhanumurthy, Savyasachi Kar, S. Sakthivel (2004). "Forecasting State Domestic Product and Inflation," *Economic and Political Weekly*, Vol. XXXIX, (31).

Bhide, Shashanka and Sanjit Pohit (1993). "Forecasting and Policy Analysis, A CGE Model for India," *Margin*, Vol 25, (3).

Bhide, Shashanka, Anushree Sinha, Sanjit Pohit, Dharma Kirti Joshi, Khursheed Anwar Siddiqui (1996). *Macroeconomic Modelling for Forecasting and Analysis*, (Mimeo), National Council of Applied Economic Research, New Delhi and Conference Board of Canada, Ottawa.

Bhoi, B.K. and S.C. Dhal (1998). "Integration of Financial Markets in India: An Empirical Evaluation," *RBI Occasional Papers*, Vol 19,(4), December.

Bryant, Ralph C., *et al.*, (Eds), (1988), *Empirical Macroeconomics for Interdependent Economics, Brookings Institution*, Washington, DC.

Bryant, Ralph C (Ed) (1993). *Evaluating Policy Regimes: New Research in Empirical Macroeconomics*, Washington, DC: Brookings Institution.

Chakrabarty, S.K. (1977). *Price Behaviour in India*. Delhi: Macmillan.

Chakrabarty, T.K. and Himanshu Joshi, (1994). *Macroeconometric Model of the Indian Economy: A Study for New-Economic Environment*, RBI Staff Studies (Mimeo).

Chakrabarty, T.K. (1987). "Macro Economic Model of the Indian Economy 1962-63 to 1983-84," *Reserve Bank of India Occasional Papers*, Vol. 8, (3).

Chakravarty, S. (1979a). "Keynes, Classics and Developing Economies," in C.H.H. Rao and P.C. Joshi (Eds.), *Reflections on Economic Development and Social Change*, Delhi: Allied Publishers.

―――. (1979b). "On the Question of Home Market and Prospects for Indian Growth," *Economic and Political Weekly*, Special Number, Vol. 14, Nos. 31,31 and 32, pp. 1229-1242.

————. (1983). "Keynes Century - Another Look at His Work," *Mainstream.*

Choudhry, N.K. (1963). *An Econometric Model of India, 1930-55*, Ph.D. Dissertation (Unpublished), University of Wisconsin.

Chowdhry, N.K., and K Krishnamurty (1968). *Towards A Post-War Econometric Model of India*, Institute for Quantitative Analysis of Social and Economic Policy, Toronto: University of Toronto, (Mimeo).

Choudhary, N.K., Meghnad Desai, D.B. Gupta, K Krishnamurty, K.L. Krishna and A.L. Nagar (1974). *Towards An Econometric Model of the Indian Economy: Part I, Plan and Focus of the Project.* A Report Submitted to the ICSSR. (Mimeo).

————. (1974). *Towards An Econometric Model of the Indian Economy: Part II, Database of the Indian Econometric Model*, A Report Submitted to the ICSSR, (Mimeo).

————. (1974). *Towards An Econometric Model of the Indian Economy: Part III, Framework of the Project and Experimental Results*, Report Submitted to the ICSSR. (Mimeo).

Desai, M.J. (1973). "Macroeconometric Models for India: A Survey," *Sankhya*, reprinted in *Survey of Research in Economics*, Vol. Seven, Econometrics (1978), Indian Council of Social Sciences Research, New Delhi: Allied Publishers.

Desai, M. (1997a). *Macroeconometric Models for Planning, Note* (Mimeo).

————. (1997b). *Macroeconometric Models for Planning, Note* (Mimeo).

Dua Pami, Nishita Raje and Satyananda Sahoo (2003). *Interest Rate Modelling and Forecasting in India*, Development Research Group, Study No. 24, DEAP, Reserve Bank of India, Mumbai.

Dua Pami and B.L. Pandit (2002). "Interest Rate Determination in India : Domestic and External Factors," *Journal of Policy Modelling*, 24.

Duesenberry, J.S., G. Fromm, L.R. Klein and E. Kuh (Eds.) (1965). *The Brookings Quaterly Econometric Model of the United States*, Chicago: Rand Mcnally.

Dutta, Manoranjan (1964). "A Prototype Model of India's Foreign Sector," *International Economic Review.*

Ghose, Devajyoti, Ashok K. Lahiri, Srinivasa Madhur and Prannoy Roy (1983). *An Outline of A Macroeconometric Model of the Indian Economy: Specifications and Estimated Results*, (Mimeo), September.

Ghose, Devajyoti, Ashok K. Lahiri and Wilima Wadhwa (1986). "Quantitative Restrictions and Indian Exports," *Journal of Development Economics*, 20.

Green, W (1993). *Econometric Analysis*, New York: Macmillan (Second Edition).

Gupta, G.S. (1973). "A Monetary Policy Model for India," *Sankhya*, Series B.

IEG-DSE Research Team (May 1996). *Macroeconometric Modelling for India Vol. I, Theory, Methodology and Model (Mimeo), Institute of Economic Growth, Delhi.*

————. *Macroeconometric Modelling for India : Vol. II, Sectoral Studies* (Mimeo), Institute of Economic Growth, Delhi.

————. *Macroeconometric Modelling for India, Vol. III, Applications* (Mimeo) Institute of Economic Growth, Delhi.

————. (1997). *Seminar on Macroeconometric Modelling for India*, (Mimeo), Institute of Economic Growth, Delhi.

————. (1997). "Background Papers," *Seminar on Macroeconometric Modelling for India*, Institute of Economic Growth, Delhi.

————. (1999). "Policies for Stability and Growth: Experiments With a Large and Comprehensive Structural Model for India," *Journal of Quantitative Economics*, Vol. N15, (12), also see Pandit and Krishnamurty (Eds. 2004).

IEG-CPB-IPC (1997). *Macroeconomic Model of the Indian Economy for Short and Medium Term Forecasting and Policy Simulation*, Institute of Economic Growth, (Mimeo).

Jadhav, Narendra (1990). "Monetary Modelling of the Indian Economy: A Survey," *Reserve Bank of India, Occasional Papers*, Vol. 11, (2), June.

————. (1994). *Monetary Economics for India*, Delhi: Macmillan.

Kalirajan Kaliappa and Shashanka Bhide (2003). *A Disequlibrium Macroeconometric Model for the Indian Economy*, Ashgate, Aldershot, England.

Kannan, R. (1985). "An Econometric Model of Foreign Trade Sector (1956-57—1979-80)," *Reserve Bank of India, Occasional Papers*, Vol. No. 6, (1), June.

————. (1989). "An Econometric Model of India's Balance of Payments," *Journal of Foreign Exchange and International Finance*, Vol. 3 (2), April-June.

Klein, L.R. (1965). "What Kind of a Macro Economic Model for Developing Economies?," *The Econometric Annual of the India Economic Journal*.

————. (1978). "The Supply Side," *American Economic Review*, March.

————. (1984). "Econometric Models, Planning and Developing Countries," *Development Perspectives*, Institute of Economic Growth Silver Jubilee Lecture, B.R. Publishing Co., 1988.

Klein, L.R, (Ed), (1991). *Comparative Performance of US Econometric Models*, New York: Oxford.

Klein, L.R., Aleksander Welfe and Wtadystaw Welfe (1999). *Principles of Macroeconometric Modelling*, Amsterdam: North Holland.

Klein, L.R., and Edwin Burmeister (Eds) (1976). *Econometric Model Performance: Comparative Simulation Studies of the US Economy*, University of Pennsylvania Press.

Klein, L.R. and T. Palanivel (1999). "An Econometric Model for India with Special Emphasis on Monetary Sector," *The Developing Economics*, Vol. 8, (3).

Krishna, K.L., K. Krishnamurty, V.N. Pandit and P.D. Sharma (1991). "Macro-Economic Modelling in India: A Selective Review of Recent Research," *Development Papers No. 9, Econometric Modelling and Forecasting in Asia*, ESCAP, U.N.

Krishnamurty, K. (1964). *An Econometric Model of India, 1948-61*, Ph.D. Dissertation (Unpublished), University of Pennsylvania.

————. (1984). "Inflation and Growth: A Model for India," *Indian Economic Review*, Vol. XIX (1), Jan-June; reprinted in K. Krishnamurty and V. Pandit. *Macroeconometric Modelling of the Indian Economy*, Hindustan Publishing Co., 1985.

————. (1987). "Inflation and Growth: Some Experiments on a Model for India," in Luigi Pasinetti and Peter Lloyd (Ed), *Structural Change, Economic Interdependence and World Development, Vol.3, Structural Change and Adjustment in the World Economy*, London: Macmillan.

————. (1992). *Status of Macroeconometric Modelling for India*, (Mimeo), Institute of Economic Growth, Delhi, A paper presented in the Workshop on Macro Modelling for Forecasting and Policy Analysis, The Conference Board of Canada, Ottawa, Canada, May 14, 1992.

————. (2000). "Economic Liberalisation and Planning in India: Perspectives and Modelling" in R.V.R. Chadrasekhar Rao, A. Prasanna Kumar and K.C. Reddy (Eds.), *Perspectives on Indian Development : Economy, Polity and Society* New Delhi: Sterling Publishers. Also see Nanda K Choudhry and K Krishnamurty (1996). *Economic Liberalisation and Planning in India: Perspectives and Modelling*, Institute of Economic Growth, Delhi, (Mimeo)

————. (2002). "Macroeconometric Models for India: Past, Present and Prospects," *Economic and Political Weekly*, Vol XXXVII, (42).

Krishnamurty, K. and V. Pandit (1996). "Exchange Rate, Tariffs and Trade Flows: Alternative Policy Scenarios for India," *India Economic Review* (Jan-Jun 1996) (Mimeo Version 1995), reprinted in *Journal of Asian Economics*, Fall, 1997

————. (1984). "Macroeconometric Modelling of the Indian Economy: An Overview," *Indian Economic Review*, Vol. XIX, (1), Jan-June; reprinted in K. Krishnamurty and V. Pandit, *Macroeconometric Modelling of the Indian Economy*, Hindustan Publishing Co., 1985. .

Krishnamurty, K., V. Pandit and P.D. Sharma (1989). "Parameters of Growth in a Developing Mixed Economy: The Indian Experience," *Journal of Quantitative Economics*, Vol. 5 (2), July.

Krishnamurty, K. and P.D. Sharma (1989). "Global Economic Prospects : Indian Scenario," *Developing Economies in Transition*, Vol. II, Country Studies, World Bank Discussion Papers No. 64, F. Desmond McCarthy (Ed.).

Krishnamurty, K., V. Pandit and T. Palanivel (1995). "Price Behaviour During the Eighties," in *Indian Economy During the Decade of Eighties*, V.N. Kothari (Ed), Baroda: The M S University of Baroda,.

Krishnamurty, K and V. Pandit, (1985). *Macroeconometric Modelling of the Indian Economy: Studies in Inflation and Growth*, Delhi: Hindustan Publishing Co.

Krishnamurty, K., K.S. Krishnaswamy and P.D. Sharma (1987). "Determinants of Saving Rate in India," *Journal of Quantitative Economics*.

Krishnamurty, K. and D.U. Sastry (1975). *Investment and Financing in the Corporate Sector in India*, New Delhi: Tata McGraw-Hill.

Krishnaswamy, K.S., K. Krishnamurty and P.D. Sharma (1987). *Improving Domestic Resource Mobilization Through Financial Development: India*, Asian Development Bank.

Lucas, Robert E.B. (1988). "Demand for India's Manufactured Exports," *Journal of Development Economics*, 29.

Madhur, Srinivasa (1987). *Forecasts and Policy Evaluations Using a Macroeconometric Model for India*, (Mimeo).

Mammen, T. (1973). "Indian Money Market: An Econometric Study," *International Economic Review*.

————. (1999). *India's Economic Prospects*, Singapore: World Scientific.

Marwah, K. (1963). *An Econometric Model of Price Behaviour in India*, Ph.D. Dissertation (Unpublished), University of Pennsylvania.

————. (1972). "An Econometric Model of India: Estimating Prices, their Role and Sources of Change," *Indian Economic Review*.

————. (1987). "On Managing the Exchange Rate of the Indian Rupee: Modelling Post-Bretton Woods Experience," *Journal of Quantitative Economics*, Vol. 3 (1), January.

————. (1991). "Macroeconometric Modelling of South-East Asia: The Case of India," in R.G. Bodkin, L.R. Klein and K. Marwah, (Eds.), *A History of Macroeconometric Model-Building*, U.K.: Edward Elgar.

Mehta, Rajesh and Narain Sinha (1991). "External Trade, Public Sector and the Indian Economy," *Development Papers No. 9, Econometric Modelling and Forecasting in Asia*, ESCAP, UN.

Nachane, D.M., Romar Correa, G. Ananthapadmanabham and K.R. Shanmugam (2004). *Econometric Models, Theory and Applications*, New Delhi: Allied Publishers.

Nagaraju, G. (2000). *Comparative Evaluation of Three Selected Macroeconometric Models for India*, (Mimeo), paper presented at to 37th TIES Annual Conference, Surat, Feb., 2-4, 2000; also see, *A Critical Evaluation of Macroeconometric Models for India, with Special Emphasis on Explanatory Power and Forecasting Ability*, Ph.D. Dissertation (2000), Osmania University, (Unpublished).

Narasimham, N.V.A. (1956). *Short-Term Planning Model for India*, Amsterdam: North Holland.

National Council of Applied Economic Research, Custom Economic Services, The Conference Board of Canada (1996). *Macroeconomic Modelling for Forecasting and Policy Analysis, Executive Summary*, Publication No. 4, April 1996, Canada—India Institutional Linkage Programme.

Panchamukhi, V.R. and Rajesh Mehta (1991). "Modelling of Trade Flows," *Development Papers No. 9, Econometric Modelling and Forecasting in Asia*, ESCAP, UN

Pandit, B.L., (1991). *Growth and Structure of Savings in India*, Bombay: Oxford.

Pandit, V. (1973). "Income and the Price Level in India, 1950-51 to 1965-66," *Sankhya*, Series B.

————. (1977). *Structural Basis for Macroeconomic Policy in India, 1950-51 Through 1974-75*, (Mimeo.), Manchester: Faculty of Economic and Social Studies, University of Manchester.

————. (1982). "Macroeconomic Structure and Policy in a Less Developed Economy," (Mimeo.), *Working Paper No. 235*, Delhi: Delhi School of Economics.

————. (1984). "Macroeconomic Adjustments in a Developing Economy : A Medium Term Model of Outputs and Prices in India," *Indian Economic Review*, Vol. XIX (1), Jan-June; reprinted in K. Krishnamurty and V. Pandit (Eds.), *Macroeconometric Modelling of the Indian Economy*, Hindustan Publishing Co., 1985.

———. (1985). "Macroeconomic Structure and Policy in a Less Developed Economy," *Journal of Quantitative Economics*, Vol. 1 (1), January.

———. (1985a). *Supply, Demand and Monetary Policy in an LDC: An Empirical Analysis of India*, (Mimeo.), Delhi School of Economics, April.

———. (1986). *A Note of the Structural Macroeconomic Model of India*, (Mimeo.), Delhi School of Economics, January.

———. (1986a). *Growth Performance of the Indian Economy Supply or Demand?*, (Mimeo.), *Working Paper No. 277*, Delhi School of Economics, March.

———. (1995). *Macroeconomic Character of the Indian Economy: Theories, Facts and Fancies in Macroeconomics* Prabhat Patnaik (Ed.), New Delhi: Oxford.

———. (1999). "Macroeconometric Modelling for India: A Review of Some Analytical Issues," *Journal of Quantitative Economics*, Special Issue on Policy Modelling, Vol. 15, No. 2.

———. (1999). "Macroeconometric Modelling for India: A Review of Some Analytical Issues," *Journal of Quantitative Economics*, Vol. 15 (2); reprinted in V. Pandit and K. Krishnamurty (Eds., 2004).

———. (2004). "Sustainable Economic Growth for India: An Exercise in Macroeconomic Scenario Building," *Journal of Quantitative Economics*, January 2004, New Series Vol. 2, (1).

Pandit, V. and B.B. Bhattacharya (1987). "Resource Mobilisation, Growth, and Inflation: A Trade-Off Analysis for India," *Asia Pacific Economies: Promises and Challenges: Research in International Business and Management*, Vol. 6, Part A.

Pandit, V. and K. Krishnamurty (Eds.), (2004). *Economic Policy Modelling for India*, New Delhi: Oxford.

Pandit, V., A. Sarma, T.C.A Anant, G. Ananthapadmanabham and K.R. Shanmugam (2002). *Data, Models and Policies*, Indian Econometric Society, Chennai: Madras School of Economics.

Pani, P.K. (1977). *A Macroeconomic Model of India*, Delhi: Macmillan.

———. (1984). "A Macro Model of Indian Economy with Special Reference to Output, Demand and Prices (1969-70 to 1981-82)," *Reserve Bank of India, Occasional Papers*, Vol. 5 (2), December.

Pradhan, B.K., D.K. Ratha and Atul Sharma (1990). "Complementarity Between Public and Private Investment in India," *Journal of Development Economics*, 33.

Rakshit, M.K. (1982). *The Labour Surplus Economy*, Delhi: Macmillan.

———. (1989). "Towards an Integration of Monetary and Real Models for Mixed Economies," (Mimeo.), a paper presented at the *International Conference on Methods of Planning and Policy Analysis for Mixed Economies*, Bombay: Indira Gandhi Institute of Development Research.

Ranjan, Rajiv and D.M. Nachane (2004). "Analysis of Capital Account in India's Balance of Payments," *Economic and Political Weekly*, July 3-9, Vol. XXXIX, No. 27; also see their monograph (2002), *An Econometric Model of the Capital Account of India's Balance of Payments*, New Delhi: Indian Economic Association Trust for Research and Development.

Rangarajan, C. (1982). *Agricultural Growth and Industrial Performance*, International Food Policy Research Institute.

Rangarajan, C. and Anoop Singh (1984). "Reserve Money: Concepts and Policy Implications for India," *Reserve Bank of India Occasional Papers*, Vol. 5 (1), June.

Rangarajan, C., Anupam Basu and Narendra Jadhav (1989). "Dynamics of Interaction between Government Deficit and Domestic," *Reserve Bank of India, Occasional Papers*, Vol. 10 (3), September.

Rangarajan, C. and A.R. Arif (1990). "Money, Output and Prices," *Economic and Political Weekly*, Vol. 25, (6)

Rangarajan, C. and M.S. Mohanty (1997). "Fiscal Deficit, External Balance and Monetary Growth— A Study of Indian Economy," *Reserve Bank of India, Occasional Papers*, December 1997.

Reserve Bank of India (2002). *Report on Currency and Finance, 2000-01*.

Rastogi, Anupam (1994). "A Rational Expectations Model of the Indian Economy," in *Economic Progress and Growth* H.M. Scobie (Ed), London: Chapmans Hill.

Sarkar, Hiren and Manoj Panda (1991). "A Short-Term Structural Macro-Economic Model for India: Applications to Policy Analysis," *Development Papers 9, Econometric Modelling and Forecasting in Asia*, ESCAP, UN.

Sinha, Narain (1986). *A Structural Model for India*, Jaipur: RBSA Publishing.

————. (1994). *Macroeconometric Modelling for India*, (Mimeo), A Report submitted to the ICSSR.

Srivastava, D.K. (1987). "Policy Simulation with a Macroeconomic Model of the Indian Economy," *Journal of Policy Modelling*.

Tinbergen, J. (1956). *Economic Policies, Principles and Design*, Amsterdam: North Holland.

Virmani, Arvind (1991). "Demand and Supply Factors in India's Trade," *Economic and Political Weekly*, February 9.

5

Shocks and Long Run Growth in Agriculture: A Macroeconomic Analysis

B.B. BHATTACHARYA
SABYASACHI KAR

1. Introduction

The share of agriculture in the total output of the Indian economy has declined secularly from more than 50 per cent at the time of independence to less than 25 per cent in the recent period. However, agriculture continues to play a very important role in the Indian economy due to a number of reasons. First, even though the share of agriculture in output is much lower than before, the total contribution of agriculture in gross domestic product (GDP) through its impact on industry and services is much higher. The agricultural sector and the rural economy sustains a great deal of demand for industrial products and, hence, the forward and backward linkages between agriculture and industry in India, is still quite strong. Agriculture and industry together also stimulate the growth in the services sector. As a result of all these linkages, any shortfall in agricultural output makes a significant impact on the performance of the economy. Secondly, a poor country with a high incidence of poverty requires a sustainable food reserve, and this can only be achieved by a healthy agricultural growth. Finally, even though the share of agriculture in GDP has declined sharply, its share in total workforce is still as high as 60 per cent. Hence, agricultural growth is also crucial for employment generation.

Since, agriculture is still a crucial sector in the Indian economy for both output and more importantly for employment, it is important to study the factors that influence agricultural growth in both short and long run. As India is a labour surplus economy—especially in the rural sector—labour supply is not a constraint on agricultural growth. In the short run, agricultural growth varies largely on account of variations in rainfall. The long run growth in agriculture however, would depend on the investment and the productivity of capital in agriculture. Hence, the rate of investment—both private and public—continues to be the crucial determinant of growth in this sector.

This study makes a macro analysis of short and long run growth prospects of agricultural GDP. In the first part of the chapter, we analyse the impact of rainfall shocks on the performance of agriculture. In the second part of the chapter, we study the effect of public investments on long run growth in the agricultural sector and the aggregate economy. The next section presents the methodological approach used in this study. Section three presents an analysis of rainfall shock and its impact on the economy. Section four presents the results of a macro-modelling exercise on the impact of rainfall shock on the agricultural growth. Following this we analyse the long run behaviour of both public and private investments in and for agriculture. Section six presents results of a macro-modelling exercise to study the impact of public investment on the long run agricultural growth. Conclusions and policy prescriptions are presented in section seven.

2. Methodological Approach

Given the objectives of this study, the most appropriate tool that can be used for an analysis of these issues is a structural macro-modelling framework. Macro-modelling is based primarily on the 'structural modelling' methodology associated with the Cowles Commission. The steps of the methodology may be summed up in terms of the following:

1. Constructing a model of the macro economy on the basis of a theoretical framework and with a chosen degree of disaggregation. The framework will incorporate the sectors and variables that are affected by the shocks as well as policy variables that can be used to counter them.

2. Acquiring time series data for all the variables (endogenous as well as exogenous) for the period to be studied.

3. Estimating the behavioral equations on the basis of the *a priori* theories and the time series data. Suitable changes can be made to the behavioural equations during the course of this exercise.

4. The whole model including the technical equations, identities and the behavioural equations are solved (simulated) using the Gauss-Seidel method in order to generate the predicted values of the endogenous variables.

5. The model is then used to simulate base-run (normal) growth rates and counterfactual situations caused by a rainfall shock or increased public investment in the agricultural sector.

Using the modelling techniques described above, we shall analyse the short- and long-run growth prospects of the agricultural sector. We shall use two models, the first one is built to analyse the rainfall shock, while the second model analyses the effect of public investment on long run growth. The complete model (including the behavioural equations) for the first model is presented in Bhattacharya and Kar (2005) while that for the second model is presented in Bhattacharya and Kar (2004). Data for the models are obtained from national accounts and other sources. A simultaneous estimation of all the equations was not found feasible in either models as the number of observations required for system solution turned out to be larger than number of observations available for estimation of the behavioural parameters. We have, therefore, estimated behavioural equations independently using ordinary least squares (OLS) method. However, the complete model is solved simultaneously using system solution method.

In order to analyse policy impact as well exogenous shocks, we have kept relevant variables as exogenous in behavioural equation. This might result in some cases omitted variable bias leading to serial correlation and poor Durbin Watson statistics. In such cases we have estimated the behavioural equations with AR(1) errors. In order to distinguish between short- and long-run effects of the shocks, we have incorporated lagged dependent variables as regressors. For these equations we have tested serial correlation through the Durbin's h statistics.

The OLS estimation of the behavioural equations suffers from the simultaneous equation bias. However, as stated before, the system solution is not possible due to degrees of freedom problem. In fact, due to this problem, most large macro econometric models estimate individual equations by OLS, and the simultaneous solution of complete model through the Gauss—Seidel simulation technique. We have also followed the same procedure. Following the convention, we have also taken care of order condition of identification in estimation of behavioural parameters.

The frameworks of the two models are based on known stylised facts about the Indian economy. It is well known that the overall macroeconomic behaviour can be portrayed following either the Neoclassical or the Keynesian approach. They differ in many respects, particularly with respect to the output and/or price adjustments in bringing about macroeconomic equilibrium. A third alternative that came up specifically in the context of developing economies is known in the literature as Structuralism. In practice, however, most macroeconomic models of developing economies have put together different aspects of all these paradigms. This is known in the literature as the eclectic approach. In this study, we shall adopt this approach. Keeping in view the liberalisation process introduced in the economy in 1991, the models have been designed to represent a market-oriented economy. The overall economy is broadly classified into the production, fiscal, monetary and external sectors, and appropriate behavioural functions are chosen for each blocks.

3. Incidence and Impact of Rainfall Shocks on the Indian Economy

In order to analyse the impact of rainfall shocks we may first look into the historical behaviour. Following from this, we shall identify the impact of these shocks on various intermediate and equilibrating macroeconomic variables in the economy. It may be noted that wherever we refer to a calendar year, it actually represents the corresponding fiscal year. For example, a reference to 1970 would indicate the fiscal year starting in April 1970 and ending in March 1971.

The Indian economy has traditionally depended heavily on agriculture. Agriculture has been an engine of growth not only due to the output from this sector but also due to the demand and supply linkages to the non-agricultural sector. The most important input in agricultural production is water, for which the country is largely dependent on rainfall. As a result, rainfall deficiency continues to be the most significant destabilising factor in the Indian economy. Figure 5.1 presents graphically the relationship between rainfall index (normal rainfall = 100) and agricultural growth (annual percentage rate of change of agricultural GDP) during the period 1975 to 2000. It may be seen that in spite of growing irrigation facility and controlled water management, year-to-year change in agricultural growth is still mainly a function of rainfall. However, the sensitivity of agricultural growth with rainfall deficiency has come down over the years. During this period 1979 and 1982 were two most severe drought years when the rainfall was 20 per cent and 15 per cent below normal respectively. The period 1984 to 1987 saw four consecutive bad rainfall years, leading to a medium term shock to Indian agriculture. The direct impact of rainfall is of course, on agriculture. However, as we have mentioned earlier, agricultural growth affects the growth of non-agricultural output through demand and supply linkages. Thus, a rainfall shock affects the growth of both agricultural and non-agricultural GDP. Figure 5.2 therefore, presents graphically the relationship between rainfall index and annual percentage rate of change of aggregate GDP. It turns out that all major rainfall shocks have resulted in very poor performance of the overall economy, such as in 1979 and 1982. But like in the case of

Figure 5.1

The Association between Rainfall and Growth of Agricultural GDP

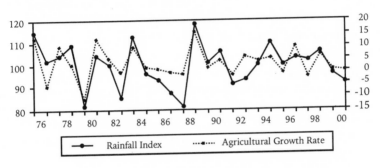

Note: Rainfall index normalises the volume of rainfall by taking the long run average (normal) rainfall to be 100. Agricultural growth is the rate of growth (per cent) of real agricultural GDP.

Figure 5.2

The Association between Rainfall and Growth of Aggregate GDP

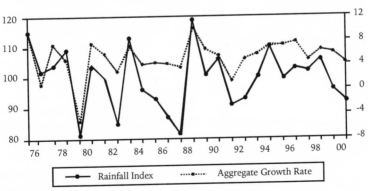

Note: Rainfall index as defined in earlier figure. Aggregate growth is the rate of growth (per cent) of real GDP.

agriculture, the impact of rainfall in the overall economy has become more and more diffused in the recent period. The turning points in the aggregate growth rate is, however, still very much dependent on rainfall performance.

4. Analysis of the Impact of Rainfall Shocks

An analysis of the impact of a shock has to provide an answer to the following questions:

- What is the origin of the shock?

- What are the intermediate variables that are affected by this shock and that in turn pass on these affects to the production sector of the economy?

- What are the equilibrating variables in the economy that adjust to the disequilibrium created by this shock?

- How do we quantify all these effects that originate in one sector and then spread to the rest of the economy through multiple channels?

- How do we differentiate between the short term and long term effects of these shocks?

- How do we assess the ability of public policy interventions in mitigating these shocks?

We shall try to answer these questions through a macro-econometric model presented in Bhattacharya and Kar (2005). In the following paragraphs, we shall give a brief description of the model that is pertinent to the present analysis.

The Indian economy is heterogeneous in terms of production, investment and price behaviour. To make a meaningful macroeconomic analysis of the economy we, therefore, need to divide the economy into three major sectors, *i.e.*, agriculture, industry and tertiary. The disaggregation is necessary to incorporate the differential behaviours of the three sectors with respect to production, demand, investment and price. We also need to distinguish between the short and long run effects, which is done through incorporation of the lagged dependent variables in the estimation of all these functions. In the case of output, this would represent the generalised distributed lag behaviour between output and capital. In the case of investment, this would represent the discrepancy between the desired and actual investment behaviour. In the case of prices, the lagged dependent variable will incorporate the adaptive expectations in price formation. In this study we present only analysis of output functions.

We postulate that agricultural output (XA) is constrained by capital stock in agriculture (KA) and rainfall (RF). The impact of all other variables at the aggregate level turns out to be quite weak and hence ignored. However, a dummy variable is included to incorporate the structural retrogression in agricultural growth since 1980s (D80S) and another dummy variable DUMXA is included to incorporate the impact of the extreme drought effect of 1979.

$$XA = EXP(-8.16 + 1.43*LOG(KA)^{***} + 0.27*LOG(RF)^{***}$$
$$(1.31) \qquad\quad (0.24) \qquad\qquad (0.05)$$

$$- 0.12*D80S^{***} - 0.14*DUMXA^{***} + 0.10*LOG(XA(-1)))$$
$$(0.03) \qquad\quad (0.03) \qquad\qquad (0.14)$$

$$R^2 = 0.99 \qquad\qquad Dh = -1.06$$

(Figures in parenthesis in all estimated equations presented are standard errors. Number of *s on the right side of regressors indicate the level of significance of the coefficients (i.e., * denotes 10 per cent, ** denotes 5 per cent and *** denotes 1 per cent level of significance). Dh gives the Durbin's h statistic.

The results indicate that capital stock in agriculture and rainfall together can explain the bulk of variation in agricultural GDP. The relatively low value of the lagged dependent variable shows that there is no significant lag in the impact of agricultural capital on agricultural output. This is consistent with *a priori* expectations because most investments in agriculture make direct impact on production immediately. However, as would be mentioned later, the conventional national accounts concept of agricultural investment in India does not include capital formation in rural roads and electrification etc. that have long gestation impact on agricultural growth.

The agricultural sector affects the growth of the economy not only through its own performance, but also through interlinkages with the other sectors of the economy. This could be traced through the behavioural equations representing the determination of industrial and the tertiary GDP. The industrial output (XI) and tertiary output (XT) are postulated to be functions of the productive capacity in the respective sectors and the capacity utilisation rates. The productive capacity is determined by the capital stock (KI and KT) while large pools of unemployed labour ensure that there are no labour constraints in these sectors. Consistent with some recent theoretical and empirical studies on

India, we postulate that output and capacity utilisation in industry and the tertiary sector are sensitive to changes in demand. In industrial output function, domestic and external demand are represented by the autonomous expenditure (RAE), defined as the sum of government expenditure and exports of goods and services. Industry also depends on agricultural demand. Moreover, Industrial output is negatively related to industrial price (PI), again reflecting the demand-constrained nature of this sector. The industrial output function has two structural dummies, DPLIB (representing the partial liberalisation of the economy in the mid-eighties) and D95 (representing the peak effect of liberalisation in 1995 following large deregulation of the economy in 1994). In the tertiary sector, the demand constraints are captured by the commodity output (XCOM), *i.e.*, the sum of the output in agriculture and industry. The tertiary output function has two dummies DPLIB (partial liberalisation) and DUMPAY (representing the impact of large hikes in the salaries and wages of public administration that inflate the value added in the tertiary sector).

$$XI = EXP(-2.57 + 0.08*LOG(KI) + 0.34*LOG(XA)***$$
$$\quad (0.83) \qquad (0.09) \qquad (0.07)$$

$$\quad + 0.18*LOG(RAE)*** - 0.06*LOG(PI) + 0.02*DPLIB$$
$$\quad\quad (0.05) \qquad\qquad (0.04) \qquad\qquad (0.01)$$

$$\quad + 0.6*LOG(XI(-1))*** + 0.04*D95**)$$

$$\quad\quad (0.06) \qquad\qquad (0.01)$$

$$R^2 = 0.99 \qquad\qquad Dh = -1.32$$

$$XT = EXP(-5.06 + 0.67*LOG(KT)*** + 0.13*LOG(XCOM)**$$
$$\quad\quad (1.02) \qquad (0.17) \qquad\quad (0.05)$$

$$\quad + 0.01*DUMPAY* + 0.02*DPLIB** + 0.52*LOG(XT(-1))***)$$
$$\quad\quad (0.006) \qquad\quad (0.008) \qquad\qquad (0.09)$$

$$R^2 = 0.99 \qquad\qquad Dh = -1.54$$

The results indicate that demand side factors like agricultural output and autonomous expenditure are the crucial determinants of industrial output. Capital stock has a small impact on current periods output but the lagged dependent variable indicates that capital has a strong lagged effect on industrial output. The output in the tertiary sector is largely determined by capital stock, which has an impact on current as well as future services output. The demand factor, *i.e.*, the output from the commodity producing sectors (*i.e.*, agriculture and industry) also affects the output in this sector. The broad inference that may be drawn from the output functions is that agriculture depends crucially on rainfall, and through agricultural output rainfall affects industry and tertiary outputs.

The complete model along with all other behavioural equations and identities are solved through the Gauss–Seidel methodology that solves for the endogenous variables corresponding to alternative assumptions about the exogenous variables. We have chosen the period 1994 to 2000 to evaluate the impact of domestic shocks. This is the period following the liberalization of the economy when most of the exogenous variables exhibited normal behaviour and the economy had a relatively high growth rate. The objective of imposing the shocks in this period is to find out the possible performance of the economy if the exogenous variables had exhibited abnormal behaviour. We have imposed the shocks in the years 1994 and 1995 (when the economy attained peak growth rate of more than 7 per cent) and, hence, the average performance in these two years will represent the short run impact of the shocks. However, our model has built-in dynamics that results in the shocks having a long run impact as well. The average performance for the period 1994 to 2000 will represent the long run impact of the shocks.

It may be noted at this stage that shocks can have an impact on various aspects of the growth process. These aspects include (i) the magnitude of the impact on growth rates, (ii) the pervasiveness of the shocks in the long run, (iii) the capability of the shock to give rise to stagflationary situations, and (iv) the capability of the shock to give rise to instability in the fiscal or external sectors. In this study, we analyse the impact of the rainfall shock according to what effect it has on each of these aspects of the growth process.

We shall now present the simulation results corresponding to the base run and the alternative scenarios. The base-run simulation assumes that the exogenous variables had their actual historical values. The alternative scenario represents a rainfall shock where the rainfall index is assumed to be 20 per cent below normal in the years 1994 and 1995. This scenario does not assume any policy reaction to the drought by the government. The results of this simulation together with the base-run are given in Table 5.1.

From this table, it is clear that in the short run, a rainfall shock would lead to a significant fall in both agricultural and overall GDP growth rate. This would result in steep rise in agricultural prices and the overall inflation rate would shoot up significantly. Thus, the rainfall shock has a short run stagflationary impact on the economy. Next, we look at the long run impact of the rainfall shock. We find that the impact on both growth and inflation is less strong, indicating that in the long run the impact of the shock is largely offset by the resilience of the economy that recovers strongly after the two bad years. Finally, there is no instability to the growth process in the short or the long run from the fiscal or external sectors due to a severe rainfall deficiency in the short run. This should be, however, interpreted with caution, because a macro-econometric model cannot incorporate the psychological and political impact of high inflation and low output and employment on the economy.

Table 5.1

Effect of Rainfall Shock

Variables	GDP Growth	Agricultural Growth	Agricultural Inflation Rate	Aggregate Inflation Rate	Government Expenditure Ratio	Gross Fiscal Deficit Ratio	Imports	Foreign Exchange Reserves	Exchange Rate
Short Run									
Base-run	7.55	4.44	10.71	9.13	24.36	5.63	38.7	23.3	32.36
Shock	5.31	-0.14	18.13	13.78	23.05	4.43	38.6	22.9	33.25
Per cent Change	-29.7	-103.2	69.3	50.9	-5.4	-21.3	-0.3	-1.7	2.8
Long Run									
Base-run	6.68	2.78	6.83	6.77	25.72	7.87	50.6	32.3	38.79
Shock	6.11	2.15	8.1	7.78	24.69	6.92	49.8	33.0	40.5
Per cent Change	-8.5	-22.7	18.6	14.9	-4.0	-12.1	-1.6	2.2	4.4

As we have mentioned earlier, the first alternative scenario does not assume any policy reaction to the drought by the government. However, a severe drought usually results in high rates of inflation and low income and consumption for the farmers. In such a situation, the government is forced to import foodgrains in order to bring down inflation. Moreover, they have to subsidise the farmers to protect them from starvation and death. All this increases the government's expenditure and may be termed as counter-shock policy response. We now present a second scenario, which represents a combination of a rainfall shock and such policy response. In this scenario, we assume that due to extreme rainfall shock the government imports food worth two billion dollars and increases government consumption and transfer payments each by half a per cent of nominal GDP at market prices in the years of rainfall shock. This simulation, thus, represents a combination of shocks and policy response. The results of these simulations together with the base-run are given in Table 5.2.

Results indicate that as a consequence of a combined rainfall shock and policy response, government fiscal worsens, but long run GDP growth improves. The higher imports also deplete the foreign exchange reserves and pushes up the exchange rate. On the positive side, however, the policy response does bring down aggregate and agricultural inflation considerably and gives a slight boost to the growth rates as well. In the long run, the negative impact of the policy response is further diminished, such that the fiscal and external sector variables have values very close to the base run. Similarly, the long run positive impact of the policy response on growth and inflation is also very marginal.

Table 5.2

Effect of Rainfall Shock with Policy Response

Variables	GDP Growth	Agricultural Growth	Agricultural Inflation Rate	Aggregate Inflation Rate	Government Expenditure Ratio	Gross Fiscal Deficit Ratio	Imports	Foreign Exchange Reserves	Exchange Rate
Short Run									
Base-run	7.55	4.44	10.71	9.13	24.36	5.63	38.7	23.3	32.36
Shock	5.31	-0.14	18.13	13.78	23.05	4.43	38.6	22.9	33.25
Shock with Policy Response	5.37	-0.05	15.5	12.16	24.71	6.03	39.6	21.4	33.21
Long Run									
Base-run	6.68	2.78	6.83	6.77	25.72	7.87	50.6	32.3	38.79
Shock	6.11	2.15	8.1	7.78	24.69	6.92	49.8	33.0	40.5
Shock with Policy Response	6.18	2.24	7.89	7.61	25.29	7.49	50.0	32.5	40.22

5. Agricultural Performance in the Long Run

As we have found in the last section, the volume of rainfall is a major factor in determining short run agricultural growth, but in the long run, agricultural growth would be unaffected by it. In this section, we will look at the long run agricultural investment and its relationship with agricultural growth. Figure 5.3 represents the annual agricultural growth rate (XAG) from the seventies. This figure also presents the long run trend agricultural growth rate (HPTREND) during this period, which has been generated by using a Hodrick-Prescott filter. From this figure, it is clear that the short run agricultural growth in India over the past three decades has fluctuated very sharply due to variations in rainfall. However, the fluctuations have reduced significantly over time and hence, the nineties experienced a much more stable agricultural growth compared to the seventies. The stability is, however, attained at the cost of lowering of the long run growth. We shall now analyse the main cause of this.

Figure 5.3

Agricultural GDP Growth Rate (%) with HP Trend

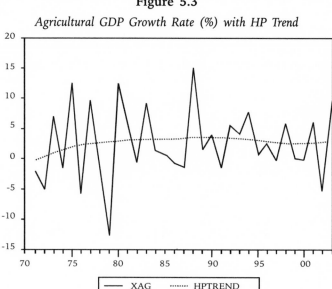

Although, the rainfall is a major factor in determining short run growth, in the long run, agricultural growth depends on investments and the productivity of capital. It is important at this stage to understand that agricultural investments can be defined in two alternative ways depending on whether we consider investments made in the agricultural sector or investments made for the agricultural sector. The Central Statistical Organisation (CSO) measures capital formation in agriculture using the conventional national accounts concept. In the case of the public sector, it becomes mainly investment in irrigation. Private capital formation in agriculture according to CSO covers construction, plantation, household, livestock, dwellings, etc. Agricultural growth, however, depends not only on capital formation in agriculture but also on various inputs like fertiliser, pesticides, seeds etc. Investments on the production of these items often contribute very significantly to the overall growth of agricultural output. Keeping in view one may measure a broader concept of capital formation for agriculture. The alternative definition developed in Bhattacharya (2002) includes not only traditional national accounts concept as well as capital formations in both public and private sectors in fertiliser, pesticides, rural electricity, roads, trade and transport, storage, communication, banking and insurance etc. The broader measure may be termed as investment for agriculture as against traditional measure of investment in agriculture. It would be interesting to analyse trends in investment and its productivity on the basis of both the definitions.

We first look at the trends in the agricultural investments in both public and private sectors. Figure 5.4 depicts the trends in public investments in agriculture as a share of GDP. In this figure, the bold line represents public investments made in agriculture (SIGA) while the dashed line represents public investments made for agriculture (SFIGA).

Figure 5.4

Share (%) of Public Investment in GDP at Market Prices in Agriculture (SIGA), for Agriculture (SFIGA)

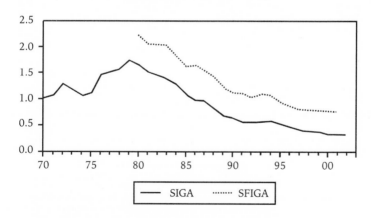

It is clear from the Figure that the share of public investment in GDP had increased during the 1970s and fallen thereafter. In the early 1980s, the public investment for agriculture was more than 2 per cent of GDP, and even in agriculture was about 1.5 per cent of GDP. Since then both the ratios have declined sharply and currently public investment in both in and for agriculture is below 1 per cent of GDP. Investment for agriculture is of course higher than investments in agriculture, but the shares of both in GDP have fallen during the nineties. No wonder, the long run agricultural growth has also come down since 1980s and virtually stagnated during the 1990s.

It is interesting to look into the reasons behind the falling public investments, particularly in the nineties. This fall is, of course, the result of a number of factors but one of the important one is the increase in subsidy (as a ratio to GDP). Figures 5.5 shows that while the public investment rates declined both in and for agriculture, the ratio of subsidy in GDP increased. Figure 5.6 shows that agricultural cash subsidy—food and fertiliser—has become larger than total agricultural investments whether in or for agriculture. The long run decline in agricultural growth is, therefore, associated with long run decline in agricultural investment and rise in agricultural subsidy.

Figure 5.5

Share (%) in GDP at Market Prices Subsidy (SSUB) Public Investment in Agricultural (SIGA) for Agricultural (SFIGA)

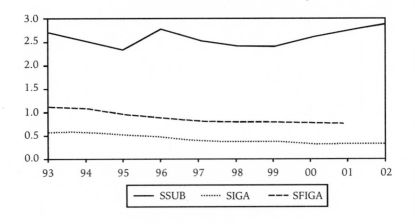

It is argued that after liberalisation government investment is expected to fall, and the fall should be more than compensated by the rise in private investment. Figure 5.7 shows that while public investment in agriculture has fallen as a ratio to GDP in the recent years the ratio of

Figure 5.6

Share (%) in GDP at Market Prices Subsidy (SSUB) Total Investment in Agriculture (SIA) for Agriculture (SFIA)

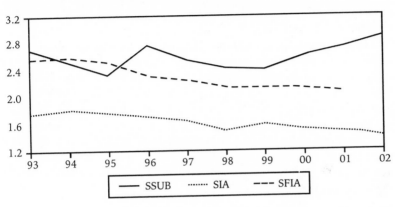

Figure 5.7

Share (%) of Private Investment in GDP at Market Prices in Agriculture (SIPA) for Agriculture (SFIPA)

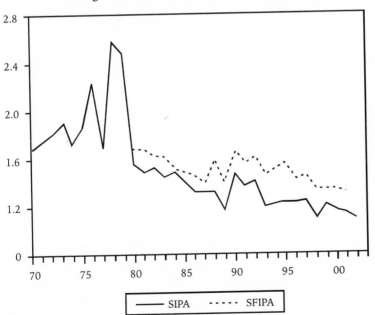

private investment in agriculture has improved marginally during the recent years. However, the rise in the latter was inadequate to compensate for the fall in the former. The relationship between public and private investments in agriculture is a matter of controversy in development economics. Most researchers have found a strong complimentarity between public and private investments in agriculture In India; see for instance, Bhattacharya and Hanumantha Rao (1986). This is also confirmed by the present analysis using latest data.

The broad behaviour of private investment in agriculture turns out to be similar to that of public investment, *i.e.*, there is a secular decline in both public and private investments as ratios to GDP since the seventies. This similarity in the behaviour of public and private investments in agriculture underscores the fact that public investments "crowd in" private investment in this sector. Like in the case of public investment, private investment for agriculture is higher than private investment in agriculture, but both have fallen during the recent years. As a result, the total investment in and for agriculture as a ratio to GDP also fell during the recent years, as would be evident from Figure 5.8.

Figure 5.8

*Share (%) of Private Investment in GDP at Market Prices
in Agriculture (SIA) for Agriculture (SFIA)*

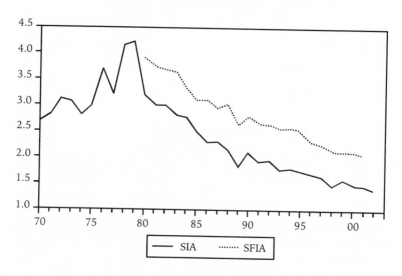

The analysis above reveals that there is a clear evidence of a decline in agricultural investment during the 1990s. The fall in agricultural growth is, however, less significant due to an improvement in productivity of agricultural capital. Figure 5.9 shows that the agricultural capital-output ratio in agriculture has declined over the years, thus partially compensating the adverse impact of decline in agricultural investment. However, in the long run the law of diminishing marginal return would prevail in agriculture. Already there is an indication that the agricultural capital-output ratio has begun to stabilise, if not rise. Thus, unless the agricultural investment rate improves in the long run the agricultural growth would suffer further.

Figure 5.9

Share (%) of Private Investment in GDP at Market Prices in Agriculture (CORA) for Agriculture (CORFA)

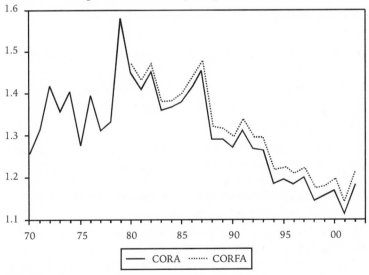

To sum up, we find that significant fall in investment rates have put a downward pressure on agricultural growth rates, while a fall in capital output ratios have partially neutralised the adverse effects, the net effect is that the fall in agricultural investment rates in public and consequently in private sectors have led to a fall in agricultural growth rates in the nineties.

6. Public Investment and Long Run Growth

It is clear from the previous section that in order to increase agricultural growth rates, we have to increase the agricultural investment rate. Since the private investment rate is induced by the GDP growth, an autonomous rise in it can be only through a step in the public investment in agriculture. This would be evident from the estimated private investment function presented below. It appears that the private investment in agriculture (IPA) is positively related to public investment in agriculture (IGA), after separating effects of agricultural output (XA) and commercial bank lending rate (LNDRN). The function also includes other determinants of private investment in agriculture such as relative price of agricultural products to general price level (RPGAR). The lagged dependent variable is introduced to represent dynamic investment behaviour and a dummy variable (DUMIPA) represents effects of irregular changes and omitted variables. The coefficient of public investment is however significant only at 10 per cent level. But the fact that it remains positive even after deregulation is an indication of persistence of crowding in phenomenon.

$$IPA = -11190.93 + 0.03*XA - 95.38*LNDRN + 102.24*RPAGR(-1)$$
$$(-3.01) \quad (11.29) \quad (-2.05) \quad (3.05)$$
$$+ 0.12*IGA + 0.34*IPA(-1) + 3214.73*DUMIPA$$
$$(1.14) \quad (5.51) \quad (13.07)$$

Adj. R^2 =0.97 D.W=2.06

To analyse the impact of increased public investment on agricultural growth we need a complete model of the economy. For this purpose we simulate the model presented in Bhattacharya and Kar (2004). We evaluate the impact of higher public investment on agricultural growth in the Tenth Plan period under alternative assumptions.

The first simulation that we present for the Tenth Plan period is based on the assumption that the exogenous factors will continue to behave according to past trends during this period. We refer to these as the base run forecasts. The base run assumes that the public investment rate in agriculture is fixed at 1.48 per cent of GDP at market price. The corresponding shares of public investment in industry and the services sectors are 3.7 per cent and 2.22 per cent of GDP at market price. Hence, the total public investment is fixed at 7.4 per cent of GDP at market price. This public investment consists of 3 per cent investment by government administration (GINV, through budgetary sources) and 4.4 per cent by public enterprises (PEINV). It may be pointed out that in our model, government administration consists of both the state and the central government. The sectoral allocation as well as the total volume of public investment is based on the behaviour for the last few years.

Other assumptions include no new structural changes apart from the ongoing reform process, normal rainfall, standard depreciation rate for the whole period, etc. In the fiscal sector, employment in public administration and defence (which excludes employment in public enterprises) increases at 0.3 per cent per annum. The average tariff rate is brought down from 23 per cent in 2001 to 20 per cent by 2006 due to the requirements of the WTO agreement. It is also assumed that tax reforms that have been initiated in 1993 will not be reversed. Budgetary subsidies as a ratio of GDP at market prices will slowly decline from 1.2 per cent in 2001 to 0.95 per cent in 2006. The various transfer payments will remain at 2.6 per cent of GDP at market prices. We also assume that there will be no pay hike during this period. In the monetary sector, it is assumed that the bank rate and CRR remain fixed at 6.5 and 5 per cent respectively, as per the monetary policy declared in April, 2002. The government's borrowing from the RBI is pegged at 0.2 per cent of GDP at market prices. In the external sector, the world trade growth, which dipped to around 1 per cent in 2001, will bounce back to 3.5 per cent in 2002 and then increase gradually to reach 5 per cent in 2006. It is assumed that there is no new oil shock destabilising the system. Rather, there is a gradual increase in oil and non-oil prices at 5 per cent and 3 per cent per annum throughout the period. The LIBOR, which dipped to 4.5 per cent in 2002 will recover to 5 per cent in 2002 and remain at that level throughout. The rupee debt slides down gradually while it is assumed that there will be no new foreign borrowing schemes like Resurgent India Bonds and India Millennium Deposits, etc., in the future. Private transfers will increase from $ 12 billion in 2001 to $ 14.5 billion in the final year of the plan. However, official transfer payments will remain frozen $ 300 million per annum. We also assume net investment income (outflow) will slowly rise from $ 3.7 billion in 2001 to $ 4 billion by 2006.

The next two simulations comprise the optimistic scenario in which we look at the effects of higher levels of public investments comparable to earlier years. In Simulation 1 (*i.e.*, **S1**), it is assumed that public investment has been increased by 2 per cent of GDP at market prices. This increase in public investment is achieved by increasing both GINV and PEINV by one per cent of nominal GDP respectively. In terms of sectoral distribution of this investment, it is assumed that from this increased investment, 20 per cent goes to agriculture, 50 per cent goes to industry and 30 per cent goes to the services sector. The increase in GINV is financed through market borrowing while the increase in PEINV is financed by extra-budgetary methods. Simulation 2 (*i.e.*, S2) assumes an increase in public investment by 4 per cent of GDP at market prices. Here, this increase is achieved by increasing both GINV and PEINV by two per cent of nominal GDP respectively. In terms of sectoral distribution of this investment, we assume the same proportions as in simulation 1.

The forecast values of the average annual growth rates for the Tenth Plan period corresponding to the base run (B) and the two alternative simulations (S1 and S2) is presented in Table 5.3 below.

Table 5.3
Base-Run and Alternative Scenarios for the Tenth Plan Period

	B	S1	S2
Aggregate Growth Rate	6.1	6.8	7.4
Agricultural Growth Rate	2.9	3.1	3.4
Industrial Growth Rate	5.7	6.5	7.5
Services Growth Rate	8.2	8.9	9.7

The table shows that under the base-run simulations, the average growth rate of aggregate output for the Tenth Plan should be 6.1 per cent. This is the result of an almost 3 per cent growth in agriculture, together with 5.7 per cent in industry and 8.2 per cent in services. The two alternative simulations show that long run growth can be increased substantially by increasing the public investment rates in all the sectors. In particular, higher public investment in agriculture leads to higher growth in that sector as well as higher growth in other sectors through the sectoral interlinkages.

7. Summary and Conclusions

We have studied the effect of rainfall shocks and increases in public investment on the performance of the agricultural sector and the Indian economy. As far as the analysis of a shock is concerned, the primary focus is to study their impact on the aggregate growth rates. In this context, it is fair to say that realistic rainfall shocks have a strong growth retarding effect, both in the short as well as the long run. The second issue of interest is the pervasiveness of the shocks, *i.e.*, their long run persistence. Here we find that the economy is somewhat resilient to the rainfall shock. The third issue that is of interest from the policy point of view is whether the shock leads to a stagflationary situation or not. This is because demand management policies can be used in non-stagflationary situations while stagflationary situations sometimes worsen with the use of such policies. We find that the rainfall shock is stagflationary in the long run. The fourth point of interest is to study whether the shock leads to some instability in the growth process by enlarging the disequilibrium in the fiscal or the external sectors. As we have mentioned, a large increase in the deficits in these sectors have the potential to destabilise future growth rates by affecting investor confidence in the economy. We find from our study that the rainfall shock does not have any significant negative impact on either the fiscal deficit or the external reserves.

Next, we have studied the impact of government intervention in the face of such a shock. The results show that in the short run, a government policy response (consisting of higher food imports, government consumption and government transfers) diminish the stagflationary impact of a rainfall shock and gives a marginal impetus to the growth rate.

Finally, we have studied the effect of public investment on the long run growth of agriculture and aggregate output. We find that increased public investment increases the long run growth rate of all the sectors as well as aggregate output.

These results are not very difficult to interpret. Any shock that affects the supply side, such as the rainfall shock, will have a big impact on GDP growth. The impact is pervasive because rainfall deficiency not only reduces agricultural output but also non-agricultural output *via* sectoral interlinkages. The long run impact of this shock depends on the magnitude of the accelerator. However, since rainfall moves in cycles, it has a tendency to restore balance in the long run and, hence, the long run impact is more muted than the short run impact.

As far as counter shock policies are concerned, rainfall shocks must be countered through contra-cyclical fiscal and monetary policies. In the short run, this may lead to higher inflation due to a tradeoff between growth and inflation. The long run effect of the counter shock policies will depend on their impact on investments. In this context our estimation results indicate that in spite of interest rate deregulation, the overall impact of interest rate or private investment is small, and hence monetary policy is not very effective as a long run counter shock policy. The alternative is, therefore, to go in for a more bold fiscal policy involving higher public investment financed by the lowering of other government expenditure.

References

Bhattacharya, B.B. (1984). *Public Expenditure, Inflation and Growth,—A Macro-Econometric Analysis For India*, Delhi: Oxford University Press.

Bhattacharya, B.B., R.B. Barman and A.K. Nag (1994). "Stabilisation Policy Options: A Macroeconometric Analysis," *Development Research Group Studies* No. 8., Bombay: Reserve Bank of India.

Bhattacharya, B.B. and S. Kar (2004). "Growth and Inflation: A Macro Modeling Exercise and Forecasts for India," in *Journal of Quantitative Economics* Vol. No. 2(2), (pp. 76-103).

Bhattacharya, B.B. and S. Kar (2005). "Shocks, Economic Growth and The Indian Economy" *Working Paper* of the Institute of Economic Growth.

Bhattacharya, B.B. and C.H. Hanumantha Rao (1986). "Agriculture-Industry Inter-Relations: Issues of Relative Growth and Prices in the Context of Public Investment," Paper Presented in the *Eighth World Economic Congress of the International Economic Association*, New Delhi 1986.

Bhattacharya, B.B. (Chairman) (2002). *Report on Capital Formation in India*, Ministry of Agriculture, Government of India.

Easterly, William (1995). "The Mystery of Growth: Shocks, Policies, and Surprises in Old and New Theories of Economic Growth," *The Singapore Economic Review* Vol. No. 40(1), (pp.3-23).

Lucas, Robert E., Jr. (1988). "On the Mechanics of Economic Development" *Journal of Monetary Economics* Vol. No. 22(1), (pp.3-42).

Pritchett, Lant (2000). "Understanding Patterns of Economic Growth: Searching for Hills Among Plateaus, Mountains, and Plains" *The World Bank Economic Review* Vol. No. 14(2), (pp.221-50).

Rodrik, Dani (1999). "Where Did All the Growth Go?: External Shocks, Social Conflict, and Growth Collapses," *Journal of Economic Growth*, Vol. No. 4, (pp.358-412).

6

Globalisation, Liberalisation and Performance of Firms: Emerging Trends from Literature

N.S. SIDDHARTHAN

1. Introduction

Studies on the impact of liberalisation on industry focus, by and large, on inter-country samples or inter-industry samples in a given country. The equivocal nature of the results of studies conducted for India and other developing countries raises several important questions relating to the usefulness of inter-country and inter-industry studies. For example, inter-industry studies assume that all firms in an industry behave alike and therefore, industry level characteristics could be attributed to all firms operating in that industry. However, during an era of liberalisation, new firms with more advanced technology are likely to enter an industry and existing firms are expected to develop a strategy to meet the challenge from the new entrants and in particular, the multinational enterprises (MNEs). Under these circumstances, the homogeneity assumption, that is, the assumption that all firms in an industry are alike, might not be valid (Liu and Tybout, 1996; Liu, 1993; Bartelsman and Doms, 2000). In an industry consisting of a variety of firms that differ in terms of their access to technology, knowledge and other intangible assets, liberalisation would result in gainers and losers and the productivity gap between firms in an industry could widen. This chapter, therefore, concentrates on the findings from inter-firm studies rather than inter-country or inter-industry studies.

In analysing the emerging trends, this chapter concentrates on three performance variables and the changing pattern of their determinants: exports, growth, and productivity. Section 2 analyses the effect of liberalisation, MNEs and SMEs on exports; Section 3 discusses the impact of liberalisation on the growth of firms; Section 4 deals with the technology and productivity spillovers from FDI; and Section 5 summarises the main findings and draws lessons from the literature survey.

2. Liberalisation, MNEs and Exports

This section is devoted to an analysis of the impact of multinational enterprises (MNEs), technology imports and liberalisation measures on exports. It will also discuss the role of small and medium enterprises and the information technology tools like e-commerce in promoting exports. Literature survey with regard to the impact of liberalisation variables on the exports of Indian firms reveals an interesting pattern during the second half of the 1980s. However, during the 1990s the relationship between exports and liberalisation was less clear. Kumar and Siddharthan (1994), have analysed the inter-firm variations in export behaviour in 13 Indian manufacturing industries using panel data for 640 firms for the period 1987-88 to 1989-90. They argue that the technology factors could be important for low- and medium-tech industries but not for high-tech ones. They have captured technology factors through R&D intensity and skill content of the workforce. R&D was statistically significant with a positive sign for firms operating in transport equipment, manmade fibres, paper and rubber products. Skill was significant in the case of firms manufacturing food and transport equipment. All these industries were classified under low- and medium-tech industries. R&D and skill variables were not significant for high-tech industries. Furthermore, they have found technology import variable significant with a positive sign in the case of paper products, rubber products, non-electrical machinery and electrical machinery. These indicate the emerging trends of the Indian engineering enterprises breaking into international markets with the help of foreign collaboration and technology imports. Capital output ratio was used as a measure of capital intensity and it had a negative sign for six industries, namely, food processing, cement, paper, rubber products and industrial and other chemicals. All these happen to be low and medium technology industries. On the other hand, in high-tech industries like electrical engineering, drugs and pharmaceuticals capital output ratio was significant with a positive sign. The results indicate that capital intensity of operations did not give a competitive advantage to exporting firms in low and medium technology industries while it was useful in breaking into export markets in high technology industries. They have captured the role of MNEs by using a MNE dummy and it was significant only in the case of one industry – non-electrical machinery, indicating that the export behaviour of MNE affiliates and Indian firms are not very different. With regard to the divergence of performance of technology and capital intensity variables in high- and low-tech industries they conclude that in low- and medium-tech industries, export competitiveness is to be obtained on the basis of indigenous technological effort and through use of labour intensive production process. In the high-tech industries, on the other hand, import of technology and, thus, affiliation with MNEs, a higher degree of automation, and modernisation appear to be important for breaking into international markets.

MNEs and Exports

Contrary to expectations, that, liberalisation would result in increased importance of R&D, MNE affiliation and technology imports in explaining the export performance of firms, Aggarwal's (2002) study does not find these variables significant in explaining export intensities of firms in India during the period 1996-2000. The only significant determinants of exports are firm size and import of capital goods, materials and components. There could be several explanations for the differences in the results for the samples drawn during the late 1980s and late 1990s. The explanation given by Aggarwal is that India has been attracting host market seeking MNEs and not efficiency seeking MNEs. For attracting export-oriented efficiency seeking MNEs, India needs to improve its infrastructure and other facilities apart from introducing liberalisation measures. Likewise, expenditures on R&D and import of technology were also targeted at domestic consumers and improving the domestic competitiveness of the firms. These explanations could very well be true, but there could also be other explanations, which are methodological in nature.

Studies for Sri Lanka (Athukorala, Jayasuriya and Oczkowski, 1995) also show that MNEs' export intensities are not higher. The study finds no significant relationship between MNE affiliation and the degree of export orientation of exporting firms. On the other hand MNE affiliation influenced the decision to export, namely, whether a firm is an exporter or not. Similarly, Willmore (1992) found mixed results for Brazil.

Siddharthan and Nollen (2004) argue that MNE affiliates behave differently from other firms and that the magnitude and sign of the coefficients of some determinants of exports will differ between the MNEs and other firms. Therefore, in order to obtain more meaningful and interpretable results, they advocate fitting separate equations for different groups of firms. Mere introduction of a MNE dummy as was done in the earlier studies may not yield satisfactory results.

Their study demonstrates that for information technology firms in India, the explanation of export performance depends in part on the firm's foreign collaboration and on the amount and type of technology that it acquires from abroad. For affiliates of MNEs, both explicit technology transfer from purchases of licenses and payments of royalties, and tacit technology transfer received from foreign ownership contribute to greater export intensity. They do so independently, without a complementary interaction to further boost export performance.

In contrast, the explanation of export performance for strictly domestic firms that have neither a foreign equity stake nor foreign licenses is different. For these firms, more imports of raw materials and components as a source of product quality improvement contribute to more exports of products, as do the larger size of a firm and greater capital intensity. These export determinants for domestic firms are unimportant for MNE affiliates, they argue, because the foreign ownership influence in the MNE affiliates makes them less necessary.

SMEs and Exports

The relationship between exports, technology and MNEs is a complex one. The Indian evidence shows that MNEs do not play a significant role in Indian exports. In recent years the export intensities of MNEs have increased but despite this their share in the Indian export is small. On the other hand, the exports of small and medium enterprises (SMEs) constitute the bulk of the Indian exports. If technology is crucial to exports, then SMEs ought to be at a disadvantage as there are sizable scale economies in in-house R&D and technology acquisition from other enterprises. This raises the question of the nature of competitive advantage of the SMEs in exports. In this context, there are some interesting results from studies on the export performance of Italian SMEs and their competitive advantages. India can draw valuable lessons from these studies.

The study by Nassimbeni (2001) based on a sample of 165 small manufacturing firms in furniture, manufacturing and electro-electronics sectors in Italy reveals a number of interesting results relating to technological and innovative capacity related factors that significantly differentiate exporting and non-exporting small enterprises. It shows the crucial role of the management of product related activities in promoting exports. Technology and more generally process innovations have played a secondary role. Thus, a mere possession of an elevated technological level does not guarantee an effective export advantage. Technology is obviously important but it is not distinctive. Product management depends on inventiveness and an ability to forge inter-organisational relationships.

The study makes a distinction between technological innovations and product inventiveness. The latter would depend on the ability of the small firms to forge vertical and horizontal networks with other firms and the creativity and inventiveness of the work force.

In this context, the role of internet and e-commerce and, in particular, business to business (B2B) commerce assumes importance. The study by Freund and Weinhold (2004) finds that internet stimulates trade. They show that internet reduces the fixed cost of entry into a foreign market which helps firms from less developed countries and SMEs. Using data on bilateral trade from 1995 to 1999 and controlling for the standard determinants of trade growth, they find that growth in the number of websites in a country helps to explain export growth in the following year. Accordingly, the success of SMEs in the export front would crucially depend on their ability to network, which in turn would depend on the infrastructure facilities for doing B2B commerce. These in turn would depend on the cost, reliability and availability of internet facilities, the band width and connectivity.

Liberalisation and Value of Exports

Liberalisation and technology imports can affect exports in two ways: first, by increasing export intensities of firms and the volume of exports, and second, by increasing the unit value of exports or the quality of exported goods. Navaretti, *et al.*, (2004) for a sample of developing countries neighbouring European Union (Central and Eastern European countries and the Southern Mediterranean Countries) has found evidence in favour of higher unit value of exports implying higher quality of products consequent to liberalisation and technology imports. Their paper argue that with declining trade barriers new sources of technological inputs become available, some directly purchased – machinery, blue prints and designs – and others acquired indirectly through spillovers. They have found that the unit values of exports to EU for the sample countries rose steadily between 1988 and 1996, relative to the unit values of world exports to EU. In other words, liberalisation and technology transfer need not increase the volume of exports but could increase the unit value of exports or the quality of exported goods. Since international trade is growing faster in high quality goods than in standardised goods, in the long run a switch over to a higher unit value exports would sustain exports growth better.

3. Liberalisation and the Growth of Firms

Studies on the growth of firms have emphasised the roles of technology acquisition, product creation and diversification in promoting growth (Siddharthan and Rajan, 2002). For the developed countries' firms, studies have shown that expenditures on product diversification, differentiation and innovative activities were mainly responsible for promoting growth (Siddharthan and Lal, 1982). However, these variables did not emerge important for a sample of Indian firms during the pre-liberalisation (pre-1985) period (Siddharthan, *et al.*, 1994).

Siddharthan, Pandit and Agarwal (1994) in their study have developed, a comprehensive econometric model to analyse growth, profit margins, investment and financial choice of the top 385 private corporate firms in India during the pre-liberalisation period (1981-84). They have used a simultaneous equations framework to highlight the inter-relationships and interactions between growth, profits, investments and financial choice variables. In analysing inter-firm differences in growth, they have considered both technology input and output variables as determinants. The technology input variables include technology purchases from abroad against royalties, lump-sum payments, technical fee payments, and foreign equity participation representing intra-firm transfer of technology from a MNE to a host country affiliate. Royalty, lump-sum and technical fee receipts, awards won for their R&D activities, and patents registered are taken as representatives of technology output variables. In their study most of these variables are not useful in explaining growth but are important in explaining profits. They attribute the unimportance of the technology variables in their growth equation to the existence of the pre-1985 strict capacity-licensing regime in India. In this regime expansion of capacity and growth depended on obtaining an industrial license and not on expenditures on innovation and technology. If these explanations are correct, then in the post-deregulation regime technology acquisition factors should influence growth.

India first introduced internal deregulation measures in 1985 and introduced external liberalisation measures progressively since 1991. Siddharthan and Pandit (1998) argue that while the growth of firms in India would be influenced by government controls, industrial and import licences in the pre-1985 period, technology acquisition factors will influence their growth rate after 1985. For their study they have used the Reserve Bank of India data tapes on "Finances of Large Public Limited Companies" and have considered three sectors: chemicals, machinery and drugs and pharmaceuticals. For the pre-deregulation period, 3-year data for the years 1982-83 to 1984-85 are used. For the post-deregulation period the years 1987-88 to 1989-90 are considered. All the variables are defined as the share of the individual firm in the industry's total. The share of the firm's investment in the industry's investment is used as the dependent variable. The explanatory variables are advertisement, age of the plant and machinery, exports, import of machinery, MNE affiliation, market share of the firm, technology payments like royalty and technology fees, and R&D.

For the pre-deregulation sample none of the technology variables emerge significant in explaining investment. The only significant variables are market share of the firm (with a positive coefficient), import of machinery (positive sign) and age of the plant (negative sign for the coefficient). The results show that a firm's share in an industry's investment in the license – permit period depended mainly on its market power and ability to apportion a share in the licences required to import capital goods. However, during the later half of the 1980s – post-deregulation period – the results dramatically changed. In addition to the three variables that were significant for the earlier period, variables representing product differentiation (advertisement), R&D, MNE affiliation, and technology purchases emerge important in explaining the investment share of a firm. The authors conclude that in the pre-deregulation period firms could successfully deter entry of rivals by pre-empting licensed capacities by acquiring a license. In other words, entry deterrence was possible without enhancing expenditures on technology acquisition on R&D and technology payments. Under the relatively liberalised policy regime of the later half of the 1980s, when a large number of industries were de-licensed, entry deterrence was no longer possible by simply pre-empting licensed capacities. They had to incur expenditures on technology.

The study by Pandit and Siddharthan (1998) examines the role of technology acquisition in influencing investment decisions of private corporate firms in the aftermath of the Indian economic reforms introduced in 1995. Using pooled cross-section data for 1987-88 to 1989-90 on a sample of 325 large corporate firms from seven industries, the study shows the crucial role played by technology in influencing investment decisions. The industries covered are textiles, metals, electrical and electronic goods, chemicals, drugs and pharmaceuticals, automobiles and machinery. Empirical tests of the model carried out for each industry separately indicate that inter firm differences in the investment rate at the firm level are due to opportunities to import disembodied technology through arms length purchase of technology and embodied technology through import of machinery. The results further show that in-house R&D expenditures promote capacity expansion. Even from the point of view of licensing technology, firms with R&D units are better placed to locate new technology and adapt it to suit Indian market conditions. In this context it is important to contrast the post-1985 findings with the findings during the controlled regime.

India introduced major liberalisation measures in the year 1991 and Siddharthan and Lal (2004) argue in their paper that with the new liberalisation measures the super environment facing Indian firms changed. With the change in policy, firms were allowed to enter into joint-ventures with multinational enterprises (MNEs) more freely, import technology from MNEs, import capital goods and expand capacities and introduce new products without obtaining an industrial license. In the early 1990s the Indian rupee was made convertible in the current account and imports were more freely allowed. These measures, they suggest would affect the firms differentially.

They identified firm-specific variables, which would have enabled the firms to grow faster/slower. These are the size of the firm, MNE affiliation as measured by the share of foreign equity in the total equity of the firm, import of technology, import of machinery, export orientation, vertical integration, and capital intensity. Furthermore, they argue that the impact of these determinants on growth will not remain constant over the years but will change during the process of liberalisation over the years. The results of the study show that during the initial years, firm size, MNE affiliation, capital intensity, vertical integration and import of capital goods had a negative impact on growth. However, in recent years the impact of these variables has turned positive and significant indicating the important changes brought about by globalisation.

Soon after the introduction of liberalisation measures there was a surge in the investment and expansion programmes of the sample firms. The average growth in capital stock during 1995 was more than 100 per cent. This was mainly due to the removal of shackles by the government and the desire of the firms to reap early entrant advantages in introducing new and better quality goods. However, this extraordinarily high investment rate could not be sustained and the investment rate settled down to more realistic levels. During the controlled regime, since expansion of capacity in a given product line was not easily granted, firms opted for product diversification rather than specialisation. After liberalisation, expansion activities became more focussed and firms turned to vertical integration aimed at improving product quality and delivery schedules. The sign of the coefficient of vertical integration changed to positive after 1995. Arm's length purchase of technology against lump-sum and royalty payments also influenced inter-firm differences in investment rates, though its impact was not strong. Perhaps liberalisation policies with regard to arm's length purchase of technology affected all firms more or less equally thereby reducing its impact. Furthermore, the sums involved in technology payments were not large. However, inter-firm differences in the import of capital goods were substantial and this variable significantly influenced the investment behaviour of the sample firms. In the case of computer aided numerically controlled machines, the software and the tacit components were in-built and the machines were also activity specific. Thus, unlike for the machines of the earlier vintage, the search, acquisition and transaction costs are high for the purchase of new machines. Firms that were successful in acquiring these machines grew faster. Thus, liberalisation policies had different impacts on different sets of firms. Also, the impact of the determinants changed over time.

4. FDI and Productivity Spillovers

When foreign enterprises with superior technology and managerial and marketing practices set-up units and joint-ventures in developing countries, the move, in addition to increasing the productivity of the FDI sector, is also likely to have spillover effects resulting in increased productivity of local firms. Studies have investigated the existence and importance of spillovers of FDI for local firms in China, India and several South American countries. In particular they have analysed the nature of spillovers and identified the main beneficiaries and possible victims of FDI enterprises.

The Chinese Experience

Buckley *et al.,* (2002) have investigated the impact of FDI on the performance of locally owned Chinese firms in manufacturing. In addition to analysing productivity spillovers the study also analyses exports and the introduction of new products. Furthermore, it distinguishes different types of productivity advantages for overseas Chinese investment and investments by non-Chinese (that is, investment mainly by developed economies). In addition the study also differentiates between the locally owned Chinese firms, namely, government owned and privately (including collectively) owned enterprises.

The study shows that overseas Chinese capital did not enhance the productivity of Chinese firms but the non-Chinese investments did. Their results further showed that while non-Chinese capital generated both technological and market access (exports) spillovers, the overseas Chinese capital enabled only market access benefits. The non-Chinese investments also contributed to the creation of new products by the local Chinese firms. The study also reveals that FDI did not contribute to productivity and export spillovers for the government owned enterprises. Consequently, the spillovers were limited to privately owned enterprises. This study, thus, brings out clearly the differential capacity of firms in absorbing technology based on ownership.

The Indian Experience

With regard to productivity spillovers the issues facing Indian firms are in some respects different from those of the Chinese as the Indian environment is not the same as that in China. The dominance of the state owned enterprises in India is less than that of China and overseas Indians have not been investing in India like the overseas Chinese have been investing in China. India also enjoys the presence of large Indian industrial houses. Many of them are also investing overseas and are in the process of emerging as MNEs in their own right. Consequently, in several industries the productivity gap between Indian enterprises and FDI enterprises is not large. Some of the Indian firms could also enjoy productivity advantages.

Siddharthan and Lal (2004) argue that in analysing the impact of liberalisation and FDI on productivity spillovers, it is essential to take into account the entry of new enterprises and the exit of older ones. Furthermore, the value of the spillover coefficients could change over time. Therefore, estimating an average coefficient (averaged over several years) many not reflect the changes in the spillover effects. In addition, labour productivity measures used by earlier studies do not take into account the heterogeneity in the skill content of the workforce. They have advocated another measure, namely, value added per unit cost of labour, which avoids the problem posed by skill diversities and the consequent wage differentials of the workers.

Their study shows the presence of significant spillover effects from FDI. During the initial years of liberalisation, namely, the early 1990s, the spillover effects were modest but later they increased sharply and stabilised towards the end of the decade. However, not all domestic firms gained equally from the spillovers. Domestic firms that possessed higher labour productivities and had lower productivity gaps with MNEs were able to enjoy higher spillovers while those with larger productivity gaps could not benefit much. As a result, firms with better endowments in terms of productivity and technology benefited from liberalisation and FDI presence. Firms with large productivity gaps became the victims.

A study by Kathuria (2002) also shows that Indian firms that invested in R&D benefited from FDI spillovers. Indian firms with low or nil R&D expenditures did not benefit from the spillovers. Furthermore, in the case of low R&D intensive industry groups the impact of import liberalisation was found to be productivity depressing. Based on these results, Kathuria concludes that spillovers were not automatic and they depended largely on the level of investment a firm made in R&D. In other words, only firms that had low productivity gaps benefited from spillovers.

Successful Indian firms did not wait for spillovers to take place. They had a positive strategy to tackle the entry of foreign firms with advanced technology. Some Indian firms entered into a series of non-equity strategic alliances with several MNEs and Indian firms. Such strategic alliances seem to have enabled these Indian firms to enhance their productivity and emerge competitive in several sectors like IT, automobiles, electronics, drugs and pharmaceuticals.

Latin American Experience

Furthermore, spillovers from MNEs need not always be positive. Studies for Latin America have reported negative spillovers. For example, a study by Aitken and Harrison (1999) using annual census data for over 4000 Venezuelan firms for the period 1976 – 1989, presents two interesting results with regard to spillovers. They have found a positive relationship between increased foreign participation and plant performance only in the case of small plants, namely, plants with less than 50 employees. For large enterprises when plant specific differences (fixed effects) are taken into account the positive foreign investment effect disappears. They argue that foreign firms are not more productive but they invest in more productive sectors. Thus, the higher productivity observed is due to sector effect and not due to FDI. Moreover, their results show that the productivity of domestic enterprises declines when foreign investment increases, suggesting a negative spillover from foreign to domestic enterprises. They consider this as market stealing effect.

While Aitken and Harrison (1999) obtained a negative spillover effect for Venezuela, Kokko *et al.*, (1996) have not found evidence of technology spillovers from FDI in Uruguayan manufacturing plants. Their regression analysis shows no signs of spillovers from FDI for a sample of 159 locally owned manufacturing plants. However, they have found positive spillovers in the case of a sub-sample of plants that had small and moderate technology gaps *vis-à-vis* foreign firms but not in the case of local plants facing large gaps. Perhaps when foreign and domestic firms operated on the same technological paradigm they experienced spillovers not otherwise. They have also found many domestic plants experiencing higher productivity levels compared to foreign firms. In their cases the spillover could be from the domestic to the foreign firm.

The impact of FDI could also depend on the trade regime, namely, import substituting or trade promoting regime. Some works (Balasubramanayam *et al.*, 1996) suggest that unlike import-substitution regimes, export-promoting regimes attract FDI which has a significant impact on the growth of GDP. Kokko *et al.*, (2001) analyse the characteristics of FDI inflows during two different trade regimes in Uruguay and examine whether FDI in the two regimes had differential impacts on Uruguay industry. Their sample consisted of 1243 private manufacturing firms distributed among 74-four digit industries. Their results suggest that foreign firms established in the import substitution regime, that is, before 1973, generate positive productivity spillovers to local firms but the impact of foreign firms established after 1973 is the opposite. Thus, the presence of import substituting MNEs had a more beneficial effect on labour productivity of local firms than the presence of export-oriented MNEs.

5. Lessons from Literature

This paper has discussed the impact of liberalisation and FDI inflows on exports, growth of firms, and productivity spillovers. While considering the influence of FDI and liberalisation policies on growth of firms some discerning trends emerged from literature. However, for exports and productivity spillovers clear-cut trends are not visible and, therefore, no generalisations could be attempted.

There has been no consensus on the role of MNEs and FDI in influencing exports. More than 55 per cent of exports in China emanated from fully owned foreign ventures or joint ventures. The share of foreign firms in the exports of high-tech industries is even higher. But for most of the other developing countries the evidence is mixed and ambiguous. For example, in India, (Aggarwal, 2002) unlike China, MNEs have not emerged as important exporters. Several reasons are given for this empirical result; MNEs came to India to seek the host-market and not exploit opportunities for export, efficiency seeking FDI is very different from host-market seeking FDI and the Indian regime is not liberal enough to attract efficiency seeking FDI. Likewise, studies for Sri Lanka (Athukorala, Jayasuriya, and Oczkowski 1995) and Brazil (Willmore, 1992) also did not find any significant relationship between MNE presence and exports. On the contrary several studies (Nassimbeni, 2001 and Freund and Weinhold, 2004) show the crucial role of SMEs in promoting exports in both developed and developing countries and in particular the vital role of internet in promoting B2B commerce.

While the studies are ambiguous about the relationship between liberalisation and export intensity of firms, some studies show that liberalisation results in an increase in the unit value of exports implying increase in the quality of products (Navaretti *et al.*, 2004). This result assumes importance in the context of higher growth of international trade in high quality goods rather than in standardised low skill intensive goods. In the long run firms that shift to a higher unit value exports would benefit by being part of a rapidly growing market. For the developing countries in particular, a shift from a stagnant to a growing segment of the market is important.

The evidence from literature shows that the determinants of a firm's growth drastically changed when the economic regime changed from a controlled to a liberal one. The Indian experience clearly demonstrated that during the controlled regime a firm's expenditures on technology acquisition and modernisation and product differentiation did not influence its growth. Instead it was its strategy to pre-empt the industrial and import licenses and its current market power that influenced its growth. However, after deregulation of the economy and industry, technology variables emerged important in determining the relative growth of firms. Liberalisation did not have an uniform impact on all firms and its influence depended on each firm's characteristics. Firms with superior technological base and firms that networked with other firms through strategic alliances performed better. Furthermore, over the years the significance and the role of the determinants changed in favour of technology variables.

Studies surveyed in this paper show that technology and productivity spillovers from MNEs to local firms are not automatic. Spillovers will depend on the nature of the investing MNE and the technological base, ownership and managerial practices of the domestic firms. In the case of China, FDI from developed countries resulted in technology and productivity spillovers to non-state owned Chinese firms. State owned firms did not benefit from spillovers nor did investments from overseas Chinese result in productivity spillovers (Buckley *et al.*, 2002).

Studies done for India (Siddharthan and Lal 2004; Kathuria 2002), and for Latin American countries (Aitken and Harrison 1999; Kokko *et al.*, 1996), show that firms that already enjoyed a good technological base, had a smaller productivity gap with regard to MNEs, and spent on in-house R&D captured spillovers. The rest did not. Furthermore, in several industries local firms also enjoyed high productivity levels, higher than the MNEs and, therefore, the assumption that MNEs always enjoyed higher productivity levels is not valid. Some studies also reported negative spillovers indicating a market stealing effect by MNEs. Some studies (Kokko *et al.*, 2001) also show a higher presence of spillovers in the import substitution regime than in the liberalised regime. In the liberalised regimes the quantity of FDI inflows could be more but in the regulated regimes the quality of FDI in terms of spillovers and domestic sourcing of components was higher (Kumar, 2002). Given this finding in the current WTO regime, which aims at elimination of regulations, the spillovers from FDI could decline. Under these conditions firms from developing countries should develop positive strategies like non-equity strategic alliances and networking with other firms to compete successfully with MNEs than passively wait for spillovers to occur.

References

Aggarwal, Aradhna (2002). "Liberalisation, Multinational Enterprises and Export Performance: Evidence from Indian Manufacturing," *Journal of Development Studies*, 38(3), (pp.119-137).

Aitken, Brian J. and Ann, E. Harrison (1999). "Do Domestic Firms Benefit from Direct Foreign Investment? Evidence from Venezuela," *American Economic Review*, 89(3), (pp. 605-618).

Athukorala, P., Jayasuriya, S. and Oczkowski, E. (1995). "Multinational Firms and Export Performance in Developing Countries: Some Analytical Issues and New Empirical Evidence," *Journal of Development Economics*, 46(1), (pp. 109-22).

Balasubramanyam, V.N. , M.A. Salisu and D. Sapsford (1996). "Foreign Direct Investment and Growth in EP and IS Countries," *Economic Journal*, 106, (pp. 92-105).

Bartelsman, Eric J. and Mark, Doms (2000). "Understanding Productivity: Lessons from Longitudinal Microdata," *Journal of Economic Literature*, 38 (September), (pp.569-594).

Buckley, Peter J., Jeremy, Clegg and Chenjqi, Wang (2002). "The Impact of Inward FDI on the Performance of Chinese Manufacturing Firms," *Journal of International Business Studies*, 33(4), (pp. 637-655).

Freund, Caroline L. and Diana, Weinhold (2004). "The Effect of Internet on International Trade," *Journal of International Economics*, 62, (pp. 171-189).

Kathuria, Vinish (2002). "Liberalisation, FDI and Productivity Spillovers – An Analysis of Indian Manufacturing Firms," *Oxford Economic Papers*, 54, (pp. 688-718).

Kokko, Ari., Ruben Tansini., Mario C. Zejan (1996). "Local Technological Capability and Productivity Spillovers from FDI in the Uruguayan Manufacturing Sector," *Journal of Development Studies*, 32(4), (pp. 602-611).

Kokko, Ari., Mario, Zejan and Ruben, Tansini (2001). "Trade Regimes and Spillover Effects of FDI: Evidence from Uruguay," *Weltwirtschaftliches Archiv*, 137(1), (pp.124-149).

Kumar, Nagesh (2002). *Globalisation and the Quality of Foreign Direct Investment*, New Delhi: Oxford University Press.

Liu, Lili (1993). "Entry-Exit, Learning, and Productivity Change: Evidence from Chile," *Journal of Development Economics*, 42, (pp.217-242).

Liu, Lili and James, R. Tybout (1996). "Productivity Growth in Chile and Colombia: The Role of Entry, Exit, and Learning," in Mark J. Roberts and James R. Tybout eds. *Industrial Evolution in Developing Countries: Micro Patterns of Turnover, Productivity and Market Structure*. NY. Oxford University Press.

Navaretti, Giorgio Barba., Marzio Galeotti., and Andrea, Mattozzi (2004). "Moving Skills from Hands to Heads: Does Importing Technology Affect Export Performance in Textiles?," *Research Policy*, 33, (pp.879-895).

Nassimbeni, Guido (2001). "Technology, Innovation Capacity, and the Export Attitude of Small Manufacturing Firms: A Logit/Tobit Model," *Research Policy*, 30, (pp.245-262).

Pandit, B.L. and N.S. Siddharthan (1998). "Technological Acquisition and Investment: Lessons from Recent Indian Experience," *Journal of Business Venturing*, (North - Holland) Elsevier Science; 13(1), (pp 43-55).

Siddharthan, N.S. and K. Lal (2004). "Liberalisation, MNE and Productivity of Indian Enterprises," *Economic and Political Weekly, Review of Industry and Management*, Vol. 39(5), (pp. 448-452).

Siddharthan, N.S. and S. Lall (1982). "The Recent Growth of the Largest US Multinationals," *Oxford Bulletin of Economics and Statistics*, 44, (pp. 1-13).

Siddharthan, N.S. and Stanley Nollen (2004). "MNE Affiliation, Firm Size and Exports Revisited: A Study of Information Technology Firms in India," *The Journal of Development Studies*, 40 (6), (pp. 148-170).

Siddharthan, N.S. and B.L. Pandit (1998). "Liberalisation and Investment: Behaviour of MNEs and Large Corporate Firms in India," *International Business Review*, 7 (5), (pp 535-548).

Siddharthan, N.S., B.L. Pandit and R.N. Agarwal (1994). "Growth and Profit Behaviour of Large Indian Firms," *The Developing Economies*, Vol. 32, (2), (pp. 188-209).

Siddharthan, N.S. and Y. Rajan (2002). *Global Business, Technology and Knowledge Sharing: Lessons for Developing Country Enterprises*, New Delhi: Macmillan.

Willmore, Larry (1992). "Transnationals and Foreign Trade: Evidence from Brazil," *Journal of Development Studies*, 28(2), (pp. 314-35).

Section II

Issues in
Agricultural Development

7

Indian Economic Strategies After Doha

YOGINDER K. ALAGH[36]

1. Introduction

The purpose of this paper is to discuss global economic strategies followed by India after the Doha WTO meetings. At Doha, India played a role to focus on the trade issues. We attempt to show that the stand India took emerged not from earlier strategies of policy in an autarchic framework, but the requirements of a policy of economic reform and integration with the global economy. India signed the Marrakesh agreement with many misgivings, having stood out till the end, but also with many expectations. The first half of the Nineties went reasonably well, but developments in the period after the East Asian crisis lead to serious questioning and India tried to engage global discussions to resolve problems. This was dimly understood initially even by Indian policy-makers at first but by now is clearly articulated. To professional economists and trade negotiators this transition should itself be of considerable interest, for the theoretical and negotiation issues it raises and the need for fresh approaches it underlines.

We show in this paper:

i) The impact of the global economy on the macro performance of the Indian economy in the Nineties, the swings in it, and a gradual understanding of them leading to the evolution of her trade responses:

ii) The reasons for the concentration largely on agricultural issues and the interesting issues raised of a conceptual and applied nature in the negotiations, for example, the recent sharp disagreement between Mr. Lamy and the Director General of WTO on the definition of subsidies and domestic support has a long history in earlier Indian debates. We describe these since the issues are bound

36. Comments by Prof. S. Bhalla are gratefully acknowledged.

to persist in the future and understanding them is central to resolving them:

iii) The approaches India is developing to adjust her policies in the agricultural sector, including less priority to direct statal interventions and use of trade policy and fiscal, technological and monetary mechanisms for 'Road Maps' for crops which directly confront the dynamics of adjustment to a trade dominated regime:

iv) The nature of the coalitions emerging in the agricultural negotiations and India's role in them, seen from the angle of the coalition building around interest groups in the context of global paradigms.

v) In each of the issues the emphasis is on describing the analytical issues involved and the Indian position that has emerged from them. Since the basic position is now trade enhancing, we believe the issues are of some relevance to her future domestic policies and larger global trade negotiations.

As is well known, the Singapore issues were in a sense taken off the fast track at Doha and at Cancun a Group of 16 countries led by Malaysia and India with the support of 30 least developed countries sought further clarification rather than agreeing to give a negotiating mandate. The Group of 74 African, Caribbean and Pacific countries (ACP) took largely the same stand. The Draft Ministerial Text issued on 13 September 2003 wanted to give a negotiating mandate on all these issues except 'competition'. India felt that from a development point of view this was the worst position since there would be binding rules on investment but not competition. The developing countries did not agree with the draft. The only other major non-agricultural issue for India was the market access commitments to textiles and clothing. This and the tariff issue were taken up and we will note it later. The most important issue was agriculture.

Paragraph 13 of the Doha Ministerial Declaration provides (WT/MIN(01)/DEC/1 refers):

13. "We recognise the work already undertaken in the negotiations initiated in early 2000 under Article 20 of the Agreement on Agriculture, including the large number of negotiating proposals submitted on behalf of a total of 121 Members. We recall the long-term objective referred to in the Agreement to establish a fair and market-oriented trading system through a programme of fundamental reform encompassing strengthened rules and specific commitments on support and protection in order to correct and prevent restrictions and distortions in world agricultural markets. We reconfirm our commitment to this programme. Building on the work carried out to date and without prejudging the outcome of the negotiations we commit ourselves to comprehen-

sive negotiations aimed at: substantial improvements in market access; reductions of, with a view to phasing out, all forms of export subsidies; and substantial reductions in trade-distorting domestic support. We agree that special and differential treatment for developing countries shall be an integral part of all elements of the negotiations and shall be embodied in the Schedules of concessions and commitments and as appropriate in the rules and disciplines to be negotiated, so as to be operationally effective and to enable developing countries to effectively take account of their development needs, including food security and rural development. We take note of the non-trade concerns reflected in the negotiating proposals submitted by Members and confirm that non-trade concerns will be taken into account in the negotiations as provided for in the Agreement on Agriculture."

As we will see, Cancun did not make progress in this direction, but between Doha and Cancun the understanding of the situation was much deeper. This may help in later negotiations.

2. Agriculture, Trade and the Macro Economy in India

In the early nineties, India borrowed somewhat uncritically a reform package for agriculture. Since there was little understanding behind it of the global context and its impact on Indian agriculture as also a strategic view of reform at home, the consequences on income, output, employment, profitability and capital formation were severe.

Output and Income Effects

For some unknown reasons there is a tradition in Indian Economics to include fertiliser imports in 'agricultural imports.' If terms of trade or intersectoral flows are to be measured then seeds and pesticides and so on must also be included. If not, agriculture should be as conventionally defined. The summary of the record of the Nineties was as shown in Table 7.1.

Table 7.1
Growth of Agricultural Trade in the Nineties

S. No.	Period	Unit	Average of Annual Growth Rates	
			Export	Import
1.	1991-92—1996-97	US$	17.04	46.20
2.	1996-97—1999-00	US$	-7.08	25.38
3.	2000-01—2002-03	Rs. crore	2.89[1]	19.41

Source: Annex Table 1, in Alagh, 2003.
   1. Growth of 2001-02 over 2000-01. Figures for 2002-03 not available.
   Row 3 not comparable with Rows 1 and 2.

The first half of the Nineties was a period of explosive growth of agricultural trade. Import growth far exceeded export growth. In the second half, substantial import growth continues *albeit* at a slower rate. Exports collapse. However, the aggregate effect of net export changes in the agricultural sector on the economy is small, but not insignificant. The opening up of the agricultural economy is beginning to matter at the margin, in terms of macro-demand effects (Table 7.2)

Table 7.2

Incremental Net Exports in Agriculture

S. No.	Variable	Percentage	
		1990-91—1996-97	*1996-97—2001-02*
1.	Incremental Net Export in Agriculture w.r.t. Incremental GDP in Economy	1.74	-0.53
2.	Incremental Net Export in Agriculture w.r.t. Gross Capital Formation in Economy	6.87	-2.19

Source: For net exports from agriculture, MoA, *Agricultural Statistics at A Glance*, 2002.
For GDP and GCF, C.S.O., *National Account Statistics*, 2002.

If the macro effect of net agricultural exports on GDP from the demand side was to be the same in the second half of the Nineties as in the first half, net agricultural exports should have grown in the later period by around 2 per cent more of GDP. Since aggregate consumption swamps macro demand, a better comparison would be with another component of GDP, say gross capital formation. If net agricultural exports were to play the same role they did in the macro economy in comparison to gross capital formation, in the second half of the Nineties, it should have grown by around 9 per cent. The point we are making is a simple one, but which has been ignored in the policy literature; in a trade dominated policy regime, macro effects of trade need tracking. The Economic Survey should discuss these issues seriously. It does not.

The experience of the first half of the Nineties, it has been argued, was on account of devaluation of the Rupee and consequent gap of global and national prices (Chand, 2002). Another argument was that the economic policy changes of the earlier years of the nineties led to removal of a very large number of domestic agro-commodity movements, restrictions and controls on investment and production of agro-based commodities. (For an amazing list of such restrictions, see Alagh, 1992). The second half of the nineties, Chand has argued was also on account of adverse price movements. Low growth in the world in this period and the East Asian crisis could also have led to this outcome on account of demand flattening out. (Alagh and Alagh, 2003).

The trends in imports were in the opposite direction. In the first half of the nineties, agricultural imports were constant. In the second half they grew by around 10 per cent annually. This could be on account of trade restrictions in the first half of the nineties being relieved in the second half. The impact of slower growth of production capacity in Indian agriculture leading to the need for large imports is again not discussed much. Capital formation in agriculture, decline in output growth rates, and fall in agricultural productivity rates in macro-economic production for larger import growth have not been discussed. It is possible that the production constraint was more severe in the later period.

Some thoughtful modellers had, however, shown that even unilateral reduction of trade restrictions would lead only to low trade expansion. Some scholars argued that the diversification of Indian agriculture at home was creating important markets and trade advantages were only at the margin (Alagh, 1994, 1995 a, 1995b). Fears concerning imports, following trade liberalisation, and on account of the distorted nature of global agricultural trade were brushed aside (See Alagh, 1995c; 1998). These studies turned out to be right.

Composition of Output

While not insignificant, the aggregate effect of agricultural trade seems marginal. The real questions lie in the composition of output and its economic and employment consequences. The historical record is that from the mid-seventies, when the economy started growing faster, the agricultural growth rate rises only marginally, but the non-foodgrains sector grows much faster as also sectors like livestock and fishing (Table 7.3).

The second half of the nineties, however, sees a slowing down of this process (Table 7.4).

Table 7.3

Growth Rate in Macro Parameters during 1960-61 to
1995-96 (per cent compound annual in 1980-81 prices)

S. No.	Item	1960-61—1975-76	1975-76—1995-96
1.	GDP at Market Prices	3.47	5.06
2.	NDP at Market Prices	3.30	4.95
3.	Agricultural GDP	1.97	2.94
4.	Non-Agricultural GDP	4.35	6.12
5.	Agricultural Value of Gross Output	2.32	2.98
6.	Non-Foodgrains crop output	2.70	4.39
7.	Livestock Value of Gross Output	1.43	4.71
8.	Fishing Value of Gross Output	4.11	5.44
9.	Forestry Value of Gross Output	2.69	1.37

Source: National Account Statistics. Row 6 from Agriculture Statistics At a Glance. (See Alagh and Alagh, 2003).

Note: Growth Rates estimated by semi-log regressions against time. All estimates significant at 99 per cent level.

Table 7.4

Production of Agriculture and Allied Products
in the Nineties (mn. Tonnes/bales for Cotton)

S. No.	Crop/Sector	1996-97	Highest 1997-99	Target Ninth Plan
1.	Foodgrains	199.44	205.91	234.00
2.	Oilseeds	24.38	25.21	30.00
3.	Sugarcane	277.56	309.31	336.00
4.	Cotton	14.23	12.18	15.70
5.	Fruits and Vegetables	141.00	122.00	179.00
6.	Milk	69.10	78.10	96.50
7.	Eggs (billion Nos.)	27.50	30.32	35.00
8.	Fish	5.35	5.80	7.00
9.	Tea	0.78	0.85	1.00

Source: Planning Commission, Annual Plan, 2000-01, p. 301.

What is the role of agriculture trade in these developments? Change in the commodity composition of output should have been expected to be a major consequence of a trade-dominated agriculture. Yet this question was not raised at an empirical level. After foodgrains, these are the most important crops in the Indian economy. They are, as they were taken for granted that agricultural trade would be a major engine of diversification since the composition of global demand would come to determine through trade, domestic production. This should not have been so, because in theory, trade can lead to specialisation and could therefore, also be seen as anti-diversification. In the classical two-commodity two-country comparative advantage case, both countries end up producing one commodity only. The hypothesis probably was that when a closed economy opens up, within agriculture, specialisation would lead resources away from the existing pattern. The story was more complex as we will see with a few crops.

The story of sugarcane and cotton in the last decade is that of horrible policy neglect if not perversity were, the flag bearers of the non-foodgrains economy growing as we saw earlier. Cotton and sugar are important crops accounting for around 7 per cent of cropped area. If the Planning Commission's labour coefficients are taken into account around 11 per cent of India's agricultural work force depended on them. But when the impact of WTO or of free trade was described in official publications initially, cotton and sugar imports were excluded to show that free trade does not matter. When the Ministry of Commerce and Industry stated that:

"Whereas prices are mainly a function of demand and supply, the demand for a particular product depends to a great extent on consumer preferences. An analysis of the import data (as shown in Table 7.5) reveals that there has been no significant surge in the import of these items. It will not be correct in general to attribute the present decline in domestic prices of such commodities except edible oils to import surges or to our WTO commitments for the domestic sector." (GoI, Ministry of Commerce and Industry, 2001, p.33).

An interesting feature of the sugar economy has been the wild swings in sugar production of a magnitude not seen earlier (Table 7.5).

Table 7.5

Fluctuations in Sugar Production

Fluctuations in Sugar Production (Range in lakh tonnes)	No. of Years 1980-81 to 1989-90	No. of Years 1990-91 to 1999-2000
0 to 10	5	2
10 to 20	2	3
20 to 30	2	3
30 to 40	1	1
40 to 50	0	1

The cane cycle is well known. Its Nerlovian nature was described way back in 1982, when I was the Agriculture Price Commission (APC) Chairman. However, in the Nineties we see that sugar production fluctuations were much sharper than the cane cycle. The larger regional swings, the larger swings in sugar as compared to cane production were bound to affect seriously the health of the Indian sugar and cane economy, its competitiveness and the sustainability of sugar production. The central consequence of this was shorter effective crushing seasons and much greater fluctuations in capacity utilisation in the factory sector. This in turn reduced the recovery rate from the level otherwise possible and raised overhead costs. The result was wasteful use of land and diminishing competitiveness of the industry at home and abroad. The import cycle was loaded on to the cane cycle. The tariff rates on sugar are given in Table 7.6.

Table 7.6
Tariff Rates on Sugar

1994-98	Nil
April 1998	5 per cent plus countervailing duty of Rs. 850/tonne
January 1999	20 per cent
Budget 1999	25 per cent plus 10 per cent surcharge
December 1999	40 per cent—surcharge abolished
February 2000	60 per cent

The reason on account of which tariff rates were kept low until 1999 is not quite clear. These were then revised and now they have gone the other way with the high tariffs.

Cotton, like sugarcane, was one of India's largest crops, affected millions of farmers, was a high cash input, risky game. The late eighties and early nineties sees the heyday of Indian cotton. Newer varieties meant lower crop cycles, less pesticides, lower costs and yields rose. India was exporting both the long and short staple varieties. The second half of the Nineties saw a collapse. Output growth which was 2.8 per cent annual in the eighties, went up in the early nineties from 9.84 million bales in 1990-91 steadily to 14.23 million bales in 1996-97, but fell to 10.85 million bales in 1997-98 and has been hovering between 9.5 and 11.5 million bales in the last few years. India imports a few thousand tonnes of raw cotton until the mid-nineties. This goes up to 0.54 lakh tonnes in 1997-98, 2.37 lakh tonnes in 1999-00, 2.12 lakh tonnes in 2000-01 and

3.86 lakh tonnes in 2001-02. Some of the highest imports, around 20 per cent of domestic consumption, (1 tonne=5.88 bales) have been in the last few years and domestic stocks of unsold cotton went up. A very nominal tariff was announced in recent years. The tariff rate for cotton was 5 per cent, that too imposed in 2001 after large imports had taken place. It was raised to 10 per cent in October 2001.

By now around half of India's edible oil requirements are imported. The import duty on edible oil was only 15 per cent in 1998. To control surges in imports, the duties have been revised many a times and the present level of duty are 65 per cent for crude palm oil, 75 per cent for refined palm oil, 75 per cent for other types of crude oil and 85 per cent for other types of refined oils. The duties on refined and crude soyabean oil are low at 45 per cent which is due to lower tariff bindings. However, the duty on non-edible vegetable oil is 30 per cent. The data on domestic availability and imports of edible oils are presented in Table 7.7.

Table 7.7

Domestic Availability and Import of Edible Oils (Quantity: Million Tonnes)

Year	Domestic Edible Oil Availability	Import of Edible Oils
1998-99	6.91	2.62
1999-2000	6.32	4.19
2000-01	5.85	4.18
2001-02	6.72	4.32
2002-03	5.54	4.26
2003-04	7.50	5.30
2004-05	7.81#	2.25 (April to September. 2004)

Based on targetted production.

Relative prices have been moving against the edible oil sector as may be seen from Table 8.

Table 7.8

Wholesale Price Index (Average of Weekly Base—1993-94)

Year	Edible Oils	Primary Products	All Commodities
1994-95	111	116	112.6
2003-04	158	182	175.9

There are also commodities like spices, horticultural crops and even 'other' oilseeds, where imports were not large enough to show up in the national basket, but created tremendous adjustment problems for a set of districts. The point of these stories is not that imports took place. A trade dominated policy must provide for imports. But Indian policy making did not anticipate or provide a policy perspective for them. We cannot get scared of this, since trade means imports also, but we have to prepare ourselves to adjust to swings and this needs quick assessments of facts. However, the official stance is that imports are marginal in the agricultural sector.

3. Composition in East Asia

The export aspect also played a role in the changing composition of output in the second half of the nineties. The diversification of the agricultural demand basket also became a significant feature of the Tiger economies from the mid-eighties onwards. FAO projected that up to 2010, GDP growth would be 7 per cent annual in East Asia and 4.4 per cent in the Near East and North Africa, with the West Asian (Near East) component growing faster (See Alexandratos, 1995) Per capita income growth was 5.7 per cent annual for East Asia. With this kind of income growth there was a shift of demand to non-cereal food items and commercial crops. Countries projected to have high volumes and growth of agricultural imports were Japan, Hong Kong, the Republic of Korea, Saudi Arabia, Singapore, Malaysia, Indonesia, the Islamic Republic of Iran, Thailand, Kuwait and Oman. These countries were estimated to be large and growing markets for fruit, vegetables, meat and fish. In fact, up to the mid-nineties the agricultural import of each of these countries was growing between 4 to 8 per cent annual and they accounted for around 40 per cent of India's agricultural exports (Alagh, 1995, 1998). The GDP growth of these countries went down to 4.7 per cent, 2.9 per cent, 0.3 per cent and 4.4 per cent and the incremental livestock to agricultural production ratio went down to minus 1.79, 1.01, minus 1.61 and minus 0.72 in these countries, from 1994 to 1999. On the other hand, countries like China which grew at around 8 per cent since 1980 and where the growth did not decelerate, had the incremental livestock to agricultural production ratio of 1.82 in the earlier period and 1.59 in the later period suggesting that the momentum of diversification and widespread agricultural growth was kept up. Data on vegetable and fruit production is available only for the nineties (FAOSTAT), and the incremental vegetable to cereal production ratio is minus 1.14 in Indonesia, minus

2.58 in Malaysia, minus 0.3 in Thailand and 1.43 in South Korea from 1994 to 1999. (I am grateful to Munish Alagh for these ideas and for a more elegant presentation see Alagh and Alagh, 2003). Trade should have meant diversification away from grains. In the Kafkaesque World of Trade Distortions in some of the Asian economies grain exports kept up. Given the subsidies that OECD countries give, there was no way of stopping grain exports. India has been advised to give up subsidies to rice and wheat exports, but there is no way of enforcing that.

The point is not that diversification reversed. The point is that it did and policy did not know. When the World was moving slowly it did not matter. But these are the days of short economic movements and short product cycles. If you don't know you suffer. To use an expression by Ricardo Petrella of the EEC, newer profitable opportunities build on the corpses of earlier ones.

4. The Indian Experience and Conceptual Issues

Recently, there has been an interesting debate on the nature of subsidies to agriculture with Mr. Lamy arguing that the Thai Director General of the WTO should not have argued that agricultural subsidies are the difference between global and national prices, but are the 'budget' figures. European Union Trade Commissioner Pascal Lamy, one of the most powerful men in global trade negotiations, lambasted Supachai Panitchpakadi, none other than the Director General of the World Trade Organisation, for engaging in 'dangerous polemic' on farm subsidies. In more sanguine times, this kind of language at this level was unthinkable but trade negotiations are no longer cricket.

Panitchpakadi had earlier in a speech in Costa Rica repeated the OECD based figure that the industrialised countries spent $300 billion on farm subsidies. Lamy called these numbers 'misleading,' 'contestable' and employing 'ideology based arguments.' He wanted actual budget numbers to be used. But budgets with a clever finance minister can be dressed up and a tariff can be an equivalent sum as compared to a subsidy, as introductory trade textbooks teach us. 'Should I remind you that this figure does not in any way correspond to budgetary outlays?' Lamy says and goes on moralising: 'The honest figure would be around $100 billion and less than $45 billion a year in the EU.'

This debate has a precursor in India. I have been arguing earlier that profitability in agriculture has been falling and that is not a happy sign in a liberalising phase (Alagh, 2003). In a market economy of the kind economic policy in India is pushing, relative profitability gives signals for resource allocation. Some of my peers whose understanding I respect highly, think otherwise—pointing out the argument we had all sworn by earlier—that, as long as land productivity is rising, we are alright. I suggested that this was no longer valid. In a market economy, profitability gives powerful signals for resource allocation, both for the short run and equally important for investment. Profitability of resource use is important, not just productivity of land. We have to move over from a Ricardian to a Haberler point of view at the micro level. Not just land productivity, but profitability of resource use gives signals at the margin for resource use. Mindsets have to change. The facts are as follows in (Table 7.9).

Table 7.9

*Per cent Change in the Prices Paid for Intermediates
and Output Prices in Nineties*

S. No.	Period	Prices Paid for Intermediates	Output Prices
1.	1990-91	104.0	112.3
2.	2000-01	223.0	224.8
3.	Per cent change 1990-91—2000-01	114.4	100.2

Source: Computed from estimates given in CACP, 2003, Table 5.1, p.297.

Agricultural profitability, therefore, falls by 14.2 per cent through the decade of economic reforms. I was hesitant in pushing this argument too far since agricultural fixed capital formation in the private sector was rising, although, it had collapsed in the public sector. I was, therefore, predicting that private investment in agriculture would go down. I was unfortunately for my country correct. In the last few years, private sector investment in agriculture collapses, although, there is some revival in public investment. The facts are as follows and they show that the policy-makers have failed in creating a positive economic regime for private investment in agriculture:

Table 7.10

Gross Fixed Capital Formation in Public and Private Sectors

S. No.	Year	Gross Fixed Capital Formation	Public	Private
1.	1997-98	14685	3929	10756
2.	1998-99	13934	3878	10056
3.	1999-00	14836	4116	10720

Source: CSO, 2002, pp.45-47, 93.

This is, as I had argued earlier, an extremely serious matter and needs a well worked out policy response. I have argued elsewhere that this needs institutional response in terms of alternative distributional channels and strengthening of markets (Alagh, 2003). But all this has to be imbedded in a positive macro regime for the agricultural sector.

To go back to the Lamy-Panitchpakadi debate, it is intriguing that while domestic profitability was going down, Indian agriculture's relative position with the rest of the world was improving. India was in earlier decades estimated to have a negative Aggregate Measure of Support (AMS) for Agriculture. This was estimated in a well-known set of studies done for the World Bank by Pursell and Gulati (1993). This was then the argument of policy taxing agriculture. In 1996, in a published report, the World Bank released new estimates. These were presented in a table which read as follows;

Table 7.11

Protection Rate for Agriculture (in Per cent)

Source of the Bias	*1970-71 to 1984-85*	*1985-86 to 1990-91*	*1991-92 to 1994-95*
Economy-wide policies	-0.26	-0.25	-0.03
Agriculture Policies	-0.04	+0.07	-0.07
Total	-0.30	-0.18	-0.09

Source: Rosenblatt, Pursell, Gupta, and Blarel, 1996.

According to the World Bank estimates, the AMS was falling and since agricultural prices in India were rising faster than the world, this trend could be accentuated further. As compared to the Pursell-Gulati estimates of negative AMS of 28 per cent, the finding for the nineties by Rosenblatt *et al.*, study is that the AMS is lower. The estimates normally discussed in India are based on the Pursell-Gulati methodology originally developed by the World Bank. The Bank has changed that as is evident in the Rosenblatt *et al.*, estimates.

The World Bank Report referred to above states the following:

'Accelerating a trend in the mid-1980s, the 1991 economy-wide reforms virtually eliminated the anti-agricultural bias implicit in the trade and foreign exchange regimes.' The World Bank Report makes this point somewhat emphatically in a Box, which we repeat, since some commentators deny this. This Box reads as follows:

Box 7.1

*Correcting for India's Large Size Reduces Significantly
the Apparent Policy Bias Against Agriculture*

The estimated mild protection of agricultural price policies contrasts with earlier studies which indicated much higher levels of relative price discrimination and deserves an explanation. The present estimates take into account the fact that India, because of its large size cannot export infinite quantities of rice on the thin rice world market without affecting the world price. Ignoring this price-depressing (or large country) effect of Indian rice exports would significantly over-estimate the extent of price discrimination imposed on rice by Indian food policies. The present estimates also treat wheat as non-traded, recognising that under free trade its equilibrium domestic price would have remained within the import-export parity band for most years.

Correcting for the large-country situation in rice, and the non-traded status of wheat, significantly lowers the price discrimination of Indian agriculture since rice and wheat alone account for about 30 per cent of the India agricultural production basket.

Source: Box 4.1 World Bank Report, 1996.

On subsidies the World Bank's position is clear as the following quotes show: 'India devotes considerable public resources (centre and state) to agriculture which totalled Rs. 685 billion (US $ 22 billion) in 1994-95, equivalent to 28 percent of agricultural GDP (8 per cent of GDP). When measured as a share of agricultural GDP, India spends at least twice as much on agriculture as some East Asian economies (Table 4.3 of World Bank, 1996).' The table reads as follows:

Table 7.12

*Agriculture Public Expenditure Expressed as a Share
of Agricultural GDP*

				(Percentage)
	India	*Indonesia*	*Malaysia*	*Thailand*
Average 1990-1993	29.1	6.9	10.1	12.9
Memo Item				
Ag. Annual GDP Growth (1980-93)	3.0	3.2	3.5	3.8

Source: Table 4.3, World Bank, 1996.

Another argument sometimes given is that the AMS has a 1988 price base. When the AoA is up for discussion, not to understand—that between DRCs, EPRs and the AMS there is a one-to-one relationship—is sad. This was happening in India and is now being repeated at the global level in the Lamy debate. The base year has now come up for discussion. The Special Committee on Agriculture had raised this issue in the deliberations after Doha and the agreement at Geneva (July/August 2004) also refers.

> 'Scheduled Total AMS commitments may be expressed in national currency, a foreign currency or a basket of currencies. In case a foreign currency or a basket of currencies is used and the final bound Total AMS in a Member's Schedule is expressed in national currency (or another foreign currency) and a participant wants to avail itself of this option, the final bound Total AMS shall be converted using the average exchange rate(s) as reported by the IMF for the year at issue.'

This is the background against which recent comments on India's Trade Policy Review must be seen. Canada, the EU, the US, New Zealand and other countries have been sharply raising these issues in the discussions on India's Trade Policy Review (See, WTO, Geneva, October 2002).

India was, therefore, under pressure to reduce explicit subsidies at least 'market distorting' ones. As Ms. Mary Whelan argued, in the Chairperson's concluding remarks in the last Trade Policy Review of the WTO on India;

> 'Members noted the importance of the agricultural sector in India and stressed the need to further liberalise it in order to develop its full potential. Concerns were expressed over subsidies for agricultural products and inputs, which have contributed to large grain stocks and export restrictions on agricultural goods.' (WTO, 2002, p. ix). Her conclusion was based on the comments of a number of countries. Canada 'encouraged the authorities to examine subsidies, particularly in agricultural production and procurement. ... assess these subsidies in order to correct the Government's fiscal imbalance, thus benefiting from removal of production distortions.' (WTO, 2002, p.198). New Zealand said, 'attempts to achieve food security had created distortions in the economy, through higher support prices and financially and environmentally unsustainable input subsidies.' (WTO, 2002, p.204). Most developed countries argued for reduction of tariffs.

The Chairperson also stated that India should clarify its stand on 'the role of State Trading Companies.' (WTO, 2002, p.x.). On this for Cancun, Stuart Harbinson the Chairman of the Special Session of the Committee on Agriculture of the WTO referred to it in the First Draft of Modalities for the Further Commitments of the Negotiations on Agriculture. This was based on work carried out by the Special Session of the Committee on Agriculture and technical and other consultations following the mandate at Doha in March 2002. Attachment 6 is on State Trading Enterprises. Since many OECD countries and others have moved away from direct government budgetary subsidies to working through commodity boards and such like arrangements and such bodies have huge reserves of money, the effort is to bring such interventions under some discipline. But the Indian price intervention programmes are also through state trading enterprises and while all the disciplines wont apply to developing country members, they will be required 'to ensure that exports of a product by a governmental export enterprise do not take place at a price less than the price paid by such an enterprise to the domestic producers of the product concerned.' (This draft is available on internet).

Two recent arguments are interesting (Hoda, 2003). This is to the effect that India never had a trade strategy and that anyway the scope for intervention in agricultural markets is limited by the fiscal crunch. There is an element of force in these arguments and yet they are to an extent shadow men. The export strategy in India in the seventies on 'supply planning' and an 'appropriate system of incentives,' gave way in the mid-eighties to export setoffs of the South Korean variety. Imports of edible oil, and at the margin of grains, edible oils and wage goods were a part of Indian policy since the mid-seventies (Writings of the late Manohar Rao, was an example of this kind of work: See the obituary of Alagh and Karnik, 2003). More generally, as Indian agricultural policy moved over from the initial emphasis in the seventies on grain self sufficiency to diversification in the early eighties and a resource based agro-climatic strategy from the late eighties, the role of regional specialisation and trade became more explicit. It has been argued, by the present author and others that agricultural diversification in India is basically driven by domestic demand, (Alagh, Shastri Memorial Lecture, 1995) International trade would also hasten the process (Alagh, First Dantwala,Memorial Lecture, 1999). This follows from trade theory and was welcomed (Alagh, U.N., Studies in International Trade, 1995). It has also been argued that the trading agricultural agroclimatic regions were also those that had more often than not, followed sustainable land and water development policies (Alagh, Inaugural Address, Indian Society of Agricultural Economics, Parbhani, 1998). The fiscal argument is overdone, since intervention in agricultural markets should be only at the margin, in some regions and in particular contexts and in any case as we will see later, tariff, tax and monetary policy instruments would also be available. There was, therefore, considerable synergy seen in trade, diversification and sustainable development. In the agro-climatic literature, for example, economists and policymakers supported the recommendations of studies on diversification and agricultural markets (See Government of India, 1989 and Basu and Guha, 1995). Hoda and others have also argued that India can impose high tariffs if it wants to. These experts (including A. Gulati) were earlier arguing that India taxes agriculture and now have switched to a high tariff regime argument. These are fairly contentious issues in any negotiation as the comments on India's Trade Policy Review bring out. Thus, on the 2002 Trade Policy Review, it was 'noted that many tariffs remained high, and hoped that high tariff and non-tariff barriers would not impede access to high quality and competitively priced imported goods for Indian consumers.' (See WTO, 2002, Geneva, WTO, 2002, p.198) Switzerland argued that 'The rather large proportion of unbound tariff lines as well as the gap between bound and applied rates provided scope for uncertainty, and diminished the predictability needed by economic operators.' Japan 'thought that India's tariff was a bit too high.' (p.199) The EU stated that 'there was still a need to cut down the high number of rates and to simplify the complex tariff structure.' (p. 201) New Zealand 'was concerned about the increase in the average MFN tariff from 35 per cent in 1997-98 to 41 per cent in 2001-02. New Zealand also had reservations about the extent of tariff escalation on agricultural forestry imports.' And again 'New Zealand looked forward to working with India in the relevant negotiations to address some of these issues.' (p.203). The US 'asked about India's plan to simplify it's tariff and excise structure, and to reduce rates, which were prohibitively high.' (p. 204). Even Norway wanted tariff simplification to 'cover fish and fish products, and hoped it would do so at the lower levels.' (p. 207).

Some Indian economists and policymakers, on the other hand, keep on repeating earlier arguments in a mechanical way, without appreciating that now the arguments are that:

1. India does not discriminate against agriculture as much as it did in the past.

2. In the case of rice and wheat a new playing field is there.

3. India subsidises agriculture.

4. Indian subsidies will be up for discussion in the next round.

A moments reflection will show that the stand that Mr. Lamy is taking is anti-reform in the Indian context and of course in the global context.

5. The Analytical Issues and India's Preparation

By the time the Cancun meeting was approaching, India having made its position clear in the Committee on Agriculture was willing to negotiate around the draft prepared by the Special Session of the Committee. On February 17, 2003, the Chairman of the Special Session of the Committee on Agriculture of the WTO released the First Draft of Modalities for the Further Commitments of the Negotiations on Agriculture. This was based on work carried out by the Special Session of the Committee on Agriculture and technical and other consultations following the mandate at Doha in March 2002 in which India had kept space for its interest. Attachment 6 was on State Trading Enterprises. Since many OECD countries and others have moved away from direct government budgetary subsidies to working through commodity boards and such like arrangements and such bodies have huge reserves of money, the effort was to bring such interventions under some discipline. But the Indian price intervention programmes are also through state trading enterprises and while all the disciplines wont apply to developing country members, they will be required 'to ensure that exports of a product by a governmental export enterprise do not take place at a price less than the price paid by such an enterprise to the domestic producers of the product concerned.' Interestingly, India was willing to negotiate around such issues. In fact, already a Committee had been set up under my Chairmanship in the Ministry of Agriculture to build up a WTO compatible strategy for agricultural price interventions in India.

The strategy the Indian policymakers were working with was to integrate monetary policy and tariff policy changes in a medium term policy reform package, which moves away from direct parastatal intervention to a crop-wise strategy which was reform and WTO compatible. The details of this have been covered elsewhere so they are not repeated here (See Alagh, 2003, Tenth Dharam Narain Lecture, Delhi School of Economics and Institute of Economic Growth). If an LRMC price is taken as a medium term target, for rice it was worked out that 23 per cent of the intervention costs would be 'saved' as compared to a direct intervention strategy. The argument, therefore, was of harmonisation of agricultural policies with reform strategies and that such policies should be worked out for major crops. This is the concept of a roadmap for each crop to be prepared and a policy which is WTO compatible to be designed and implemented. This has now been advocated in the Budget for 2005, which explicitly argues for a roadmap for crops. This policy would consist of tariff policy support, monetary policy support and tax policies on the side of economic policies and technology and marketing support. Details of a roadmap for paddy are contained in my Dharam Narain lecture. In this paper, we also present the concept of a 'shifter,' namely, the dynamic policy required for a 'gap' to be covered if the Indian farmer in that crop is to be made globally competitive. The farmer must be supported to shift to a competitive cost regime through technology and economic support. For that his capital cost will be higher, although current costs will be lower. This will then be an adjustment problem.

In my Dharam Narain Lecture, an example was given from paddy. We collected data from a watershed project on the River Pravara to build up a crude, but working example to illustrate the ideas being advocated. The contours of the capital project were around Rs. 35000/hec. It may be recalled that the LRMC principle requires the capital cost to be worked out in real and not accounting terms and the current costs to be worked out for the efficient technology. We had limited access to cost of cultivation data for paddy for Punjab in 1999-2000. The average cost of cultivation per hectare was Rs. 21119 ranging between Rs. 13077 and Rs. 51310 with a C.V. of 27.06 per cent. Out of 30 *tehsils* for which we had data, 14 had higher costs than the State average. But we had no way of knowing if the costs were higher on account of technical superiority or poor natural resource endowments. The average cost per kg of paddy was Rs.3.84. This could range between Rs.2.24 and Rs. 18.12 per kg. Interestingly out of the 14 *tehsils* with per hectare costs higher than the State average, three *tehsils* had per kg costs less than the State average. These *tehsils* also had per hectare seed costs higher than the state average, suggesting a possible technical superiority leading to a cost and productivity advantage.

We worked out the desirable economic profiles for paddy under two assumptions—an interest rate for long term investments of 7.25 per cent which would follow from RBI Governor Y. Venugopal Reddy's monetary policy announcement, if operationalised on the field and an existing BAU rate of 14.5 per cent. Similarly, the interest rate for working capital is ideally 9.75 per cent and a BAU rate of 19.5 per cent (Table 7.13).

We can illustrate the concept of a 'Shifter' now:

In the years we were talking about the procurement price was around Rs. 6/kg. In the framework being discussed a low procurement price is consistent with government support as a matter of last resort. The road map has to be for monetary, tax and technology policy support for competitive agriculture. The argument is that these have to be used as

Table 7.13

Desirable Economic Profiles for Paddy Under Two Assumptions

S.No.	Cost Item	Normative Monetary Policy	BAU
1.	Return on Net Worth	77.30	77.30
2.	Return on Term Loan	27.05	54.10
3.	Interest on Working Capital	26.00	52.10
4.	Depreciation	129.20	129.12
5.	Input Cost	400.00	400.00
6.	Total	659.61	712.66

shifters to permit farmers to move to a globally competitive agriculture. If a credible support system is not there, a WTO compatible agriculture will remain a dream. The figures in the case of rice are illustrative. Another way of building up the empirical argument was to work with capital related cost data. In Punjab for example, in the case of paddy, rent (reflecting land development costs) and machinery costs were the items included in capital related costs. The modal cost on these items was found to be around Rs. 8000 per hectare. Figure 7.1 shows the farm categories, which are above and below the modal costs. In the figure, the circles are the averages used by the CACP for support price calculations. The dynamics of shifting the agrarian economy from squares to the triangles curves is the problem now.

Figure 7.1

Yield versus Cost of Machinery and Land

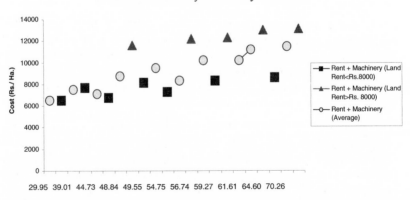

It was interestingly on the growth aspects that the drafts after Doha had laid a basis for further discussion. This was important to India, since by now it was committed to trade as policy tool. In the growth aspects many of India's general propositions were recognised. There will be great difficulty in giving direct income support to farmers but there was full recognition of a point we made in Doha namely that there has to be support for community based institutions of farmers and producers associations for land and water development, development of markets, agroprocessing and diversification of agriculture to support broad based development of agriculture. Some of these concepts developed in India (See, Alagh, World Food Day Lecture, FAO, Bangkok, 15 October, 2002) have entered the post RIO dialogues and now the arguments find a way in the WTO debates. Attachment 9 to the draft provided, for example, subsidies for concessional loans through established credit institutions or for the establishment of regional and community cooperatives, capacity building measures with the objective of enhancing the competitiveness and marketing of low income and resource poor producers, government assistance for the establishment and operation of agricultural cooperatives and government assistance for risk management of agricultural producers and savings instruments to reduce year-to-year variations in farm incomes.

Paragraph 13 of the Doha Ministerial Declaration provided (WT/MIN(01)/DEC/1 refers) as we saw earlier:

'We agree that special and differential treatment for developing countries shall be an integral part of all elements of the negotiations and shall be embodied in the Schedules of concessions and commitments and as appropriate in the rules and disciplines to be negotiated, so as to be operationally effective and to enable developing countries to effectively take account of their development needs, including food security and rural development. We take note of the non-trade concerns reflected in the negotiating proposals submitted by Members and confirm that non-trade concerns will be taken into account in the negotiations as provided for in the Agreement on Agriculture.'

India was willing to treat the earlier Drafts as a base for discussion, since its interests were in laying the foundation of more open trade as a part of a widespread growth process. Issues of rural growth, employment and food security were important to it in the emerging trading World. The issue was not grain, but access. You need money to buy food, even if your farmers produce it and your shops have it. You need agricultural growth, not to grow grain, but to create a source of income on a widespread basis. When a large number of people live in rural areas, only widespread agricultural growth can trigger broadbased rural growth and this is the only guarantee of reducing hunger. The State can feed a few people and

it must do so. The really starving are the destitute. Women headed
households, disabled wage earners, and the destitute old. They have to be
given grain. You have to give the poor girl child a free lunch to keep her
in school and the poor pregnant or lactating mother needs assistance.
There are also sharply defined geographical pockets of starvation placed
there by the atrocities of man on nature and the environment and they
need special attention. More generally, however, paradoxically to grow on
a widespread basis, grain growth will slow down more than in the past.
In fact livestock production grew by 4.3 per cent in South Asia and
generally the pattern is that non-grain crops grow faster than grain crops
and animal husbandry and fish even faster. Diversification is the name of
the game and incomes grow fast in response to demand changes, only this
way. But it is not happening fast enough. You need investment in land and
water and as the FAO's Bangkok Declaration says, there is synergy in land
and water investment when it is made together. You need reform and
investment in rural infrastructure. This reform is more difficult. For, it
runs into problems, because the rural economy is complex.

There have to be well identified shelves of a large number of small
projects on land, water and other infrastructure projects available for
financing. Financial institutions have to design structures such that
community collateral by farmers and their organisations is possible for
viable projects. Self-help financing groups are only one such group. Farmer
organised and run market and rural infrastructure facilities, land and water
development groups, local infrastructure projects, in road or
communication sectors, productionising products developed in R&D
institutions, training for production with improved techniques, market
development schemes would be other examples.

Some of the policy reform required for the replication on a required
scale of such projects includes: lending through a weather or project cycle,
NABARD had started a scheme of this kind as a part of the agro-economic
rationalisation strategy of Rajiv Gandhi, gave it up in 1993 and is again
starting it now (See Kapur Committee, Reserve Bank of India, 2000 for
details); Financial institutions have to design structures such that
community collateral is possible for viable projects. Policy 'champions' are
necessary in the State administration and political leadership for sorting
out administrative, financial and procedural issues at local, regional and
national levels, when problems arise with these kind of development
strategies. It is reasonably certain that problems are going to arise in
development experiments which are off the beaten track. The question
then is, is there somebody in the policy decision-making structure who

will sort out the problem. ADB reports in a detailed study of farmer managed irrigation systems, that the failure cases were those where such support did not exist. Failure here is defined as performance levels in water delivery lower than by government agencies

Markets and their development and processing are the key. Strategic alliances must be encouraged. The Companies Second Amendment Bill, 2002 in India, for example lets Farmers Producers groups and coops register as companies. Targeted employment and food distribution programmes for poor populations have a role, but only as a part of a strategy and a policy. A large part of the poor and hungry segments of the work force are low productivity food producers. Demarcation of 'hunger zones' – and targeted programmes, has to take a larger context into account. A hunger removal programme, embedded in a food security strategy will have to be a part of the wider process of diversification and growth of agriculture.

These arguments were started by India, but there is by now considerable acceptance of these needs in the global debates. For example, one of the more serious preparatory meetings for the World Summit on Sustainable Development at Johannesburg was the Expert Thematic Round Table on Promoting Sustainable Development in A Globalising World, February 2002. This Expert group squarely addressed the issues we have been pleading for as listed above. The Former Swedish P.M. Ulsten, the present author and the Former Environment Minister of New Zealand were the monitors for the different sections of the discussion.

Amongst others, the following proposals for action emerged from the discussion of the Round Table are important, because with minor changes they have been incorporated in the Johannesburg Declaration:

- *Improve* investment processes in developing countries and countries with economies in transition to facilitate access to credit lines as well as to preferential terms of financing and of providing funds for collateral support systems and sharing of investment risk. In this context, provide securities for local institutions involved in infrastructure development and specific knowledge based activities to support sustainable economic growth, through, for example, creation of collaterals, interest differentials and trading of financial papers. These processes should be targeted, amongst others, to artisan and producer groups linked with local and global markets, local government agencies providing social and economic infrastructure, and farming and rural communities.

- *Improve* coordination among international financial institutions and redirect funds to sustainable development projects.

- *Develop* new or *strengthen* existing mechanisms such as the Clean Development Mechanism (CDM), to finance or re-finance community projects in rural areas aimed at land and water development, agricultural diversification and agro-processing, development of infrastructure, trade, and rural energy supply.

- *Strengthen* international support to developing countries for efforts of sustainable agricultural practices, while the global agricultural markets are being reformed.

- *Study* for the purpose of replication, existing models for providing access of rural communities to ICTs in order to enhance the level of information in rural communities on productions, crops, markets, prices and technologies as well as in support of medical services and education.

- *Use* debt swap mechanisms to finance sustainable development projects including projects for environmental conservation.

- [For this text and incorporation in the Johannesburg Declaration See (WSSD Secretariat at *www.johannesburgsummit.org*)].

From the Delhi Expert meeting these kinds of arguments entered the Monterrey discussions and then the Johannesberg Declaration. It is to India's credit that they find expression for the first time in the WTO negotiations.

On the development side the only major concession the draft of negotiations of the Special Committee on Agriculture after Doha was support to Farmers Producer and Cooperatives in rural development infrastructure. As compared to the above the opportunities in the Draft were as follows:

Attachment 9
Article 6.2 of the Agreement on Agriculture

Possible Amendments for Further Consideration (changes in italics)

In accordance with the Mid-Term Review Agreement that government measures of assistance, whether direct or indirect, to encourage agricultural and rural development are an integral part of the development programmes of developing countries, *and in accordance with paragraph 13 of the Doha Ministerial Declaration the following measures* in developing country Members shall be exempt from domestic support reduction commitments to the extent that these commitments would otherwise be applicable to such measures:

i.   investment subsidies which are generally available to agriculture;

ii.   agricultural input subsidies generally available to low-income or resource-poor producers;

iii. domestic support to producers to encourage diversification from growing illicit narcotic crops or those whose non-edible or non-drinkable products, being lawful, are recognised [by WHO] as harmful for human health;

iv.   subsidies for concessional loans through established credit institutions or for the establishment of regional and community credit cooperatives;

v.   transportation subsidies for agricultural products and farm inputs to remote areas;

vi.   on-farm employment subsidies for families of low-income and resource-poor producers;

vii. government assistance for conservation measures;

viii. marketing support programmes and programmes aimed at compliance with quality and sanitary and phyto-sanitary regulations;

ix.   capacity building measures with the objective of enhancing the competitiveness and marketing of low-income and resource-poor producers;

x.   government assistance for the establishment and operation of agricultural cooperatives; and

xi.   government assistance for risk management of agricultural producers and savings instruments to reduce year-to-year variations in farm incomes.

Domestic support meeting the criteria of this paragraph shall not be required to be included in a Member's calculation of its Current Total AMS.

On Negotiations

It is obvious that by the time of the Cancun meetings, countries like India were better prepared and on agriculture developing countries like Brazil, India, South Africa and China formed an effective coalition that submitted a counter proposal in Geneva to the EU-US proposal. The coalition kept growing and became the Group of 20 at the start of the

Ministerial and 23 by the end The Draft Ministerial Text as we know did not reflect the concerns of the earlier negotiations and followed the US-EU proposals in the main. This time as we have seen there was substantial preparation in terms of interests and in addition to China and India with livelihood concerns, Countries like Brazil and South Africa had their trading agendas. The collapse at Cancun was inevitable, but it is interesting that in the subsequent discussions, and as this is being written the issues raised are back on the table again. This was evident at the London meeting (May, 2004) organised by the US. The analytical issues raised in this chapter emerging from India's experience will, I believe, keep on recurring as we move forward. Since Cancun we were running up the Downstairs Case and in 2005 we are back to Cancun, but creatively. At the global level the problem is not that Cancun happened, but that it did and we did not know that it would. The Geneva Agreement (July-August 2005) went along the lines discussed. The G 23 has become a force and India backstops it in the G3/5.

Another interesting aspect is the regional arrangements which are coming up. In South Asia regional discussions after phase out of the MFA quota regime in textiles is gaining urgency. India's agreement with the Mercosur, South Africa and others on agriculture and the implementation issues is important.

It is obvious that given the long haul nature of the problem, and the complexity of issues discussed in this chapter, a Watch Dog body of developing countries is important as also technical assistance, on the way to the strengthened G-20 we are discussing (See Alagh's proposal in the G20 discussion in English, Cooper, Thakur, 2005, Ch.19). The recent meeting of the G23 in Delhi has emphasised this (Delhi, March, 2005).

The global trade negotiations will have to be placed in the context of broad based rural growth in poor countries and the concepts and instruments developed accordingly. This chapter is a step towards that understanding.

References

ADB (2000). *Rural Asia: Beyond the Green Revolution*, Manila, ADB.

————. (2000) *Rural Asia: Companion Volumes (I-III)*, Oxford University Press.

Alagh, Y.K (1989). "The Newly Industrialising Economies and India," *Asian Development Review*, Vol. 7(2).

————. (1991). "Indian Development Planning and Policy," *Wider Studies in Development Economics*, Helsinki and Delhi, Vikas.

————. (1994). "Macro Policies for Indian Agriculture, in FAO," *Economic Liberalization and Indian Agriculture*, New Delhi, ISID.

————. (1995a). "Agriculture, Industrialisation and Development," *ILO India Brazil Round Table, ILO/ JNU Working Paper*.

————. (1995b). "Planning and Policies for Indian Agricultural Research," Shastri Memorial Lecture, Reprinted in ICAR. *Landmarks in Indian Agriculture*.

————. (1995c). "India's Agricultural Trade with the ESCAP Region," in, U.N., *Agricultural Trade with the ESCAP Region*, Studies in International Trade, Vol. 10, U.N. New York. .

————. (1996). *Land and Man: Essays in Sustainable Development*, Delhi, Har Anand.

————. (1998). "Agricultural Trade and Policies," *Indian Economic Journal*, First Dantwala Memorial Lecture, Vol. 46(3), (pp.56-65).

————. (2000). "Global Sustainable Future and Developing Countries," in, Fu chen Lo , H. Tokuda and N.S. Cooray (ed), *The Sustainable Future of the Global System*, Tokyo, OECD-UNU, ch.19,pp.323-333.

————. (2000). *Report of the High Level Committee on Legislation for Corporatisation of Cooperatives*, New Delhi: Ministry of Company Affairs.

————. (2000). *Sustainable Development: India 2020*, Tokyo:UNU/IAS

————. (2001). *Development and Governance*, in Hans van Ginkel and Ramesh Thakur, UNU Millennium Series, *Embracing the Millennium*

————. (2001). "Working Out Power Economics," *Indian Express*, Jan.16

————. (2002a). "Emerging Institutions and Organisations: Some Aspects of Sustainable Rural Development," reproduced in in G.C. Malhotra (Ed.), *Fifty Years of Indian Parliament*, New Delhi, Lok Sabha Secratariat, 2002, pp.491-504.

————. (2002b). "Poverty Food Security and Human Security," Rajiv Gandhi Foundation, Special Issue, *Journal of Global Management*.

————. (2002c). "Water: Source of Food Security," *World Food Day Lecture*, 15th October, FAO, Bangkok

————. (2003). "Agricultural Price Policy in An Open Economy," Tenth Dharam Narain Lecture, Delhi School of Economics and Institute of Economic Growth, forthcoming *Indian Economic Review*.

————. (2005). "On Sherpas and Coolies," in J. English, A Cooper and R. Thakur, *The L 20*, UNU and CIGI, Ch.19.

Alexandratos, Nikos (1995). "World Agriculture Towards 2010" An FAO Study, Chichister, Wiley.

F.A.O. (1993). *Agriculture Towards 2010*, Rome, F.A.O., for final published version see, N. Alexandratos.

Government of India (1989). "Agro-Climatic Planning: An Overview," New Delhi, Planning Commission (authorship, Y.K. Alagh, *et al.*)

————. (2001), *WTO: Agreement on Agriculture; India's Proposals*, New Delhi: Ministry of Commerce and Industry.

Gulati, A. and A. Sharma (1994). "Agriculture Under GATTS: What it Holds for India," *Economic and Political Weekly*, July 16, pp. 1861.

Hoda, A. (2003). *The Dragon and the Elephant*, JNU-IFPRI Workshop, New Delhi.

Krugman, P. and M. Obstfeld (2000). *International Economics: Theory and Policy*, New York, Addison Wesley.

Munish, Alagh and Yoginder K. Alagh (2003), "Trends in Crop Diversification: Need For A Policy Shift," *Agricultural Situation of India*, Special Number, October.

Nayyar, D. and Sen, A. (1994). "International Trade and Agricultural Sector," in G.S. Bhalla, ed., *Economic Liberalisation and Indian Agriculture*, New Delhi, ISID, pp.61-106.

Planning Commission (1979). *Annual Plan 1979-80*, New Delhi: Manager of Publications, Government of India.

Pursell, Garry and Ashok Gulati (1993). *Liberalising Indian Agriculture: An Agenda for Reform*, World Bank Working Paper, WPS 1172.

Reserve Bank of India (2000). *Report of the Expert Committee on Agricultural Credit, (Kapur Committee)*, New Delhi.

Rosenblatt, D., Garry Pursell, A. Gupta and B. Blarel (1996). Have Economy-wide Reforms Helped Indian Agriculture? World Bank, Washington. Also quoted in World Bank (1996), P. 77.

Vyas, V.S. (2002). "Changing Contours of Indian Agriculture," in R. Mohan, Ed., *Facets of the Indian Economy*, New Delhi, Oxford

World Bank (1996). "India: Country Economic Memorandum," *Five Years of Stabilisation and Reform*, The Challenges Ahead, Washington, World Bank.

World Summit (2002). *The Expert Thematic Round Table on Promoting Sustainable Development in a Globalising World*, Johannesburg,

WTO (2002). *Trade Policy Review: India 2002*, Geneva.

8

Pro-Poor Growth—The Relation between Agricultural Growth and Poverty Reduction

JOHN W. MELLOR

1. Introduction

Asian countries have seen extraordinary reduction in poverty in the past few decades. Food insecurity as famine has left the stage (Mellor and Gavian, 1987). In Africa, poverty is steadily growing, famine is so ubiquitous that complex, and permanent famine early warning systems have been developed in apparent disbelief that Africa can ever prosper. Meanwhile, the pace of poverty reduction has declined in Asia and the remaining problems seem more intractable (Cornea, 1999). Certainly, large areas of rural India have yet to participate in extraordinary reduction in poverty.

This paper shows the importance of agricultural growth to poverty reduction, particularly through its effect on employment in the small-scale rural non-agricultural sector. It then shows the importance of public expenditure on agricultural growth and hence on poverty reduction and draws conclusions with respect to development expenditure and particularly for foreign-aid.

2. The Connection—Agricultural Growth and Poverty Reduction

We now have data confirming the existing theory that high rates of agricultural growth greatly reduce poverty. The data also suggest that the connection is complex, working indirectly through stimulus of the large, rural and market town, small-scale and non-formal sector. The following sections review those data, relate them to the underlying theory, and set the stage for stating a policy package for drastic reduction in poverty.

2.1 The Basic Data

Until recently, there were insufficiently long periods of rapid increase in incomes in a sufficient range of contemporary low-income countries to study causes of poverty change. The exceptions were isolated micro studies. A decade or more of rapid growth in a wide range of countries has changed that situation. Recent compilations of data on poverty levels for a large number of countries allows study of factors associated with changes in poverty levels and facilitates conclusions about causality. Improvements in methodology have helped extract more information from the data than was previously possible.

The initial basis for current cross section analysis was the continuing set of large scale sample surveys, carried out throughout India by the Indian Statistical Institute, over very diverse physical, economic, and social conditions, and finally extending into a recent period of rapid growth. This data set, using a similar methodology over time and across large areas provides a truly unusual opportunity for analysis of poverty relationships.

Reinforcing the Indian data, is a large, cross national, inter-temporal data set developed by Klaus Deininger and Lyn Squire (1996) that also includes ample number of countries with rapid economic growth and with a wide range of structures of that growth. In addition, data for a few Southeast Asian countries that have experienced rapid growth has become available, as has data for China covering its recent rapid growth. Together these data sets tell a detailed story of the sources of poverty and its decline in the context of growth.

Initially, only the relation between overall growth and poverty was analysed. The breakthrough in knowledge that shows it is the structure of growth that matters came from a series of empirical studies by Martin Ravallion and his colleagues at the World Bank. These studies examine the separate effect on poverty of growth by sector of the economy. Further, studies using a quite different methodology, by Peter Timmer, then at Harvard University, and his colleagues, provide independent corroboration of the basic relationships in the Ravallion studies as well as additional insights.

It is the consistency of results from varied studies with each other and with earlier micro studies and the further consistency with prior theory that gives such power to the findings.

In this section, the data will be briefly summarised for the general relationship between growth and poverty; then the effect of different structures of growth will be examined, with particular emphasis on the role of agricultural growth; next is review of the modifying effect on these relationships arising from differing initial income distributions and the presence of lags in the relationship; that will be followed by data on the geographic aspects of poverty and growth and on transient poverty.

The data will underline the importance of indirect effects of agricultural growth to poverty reduction. Therefore, attention will be given to data on the size of income and employment multipliers from agricultural to non-agricultural growth. Government expenditure is of special importance to the growth of the small-scale agriculture that is particularly important to poverty reduction. And so, the role of public expenditure in agricultural growth will be analysed. That will lead to important conclusions about the composition of poverty reduction focused foreign-aid.

Following presentation of the data on these many related issues will be discussion of the theory behind these data that explains the otherwise surprising relationships. A brief review of data for Egypt will be presented. Finally, policy conclusions will be drawn for achieving rapid reduction of poverty.

2.2 Defining Poverty

The contemporary focus on poverty in high-income countries is on the relation between growth and the distribution of income. The concern is with inequality of distribution, rather than on the proportion of the population falling under some absolute poverty line. For low-income countries, the focus is on the number and proportion of people falling under an absolute poverty line.

The choice of focus is a philosophical one. Amartya Sen makes the case that in very poor countries it is the incidence of absolute poverty that most matters (Sen, 1976). In any case, support for foreign-aid and mass concern about poverty in low-income countries is on famine, inadequate food intake, and levels of absolute poverty considered unacceptable. Hence this paper focuses on reduction of absolute poverty, although at several points data on change in distribution of income will be presented.

Absolute poverty has long been defined in terms of the income required to provide a minimal food intake for a healthy life and the associated consumption of those so poor that the minimum food intake is all they achieve (Dandekar and Rath, 1971). The traditional measurement of absolute poverty is the proportion of the population falling under the defined poverty line. Refinements examine the distribution of those under the poverty line. Generally little difference is found in the relation between growth and the variant measures.

This analysis will, therefore, concentrate on the simpler measure—the proportion of the population falling under the poverty line. That is, we will ask to what extent has the proportion of the population obtaining inadequate food intake and associated essentials for a healthy life changed.

2.3. Growth and Poverty Reduction—General Relations

The traditional interpretation of basic data on economic growth led to the conclusion that in the early stages of economic growth inequality tended to increase. Inequality decreased only during later stages of growth. This pattern is often called a J curve, for its distinctive shape, or the Kuznets curve, for the data generated by Simon Kuznets that was thought to document this relationship (Kuznets, 1955). Most of the analysis that led to this conclusion was based on historical data for the currently high-income countries.

Even before the current wealth of data on poverty reduction, time series for Taiwan showed that its pattern of growth provided decreased inequality right from the start (Lee, 1971). Now that the relation of agricultural growth to poverty reduction is better understood and documented, the Taiwan case is important for lessons about the processes that rapidly reduce poverty.

Taiwan to the contrary, a range of literature from 1971 to 1995, covering developing countries, seemed to support the Kuznets hypothesis about worsening of income distribution in early stages of growth. More recent literature, based on more sophisticated data analysis finds contrary results.

Bruno, Ravallion and Squire (1996) reviewed 63 surveys for 44 countries spanning 1981-92 and found no support for the worsening of income distribution. They further reviewed data from 45 countries for which time series data were available and found the bulk of variation in income distribution accounted for by differences among countries and only seven per cent accounted for by variation over time within countries. From these data, the distribution of income is quite stable overtime within countries.

India has the best, and perhaps only long term set of comparable data on income distribution in a large developing country encompassing considerable geographic variation in the various poverty related variables.

These data give 'no sign that higher growth rates in India put upward pressure on overall inequality' (Bruno, Ravallion and Squire, 1996). A large number of other studies confirm that growth does not worsen income distribution and, therefore, it does reduce absolute poverty (Fields, 1989; World Bank, 1990; Squire, 1993; Lipton and Ravallion, 1993; Ravallion, 1995).

If the distribution of income does not change with growth then a simple calculation shows to what extent population is lifted above any given absolute income line. It is on this basis that the World Bank estimates the poverty reducing effect of growth. As we will see later such simple estimates ignore the substantial variance in this average relation and shift attention away from the critical policy requirements for poverty reduction. In particular, it distracts attention from the requisites of pro-poor growth.

Timmer shows, based on analysis of the Deininger Squire (1996) data that 'each one per cent increase in per capita income for the overall population is matched by a one per cent increase in income of the bottom forty per cent in the income distribution' (Timmer, 1997). That is, growth is neutral to the distribution of income. All income classes participate equally.

Datt and Ravallion (1998) contrast for India the period 1958-75 when real consumption per person declined at the rate of 0.93 per cent per year with 1976-94 when real consumption grew by 1.76 per cent per year. In the former period, the proportion of the population in poverty increased at a rate of 1.18 per cent per year, while in the latter period it declined at 1.91 per cent per year.

Timmer (1996) also shows for Indonesia that between 1970 and 1995, a 25-year period, the income of the lowest quintile in income distribution rose from a level equal to half the poverty line to more than twice the poverty line. The two lowest quintiles had a rate of growth of income of 6.1 and 6.8 per cent per year, while the average was 4.9 per cent. Thus, not only was absolute poverty reduced rapidly but also the distribution of income became more equal.

With a quite different measure, analysis of 20 countries shows an elasticity of poverty reduction with respect to income increase of -2.12 (Bruno, Ravallion and Squier, 1996). Ravallion estimated the elasticity of poverty reduction (proportion of the population below the poverty line) with respect to income for India as -2.2 (Datt and Ravallion, 1989, 1983 data) and for Indonesia as -2.1 (Ravallion and Huppi, 1989, 1984 data).

A figure of -2 means that starting with 40 per cent of the population below the poverty line and a one per cent rate of increase in the per capita income the ratio would drop to 39.2 per cent in the first year. It would drop to 36 per cent with a five per cent growth rate, and would drop in half in seven years.

Ravallion and Huppi (1989) show for Indonesia between 1984 and 1987 the proportion of the population under the poverty line declined from 33 per cent to 22 per cent—that is a drop of one-third in three years.

Ravallion and Chen (1996) show for China a generally higher elasticity of poverty reduction with respect to average consumption. Using the World Banks $1.00 per day, which is comparable to the measures that start with minimal calorie intake and the goods and services that go with that in the consumption basket of the poor, the elasticity is -3.1. That is a 10 per cent increase in average consumption drops the proportion in poverty by 31 per cent.

A broader definition that brings half the population under the poverty line drops the elasticity to -2.6—that is a 10 per cent increase in average consumption brings about a 26 per cent decrease in poverty. The elasticity drops substantially for definitions that place a higher proportion of the population in poverty—in half for one that places 75 per cent of the population in poverty, compared to the 2.6 for 50 per cent in poverty. Thus, growth brings disproportionately large reductions in poverty for the groups furthest below the poverty line.

All the preceding studies calculate relations between growth and more complex definitions of poverty and in every case the impacts are roughly the same, or somewhat more favourable for the very poorest.

It is notable that while studies for all countries show a major impact of growth on poverty reduction there is nevertheless substantial variation in the magnitudes of the poverty decline. In relating growth to poverty reduction, the most widely used number is the average relationship, with the conclusion that growth is good for poverty reduction. But, the variation suggests that something important is being hidden. That is the subject of the next section.

2.4 *The Structure of Growth—Poverty and Agriculture*

The structure of growth matters very much to the extent of poverty reduction. If poverty reduction is the objective, then certain structures, or sectors, must form the core of that growth. Two recent studies give detailed data on this issue. They confirm similar results from earlier but much less comprehensive data. The two recent studies are by Ravallion and Datt (1996) for India and Timmer (1997) for a cross section of a large number of countries.

The two studies are quite different methodologically and in source of data, but find the same striking relationship. Several for individual countries reinforce these studies. While this paper draws on all the studies shedding light on the structural issues, it does draw particularly heavily from India. That is advantageous because it does allow the picture to be drawn from a single basic source without the weakness of cutting across very different countries. However, the Indian experience, like that of any one country has specifics of its own. In any case, the India data is confirmed by the cross-national study from Timmer, individual studies for other countries, and by the theory. Thus, the Indian data do end up being compelling.

Preceding the studies of Timmer and Ravallion, Montek Ahluwalia (1978) presented data showing that increased agricultural output per head of the rural population decreased poverty. Dharm Narian furthered this analysis with important conceptual additions (Mellor and Desai, 1985). He too shows a major effect of agricultural growth in reducing poverty. Mellor and Desai (1985) elaborate at length on the relations, the supporting data, and alternative views.

For both Ahluwalia and Narian, the data cover a period when both agricultural growth and poverty fluctuated considerable but there was not sustained agricultural growth or poverty reduction.

Thus, their analyses essentially deal with a situation not of steady growth but of fluctuations in income. In practice, those fluctuations were substantially driven by the varying effect of weather on agricultural production.

It is the Ravallion and Datt (1996) work for India that is recent enough to include periods with far higher agricultural growth rates than the earlier studies as well as sustained growth beyond previous peaks and declines in poverty far beyond previous troughs.

Ravallion and Datt relate change in yields of crops to poverty. They show that reduction in poverty is a result of growth within sectors, not the transfer of labour from a low earning sector to a high earning sector. The latter is the basis for the Kuznets J curve. But what is truly striking is that agricultural growth and tertiary sector growth have a major effect on poverty reduction and manufacturing growth does not. Further, the service sector growth that has the favourable effect is the small-scale portion of that sector, which we will show later is itself closely related to agricultural growth.

The Ravallion and Datt data show that 84.5 per cent of the substantial poverty reduction in India in the period of analysis was due to agricultural growth. That is truly startling data. They also show little effect of the many programmes that directly target the poor.

Growth of manufacturing in India has historically been biased towards large-scale capital intensive industry, so the manufacturing data may be somewhat biased as compared to a market oriented structure (Mellor, 1976). But, the Timmer (1997) data confirm the Ravallion Datt findings for a large cross section of countries.

The various studies show that industrial growth does reduce poverty from the direct effect of income increase, but it concurrently has an unfavorable effect on the distribution of income thereby reducing the effect on the poor. Agricultural growth, including its indirect as well as direct effects, does not have the unfavourable distributional effect.

In a later article Datt and Ravallion (1998b) also relate rural wage rates and food prices to poverty. All three have a substantial effect. Of course, rural employment and hence wages are importantly influenced by the volume of agricultural production, as we will point out later. Food prices are also related to agricultural production.

Ravallion and Datt show that wage rates are important to poverty reduction and that higher farm productivity is closely associated with higher wage rates. Similarly, food prices are important and higher farm productivity reduces food prices. Thus, it is farm production that drives poverty reduction. In a later section, we will elaborate on this relation of agricultural growth to non-farm employment and hence to wage rates.

Peter Timmer (1997) uses the Deininger-Squire data set for poverty and purchasing power for 35 developing countries and relates those data to agricultural Gross Domestic Product (GDP) per capita. 'A one per cent growth in agricultural GDP per capita leads to a 1.61 per cent increase in per capita incomes of the bottom quintile of the population' (p.3). Unlike Ravallion, Datt, Timmer shows a positive elasticity for industrial GDP, but the agriculture elasticity is 38 per cent larger than the industrial elasticity.

The 27 countries and 181 observations (studies) from 1962 to 1992 in the Timmer sample of the Deininger-Squire data include 3.3 billion people in 1995 or two-thirds of the population of low and middle-income countries as classified by the World Bank (Timmer, 1997). On average, agriculture accounted for 25 per cent of GDP and 51 per cent of the labour force. Countries are roughly equally divided among regions of the world, with some under-representation of Africa.

Note that Ravallion and his colleagues relate agricultural output per unit of land to poverty reduction while Timmer relates agricultural output per worker. Ravallion provides a sound theoretical argument for his approach. And, the mechanism of agricultural output growth is largely increased yields of specific crops and increased intensity of agricultural production, consistent with Ravallion's argument.

However, since this paper focuses on the linkage to non-agricultural growth both in interpreting the Ravallion and Timmer data and in employment calculations it is what is happening to incomes for farm families that is important. That is better measured by income per worker.

Ravallion (1998) focuses on the real labour earnings per acre and agricultural productivity. His model brings in four variables, the productivity of labour in agriculture, yields in agriculture, agricultural wage rate, and food prices. The former two have about equal weight and the food price elasticity is also high. Of course, all four are related to agricultural production and incomes, as we will elaborate later.

Yield is shown to have a major effect on the real wage rate, and the effect is eight times larger in the long-run than the short-run, showing that it takes time for this important component of poverty reduction to show itself.

As we will point out below, this lag is too much if the wage effect is entirely from agricultural labour where the tightening of the labour market would be immediate. It is consistent with the argument presented below, that the wage effect comes from the agricultural stimulus to non-farm employment. This point is neglected in the empirical data but not in the theoretical arguments.

While the emphasis here is on the simple measure of the proportion of the population under the poverty line, it is notable that agricultural growth reduces inequality among the poor as well as lifting the poor above the poverty line.

Ravallion's data do show that non-agricultural output growth explains decrease in poverty, but only if agricultural output per acre is excluded as a variable. That means that the non-agricultural output stimulated by the agricultural output is important but gets picked up by the agricultural yield figure when the latter is included. That implies that the non-agricultural growth that reduces poverty is that part stimulated by the agricultural growth.

In the Timmer (1997) sample of countries output per capita is three times higher in non-agriculture as agriculture. This means that agricultural growth does much more for employment and poverty reduction than non-agricultural growth while non-agricultural growth has much more of an impact on over-all growth rates.

Datt and Ravallion (1998) do not find a declining trend in the elasticity of employment with respect to agricultural output. The power of the relationship holds up over time. Thus, the current decline in the rate of poverty reduction is due to decline in the agricultural growth rate, not due to declining power of that variable.

Huppi and Ravallion (1990) find that wage earnings of poor self-employed farmers grew faster than earnings from any other source and were a major cause of decreased poverty. Wage earnings of poor farmers in Central Java doubled over three years. Since wage rates changed little in the period the effect was largely from increased employment. Most of the employment growth came from a booming rural non-farm sector. Growth in cash crop income was more important to the non-poor than the poor (strengthening the case that it is the indirect effects of agricultural growth that affects the poor).

Ravallion (1989) shows that the poor lose from agricultural price increases in the short run, but not in the long-run. That is consistent with price increase stimulating increased demand for labour through increased agricultural production in the long-run (See also Mellor (1978, 1968).

Gini coefficients for sub-sectors of the economy tend to be unstable. However, the following data from Sharma and Poleman (1993) corroborate other evidence on the high degree of equality in specific agriculture related sub-sectors. They show increments to crop income alone skews the distribution towards the well to do, with a Gini coefficient of 0.86, far above the Gini coefficient for the economy in total. That finding is, of course, consistent with early critics of the green revolution (See also Adams (1999) on this point).

In sharp contrast to crop income, the Gini coefficient for dairy production, which is very important to the poor in India because of its labour intensity, is 0.11. That is an extraordinarily low Gini coefficient, but is quite consistent with the observation that dairy animal numbers vary little by size of farm, sales of dairy products are inverse to size of farm, and the well-known impact of increased dairy production on the poor. The

Gini coefficient for off-farm work in rural areas is a still low 0.22. That also reinforces the data that show off-farm income of the rural poor is an important source of poverty reduction (Adams, 1999). Thus, when rising agricultural incomes are spent in those sectors they redistribute income towards the poor.

The data show clearly that it is growth of agriculture that reduces poverty, not growth in general. One misleading interpretation should be avoided. Typically high overall growth rates are achieved when agriculture grows rapidly. That is because the resources used for agricultural growth are only marginally competitive with other sectors and so fast agricultural growth tends to be additive to growth in other sectors, as well as being a stimulant of growth in the labour surplus non-tradable sector (Mellor, 1976).

The countries that grew the fastest from 1985 to 1995 experienced a narrowing of the income gap (Timmer, 1997). That means that agricultural growth resulted in faster over-all growth and an improvement in the income distribution. Thus, emphasising agriculture in order to improve income distribution does not result in slow growth. The sectors are more complementary than competitive. Conversely, leaving out the forces that accelerate agricultural growth, as has been increasingly the case in the past decade provides slower growth and leaves out the poor.

The average elasticities cited at the beginning of this section are strongly influenced by high agricultural growth rates. Thus, it is grossly misleading to think of those elasticities as applying to some average growth rate. Those are substantially the elasticities when agriculture grows rapidly. In the 1990's, prior to the economic setback in East and Southeast Asia, overall growth rates were high, but agricultural growth rates had slowed, and hence the pace of poverty reduction declined.

Thus, agricultural productivity increase has a major effect in reducing poverty, and the effect is relatively greater in its impact on the poorest and the distribution of income among the poor. Industrial growth has much less or even no effect in reducing poverty (Ravallion and Datt 1996 and Timmer, 1997). Service sector growth has no effect for the large-scale part and a substantial positive effect for the small-scale portion (*Ibid*).

If growth occurs leaving the agricultural sector out, two onerous burdens fall on the poor. First the over-all growth rate will be lower and secondly the part that reduces poverty will be missing. As we will show later, rapid agricultural growth is more easily achieved now than some decades ago, but it does require overt actions by government.

2.5 The Structure of Growth—Rural and Urban

Ravallion and Datt (1996) also analyse the Indian data according to urban and rural income. They find that the rural-urban population shift (the Kuznets effect) has little effect in reducing poverty. Neither does urban growth.

Urban consumption growth increases inequality in urban areas, while rural growth improves the *urban* distribution. The impact of rural growth on poverty reduction is nearly three times as great as urban growth. The point, as we will emphasise later is not that rural growth should be pursued in place of urban growth, but rather that agriculture and the rural sector should not be neglected. If it is neglected, employment will increase little and poverty will increase substantially.

That is presumably because increased rural incomes reduce the queue of urban unemployed waiting for jobs (see Todaro, 1969, Harriss and Todaro, 1970). Rural growth, of course, has a major impact on reducing rural poverty. Ravallion and Datt (1996) find that rural growth reduces urban poverty even more than does urban growth. Urban growth does not reduce rural poverty.

2.6. Lags

Datt and Ravallion (1998) find significant lags in the impact of agricultural growth on poverty. The effect on rural wage rates is eight times as large in the long-run as the short-run and the over-all effect on poverty reduction is five times as large. The over-all lag is importantly influenced by the lag in adjustment of wage rates. The wage rate adjustment presumably lags because of lag in increased employment, which is in turn due to the expenditure patterns for increased farm incomes.

About half of the long-run effect of increased agricultural output on the welfare of the poor occurred within three years of an initial gain in farm yield (Ravallion and Datt, 1996). As we shall see later this is powerful evidence to support that it is the agricultural stimulus to non-farm employment that is driving the poverty decline.

2.7 Asset Distribution

The literature generally notes the impact of skewed distribution of income and of assets in slowing growth. That in turn is seen as slowing poverty reduction. The more detailed data show that agricultural distribution is at the heart of the problem.

Timmer finds a major effect of income distribution on the effect of agricultural growth on poverty reduction. In the most revealing part of his exposition, Timmer shows that if agriculture grows at (the relatively slow) rate of three per cent per year, and non-agriculture grows at a rate to give overall growth at five per cent, then for countries with small gaps between the top and bottom quintiles the bottom fifth in the income distribution experiences a 241 per cent increase in income after 25 years, while the top fifth experiences a 211 per cent increase. However, if the income gap between these quintiles is large, more than twice the average per capita income, the incomes of the poorest quintile increase by only 75 per cent while the top quintile increases by 273 per cent.

'Agricultural growth, when the distribution of income is quite equitable, raises the average contribution to growth for the five income level quintiles by 5.5 per cent, and the elasticities decline for each successively higher income quintile, confirming an improvement in the distribution of income' (Timmer, 1997). In contrast, the rich in countries with large income disparities benefit considerably from agricultural growth, while the poor are not reached by growth in either the agricultural or non-agricultural sectors (Timmer, 1997). Indeed, with such inequitable asset distribution, the 95 per cent confidence interval includes zero response of income of the poor to growth from either sector.

When income growth is highly skewed to the rich, growth in agricultural productivity is no more successful in reducing poverty than growth in other sectors (Timmer, 1998). Again, this finding is important to understanding process as developed later in this paper.

Ravallion (1997) shows that high inequality provides lower growth and even lower reduction of poverty. The elasticity of poverty reduction with respect to growth declines sharply with increasing inequality. With a very low Gini coefficient of 0.25 the elasticity is a very high 3.33; while it drops almost in half to 1.82 with a Gini coefficient of 0.59. Birdsall, *et al.*, (1995) show similar results.

Despite his pioneering work on the impact of agricultural growth on poverty, Ravallion did not bring that structure into analysis of the effect of inequity on poverty. We will show later that the importance of income distribution confirms an important part of the relation between agricultural growth and poverty reduction.

2.8 Poor Areas

Ravallion and Wodon (1997) find that in Bangladesh investment in poor areas gives low returns. In a study of southern China, Jalan and Ravallion (1996) find that returns to household investment are lower in poor areas than less poor areas. Again, our later discussion will relate this to agriculture and its effect on poverty and draw policy conclusions for dealing with poor areas.

2.9 Transient Poverty

Jalan and Ravallion (1997) show that the poor are least able to buffer adversity. Fluctuations in agricultural production (affecting employment and prices) are a major source of transient adversity. They show that the lower a households wealth the least well are they ensured against fluctuations in income and hence in food security. Mellor's earlier analysis of production induced food price fluctuations reached similar conclusions (Mellor, 1968; Mellor, 1978).

Most striking, Jalan and Ravallion note that transient poverty is so large, that targeting on current consumption as a means of redressing chronic poverty is no more efficient than no targeting at all. This suggests that targeting the poor is not likely to be an efficient means of reducing poverty. That turns the emphasis even further to achieving a pro-poor structure of growth as the principal means of reducing poverty.

2.10 Multipliers

The multipliers to output and employment from increased agricultural incomes are important because they tend to be oriented towards non-tradable goods and services that use underemployed labour. Thus, they stimulate a sector that cannot be stimulated by increased foreign demand and mobilise resources that would otherwise be idle.

Block and Timmer's model of the Kenyan economy shows the domestic multipliers from agricultural growth to be three times as large as those for non-agricultural growth (Block and Timmer, 1994). That is because the linkages from agricultural growth are much more towards the domestic economy and within that to use of resources that are underemployed, as compared to the non-agricultural sector.

In the Timmer study, the multiplier effects are largely worked out within four years. The multiplier he finds for agriculture is 1.64; that for non-agriculture is 1.23. Note that the multiplier to the sectors directly stimulated by agriculture will be much larger than the over-all multiplier since they occupy a smaller proportion of the economy and receive a large impact.

Multipliers for agriculture from data for Malaysia are 1.8, and 1.5 for Sierra Leone and Nigeria (Hazel and Roll, 1990); for India 1.6 (Hazel, Ramaswamy and Rajagopalan, 1991)(see also Bell, Hazel and Slade, 1982; Hazel, 1984; Haggblade, Hazel and Brown, 1987; Dorosh and Haggblade, 1993). Rangarajan (1982) using the same model as Timmer found a multiplier of 1.7 for agriculture, compared to 1.5 for industry (Rangarajan, 1982). Delgado (1998) notes a finding of Hazel and Roll (1983) that because of the low level of commercialisation in African agriculture, the multipliers to the non-farm sector are much weaker than in Asia. Delgado then goes on to show that a high proportion of agricultural output in Africa is comprised of non-tradables and the multipliers to the non-tradable sector as a whole are indeed as high as in Asia.

Delgado (1985) points out that because of the high transactions costs, particularly for transport, the high-income elastic, high value commodities such as livestock and horticulture are largely non-tradables, particularly outside the region—in this case West Africa. He also finds that much of the basic cereal production is non-tradable because of specifications that are not well suited to international markets. Thus, increased farm incomes from increased productivity of resources from technological change cause income increases that are largely spent for goods and services that otherwise lack effective demand and that mobilise underemployed local resources.

The conclusion from the Delgado analysis is the multipliers to non-tradables from agricultural income growth ranges from 1.96 for Niger to 2.88 for Burkina Faso. The impact of getting agriculture moving is two-three times as large as the initial agricultural growth.

2.11. Public Sector Investment

Later we argue that agriculture requires substantial public sector investment and hence that the indiscriminate, or perhaps more correctly the bias against agricultural sector investment associated with the structural changes of the 1990's has slowed agricultural growth and hence slowed poverty reduction. The following data confirm that public investment is far more important to agriculture than to other sectors.

The Block Timmer analysis of Kenya shows that the multiplier of public sector investment in agriculture is far greater than for non-agriculture - 1.96 compared to 0.37 (Block and Timmer, 1994). This is consistent with the data for Latin America from Victor Elias showing high rates of return to public sector investment in agriculture (Elias, 1985).

Datt and Ravallion (1998) show that public investment is important to agricultural growth. In a regression they showed that the elasticity of yield with respect to public expenditure was 0.29—a high figure given the large size of agriculture relative to State spending. Thus, State spending reduces poverty through its effect on farm yields.

These data show that recent pressures to reduce public sector deficits when applied across the board have a disproportionate effect on agricultural growth. This means that there is a disproportionate effect on the reduction of poverty. Poverty reduction efforts must address this complex issue.

It has been common for the reformers whose policies do so much for industrial growth to insist on drastic reductions in public expenditure, which in effect hits agriculture very hard. An even handed approach to development that makes the public expenditures that agriculture requires will foster employment creation and poverty reduction from the agricultural side as well as increasing the rate of GDP growth. That is a further argument for balanced growth.

Price discrimination against agriculture also has important multiplier effects. Lipton (1977) has emphasised this point in a general argument, quite aside from specific effects on poverty. Although, this exposition emphasises increased agricultural production through technological change and mobilising underemployed resources to produce high value commodities, a transfer of income from non-agriculture to agriculture has a favourable effect in reducing poverty. That is because the multipliers to growth and even more to employment are more powerful in the agricultural sector.

Conversely, price policies that discriminate against agriculture are inimitable to poverty reduction. See the earlier citation of Ravallion's data that show in the short-run higher agricultural prices hurt the poor and in the long-run benefit them. That is consistent with this analysis. Having said that, technological change and mobilising underemployed resources are a preferable means of accelerating agricultural growth and poverty reduction. Thus, the Washington consensus policy reforms are very helpful to agricultural growth and poverty reduction through their price effect but very deleterious through the effects of indiscriminate reduction of public expenditure, which strikes agricultural growth very hard.

3. The Explanatory Theory

The preceding data make a powerful case that it is agricultural growth and essentially only agricultural growth that brings about poverty decline in low-income countries with a substantial agricultural sector. However, what is shown is a strong association. We need an explanation of that association to have confidence in a conclusion that has such powerful policy implications. That explanation greatly predates the data (see Johnston and Mellor, 1961, Mellor and Johnston, 1984, Mellor and Lele, 1973, Mellor, 1976, Mellor, 1992). It depends very much on multipliers of agricultural growth on the employment intensive rural non-farm sector.

The following associations require explanation. First, the decline in poverty with agricultural growth (and by indirection the lack of decline with manufacturing and large-scale service sector growth). Second, the substantial lags in the full effect of the agricultural growth on employment and poverty reduction. Third, the lack of impact of agricultural growth on poverty reduction when income and assets are highly skewed towards the rich. Fourth, large increase in wage rates in response to high agricultural growth rates—increases that are far larger than can be explained by increased labour requirements in traditional agriculture.

We will deal with these associations by discussing food as a wage good, employment directly in agriculture, and employment created by the expenditure of increased farm incomes on non-farm goods and services. It is the latter that is most powerful and helps explain all four of the associations noted here. It should also be noted that the knowledge of the details of the rural and small town non-farm sector stimulated by agriculture is incomplete. The following pages will review the current state of knowledge of this sector and make a strong circumstantial case for its importance. But, the definitive set of facts on this sector is lacking.

The wage goods argument for the relation between agricultural growth and poverty reduction has merit in the context of a closed economy in which domestic food production affects domestic food prices, with no mitigation from the impact of global supply and demand. It is further strengthened in an economy with large amounts of unemployment. In a neo-classical world of open trade for food and with poverty related to the wage rate rather than unemployment, the argument depends on the expenditure patterns of farmers for the employment intensive rural non-farm sector, as explained below.

3.1 The Wage Goods Argument

The wage goods argument that so dominated the literature on development in the 1950's is of course still valid (e.g. Lewis, 1954, Johnston and Mellor, 1961). However, it will be dealt with only briefly here, since the literature itself is accessible and clear and because the arguments below on employment are so powerful that they dominate the wage goods argument. If agriculture grows fast enough to play its full employment role it can be shown that food prices will in fact decline slightly (Lele and Mellor, 1981).

The wage goods argument in brief is that when the poor become employed they spend on the order of 80 per cent of their incremental income on food (Lipton, 1972). If agricultural production is stagnant and employment increases rapidly, food prices will rise, pushing up wage rates and hence the cost of producing labour intensive goods and services and so the employment growth will slow.

This approach has sometimes been incorrectly described as a closed economy approach that is trade is not allowed to fill the wage goods gap. International prices are thought not to be influenced by the growth in employment and demand for food from individual developing countries. If domestic food prices rise, exports can be increased to pay for food imports. There are two reasons why this argument is not correct.

First, the collectivity of developing countries, or even China or India alone will influence World food prices if their employment grows rapidly and agriculture stagnates. Second, food is so large an item in national consumption that rapid employment growth with stagnant agriculture will soon result in such large food imports that it is highly unlikely that exports can generate sufficient foreign exchange. In that case, the currency will devalue pushing up food prices in domestic currency even though international prices may be constant. Of course, export led growth, where the bulk of additions to GDP come from exports, will generate sufficient foreign exchange to meet the needed food imports.

In any case, the wage goods theory is unlikely to be tested because, as indicated below and by the data above, employment is unlikely to grow rapidly as a per cent of the total labour force unless agriculture is also growing rapidly. For the reasons shown below, agricultural production growth and employment tend to go together.

Fast agricultural growth countries do in fact increase their agricultural imports. That is to say they generate so much employment (and poverty reduction) that their own agriculture cannot keep up. However, that is primarily because of rapid growth in consumption of livestock and the inability to keep up with the demand for livestock feed (e.g. Taiwan, China).

3.2. Employment in Agriculture

Agriculture is, of course, by far the largest employer in essentially all low income countries. Development may be usefully described as an economic transformation in which the size of the agricultural sector declines—indeed the next section will point out that rapid agricultural growth itself accelerates its own relative decline (Mellor, 1966).

For poor countries, with well over half the labour force directly engaged in agriculture, it will be many decades before agriculture ceases to be a major factor in employment. The major sources of employment growth in agriculture are: (a) yield increasing technology; (b) increased land area; and (c) change in the composition of output to high value commodities.

3.3. Technology

A major source of growth in poor countries must be technological change in its dominant basic food production sector. Because of land limitations it is yield increasing improved technology that dominates (Hayami and Ruttan 1985). Such technology increases labour productivity as well as land productivity. Most obviously, it takes much less labour to harvest the increased production than the original level of production.

Many studies have been made of the impact on agricultural employment of yield increasing technology. The work of Hanumantha Rao for India is representative (Rao, 1975). The elasticity of employment ranges from a high of 0.6 to a low of 0.3. That is for each 10 per cent increase in output employment at best increases six per cent and may be as little as three per cent. Since an increase of 10 per cent from yield increasing technology alone is likely to take up to three years, and population may have grown by six to nine per cent, such increase in employment cannot even take care of the natural increase in the farm population let alone tighten labour markets—there will not be an impact on poverty reduction.

If the elasticity of employment with respect to output is only 0.3 then the situation is far worse. In practice in labour surplus countries with very poor labourers, i.e. much poverty, the elasticity is more likely to be at 0.6

representing no substitution of improved labour saving methods for labour. However, as soon as real wages begin to rise, low cost labour savings will occur and the elasticity will decline. The point here is that even assuming the elasticity at the higher end of the range of experience, direct employment in agriculture will not be a major source of poverty reduction.

3.4 Land Area

If the land area can be increased and the poor are large in number then production will be increased symmetrically—that is just as much labour will be used on the additional area as on the base area. That provides an elasticity of employment of one—for each 10 per cent increase in production; employment will increase by 10 per cent. From an employment point of view that is good, from a growth point of view it is not so good since resource productivity is not increasing. In any case, for most countries it is of at most modest relevance.

Throughout Asia, essentially all the land that can be brought into agriculture has already been brought in. In the 1950's, production did grow substantially from increased land area, even in India, but that ran out by the mid 1960's and land expansion is not now an important source of agricultural growth. Even in Africa, often thought of as land rich, the additional land that can be brought into agriculture is generally much less productive than old lands. In any case, the average amount of land per farmer is declining in Africa.

An exception to land scarcity in Africa is in the traditionally disease prone areas, where disease control can open large areas for high productivity cultivation—as happened a few decades ago in malaria infested areas of Asia.

3.5 High Value Commodities

A much more likely possibility for increasing employment in agriculture is increased production of high value commodities—particularly horticulture and livestock. These commodities are highly labour intensive. Transfer of area from field crops results in a large increase in labour requirements. As long as real wages are constant, increased production of these crops is likely to occur with little increase in labour productivity. The increased production occurs because of increased demand and, hence, it is profitable without increased factor productivity. That is in contrast to basic field crops in which the incentive to increase production comes not from increased demand but from decreased cost of production.

Thus, the elasticity of employment with respect to high value commodities may be close to unity—say 0.9 to allow for some scale economies.

One of the major changes of the past few decades with respect to agriculture in low-income countries is the increase in potential for rapid growth in production of high value commodities. This increased potential comes from two sources. The major opening of trade potentials with structural adjustment in low-income countries and the GATT rules allowing low-income countries to exploit there potentially powerful comparative advantage in labour intensive agricultural commodities. For horticulture, recent health trends in high-income countries have further expanded this market.

Concurrently, accelerated growth in low-income countries rapidly expands the domestic market for income elastic commodities, particularly livestock products, but also horticulture. These two tendencies feed on each other—larger domestic markets encourage increased output, a portion of which can then be shifted to the high quality export markets.

The result is potential for six to ten per cent growth rates for a major portion of agriculture. Those are rates comparable to what a vigorous non-agricultural sector achieves—and for a very large sub-sector. That makes possible much higher over-all rates of growth in agriculture—more nearly four to six per cent than the three to four per cent that was considered exemplary a few decades ago. See for example the four to six per cent agricultural growth rates achieved by high growth rate countries (Mellor, 1991).

It is notable that the high value commodities generate large incomes per hectare with consequentially large employment impact on the rural non-farm sector. So, as is discussed in the next section, even though direct employment in agriculture may be substantial from the high value commodities, the multipliers to the rural non-farm sector will be far larger.

3.6 Agriculture-Led Non-Farm Growth

The circumstantial evidence is strong that agricultures powerful poverty reducing effect comes substantially through its impact on the rural, non-agricultural, small-scale sector. There is considerable knowledge of this sector from the studies of Liedholm and his colleagues (Liedholm and Meade, 1987). They conclude that this sector is large, employment intensive, expands readily in response to increased demand, and is largely driven by agricultural demand.

Nevertheless, the evidence about the size of the sector, the proportion of incremental farm income spent in this sector, and the employment intensity is meager. The evidence of its links to agriculture and its importance to employment calls for intensive study. The following paragraphs summarise the current state of knowledge of this sector.

Because the agricultural sector in low-income countries is so large, accelerated growth into the four to six per cent range adds immense purchasing power (Mellor, 1992). That is because this growth is substantially driven by improved technology (yield increasing crops of the green revolution) and mobilises previously under-utilised farm family labour resources within agriculture.

Several empirical studies cited above document that farmers spend a substantial proportion of incremental income on locally produced non-farm goods and services. Liedholm and Meade turn that around and state that the rural non-farm sector derives a high proportion of its demand from farmers. Since this is a large employment intensive sector it is logical to turn to these forces to explain the powerful effect of agriculture in increasing employment and reducing poverty.

This argument is also consistent with the lag in the effect of agricultural growth, the fact that highly skewed distribution of income from land removes the poverty reducing effect, and the important wage increasing effect of agricultural growth. Further, the power of this income effect causes a tightening of the labour market that cannot be explained by the agricultural growth alone. Because it is the income growth that drives the process it does not matter that the initial income effect is concentrated in the hands of the middle peasant rather than the poor. The poor benefit in the next round.

Three questions arise about this process. How large is the sector that is driven by agricultural incomes and is it a tradable or non-tradable sector? How employment intensive is this sector? And, to what extent is it driven by purchase of production goods and to what extent by consumption goods?

3.7 Size of the Rural Non-Farm Sector

There are two ways measure the size of the agriculture driven non-farm sector. One is by surveys of the production pattern and source of demand for output for the sector thought to serve agriculture and the other is through analysis of the consumption patterns for incremental income of farmers. Neither type of information is well developed. Farmer expenditure data rarely give sufficient breakdown to allow analysis of the relevant parts of expenditure. Surveys of small business in rural and market town areas are infrequent and usually lacking in detail with respect to sources of demand.

Delgado spells out in some detail why it is the non-tradable sector that is important to the employment increasing poverty-reducing impact of agricultural growth (Delgado, 1999). The non-tradable (products and services that do not enter international trade) sector cannot be stimulated to growth by international exports. The labour force and production systems are such that they are not employable in the short run producing goods and services for other than the rural market.

Of course, in the long-run with education and gradual integration of markets labour will move into tradable sectors. The story of low incomes is the slow pace at which that changes occurs. In the meantime, rapid growth in demand for such output provides employment, expands the number of entrepreneurs, and creates a favorable environment for the transition to tradable. The interaction between agriculture and this large sector is an important part of the transition to a modern economy.

Currently a major emphasis on stimulating growth in low-income countries is on exports and the question arises why cannot any stimulus provided by agriculture to employment growth be more easily provided by foreign demand. In some respects the very thought is somewhat silly. Is it reasonable to think that all or even the bulk of incremental demand for the vast labour resources of all low-income countries can come from the high-income countries?

Of course, an important supplement can come from exports and that increment is apt to make the difference between moderate and rapid growth. Also, exports of labour intensive commodities provide the foreign exchange to allow import of capital-intensive commodities thereby allowing domestically available capital to concentrate on labour intensive goods and service. But, in general, much of incremental demand must come from domestic sources.

One might ask also how reasonable it is to think that the bulk of the now widely dispersed population with already existing housing infrastructure can be accommodated in the short-run in the major cities near ports that are essential for competition in international markets? Thus, the issue is not one simply of tradable *versus* non-tradable.

In any case peasant farmers spend a high proportion of incremental income on low quality goods and on non-exportable goods and services. Examples are expanded housing, personal services, increased lower level education, increased health services, local transport. Note that where labour is cheap, prospering farmers hire a substantial addition of labour so as to devote family labour away from farm production to education, leisure, and marketing activities (Hayami and Kikuchi, 1999). These are all non-tradable and are produced primarily by labour with very little capital.

Consumption studies suggest that in middle-income countries, e.g. Egypt, this sector, located in market towns and rural areas has an initial GDP roughly equal to that of agriculture (Mellor, 1999). It is striking that even at this stage of development the sector is large and non-tradable. In Africa, with very low incomes, it may be only one-fifth the size of agriculture (Delgado, 1999).

In very low income societies, with minimal commercial differentiation, as in most of Africa, the multipliers from agricultural growth to the non-farm sector are much weaker than in more differentiated societies. However, Delgado, in a careful analysis for sub-Saharan Africa points out that marginal propensity to consume non-tradable agricultural commodities is very high.

In rural Africa with high transaction costs derived from poor communications systems much of agriculture is non-tradable. That is certainly true of much of livestock and horticulture sub-sectors, but it may well apply to the coarse grains as well. Since these are labour intensive sectors, with high propensities to consume them, considerable employment is generated within agriculture itself. Thus, an initial boost to income from yield increasing technological change may greatly increase employment through multipliers back into agriculture itself.

In this review the high value, high-income elastic parts of agriculture are counted as agriculture, *albeit* a part of agriculture the demand for which may come importantly from rising farm incomes. Thus, the non-farm sector is seen as more limited, but nevertheless large. But, with this more restricted definition it should be recognised that in very poor societies the employment multipliers from agricultural growth might be quite large because of this circularity back into agriculture.

In middle-income countries the agriculture driven non-farm sector may be as large as agriculture (Mellor, 1998). The incremental income in farmer's hands will be spent more than proportionately in that sector. That is the income elasticity of demand is well above 1.0.

3.8. Employment in the Rural Non-Farm Sector

Employment elasticities in the agriculture driven non-farm sectors are high, close to one. Increased output is driven by increasing demand, As long as real wages are constant, there is little incentive to increase labour efficiency. Since very little capital, or land, is employed in this sector virtually all the gross income is return to labour.

Empirically, compared to farming, with half as much GDP in the sector, twice the labour intensity, the initial labour force is the same size as for agriculture. Typically in low-income countries, about half of farmers base income is spent on production services and locally produced consumption goods (Bell *et al.*, 1980, Hazel and Roll, 1983).

Commonly used statistics overstate employment in agriculture and thereby understate employment in the rural non-farm sector. Persons with even small plots of land tend to be counted as farmers, even though a high proportion of those with land have plots so small that they earn less then half their income and gain less than half of their employment from farming. Such persons should be counted as rural non-farm rather than farm or agriculture. Such a calculation tends to confirm that a norm is for on the order of half the rural population to be rural non-farm.

With an average income elasticity of demand for goods and services produced in the rural non-farm sector of 1.5, employment expands at 1.5 per cent of the base output for each per cent increase in the rate of growth of agricultural income. With a 4 per cent growth rate in agriculture the growth rate of employment is 6.5 per cent. That compares with agriculture at a four per cent growth rate and an employment elasticity of 0.3 of 1.2 per year—the additions to employment in the agriculture stimulated local non-farm sector is several fold that directly in agriculture. That is the key point about the agricultural growth impact on poverty.

The critical point on employment growth is that the rural non-farm sector is employment intensive with elasticities of employment with respect to output on the order of 1.0 that is, in that sector output growth is driven by rising demand not by technological change as in agriculture. In contrast, both agriculture and urban industry have employment elasticities that are very low and may even be close to zero judging by much of recent Indian experience (Bhalla, 2004). If employment is to rise and poverty decline agricultural income growth must stimulate growth in the rural non-farm sector.

3.9 Agribusiness and Consumption Goods

Fertiliser and other chemical and mechanical inputs to agriculture take place in the tradable sector and tend to be imported or produced by capital-intensive processes. Increased demand for such goods does not add much to employment and that demand could have been provided from sources other than domestic agriculture.

In contrast, the local marketing service for these inputs and for output are labour intensive non-tradable and the increase in demand from agriculture stimulates production and employment that are net additions to the economy that could not come from other sources. That will remain true as long as there is poverty representing inadequate employment opportunity for the wage earning classes.

Studies of marketing margins suggest that the stimulus to the rural and market town non-tradable sector is equal to about 10 per cent of the value of incremental agricultural production since a high proportion of incremental production depends on purchased inputs and is marketed.

Consumption studies in Asia show about 40 per cent of incremental income are spent on locally produced non-farm goods and service (Hazel *et al.,*). These are all highly labour intensive in their production.

Thus, consumption goods comprise about three-quarters of incremental demand for non-tradable and production services about one-quarter. It is the consumption expenditure that is dominant (Mellor and Lele, 1972).

3.10 Rich Peasants and Income Distribution

A substantial literature in the immediate post-green revolution period stated that the green revolution concentrated incremental income in the hands of the land owning classes, including the middle peasant or *kulak* to use the Marxian term. Consequently the poor did not participate in income growth. The concentration of income led to further concentration of land ownership. That was the basis for much of the anti-green revolution spirit of the 1970's.

This exposition points out that in fact increased agricultural incomes in the hands of the middle peasant or *kulak* has powerful employment linkages, but they take time to operate. The initial studies did not allow for that time and in any case were only concerned with the direct affect of income growth.

The important point is that an initial skewing of the benefits of agricultural growth towards the higher income rural people is not antithetical to poverty reduction. The issue is not the initial distribution of the increased income but the expenditure patterns from that income. Middle peasants in low-income countries spend a high proportion locally on non-tradables thereby providing a stimulus to production and particularly to employment that cannot be obtained in any other manner.

Delgado carefully documents that in Africa, incomes and commercial differentiation are so low that the non-farm goods and services receive relatively little stimulus but that the increment to demand for agricultural non-tradables is very large. That stimulates a large increase in demand driven production of high value agricultural products (livestock and fruits and vegetables) and even for some non-tradable basic staples. Thus, an initial stimulus to agricultural growth from technological change (high yielding varieties of basic staples) has strong multipliers back to other sectors of agriculture that are highly labour intensive. The effects are precisely as described for the rural and market town non-farm sectors.

3.11 When Do Real Wages Rise and Employment Elasticities Decline?

The empirical data show rising real wage rates as a significant factor in declining poverty. In practice, the statistical techniques do not catch employment quantity since there are no measures available. They catch the effect of employment separately only through the increment in real wages.

As long as there is underemployment in rural areas, roughly synonymous with poverty, real wages will not rise. Thus, it is surprising that the data catch real wage increases at such an early stage.

Increased production of basic agricultural commodities that are non-tradable will result in declining real price of that output unless effective demand increases through increased employment. The statistical studies do catch an effect of declining real prices of basic food staples. That is because much of the change in production is large annual fluctuations due to weather rather than the steady effect of technological change. In the case of the former, employment cannot increase sufficiently rapidly to make effective demand for all the increment in production. But, the steady increase of technology driven output growth can be matched by roughly commensurate increase in demand through increased employment of the poor who spend a high proportion of increased income on basic food.

Thus, the poor benefit from increased basic food staple output either through lower prices or increased employment. The latter is in fact more certain in peasant agriculture because the basic food may in fact be tradable (although trade economists like to exaggerate that for low-income countries) eliminating the price decline.

Let me return to the real wage story. What the data are telling us is that the labour market tightens surprisingly quickly. Why? Because of the immense increase in employment in the local non-farm sector, the poor benefit as employment increases and then again as real wages rise. That is why poverty declines so rapidly with high agricultural growth rates.

When real wages rise it pays to increase labour productivity. That will happen in both the farm production sector and the rural and market town non-farm sector. In practice, raising labour productivity is low cost in both these sectors. So again, we find that statistical evidence of steadily rising real wages with agricultural growth shows how powerful the employment multipliers must be. For that to be the case the effect must come substantially from the non-farm sector because the increase in labour productivity is so automatic in food staples production.

Of course, it is per capita farm income that drives the rural non-farm sector. Thus, for a major impact, agricultural production must grow considerably faster than the farm population. It is the four to six per cent agricultural growth rate that is characteristic of fast growth economies that bring rapid employment growth. Such growth rates require substantial growth in exports or middle-income status with rapid growth in domestic demand for high value agricultural commodities on a large base of production of such commodities.

4. Employment Numbers

It is difficult to estimate the actual employment numbers for the indirect effects of agricultural growth because statistics are not kept for the composition of the rural and market town non-farm sectors. What data there are not broken down by sources of effective demand? Hence, we have little data on the size of the sector in GDP terms or of the employment content. However, a rough approximation can be made of these numbers. Such estimates are large and fully in keeping with the clearly measured impact of agricultural growth on poverty reduction.

A careful estimate of the relative impact of agriculture and urban industry on employment has been made by Mellor and Gavian (1999) for

Egypt. These estimates of the impact on poverty of the structure of growth in a pre-reform period (early 1980's) when agricultural output growth was slower than the labour force growth (-0.2 per cent per capita); for an early reform period when the agricultural growth rate significantly exceeded the labour force growth rate (1.0 per cent per capita); and a projected future period of full implementation of reforms, providing an agricultural growth rate of 2.7 per cent per capita. Calculations were made of the size of the farm income driven non-farm sector, the incremental expenditure on farm driven non-farm production, and the effect on employment.

Table 8.1 summarises the results from those calculations. When agricultural growth was less than the labour force growth rate, the annual increments to employment from agricultural growth were small and total employment growth was far less than the labour force growth. Poverty increased. In the full reform period of high agricultural growth, employment increases far faster than labour force growth so that real wage rates would rise.

Table 8.1

Annual Increments to Employment, by Sector, 1980-81–2005-06

Sector	Pre-Reform 1980-81–1985-86 (Slow Agricultural Growth)	Early Reform 1997-98, (Medium Rate of Agricultural Growth)	Mature Reform 2001-02–2005-06 (Fast Rate of Agricultural Growth)
Agriculture	37,950	100,122	146,164
Agri. Driven non-agr.	108,810	340,875	581,175
Autonomous non-agr.	17,707	43,350	45,084
Total Employment	164,467	484,347	772,423
Annual Additions to Labour Force @ 2.7%	480,060	48,006	549,080

Source: (Mellor and Gavian 1999) See original source for full explanation of derivation of numbers in the table.

In the fast growth period when agriculture and non-agriculture were growing rapidly, agricultures direct and indirect effects accounted for 70 per cent of employment growth, while the sectors autonomous from agriculture generated 77 per cent of GDP growth. Since these are all market price driven forces they are all in economic equilibrium and one cannot in a neo-classical context say that one form of growth is better than others; but the agricultural growth contributes most to employment growth. And, the agricultural growth does require government interventions.

4.1 Programmes to Reduce Poverty

An important current widely accepted target is to reduce the number of persons under the poverty line by half over the next 15 years. That is an ambitious target but not unprecedented for individual countries. It is clear from the data and the theory that the core of achieving large macro targets of poverty reduction must be major acceleration of the agricultural growth rate and concurrent facilitation of the growth of small-scale non-farm enterprises, largely producing non-tradable goods and services in rural and market town areas. Conversely, poverty does not decline, even with large direct action programmes without rapid agricultural growth (Ravallion and Datt, 1996).

4.2. Agricultural Growth

It is now feasible to achieve much higher agricultural growth rates than were considered the norm only a few decades ago. Then growth rates of 3.0 to 3.5 per cent were considered quite substantial. That only gave 1.0 to 1.5 per cent rates of growth per capita. Now fast agricultural growth would be considered more nearly 4.0 to 6.0 per cent (Mellor, 1992).

4.3 Increased Potential

Three major changes explain this greatly increased potential for agricultural growth—greater knowledge, greater capital availability, and more open global markets and rapid growth in domestic demand for high value agricultural commodities.

4.4. Knowledge

First, the knowledge of how to develop agriculture has burgeoned since the 1950's. We not only have a clearer view of the strategic needs but immense detail on how to run credit programmes, what works and what doesnot, the appropriate role for government *vis-à-vis* the private sector, and of course far greater knowledge of the basic science for bringing about yield increasing technological improvements.

The potentials for biotechnology are immense and just beginning to be tapped, *albeit* particularly under-funded for the problems of low-income countries (Mann, 1999, Science, 1999). On the Social Science side the American Agricultural Economics Association review of post-war literature on agricultural development has over 4000 references divided over Asia, Africa, and Latin America (see Eicher and Doyle, Mellor and Mudahar, and Schuh and Brandao respectively in Martin, 1992). With the slackening of foreign aid interest in agriculture and support for research, the pace of knowledge generation for agricultural and rural development has, of course, slowed, but there is an immense backlog of under-utilised knowledge and new knowledge generation has not halted.

4.5 Capital

Second, international capital flows are now at levels undreamed of when the Asian countries began their takeoff. Although, international capital is not likely to cover a significant portion of the direct needs of the agricultural sector, it can so relieve other financial pressures on low-income country governments that much greater resources can be freed for investment in agricultural research and infrastructure than was possible in the early days of the Asian breakthroughs.

Of course, to say that capital need not be limiting is not say that it is not limiting. Governments must recognise the importance of agriculture, follow liberal policies to encourage capital flows, and then invest fully their own funds in agriculture. Foreign aid can do much and may indeed be critical in strengthening the national forces that understand these relationships. It used to do that in Asia, it needs to start doing it in Africa.

Low-income countries with large natural resource exports, *e.g.* oil, diamonds, cannot expect simply the generation of those resources to result in the employment growth rates that reduce poverty, particularly rural poverty. Such resources are valuable for reducing poverty if they are invested in agricultural growth that in turn creates the employment multipliers that reduce poverty. The contrast between Indonesia that used oil revenues at least in part for massive investment in rural roads and education and Nigeria that did not is instructive.

4.6 High Value Commodities

Third, and perhaps most important in quantitative terms, production of high value commodities, particularly horticulture and livestock can grow more rapidly than in the past. That is important to agriculture, which tends to be land constrained and, hence, increasing yields through technology and value of output per unit through enlarged markets lessen that constraint.

As domestic growth reaches high levels the high income elasticities for these commodities result in rapid growth in demand. But, now with international trade far more free than in the past, and promising to become more open, domestic production of high value commodities can grow far more rapidly than domestic demand.

By definition, high value commodities use little land and so abundant labour can result in growth rates of output of 6.0 to 8.0 per cent. Since they initially comprise some 20 per cent of the value of agricultural output and gradually rise to well over 50 per cent that is a cause of major acceleration in the agricultural growth rate.

Tremendous growth in the global economy, in substantial part because of the takeoff in Asia has greatly increased the market and the price responsiveness of demand for traditional high value tropical exports. Hence, that potential is also now greater than it used to be. Africa has been the great loser from not exploiting these potentials, while Asian countries, particularly Malaysia and Indonesia have benefited immensely from rapid growth in exports of these commodities.

4.7 Realising the Potential

The requisites of high agricultural growth rates are three: cost reducing technology; low transaction costs; and an open economy. Foreign aid oriented towards poverty reduction can be important to each.

4.7.1 Infrastructure

Rapid growth in agriculture requires specialisation and trade. That in turn requires massive investment in rural roads, electrification and communications. Agricultural growth cannot occur on the cheap. An accelerated pace of agricultural growth can occur for a few years in proximity to existing infrastructure. But, longer term growth and, hence, continued employment growth and poverty reduction require that the infrastructure network be pushed back to cover the bulk of the productive resources of the country. That requires a massive long-term plan.

There is no possibility of a high productivity agriculture producing its own nutrients. Too much is taken off the land. Thus, dependence on purchased plant nutrients is inevitably immense. The situation for pest control is more complex. Particularly in tropical climates chemical pest control is far too expensive as the sole means of pest management. Biological controls are important but they require some chemical complements. Weed control is even more likely to require some chemical input, particularly if low or no tillage systems are used to improve soil retention.

Even more important than purchased inputs is the specialisation in production that allows fine-tuning of the production system to the environment. That requires specialisation and trade.

If transaction costs are high, due to poor transport and communication systems then specialisation and trade cannot occur and agriculture cannot modernise and increase farm incomes to drive anti-poverty programmes. Thus, large investment in rural infrastructure is crucial to poverty reduction.

Most important of all, rapid agricultural growth requires institutions staffed by educated people—extension, credit, marketing organisation, and educated people in general will only live where all weather roads favour well staffed schools and clinics and ready movement back and forth to major population centres.

Of course, there are immense direct benefits to the poor from improved infrastructure—better access to medical services for example. But, more important practitioners in health, education, and other services important to the poor are only willing to live in rural areas if they become decent places to live. For the rich travel, even for long periods, to these services is a reasonable alternative. It is not an alternative for the poor. They go without.

Sachs (1998) and Krugman (1998) underrate the effect of agricultural specialisation making high productivity use of resources that were low productivity in subsistence agriculture. For example, the old tropical soils are of low productivity in annual food crops, but produce a high level of output per unit area and per worked in tropical tree crops such as oil palm, or cacao.

4.7.2 Technology

Agricultural growth at rates significantly faster than population growth rates is technology driven to a far greater extent than other sectors. That was markedly so for the United States in the slow technological advance period up to 1990, when agriculture accounted for 80 per cent of productivity increase (Ball *et al.,*).

Agricultural technology must in significant part be driven by domestic research even while it draws very heavily on international research (Evenson and Kislev, 1975). The domestic systems provide the basis for drawing on the international. Of course, education of farmers must move in tandem with the research system and systems of credit are needed to finance the inputs and capital requirements of improved technology.

4.7.3 Broad Participation

Ensuring broad participation in agricultural growth is one of the most effective anti-poverty programmes in the context of growth. Such participation has two advantages: it involves the poor directly in increased incomes, and, it results in faster over-all growth. Broadening participation means spending more than pure economics would call for on women's participation, small farmer participation, disadvantaged ethnic groups participation, and possibly in poor areas. Each of these has additional costs beyond including the bulk of middle farmers in the best areas. Those costs can be justified on the basis of poverty alleviation.

Women generally participate fully in most aspects of traditional agriculture. When agriculture modernises traditional role differentiation tends to deny women access to modern information, inputs, and marketing. Emphasis needs to be given to ensuring their participation not only for increasing agricultural incomes and participation of the poor, but to use modernising agriculture as a means to bring women into the totality of modern society.

Small farmers are more costly to reach per unit of output and so may be left out of agricultural growth. That tendency may be reinforced by greater conservatism rooted marginal incomes for subsistence. Ingenuity is needed to bring small farmers into the process.

Disadvantaged ethnic groups may also be left out of the modernisation process. The special problems and needs of such groups need to be part of anti-poverty and agricultural growth programmes.

Poor areas are a more complex problem. It is sometimes argued that once substantial progress has been made in the favourable areas that the returns to investment are then better in the poor areas. That however is based on a static view of technology. In practice, improved technology is constantly being generated so the issue is not the movement along a static production function but the pace at which the function is being shifted up and to the right. Areas with favourable soil structure, moisture and sunlight conditions will generally continually respond better to improved technology and the gap will become larger and larger with the less responsive areas.

Having said that, some technology does reverse the income situation for some conditions. For instance, chemical fertiliser greatly reduces the costs of adding nutrients so that conditions that are favourable in all respects except initial nutrient situation may improve their relative position with commercialisation. Improved communications may allow specialisation in commodities that do have a comparative advantage under new conditions—tree fruit crops in Nepal, tropical perennial exports in Africa.

Thus, the potentials for poor areas must be examined carefully and the changes needed to bring some of them along made. But, given potentials to migrate to burgeoning market towns in prospering agricultural areas a harsh decision not to invest in the agriculture of unresponsive areas needs to be made. Concurrently investments that assist migration (*e.g.* education) and mitigate the problems of the remaining people are sound anti-poverty programmes.

4.7.4 Small Enterprise

The importance of micro-enterprise to the poor has been well recognised. What have not been recognised is that the demand for the products of micro-enterprise must expand and that the output is largely non-tradable.

Export markets for the products of micro-enterprise exist, e.g. for handicrafts, but the total is a small proportion of what is needed to solve poverty problems through employment growth.

The problem is well exemplified by study of the Grameen Bank in Bangladesh where in areas with little agricultural expansion financing of micro-enterprise for the very poor tended to be at the expense of the livelihood of the poor (Hossain, 1988). However, where agriculture was expanding rapidly, income was rising and demand expanding for such goods and services and so total employment in these enterprises expanded.

Thus, the growth in income from agriculture provides effective demand for service weighted, relatively low quality goods and services that characterise the bulk of micro enterprise. Of course, as such firms multiply some will have the entrepreneurial leadership to expand into urban and foreign markets. Taiwan' current pattern of small-scale geographically dispersed industrialisation, in such sharp contrast with the entirely different pattern in South Korea, exemplifies the process.

Thus, the first step in ensuring rapid growth of micro enterprise is expanding effective demand through growth in agricultural incomes.

Credit is important for the poor to participate in micro-enterprise as entrepreneurs. That has been the source of success of the major examples of credit to assist low-income persons, e.g. the Grameen Bank in Bangladesh. But, it is even more important to expansion to the next stage of middle-sized business with large increase in employment opportunities a la Taiwan (Liedholm and Meade, 1987).

The poor are of course highly vulnerable to all sources of uncertainty and fluctuations. Most onerous are fluctuations in food prices, but fluctuations in crop production from weather fall heavily on the poor as farm incomes are reduced and are leveraged in their impact on non-farm employment.

4.7.5. Unresponsive Areas

The problem of geographic areas that are unresponsive to improved crop technology and ill suited to high value products is currently intractable. Every effort needs to be found for adapting such areas to improved technology and high value commodities, but for those that cannot be so adapted, the data are clear that the returns to investment are far lower than in the more responsive areas. In that circumstance it is better to invest where the returns in increased incomes are higher. Since the job formation from such increased incomes is disproportionately in the market towns the scope to absorb migrants from less advantaged areas is great. Thus, what is needed is increased education in the less responsive areas to facilitate migration. See the work of Ravallion on this issue (1998).

4.7.6 Skewed Income Distribution

The most intractable poverty problem occurs where incomes are highly skewed to the rich. Agricultural growth does nothing for the poor in such circumstance, nor does any other growth related approach. What is most needed is radical redistribution of assets. Failing that education will assist the poor to leave for other countries, or eventually for increasing job opportunities in their own urban areas. That however, for the poor countries will take a long time. This is the only discouraging feature on the poverty mitigation front.

4.7.7 Foreign-Aid

A recent Overseas Development Institute (ODI) report done for the British foreign assistance programme (DFID) notes the general decline and specifically the USAID reduction in assistance to agriculture from $1.2 Billion in 1986 to $240 million in 1997, an astounding 80 per cent reduction (ODI, 1999). This is of course a radical turn away from pro-poor growth.

The importance of foreign-aid to pro-poor growth derives from the strong urban bias of low-income country governments (Lipton, 1977). Given that bias, foreign-aid played a major role by steady effort, in Asia, to strengthen nationals in low-income countries who saw the important role of agriculture. The result was major progress in agriculture. It has slackened since foreign-aid turned away from agriculture. In Africa, foreign-aid has given little attention to agricultural growth. Ruttan (1996) has documented why this has happened. If pro-poor growth is to occur, foreign-aid must return its attention to agriculture.

5. Conclusions

Thus, we provide explanation of the conundrums of why growth does not always bring down poverty levels—it is the wrong structure; why the right structure takes time—the effects are indirect they must work their way through the system; why so much of the world is finding its way out of poverty (all of Asia for example)—because agriculture got going in those areas; why poverty reduction is slowing in those same areas—agricultural growth has received much less attention in the last decade and despite considerable institutionalisation it has slowed, a slowing reinforced by foreign-aid pressures for indiscriminate budget cuts; why Africa has been such a disaster from a poverty reduction point of view—national governments are urban oriented and biased and, in contrast to the record in Asia, foreign-aid stopped pressuring for emphasis on agriculture over the past two decades; and, why foreign-aid is so important to getting agriculture going—because government actions are critical to agriculture and low-income country governments tend to be strongly urban.

References

Ahmed, Raisuddin and Mahabub Hossain (1990). *Developmental Impact of Rural Infrastructure in Bangladesh*, Washington, International Food Policy Research Institute, Research Report No. 83

Acharya, Sarthi and V.G. Panwalkar (1988). *The Maharashtra Employment Guarantee Scheme: Impacts on Male and Female Labour*, New York: Population Council.

Adelman, Irma and Morris, C.T. (1973). *Economic Growth and Social Equity in Developing Countries.* Stanford: Stanford University Press.

————. and S. Robinson (1988). "Income Distribution and Development" eds Hollis Chenery and T.N. Srinivasan in *Handbook of Development Economics*, Volume 2, Amsterdam: North Holland.

Ahluwalia, Montek S. (1985). "Rural Poverty, Agricultural Production and Prices: A Re-Examination," in Mellor and Desai (ed).

————. (1978). "Rural Poverty and Agricultural Performance in India" *Journal of Development Studies*, 14: 298-323.

————. (1976). "Inequality, Poverty and Development" *Journal of Development Economics*, 3:307-342.

Ahmed, Raisuddin and Mahabub Hossain (1990). *Developmental Impact of Rural Infrastructure in Bangladesh*, Washington, International Food Policy Research Institute, Research Report No. 83.

Anand, Sudhir and Ravi Kanbur (1993). "The Kuznets Process and the Inequality Development Relationship," *Journal of Development Economics*, 40: 25-52.

Atkinson, Anthony B. (1977). "Bringing Income Distribution in from the Cold," *Economic Journal*, 107 (March): 297-321.

Ball, V. Eldon, *et al.*, (1999). "Patterns of State Productivity Growth in the U.S. Farm Sector: Linking State and Aggregate Models," *American Journal of Agricultural Economics*, 81.

Behrman, Jere (1991). *Nutrient Intake Demand Relations: Incomes, Prices, Schooling*, mimeo, Department of Economics, University of Pennsylvania.

————. and Anil Deolalikar (1987). "Will Developing Country Nutrition Improve with Income? A Case Study for Rural South India," *Journal of Political Economy*, 95:108-138.

Bell, C.L., P.B. Hazell and R. Slade (1982). *Project Evaluation in Regional Perspective: A Study of an Irrigation Project in Northwest Malaysia.* Baltimore, MD: John Hopkins University Press.

————. and P.B.R. Hazell (1980). "Measuring the Indirect Effects of an Agricultural Investment Project on its Surrounding Region" *American Journal of Agricultural Economics*, 62:75-86.

Bhalla, Sheila (2004). "Employment Density and Linkages of Rural Non-farm Enterprises in Andhra Pradesh and Haryana" *Indian Journal of Labour Economics*, Vol. 47 (4).

————. (2004). "A Perspective on Employment in India's Non-farm Sector," Paper for the National Commission on Farmers - 2005, Delhi: JNU.

Bidani, Benu and Martin Ravallion (1985). *Decomposing Social Indicators Using Distributional Data,* Washington, DC: The World Bank.

Binswanger, Hans P., Klaus Deininger and Gershon Feder (1993). *Power, Distortions, Revolt, and Reform in Agricultural Land Relations*, Washington, DC: The World Bank.

Block, Steven and C. Peter Timmer (1994). *Agriculture and Economic Growth: Conceptual Issues and the Kenyan Experience* mimeo, Cambridge, MA: Harvard Institute for International Development.

Bouis, Howarth E., and Lawrence J. Haddad (1992). "Are Estimates of Calorie-Income Elasticities too High? A Recalibration of the Plausible Range," *Journal of Development Economics*, 39: 33-364.

Bourguignon, Francois and Christian Morrison (1998). "Inequality and Development: The Role of Dualism," *Journal of Development Economics*, 57(2): 233-257.

————. and C. Morrison (1990). "Income Distribution, Development and Foreign Trade: A Cross-Sectional Analysis" *European Economic Review*, 34: 1113-1132.

————. and Gary Fields (1990). "Poverty Measures and Anti-Poverty Policy," *Recherches Economiques de Louvain* 56: 409-428.

Bruno, Michael, Martin Ravallion and Lyn Squire (1998). "Equity and Growth in Developing Countries: Old and New Perspectives on the Policy Issues," ed. by Vito Tanzi and Ke-young Chu in *Income Distribution and High-Quality Growth*, Cambridge, Mass: MIT Press.

Chen, Shaohua, Gaurav Datt and Martin Ravallion (1993). *Is Poverty Increasing in the Developing World?*, Washington, DC: The World Bank.

Chuta, E. and C. Liedholm (1981). *Rural Non-Farm Employment: A Review of the State of the Art*, East Lansing: Michigan State University.

Clarke, Colin (1940). *The Conditions of Economic Progress* London: Macmillan.

Clay, Don (1999). "Food for Work and Food Security," *Food Policy*.

Cornea, Giovanni Andrea (1999). "Policy Reform and Income Inequality" mimeo, Helsinki, WIDER,

Dandekar, V.M. and N. Rath (1971). "Poverty in India," Bombay: *Economic and Political Weekly*.

Datt, Gaurav (1997). *Poverty in Indian 1951-1994: Trends and Decompositions*, mimeo, Washington, DC: World Bank and IFPRI.

————. and Martin Ravallion (1998a). "Why Have Some Indian States Done Better than Others at Reducing Rural Poverty?" *Economica*, 65: 17-38.

————. (1998b). "Farm Productivity and Rural Poverty in India," *Journal of Development Studies*, 34: 62-85.

————. (1997). "Macroeconomic Crises and Poverty Monitoring: A Case Study for India" *Review of Development Economics*, 1(2): 135-152.

————. (1990). *Regional Disparities, Targeting, and Poverty in India*. Washington, DC: The World Bank.

Deininger, Klaus, Lyn Squire and Tao Zhang (1995). *A New Data Base on International Income Distribution*, mimeo. Policy Research Department, World Bank.

Delgado, C. et al., (1998). *Agricultural Growth Linkages in Sub-Saharan Africa*. Research Report No. 107, Washington, DC: International Food Policy Research Institute (IFPRI),

Dev, S. Mahendra (1988). "Regional Disparities in Agricultural Labour Productivity and Rural Poverty," *Indian Economic Review* 23(2): 167-205.

Dev S. Mahendra, K.S. Parikh and M.H. Suryanarayan (1991). "Rural Poverty in India: Incidence, Issues and Policies," *Discussion Paper No. 55*, Ahmedabad: Indira Gandhi Institute of Development Research.

Dorosh, Paul A., and David E. Sahn (1993). *A General Equilibrium Analysis of the Effect of Macroeconomic Adjustment on Poverty in Africa*, mimeo, Cornell University Food and Nutrition Policy Programme.

Elias, Victor (1985). *Government Expenditure and Agricultural Growth in Latin America*, Washington, International Food Policy Research Institute, Research Report No. 50.

Evenson, R.E., and Y. Kislev (1975a). "Investment in Agricultural Research and Extension: A Survey of International Data" *Economic Development and Cultural Change* 23:507-522.

Fields, Gary (1989). "Changes in Poverty and Inequality in Developing Countries," *World Bank Research Observer*, 4:167-186.

————. (1980). *Poverty, Inequality and Development*. New York: Cambridge University Press.

————. (1994). "Data for Measuring Poverty and Inequality Changes in the Developing Countries," *Journal of Development Economics*, 44: 87-102.

Foster, James, J. Greer and Erik Thorbecke (1984). "A Class of Decomposable Poverty Measures," *Econometrica*, 52: 761-765.

Haggblade, S., P. Hazell and J. Brown (1989). "Farm-Nonfarm Linkages in Rural Sub-Saharan Africa," *World Development* 17(8): 1173-1202.

Harris, John R., and Michael P. Todaro (1970). "Migration, Unemployment and Development: A Two Sector Analysis," *American Economic Review*, 126-142.

Hayami, Yujiro and Masao Kikuchi (1999). *Does Modernization Promote Inequality? A Perspective from a Philippine Village in the Three Decades of the Green Revolution*, mimeo, Manila, International Rice Research Institute

Hayami, Y. and V.W. Ruttan (1985). *Agricultural Development*, Baltimore: John Hopkins University Press.

Hazell, Peter B.R. and Ailsa Roell (1983). *Rural Growth Linkages: Household Expenditures Patterns in Malaysia and Nigeria*, Washington: International Food Policy Research Institute, Research Report No. 41

Hossain, Mahabub (1988). *Credit for the Alleviation of Rural Poverty: The Grameen Bank in Bangladesh*, Research Report No. 65, Washington, DC: IFPRI.

Huppi, Monika and Martin Ravallion (1991). "The Sectoral Structure of Poverty During an Adjustment Period: Evidence for Indonesia in the Mid-1980s," *World Development*, 1653-1678.

Jalan, Jyotsna and Martin Ravallion (1998). "Are There Dynamic Gains from a Poor-Area Development Programme?" *Journal of Public Economics.*

————. (1998). *Geographic Poverty Traps? A Micro Model of Consumption Growth in Rural China.* Indian Statistical Institute, Delhi and The World Bank, Washington, DC.

————. (1998). *Determinants of Transient and Chronic Poverty, Evidence from Rural China*, Washington DC: The World Bank.

————. (1998). *Behavioral Responses to Risk in Rural China*, Washington D.C: The World Bank.

————. (1997). *Spatial Poverty Traps?* Washington, DC: The World Bank.

————. (1997). *Are the Poor Less Well-Insured? Evidence on Vulnerability to Income Risk in Rural China.* Washington, DC: The World Bank,.

Johnston, Bruce F. and John W. Mellor (1961). "The Role of Agriculture in Economic Development," *American Economic Review* 51 (4), 566-93.

————. and Peter Kilby (1975). *Agriculture and Structural Transformation: Economic Strategies in Late-Developing Countries*, (New York: Oxford University Press.

Kuznets, Simon (1966). *Modern Economic Growth*, New Haven: Yale University Press.

————. *(1955).* "Economic Growth and Income Inequality," *American Economic Review* 45:1-28.

Lanjouw, Peter and Martin Ravallion (1994). *Poverty and Household Size*, Washington, DC: The World Bank.

Lee, T.H. (1971). *Intersectoral Capital Flows in the Economic Development of Taiwan*, 1895-1960, Ithaca: Cornell University Press.

Lele, Uma (1979). *The Design of Rural Development: Lessons from Africa*, Baltimore: John Hopkins University Press.

————. and John W. Mellor *(1981).* "Technological Change, Distributive Bias and Labour Transfer in a Two Sector Economy," *Oxford Economic Papers*, Vol. 33 (3), 426-41.

Lewis, W.A. (1954). *Economic Development with Unlimited Supplies of Labour*, Manchester School: 139-191.

Liedholm, Carl and Donald Meade (1987). *Small Scale Industries in Developing Countries: Empirical Evidence and Policy Implications*, East Lansing: MSU International Development Papers

Lipton, M. (1977). *Why Poor People Stay Poor: Urban Bias in World Development, London*: Temple Smith.

————. and Jacques van der Gaag (eds). (1993). *Including the Poor*, Baltimore: Johns Hopkins.

————. and S. Maxwell (1992). *The New Poverty Agenda: An Overview*, mimeo, Brighton: Institute of Development Studies.

————. and Martin Ravallion (1995). "Poverty and Policy," in Jere Behrman and T.N. Srinivasan (eds) *Handbook of Development Economics*, Vol. III., Amsterdam: North-Holland.

Love, Alexander R. (1999). *Food Security and Donor Collabouration - Next Steps 1999*, Research Report No. 1070. Abt Associates Inc., Bethesda, MD.

Mann, Charles C. (1999). "Crop Scientists Seek a New Revolution" *Science.*

Martin, Lee R. (1992). *Survey of Agricultural Economics Literature - Volume 4 - Agriculture and Economic Development 1940's to 1990's*, Minneapolis: University of Minnesota Press.

Mellor, John W. (1995). *Agriculture on the Road to Industrialization*. Baltimore: John Hopkins University Press.

————. (1978). "Food Price Policy and Income Distribution in Low-Income Nations" *Economic Development and Cultural Change* 27:1-26.

————. (1976). *The New Economics of Growth*, Ithaca, NY: Cornell University Press.

————. (1974). "Models of Economic Growth and Land-Augmenting Technological Change in Foodgrain Production" ed. Nural Islam in *Agricultural Policy in Developing Countries*, London: Macmillan.

————. (1968). "The Functions of Agricultural Prices in Economic Development" *Indian Journal of Agricultural Economics*, 23(1), 23-37.

————. (1966) *The Economics of Agricultural Development*, Ithaca: Cornell University Press.

————. Christopher L. Delgado, and Malcolm J. Blackie, eds. (1987). *Accelerating Food Production Growth in Sub-Saharan Africa*. Baltimore: John Hopkins University Press.

————. and G.M. Desai (eds) (1985). *Agricultural Change and Rural Poverty*, Baltimore: John Hopkins University Press.

————. and Sarah Gavian (1999). *Impact Assessment of Agricultural Policy Reform on Employment and Productivity in Egypt*, Bethesda, MD: Abt Associates Inc.

————. (1987). "Famine: Causes, Preventions, and Relief," *Science* 235:539-545.

————. and B.F. Johnston (1984). "The World Food Equation: Interrelations Among Development, Employment, and Food Consumption," *Journal of Economic Literature* 22:531-574.

————. and U.J. Lele (1973). 'Growth Linkages of the New Foodgrain Technologies' *Indian Journal of Agricultural Economics*, 28(1):35-55.

————. and W.A. Masters (1991). "The Changing Roles of Multilateral and Bilateral Foreign Assistance" ed. by Uma Lele and Ijaz Nabi in *Transitions in Development: The Role of Aid and Commercial Flows*, San Francisco, Calif.: ICS Press.

————. and Rajul Pandya-Lorch (1992). "Food Aid and Development in the MADIA Countries" ed. by Uma Lele, in *Aid to African Agriculture: Lessons from Two Decades if Donor Experience*, Baltimore: John Hopkins University press.

Myrdal, Gunnar (1988). in G. Meier and D. Seers (eds) *Pioneers in Development*, New York: Oxford University Press.

Nepal, Government of (1995). *The Agricultural Perspective Plan*, Kathmandu: APROSC.

Overseas Development Institute (ODI) (1999). *Poverty Briefing 2*, London: Overseas Development Institute.

Papanek, Gustav and Oldrich Kyn (1986). "The Effect on Income Distribution of Development, the Growth Rate and Economic Strategy," *Journal of Development Economics*, 23:55-65.

Piriou-Sall, Suzanne (1998). *Decentralization and Rural Development: A Review of Evidence*, Washington, DC:.The World Bank.

Pradhan, Menno and Martin Ravallion (1998). *Measuring Poverty Using Qualitative Perceptions of Welfare*, Washington, DC: The World Bank.

Rangarajan, C. (1982). *Agricultural Growth and Industrial Performance*, Washington: International Food Policy Research Institute, Research Report No. 33

Rao, C.H. Hanumanthan (1975). *Technological Change and Distribution of Gains in Indian Agriculture*, Delhi: Macmillan Company of India.

Ravallion, Martin (1998). *Appraising Workfare Programmes*, Washington, DC: The Word Bank.

————. (1998). *Reaching Poor Areas in a Federal System*, Washington, DC: The World Bank.

————. (1998). *Do Price Increases for Staple Foods Help or Hurt the Rural Poor?*, Washington, DC: The World Bank.

————. (1997). *Can High-Inequality Developing Countries Escape Absolute Poverty?*, Washington, DC: The World Bank.

————. (1996). *Issues in Measuring and Modeling Poverty*, Washington, DC: The World Bank.

————. (1996). *Famines and Economics*, Washington, DC: The World Bank.

————. (1995). "Growth and Poverty: Evidence for the Developing World," *Economics Letters*

————. (1994). *Poverty Comparisons*. Harwood Academic Press.

————. (1993). "Poverty Alleviation Through Regional Targeting: A Case Study for Indonesia" *The Economics of Rural Organisation*, Oxford: Oxford University Press for the World Bank.

————. (1991). *The Challenging Arithmetic of Poverty in Bangladesh*, Washington, DC: The World Bank.

————. (1991). *Hunger and Public Action*, Washington, DC: The World Bank.

————.(1989). *Is Undernutrition Responsive to Changes In Incomes?*, Washington, DC: The World Bank.

————. and Shaohua Chen (1989). *When Economic Reform is Faster than Statistical Reform, Measuring and Explaining Inequality in Rural China*, Washington, DC: The World Bank.

————. et al., (1991). *Quantifying the Magnitude and Severity of Absolute Poverty in the Developing World in the Mid-1980s*, Washington, DC: The World Bank.

————. and Shaohua Chen (1997). "What Can New Survey Data Tell Us About Recent Changes in Distribution and Poverty," *The World Bank Economic Review*. Vol. 11 (2), 1997.

————. and Benu Bidani (1993). *How Robust Is a Poverty Profile?*, Washington, DC: The World Bank.

————. (1998). *Do Price Increases for Staple Foods Help or Hurt the Rural Poor?*, Washington, DC: The World Bank.

————. and Shaohua Chen (1998). *Economic Reform is Faster than Statistical Reform, Measuring and Explaining Inequality in Rural China*, Washington, DC: The World Bank.

————. and Gaurav Datt (1996). "How Important to India's Poor is the Sectoral Composition of Economic Growth," *The World Bank Economic Review*, Vol. 10 (1).

————. Gaurav Datt and Shubham Chaudhuri (1991). *Higher Wages for Relief Work Can Make Many of the Poor Worse Off, Recent Evidence from Maharashtra's Employment Guarantee Scheme*, Washington, DC: The World Bank.

————. and Monika Huppi (1989). *Poverty and Undernutrition in Indonesia during the 1980s*, Washington, DC: The World Bank.

————. and Binayak Sen (1994). *When Method Matters, Toward a Resolution of the Debate About Bangladesh's Poverty Measures*, Washington, DC : The World Bank.

————. and Binayak Sen (1994). *How Land-Based Targeting Affects Rural Poverty*, Washington, DC: The World Bank.

————. and Quentin Wodon (1998). *Evaluating a Targeted Social Programme When Placement Is Decentralized*, Washington, DC: The World Bank.

————. and Quentin Wodon (1997). *Banking on the Poor? Branch Placement and Non-farm Rural Development in Bangladesh*, Washington, DC: The World Bank.

————. and Quentin Wodon (1997). *Poor Areas, Or Only Poor People?* Washington, DC: The World Bank.

Reardon, T., C. Delgado and P. Matlon (1992). "Determinants and Effects of Income Diversification Among Farmer Households in Burkina Faso," *Journal of Development Studies*, 28(2): 264-296.

Ruttan, Vernon W., ed. (1993). *Why Food Aid?* Baltimore: John Hopkins University Press.

————. (1996). *United States Development Assistance Policy: The Domestic Politics of Foreign Economic Aid*, Baltimore: John Hopkins University Press.

Sahn, David and Harold Alderman (1992). "The Effect of Food Subsidies on Labour Supply," Paper presented to the *World Bank Conference on Public Expenditures and the Poor: Incidence and Targeting*, Washington, DC: World Bank.

Sharma, R. and Thomas Poleman (1993). *The New Economics of the Green Revolution*, Ithaca: Cornell University Press.

Schultz, Theodore W. (1953). *The Economic Organisation of Agriculture*. New York: McGraw Hill.

Science (1999) "Plant Biotechnology: Food and Needs," *Science*.

Sen, Amartya (1992). *Inequality Re-Examined*. Oxford: Oxford University Press.

———. (1981). *Poverty and Famines: An Essay on Entitlement and Deprivation*, Oxford: Oxford University Press.

———. (1976). "Poverty: An Ordinal Approach to Measurement," *Econometrica*, 46:437-446.

Siamwalla, Ammar (1983). *The World Rice Market: Structure, Conduct, and Performance*, Washington International Food Policy Research Institute, Research No. 30.

Singer, H.W., with S.J. Maxwell (1983). "Development Through Food Aid: Twenty Years' Experience," *Report of the World Food Programmeme*, 31-46. The Hague: Government of the Netherlands.

Stryker, J. Dirck and Jeffrey C. Metzel (1998). *Meeting the Food Summit Target the United States Contribution - Global Strategy*, Research Report No. 1039. Abt Associates Inc., Bethesda, MD.

Squire, Lyn (1993). "Fighting Poverty," *American Economic Review*, 83(2): 377-382.

Sukhatme, P. (1981). *Relationship between Malnutrition and Poverty*, Delhi: Indian Assn. Of Social Science Institutions.

Thorbecke, Erik (1991). "Adjustment, Growth and Income Distribution in Indonesia," *World Development* 19:1595-1614.

Thorbecke Erik, Jung Hong-Sang (1996). "A Multiplier Decomposition Method to Analyze Poverty Alleviation," *Journal of Development Ecˀnomics*, (48):279-300.

Timmer, C. Peter (1997) "How Well do the Poor Connect to the Growth Process," CAER Discussion Paper No. 178. Cambridge, MA: .Harvard Institute for International Development (HIID).

———. (1996). *Food Security Strategies: The Asian Experience*, Cambridge, MA: Harvard Institute for International Development.

Todaro, Michael P. (1969). "A Model of Labour Migration and Urban Unemployment in Less Developed Countries," *American Economic Review* 59:138-148.

Viner, Jacob (1953). *International Trade and Economic Development*, Oxford: Oxford University Press.

World Bank (1991). *Assistance Strategies to Reduce Poverty*. A World Bank Policy Paper, Washington, DC: The World Bank.

———. (1990.) *World Development Report* 1990, New York: Oxford University Press.

9

Some Aspects of Total Factor Productivity in Indian Agriculture

K.L. KRISHNA

1. Introduction

Nearly 50 years ago, Abramovitz (1956) and Solow (1957) highlighted the large contributions of total factor productivity (TFP) to output growth. Since the causes of TFP growth (TFPG) were not known, a debate started which has not so far been fully resolved. Much of the research involving TFP growth has been concerned with attempts to reduce the size of the measured residual (TFP) or to find an explanation for it.

During the past 15 years or so, the literature on TFP growth in Indian agriculture has evolved. Estimates are available for aggregate agriculture, crop sector, livestock sector and even individual crops such as rice, wheat, maize and sugarcane.[37] Estimates have been worked out at the state level for major crops. Concerns have been expressed on the basis of available evidence that agricultural growth is becoming unsustainable as a result of resource degradation. There is a case for policy reform to deal with the problem of resource degradation.

This paper has a limited scope. Using the results of available studies, we deal with three themes:

(i) Assessment of the TFP growth performance of the aggregate agriculture sector in India, relative to that of the non-agriculture sector over the long-term of 50 years, 1950-2000; also relative to the manufacturing sector over the post-green revolution period, 1967-92, when public policy in India attempted to promote both agriculture and manufacturing,

(ii) Comparison of India with a few other developing countries in regard to TFP growth in agriculture and its components, technical change and change in technical efficiency, and

---

37. See Kumar and Hussain, 2004, and Pingali and Heisey, 2001, for a review of studies.

   (iii) Brief review of the determinants of TFP growth in Indian agriculture

The paper is structured as follows. In section 2, issues in the interpretation and explanation of TFP growth are discussed. The different methods of estimating TFP growth are introduced in Section 3. We address theme one of the paper in Section 4. Apart from presenting the long-term assessment of relative productivity performance of agriculture over the period 1950-2000, we examine the performance over shorter periods on the basis of Sivasubramonian's (2004) work. We then take up Dholakia's comparison of the productivity performance between pre-liberalisation period (1960-85) and post-liberalisation period (1986-2001) and finally, the more meaningful comparison between agriculture and manufacturing will be attempted. Section 5 deals with the second theme of the paper: Indian performance is compared with that of China and that of other countries in South Asia. This section contains also a somewhat detailed comparison between Indian Punjab and Pakistan Punjab. The evidence on the determinants of TFP growth is summarised in Section 6. Summary and conclusions of the paper are presented in Section 7.

2. Issues in Interpretation and Explanation of TFP

Problems in the interpretation of measured TFPG have received considerable attention in the literature. There are at least three different interpretations of TFPG (Carlaw and Lipsey, 2003).

   (1) TFPG is technological change (Solow, 1957).

   (2) TFPG is the "Manna from Heaven," reflecting costless spillover externalities from research projects (Jorgenson and Griliches, 1967).

   (3) TFPG is a residual and it is a "measure of our ignorance" (Abramovitz, 1956).

The first interpretation is valid only if technical efficiency does not change and other sources of bias are absent. Since 1957 researchers have tried to reduce the magnitude of the residual.

There are several measurement problems associated with TFPG. Griliches (1987) outlines the following problems/issues: errors in the measurement of inputs, errors in the weights for the different inputs, non-constant returns to scale, omitted inputs (private or public). In view of the clear possibility that some of these errors and omissions may cause large bias in the TFPG estimates, abundant caution is needed in interpreting them.

Prescott (1998) highlighted the need for a theory of total factor productivity. Thanks to the empirical importance of TFP, several models of TFP have been developed. These focus on technological change (e.g. Aghion and Howitt, 1988), externalities including spillovers, economies of scale (Romer, 1900), changes in the sector composition of output and the adoption of lower cost production methods (Harberger, 1998). The relative importance of each of these conceptions of TFP needs to be assessed empirically. But the models suggested provide some guidance in accounting for the measured TFP.

The TFP residual includes the effects of not only technological and organisational innovations but also measurement errors, effects of omitted variables and model misspecification (Hulten, 2000). Jorgenson and Griliches (1967) hypothesised that accurate measurement of relevant variables, for example, correcting inputs for quality changes, correcting capital input for capital utilisation, would help reduce the residual substantially. They produced empirical evidence in support of their hypothesis. They pursued an integrated approach to data adjustments and growth accounting in the light of production theory.

The econometric approach in which appropriate flexible production or cost functions are estimated enables the relaxation of some restrictive assumptions of the growth accounting approach and helps to eliminate certain biases in the TFP residual. The two approaches can be fruitfully combined for the purpose of explaining the residual.

In the wake of "New growth theory," some methodological improvements have occurred (Hulten, 2000):

a. Incorporation of non-competitive models of firm behaviour,

b. Shift in attention to analysis at the firm level,

c. Use of firm–level R&D and patenting data, and

d. Adjustments for product quality improvement.

3. Methods of TFPG Measurement

The literature on the methodology of measurement of productivity and efficiency is very rich and vast. Here we outline three approaches which have been applied in studies reviewed in the paper.

A. The Non-Parametric Growth Accounting (Index Number) Method

Total factor productivity (TFP) is defined as an index of output divided by an index of total factor input (TFI). TFP growth (TFPG) is the rate of change in TFP over time. An important issue is the selection of the appropriate index. Different indexes correspond to different forms of the underlying production function. The Tornquist index is the one most commonly used. It is "exact" for the constant returns to scale (CRS) translog aggregator function and is referred to also as the translog index. The weights in the Tornquist index are averages of the factor shares for the two periods under comparison.

This non-parametric approach requires data on quantities and prices of outputs and inputs. Its chief attraction is the ease of calculation. Its limitations are: (1) it ignores possible technical inefficiency, and (2) in using input shares as weights to aggregate inputs it assumes that there is no allocative inefficiency. For these reasons, the TFPG measure may be biased and there is no way of assessing the precision of the estimated TFPG. The growth accounting definition of TFPG is output growth minus growth of total factor input.

B. The Non-parametric Malmquist Method

The Malmquist index of productivity has come to be used extensively in recent years. It does not require price data. It allows for the presence of technical inefficiency. It is constructed from distance functions. It can be calculated easily by exploiting the property that the distance functions are reciprocals of the Farrel measures of technical efficiency.

A Malmquist output-oriented productivity index is defined as the geometric mean of a pair of ratios of output distance functions. The first ratio compares the performance in periods t and (t + 1) relative to technology of period t, and the second compares the performance of the same data relative to the technology in period (t + 1) (see Grosskoff, 1993). It is the geometric mean of two TFP indices. The first is evaluated with respect to period t technology and the second with respect to period (t + 1) technology.

This productivity index can be expressed as the product of change in technical efficiency and technological change. The technological change term is the geometric mean of the shifts in technology observed in periods t and (t + 1).

The distance functions in terms of which the Malmquist productivity index is defined can be calculated by the linear programming technique.

When the technology has the translog form, the Tornquist and Malmquist approaches yield the same result. However, the two approaches may yield different results if the efficiency differences are not Hicks neutral, or if there are increasing return to scale (Hulten, 2000).

C. The Econometric Method

Depending on the nature of the available data and its properties, a production function or cost function is algebraically specified and estimated econometrically by a suitable procedure. The estimated parameters are used to obtain a measure of technical change. If there is no change in technical efficiency, this measure is equivalent to TFPG. Alternatively, from the estimated parameters, the marginal products of the inputs can be estimated and used in the calculation of a Tornquist index, for example.

The econometric approach has the merit of allowing for measurement error, but it may be subject to specification error. The approach does not allow for technical inefficiency.

Most of the studies on agricultural productivity for India have relied on the growth accounting approach. Some of the studies have interpreted the calculated TFPG estimates as rates of technological change, and this interpretation is erroneous if there is a change in technical efficiency. Some of the studies dealing with several countries, including India have used the Malmquist index. A few studies reviewed in this paper have relied on the econometric approach.

4. TFP Growth in the Agriculture Sector Relative to Other Sectors

The assumption that productivity growth in agriculture is lower than that in manufacturing has pervaded the literature on economic development. This premise is largely responsible for strong policy biases against agriculture and in favour of manufacturing. What is the empirical evidence on this important issue? This issue is addressed in this section. In sub-section 4.1 agriculture and non-agriculture sectors are compared and in sub-section 4.2 agriculture and manufacturing are compared.

4.1 Agriculture-non-Agriculture Comparison

We have two recent studies, which report estimates of TFPG for the agriculture sector, non-agriculture sector and the total economy, making it possible to compare the productivity performance of the agriculture and non-agriculture sectors. Sivasubramonian (2004) and Dholakia (2002) cover the periods 1950-2000 and 1960-2001, respectively. They rely mainly on National Accounts Statistics (NAS) for the basic data for their analyses. GDP in constant prices is the measure of output. Labour, capital and land are the inputs. Sivasubramonian has meticulously documented all the data adjustments and the GDP and input series. He has adjusted the labour input for changes in age-sex composition and education. Both studies have closely followed the Denison (1962) methodology in constructing the time series on total factor input (TFI). TFP index is obtained by dividing the sectoral GDP index by the sectoral TFI index. We shall review the evidence from these two important studies.

Sivasubramonian's TFP growth rate estimates for the two sectors are presented in Table 9.1. Estimates for the period 1950-51 to 1999-2000, and four sub-periods 1950-51 to 1964-65, 1964-65 to 1980-81, 1980-81 to 1990-91 and 1990-91 to 1999-2000 are provided. Comparison between the last two sub-periods may be particularly instructive. The author in his earlier book (2000) on National Income of India in the 20th century reported TFPG estimates for the pre-independence period. These are also given in Table 9.1, although, they may not be strictly comparable with those for the period 1950-2000 on account of the differences in the base period for the output and input series and geographical coverage.

Over the 50 year period 1950-2000 (See columns (2) and (8) of Table 9.1) the two sectors achieved identical rate of TFPG of 1.13 per cent per annum, although the GDP growth of 2.64 per cent in agriculture was less than half that in the non-agriculture sector (5.75 per cent). The contribution of TFP to output growth in agriculture was 43 per cent, compared to 20 per cent in non-agriculture. The dependence of the non-agriculture sector on factor accumulation (80 per cent of output growth) far exceeded that of the agriculture sector (57 per cent).

During the sub-periods 1980-90 and 1990-2000 the non-agriculture sector experienced marginally higher rates of TFPG than the agriculture sector. It is noteworthy that TFPG's contribution to output growth in agriculture was above 55 per cent in both sub-periods. Thus, TFPG seems to have played a bigger role in the growth of agriculture than in that of non-agriculture.

In agriculture, both output growth and TFP growth decelerated in the 1990s relative to 1980s. Such a tendency is not observed in non-agriculture.

In the pre-independence era, 1900-47, output growth and TFP growth were very low in both the sectors. TFP growth was almost zero in agriculture, while it was about 0.6 per cent per annum in non-agriculture (Columns 1 and 7 of Table 9.1).

Table 9.1

Estimates of Growth of GDP and TFP in Agriculture and Non-agriculture Sectors of Indian Economy: 1900-47, 1950-2000

(Per cent per annum)

Item	Agriculture Sector						Non-Agriculture Sector					
	1900-01 to 1946-47	1950-51 to 1999-00	1950-51 to 1964-65	1964-65 to 1980-81	1980-81 to 1990-91	1990-91 to 1999-00	1900-01 to 1946-47	1950-51 to 1999-00	1950-51 to 1964-65	1964-65 to 1980-81	1980-81 to 1990-91	1990-91 to 1999-00
	(1)	(2)	(3)	(4)	(5)	(6)	(7)	(8)	(9)	(10)	(11)	(12)
GDP Growth	0.44	2.64	2.83	1.80	3.43	2.97	1.69	5.75	5.84	4.29	6.77	7.14
TFP Growth	0.03	1.13	1.47	0.08	1.89	1.69	0.57	1.13	1.21	0.07	1.98	2.04
TFPG (per cent) GDPG	6.8	42.8	51.9	4.4	55.1	56.6	33.7	19.5	20.7	1.4	29.2	28.6

Sources: Columns (1) and (7): Sivasubramonian (2000), Table 7.21.
Columns (2) to (6) and (8) to (12): Sivasubramonian (2004), Tables 7.7, 7.8, 7.11, and 7.12.

Notes: TFP index is computed as the ratio of GDP index to total factor input index (TFI). For computing TFI index, land, labour and capital input are weighted by respective income shares.

Dholakia (2002) focuses on the comparison of TFPG in the sectors between pre-liberalisation (1960-61 to 1985-86) and post-liberalisation (1986-87 to 2000-01) periods. His results are summarised in Table 9.2. The performance in the post-liberalisation period was decisively superior in both the sectors. During both periods, non-agriculture witnessed higher TFPG than agriculture, lending credence to the hunches of early development economists. The TFPG in non-agriculture was as high as 3.4 per cent per annum. In both sectors, the acceleration in TFPG in the post-liberalisation period was much steeper than that in output growth.

Given the differences in periodisation, it is not easy to compare Dholakia's estimates to Sivasubramonian's. However, it is clear that Dholakia's estimates indicate a greater divergence between the two sectors, particularly in the post-liberalisation period.

Table 9.2

Estimates of Growth of GDP and TFP in Agricultural and Non-agricultural Sectors of the Indian Economy During Pre-Liberalisation and Post-Liberalisation Periods

(Per cent per annum)

Item	Agriculture Sector		Non-agriculture Sector	
	1960-61 to 1985-86 (Pre-Lib)	*1986-87 to 2000-01 (Post-Lib)*	*1960-61 to 1985-86 (Pre-Lib)*	*1986-87 to 2000-01 (Post-Lib)*
Sectoral GDP	2.13	3.16	4.89	7.17
TFP	0.36	1.34	0.62	3.39
TFPG (per cent) GDPG	16.90	42.40	12.70	47.30

Source: Dholakia (2002).

4.2 Agriculture-Manufacturing Comparison

Martin and Mitra (2001) provides estimates of TFP growth in agriculture and manufacturing for about 50 countries, majority of them belonging to the developing world. India is among them. The extent to which productivity growth converges in each sector is also addressed. In this study, the Cobb-Douglas and translog productions with real value added as the measure of output, land, labour and capital as inputs for the agriculture sector and labour and capital as inputs for manufacturing are estimated from country panel data for the years 1967 to 1992. The efficiency parameter is allowed to vary with country and over time. The data series for the exercise are constructed from the Larson – Mundlak data set developed at the World Bank; supplementary data sources are ILO and FAO.

Relevant results from Martin and Mitra (2001) are given in Table 9.3. For each country and group of countries three alternative estimates were obtained.

Table 9.3

TFP Growth in Agriculture and Manufacturing in Selected Countries: 1967-92

(per cent per annum)

Country	Translog CRS		Cobb-Douglas CRS		Growth Accounting	
	Agri	*Manuf.*	*Agri.*	*Manuf.*	*Agri.*	*Manuf.*
India	1.90	-0.20	1.52	-0.33	2.29	-0.39
Sri Lanka	2.38	-2.00	1.94	-2.00	1.77	-0.11
Pakistan	2.30	2.33	1.70	1.40	3.05	1.85
Low Income (10) country average	1.80	0.93	1.44	0.22	1.99	0.69
Developing (23) country average	2.29	1.74	2.26	0.93	2.69	1.41

Source: Martin and Mitra (2001), Table 1.

Note: CRS=Constant returns to scale.

In each of the three pairs of estimates for India, TFPG in agriculture is positive while TFPG in manufacturing is negative, with TFPG for agriculture ranging from 1.52 to 2.29. The estimates for other countries in the table also establish that TFPG in agriculture exceeds that in manufacturing.

In the Martin-Mitra study, based on a sample of 36 countries, the null hypothesis of equal TFPG in the two sectors is rejected against the alternative of (TFPG) agriculture greater than (TFPG) manufacturing.

5. Productivity in Indian Agriculture in an Inter-Country Perspective

In this section we seek to review the agricultural productivity experience of India in an inter-country perspective. We look at the evidence from recent studies.

Kumar and Hossain (2004) puts together TFP growth estimates for 1961-80 and 1981-2001 for five countries in South Asia. The estimates for four countries for crops and livestock are presented in Table 9.4. The estimates are derived from studies undertaken by Avila and Evenson (2004) and Coelli and Rao (2003).

Coelli and Rao (2003) estimates for the crops and livestock sectors combined show that India and Bangladesh experienced a modest TFP growth of 0.90 per cent per annum during 1980-2000. Nepal and Sri Lanka with growth rates of 0.50 per cent and 0.20 per cent fared even worse. The estimates appear to be based on gross output (rather than value added) version of the production function, and hence should be lower than those based on the value added version. Sivasubramonian's and Dholakia's estimates correspond to the value added version.

Avila and Evenson's estimates for crops, livestock, crops and livestock combined are quite high in most cases. They do not suggest any deceleration in TFP growth in the recent period 1981-2001 compared to 1961-80. Indian performance appears to be the best.

Table 9.4

Estimates of TFP Growth (Tornquist Index) in Crop Sector, Livestock Sector in Four South Asian Countries: 1961-80, 1981-2001

Sector	Period	Bangladesh		India		Nepal		Sri Lanka	
		TFPG	TFPG (per cent) OG	TFPG	TFPG (per cent) OG	TFPG	TFPG (per cent) OG	TFPG	TFPG (per cent) OG
Avila and Evenson (2004)									
Crops	1961-80	-0.23	Negative	1.54	68.1	0.20	13.2	-0.39	Negative
	1981-01	1.06	49.3	2.33	85.7	2.42	66.1	-1.21	Negative
Livestock	1961-80	0.75	42.9	2.63	92.6	1.36	51.3	-2.19	Negative
	1981-01	2.65	71.8	2.66	69.3	1.11	48.5	1.30	1.54
Crops and Livestock	1961-80	-0.01	Negative	1.92	78.7	0.50	27.0	-0.93	Negative
	1981-01	1.30	54.8	2.41	80.3	2.10	64.4	-0.92	Negative
Coelli and Rao 2003									
Crops & Livestock	1980-00	0.90	Na	0.90	Na	0.50	Na	0.20	Na

Source: Kumar and Hossain (2004).

Note: (1) OG=output growth (2) Na=not available.

Rao and Coelli (2004) examines growth in agricultural productivity in 97 developed and developing countries over the period 1980 to 1995. Data from the FAO are utilised. Due to the non-availability of reliable input price data, the study uses Data Envelopment Analysis (DEA) method to construct Malmquist productivity indices. Two major output variables, namely, crop output and livestock products are covered. Five input variables—land, tractors, labour, fertiliser and livestock are in the input vector. Table 9.5 below gives mean technical efficiency (TE) change, technical change (TC) and TFP change over the period 1980 to 1995 for selected countries, Asia and all 97 country aggregate.

Table 9.5

Mean Technical Efficiency (TE) Change, Technical Change and TFP Change in Agriculture-Selected Countries – 1980 to 1995

Country	TE Change	Technical Change	TFP Change
China	1.051	1.016	1.068
India	1.009	1.006	1.016
Pakistan	1.012	1.004	1.016
Bangladesh	1.009	1.002	1.012
Nepal	1.007	0.997	1.004
Sri Lanka	0.998	0.999	0.996
USA	1.000	1.020	1.020
Asia (22 Countries) excluding USSR	1.022	1.009	1.031
All 97 Countries	1.015	1.012	1.027

Source: Rao and Coelli (2004).

The global average annual rate of growth of TFP over the period 1980 to 1995 was 2.7 per cent, the technical efficiency change and technical progress components being 1.5 per cent and 1.2 per cent, respectively. Among all continents, Asia excluding USSR, registered the highest TFP growth of 3.1 per cent per annum, with TE change (2.2 per cent) being the major contributor and technical change (0.9 per cent) playing a relatively minor role. The performance of China was the most impressive, with a TFP growth of 6.8, TE change of 5.1 and technical progress of 1.6 per cent per annum. Both India and Pakistan registered modest TFP growth of 1.6 per cent per annum. In both cases, the contribution of technical progress was secondary: 0.6 per cent in the case of India and 0.4 per cent in the case of Pakistan. Bangladesh with TFP growth of 1.2 per cent fared much better than Nepal (0.4 per cent) and Sri Lanka (-0.4 per cent).

The study finds little evidence of technological regression in developing countries, a phenomenon highlighted by earlier studies. Subject to data and methodological limitations, the study helps to place the productivity performance of Indian agriculture in a global perspective. Although, India did as well as Pakistan and better than other South Asian countries, it fared much worse than China. The Asian average TFPG was high at 3.1 per cent, because of China's dominant position. India's performance was inferior to that of the 97 country average of 2.7 per cent.

The paper addresses the issue of catch-up and convergence in agricultural productivity. Countries, which were below the frontier in 1980 with TE of 0.6 or less experienced TFP growth rate of 4.2 per cent, and countries, which were on the frontier in 1980 achieved a low, 0.6 per cent growth of TFP. These results are indicative of a catch-up in productivity levels during 1980-95, and of a reversal of negative productivity growth and technological regression trends reported in some of the studies for the period 1961-1985.

The results of this study appear quite plausible. As pointed out by the authors, several issues need to be further examined (i) robustness of the results to shifts in the base period for the calculation of output aggregates; (ii) accounting for the effects of land quality, irrigation and rainfall; and (iii) inclusion of pesticides in the input set.

Suhariyanto and Thirtle (2001) reports Malmquist indices of agricultural TFP for 18 countries over the period 1965 to 1996 and then tests for convergence. The sequential Malmquist index, which accumulates data, is used in place of the conventional contemporaneous approach, in which the frontier in year (t + 1) is compared only with that for the previous year, t, ignoring all past history.

Agricultural TFP is calculated using one output, five input technology. Output data are from the USDA World Agriculture Trends and Indicators (WATI VIEW) database and were updated by the FAO Agrostat database, which was also the source for input data. The input variables are the same as in Rao – Coelli (2004) study. Output is defined as total value of agricultural production expressed in 1979-81 international (PPP) dollars, including food and non-food items.

The TFP growth rates for the sequential Malmquist TFP indices and their components EC (efficiency change) and TC (technical change) are given in Table 9.6 for countries in South Asia, for China, and Asia.

Table 9.6

Starting Level and Annual Growth Rate of the Malmquist Index of Agricultural TFP and its Components (per cent per annum) 1965-96

Country	1965 Level	1965-96 Growth			1981-90 Growth			1991-96 Growth		
	TFP	TFP	EC	TC	TFP	EC	TC	TFP	EC	TC
India	0.72	-0.50	-1.05	0.55	1.74	1.73	0.01	2.21	0.86	1.34
Bangladesh	1.00	-0.42	-0.77	0.35	-0.90	-0.99	0.10	0.63	0.36	0.27
Nepal	1.00	-0.70	-0.89	0.20	1.65	1.47	0.18	-1.50	-2.14	0.66
Pakistan	0.98	-0.48	-1.29	0.82	1.88	1.56	0.31	1.46	0.26	1.20
Sri Lanka	0.72	0.67	-0.62	1.29	0.14	-0.08	0.22	-0.41	-3.00	2.67
South Asia	0.77	-0.40	-0.98	0.58	1.59	1.53	0.06	1.97	0.72	1.26
China	0.99	0.47	-0.41	0.88	1.57	0.79	0.77	1.17	0.73	0.44
Asia	0.91	0.31	-0.65	0.94	1.38	0.74	0.63	1.63	0.71	0.92

Source: Suhariyanto and Thirtle (2001).

Note: The efficiencies for South Asia and Asia are calculated using the constituent country's share in the value of total output as weight.

The first column gives the starting values, which are the 1965 efficiency levels, calculated from the sequential frontier constructed from pooled data from 1961 to 1965. In 1965, Bangladesh and Nepal were on the frontier. Agriculture in India and Sri Lanka was only 72 per cent efficient. Pakistan and China had efficiency scores of 98 and 99 per cent, respectively.

All the five countries in South Asia experienced decline in TFP over the long period of 1965-96 while China registered an increase of 0.47 per cent. Asia as a whole registered TFP increase of 0.31 per cent per annum.

India's productivity growth performance in agriculture during 1981-90 and 1991-96 was impressive, the average annual rates of growth being 1.74 per cent and 2.21 per cent, respectively. During 1981-90, change in technical efficiency (1.73 per cent) accounted for most of the TFP growth, technical change (0.01 per cent) being negligible, while during 1991-96, technical change (1.34 per cent) was the dominant contributor, technical efficiency change (0.86 per cent) playing a relatively minor role.

According to these results, agriculture in Asia registered TFP growth of 1.38 per cent per annum during 1981-90 and 1.63 per cent per annum during 1991-96. China's productivity growth performance was quite inferior to that of India especially during 1991-96, although, China was very close to the production frontier in 1965. The results of this study are not in agreement with those reported by Rao and Coelli (2004). They do not appear plausible in some respects. For example, the results depict a secular decline (-0.50 per cent per annum) in TFP in Indian agriculture during 1965-96, due to fall in TE. This finding does not accord with those of Sivasubramonian and Dholakia.

Comparison of Indian Punjab and Pakistan Punjab

Murgai et al., (2001) compares the productivity performance of irrigated agriculture in the Indian and Pakistan Punjabs over the period 1966-94, and addresses the important issue of sustainability. The study pays careful attention to quality aspects of the different inputs in constructing the input index. Crop output and livestock products are aggregated into an output index. The Tornquist index of TFPG is calculated from district level data, for different agro-ecological regions defined in terms of cropping systems-wheat-rice, wheat-cotton etc. Three technological phases were distinguished: green revolution phase, input intensification phase and post-green revolution phase.

Growth rates of three partial productivities and TFP for the different technological phases are presented in Table 9.7. In terms of output growth, growth of land productivity and labour productivity in Indian Punjab fared much better than in Pakistan Punjab in almost all cases. Over the period

Table 9.7

Growth Rates of Partial and Total Factor Productivities for the Three Phases of Technical Change: Indian and Pakistan Punjabs: 1966-94

(Per cent per annum)

Technological Phase	Partial Factor Productivities			Total Factor Productivity		
	Land	Labour	Water	Output	Input	TFP
INDIAN PUNJAB (1966-94)	4.4	4.9	-8.1	5.0	3.0	1.9
Green Revolution (1966-74)	4.9	5.4	-22.1	5.9	4.6	1.3
Input intensification (1975-85)	4.5	3.8	0.6 ns	4.3	2.4	1.8
Post-GR (1986-94)	2.9	5.6	0.6 ns	4.5	3.0	1.5
PAKISTAN PUNJAB (1966-94)	2.4	2.5	-1.4	3.2	1.9	1.5
Green Revolution (1966-74)	2.0	-3.9	-5.9	3.2	4.6	-1.4 ns
Input Intensification (1975-84)	2.3	3.0	-1.3	2.8	1.4	1.4
Post-GR (1985-94)	2.9	6.2	1.5	3.9	1.0	2.9

Source: Murgai et al., (2001).

Note: ns = not significant from zero at 10 per cent level of significance.

1966-94, Indian Punjab achieved TFPG of 1.9 per cent per annum, while Pakistan Punjab achieved 1.5 per cent. In the post–green revolution phase, Pakistan Punjab stole a decisive march over Indian Punjab in labour productivity growth and TFPG. Both Punjabs registered higher TFPG in the input – intensification phase compared to green revolution phase, due to time lag between adoption of new technologies and realisation of productivity gains, and better utilisation of capital investments over time.

Productivity performance of different cropping systems varied considerably (Table 9.8). In both states, the wheat-rice system had the lowest rate of growth of TFP. The wheat-cotton system fared best in Indian Punjab with a TFPG of 2.5 per cent, fared very well in Pakistan Punjab too with TFPG of 1.9 per cent. Wheat-maize system in Indian Punjab and wheat–mungbean system in Pakistan Punjab too were at the top in the performance scale.

Table 9.8

Growth Rates of Output, Input and TFP by Cropping System in Indian and Pakistan Punjabs: 1966-94

(Per cent Per annum)

Cropping System	Output	Input	TFP
		Indian Punjab	
Wheat-rice	5.1	3.7	1.4
Wheat-cotton	5.0	2.5	2.5
Wheat-maize	3.6	1.2	2.4
Overall	5.0	3.0	1.9
		Pakistan Punjab	
Wheat-Rice	2.4	2.3	0.1
Wheat-cotton	4.1	2.1	1.9
Wheat-mungbean	4.3	2.3	2.0
Wheat mixed crops	2.6	1.6	1.0
Overall	3.2	1.9	1.5

Source: Murgai *et al.*, (2001).

The study shows that input intensification, especially in the wheat-rice cropping system, resulted in resource degradation in both Punjabs. The impact of resource degradation on productivity growth is assessed by estimating a cost function for Pakistan Punjab with human and physical infrastructure, technical change and resource quality as explanatory variables. Resource degradation is estimated to reduce productivity growth by one-third overall. In the case of wheat-rice system, the negative impact of resource degradation is nearly equal to the positive impact of technological change.

The findings of the study point to the need for policies (1) to promote agricultural productivity and sustainability through public investments in human development, rural infrastructure and research and extension, and (2) to reduce resource degradation by decreasing subsidies that encourage excessive use of inputs.

6. Determinants of TFP Growth in Indian Agriculture

TFP growth is shown to be the product of technological change and change in technical efficiency and evidence on the two components has been reviewed earlier. Pingali and Heisey (2001) review the results of studies on the sources of growth in agricultural TFP conducted for China, India, Pakistan, Brazil, Sub-Saharan Africa and Zimbabwe. Eight of the twelve studies reviewed are for Indian agriculture. Seven of them are for the crop sector or individual crops, namely, rice and wheat.

Agricultural research, infrastructure, agricultural extension and improvements in efficiency were found to be the major sources of TFP growth in agriculture.

Recently, Kumar (2001) investigated through regression analysis the determinants of TFP, in the case of four major cereal crops, namely, rice, wheat, sorghum and maize. His results are given in the Table 9.9. The relative importance of the listed sources are crop specific. Agricultural research is found to be quite important for every crop.

Table 9.9

Crop-wise Determinants of TFPG in India, 1971-95

Source of TFPG	Per cent Share of TFPG Explained			
	Rice	*Wheat*	*Sorghum*	*Maize*
Agr. Research	20.0	54.5	26.6	57.9
Agr. Extension	7.3	1.0	16.8	0.4
Rural literacy	12.9	0.0	26.6	0.0
Rural electrification	47.3	6.8	30.0	21.8
Surface irrigation	12.5	1.9	0.0	19.9
Tubewell irrigation	0.0	35.7	0.0	0.0

Source: Kumar and Hossain (2004).

7. Summary and Conclusions

This paper has three main objectives:

(i) to assess the relative productivity (TFP) growth performance of the agriculture sector within the Indian economy,

(ii) to analyse the productivity (TFP) growth performance of Indian agriculture in an inter-country perspective, and

(iii) to summarise the evidence on the determinates of TFP growth in Indian agriculture.

Recently some very useful empirical evidence on the productivity (TFP) performance of the Indian economy and its two broad sectors, agriculture and non-agriculture, for the period 1950-2000 has become available (Sivasubramonian, 2004). Agriculture with a TFPG of 1.13 per cent annum fared as well as non-agriculture during the post-independence era of 1950-2000. During the first 15 years, 1950-51 to 1964-65, agriculture (1.47 per cent) scored better than non-agriculture (1.2 per cent). In 1980s agriculture (1.89 per cent) was slightly behind non-agriculture (1.98 per cent). During 1990s when agricultural output growth decelerated, non-agriculture (2.04 per cent) went far ahead of agriculture (1.69 per cent).

Dholakia (2002) is another important source of information on the relative productivity performance of agriculture and non-agriculture sectors in India. His perodisation was designed to bring out the contrast between pre-liberalisation and post-liberalisation periods. In both the periods, and more sharply in the post-liberalisation period, agriculture was found to be far behind non-agriculture in TFP growth. In agriculture, TFPG improved from 0.36 per cent in the first period to 1.34 per cent in the second, while in non-agriculture it improved quite phenomenally from 0.62 per cent to 3.39 per cent. Thus, the divergence between the two sectors was very sharp, contradicting the evidence from Sivasubramonian study. The differences between the two studies need to be reconciled.

Using the material in Martin and Mitra (2001) we have compared the performance of agriculture and manufacturing sectors in India over the period 1967-92. While Indian agriculture achieved a TFP growth rate of 1.90 per cent, per annum, manufacturing with a TFPG of -0.20 per cent fared very badly. There is little evidence in this study in support of the premise of early development economists that agriculture is characterised by lower productivity compared to manufacturing.

To examine productivity in Indian agriculture in an inter-country perspective we have reviewed the evidence from four studies. Two studies relied on Malmquist index and provided a decomposition of TFP growth into technical change and change in technical efficiency. Indian agriculture appears to have performed relatively well in the post-green revolution period. Change in technical efficiency was quite large in some periods, so that TFP growth and technical change cannot be treated as synonymous. The results are quite interesting, although, they are not always robust. The results based on the Malmquist index appear to be sensitive to measurement errors.

We have reviewed comparative agricultural productivity performance in Indian Punjab and Pakistan Punjab. Indian Punjab fared better in terms of output growth and TFP growth. In both Punjabs in the post-green revolution phase (1985-94) growth showed signs of unsustainability especially in the wheat-rice cropping system, because of resource degradation. Suitable policy measures to discourage input intensification and to expand infrastructure facilities would facilitate sustainable growth.

One attractive feature of research studies on agricultural productivity is that several of them have addressed the issue of explaining the measured TFP growth. The available evidence shows that agriculture research is an important determinant of TFP growth for each of the four important crops, rice, wheat, sorghum and maize. Next in importance are agriculture extension and rural infrastructure.

Productivity and in particular total factor productivity continues to be an important research area in view of the important role of productivity in the growth process. The pitfalls in productivity measurement and difficulties in the interpretation of the empirical measures should be kept in mind in drawing conclusions from productivity studies. There is considerable scope for improvement in the quality of data needed for productivity research. The differences in productivity growth estimates of different studies need to be reconciled. The substantive concern about resource degradation and sustainability of agricultural growth warrants urgent policy attention, so that productive potential of the sector is fully realised.

References

Abramovitz, M. (1956). "Resource and Output Trends in the US since 1970," *American Economic Review*, 46, 5-23.

Aghion, P. and P. Howitt (1998). *Endogenous Growth Theory*, Cambridge Mass: MIT.

Avila, A.F. and R.E. Evenson "TFP Calculations from FAO Data" unpublished, citied in Kumar and Hossain.

Carlaw, K.I. and R.G. Lipsey (2003). "Productivity, Technology and Economic Growth: What is the Relationship?" *Journal of Economic Surveys*, Vol. 17, No. 3, 453-495.

Coelli T.J. and D.S. Prasada Rao (2003). "Total Factor Productivity Growth in Agriculture: A Malmquist Index of 93 Countries, 1980-2000" cited in Kumar and Hossain (2004).

Denison, E.F. (1962). *The Sources of Economic Growth in the United States and Alternative Before US*, New York: Committee for Economic Development.

Dholakia, B.H. (2002). "Sources of India's Accelerated Growth and the Vision of Indian Economy in 2020" *Indian Economic Journal* Vol. 49, No. 4.

Easterly, W. and R. Levine (2001). "Its not Factor Accumulation: Stylized Facts and Growth Models," *World Bank Economic Review*, Vol. 5, No. 2.

Griliches, Z. (1987). "Productivity: Measurement Problems" in Eatwell *et al.* (eds) *The New Palgrave, A Dictionary of Economics*, London: Macmillan.

Grosskopf, S. (1993). "Efficiency and Productivity," in H.O., Fried, C.A.K. Lovell, S.S. Schmidt (eds). *The Measurement of Productive Efficiency: Techniques and Application*, New York: OUP.

Harberger, A.C. (1998). "A Vision of the Growth Process," *American Economic Review*, 88 (1): 1-32.

Hulten, C.R. (2000). *Total Factor Productivity: A Short Biography*, NBER Working Paper 7471.

Jorgenson, D.W. and Z. Griliches (1967). "The Explanation of Productivity Change," *Review of Economic Studies* 34: 349-83

Kumar, P. (2001). "Agricultural Performance and Productivity" in S.S. Achrya and D.P. Chaudhry (eds.) *Indian Agriculture at the Cross Roads*, New Delhi: Rawat Publications.

Kumar, P. and M. Hossain (2004). "Agriculture Development in South Asia" in R.E. Evenson, P. Pingali, and T.P. Schultz (eds.), *Handbook of Agricultural Economics: Agriculture Development, Farmers, Farm Production and Farm Markets*, mimeo.

Martin, W. and D. Mitra (2001). "Productivity Growth and Convergence in Agriculture *versus* Manufacturing," *Economic Development and Cultural Change*, Vol. 49, No. 2,

Murgai, R., M. Ali and D. Byerlee (2001). "Productivity Growth and Sustainability in Post-Green Revolution Agriculture: the Case of the Indian and Pakistan Punjabs," *The World Bank Research Observer* Vol. 16, No. 2 (Fall): 199-218.

Pingali P.L. and P.W. Heisey (2001). "Cereal Crop Productivity in Developing Counties; Past Trends and Future Prospects," in J.H. Alston *et al.* (eds.). *Agricultural Science Policy: Changing Global Agenda*, Johan Hopkins University Press, Baltimore.

Prescott, Edward (1998). "Needed a Theory of Total Factor Productivity," *International Economic Review*, 39 (3): 525-32.

Rao, D.S.P. and T.J. Coelli (2004). "Catch-up and Convergence in Global Agricultural Productivity in Special Issues on Productivity" in Special Issue on Productivity of *Indian Economic Review*, (forthcoming).

Romer, P.M. (1990). "Endogenous Technological Change," *Journal of Political Economy*, 98: pp. 71-102.

Ruttan, V.W. (2002). "Productivity Growth in World Agriculture: Sources and Constraints," *Journal of Economic Perspectives*, 16, 161-184.

Solow, R.M. (1957). "Technical Change and the Aggregate Production Function," *Review of Economics and Statistics*, 39, 312-50.

Suhariyanto, K. and C. Thirtle (2001). "Asian Agricultural Productivity and Convergence," *Journal of Agricultural Economics* 52, 96-110.

Sivasubramonian, S. (2000). *The National Income of India in the Twentieth Century*, New Delhi: OUP.

————. (2004). *The Sources of Economic Growth in India: 1950-51 to 1999-2000*, New Delhi: OUP.

Section III

Equity and Emerging Institutions in Agricultural Development

10

Agrarian Communities Across Asia:
A Provisional Framework for Comparison

YUJIRO HAYAMI

1. Introduction

Social and institutional characteristics of communities, such as tribes and villages, are the basic determinants of production and resource use in agrarian economies. This chapter represents an attempt toward building a conceptual framework for comparing the community characteristics across major regions in Asia. In a previous paper, Platteau and Hayami (1998) advanced a hypothesis to explain the differences in community relationships and structures between Africa and Asia in terms of differences in agricultural production modes corresponding to different resource endowments. Here, I try to examine the applicability of the Platteau-Hayami hypothesis to the explanation of differences and similarities among the agrarian communities of three major regions in Asia, namely, South, South-East and North-East Asia

Needless to say, since community structures vary greatly even within each region, it is audacious to characterise communities in one region commonly in distinction from those of other regions. Therefore, the hypotheses to be advanced necessarily involve broad and conjectural generalisation relative to hard evidence. Moreover, my attempt to build a framework for the three-region comparison is seriously constrained by my ignorance about the communities of South-Asia relative to my knowledge regarding East Asia. It is quite possible that my theorising based on casual observations may sound irrelevant or even absurd to scholars specialising in the study of agrarian communities in India and other South-Asian countries. Nevertheless, I dare to present my "provisional framework" at this stage for the sake of inviting criticism for the input of my future research and, at the same time, to promote the efforts of critics toward constructing a truly relevant framework for comparative analysis.

Following this introduction, section 2 explains the ready applicability of the Platteau-Hayami hypothesis to the differences between South-East and North–East Asia, while section 3 identifies the unique characteristics of communities in India that defy its applicability to comparisons including South-Asia, especially India. Finally, section 4 concludes with the specification of the research agenda for the future.

2. Africa, South-East and North-East Asia: A Continuous Spectrum

In my mind, agrarian communities in South-East Asia lie in the midst of a continuous spectrum ranging from Africa to North-East Asia. Differences in the community characteristics across those three regions seem to be largely explainable in terms of differences in the endowment of natural resources relative to population that is crudely measurable by population density—the lowest in Africa and the highest in North-East Asia such as China, Japan and Korea, while South-East Asia such as Indonesia, Malaysia and Thailand lies in-between. Correspondingly, different modes of agricultural production prevailed traditionally. (The word "traditionally" here means the situation before population explosion in developing economies began in the 1920-30s.) Africa was based predominantly on mobile agriculture including hunting-gathering, nomadic grazing and shifting cultivation with little investment in land infrastructure, while North-East Asia was based on sedentary agriculture with heavy investment in land infrastructure, especially irrigation, represented by irrigated rice cultivation. On the other hand, South-East Asia's dominant traditional mode of production was rain-fed rice cultivation in lowland plains/valleys and shifting cultivation in population-sparse hills/mountains, though irrigated rice cultivation has also been long practiced in several locations such as Java and North Thailand.

Rural communities in Africa based on mobile production systems are tribal, lineage-based societies (Throughout this chapter, Africa refers to sub-Saharan Africa). Production based on direct extraction from natural resources is highly hazardous to fluctuations in environmental conditions, which tend to overshadow the effects of human efforts to increase output. High production risk as well as a weak linkage between efforts and outcomes in agricultural production is considered to underlie "redistributive norms," by which "lucky guys" are forced to distribute their incomes and wealth to other members in the same community. As such, the community norms are detrimental to capital accumulation and economic growth.

Communities in North-East Asia based on irrigated rice cultivation represent an opposite polar case to the African case. A rural community is usually consisted of small family farms or peasants. Because people's settlement is stable in one location where their efforts have been allocated over generations to the improvement of land infrastructure, communities tend to be organised more strongly on locational affinity than blood ties, as appropriately called "village communities." in contrast to "tribal communities" in Africa. Production risk is relatively low under irrigation. However, they are constantly faced with the danger of population pressure on severely limited land resources to culminate in subsistence crisis, especially for poor members in the village community. How to organise collective actions to conserve and augment local commons, especially irrigation systems, has thus, become their central concern. Community norms have been developed to penalise free-riders in the enhancement and maintenance of critical local infrastructure needed to increase output and employment at a pace consistent with population growth. Communities are "tightly structured" (Embree, 1950) in the sense that both the geographical and social borders between one village and others are unambiguously demarcated and that rights and obligations are clearly assigned to individual households relative to others within the village.

Communities in North-East Asia, especially in Japan, used to be rather highly stratified according to differential claims to property rights established on arable land. Accumulation of land property by an individual is not something to be blamed if accomplished by his efforts in both production and investment activities. He is, however, expected to allocate his time and effort to construct and maintain infrastructure vitally needed to his community, including drafting villagers for communal work projects as well as lobbying to the state for the provision of infrastructure. As one accumulates land more than cultivable by his family labour, he usually rent out the excess portion to poorer villagers, while continuing self-cultivation of the rest. To establishing himself as legitimate elite, he must behave as a benevolent patron to his tenant and, at the same time, he himself should work hard on his own operational plot with the best use of available farm practices to serve as a model to his tenants.

It is my impression that the communities of mountain tribes in South-East Asia are similar to those in Africa. On the other hand, communities in lowland rice areas where the majority of population live are similar to those in North-East Asia—village communities consisted of peasant households (except large agribusiness plantations for export cash crops). However, as natural resources have traditionally been much more abundant, the need for conserving and augmenting local commons was lower. Also, until rather recently, an option has been open for villagers to migrate to frontier lands for new land opening. As population was more mobile and the need to construct and maintain local infrastructures by communal efforts was smaller, villages in South-east Asia was "loosely structured" as compared with North-East Asia. Typically, obligations to participate in collective actions for enhancement and maintenance of local commons including irrigation systems have not been established as social norms.

Yet, villages in South-East Asia have their own mechanism of guaranteeing subsistence to poor members in the same community. Similar to the case of North-East Asia, village communities in lowland rice areas in South-East Asia are stratified according to claims to land property rights. The difference is that, instead of taking leadership in the construction and maintenance of local infrastructure vital for increasing output and employment under limited land resources, well-to-do members in South-East Asian villages tend to retreat from doing manual work by themselves on their farms and employ poor neighbours instead even if they have sufficient family labour, while the better-off villagers develop patron-client relationships with landless tenants/labourers. This system of sharing income through sharing work as a guarantee of subsistence to the poor seems to have established as a basic norm in the peasant communities in South-East Asia. Indeed, the rates of dependency on hired labour by small rice farmers in South-East Asia are incomparably higher than in North-East Asia (Hayami, 1998a). While this work- and income-sharing norm had its merit under the traditional condition of relative land abundance and high risk inherent to rain-fed farming, it has been creating conflicts with the need to increase investment and output under the new condition of continued population pressure on limited land resources with closed frontiers.

3. South *vs.* East Asia: A Discontinuity?

It does not appear to me that communities in South Asia, especially India, are located on the same spectrum as those of Africa, South-East and North-East Asia. India is a big country characterised by large inter-regional variations. Yet, it should be safe to assume that, on the average, India's land endowment relative to population and labour force has traditionally been in-between South-East and North-East Asia. Its rural communities are villages with people living on sedentary agriculture. It is difficult to develop irrigation systems in flat flood-plains in the Gangetic delta, such as East UP, Bengal and Orissa. In South-India where decent undulation exists, irrigation systems based on gravity flows, tanks and wells were traditionally developed more commonly than in South-East Asia though less commonly than in North-East Asia. In this region it is my impression that rural communities' capacity of maintaining the local infrastructure is in-between South-East and North-East Asia. In these respects, India appear also belonging to the same spectrum determined by relative resource endowments.

However, the major difference seems to exist in the social organisations of village communities. In East Asia, inter-class differences are economic but not social; in principle (though rare in practice), it is possible for landless agricultural labourers and tenant farmers in the bottom of social strata to ascend to owner farmers and landlords. In fact, many agricultural labourers and tenants are relatives, even sons, of farm operators and landlords. It should be easy to imagine that labour employment and land tenure contracts in such a society tend to be embraced and enforced by the patron-client relationship within a relatively homogeneous group. In this regard, the situation in India seems sharply different, as its class differentiation is based on castes rather than land asset holdings (though these two factors are usually correlated). Typically, farm operators and agricultural labourers belong to different castes across which no agricultural ladder is bridging for both ascension and descension.

It is my impression that the patron-client relationship that characterises employment relations in rural South-East Asia is significantly different from that of Indian villages. In the patron-client relationship in East Asia a landless labourer worked for a certain patron farmer on a number of tasks, often involving domestic work and political supports, over an indefinite period of time under an implicit contract or tacit understanding. Alternatively, the landless cultivates lands in submitting a share of outputs to a landowner, while rendering a multitude of faithful services to the patron. In return, the patron is supposed to guarantee the subsistence of his poor client by giving gift, credit and other forms of assistance in the event of the client's crisis such as sickness, crop failure and troubles with police. In this implicit contract, contents of exchange are not very clearly specified and the balance is cleared in the long run (Scott, 1976). The contract is enforced by mutual trust between the patron and the client as well as their fear of social opprobrium or ostracism against their committing moral hazards and opportunism within a socially homogeneous community (Hayami, 1981; Hayami and Kikuchi, 1981; 2000).

In contrast, according to my limited observation, a labour contract involving a single transaction for one task in one spot of time seems to be more common for farm work in India. Of course, there are permanent labourers who are employed on an annual or seasonal basis. Typically, living in a hut in the backyard of an employer's house, a permanent labourer and his family members look after not only farming but also domestic work. Still, it appears to me that, while he is more strongly subordinate to his master in a high caste, his obligations and compensations are more clearly specified than in the patron-client relationship of the East Asian type involving a complex of unspecified transactions for which the balance will be cleared over an indefinite period of time. Outside the employment for farm work, the *Jajimani* system in which a person or household in a land-owning high caste provides a share of his agricultural produce and some other subsistence allowances to landless low-caste workers in exchange for certain craft and menial services, such as potters, sweepers and laundrymen, is often cited as a typical form of the patron-client relationship in Indian villages (Wiser, 1936; Gould, 1958). However, compared with the case in East Asia, the obligations and benefits expected from the *Jajimani* contract are more explicitly specified and the balance is cleared largely within each year, such as a certain number of pots to surrender in exchange of a certain amount of food per year, even though the contract is expected to be repeated indefinitely. Moreover, the contract enforcement appears to be more strongly based on the coercive power of the high castes on the low castes backed by both religious taboos and the political domination of the high castes in village *panchayats* than mutual trust within a socially homogeneous community (Beidelman, 1959).

Overall, my impression is that there is a sharp contrast between village community structures between East and South Asia—a relatively homogenous community consisted of peasant sub-classes with class differentiation largely based on economic factors *versus* a heterogeneous community, which is socially differentiated by castes. Corresponding to such a difference in community structure, there is a major difference in agrarian structure as measured by the distribution of operational farm sizes, *i.e.*, the dominance in small-scale family farms in East Asia *vs.* coexistence of small farms and large farms based in hired labour even in the food crop sector excluding plantations. This contrast is succinctly expressed by Raj (1988) as follow:

"In Japan, Taiwan and most parts of mainland China, the land-lease markets seem to have functioned for a long time in a manner that inequalities in the size distribution of operational holdings were relatively small and few rural households, dependent on agriculture for their livelihood, were left totally landless. Under these conditions it was in the interest of tenants to raise the productivity of land through more intensive input of labour, even if it helped landlords to increase rent; it was also in the interest of landlords to help them do so through advances of working capital on a selective basis and, where they were far-sighted, through various other initiatives for improving the infrastructure and related farm practices. In South Asia, however, high proportions of rural households have received no land at all or only very small parcels of it through the leasing process and have been, therefore, wholly or largely dependent on wage labour. Most of the land leased out by owners even appears to have gone to relatively privileged categories of households (with often holding some land of their own), which could thereby operate larger holdings employing such labour. (Although, leasing of land to tenants with smallholdings has been widespread in the traditional rice growing regions of India, combined also with systems of crop-sharing, relatively large holdings dependent primarily on wage labour persisted in such regions on an extensive scale). Neither the landlord-tenant nor the employer-employee relationships in such situations have been favourable to intensive use of labour on the available land."

The above statement by Raj finds an empirical support from a comparison between India and Japan. Agrarian structures in both countries underwent major changes due to land reform programmes after the Second World War. Data for 1953-54 in India and 1935 in Japan in Table 10.1 are supposed to represent traditional patterns, whereas those of 1971-72 in India and 1955 in Japan represent post-reform patterns. The traditional pattern in India shows that the concentration of operational land holdings in the hands of large farms was about the same as that of land ownership, measured by either the shares of farms above 3 hectares or Gini coefficients. In contrast, the concentration of operational holdings was distinctively smaller than that of owned land areas in Japan. This difference corresponded to the very high incidence of tenancy in Japan compared with India, as envisioned by Raj. It is interesting to observe that about equal concentration continued in India after land reform between operated and owned areas despite a major reduction in the incidence of tenancy. In Japan, although, data are not available, it is safe to infer that the concentration of land ownership was reduced by the drastic redistributive reform to a level equal to that of operated land under the very low incidence of tenancy.

Table 10.1

Agrarian Structures in India and Japan Before and After Land Reforms

	India		Japan	
	1953-54	1971-72	1935	1955
Share of farms above 3ha (%):				
Operated area	74.5	63.0	24.1	12.7
Owned area	75.8	64.7	50.3	n.a.
Rented-in area	69.6	49.0	n.a.	n.a.
Gini coefficient of land concentration:				
Operated area	.67	.66	.48	.43
Owned area	.69	.66	.65	n.a.
Share of farmland under tenancy (%)	20.3	10.6	47.1	8.9

Sources: 1. India: Fujita (1993, p.93) based on National Sample Surveys of India, no.74 and 215.
2. Japan: Kayo (1977,p.p, 66, 68, 100).

According to Raj, the environmental/technological factors that require an indivisible input in the form of a pair of bullocks in Indian farming may partly explain the dominance of large farms. However, he considers that a more important factor is likely sociological, especially "the privileges and discriminations associated with the caste system and with hierarchies in rural society created by various systems of collection of land revenue in the past" (p. 268). In my interpretation, the major factor that has prevented land-rental market from equalising operational farm sizes could be the lack of mutual trust between the land-owning and the landless classes bifurcated socially, making land-rental transaction costs excessively large. In any case, the bifurcation between mini- and large-scale farms should have a serious implication on agricultural productivity under the condition of negative correlation between farm sizes and land productivity observed commonly in Indian data.

The major difference in community structures between South Asia (typically India) and East Asia (typically Japan), which does not seem explainable in terms of differences in relative resource endowments, might be attributed to different historical paths created by *ad hoc* historical accidents such as inter-ethnic confrontations and wars. Deepak Lal (1991), for example, sought the origin of the caste system to the conquest of Indian Subcontinent by the Aryans; as they invaded from semi-arid winter-crop areas to humid areas growing summer crops requiring more intensive use of labour such as for furrowing, they were confronted with serious labour shortage; the Hindu belief on incarnation and the determination of one's present social status based on his conducts in the previous life was developed as a convenient doctrine for the Aryan conquerors to subdue original inhabitants into dependable attached labourers.

It might be dangerous to emphasise the uniqueness of India too much. I must point out that the agrarian structure in Japan in the early Tokugawa period (17th century) was somewhat similar to that of India with the dominance of large farms based on the labour of extended family members and hereditary servants. Later, with the development of both market and irrigation infrastructure, which induced the diffusion of multiple cropping with commercial crops requiring more intensive care and judgment, the advantage of small family farms increased (Hayami and Yamada, 1991). Scale economies associated with the use of bullock for land preparation was also reduced by the introduction of long-handled spades with steel edges (*kuwa*) for hand hoeing. Subsequently, large farms were subdivided into small family farms through the *de facto* practice of tenancy contracts (which were illegal during the Tokugawa period) to have resulted by the mid 19th century in an agrarian structure similar to that observed for 1935 in Table 10.1. A major question is if the developments of market and irrigation systems have been inducing a similar structural change in Indian agriculture. How strong is the grip of the caste system in preserving Indian agriculture in the traditional Hindu equilibrium? How is the land-to-tillers legislation that by nature discourages the practice of tenancy working as a block to the structural transformation in addition to the caste system?

4. Research Agenda

Besides more intensive data collection on community relationships and structures, a major research agenda appears to be about how the differences in community structures as observed above is related with differences in market and state governance structures. Platteau and Hayami (1996) advanced a hypothesis that densely-populated rural communities with low mobility in Asia motivated rulers to protect peasants as the stable source of expropriating tax; the peasant fundamentalism to consider the protection of peasants the obligation to legitimate rulers seems to have underlain decent provision of public goods to agriculture in Asia relative to other regions in the Third World. This hypothesis seems rather plausible to me in the context of North-East Asia especially, and also of South-East Asia to some extent. I wonder how valid it is in the context of South Asia.

It appears that rural community structures have major implications on market development and performance. High trust accumulated in tightly-structured villages in Japan seems to underlie not only the remarkable development of rural-based commerce and industry in the late Tokugawa to the early Meiji period but also the rather unique, productive industrial organisation today (Hayami, 2001). Japan's experience seems to be replicated in South-East Asia in recent years (Hayami, 1998). I would like to know how this mechanism is working in the recent development of rural industries in South Asia.

References

Beidelman, T.O. (1959). *A Comparative Analysis of the Jajimani System.*, Monograph of the Association for Asian Studies VII. New York: J.J. Augustin.

Embree, J.F. (1950). "Thailand—A Loosely Structured Social System," *American Anthropologist* 52 (April-June), (pp.181-93).

Gould, H. (1958). "The Hindu *Jajimani* System: A Case of Economic Particularism," *Southern Journal of Anthropology*, 14, (pp. 428-37).

Fujita, K. (1993). *Bangladesh Nogyo Hattenron Jyosetsu* (An Introduction to Agricultural Development in Bangladesh Agriculture). Tokyo: National Research Institute of Agricultural Economics.

Hayami, Y. (1981). "Agrarian Problems of India from an East and Southeast Asian Perspective," *Economic and Political Weekly*, Vol.16, (16), (pp. 707-12).

———. (2001). *Development Economics: From the Poverty to the Wealth of Nations*. Second edition, Oxford: Oxford University Press.

———. (1998 a). "Norms and Rationality in the Evolution of Economic Systems: A View from Asian Villages," *Japanese Economic Review* 49 (March), (pp.36-53)

———. ed., (1998b). *Toward the Rural-Based Development of Commerce and Industry: Selected Experiences from East Asia*. Washington D.C.: World Bank.

———. and Kikuchi (1981). *Asian Village Economy at the Crossroads*. Tokyo: University of Tokyo Press (published for North America by Johns Hopkins University Press, 1982)

———. and Kikuchi (2000). *A Rice Village Saga: Three Decades of Green Revolution in the Philippines*. London: Macmillan.

———. and S. Yamada, eds., (1991). *The Agricultural Development of Japan: A Century's Perspective*. Tokyo: University Tokyo Press.

Kayo, N., ed., (1977). *Kaitei Nihon Nogyo Kisotokei* (The Basic Statistics of Japanese Agriculture, Revised edition), Tokyo: Norin Tokei Kyokai.

Lal, D. (1988). *Cultural Stability and Economic Stagnation; India, C. 1500 BC-AD*. Oxford: Clarendon Press.

Platteau, J.P. and Y. Hayami (1998). "Resource Endowments and Agricultural Development: Africa vs. Asia," in Y. Hayami and M. Aoki, eds., *The Institutional Foundation of Economic Development in East Asia*. London: Macmillan.

Raj, K.N. (1988). "Mobilization of the Rural Economy and Asian Experience," in G. Ranis and T. P. Schultz, eds., *The State of Development Economics: Progress and Perspectives*. Oxford: Basil Blackwell.

Scott, J.C. (1976). *The Moral Economy of the Peasant*. New Haven: Yale University Press.

Wiser, W.H. (1936). *The Hindu Jajimani System*. Luckow, India: Lucknow Publishing House.

11

Agricultural Growth and Regional Variations

G.S. BHALLA

1. Introduction

In a sub-continental country like India with wide differences in agro-climatic conditions across various regions it is but natural that there would be marked regional differences in cropping pattern, in productivity levels of various crops and in the levels of overall agricultural development. Crop selective technological innovations can further accentuate these variations. Furthermore, should the rural infrastructural investments also get concentrated in selected regions to the exclusion of a large number of disadvantaged regions; regional variations in agricultural development can get highly accentuated.

Variations in productivity levels in agriculture also lead to significant differences in income levels of a large number of workers engaged in agriculture. This results in large inter-regional variations in the living standards and poverty levels of rural population primarily dependent on agriculture. Further, since quite often agricultural growth is also associated with the growth of secondary and tertiary sectors through input-output and consumption linkages, regional variations in agricultural development also go a long way in influencing the pattern of regional variations in the levels of overall economic growth.

In addition, the policy framework regarding price policy, trade policy and fiscal policies are also influential in determining the growth rates as well as terms of trade of agriculture *versus* other sectors of the economy. The administered price policy also tends to favour those regions that specialise in the production of crops that are covered under guaranteed price regime specially when minimum prices are fixed at highly remunerative levels.

The initiation of economic reforms in 1991 with the aim of liberalisation of the economy and its integration with the world economy marks the beginning of a new policy framework for India. Several elements of new economic policy had important implications for the agricultural sector. First, changes in trade policy and in particular the devaluation of the rupee made many tradable agricultural commodities competitive in the world market. Other strands of new economic policy were gradual withdrawal of input subsidies and raising the output prices with a view to ending discrimination against agriculture and improving the terms of trade of agriculture *vis-à-vis* other sectors of the economy. This, it was expected would provide necessary incentive to agricultural producers to increase their production and exports.

But the main beneficiaries of the new economic policy are also likely to be the well-endowed regions which could diversify their agriculture and increase exports. Contrary to expectations, agriculture failed to show any buoyancy after the introduction of economic reforms. As a matter of fact, agricultural income and output recorded a visible deceleration in their growth rates during the nineties as compared with the eighties.

The objective of this chapter is to review the pattern of agricultural growth at the national and regional level and to examine the main reasons for regional variations in levels and rates of agricultural growth. The chapter also briefly examines how far the new policy framework has succeeded in ensuring higher growth of agricultural output and income by improving the incentive structure in agriculture. If not what have been the main reasons for its limited success? India is characterised by very large regional variations in agricultural development which can be traced to both the difference in agro-climatic conditions and large differences in infrastructural investments including investments in R&D and crop specific technologies over the years. The chapter analyses changes in the regional levels and growth of agriculture. It also examines how far the differences in regional patterns of overall and agricultural growth explain regional differences in standards of living, in poverty levels and levels of labour force diversification.

The chapter is divided into six sections. After the Introduction in section 1 which sets out the main objectives of the paper, section 2 is devoted to a brief review of the performance of Indian economy in general and Indian agriculture, in particular, at the national level. The review covers the entire post-independence period 1950-51 to 2003-04 with a focus on the comparison between the pre-reform period of 1980-81 to 1990-91 and the post-reform period 1991-92 to 2003-04.

Section 3 is devoted to a discussion of the consequences of deceleration of agricultural growth at the national level during the nineties as compared with the eighties. The main issues covered include trends in growth of GDP and Output and deceleration during the 1990s; export boom and its subsequent slow down; and stagnant terms of trade for agriculture. The main reason for deceleration of agricultural growth namely decline in agricultural investment is also highlighted.

Section 4 is then devoted to a discussion of agricultural growth at the regional level. This includes an analysis of regional variations in growth of GDP and output and more important regional variations in per worker GDP in agriculture.

Using recent data on the state level growth of overall and agricultural GDP and incidence of poverty, Section 5 is devoted to an examination of various alternative hypotheses that explain the incidence of total and rural poverty. These include the well-documented relationship between growth of GDP and incidence of overall poverty and growth of agriculture and incidence of rural poverty. An alternative hypothesis that is tested is the relationship of labour productivity in agriculture with the incidence of rural poverty. Finally, this section also looks at the relationship between labour productivity in agriculture and growth of non-farm sector.

Finally, section 6 contains the main conclusions arrived at in the paper and offers some suggestions for reducing regional inequalities.

2. Performance of Indian Economy and Indian Agriculture since Independence

Growth of GDP and Agricultural Growth at the National Level

A perusal of the available data of the first half of the 20th century under British rule brings out that the Indian economy in general and the agricultural sector in particular, recorded rather low growth during this period. Indian economy achieved a major acceleration in its growth rate after independence.

Taking the entire period 1950-51 to 2003-04, whereas gross domestic product (GDP) of India recorded a growth rate of nearly 4.33 per cent per annum at 1993-94 prices, the per capita income grew at an annual rate of 2.12 per cent (Table 11.1(a) and 11.1(b)). This was several times higher than the growth rate of GDP recorded during the first half of the century. Along with GDP growth, growth rate of agriculture also recorded a notable acceleration after independence.

For analysis of overall and agricultural growth, entire period is divided into four sub periods, namely, 1950-51 to 1964-65, 1967-68 to 1979-80,

1981-82 to 1990-91 and the post-reform period of the nineties. Table 11.1(a) and 11.1(b)) below gives details.

Table 11.1(a)

Growth Rates of GDP and Per Capita Income 1993-94 Prices

Years	GDP	GDP Agr.	Secondary	Tertiary	Per Capita Income
1900-01 to 1946-47	1.05@	0.46	1.82	1.66	0.22
1950-51 to 1964-65	3.94	2.54	6.88	4.76	1.86
1967-68 to 1979-80	3.44	2.05	4.23	4.54	1.23
1981-82 to 1990-91	5.62	3.08	7.10	6.72	3.50
1992-93 to 2003-04	6.10	2.38	6.29	8.22	4.21
1950-51 to 2003-04	4.33	2.54	5.54	5.54	2.12

@ Refers to growth rate of National Income at 1938-39 prices.
Source: Sivasubramonian, 2000 and National Accounts Statistics, 2004.

Table 11.1(b)

Growth Rates of GDP and Per Capita Income 1980-81 Prices

Years	GDP	GDP Agr.	Secondary	Tertiary	Per Capita Income
1980-81—1990-91	5.46	3.94	6.86	6.58	3.01
1990-91—1998-99	6.23	1.95	7.45	8.24	4.30

Source: National Accounts Statistics, Various Issues.

During 1950-51 to 1964-65 (the First, Second and Third Plan periods), the overall GDP recorded a growth rate of about 3.94 per cent per annum and per capita income grew at a rate of 1.86 per cent per annum. The growth rate of income from the agricultural sector was 2.54 per cent per annum and that from the secondary and the tertiary sectors was 6.88 per cent and 4.76 per cent per annum, respectively.

The period 1967-68 to 1979-80 is characterised by a perceptible deceleration of growth of the overall and sectoral GDP (Table 11.1(a) and 11.1(b)). This happened primarily because of severe drought and also the after effects of wars and conflicts with neighbours that resulted in a big decline in pubic and overall investment.

The severe drought during 1964-65 and 1965-66 led to a sharp decline in foodgrains production thereby necessitating large-scale food imports under PL 480. Although, the late 1960s marked the initiation of green revolution in the north-western states of India but because of its limited spread, its impact in increasing national food output was only partial. It took considerable time for the new technology to expand to new areas.

The eighties mark a watershed in the history of economic development of India as the growth rates of GDP and the main sub-sectors of the economy recorded unprecedented acceleration during this period. Because of the rapid spread of the new technology to new crops and new areas the agricultural sector which had gone through a serious crisis earlier, showed a marked revival during the eighties. The GDP recorded a growth rate of 5.62 per cent per annum during 1980-81 to 1990-91 compared with a GDP growth rate of only 3.45 per cent during the seventies. Agricultural GDP also grew at a rate of 3.08 per cent per annum compared with only 2.05 per cent during the earlier period 1967-68 to 1979-80.

The Indian economy continued with its high growth of GDP during the post-reform period 1992-93 to 2003-04. At 1993-94 constant prices, the growth of GDP accelerated from 5.6 per cent during the 1980s to 6.1 per cent per annum during the latter period. However, despite a high growth of GDP as well as of secondary and tertiary sectors during 1992-93 to 2003-04, there was a deceleration in the growth rate of gross product from agriculture which decelerated from 3.08 per cent per annum during 1980-81 to 1990-91 to 2.38 per cent per annum during the latter period. The deceleration of growth rates in agriculture was much steeper at 1980-81 constant prices.[38]

Crop Production

Crop production data have been analysed for the period 1949-50 to 2000-01 and various sub-periods namely 1949-50 to 1964-65, 1967-68 to 1979-80, 1980-81 to 1990-91 and 1991-92 to 2000-01 (Table 11.2). The trend growth rate of agricultural output at 3.15 per cent per annum was sufficiently during 1949-50 to 1964-65. But the demand for foodgrains exceeded the supply during this period because of high population growth rate combined with very high income elasticity of food consumption. This combined with serious year-to-year fluctuations necessitated large food imports. Thus, India imported a yearly average of 2.6 million tonnes during the 1950s and as much as 5.9 million tonnes a year during the

---

38. The Statistical Commission of India has expressed serious doubts about the validity of data on fruits and vegetables (GoI, Statistical Commission of India- Report, 2002).

A comparison of NSS data on consumption and production figures for vegetables and fruits by the NHB shows that the given output of vegetables and fruits in 1999-00 was 134.83 times and 258 per cent times the NSSO estimates of consumption for the 55th Round (1999-00).

Table 11.2

All India Compound Growth Rates of Area, Production and Yield of Major Crops

Crop	1949-50 to 1964-65			1967-68 to 1980-81			1980-81 to 1990-91			1990-91 to 2000-01		
	Area	Prod	Yield	Area	Prod	Yield	Area	Prod	Yield	Area	Prod	Yield
Rice	1.21	3.5	2.25	0.77	2.22	1.46	0.40	3.56	3.47	0.81	1.74	0.92
Wheat	2.69	3.96	1.27	2.94	5.65	2.62	0.46	3.57	3.10	1.03	3.27	2.21
Coarse Ce	0.90	2.25	1.23	-1.03	0.67	1.64	-1.34	0.40	1.62	-2.07	-0.54	1.18
T. Cereals	1.25	3.21	1.77	0.37	2.61	1.70	-0.26	3.03	2.90	-0.06	1.86	1.38
T. Pulses	1.72	1.41	-0.18	0.44	-0.40	-0.67	-0.09	1.52	1.61	-0.79	-0.04	0.55
Foodgrains	1.35	2.82	1.36	0.38	2.15	1.33	-0.23	2.85	2.74	-0.19	1.66	1.28
Sugarcane	3.28	4.26	0.95	1.78	2.60	0.80	1.44	2.70	1.24	1.87	2.70	0.82
Oilseeds	2.67	3.2	0.30	0.26	0.98	0.68	1.51	5.20	2.43	0.88	1.62	1.04
Cotton	2.47	4.55	2.04	0.07	2.61	2.54	-1.25	2.80	4.10	2.33	1.37	-0.94
Non-Foodg	2.44	3.74	0.89	0.94	2.26	1.19	1.12	3.77	2.31	1.19	2.41	0.86
All Crops	1.58	3.15	1.21	0.51	2.19	1.28	0.10	3.19	2.56	0.19	1.96	1.09

Source: GoI, 2001, *Agricultural Statistics at a Glance*, Ministry of Agriculture.

1960s. The country had to import 8.8 million tonnes each during the three years from 1965-66 to 1967-68 due to one of the severest droughts faced by the country. This brought home the urgency of augmenting domestic production of foodgrains in the country.

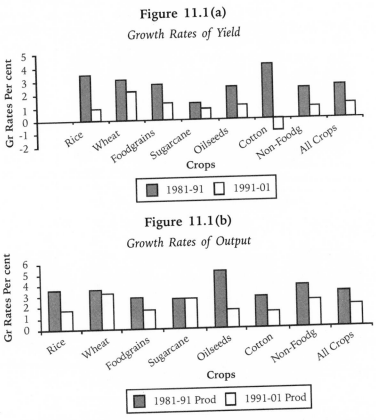

Figure 11.1(a)

Growth Rates of Yield

Figure 11.1(b)

Growth Rates of Output

The introduction of new seed fertiliser technology during the mid-sixties resulted in spectacular increases in output and yield of wheat in the north-western region of India. But since wheat output constituted a very small proportion of total foodgrains output, consequently, in the earlier phase during 1967-68 to 1980-81, the influence of green revolution in the growth of total foodgrains output was at best marginal. But with the maturing of new technology and its extension in most parts of India, growth rate of agriculture recorded a spectacular increase during the 1980s. Taking all crops together, crops output registered a growth rate of

3.19 per cent during the period 1980-81 to 1990-91 compared with a growth rate of 2.15 per cent during 1967-68 to 1980-81.

The new technology was specially successful in raising the output and yield levels of wheat and rice although some other crops also recorded significant increases in their output. Till the mid-sixties the main source of output growth in agriculture was area increases. One of the main contributions of new seed–fertiliser technology was that yield growth increasingly became the dominant source of growth of output after 1966-67. By the eighties yield growth accounted for as much as 80 per cent of the growth of total crop output.

Table 11.3

Use of Major Inputs and Increase in Yields
of Major Crops During 1970-71 to 1999-00

Input Use	1960-61	1970-71	1990-91	1999-00	2001-02
Net Area Sown (mn Hect.)	133.20	140.27	142.82	141.10	..
Gross Crop Area (mn Hect.)	152.77	165.79	188.15	190.32	..
Land Under Forests (mn Hect.)	54.05	63.91	68.39	68.97	..
Cropping Intensity	114.69	118.19	131.70	134.9	..
Net Irrigated Area (mn Hect.)	24.66	31.10	53.00	56.76	..
Area Under HYV (mn Hect.)	1.89	15.38	65.02	76.0	..
Area Under Soil Cons (mn Hect.)	1.58	13.37	35.70	40.23	..
Fertiliser Consumption (mn tonnes)	0.292	2.177	12.550	14.308	19.306
Fertiliser Consmp (Kg per Hect.)	1.90	13.13	66.70	76.05	101.43
Yield Levels (Kg- Hect.)					
Rice	1013	1123	1740	1990	2077
Wheat	851	1307	1740	2778	2761
Oilseeds	507	579	771	853	912
Cotton	125	106	225	225	186
Sugarcane (tonnes-Hect)	46	48	65	71	67
Tea	971	1182	1794	1702	1663

Source: GoI (2001), Agricultural Statistics at a Glance Ministry of Agriculture.

The main strategy adopted to increase the growth rate of agriculture in the post-green revolution period was to increase yields through the use of modern inputs and improved methods of production (Table 11.3). The role of technology as a major input in agriculture was accorded explicit recognition. That major crops like rice and wheat and to some extent some non-food crops recorded very large increases in yields is brought out in the table. The table also gives details about very large increase in the use of modern inputs like HYV's, fertilisers and irrigation. The introduction of positive price policy during the mid-sixties provided the necessary incentive to the farmers to adopt new technology on a large scale.

Deceleration of Growth During the '90s

The beginning of the nineties marked the beginning of new policy framework for India when it launched its policy of economic liberalisation and integration with the world economy. The structural adjustment programme had the objective of bringing macro-economic stability through reducing fiscal deficit, gradually reducing the role of the public sector through privatisation, abolition of controls and licences thereby ending protection to industry and freeing the labour market through cutting the strength of trade unions and also bringing reforms in the monetary and fiscal areas.

The macro-policy package and in particular the trade and exchange rate reforms including the devaluation of the rupee made many tradable agricultural commodities competitive in the world market. Other strands of new economic policy were gradual withdrawal of input subsidies and raising the output prices with a view to ending discrimination against agriculture and improving the terms of trade of agriculture *vis-à-vis* other sectors of the economy. This was expected to give a big incentive to agriculturists to increase their production and exports.

Contrary to expectations, agriculture failed to show any buoyancy in its growth rates after the introduction of economic reforms. For example the growth rate of GDP from agriculture decelerated from 3.95 per cent per annum during 1980-81 to 1990-91 to 2.38 per cent during 1990-91 to 2003-04 at 1993-94 constant prices (Table 11.1(a) and 11.1(b)). As noted earlier, the deceleration works out to be much steeper if calculated at 1980-81 constant prices.

The crop output data also confirm that growth rates of output of major crops recorded a visible deceleration in the post-reform period (Table 11.2). The growth rate for all crops taken together decelerated to 1.96 per cent per annum during 1990-91 to 2000-01 compared with a growth rate of 3.19 per cent per annum during 1980-81 to 1990-91.

A more serious problem was gradual decline in the yield levels of various crops. Thus, whereas the yield growth for all crops taken together decelerated from 2.56 per cent per annum during the eighties to 1.09 per cent per annum during the latter period, that for rice yield growth rate decelerated from 3.47 per cent to 0.92 per cent and for wheat from 3.10 per cent to 2.21 per cent per annum. In the case of cotton yield growth rate has gone down from 4.10 per cent per annum during the eighties to -0.94 per cent during the nineties. In this case the effectiveness of pesticides is declining and the spurious nature of these has failed to prevent complete loss of the crop leading many farmers to a state of distress and driving some of them to commit suicides.

New Economic Policy—Growth of GDP and Per Capita Income

The analysis of data on growth rates of GDP and per capita income brings out that the new economic policies introduced in 1991 were instrumental in accelerating the growth of the Indian economy. Both the GDP and per capita income registered significant acceleration during 1990-91 to 2000-01 compared with all the earlier decades. The growth rate of Indian economy accelerated from about 3.5 per cent per annum during 1950-51 to 1979-80 to 5.5 per cent during the eighties and further to 6 per cent per annum during the 1990s.

Another positive feature was that along with the growth of GDP and per capita income there was a significant reduction in the *incidence of poverty* compared with the earlier periods (Table 11.4).

Table 11.4

Percentage of People Below Poverty Line 1983-2000

NSS (Round) Rounds - Year	Rural	Urban	Combined	Absolute Numbers in Millions	
				Rural	Urban
27 (LS) 1973-74	56.40	49.00	54.90	261.29	60.31
32 (LS) 1977-78	53.10	45.20	51.30	264.25	67.74
38 (LS) (1983)	45.65	40.79	44.48	251.72	75.29
43 (LS) (1987-88)	39.09	38.20	38.86	229.40	83.35
50 (LS) (1993-94)	37.27	32.36	35.97	242.10	76.30
55th (LS) (1999-00) 30 days Recall	27.09	23.62	26.10	194.44	67.48
55th (LS) (1999-00)7 days recall*	24.02	21.59	23.33	172.54	61.68

LS = Large Sample;

* Because of the changes in the methodology of data collection, these two sets of estimates may not be strictly comparable to the earlier estimates of poverty. Economic Survey, 2000-2001, Page 194.

Source: NSS, Household Consumption Surveys, Government of India. Various Rounds.

Deceleration of Growth in Agriculture in the Post-Reform Period

This notwithstanding, it is growth of agricultural GDP that has a more direct impact on the living standards of the peasantry. As discussed earlier, instead of showing expected buoyancy after the introduction of economic reforms, there was a noticeable deceleration in the growth rate of agriculture. At 1980-81 constant prices, the growth of agricultural GDP decelerated from 3.94 per cent per annum during 1980-81 to 1990-91 to only 1.95 per cent per annum during 1990-91 to 1998-99. However, the revised series of GDP at 1993-94 prices show that the growth rate of total GDP originating from agriculture only declined from 3.08 per cent during the eighties to 2.38 per cent per annum during 1992-93 to 2003-04 (Table 11.1 (a) and 11.1 (b)). As pointed out earlier, the main reason for the discrepancy in the two estimates is much higher GDP contribution attributed to fruits and vegetables in the 1993-94 series. But the National Statistical Commission (2001) has expressed serious doubts about the validity of the income data from fruits and vegetables.

Slowing down of growth rates in agriculture has had many serious consequences for peasantry in the country. *Firstly,* a significant deceleration in the growth of crop output and yields has adversely affected the farmers by reducing their income and profitability and has resulted in further deterioration of relative incomes of the agricultural workers. *Secondly,* agricultural exports which had started increasing rapidly after 1991, started slowing down after 1997. *Thirdly,* although the incidence of poverty has declined at the national level, however, the employment situation has deteriorated during the post reform-period. *Finally,* the macro-economic reforms and in particular the trade and exchange rate reforms initiated in 1991 were particularly designed to improve the terms of trade for agriculture. But, hardly any improvement has taken place in terms of trade in favour of agriculture.

Export Boom and Slow Down

One of the main rationales of economic liberalisation was the expectation that the trade and exchange rate reforms would result in significant increases in exports of tradable agriculture. Exports of agricultural commodities did register an increase up to 1996-97, but started decelerating afterwards and the export boom was short lived (Table 11.5). After 1991, growth of exports again accelerated to 6.91 per cent per annum compared with a growth rate 2.24 per cent per annum during 1980 to 1990. Many commodities like rice, meat products, processed foods, fish and fruits and vegetables whose demand is more elastic, registered very high rates of growth during the nineties. On the other hand, some traditional exports like tea and cotton, were not able to sustain their growth rate after liberalisation. Marine products are the largest export earner while oil meals were also a major item in a early 1990s. Recently, oil meal exports have suffered and cotton exports have collapsed (due to shortage of supplies). Sugar has also fared in the same manner, although, its exports increased from 2001 onwards. Exports of spices have shown some buoyancy (Bhalla, 2004).

The growth rate of exports flattened after 1997 primarily because of large decelertaion in the growth of international trade in agriculture consequent to the East Asian crisis. Thus, the world trade in agricultural products recorded a decline of one per cent in 1997, five per cent in 1998 and three per cent in 1999. After recovering in 2000, it again stagnated in 2001. Simultaneously, the international prices started falling for most of the commodities making Indian exports non-competitive. For example, wheat was quoted at $ 90 a tonne that is about Rs. 4000 per tonne as against a procurement price of Rs. 5500 per tonne fixed for the *Rabi* season of 1999-00. Exports also became unviable because of large hikes given to administrative prices of many commodities. India's exports are highly elastic to prices received for exports and have grown faster than world trade when prices are favourable and *vice-versa*. This has damaged India's image as a stable export as the supply declines disproportionately when prices are depressed.

On the other hand, agricultural imports recorded a sharp rise after 1997-98 (Figure 11.2).

Although, India abolished its QR's in 2001, this has not resulted in any surge of agricultural imports. There is an increase in import growth but this is mainly because of large imports of edible oils. Recently, there was also sharp increase in imports of cotton, (because of persistent failure of rains) raw wool and rubber.

To conclude, the trade scenario in agricultural commodities after 1991 reflects the impact of economic liberalisation and steep devaluation of the rupee. Although, the country was able to accelerate its growth rate of agricultural exports, the boom was short lived. After 1996, while there was a deceleration in export growth and imports tended to increase.

Collapse of Agricultural Employment

Another serious development was a notable deceleration in employment growth in the economy from 2.20 per cent per annum during

Table 11.5

Agricultural Exports and Imports and Their Share in Total Exports and Imports

Year	Agr Exports	Agr Imports	T. Exp	T. Imports	Per cent Share Agr Exp	Per cent Share Agr Imp
1990-91	3354.4	1170	18145.2	24075	18.49	4.86
1991-92	3202.5	723	17865.4	19411	17.93	3.72
1992-93	3135.8	892	18537.2	21882	16.92	4.08
1996-97	6862.7	2171	33469.7	39133	20.50	5.55
1999-00	5608	3708	36822	49671	15.23	7.47
2000-01	6256	2611.6	44560	50536	14.04	5.17
2001-02	6146	3049	43827	51413	14.02	5.93
2002-03	6734	3885.4	52719	61412	12.77	6.33
2003-04P	7533	4411	61718	75400	12.21	5.85

Source: *Economic Survey, Various Issues.*

Figure 11.2

Agricultural Exports and Imports in $ million

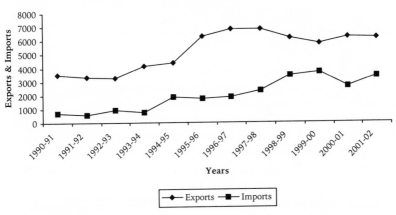

1987-88 to 1993-94 to only 1.03 per cent per annum during 1993-94 to 1999-00. During the nineties, employment growth has decelerated in all sectors of the economy and has almost collapsed to zero in the agricultural sector.

Table 11.6(a)

Growth of Workers UPSS — 1972-73 to 1999-00: Rural plus Urban

	1994-2000	1988-94	1973-94
Agriculture etc. & allied	0.02	2.18	1.49
Secondary	2.43	1.34	3.60
Tertiary	3.01	4.09	3.99
All UPSS Workers	1.03	2.40	2.20

UPSS: Usual Principal and Subsidiary Status

Source: NSSO Surveys for 1972-73, 1977-78, 1983, 1987-88, 1993-94 and 1999-2000.

Table 11.6(b)

Per cent Distribution of Usually Working (UPSS)
by Broad Group of Industry: Rural India

	Male			Female		
	Primary	Secondary	Tertiary	Primary	Secondary	Tertiary
1983	77.5	10.0	12.2	87.5	7.4	4.8
1987-88	74.5	12.1	13.4	84.7	10.0	5.3
1993-94	74.1	11.2	14.7	86.2	8.3	5.5
1999-00	71.4	12.6	16.1	85.4	9.0	5.8

Source: GoI (1999), "Household Consumer Expenditure and Employment Situation in India", NSS Report No. 442 and 55th Round of NSSO.

Second, despite slowing in the growth in the labour force, there was visible increase in open unemployment during 1993-94 to 1999-00. According to NSS, there were 3.98 million unemployed in India in 1973-74 and their number had increased to 7.49 million by 1993-94 and to as much as 9.15 million by 1999-00. In the meantime, the incidence of unemployment (defined as the ratio of unemployed persons to the labour force) increased from 1.64 per cent in 1973-74 to 1.96 per cent in 1993-94 and to 2.25 per cent in 1991-00.

The increase in both the number and percentage share of unemployed is direct consequence of collapse of employment in agriculture. This is more so because the higher growth of employment in the non-agricultural sectors has not been sufficient to compensate for decline in agricultural employment.

Table 11.7

Number Unemployed and the Incidence of Unemployment, 1973-74 to 1999-00

	1973-74	*1978*	*1983-84*	*1987-88*	*1993-94*	*1999-00*
Unemployed (mn)	3.98	7.14	5.95	9.14	7.49	9.15
Incidence of Unemployment (%)	1.64	2.58	1.93	2.74	1.96	2.25

Source: NSSO, Survey on Employment and Unemployment, Various Issues.

Terms of Trade

Finally, in terms of per worker productivity, the relative terms of trade for agriculture have been continuously deteriorating. This is brought out by the fact that whereas agriculture's share in GDP declined from 57.71 per cent in 1950-51 to 24.99 per cent in 1999-00, the proportion of workers engaged in agriculture only declined from about 66 per cent in 1950 to about 60 per cent in the mean time. Consequently, the per worker productivity in non-agriculture which was 1.8 times that of agricultural worker in 1950 had risen to 4.3 times that of agricultural worker by 1999-00. The persistent decline in the relative productivity and income of agricultural workers should be a matter of grave concern for the policymakers in India.

Table 11.8 brings out that no visible change has taken place in the terms of trade for agriculture. The relative terms of trade for agriculture *vis-à-vis* non-agriculture are continuously deteriorating.

Many scholars in India have studied barter terms of trade in detail by comparing the prices paid and the prices received by agriculture relative to non-agriculture. One of the problems with barter terms of trade is that it only refers to higher or lower relative prices received by agriculture. It does not in any way determine the relative movements in income terms of trade. Since income depends not only on relative prices but also on productivity, one way to correct would be to look at the relative movement in productivity along with prices. Or alternatively, implicit price deflators derived from GDP in agriculture and non-agriculture from current and constant prices series could give a rough idea of the movement in income terms of trade. Both barter and income terms of trade are presented below by using these two methods (Table 11.8).

Table 11.8

Index of Terms of Trade Between Agriculture and Non-agriculture

(Base: Triennium ending 1990-91=100)

Year	Combined Index of Prices Paid	Index of Prices Received	Index of Terms of Trade (DES)*A	Index of Terms of Trade (DES)**B
1981-82	61.9	54.9	88.7	91.7
1990-91	110.2	112.3	101.9	95.8
1991-92	123.8	130.8	105.6	101.1
1995-96	173.7	182.9	105.3	101.2
1999-00	214.0	223.1	104.2	105.4

Notes: * A. As compiled by the DES, Ministry of Agriculture.
        ** B. Derived by the author from National Income and NSS.

Figure 11.3

Terms of Trade Prices Received and Paid, DES

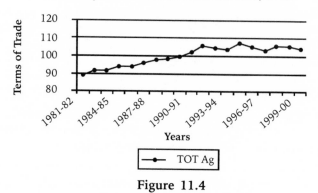

Figure 11.4

Terms of Trade–GDP Deflators

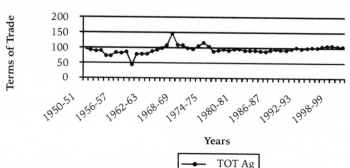

Source: National Accounts Statistics, Various Issues.

The barter terms of trade bring out that there was some improvement in agriculture's terms of trade during the 1990s. But the degree of this improvement was much smaller than that during the 1980s. Furthermore, unlike during the 1980s when a notable improvement in terms of trade was accompanied by a significant increase in productivity, during the 1990s, a small improvement in terms of trade was accompanied by a decline in productivity. Therefore, nothing conclusive can be said about improvements in income terms of trade during the 1990s. It once again comes out that there was only a marginal increase in agriculture's terms of trade *vis-à-vis* non-agriculture. Hence, contrary to expectations and despite large increases given to administered price of important agricultural commodities, economic liberalisation during the 1990s did not lead to any perceptible increase in the fortunes of the agricultural sector.

Reasons for Deceleration of Growth

There are many reasons for the recent deceleration in the growth of agriculture in India. The most important reason is the sharp deceleration in total investment and more so in public sector investment in agriculture (Table 11.9).

Table 11.9

Capital Formation in Agriculture (Rs. Crore)

Year	Total	Public	Private	Per cent Share		GCF in Agr as per cent TGDP	GCF in Agr as per cent GDP Agr
(At 1980-81 Prices)							
				Public	Private		
1960-61	1668	589	1079	35.3	64.7	2.7	5.1
1970-71	2758	789	1969	28.6	71.4	3.1	6.7
1980-81	4636	1796	2840	38.7	61.3	3.8	9.9
(At 1993-94 Prices)							
1990-91	14836	4395	10441	29.6	70.4	1.92	6.6
1995-96	15690	4848	10842	30.9	69.1	1.57	6.2
1999-00	17304	4221	13083	24.4	75.6	1.37	6.0
2000-01	16906	3927	12979	23.2	76.8	1.28	5.9
2002-03	18240	4539	13881	23.9	76.1	1.27	6.4
2003-04*	20510	5249	15261	25.6	74.4	1.31	6.0

* Provisional.

Source: GoI, CSO, National Accounts Statistics, Various Issues.

This has resulted in reducing the potential for future growth. A decline in research investment has had more serious consequences and seems to be the main cause for stagnation and deceleration of yields of major crops. The increased private investment has not benefited agricultural research either. The major reason for decline in public sector investment has been fiscal compression, which has mainly fallen on investment. In India expenditures on interest, salaries, defence and subsidies take away a major proportion of the total revenues. Some half-hearted efforts are made to increase user charges, but many inputs continue to be subsidised. Again, very little success has been achieved in containing and reducing other components of expenditure and raise revenues.

Having discussed the overall pattern of growth of agriculture, the next section is devoted to a discussion of regional pattern of agricultural growth.

3. Regional Patterns of
Agricultural Growth—State-wise Growth

The state-wise income data for the eighties are available at the 1980-81 prices and this series terminates in 1997-98. Data from 1993-94 to 2001 are now available at the 1993-94 prices. We have used both these series. First, 1980-81 constant price data are used for working the state-wise growth rates during 1983-84 to 1993-94. Again data at 1993-94 prices are used for calculating growth during 1993-94 to 2003-04. Strictly speaking to be comparable data should be at the same constant prices. But such comparable series have not been made available by the CSO. The two sets of data are, therefore, at different constant prices. Nevertheless while absolute data are not comparable, the comparison of sector-wise and overall growth rates at different constant prices may not lead to a major error.

Table 11.9 brings out that compared with the eighties, there was some acceleration in the growth rate of GDP and per capita income, during the 1990s both at the national level and for most of the states. Again, most of the states also registered a notable rise in the growth rates of the secondary and tertiary sectors during the 1990s. However, one of the disturbing feature of growth during the 1990s was that as compared with the 1980s, the growth rate of gross product from agriculture decelerated significantly for both India as a whole and for most of the states.

At the all India level, the growth rate of GDP accelerated to 6.01 per cent per annum during the period 1993-94 to 2003-04 compared with a growth of 5.32 per cent per annum during 1983-84 to 1993-94. The growth rates of the secondary and the tertiary sectors also recorded a visible acceleration during the 1990s compared with the 1980s.

Only about half the states of India were able to register an acceleration in their growth rate of GDP during 1993-94 to 2003-04 as compared with 1983-84 to 1993-94. These states were AP, Bihar, Gujarat, Himachal, Karnataka, Orissa, and West Bengal. All the other states registered a decline in their growth rates of GDP during this period.

Basing themselves on the growth rates during 1980-81 to 1990-91 and 1990-91 to 1997-98, at 1980-81 prices, Sachs *et al.*, had come to the conclusion that the best performance in terms of growth of GDP has been recorded by those states that had liberalised their economy the most. The performance of Andhra Pradesh, Gujarat and Maharashtra which registered very high growth during the early 1990s was cited as an example (Sachs *et al.*, 2002). However, the evidence to prove the hypothesis was very weak even on the basis of their own data. Growth rates based on GDP growth data at 1993-94 prices brings out that five states namely AP, Gujarat, Maharashtra, Karnataka and Kerala had done better in terms of GDP growth during 1990-91 to 1997-98 as compared with 1980-81 to 1990-91 as per the 1980-81 series. Out of these five states also, only three had undertaken economic reforms worth the name. Both West Bengal and Kerala, which did not undertake any radical reforms, had also done better during the 1990s.

As per the revised series at 1993-94 prices the states that have performed better in the post-reform period than the all-India average in terms of GDP growth are West Bengal, Karnataka, Himachal Pradesh and Gujarat. Out of these, only Gujarat and to some extent Karnataka can be credited to have undertaken meaningful economic reforms. On the other hand, the growth rates of Maharashtra recorded a significant deceleration in spite of the fact that this state was in the forefront of undertaking reforms. A similar picture obtains in terms of growth of per capita income recorded by various states. The states that recorded a higher than all-India growth in terms of PCY during 1993-94 to 2003-04 were West Bengal, Karnataka, Himachal Pradesh and Andhra Pradesh. The level of per capita income growth in Tamil Nadu and Gujarat was almost equal to the national average. Once again the hypothesis about the positive relationship between the degree of reforms and growth performance of states does not hold. Obviously, instead of making simple generalisations, there is a need to undertake an indepth study of the complex process of growth at the state level in India.

But this apart, a very disturbing development during 1993-94 to 2003-04 was that as compared with the 1980s, agricultural growth rates decelerated significantly both at the all-India level and for most of the states (Table 11.10). For India as a whole, growth rate of agricultural GDP decelerated from 3.05 per cent per annum during 1982-83 to 1993-94 to 2.19 per cent per annum during 1993-94 to 2003-04. The deceleration was very marked in the developed northwestern states of Punjab, Haryana, and Himachal Pradesh. Many other states also registered decline in growth rates of agricultural GDP. The only state where the growth rate of agriculture was significantly higher during 1993-94 to 2003-04 compared with 1982-83 to 1993-94 was Bihar. Although, growth rates were higher in Gujarat and Orissa also, but in their case the results were insignificant.

Table 11.10

Percentage Annual Compound Growth

	1983-84 to 1993-94 At 1980-81 Prices					1993-94 to 2003-04 At 1993-94 Prices				
	Agricult	Secondry	Tertiary	GDP	PCY	Agricult	Secondary	Tertiary	GDP	PCY
AP	3.05	4.79	5.93	4.58	2.42	2.78	5.62	7.26	5.63	4.50
Assam	2.12	3.24	5.10	3.51	1.25	0.51	2.54	5.42	2.93	1.47
Bihar	-0.45***	4.0	4.9	2.69	1.98	2.50	7.70	7.59	5.34	2.74
Gujarat	0.84***	6.9	6.56	5.0	3.11	1.13	7.34	8.03	6.19	4.08
Haryana	4.86	7.35	7.36	6.18	3.66	1.76	6.49	9.75	5.96	3.46
HP	3.08	9.34	6.78	5.89	3.94	1.30	8.85	7.99	6.53	4.74
J & K						3.73	1.50	6.71	4.69	2.13
KAR.	3.54	7.15	7.41	5.86	3.99	3.12	6.95	9.96	7.10	5.91
KERALA	4.4	5.63	5.78	5.33	3.94	-2.00	4.65	7.97	4.85	3.99
MAHA.	5.39*	7.09	8.73	7.42	5.20	1.27	7.00	5.61	4.14	1.97
MP	2.82*	8.02	6.4	5.21	2.73	0.23***	2.87	7.33	4.92	2.96
Orissa	-0.57***	5.95	6.04	3.39	1.51	0.17***	3.13	6.72	3.96	2.55
Punjab	4.62	7.1	4.4	5.13	3.11	2.15	5.11	5.92	4.13	2.44
Rajasthan	3.93	7.85	8.42	6.19	3.71	1.21***	6.54	7.39	5.32	2.69
T Nadu	4.43	5.18	10.29	7.45	6.10	-0.60***	4.08	8.09	5.08	4.06
UP	2.8	6.38	5.95	4.66	2.61	2.18	4.42	4.74	3.76	1.44
WB	4.45	4.57	5.17	4.73	2.47	3.45	6.21	9.70	7.03	5.46
India	3.05	6.17	6.67	5.32	3.50	2.19	6.07	8.21	6.01	4.16
C V	58.72	25.92	23.77	25.43	39.49	102.88	38.33	20.29	22.75	40.24

* Significant at 5-10 per cent; ** Significant at 10-20 per cent; *** Insignificant
All figures without * are significant at 1 per cent.

Source: CSO.

Regional Patterns of Agricultural Growth—Crop Output

State-wise data on crop production confirms the above trend. Data on levels and growth of aggregate crop output of 44 crops at the state and the regional levels are available for 1962-65 to 1996-99 (Bhalla, *et al.*, 2001). Table 11.11 gives details about regional pattern of agricultural growth during 1962-99 and the three sub-periods, namely 1962-65 to 1970-73, 1970-73 to 1980-83, 1980-83 to 1990-93 and 1990-93 to 1996-99.

Taking the entire period 1962-65 to 1996-99, total crop output in India increased at a compound annual growth rate of 2.71 per cent at constant 1990-93 prices. But important changes took place in the regional pattern of agricultural development during the various sub-periods.

Firstly, during the first phase of the Green Revolution 1962-65 to 1970-73, the new technology was only confined to wheat and the main beneficiaries were the irrigated north-western states of India, in particular Punjab, Haryana and Western Uttar Pradesh. Another state that benefited from wheat revolution was West Bengal. The new technology had hardly any impact on rice, the main foodgrains crop, with the result that the rice growing eastern states were not able to derive appreciable gains from the new technology. The southern states of Karnataka, Kerala and Tamil Nadu also registered medium to high growth, but in their case also the new technology could make any appreciable contribution only in limited areas. Crop output in the dry rainfed states in the central region was hardly influenced by new technology and agricultural production in that region was characterised by sharp weather-borne year to year fluctuations.

The second period from 1970-73 to 1980-83 is characterised by the extension of new seed-fertiliser technology from wheat to rice and its spread from Punjab and Haryana not only to eastern Uttar Pradesh but also to the rice producing states in the southern region. Along with Punjab and Haryana, Uttar Pradesh, the largest state of India, also registered an acceleration in its growth from 2.54 per cent during 1962-65 to 1970-73 to 2.77 per cent per annum during 1970-73 to 1980-83.

The third period 1980-83 to 1992-95 marks a turning point in India's agricultural development. At the all-India level, the growth rate of crop output accelerated from 2.38 per cent during 1970-73 to 1980-83 to 3.38 per cent during 1980-83 to 1990-93. An important development was the permeation of new technology to all the regions including the eastern region and the rainfed regions of India. Specially creditable was the performance of eastern states in general and West Bengal, in particular, where the growth rate increased to an unprecedented level of 5.4 per cent per annum. Another important development was a significant acceleration in the growth rates of agricultural output in the rainfed states of Madhya Pradesh and Rajasthan primarily as a result of large shifts of areas from coarse cereals to oilseeds. Thirdly, Tamil Nadu, which had a negative growth during the seventies also, recorded high growth rate of 4.6 per cent during this period.

Widespread growth over all the regions led to a notable reduction in inter-state inequalities in yield levels as also in growth rate of output during the 1980s. The coefficient of variation of yields which had increased from 56.9 in 1962-65 to 58.2 in 1970-73 declined to 46.3 during 1990-93. The coefficient of variation for growth rates declined from 88 during 1962-65 to 1990-93 to 50 during 1980-83 to 1992-95, but increased again to 112 during 1996-99.

Table 11.11

State-wise Growth of Agricultural Output, 1962-65 to 1996-99

State	1970-73 Over 1962-65	1980-83 Over 1970-73	1990-93 Over 1980-83	1996-99 Over 1990-93
Haryana	4.65	3.02	5.04	1.98
Himachal Pradesh	3.33	0.96	2.74	-0.11
Jammu & Kashmir	5.37	3.47	0.17	0.49
Punjab	6.63	4.74	4.22	0.73
Uttar Pradesh	2.54	2.77	3.06	2.47
North West Region	3.60	3.21	3.55	1.91
Assam	1.85	2.80	2.42	1.31
Bihar	1.12	-0.41	2.12	3.33
Orissa	0.99	2.65	2.92	-5.14
West Bengal	2.37	0.68	5.97	2.99
Eastern Region	1.57	1.09	3.63	1.25
Gujarat	1.78	3.12	0.86	6.83
Madhya Pradesh	1.97	1.28	4.53	3.86
Maharashtra	-3.64	6.57	2.12	3.29
Rajasthan	4.29	1.26	6.06	4.90
Central Region	0.73	3.13	3.33	4.50
Andhra Pradesh	0.93	3.61	3.42	1.52
Karanataka	2.64	2.32	3.68	3.62
Kerala	4.09	-0.91	1.92	3.60
Tamil Nadu	2.76	-0.57	4.00	3.25
Southern Region	2.40	1.38	3.43	2.19
All States	2.08	2.38	3.44	2.83
C. V.	**88**	**89**	**50**	**112**

Source: GoI, *Area and Production of Principal Crops in India, Various Issues*, Ministry of Agriculture.

4. Regional Agricultural Growth, Labour Productivity and Rural Poverty

Agricultural Growth and Rural Poverty

The growth of the economy and that of per capita income is accompanied by a significant reduction of poverty in India over a period of time. This notwithstanding even now, India along with China has the largest number of poor in the world. The following section briefly reviews the performance of Indian economy in general and that of agriculture in particular with a view to analyse the relationship if any between growth and poverty reduction.

Several hypotheses are examined below. The first is that state-wise incidence of poverty is negatively related to the growth of GDP. The second is that rural poverty is negatively related with agricultural growth. The third hypothesis is that the state level incidence of rural poverty is inversely related to the level of per worker productivity in agriculture.

These hypotheses have been tested by using the relevant data on state-wise GDP growth and agricultural growth, as well as, state-wise per worker productivity and data on state-wise incidence of overall and rural poverty during different periods. For example, to test the first hypothesis, the state-wise incidence of poverty (rural and urban combined) during 1993-94 was regressed against state-wise growth of GDP during 1983-84 to 1993-94 and similarly, the state-wise incidence of poverty during 1999-00 is regressed against state-wise growth of GDP during 1993-94 to 1999-00. Similarly, the second hypothesis was tested by using the relevant data for agricultural growth and rural poverty and the third one is examined by using the data on incidence of rural poverty and per worker productivity in agriculture during different periods. The results of linear regression are summarised below:

Table 11.12

Hypotheses Test: Results of Linear Regression

Hyp	Dependent Variable	Independent Variable	Constant	Reg. Coeff.	R^2	Sig t
I a	Rural Poverty 1993-94	GDP Gr. 1983-84 to 1993-94	52.39	-3.67	0.198	0.084
I b	Rural Poverty 1999-00	GDP Gr. 1993-94 to 1999-00	37.68	-2.66	0.108	0.214
II a	Rural Poverty 1993-94	Agr Gr. 1983-84 to 1993-94	44.759	-3.620	0.2836	0.034
II b	Rural Poverty 1999-00	Agr Gr. 1993-94 to 1999-00	22.189	-0.039	0.00001	0.990
III a	Rural Poverty 1993-94	PW Prod. in Agr 1993-94	30460	-465.37	0.253	0.040
III b	Rural Poverty 1999-00	PW Prod. in Agr 1999-00	26316	-441.17	0.259	0.037

The data tables and the graphs of these relationships are given below.

It is now increasingly appreciated that it is labour productivity in agriculture that plays an important role in raising rural incomes and in reducing rural poverty. The third hypothesis that is tested by us is that per worker productivity in agriculture is negatively related with rural poverty.

The argument is that increased labour productivity in agriculture results in higher wages and incomes for agricultural workers. Since agricultural workers constitute a very high proportion of work force, the increased income is very widely spread among a large number of workers. This leads to reduction in rural poverty. Furthermore, higher incomes of this mass of workers result in rapid growth of manufacturing and service sectors because of very strong input, output and consumption linkages. The overall result is both a decline in rural poverty as well as in diversification of the economy.

Table 11.13

Growth of GDP and Incidence of Poverty

	GDP Gr. 1980-81 P 1983-93	T. Poverty 1993-94	GDP Gr. 1993-94 P 1994-00	T. Poverty 1999-2000
Andhra Pradesh	4.58	22.19	4.39	15.77
Assam	3.51	40.86	2.33	36.09
Bihar	2.69	54.96	4.45	42.60
Gujarat	5.00	24.21	7.39	14.07
Harayana	6.18	25.05	6.04	8.74
Himachal Pradesh	5.89	28.44	7.06	7.63
Karanataka	5.86	33.16	5.05	20.04
Kerala	5.33	25.43	8.05	12.72
Madhya Pradesh	5.21	42.52	4.93	37.43
Maharashtra	7.42	36.86	5.14	25.02
Orissa	3.39	48.56	6.00	46.15
Punjab	5.13	11.77	4.10	6.16
Rajasthan	6.19	27.41	4.77	15.28
Tamil Nadu	7.45	35.03	8.17	21.12
Uttar Pradesh	4.66	40.85	6.22	31.15
West Bengal	4.73	35.66	4.62	27.02
	$y=52.39-3.67 x$ $R^2=0.198$		$y=37.68-2.66x$ $R^2=0.108$	

We have tried to look at both these relationships. Our results show that both during 1993-94 and 1999-00 per worker productivity in agriculture do have a significant negative relationship with the incidence of rural poverty.

The results of the first hypothesis regarding relationship between GDP growth and incidence of poverty is that the state-wise growth of GDP during 1983-84 to 1993-94 did have a negative and significant (at 92 per cent level of probability) relationship with the incidence of poverty. However, contrary to the often stated proposition, state-wise growth of GDP during 1993-94 to 1999-00 did not make any significant impact on poverty reduction in the states.

Figure 11.5(a)

GDP Growth 1983-84 to 1993-94 and Poverty 1993-94

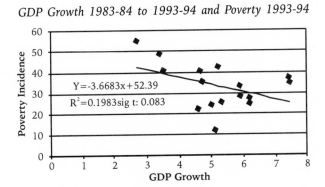

Figure 11.5(b)

GDP Growth 1993-94 to 1999-00 and Poverty 1999-00

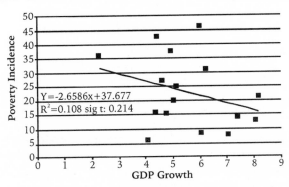

The results of the second hypothesis regarding the relationship between growth of agriculture and incidence of rural poverty are also quite puzzling. Many earlier studies in India based on state-wise data have conclusively established an inverse relationship between rural poverty at the state level and state-wise agricultural growth (Ahluwalia, 1976).

It is interesting to note that during 1993-94 also, the incidence of rural poverty in various states is found to be inversely related to the state-wise growth of agriculture during 1983-84 to 1993-94 and the relationship was statistically significant at about 97 per cent level of probability. But during 1999-00, the incidence of rural poverty was not at all significantly related to the state-wise growth of agriculture during 1993-94 to 1999-00 (R2= .00001, and Significance of t is .990). This needs some explanation.

Table 11.14

Agricultural Growth and Rural Poverty

State	Per cent Annual GR 1983 to 1993-94	Rural Poverty 1993-94	Per cent GR pa 1993-94 to 1999-00	Rural Poverty 1999-00
Andhra Pradesh	3.05	15.92	0.74	11.05
Assam	2.12	45.01	**0.83**	40.04
Bihar	-0.45	58.21	1.04	44.3
Gujarat	0.84	22.18	2.48	13.17
Haryana	4.86	28.02	**1.64**	8.27
Himachal Pradesh	3.08	30.34	0.56	7.94
Karnataka	3.54	29.88	**4.09**	17.38
Kerala	4.40	25.76	0.96	9.38
Madhya Pradesh	2.82	40.64	**2.17**	37.06
Maharashtra	5.39	37.93	1.68	23.72
Orissa	-0.57	49.72	0.33	48.01
Punjab	4.62	11.95	2.01	6.35
Rajasthan	3.93	26.46	**0.50**	13.74
Tamil Nadu	4.43	32.48	1.39	20.55
Uttar Pradesh	2.80	42.28	2.89	31.22
West Bengal	4.45	40.80	4.04	31.85
	y = -3.6197x+44.759 R^2=0.2836		y= -0.0392x+22.189 R^2=0.0000107	

Source: CSO; GSDP Various years.

It is now well-known that there are serious problems with regard to the data on growth of gross product from agriculture at 1993-94 prices, primarily because of very high growth attributed to fruits and vegetables during this period compared with the 1980s. We have already commented about this regarding growth of GDP in agriculture at the all-India level. There is strong reason to believe that this error is also present in the state-wise data on gross product data from agriculture at updated 1993-94 prices.

Questions have also been raised regarding the all-India and state-level data on incidence of poverty during 1999-00. The main reason attributed is the fact that the schedule for weekly recall and monthly recall was canvassed to the same household in many cases. This, it is argued, has introduced a non-sampling error in the estimates. Some authors feel that the extent of poverty reduction during 1999-00 as compared with 1993-94 is much lower than indicated by the official estimates (Sen, 2002).

Figure 11.6(a)

Agricultural GDP Growth 1983-84 to 1993-94
and Rural Poverty 1993-94

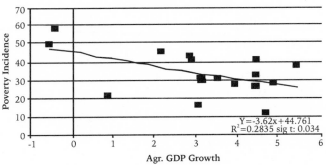

Figure 11.6(b)

Agricultural GDP Growth 1993-94 to 1999-00
and Rural Poverty 1999-00

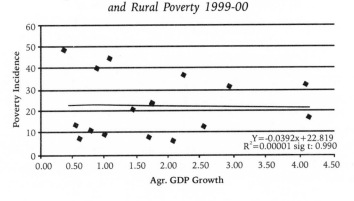

The third hypothesis is that the state-level incidence of rural poverty is inversely related to the level of per worker productivity in agriculture. This relationship turns out to be statistically significant at above 95 per cent level of probability for both 1993-94 and 1999-00.

Table 11.15

Per Worker Productivity and Incidence of Poverty

States	Per Worker Prod. in Agr. in Rs.		Rural Poverty Ratio	
	1993-94	*1999-00*	*1993-94*	*1999-00*
Andhra Pradesh	7,972	9,103	15.92	11.05
Assam	10,461	11,418	45.01	40.04
Bihar	5,413	4,634	58.21	44.3
Gujarat	9,774	9,106	22.18	13.17
Harayana	25,362	28,695	28.02	8.27
Himachal Pradesh	6,960	7,792	30.34	7.94
Jammu & Kashmir	9,243	10,940	30.34	3.97
Karnataka	10,131	13,390	29.88	17.38
Kerala	14,536	18,983	25.76	9.38
Madhya Pradesh	7,792	10,391	40.64	37.06
Maharshtra	9,828	9,251	37.93	23.72
Orissa	7,072	6,856	49.72	48.01
Punjab	30,816	32,425	11.95	6.35
Rajasthan	7,414	9,788	26.46	13.74
Tamil Nadu	9,359	11,476	32.48	20.55
Uttar Pradesh	8,427	10,474	42.28	31.22
West Bengal	13,588	16,932	40.80	31.85
India	11,739	13,495	37.27	27.09
C V	59.01	57.00	33.65	62.57
	For 1993-94; $y=-0.00055x+41.67$; $R^2=0.251$; Sig t$=.040$		For 1999-00: $y = 33.197-0.0009x+$, $R^2=0.21$, Sig t$=.064$	

It may be noted that there were very large differences in per worker agricultural productivity across states. During both 1993-94 and 1999-00, Punjab recorded the highest per worker productivity in agriculture followed closely by Haryana. During 1999-00, Punjab's productivity at Rs.32,000 per agricultural worker was twice that of India, 3.5 times that of Gujarat and Maharashtra and as much as 7 times that of Bihar.

To conclude, per worker productivity differences in labour productivity are the main determinants of differences in the standard of living in rural areas of different states. The analysis has brought out that per worker agricultural productivity had a significant negative relationship with incidence of rural poverty both during 1993-94 and 1999-00.

Figure 11.7(a)

Per Worker Agricultural GDP 1993-94 (Rs. '000) and Rural Poverty 1993-94

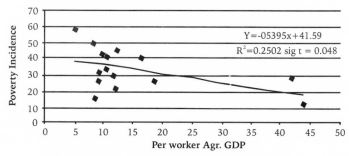

Figure 11.7(b)

Per Worker Agricultural GDP 1999-00 (Rs. '000) and Rural Poverty 1999-00

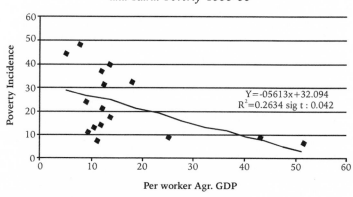

5. Per Worker Productivity in Agriculture and Labour force Diversification

One of the disturbing developments in the Indian economy is that despite a very significant diversification in the sources of income (gross product) generation, there is very little diversification of work force in the economy.

For the national economy, the following Table gives details:

Table 11.16

Share of Agriculture in GDP (at 1993-94 prices) and Employment

Year	Per cent Share in GDP	Per cent Share in Employment (UPSS)
1972-73	44.8	73.9
1993-94	33.5	63.9
1999-00	27.6	60.2

Source: National Accounts Statistics and Survey on Employment and Unemployment—Various rounds.

Thus, even by 1999-00 when the share of agriculture in the GDP had declined to only 27.6 per cent, as many as 60.2 per cent of total workers were still working in the agricultural sector. This implies that the average income of agricultural workers was less than one-fourth of that in on non-agricultural workers indicating a very high inequality among the two groups.

State-wise data indicate that there were large inter-state differences in the extent of work force diversification and per worker income generated from agriculture across various states of India (Table 11.15).

Figure 11.8

Per Worker Productivity in Agriculture in Rupees 1998-99

PW Pr. Agr.

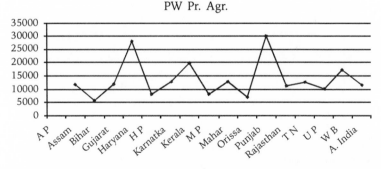

We have already noted a very slow process of work force diversification in India over time even though the diversification in terms of generation of GDP is fairly rapid. It needs to be stressed that real diversification

Table 11.17

Per Worker (UPSS) GSDP by Sectors in Rupees per year 1999-00 at Constant 1993-94 Prices

State	Agri.	Mining Qua.	Manufg.	Elect. etc.	Constn.	Trade	Trampt. etc.	Finan. Servi.	Comy. Serv.	All Sec.
A P	9103	71051	39191	421788	30865	34096	51470	258478	35542	21806
Assam	11418	482567	37054	209019	45071	30894	24916	173252	13535	19233
Bihar	4634	1848	5866	77828	16888	17820	21996	111534	24684	8326
Gujarat	9106	165552	92894	356127	44764	36522	65767	341340	44167	34458
Haryana	28695	17268	86775	35149	46292	44642	83554	292819	39365	44748
H P	7792	0	83019	112385	36277	47574	39149	329186	64340	24917
Karnataka	10940	534358	25981	69194	24343	29149	59805	381592	46157	21574
Kerala	13390	28309	45883	314680	49169	33392	52587	205678	47557	27861
M P	18983	5550	24782	196460	19177	32673	44757	161579	41803	29917
Maharshtra	10391	58096	183905	981653	69409	79185	195936	1729034	82653	47731
Orissa	9251	305878	23937	193495	19757	16865	22167	66292	17488	16268
Punjab	6856	199023	21752	176997	25024	22361	68801	286843	38862	16083
Rajasthan	32425	0	62679	124482	35977	39180	40904	318595	40927	42548
T N	9788	34732	52454	349890	24592	45704	44288	236859	47001	23121
U P	11476	35626	37613	238830	38063	35609	49531	219241	38076	29954
W B	10474	167422	24223	284558	28539	24015	34758	227610	27657	18473
All India	16932	71997	25834	124039	36310	27156	37821	351738	35596	29065
Mean	13038	128193	51403	250975	34736	35108	55189	334804	40318	26828
Stdev	7445	166746	42344	218472	13492	14500	39923	369607	16229	10770
CV	57.10	130.07	82.38	87.05	38.84	41.30	72.34	110.39	40.25	40.14

Source: CSO, Gross State Domestic Product< Various Issues, and NSSO; Survey on Employment and Unemployment.

consists of shifting of increasing labour force from agriculture to non-agriculture activities. In this context, a very pertinent question is to find out what causes diversification of workforce away from agriculture to non-agriculture occupations.

Ishikwa (1996) in one of his seminal papers on China experience of industrialisation put forward the hypothesis that it is per worker productivity in agriculture that constitutes the motive force for diversification of workforce in the economy. The logic given was that an increase in per worker productivity in agriculture leads to widespread creation of income in the hands of millions of workers engaged in agriculture. This in turn leads not only to increased demand for agricultural inputs for sustaining high growth of agriculture but also emergence of agro-processing industries to process increased agricultural and animal husbandry production. But above all, increased incomes of agricultural workers lead to generation of very large demand for consumption goods like processed foods, clothing, footwear, housing, educational and health services and recreational activities. Thus, agricultural growth that leads to higher per worker productivity in agriculture results in the generation of non-agricultural activities on large scale through the creation of input-output and above all consumption linkages.

We have tried to test the relationship between per worker agricultural productivity and extent of diversification in different states of India.

The results are as follows:

Table 11.18

Results of Linear Regression

Hyp.	Dependent Variable	Independent Variable	Constant	Reg. Coeff.	R^2	Sig t
I a	Per cent Share Secondary workers 1993-94	Per Worker Agriculture GDP 1993-94	12.45	0.187	0.178	0.155
I b	Per cent Share Secondary workers 1999-00	Per Worker Agriculture GDP 1999-00	13.71	0.227	0.260	0.044
II a	Per cent Share Non-Agriculture workers 1993-94	Per Worker Agriculture GDP 1993-94	31.07	0.600	0.406	0.008
II b	Per cent Share Non-Agriculture workers 1999-00	Per Worker Agriculture GDP 1999-00	32.71	0.634	0.496	0.002

Figure 11.9

Per Worker Agricultural GDP and Per cent Share Secondary Workers 1993-94 and 1999-00

Figure 11.9(a) Per Worker GDP in Agriculture and Share of Secondary Workers: 1993-94

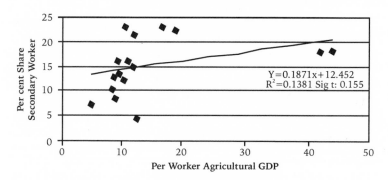

Figure 11.9(b) Per Worker GDP in Agriculture and Share of Secondary Workers: 1999-00

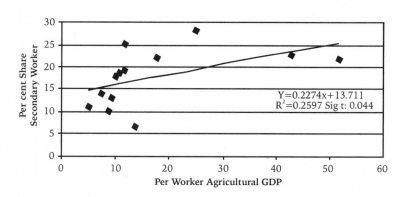

It clearly comes out that per worker agricultural productivity turns out to be a significant factor that determines the diversification of labour force to the secondary and more so to the non-farm sector. This has important policy implications. It clearly indicates that for rapid growth of the economy and its diversification, a very high priority ought to be accorded to a strategy that aims at raising labour productivity in agriculture across the country through large scale investment in rural infrastructure and in scientific research and technology.

Figure 11.10

Per Worker Agricultural GDP and Per cent Share
Non-Agriculture Workers, 1993-94 and 1999-00

Figure 11.10(a) Per Worker GDP in Agriculture and
Share of Non-Agriculture Workers, 1993-94

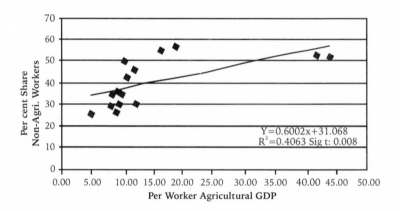

Figure 11.10(b) Per Worker GDP in Agriculture and
Share of Non-Agriculture Workers, 1999-00

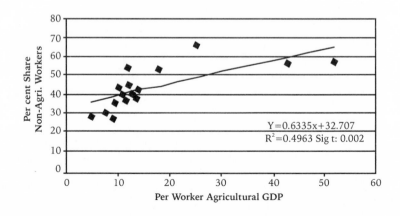

6. Summary and Conclusions

This paper has attempted to analyse the performance of Indian economy in general, and that of agriculture, in particular, at both the national and regional level since independence. For analysis, the period 1950-51 to 2003-04 has been divided into four sub-periods namely 1949-50 to 1964-65 (the pre-Green Revolution period), 1967-68 to 1980-81 (the initial stage of green revolution), 1980-81 to 1990-91 (the maturing of green revolution), and 1991-92 to 2003-04 (the post-reform period).

After independence, the strategy adopted by the policymakers to step-up agricultural growth was first to bring about land reforms and secondly, to increase investment in irrigation and other rural infrastructure. The land reforms by and large succeeded in abolishing landlordism and making self-cultivation the dominant mode of production. But the reforms failed to protect the tenants and most importantly these failed to bring about equitable distribution of land due to imperfect implementation of the land ceiling acts. Consequently, the small and marginal farmers that constitute nearly three-fourth of the total cultivators, account for only about a quarter of the operated (owned) land.

The performance of agriculture during various periods has been analysed here by using both the gross domestic product data as well as the crop output data. Taking the entire post-independence period, the performance of Indian agriculture was quite satisfactory. It was able to meet the food security needs of the population through expansion of its own production capabilities supplemented by imports up to 1980-81. Since then the country became more or less self-sufficient in foodgrains production. Increased agricultural growth also succeeded to some extent to raise the standard of living of the peasantry by raising the productivity levels in agriculture.

But this aggregative picture not withstanding, the performance of agriculture has varied during different period and in various regions.

During 1950-51 to 1964-65 (the First, Second and Third Plan periods), the overall GDP recorded a growth rate of about 3.94 per cent per annum and per capita income grew at a rate of 1.86 per cent per annum. The growth rate of income from the agricultural sector was 2.54 per cent per annum and that from the secondary and the tertiary sectors was 6.88 per cent and 4.76 per cent per annum, respectively. Indian economy registered a significant acceleration of growth after 1980-81 and even more so after 1992-93. But despite an increase in GDP growth, growth of agriculture decelerated during the post-reform period.

A similar story comes out of analysis of crop output data. The growth of output was 3.15 per cent during 1949-50 to 1964-65. But there were large inter-year fluctuations. The demand of foodgrains was very high and, therefore, the country had to undertake large food imports during this period. There was a deceleration of growth during the second period of 1967-68 to 1980-81. The new technology in agriculture, which was initiated during the late 1960s had not yet made its full impact on accelerating agricultural growth. It was only during 1980-81 to 1990-91 that there took place a distinct acceleration in the growth of agriculture. But the tempo of agricultural growth achieved during the 1980s could not be sustained during the 1990s because of failure to undertake adequate investment in agriculture infrastructure and in research and technology. There was a deceleration of growth both in terms of agricultural GDP as well as agricultural output. In terms of crop output the deceleration of growth during the post-reform period was even steeper and in fact the foodgrains production during this period was lower than that of population growth, thereby, adversely affecting the per capita availability of foodgrains in the country.

The deceleration of agricultural growth had some serious adverse consequences. First, this has led to reduced incomes for the workers engaged in agriculture. The second consequence was a slow down in employment growth in all the sectors of the economy and collapse of employment growth in agriculture. A third consequence was that although agricultural exports recorded a high growth rate after the devaluation of the rupee in 1991, the growth rate of exports decelerated significantly after 1997 and has only recovered recently in 2003. Finally, the macro-economic policy changes brought about after 1991, failed to decisively turn the terms of trade in favour of agriculture. There is hardly any improvement either in barter or income terms of trade for agriculture *vis-à-vis* the non-agricultural sector.

Our analysis has also brought out a few interesting features regarding the relative performance of states and relationship between growth and poverty.

One of the popular propositions advanced by some authors was that the states that have performed best in the post-reform period are the ones that have reformed the most. This proposition is not borne out by facts. The only states that have done better during the post-reform period are Bihar, HP, Karnataka and West Bengal and to some extent AP. Out of these only two states namely AP and Karnataka could be credited with having undertaken reforms. Actually it is some of the states like W. Bengal, and Bihar that are big laggards in the matter of economic reforms that seem to have performed better.

We have also tried to find out relation if any between state-wise growth of GDP and incidence of poverty. Similarly the impact of agricultural growth on state-wise incidence of rural poverty is examined.

It comes out that although GDP growth during 1980-81 to 1993-94 was inversely related with the incidence of poverty during 1993-94, such a relationship is found to be insignificant during 1999-00. Thus, the popular belief that GDP growth reduces poverty is not borne out by the available data on growth during 1993-94 to 1999-00 and incidence of poverty during 1999-00 does not seem to hold during 1999-00.

All empirical studies so far had brought out an inverse relationship between agricultural growth and rural poverty. But strangely enough even though this relationship does hold true for 1993-94, agricultural growth during 1993-94 is not significantly related with incidence of rural poverty among the states.

But a very important result that comes out is that it is not agricultural growth *per se* but per worker productivity in agriculture, which is significantly related with poverty reduction in rural areas during both 1993-94 as well as during 1999-00. The relationship is statistically significant during both the periods.

Finally, it also comes out that increased per worker productivity in agriculture is not only instrumental in making a dent on rural poverty it is also the main causal factor in promoting much needed diversification of labour force to non-agricultural occupations. This implies that a great deal of emphasis should be laid on policies that augment labour force productivity in agriculture.

To sum up, despite the fact that as per official data the incidence of rural poverty has declined during the 1990s, the deceleration of agricultural growth during 1993-94 to 1999-00 has adversely affected the income levels and fortunes of a vast majority of agricultural workers in India. The need is to reverse the trend and to accelerate growth of agricultural output. In particular, efforts have to be made to improve production technologies that help the farmers to increase yields and diversify to higher value added crops. The attempt should be focussed on raising labour productivity in agriculture which is woefully low in some states of India.

The new policies introduced in 1991 primarily depend on creating incentive structures for augmenting private investment. These policies were successful in promoting private investment in agriculture but this in itself was not enough to reverse the trend of deceleration in total investment in agriculture. The main cause of agricultural stagnation was a steep deceleration in public investment in agriculture primarily caused due to resource constraints of the central and state governments and policies of fiscal compression.

It would not be possible to regenerate Indian agriculture and enable it to meet the challenges of economic liberalisation and globalisation without accelerating public investment in rural infrastructure and without creating appropriate institutional structures like service cooperatives, trading houses, and market intelligence services that serve the interests of the vast majority of marginal and small farmers.

References

Ahluwalia, M.S. (1978). "Rural Poverty and Agricultural Performance in India," *Journal of Development Studies*, Vol. 14(3), (pp. 298-323).

Bhalla, G.S. (2004). "Globalisation and Indian Agriculture," Volume 19 – *State of the Indian Farmer: A Millennium Study* (27 Volumes plus CD-Rom, Ministry of Agriculture, Government of India), Academic Foundation, New Delhi.

GoI, *Household Consumption Surveys*, Various Rounds. NSSO.

———. (2000). *Cost of Cultivation of Principal Crops in India*, ESA, Ministry of Agriculture.

———. (2002). *Report of the National Statistical Commission*, Ministry of Statistics.

———. *Agricultural Statistics at a Glance*, Various Issues, Ministry of Agriculture and Cooperation.

———. *Area and Production of Principal Crops in India*, Various Issues, Ministry of

———. *National Accounts Statistics – Various Rounds*, Central Statistical Organisation (CSO).

———. *National Accounts Statistics*, Various Issues. CSO.

———. *Survey on Employment and Unemployment – Various Rounds*, National Sample Survey Organisation (NSSO).

Ishikawa, Shigeru, "China's 'Open door' and Internal Development in Perspective of the Twenty-First Century, in Ito,

Sachs, Jeffrey D., Nirumam Bajpai and Ananthi Ramiah (2002). "Understanding Regional Economic Growth in India," *CID Working Paper* No. 88, USA:Centre for International Development at Harvard University.

Sen, Abhijit (2000). "Estimates of Consumer Expenditure and its Distribution: Statistical Priorities after the NSS 55th Round," *Economic and Political Weekly*, December 16.

Sivasubramonian, S. (2000). *The National Income of India in the Twentieth Century*, New Delhi: Oxford University Press.

12

Trade Policies, Incentives, Investments and Institutions in Indian Agriculture

ASHOK GULATI

1. The Question of Farmers' Incentives: Getting Prices Right

It is widely recognised that farmers' incentives are critical for spurring growth in agriculture and alleviate poverty fast. But incentives alone, how-so-ever necessary, may not be sufficient to promote growth and end hunger and poverty. Two other components of the policy package that may be necessary to obtain results are investments and institutions. It is a combination of these three I's – Incentives, Investments and Institutions, that is likely to succeed in getting the growth process on a higher trajectory and finally end hunger from this land.

On the issue of farmers' incentives, Indian policy debate hitherto had been largely dominated by domestic terms of trade. Getting the prices right for agriculture was very much debated, but the debate was largely confined to an autarkic environment. It was presumed that Government had to ensure 'remunerative prices,' to farmers through the price support policies being recommended by the Agricultural Prices Commission (later re-designated as Commission for Agricultural Costs and Prices), which considered several factors in its recommendation of support prices. These factors range from the cost of production to terms of trade, and even international prices, at least in theory.

But a major study by Krueger, Schiff and Valdes (1992), which covered a sample of 18 developing countries from Africa, Asia and Latin America over a period of 1960 through 1985 opened up a new dimension to this debate on incentives. It brought to the forefront how trade and exchange rate policies affect farmers' incentives and thereby potential growth in these countries. They pointed out how the overvalued exchange rate and protection to manufacturing sector had discriminated against agricultural sector in these countries by imposing 'implicit taxation,' of large proportion. This anti-agriculture bias in the trade and exchange rate policies had constrained the growth of agricultural sectors in these countries substantially, by as much as 90 per cent in case of those where implicit taxation was high (-46 per cent) in comparison to those where implicit taxation was light (-8 per cent). India was not covered in their study. But the research done on India by Pursell and Gulati (1993) clearly revealed that India was no exception to this and India too was implicitly taxing its agriculture heavily through overvalued exchange rate, high protection to manufacturing sector compared to agriculture, and by imposing export restrictions on much of agriculture.

What was hypothesised in Rao and Gulati (1994) paper was that with trade and exchange rate reforms, the protection on manufacturing sector would come down which would help bring down the real prices of manufactured goods *vis-à-vis* agriculture, and with gradual removal of export restrictions on agricultural products, agricultural prices would go up relative to prices of manufactured products. This should help move the terms of trade (price incentives) in favour of agriculture and that should help promote investments in agriculture and thereby growth in agriculture. Did that happen?

Figure 12.1 shows how the nominal protection coefficient (NPC) on manufactured products decreased successively during the reform period since 1991 and how agricultural prices improved. Improvement in agricultural prices was partly in response to removal on export restrictions, partly as a result of higher support/procurement prices of wheat and rice, and partly perhaps by increasing tariff on agricultural products.

In fact, if one looks only at the tariff structure in India for the latest years (2002-03, 2003-04 and 2004-05), one would be surprised to see that the average tariff on agricultural products is much higher (47 per cent in 2002-03, 47 per cent in 2003-04, and 40 per cent in 2004-05) than on non-agricultural products (33 per cent in 2002-03, 30 per cent in 2003-04 and only 20 per cent in 2004-05) (World Bank, 2004; vol. II, p.30). This is totally opposite of what was before the reforms began. Indian agriculture in 2004-05, thus, has 7th highest protection in a group of 134 countries (*ibid*, p.35).

Does that mean that Indian agriculture is very uncompetitive? Those who are not very familiar with the political economy aspect of tariffs in India may very well conclude so. But this would be quite far from reality. To know the true price competitiveness, one should at least work out

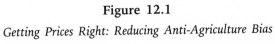

Figure 12.1

Getting Prices Right: Reducing Anti-Agriculture Bias

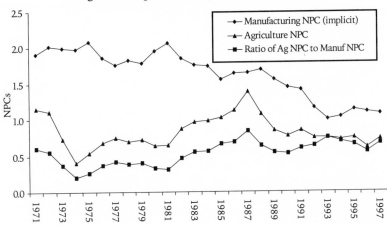

NPCs[39] of major agricultural products for a reasonably long period of time as competitiveness is a dynamic concept and keeps changing with changes in technology, costs and prices. A long term view of comparative prices can capture the impact of these changes in technology on costs and prices. Figure 12.2 (from a to m) presents NPCs of some selected major commodities over a period of 1965 to 2002 under importable or exportable or both hypotheses. For soybean the estimates are for 1974-2002 and for sunflower for 1976-2002 due to data limitations. The crop-specific all India NPCs are derived from state-level NPCs of the relevant crop for major producing states.

The results presented in the figure are self-explanatory: those below unity are price competitive, and those above unity not so. It is quite possible that one commodity is import competitive but not export competitive due to high transportation and other marketing costs, etc. It is also possible that a commodity at all India level (weighted average of state level NPCs) is competitive but is still imported at one port or another due to freight advantage on that port, etc. But broadly, the results of this NPC study do support the actual trade flows that one would expect on *a priori* basis from an analysis of NPCs (Hoda and Gulati, 2004).

39. NPC is defined as the ratio of domestic price of a commodity to its external reference price (cif or fob, depending upon whether the commodity in question is an import substitute or export commodity). The external reference price is duly adjusted for freight and other marketing costs and margins and for quality variation (Gulati and Kelley, 1999 for more details).

Figure 12.2

NPCs of Selected Commodities in India – 1965-2002

Figure 12.2(a) Nominal Protection Coefficients
for Wheat in India 1965-2002

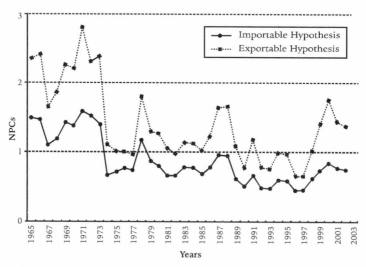

Figure 12.2(b) Nominal Protection Coefficients
for Rice in India 1965-2002

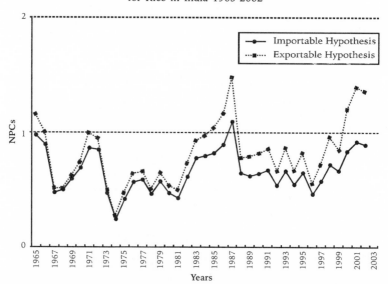

Figure 12.2(c) Nominal Protection Coefficients
for Maize in India 1965-2002

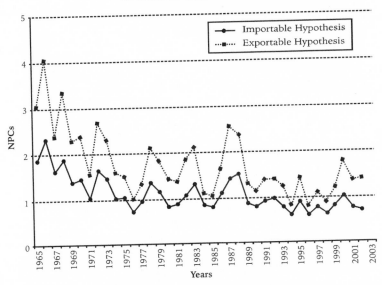

Figure 12.2(d) Nominal Protection Coefficients
for *Jowar* in India 1965-2002

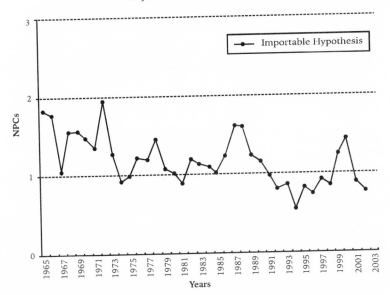

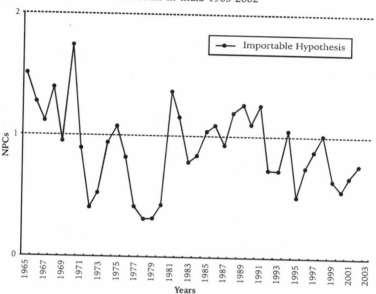

Figure 12.2(e) Nominal Protection Coefficients for Gram in India 1965-2002

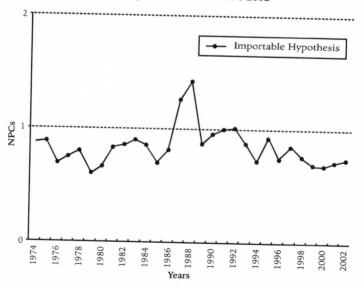

Figure 12.2(f) Nominal Protection Coefficients for Soyabeans in India 1974-2002

Figure 12.2(g) Nominal Protection Coefficients
for Mustard in India 1965-2002

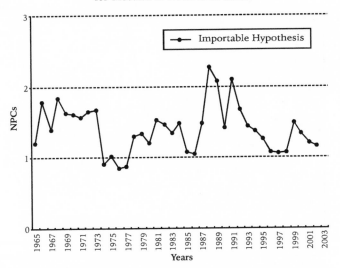

Figure 12.2(h) Nominal Protection Coefficients
for *Copra* in India 1965-2002

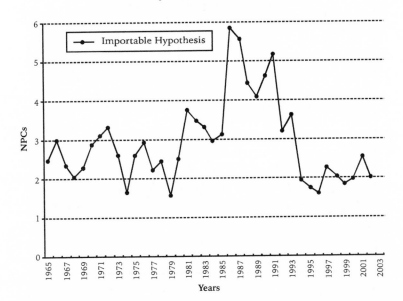

Figure 12.2(i) Nominal Protection Coefficients
for Groundnut in India 1965-2002

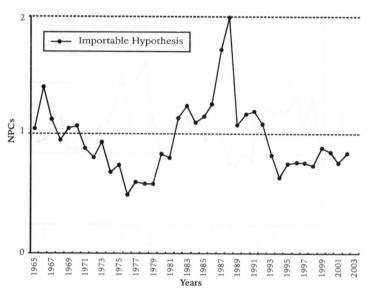

Figure 12.2(j) Nominal Protection Coefficients
for Sunflower in India 1976-2002

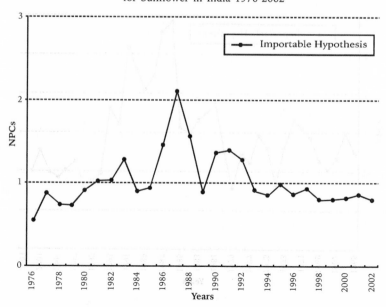

Figure 12.2(k) Nominal Protection Coefficients
for Sugar in India 1965-2002

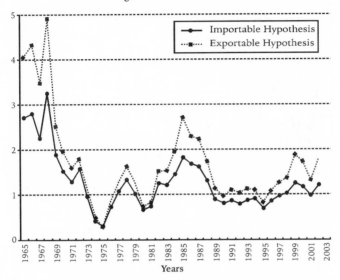

Figure 12.2(l) Nominal Protection Coefficients
for Rubber in India 1965-2002

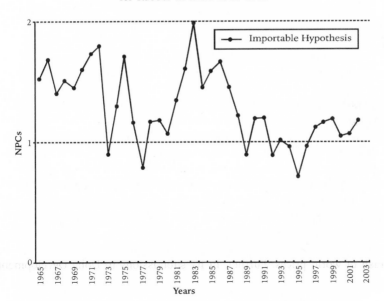

Figure 12.2(m) Nominal Protection Coefficients
for Cotton in India 1965-2002

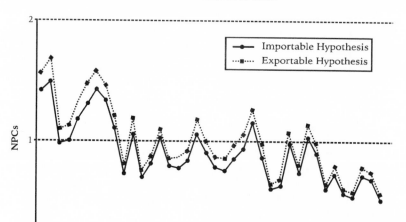

So, as per our NPC analysis of price competitiveness, much of
agriculture is reasonably competitive. Then why does India have high
tariffs for agriculture?

While high tariffs do indicate in general high inefficiency and low
competitiveness, in Indian case, there are a large number of commodities
that are either exportable or efficient import substitutes but still have a
high tariff. The reason for jacking up tariffs was that in April 2001, India
was forced to remove quantitative restrictions (QRs) on imports of
agricultural products as it could not get a waiver under BoP clause any
more under the World Trade Organisation (WTO) rules (Hoda and Gulati,
2004). As a precautionary move, India raised tariffs to very high levels
when QRs were being removed. Also, in 2000-01, one needs to keep in
mind that the world prices of most of agricultural products were still
ruling very low, almost at a bottom since 1987. And OECD countries like
the US were giving emergency payments (market loss assistance) to their
farmers in an effort to compensate them from the losses resulting from the
crash of world prices. Further, in its submissions to Doha Development

Round for negotiations on Agreement on Agriculture, the US had put forth an idea that the negotiations should start from applied tariffs and not bound tariffs. For India, this resulted in raising tariffs to high levels just to ensure enough manoeuvring space in negotiations on market access in case the negotiations really start from the applied tariffs. So, the reality is that there is lot of water in those tariffs. Nevertheless, it must be mentioned that if these high tariffs persist for long, it would surely breed inefficiency on the one hand and hurt the poor consumers on the other.

2. Incentives and Investments in Indian Agriculture

The main role of trade and exchange rate policies launched in the package of 1991-93 was to set the prices right. This meant that prices of manufactured goods would come down and those of agriculture would go up, improving the terms of trade in favour of agriculture. This did happen, as was expected, and also led to rising investments (gross fixed capital formation) in agriculture on private account (Gulati and Bathla, 2002; Landes and Gulati, 2004). It is important to observe that the private sector investments in agriculture, which used to be marginally less than the public sector investments in agriculture during early 1980s are today more than three times the level of investment coming from the public sector at 1993-94 constant prices (Gulati and Bathla, 2002; GoI, 2004). The public sector investments, as measured in National Accounts, in fact have been coming down since early 1980s from more than Rs.70 billion to less than Rs.50 billion at the beginning of this century, at 1993-94 constant prices (GoI, 2004). Even if one adjusts for the investment in and for agriculture, the share of private sector investments in agriculture (GFCF) still remains more than double of that coming from the public sector (GoI, 2003) (Figure 12.3). This seems to have helped some sub-sectors of agriculture, like horticulture and poultry, where demand is growing fast (Landes and Gulati, 2004). But on the whole, the share of agriculture in GFCF has remained weak: on-farm GFCF was only about 6 per cent of the agricultural GDP, while estimated GFCF on agriculture related activities was about 10 per cent, taking the two together to 16 per cent of agricultural GDP, which was still lower than the economy wide GFCF at 26 per cent of GDP in 2000-02 (Landes and Gulati, 2004; GoI, 2003).

Figure 12.3

Relative Prices of Agricultural and GFCF

Agricultural TOT. and GFCF in India

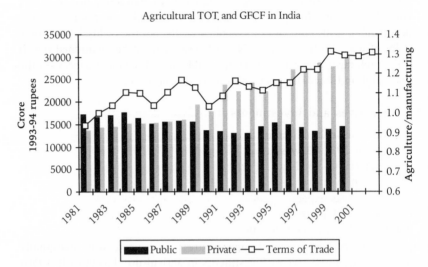

GFCF = Gross fixed capital formation in and for agriculture.
Source: Economic Survey, GoI; Ministry of Agriculture, GoI.

Private sector investment responds positively not only to improved price incentives (terms of trade), but also to public sector investments in agriculture as the latter has an inducement effect on the former (Gulati and Bathla, 2002). This implies that if public sector investments in agriculture had not declined, or had marginally improved, the private sector investments would have increased even faster. So the positive impact of improving terms of trade on private sector investments in agriculture was somewhat dampened by the declining public sector investments.

What has been the impact of this improvement in incentives and private sector investments on the overall growth of agriculture? If one looks at the growth of agricultural GDP during the pre-reform period of say 1980s and compares that with the post-reform period since 1991, statistically, there is hardly any difference. The average annual rate of growth in agricultural GDP during 1992-93 to 2003-04 was 3.17 per cent (GoI, 2004; p.155) as against about 3 per cent during 1980 through 1991. But if one splits the post-reform period into two phases, 1992-93 to 1996-97 as the first phase of reforms and then 1997-98 to 2003-04 as the second phase, one gets very different results. In the first phase of reforms, when the overvalued exchange rate was corrected and tariffs on manufactured goods dramatically reduced, and agricultural exports marginally opened, the agricultural GDP grew by an average annual rate of 4.7 per cent, a remarkable improvement over its performance of about 3 per cent during the 1980s. But this growth could not be sustained and it slumped to 2.1 per cent during the second phase of post-reform era, 1997-98 to 2003-04. Almost similar thing happened to exports and imports. The agricultural exports having surged ahead of imports by a wide margin during 1992-96 came down substantially in the later years primarily as a result of crashing world prices. This necessitated raising of tariffs on imports to stem the flow of imports (Figure 12.4), (Gulati, Pursell and Mullen, 2003). What caused this slump in agriculture growth rate, and in agricultural exports, is yet an open question to be settled in Indian policy debate.

Figure 12.4

Agricultural Tariffs and Trade Flows

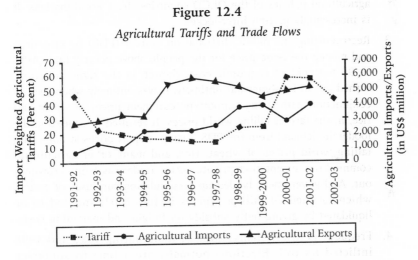

I propose a few hypotheses below that can be tested by rigorous research by anyone interested in this debate. I do not have any firm answers to these hypotheses yet, but I do intend to launch some research on this issue. The proposed hypotheses are:

1. The crash in world agricultural markets, triggered by the east-Asian crisis in 1997, hit Indian agriculture hard. Most of the agricultural prices in the world markets crashed by 40 to 50 per cent during the 1997-2000 period. For India it happened exactly when it was opening up its agriculture to world economy. For emerging export

crops, like rice and wheat, it meant loss of competitive strength in the world markets and confronting a demand constraint, while for import crops, like edible oils, it meant a deluge of imports. This adversely affected the performance of both export crops as well as import substituting crops.

2. The OECD countries, notably USA, resorted to emergency payments to their farmers in an effort to keep their export shares intact in global markets. In 2000, e.g., US support to its rice farmers exceeded the fob price of rice (Munisamy, Mullen and Gulati, 2004). This meant that farmers in developing countries like India, Thailand, Vietnam, Brazil, etc. had to bear the brunt of crisis in global agricultural markets. It is clear that Indian agriculture is no more insulated to what happens in global markets and how the agricultural policies of the OECD countries affect world markets. It is increasingly getting inter-locked.

3. Restructuring the public distribution system (PDS) by targeting, and raising the issue price for the people above poverty line (APL) to 90 per cent of economic cost, though in the right direction, turned out to be somewhat untimely. It was untimely when seen in conjunction with rising support/procurement prices of wheat and rice, in the face of falling world prices. It resulted in squeezing the foodgrain demand from the PDS. Rising support prices at home and falling world prices of wheat, rice, and many other agricultural commodities meant that private sector trade was being crowded-out. And government landed up accumulating surpluses of grains, which touched 64 million tonnes in July 2002, and had to be liquidated by giving hefty subsidy on freight and marketing costs.

4. Frequent political change-over in India during 1996 and 1998 inflicted its toll. Elections normally are a time to announce subsidies to win over votes and as a result, public investments suffer. In fact, subsidies on farm inputs like fertilisers, power and water for irrigation, started going up towards the end of the reformist Congress government in 1995-96. The public sector investment in agriculture (GCFA), however, suffered seriously with the demise of Congress government in 1996. It dropped by more than 20 per cent in real terms during 1995-96 to 1998-99 (from Rs.48.5 billion in 1995-96 to Rs.38.7 billion in 1998-99 at 1993-94 constant prices) (GoI, 2004; p.167) (Figure 12.5). Even private sector investment could not fill this gap and, as a result, total

investment in agriculture suffered during this period slowing down the impetus for growth during late 1990s.

5. For four successive years, especially from 1999 through 2002, at least one-third of the districts in India suffered from below normal rainfall. In 2002, particularly, more than half the districts (56 per cent) received below normal rainfall, which was presumably the main cause for negative growth of agricultural GDP that year.

Figure 12.5

Public Investments and Subsidies in Indian Agriculture

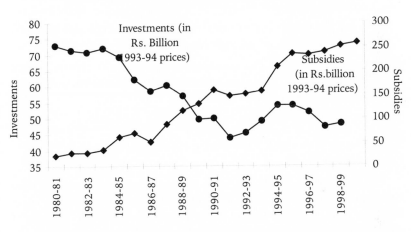

A dispassionate analysis of all these factors is required to understand why Indian agricultural performance dropped so dramatically during the 1997-2003 period. While the first three factors resulted in constraining demand for agricultural products, especially cereals, the last two factors acted as supply bottlenecks. One often hears a lot about point 3 in Indian policy debates, but a discussion on the other points is missing and they may be equally responsible, if not more, for poor performance of Indian agriculture during 1997-2003 period.

3. Building Institutions: A Neglected Area that Needs Immediate Attention

Indian policy debate is largely focused on either 'getting the prices right' for outputs and inputs (subsidies) or getting more investments for agriculture. There is much less focus on building appropriate institutions that can cut costs, promote efficiency, and propel growth that is widely shared. It is this neglected area that needs to be put on the same priority agenda as the discussion on prices or investments. But what sort of institutions are we talking about? The issue of institutions, defined as 'rules of the game,' is a vast field in itself, but in this chapter I would concentrate particularly on three institutions, which I feel are very critical for spurring growth in Indian agriculture, making it globally competitive and also ensuring that the benefits of that growth are shared by the small holders. These institutions are:

(1) Marketing institutions that help promote vertical integration, especially in high value agriculture, mitigate market risk and lower transaction costs.

(2) Land and credit institutions that can help small and marginal farmers to move up on high value agriculture.

(3) Institutions that can promote a fundamental reform in the management of state dominated agricultural research, power and water supplies for rural areas.

These are discussed briefly in the following sub-sections.

3.1 Marketing Institutions: From Getting Prices Right to Getting Markets Right

The trade and exchange rate policy reforms of early reform period were largely focused at getting prices right. But getting markets right is a bigger challenge as it involves a host of 'behind the border' reforms. The idea of efficient markets is to connect the producers with the consumers at the lowest possible transaction costs and with minimum risk. Given the heterogeneity of farmers in India, there is no one solution that would be applicable to all of them. It would be worthwhile to visualise at least three categories of farmers:

(a) Those who largely produce for self consumption called subsistence farmers and face a situation of 'missing markets' or 'market access gap.'

(b) Farmers who do produce for provincial and national markets, but face 'imperfect markets' ('efficiency gap').

(c) Those who produce for global markets and face the challenge of global grades and standards, including sanitary and phyto-sanitary standards (SPS).

Though, each category of farmers face different set of problems, and their solutions are bound to differ too, two pillars that are needed to link the farmers to efficient markets and make them globally competitive are institutions and infrastructure (Figure 12.6; Torero and Gulati, 2004). The nature of these institutions and infrastructure required for each category of farmers, however, would be different, and so would be the role of government and private sector. While these issues are discussed in detail in Torero and Gulati (2004), let me take up the case of small holders here as an illustration and what can be done to link up these small holders to markets.

Figure 12.6

Farmer Heterogeneity and Market Access and Efficiency Gaps

■ No Access Gap
▨ Market Efficiency Gap
☐ Real access Gap

Source: Torero, and Gulati (2004).

It is widely acknowledged that transaction costs are particularly high for small holders due to asymmetry in market information, small surpluses and poor infrastructure that they normally come across during the course of selling their produce. As a result, they are often faced with 'missing markets' and produce largely for self-consumption. Exposed to high risk, investors (bankers), therefore, remain shy from such farmers and the latter remain in their vicious circle of poverty. How do we break this vicious circle? The point of intervention has to be the weakest link in the market chain analysis, which in the Indian case seems to be quite often the missing institutions (rules of the game) that could promote organisational structures to keep transaction costs and market risks low and yet connect the small holders with the demand centres. (At times, it is also the missing infrastructure. But let us concentrate on institutions here).

India need not look around the world to learn how to do it. In fact Indians have done that in the past under the 'Operation Flood,' which ultimately led to the White Revolution in the country and today India stands as the largest producer of milk in the world with production figure touching 90 million tonnes. One may question this model saying that it was based on cooperatives, which got hidden capital subsidy from the government and, therefore, such a model can not be scaled up. In that case, have a look at the private sector, say a multinational like Nestlé operating in district Moga in Punjab, which procures fresh milk from more than 85,000 farmers spread over more than 1,000 villages, processes that into various dairy products and then distributes them to several towns in India through a distribution network of more than 4,000 distributors. NCAP-IFPRI study (Birthal *et al.*, 2004) on the transaction costs of the contract farmers *vis-à-vis* others in the same villages found that those under contract saved their transaction costs to the tune of as much as 94 per cent (Gulati and Mullen, 2004). If one questions even this saying that it is a multinational with not much constraints on capital, etc., one may consider the results of some domestic players in high value agriculture such as Venkateshwara Hatcheries Limited (VHL) in poultry and Safal experiment of the Mother Dairy in vegetable supplies to retail chains in Delhi. The NCAP-IFPRI study (Birthal, *et al.*, 2004) found that even in case of contracted poultry farmers, the transaction costs were 59 per cent lower and in case of vegetable farmers 92 per cent lower than their counterparts who were not under any contract in the same villages. It was also interesting to find out, at least in case of poultry, that those farmers who came under contract expanded their business much faster than those outside the contract indicating the willingness and ability to invest and expand once the market risk is reduced (Birthal, *et al.*, 2004). This is really the crux of vertical integration: those who are hooked to this vertical chain, climb the ladder fast and get out of poverty.

What is it that the Government Policy Needs to do in this Regard?

First, it must be recognised that such vertical integration between the farms and firms or retail chains takes place when processors or retail chains are big in size, which demand large volumes, assured supplies and homogeneous products. From that point of view, all restrictions on investments, both domestic and foreign, on agro-processing and organised retailing should be taken off immediately. These large processors and retailers bring not only more financial capital and risk bearing capacity, but also new technology and new institutions of doing business, creating spill over effects in the rest of the economy. They create backward and forward linkages, which are critical for their own success. Normally, given an option, they would like to source their material from large farmers, as has been the case in Latin America, but given the preponderance of small holders in South Asia, with an average holding size of just 1.6 ha., *vis-à-vis* 67 ha. in Latin America, the experience is likely to be different in this part of the world. These large processors and retailers don't have many options but to source their supplies from scores of farmers, both small and large, as there aren't enough large farmers to meet their demand. And herein lies an opportunity for the small holders to participate in this booming business.

Second, the existing market laws which do not permit direct buying from the farmers need to be amended. The new model APMC Act is moving in the right direction but most of the states are going very slow in adopting this. This needs to be expedited (GoI, 2002; Landes and Gulati, 2004).

Third, opening up gates for futures marketing in 54 commodities was long overdue, but now it is important to see that conditions are created for their smooth functioning and they do not fail due to some other hurdles. In particular, it needs to be realised that futures markets can not function smoothly if government intervenes heavily in some commodity sectors, ignoring the basic principles of markets. And this is true of commodities like wheat and rice where government intervenes in procurement and distribution through its biggest parastatal, Food Corporation of India. The prices at which the government transacts business often do not correspond to the realities of demand and supply. This also drives out private sector investments needed to modernise the entire marketing operations, ranging from procurement, movement, to stocking by big private sector grain companies. Similar problems may arise in case of cotton and sugar so long as the government intervention remains significant in these commodity sectors. The government needs to realise that for the success of future markets, it must reduce its role to just regulation and not be too heavily involved in doing actual business.

To reiterate, innovative institutions of vertical integration are particularly critical in high value agriculture (HVA) such as fruits and vegetables, milk and dairy products, poultry and meat, fish and floriculture, etc. and for the small holders. The demand for such HVA is increasing at a much faster pace, almost two to three times the rate at which cereal demand is increasing.[40] Generally, HVA is also labour intensive compared to cereals (Joshi, *et al.*, 2004). Thus, it offers unique opportunity for small holders to exploit this potential provided they can overcome other constraints of higher working capital requirements, highly perishable nature of HVA, small surpluses and need to ensure necessary grades and standards and food safety norms, and fast moving infrastructure. While at times it looks a really daunting task to make sure that small holders participate in this game, but looking at what is happening in South-east Asia and China, there is reason to be optimistic. Ongoing research at IFPRI on this issue, especially in Indonesia, Vietnam, China, Philippines and Thailand suggests that small holders can be integrated into these vertical chains and still be globally competitive.

3.2 *Land and Credit Institutions to Help the Small and Marginal Farmers*

Land markets in India are highly distorted by public policy. As a part of the Land Reforms policy, there is a ceiling on ownership of land beyond a particular size (roughly 8 ha. of irrigated land). Many states also restrict the leasing of land. Even if one appreciates the need to keep land ceilings for the sake of wider distribution of land assets in rural areas, it is hard to find a sound reasoning for controls on leasing of land. Freeing lease markets could be the beginning of some positive change in this area that could promote emergence of optimal holding size in rural areas. If it is combined with a major drive towards reforming rural credit system whereby small and marginal farmers can have easy access to credit at reasonable rates, one may find the small holders leasing in good amount of land to scale up their operations. At present, organised formal credit institutions (commercial banks, RRBs, PACs, etc.) do not provide more than 60 per cent of the credit needs of rural India. The remaining 40 per cent is still coming from informal sources at exorbitant rates that are two to four times the rates being charged by the formal sector. This is a major failure of Indian rural financial system.

Small holders, if they have less land, must have easy access to good amount of working capital if they have to come out of poverty. Banking

---

40. This is true even with the bottom 30 per cent of population, although their base level consumption of HVA is small. For example, during 1983 to 1999-2000, the demand for milk by this low-income category increased by 31 per cent, of vegetables by 50 per cent, of fruits by 162 per cent, and of meat, eggs and fish by 100 per cent.

system at present finds it very difficult and costly to reach each and every small holder. The transaction costs of small accounts are simply prohibitive. It could not be done even when banks were nationalised and agriculture was stipulated to get 18 per cent of bank credit on priority basis. Now with mushrooming of private banks, it is going to be even more difficult. In the past, government used this stipulation to allow banks to deposit a part of their unfulfilled commitment to NABARD under the Rural Infrastructure Development Fund (RIDF), which the states can then borrow and use. This is simply skirting the problem of small holders' access to institutional credit. A much better approach would be to use these vertical chains to funnel money through the processors and major retailers, vendors, input dealers, etc. to the small holders by making many of these agri-business players as non-banking financial intermediaries (NBFIs). The reason is that the small holders are already in touch with them either for their inputs or outputs, and there is enough social capital that exists between these actors. The government policy can take advantage of this and use these existing business and social structures to make credit available to small holders by allowing a small commission to these NBFIs, or even freeing up interest rates with in a reasonable band for them to charge to small holders. These NBFI can act as rural counters of banks, who would refinance the loans of these NBFIs. This would be much more efficient than banks directly trying to reach the small holders.

Experiments with Self Help Groups (SHGs) in microfinance are good, but they can not be used for large scale demand of a productive agriculture. The Kisan Credit Cards are a step in the right direction, but they also do not cut down the transaction costs of banking for small accounts.

3.3. Institutions to Better Manage Agricultural Research, Power and Water Supplies to Rural Areas

The other areas that require institutional changes on urgent basis are agricultural research, power supplies to rural areas, and canal irrigation. There is lot of talk in terms of raising investments in agricultural research, power sector and canal irrigation, as the initial steam of technology is cooling down, and as rural areas are facing increasing shortage of water. But a policy of higher investments without commensurate reforms in their institutions for better management of these resources is not likely to be very cost effective or even successful. These sectors, which are critical to raise the supply response in agriculture, are mired with problems typical of state-owned enterprises: lack of appropriate incentives, transparency and accountability. As a result, their productivity levels are way below their potential and it would be far more rewarding to concentrate on carrying suitable institutional reforms in these sectors than simply pumping in more money in the name of investments. Much of this money in mega schemes that are being dreamt today in some policy circles, such as linking of rivers through a massive canal network (old idea of garland canal), may disappear as water disappears in sand, if such investments are not accompanied by changes in institutional structures bringing more transparency and accountability. Many of these issues have been discussed at length in Gulati and Narayanan (2003) in the context of input subsidies, especially power and water, and in Gulati, Meinzen-Dick and Raju (2004) for institutional changes in canal irrigation at macro, meso and micro levels. The space constraint in this essay does not permit me to go in detail here, but very briefly, the idea is to turn these organisations from top down structures to somewhat bottoms up, which are accountable to their clients. And if they don't perform, there has to be a mechanism to fix responsibility and take action. Some beginning was made in canal irrigation with the idea of participatory irrigation management (Water User Associations) with some mixed results (see Gulati, Meinzen-Dick and Raju, 2004). But power sector has escaped any major reforms in terms of its supplies to rural areas. The whole debate is stuck up at guarantees and counter-guarantees to foreign investors and somewhat on regulatory commissions. The question of how to ensure reliable and good quality power to rural areas has never come up high on the agenda of power sector reforms. And my hunch is that power sector reforms for rural supplies alone can bring rich harvest. A reliable, good quality and appropriately priced power supplies to rural areas can unleash a revolution in cold storage chain, agro-processing in rural areas, and also raise productivity in agriculture, making it globally much more competitive than it is at present. Remember, in the absence of reliable power, farmers have to resort to diesel driven pump sets which cost a multiple of power cost. A number of surveys have revealed that farmers are wiling to pay a much higher price for power, provided they get reliable and good quality power. This is a potential win-win situation, but somehow Indian policymakers have not been able to make a dent in this area even after a decade of reforms. Often, there is a strong resistance from the vested interests that are benefiting from large leakages (theft) of power in the name of supplying free power to agriculture. Currently, roughly half of power generated in India is not fetching any revenue. No wonder, therefore, much of the power sector is bankrupt, with negative rates of return, and has no resources to upgrade and modernise the existing facilities. This is a sure sign of high inefficiency, and impending crisis.

The Indian research system, which is basically a state monopoly, is starving from funds for real research but also getting strangulated by its typical bureaucratic top down structures. While it is true that R&D expenditure in Indian agriculture is not more than 0.5 per cent of agricultural GDP, as against about 0.7 per cent for all developing countries, and 2-3 per cent in developed countries, yet I feel there is greater need for a major shake up in the research system from institutional point of view. It is amazing to see the extent of centralisation in the system.[41] There is lot of talk on decentralisation of agricultural research, but much less has been achieved on the ground. Same is the case with public-private partnership in agricultural research. And now the complex issues of bio-technology, bio-safety, and IPR, etc. are staring at face, and Indian system of research is moving quite slow on these issues.

4. Concluding Remarks

To wrap up, it may be worth speculating the shape and structure of Indian agriculture by say 2015 or 2020. Given the forces of change at national and global level in terms of higher incomes, increasing urbanisation, and greater integration with world economy, one can safely predict an increasing share and role of HVA in India. This HVA comprising of fruits and vegetables, livestock (dairy and meat, including poultry) and fishery, already has a relatively larger share (more than 40 per cent) in gross value of output than cereals. And given that their expenditure elasticity is two to three times higher than that for cereals, this share of HVA is going to increase even more in the years to come. But the policy environment in agriculture is still hung up with the priorities of 1960s and 1970s.

This HVA is highly perishable, more labour intensive and requires higher working capital. Here in lies the challenge and opportunity for Indian agriculture, especially its small holders, to play a pivotal role in poverty alleviation. Unlike the Green Revolution, which needed heavy support from government in terms of technology (seed, water and fertilisers) and prices, HVA is largely driven by the initiatives of the

---

41. To illustrate, take a simple case of a scientist from say IARI who would like to go to Nepal to participate in a two day conference on the topic on which s/he is working. The request of this scientist to go for this conference is supposedly to be cleared by the Union Minister for Agriculture! And the poor scientist has to keep guessing till last day whether s/he would be allowed to go.

private sector and is demand led. If that is the case, what is it that public policy can do in this regard?

The minimum that public policy can do in this regard is to remove any negative elements that discriminate against HVA, i.e, provide a level playing field. This could range from the allocation of resources in public research between cereals and HVA and to reduce restrictions on size, scale and location of private sector investments for processing of HVA. Being perishable in nature, HVA obviously needs a different type of infrastructure and institutions than what were created for cereals. A fast moving infrastructure and a cold chain becomes necessary to reduce post-harvest losses. The cold chain can not be viable without a meaningful reform of the power sector with a view to provide reliable power supplies at reasonable prices to rural areas. HVA also needs more working capital, and therefore, reforms in the credit sector would be very useful. Further, the institutions that vertically integrate or connect consumers to producers (plate to plough) through supermarkets, processors and farmers' organisation will become increasingly important. The policy environment needs to facilitate, not block, this coordination, and therefore any restrictions that block investments in supermarkets, processing and direct buying from the farmers must be taken away. If along with this, government policy can encourage fast moving roads, ports and airports, this HVA can play a similar role in bringing down poverty in rural areas as was played by the Green Revolution in the 1970s and 1980s. Finally, on trade policy front, the issues of food safety are going to be increasingly important in HVA and, therefore, policymakers need to pay greater attention to building appropriate institutions and infrastructure to achieve these goals.

References

Ahluwalia, M. (2002). "Economic Reforms in India Since 1991: Has Gradualism Worked?," *Journal of Economic Perspectives*, Vol. No. 16 (3) (Summer).

Birthal, P.S., P.K. Joshi and A. Gulati (2004). *Vertical Coordination in High Value Food Commodities – Assessing Implications for the Smallholders*. Washington, DC, Mimeo, International Food Policy Research Institute,.

Government of India (2004). *Economic Survey, 2003-04*, New Delhi: Ministry of Finance,

———. (2002). *Report of Inter-Ministerial Task Force on Agricultural Marketing Reforms*. New Delhi: Department of Agriculture and Co-operation.

———. (2003). *Report of the Committee on Capital Formation in Agriculture*, Department of Agriculture and Cooperation, New Delhi. Available at http://agricoop.nic.in/ statistics2003/FinalReport. doc [March 2003].

Gulati, Ashok and Kathleen Mullen (2004). "High Value Agriculture in India: Prospects for the Smallholder," paper presented at the Conference on *Economic Reforms, Human Development and Governance in India: Changes in Institutional Structures and Incentives Since 1991* organised by The Centre for the Advanced Study of India (CASI), June 13-15, 2004, at The University of Pennsylvania, USA.

Gulati, Ashok and Seema Bathala (2002). *Capital Formation in Indian Agriculture: Trends, Composition and Implications for Growth*, Occasional Paper 24, National Bank for Agriculture and Rural Development, Mumbai, India.

Gulati, Ashok, Ruth Meinzen-Dick and K.V. Raju (2004). *Institutional Reforms in Indian Irrigation*, Delhi: Sage Publications.

Gulati, Ashok and Tim Kelley (1999). *Trade Liberalisation and Indian Agriculture*, New Delhi: India, Oxford University Press.

Gulati, A.G. Pursell amd K. Mullen (2003). *Indian Agriculture Since Reforms: Performance, Policy Environment and Incentives*. (Mimeo, International Food Policy Research Institute, Washington, DC).

Gulati, A. and K. Mullen (2003). "Responding to Policy Reform: Indian Agriculture During the 1990s and After," Paper prepared for the *Fourth Annual Conference on India Economic Policy Reform*, The Center for Research on Economic Development and Policy Reform, Stanford University, Palo Alto, June.

Gulati, A. and S. Narayanan (2003). *Subsidy Syndrome in Indian Agriculture*, New Delhi: Oxford University Press.

Hoda, Anwarul and Ashok Gulati (2004). *WTO, Agricultural Negotiations and Developing Countries: Lessons from the Indian Experience*, Book Manuscript (mimeo), International Food Policy Research Institute, Washington, D.C.

Joshi, P. K., A. Gulati, P.S. Birthal and L. Tewari (2004). "Agriculture Diversification in South Asia: Patterns, Determinants, and Policy Implications," *Economic and Political Weekly*, June 12, 2004.

Landes, Rip and Ashok Gulati (2004). "Farm Sector Performance and Reform Agenda," *Economic and Political Weekly*, Vol. XXXIX (32).

Munisamy, Gopinath, Kathleen Mullen and Ashok Gulati (2004). "Domestic Support to Agriculture in the European Union and the United States," MTID Discussion Paper (forthcoming), International Food Policy Research Institute, Washington, D.C., USA.

Rao, C.H. Hanumantha and Ashok Gulati (1994). "Indian Agriculture: Emerging Perspectives and Policy Issues," *Economic and Political Weekly*, Vol. No. XXIX (53).

Torero, Maximo and Ashok Gulati (2004). *Connecting Small Holders to Markets: Role of Infrastructure and Institutions*, Policy Brief, International Food Policy Research Institute, Washington, D.C., USA.

World Bank (2004). *Trade Policies in South Asia, An Overview*, Report No. 29949, Poverty Reduction and Economic Management Sector Unit, South Asia Region, Washington, D.C., USA.

13

Withdrawal of Subsidies from Irrigation and Fertiliser: Impact on Small and Marginal Farmers

KANCHAN CHOPRA

1. Introduction

A large number of studies on subsidies in Indian agriculture have been undertaken in particular in the last decade or so.[42] Most of these studies are the outcome of a focus on structural adjustment and liberalisation and their impact on the magnitude of subsidies. The global context to the debate has been added by the discussions on the Agreement on Agriculture in the World Trade Organisation (WTO). However, the strongest case for a progressive removal of subsidies continues to be based on the increasing burden they constitute for the exchequer at a time when fiscal deficits need to be contained.

In this connection it is interesting to review the discussion following from a paper of the Ministry of Finance, which made estimates of the financial burden imposed by the major subsidies in 1997. It drew a distinction between public goods, merit goods and non-merit goods in examining the magnitude of subsidies and their burden on the government. Adopting the above classification, it was then argued that 'non-merit goods,' do not justify subsidisation. However, it was later pointed out that the classification was somewhat biased and that a significant part of the goods classified as non-merit goods did in fact have significant externality impacts.[43] Such an assessment strengthens the lurking argument that any reduction in subsidies will harm the small and marginal farmers and hence be politically incorrect. The distributive

---

42. For a survey of the studies, see Gulati and Narayanan (2000).

43. See EPW Research Foundation (1997) for details of the possible bias in classification. This paper estimated that 51 per cent of the Rs. 87,386 crore of subsidies estimated for the non-merit goods and services clearly fell outside this category, consisting as they did of social and economic services.

impact of subsidies remains a major question in the minds of policy-makers. Will the small and marginal farmer be affected more adversely than the large farmer by the withdrawal of subsidies? The present study is an attempt to respond to this question. It examines subsidies given to irrigation water (both surface and groundwater irrigation) and to fertilisers with the 'explicit objective' of determining whether their phased withdrawal will impact the small and marginal farmer more than it will the large farmer.

Agricultural subsidies in India are of two kinds: direct and indirect. Direct subsidies consists of those that are intended to encourage the adoption of particular kinds of cultivation practices such as mechanisation, use of better input saving technology and so on. Indirect subsidies, on the other hand are subsidies on generic inputs such as water, fertiliser or credit. Over the years, the indirect subsidies have come to occupy a significant part of total budgeted amount on subsidies. In 2001-02, input subsidies on irrigation, power, and fertiliser for India as a whole are estimated at Rs.35,246 crore at current prices accounting for almost 8.2 per cent of Gross Domestic Product (GDP) in Indian agriculture. The next section, examines how differential impact of their withdrawal could arise for large and small producers. Section 3 provides the broad parameters of the methodology to be followed and the data sources used in the study. Section 4 discusses the findings and Section 5 concludes with a focus on policy implications.

2. Modelling the Impact of Subsidy and its Withdrawal

Consider the case of two cultivators with landholding size C_1 and C_2 producing output Y (sold at price p) using an input such as irrigation water, w, available at price p_1 and p_2. Net output in the two cases is defined as $(p^*U - p_1^*w_1)$ X1 and $(p^*Y - p_2^* w_2)$X2. If the water is supplied, say, by canal irrigation at a subsidised price, it implies that p_1 and p_2 are replaced by $(p_1 - p')$ and $(p_2 - p')$ where p' is the per unit subsidy. This subsidy has, like any other price change, an income effect and a substitution effect. The real income of the two cultivators increases with the result that they can demand more of the subsidised input. Simultaneously, a substitution effect also takes place. More of irrigation water will be used relative to other inputs such as for instance, labour. Differences in the impact of the subsidy on the two cultivators depend on the relative value of the income and the substitution effect in the two cases.

Assuming that cultivators' only income is from agriculture, the increase in real income in the two cases depends on the relative landholding and the productivity per unit land. Taking note of the fact that farmers have different productivities per unit of land, this income effect may not be proportional to the relative size of the landholdings. The substitution effect also adds to the demand for the subsidised input relative to that for others. A cheaper access to water is expected to result in a substitution of water for labour or other factor inputs such as energy. The extent to which this takes place depends on the differential access to other inputs. Small farmers may substitute water for labour and larger farmers water for energy. Such substitution between inputs is in evidence when water is subsidised. Labour intensive maintenance of water channels is neglected and more water saving innovations is not adopted. The nature of substitution differs in the case of different categories of cultivators. It shall depend on their relative resource endowment. Further, a continued subsidy of certain inputs shall, in all cases, act as a disincentive to innovations to substitute for it in the long run. Higher levels of use of the input by all categories of cultivators are expected, and an extended subsidy regime shall imply higher use levels in the long run as well.

The impact of a change in price of an input, consequent on a withdrawal of subsidy, on its use by different sets of producers can be estimated by setting up and estimating demand functions for the inputs.

A typical demand function for input i by household j could be set up as follows:

$$D (i, j) = f (P_{ij}, ACC_{ij}, L_j, TR_{cj}) \dots\dots (1)$$

Where D (i j): demand for input i by household j

P_{ij} : price of input i paid by household j

ACC_i j: Access to input i of household j

L_j: Land owned/operated by household j

TR_{cj}: Technical input requirements of crop mix grown by household j.

The above specification states that levels of use of an input are impacted by price, access, landholding size and the technical requirements of the crop mix grown. Whereas the price variable is easily understood, others may need some explanation. Access is one such factor. For inputs such as fertiliser, the variable, $ACC_{i,j}$ can be interpreted as distance from outlet and quality of the transport infrastructure. For inputs such as canal irrigation and power, which are perceived to have characteristics of public goods, access depends on location in a canal command or within the ambit of a power grid. Further, access to groundwater is a function of ability to invest in extraction of water or the ability to hire services of tubewells, tractors or other agricultural machinery which in turn depends on resources such as income, represented in this specification by Lj.

The variable Lj land owned or operated also determines the level of demand. The significance or otherwise of this variable may be a pointer towards the presence of a differential impact of subsidy on different size class of cultivators.

TRcj, the next explanatory variable, indicates the average input requirements of the crop mix grown by the cultivators in a region: it may for instance stand for optimal water or fertiliser requirement of crops grown.

The input demand function specified above can be estimated for households belonging to the specified group (small and marginal farmers, for instance) and in general for the complete set of households to arrive at differential demand for subsidised inputs. The results can then be used to assess the distributional impact of the subsidy being considered.

This specification with land ownership category as an additional variable is also more appropriate keeping in view the nature of data available. It shall have the following specification

$$Dij = f (Pij, ACCij, Lj, TRcj)................................(2)$$

with Lj as the holding size category. The variation in response of demand to each of the variables is then examined to determine whether or not small and marginal farmers are impact differently by price increases consequent on a withdrawal of subsidy.

3. Data Aspects and Sources for the Nineties

Estimation of the above input demand function requires input use data by size class of holdings. The following data sources provide some such estimates for different points of time in the nineties:

- Government of India (GoI), Agricultural Census 1990-91.
- GoI, Ministry of Agriculture, Input Survey 1991-92.
- GoI, Agricultural Census 1995-96.
- National Sample Survey Organisation (NSSO), 54th Round Cultivation Practices in India, January-June 1998.

The two agricultural censuses are based on complete enumeration of all holdings. The Input Survey is part of Phase III of the Agricultural Census (1990-91 and 1995-96). It is conducted on a sample basis, with the sample consisting of seven per cent of 20 per cent of the holdings surveyed in Phase II. It constitutes a subset of the Agricultural Census set of holdings but gives the input use information. The NSSO survey constitutes an independent data category with 10,978 villages and therefore, 78,990 households selected on the basis of a two stage stratified sampling design.

In all the data sources listed above, operational holdings are divided into five size classes. These are marginal (below 1 ha), small (1-1.9 ha), semi-medium (2-3.99 ha), medium (4-9.99 ha) and large (above 10 ha). The data is available for four years i.e. 1990-91, 1991-92, 1995-96 and 1997-98 and for 14 major States in India. We categorise the first two size classes put together as small and marginal holdings (i.e. those operating less than 1.9 hectares of land). We shall refer to these two together as the 'smaller' holdings as against 'the rest' which are defined to include semi-medium, medium and large holdings.

4. Background Information: All States 1990-91 (Agricultural Census) to 1997-98 (NSSO): A Comparison with 1995-96 (Some States)

As expected, the distribution of operational holdings across the five size classes indicates that marginal holdings constitute a large part of the total at all points of time. Their share increased from 59.4 per cent in 1990-91 to 62 per cent in 1997-98. Further, put together, marginal and smallholdings account for more than three-fourth of the total number of operational holdings (78.2 per cent).

The picture is similar across most of the fourteen major States selected for analysis. 'Smaller' holdings as defined above comprise a significant share of the total number of operational holdings in 1990-91 ranging from a minimum of 44.8 per cent in Punjab to a maximum of 91.4 per cent in West Bengal. From 1990-91 to 1997-98, with the exception of Uttar Pradesh, the share of smaller holdings in total operational holdings has increased in all the States. This increase has ranged from a minimum level of 0.3 percentage points in Bihar to 16.3 percentage points in Karnataka. Some part of this difference could be attributed, however, to error arising out of differences in coverage in the two sets of data i.e. complete enumeration followed in 1990-91 as against sampling followed by the NSSO in 1997-98. The increase in the proportion of smaller holdings is not so high when we compare 1990-91 and 1995-96 data, both of which are based on similar methodology i.e. complete enumeration. Nevertheless, the share of small and marginal holdings in the total operational holdings increased from 1990-91 to 1995-96 for almost all the States with the exception of Punjab.

Smaller holdings then constitute a large part of the total operational holdings. It follows, therefore, that in absolute terms a large part of the input subsidies, are in fact accruing to them. This is true for both fertiliser and water. It is also the reason for their continued political attractiveness.

Further, in 1991-92, based on Input Survey data, they irrigated 41 per cent of their gross cropped area as compared to 37.6 per cent irrigated by larger farmers. The variation is also lower (with standard deviation being 0.229 for smaller size class of holdings as compared to 0.26 for the larger size class). However, in 1997-98, (as indicated by NSSO data on Cultivation Practices), small and marginal farmers irrigated less (62.7 per cent) of their gross cropped area as compared to that irrigated (68.5 per cent) by larger cultivators. Be that as it may, the policy question that we address is: what shall be the effect of a withdrawal in subsidies on the smaller and larger farmers? Shall the relative impact of the price rise be different for the two categories? How shall it affect irrigated area (as a percentage of gross cropped area) in the case of the two categories of cultivators?

5. Impact of Phased Withdrawal of Irrigation Subsidy on Small and Marginal Farmers

5.1 The Model, Variables and Data

As explained in Section 2, the input demand function, which determines demand for irrigation, as approximated by irrigated area as percentage of gross sown area, has the following explanatory variables:

- Price of irrigation water. This is measured, in the case of surface irrigation by per hectare irrigation charges. For groundwater irrigation, it is approximated by the cost per unit of power used, assuming that this is the major component of the variable cost.

- Technology related factors in this case approximated by adoption of improved seeds for crops grown.[44]

- Access to irrigation, as approximated by location in or outside a canal command area.

---

44. The assumption is that adoption of better quality seeds constitutes technological change since it usually requires changes in other inputs and higher outputs.

- Size of holding measured either by holding size or by a dummy variable.

State level analysis for the five-size class of holdings is undertaken using data from NSS (1997-98) and Cost of Cultivation Surveys. Descriptive Statistics on variables used is given in Appendix 13.1. Data on irrigation charges per hectare (for surface irrigation) are averages of crop-specific charges weighted for the proportion of area under the crop to total gross cropped area in the State. Data on power price (a surrogate for the one significant factor impacting variable cost of groundwater irrigation) is obtained from State Electricity Boards and is assumed to vary only across States. Variation in price of both surface irrigation water and power is high. Also, irrigation charges for surface water with an average of Rs.748 per hectare are at higher levels as compared to 1991-92. Also to be noted is that power price on average is Rs.35.88 per unit, with a high degree of variation from 0 in some States to Rs.151.26 per unit in others. On average, 66.23 per cent of gross cropped area is irrigated and 63.31 per cent of area is under improved seeds.

We use different specifications of the model to determine, in alternative ways, the impact of technology, price and land-ownership variables on area irrigated, both by groundwater or by surface water.

In the first specification two separate equations are estimated for groundwater irrigation and for surface irrigation. In the equation relating to groundwater, proportion of farms located outside canal commands is taken as one of the explanatory variables and assuming that these are groundwater irrigated, the price of power, a complementary input is taken as one of the independent variables. In a similar fashion, the surface water equation takes location within canal commands and surface irrigation charges as the two independent variables.

Further, three equations each are estimated for groundwater and surface water irrigation to correspond to the total sample, the subset of large and medium farmers and of small and marginal farmers. The linear specification, found to give the best fit is used. The results for these are tabulated in Tables 13.1 and 13.2 respectively.

Table 13.1 gives the results for three estimates corresponding to the complete sample including all size classes of holdings, the larger holdings and the smaller holdings. Since both power price and location outside canal commands are taken as explanatory variables, this set of equations explains the situation mainly with respect to tubewell irrigated areas. It is found that the technology variable, approximated by use of improved seeds, the vocational variable and the power price variable are all significant in determining the ratio of irrigated area to gross cropped area. Holding size does not seem to be significant, however. This is true for all three sets implying that both for the set of 70 holdings and within each subset, the holding size are not an important determinant of access to groundwater irrigation.

Table 13.1

Groundwater Irrigation: Dependent Variable: Gross Irrigated Area/Gross Cropped Area: 1997-98

	Coefficient	t-Statistic	Prob.	Adjusted R2
All Size-classes				
C	0.1162	1.5218	0.133	0.7228
Improved Seed	0.0050	4.9494	0.000	
Non-Canal	0.4468	8.0346	0.000	
Power Price	-0.0010	-2.3795	0.0203	
Holding Size	-0.0007	-0.2132	0.8318	
Larger Holdings				
	Coefficient	t-Statistic	Prob.	Adjusted R2
C	0.1175	1.1148	0.2721	0.7145
Improved Seed	0.0053	4.2104	0.0002	
Non-Canal	0.3845	5.3826	0.000	
Power Price	-0.0012	-1.9769	0.055	
Holding Size	0.0017	0.3165	0.7533	
Smaller Holdings				
	Coefficient	t-Statistic	Prob.	Adjusted R2
C	0.0846	0.6196	0.5416	0.7127
Improved Seed	0.0047	2.6595	0.014	
Non-Canal	0.5678	6.02339	0.000	
Power Price	-0.0009	-1.24442	0.0140	
Holding Size	-0.02672	-0.5287	0.6020	

The above analysis suggests that access to improved seeds in the absence of access to canal irrigation shall substantially increase groundwater irrigation. It will result, presumably in more private invest in tubewells. Further, in areas outside of canal commands, an increase in power tariff will affect the spread of groundwater-based irrigation adversely. However, 'the adverse impact' shall be felt more or less uniformly by holdings belonging to different size groups. The small and marginal farmers are not likely to be particularly adversely impacted due to the smallness of their holdings *per se*.

Regression results analysing factors that are likely to affect the proportion of irrigated area to sown area as they operate in the context of surface irrigation are given in Table 13.2. The explanatory power of the model is less (43 to 44 per cent) as compared to the corresponding model in the case of groundwater irrigation (71 to 72 per cent). However, the direction of the results is similar. Adoption of better technology as exemplified by the adoption of improved seeds and location in canal command are the important factors determining proportion of area irrigated. In this instance, both irrigation charges and holding size turn out to be insignificant in determining the variation in the dependent variable. Further, this is uniformly true, whether we pool the data from holdings of all size classes or we consider small and larger holdings in separate subgroups.

Table 13.2

Canal Irrigation Dependent Variable: GIA/GCA: 1997-98

All Farms

Variable	Coefficient	t-Statistic	Prob.	Adjusted R2
C	-0.09858	-0.9510	0.3451	0.446
Improved Seed	0.008697	5.7217	0.0000	
Canal Command	0.26952	3.4211	0.0011	
Irrigation Charges	-6.38 E-06	-0.1259	0.9001	
Holding Size	0.000293	0.05674	0.9549	
Larger Farms				
	Coefficient	t-Statistic	Prob.	Adjusted R2
C	-0.06725	-0.47336	0.6387	0.431995
Improved Seed	0.008773	4.772927	0.000	
Canal Command	0.192212	1.99053	0.0540	
Irrigation Charges	-1.30 E-05	-0.201358	0.8415	
Holding Size	0.00335	0.4386	0.6635	
Smaller Farms				
	Coefficient	t-Statistic	Prob.	R2
C	-0.25228	-1.2986	0.2069	0.4233
Improved Seed	0.009288	3.190346	0.0041	
Canal Command	0.475066	3.235844	0.0037	
Irrigation charges	6.40E-06	0.073732	0.9419	
Holding Size	-0.03579	-0.49756	0.6235	

It can be concluded that for increasing area under surface irrigation, technology and location in a canal command are the important policy variables. In other words, if access were ensured in terms of appropriate location in canal commands and improved technology were to be made available (in the form of improved seeds for example), an increase in irrigation charges is not likely to have an adverse effect on access to irrigation. This holds uniformly for 'all categories' of farmers, large medium, small and marginal. A large number of micro-studies have found that relative location, at the head or the tail is also significant in determining access to irrigation. Whereas such in-depth micro observation is outside the framework of the present study, policy formulation exercises need to take account of both kinds of studies.

5.2 An Alternative Specification

In the above specification of the model, ground and surface irrigation is studied separately: the variable proportion of holdings located within or outside canal commands was treated as proxy for primary irrigation source (groundwater or surface water), the argument being that those located in non-canal areas shall have to depend in a large way on tubewells. In the alternative specification in this section, both variables specifying location and both sets of prices, (i.e. The per unit power price and the per hectare irrigation charge) are introduced into the same equation. The other two independent variables, holding size and adoption of improved seeds are also retained. The results for the combined set as obtained from this specification are tabulated in Table 13.3

Table 13.3

All Irrigation Dependent Variable: GIA/GCA

All Farmers

Variable	Coefficient	t-Statistic	Prob.	R2
C	-1.913844	-7.837736	0.000	0.701582
Improved Seed	0.017767	5.495756	0.000	
Non-Canal	0.502348	2.238258	0.0287	
Canal	0.395771	1.765067	0.0824	
Irrigation Charges	-8.00E-05	-0.795648	0.4292	
Price of Power	-0.005780	-4.447860	0.000	
Holding Size	-0.021534	-2.115117	0.0384	

The combined regression following the new specification yields interesting results. It has a high explanatory power of some 70–72 per cent for the full sample of observations. Adoption of new technology in the form of new seeds, location within canal command or otherwise and power price turn out to be significant in determining the proportion of area irrigated. Irrigation charges for surface irrigation are not a significant determinant. However, the price of power is significant in determining area irrigated and any increase in its price shall impact the irrigated area significantly. Further, holding size appears as a significant factor but with a negative sign. This implies that if all other factors are accounted for, smaller holdings tend to have a larger percentage of their land under irrigation. In other words, smaller holdings tend to use their land more intensively, other factors being the same. This conclusion is somewhat similar to the situation in the context of the mid-sixties discussions on size productivity.

The above analysis leads us to conclude that a farmer not among the factors that have a significant impact on percentage of cropped area irrigates irrigation charges for canal water. Location of the holding and the requirement of the technology he uses are far more significant determinants of how much land he decides to irrigate. Further, this is true for all categories of farmers, large and small. However, the case of groundwater is different in so far as the price of power is significant in determining area irrigated. It is important to point out however, that this is uniformly true for all categories of farmers, large and small. The smaller farmers shall not be negatively discriminated against by the withdrawal of subsidies on power. It is clear that the case for irrigation subsidies, both for canal and groundwater, cannot be built on the egalitarian argument of supporting the small and marginal farmers. If the objective of policy is to improve access of this disadvantaged lot to irrigation, 'the focus has to be on physical access and technology related variables, not on price of water'.

6. Fertiliser Use, Impact of Fertiliser Subsidy Withdrawal on Small and Large Farmers

The second major input subsidy in India is that on fertiliser. According to evidence from the Input Use Survey (1991-92), small and marginal farmers fertilise a larger proportion of their cultivated area and also use larger amounts of fertiliser per hectare of fertilised area. As in the case of irrigation, the question posed is: what are the factors impacting the relative impact of withdrawal of fertiliser subsidy on large and small farmers? In other words, what is the relative impact of different price and non-price factors in influencing levels of fertiliser use? By including holding size as an independent variable, we shall also be able to determine how this will vary across size group of holdings.

An analysis of input survey data and cost of cultivation data (for 1991-92) indicates that the demand for fertiliser is negatively and insignificantly related to its price in case of total size groups of farmers and for large farmers. In the case of small farmers, the price coefficient turns out to be positive though again insignificant. Credit availed of is significant at five per cent level of significance. The size of the holding is also found to be insignificant throughout, irrespective of whether it is approximated by the mid-point of the class interval or by a dummy variable.[45]

Further, it is seen from the analysis of data for 1991-92, that the impact of variables relating to price, technology and holding size on fertiliser use suggests some degree of interdependence between the use of fertiliser and the proportion of area irrigated as a proxy for adoption of new technology. Similarly, the decision of farmers on the proportion of area to irrigate is impacted by technology adoption as approximated by the use of improved seeds, as illustrated by the analysis of NSSO data of 1997-98. In such a situation of interdependence, it seems appropriate to use a simultaneous equations model to examine the factors affecting input-use. Ideally, a three-equation model with technology, fertiliser use and adoption of irrigation would have been most appropriate. However, the two-equation specification we have selected has been determined partly by the data availability. Using the two sets of data, for 1991-92 and 1997-98 respectively, the simultaneous equation specification gave interesting results. We discuss these in turn.

In the model for 1991-92, the endogenous variables in the simultaneous equation model are: fertilsed area as proportion of cropped area and irrigated area as proportion of cropped area as endogenous variables, the latter as proxy for technology.

The exogenous variables are:

*   fertiliser price,

---

45. For details, see Chopra and Kapuria (2001). The variables used to capture price, access to input, technology and farm-size in the regression are: weighted fertiliser price (Rs. per kg. of nutrient) as calculated from Cost of Cultivation data for the relevant year, Number of fertiliser sale points as on 31.3.92. per '000 sq. kms. of area in the state; Short-term institutional credit taken for purchasing fertiliser by major size groups of holdings across 14 states in Rs/hectare; Total irrigated area as percentage of gross cropped area by major size groups of holdings across 14 states; Mid-point of the interval of farm size representing different categories of farmers namely, marginal, small, semi-medium, medium and large.

- holding size,
- price of power, as proxy for groundwater cost,
- canal Irrigation charges, and
- roads per unit area in State, as a general infrastructure or access capturing variable.

The results of the simultaneous equation model estimated using 3SLS method are given in Table 13.4. It is clear that irrigation and fertiliser use are important explanatory variables in the two-equation model. Neither the holding size variable nor the respective price variables turned out to be significant in determining area fertilised or area irrigated as a proportion of gross cropped area. It follows, therefore, that 'irrigation and fertiliser' need to be provided as 'joint-inputs' and the 'holding size is not' an important determinant of access to these inputs.

Next, the 1997-98 data set from NSSO is used to set up a simultaneous equation model with technology adoption (as exemplified by the use of improved seeds) and irrigated area as the two endogenous variables. The exogenous variables are:

- number of sales points for fertilisers,
- holding size,
- price of power, as proxy for cost of groundwater irrigation,
- canal water charges,
- area located in canal command,
- area not located in canal command, and
- road density in the State.

Table 13.5 gives the results of the simultaneous equation model based on 1997-98 data the results of the simultaneous equations model for 1997-98 also corroborate those of the earlier ones. The adoption of better technology is facilitated by the presence of more area under irrigation and *vice-versa*. None of the exogenous variables postulated to impact improved seed adoption as proxy for technology turn out to be significant. Further, holding size is also not a significant variable determining irrigated area. Location both within and outside of canal commands is significant, capturing the effect for canal and groundwater access respectively.

Further, of the price variables, canal irrigation charges are not significant. Power price is marginally significant at the 10 per cent level. An increase in it would impact groundwater irrigation negatively whereas

Table 13.4

3SLS Estimates of Simultaneous Equations Model: 1991-92

Endogenous Variables	Fertiliser Area/GCA	Irrigated Area/ GCA
Fertiliser Area/GCA	—	0.918
		(4.844)
IrrigatedArea/GCA	1.146	—
	(5.131)	
Exogenous Variables		
Price of Fertiliser	0.007	—
Holding Size	0.008	-0.0075
	(0.2097)	(-0.245)
Power Price		0.0012
		(0.7709)
Canal Irrigation Charges		-9.34 E-06
		(-0.469)
Roads		3.33E-05
		(0.876)
R bar **2	0.301	0.594

Table 13.5

3SLS Estimates of Simultaneous Equations Model: 1997-98

Endogenous Variables	Area Under Improved Seed/GCA	Irrigated Area/GCA
Area Under Improved Seed/GCA		0.0088
		(2.333)
Irrigated Area/GCA	48.65	
	(6.554)	
Exogenous Variables		
Sales-points	0.0055	
	(0.4191)	
Holding Size	0.4284	-0.0025
	(1.1271)	(-0.7103)
Price of Power	—	-0.0009
		(-1.693)
Canal Irrigation Charges	—	-3.49E-05
		(-0.561)
Non-Canal Location		0.4344
		(4.677)
Canal Command Location		0.129
		(1.61)
Road Density		-1.522E-05
		(-0.307)
R bar **2	0.35	0.657

increased canal water charges do not have a similar impact on irrigation by canals.

7. Concluding Remarks

This paper uses data sets from the 1990s to investigate into the likely effects of a withdrawal of irrigation and fertiliser subsidies on small and marginal farmers. Both single equation and simultaneous equation models are used to analyse data for 1991-92 and 1997-98.

It is found that the factors significant in determining demand for fertiliser are similar for farmers operating different size of holdings. Irrigated area per hectare of gross cropped area (representing technological requirement of the crop mix) is highly significant in determining the fertilised area, and hence, the demand for fertiliser. Access to credit also plays an important role in determining fertiliser demand.

The elasticity of demand for fertiliser with respect to significant variables is estimated. Increasing prices by 10 per cent shall decrease area fertilised by all farmers by 0.1 per cent. Small and marginal farmers' area fertilised shall decrease negligibly while that of larger farmers shall decrease by 0.7 per cent. Increasing area irrigated shall increase area fertilised by 4.4 per cent for all farmers, 4.6 per cent for small farmers and 4.2 per cent for large farmers. This implies that investment in irrigation infrastructure is preferable to subsidising irrigation water from the viewpoint of the small and marginal farmers. Their demand for fertiliser would increase more by increased investment in irrigation infrastructure than from a continuation of the subsidy regime. When looked at in conjunction with the finding (from NSSO 1997-98) that small and marginal holdings have a smaller proportion of their area located within canal commands, this finding points towards the need to improve physical access to water through more infrastructure investment

Independent results obtained from OLS regressions for groundwater-based irrigation suggest that access to improved seeds (as a technology representing parameter) increase groundwater irrigation. Better technology shall presumably result in more investment in tubewells and hiring of tubewell water. It is also found that a withdrawal of subsidy and a consequent rise in power tariff will have an adverse effect on spread of groundwater irrigation. However, the adverse effect will be felt more or less uniformly by holdings of different size groups. Small and marginal farmers are not adversely impacted due to the smallness of their holdings per se.

For surface water too, adoption of better technology as exemplified by improved seeds and location in canal command are the important factors determining proportion of area irrigated by a holding. Irrigation water charges and size of the holding are insignificant. This is uniformly true for the set of small, large and all holdings.

The results of the simultaneous equation models for both 1991-92 and 1997-98 corroborate the above findings with adoption of better technology being facilitated by the presence of more area under irrigation and this being accompanied by higher levels of fertiliser use. By way of conclusion, it can be said that:

- Policy must concentrate on providing equitable access for smaller farmers to location with respect to canal irrigation.

- A gradual withdrawal of fertiliser subsidy shall not have an adverse impact on fertiliser use by smaller farmers if such infrastructure by way of access to irrigation and credit is created. Their consumption would in fact increase.

- Increases in canal irrigation charges shall not reduce use of irrigation by smaller farmers, provided they are located in canal commands.

- Power price increases shall result in a decreased access to groundwater irrigation by all farmers; here again smaller farmers are not more adversely affected.

Appendix 13.1

Descriptive Statistics

	IMPSEED	IRRCHRG	IRRGCA	NCANAL	POWER	CANAL
Mean	63.51	748.80	0.66	61.24	35.90	78.52
Median	66.90	744.00	0.70	70.20	19.07	89.90
Maximum	100.00	2057.02	1.00	100.00	151.26	100.00
Minimum	0.01	0.03	0.01	0.01	0.00	0.01
Std. Dev.	18.20	544.70	0.25	31.85	40.55	29.36
Skewness	-0.74	0.81	-0.56	-0.56	1.70	-1.84
Kurtosis	3.62	3.30	2.36	2.10	5.21	5.38
Jarque-Bera	7.52	7.94	4.90	6.06	48.05	56.47
Probability	0.02	0.01	0.08	0.05	0.00	0.00
Observations	70	70	70	70	70	70

Note: Variables are defined as follows

IMPSEED: Percentage of area under improved seeds

IRRCHRG: Canal Irrigation charges in Rupees per hectare

IRRGCA: Irrigated area as proportion of Gross Cropped Area

NCANAL: Percentage of irrigated holdings located outside of canal commands

POWER: Price of Electric Power in Rupees per Kilowatt-hour

CANAL: Percentage of Holdings located in canal commands

References

Chopra, Kanchan and Kapuria, Preeti (2001). *Agricultural Input Subsidies in India: Impact on Small and Marginal Farmers*, Monograph, Institute of Economic Growth, Delhi.

EPW Research Foundation (1997). "Distorted Perceptions: Government Subsidies and Fiscal Crisis" *Economic and Political Weekly*, Vol. XXXII, No. 22, May 31, pp. 1234-1235.

Fertiliser Association of India, The (1992). *Fertiliser Statistics 1991-92*, December.

Government of India, *Bulletin of Food Statistics*, Directorate of Economics and Statistics, Ministry of Agriculture, Various Issues.

————. (1992). *Report of the Committee on Pricing of Irrigation Water, Planning Commission*, New Delhi (Chairman: A. Vaidyanathan).

————. (1991). *Costs of Cultivation of Principal Crops in India*, Directorate of Economics and Statistics, Department of Agriculture and Cooperation, Ministry of Agriculture, New Delhi.

————. (2000). *Input-use Survey, 1991-92*, Ministry of Agriculture.

————. (1998). *All India Report on Agricultural Census, 1991-92*, Ministry of Agriculture

————. (2000). *Preliminary Result of Agricultural Census, 1995-96*, Ministry of Agriculture.

Gulati, Ashok and Narayanan Sudha (2000). "Subsidy Syndrome in Indian Agriculture," Mimeo, Institute of Economic Growth, Delhi.

Gulati, Ashok and Sharma Anil (1995). "Subsidy Syndrome in the Indian Agriculture," *Economic and Political Weekly* (Review of Agriculture), September 30, 1995.

Gulati, Ashok and Chopra Kanchan (1999). *Consolidated Report of IEG, ISEC and IIMA Studies on Reform of the Subsidy Regime: Implications for the Agricultural Sector*, September.

Gulati, Ashok (1989). "Input Subsidies in Indian Agriculture: A State-wise Analysis," *Economic and Political Weekly*, Vol. 24, No. 25, A-57.

Gulati, Ashok, Mark Svendsen and Nandini Roy Choudhury (1995). "Capital Costs of Major and Medium Irrigation Schemes in India," edited by Mark Svendsen and Ashok Gulati, in *Strategic Change in Indian Irrigation*, Delhi: Mac Millan India Ltd.

Gulati, Ashok, Kanchan Chopra, and Padmeje Sexena (1998). "Reform of the Subsidy Regime: Implications for the Agricultural Sector Irrigation and Power," Mimeo, Institute of Economic Growth, Delhi.

Gulati, Ashok, Ruth Meinzen-Dick and K.V. Raju (1999). "From Top-down to Bottoms- up: Industrial Reforms in Indian Irrigation," Mimeographed, Report of IEG-NCAER Project.

Kumar, P. and G.M. Desai (1995). "Fertiliser Use Patterns in India During the Mid-1980s: Micro Level Evidence on Marginal and Small Farmers," in Desai, G.M. and Vaidyanathan, A. (1995) edited *Future Growth of Fertiliser Use in India*, Macmillan India Ltd.

NSSO (1999). *Cultivation Practices in India*, Report No. 451.

14

Globalisation: Neo-Liberal Economic Policies and Small Farmer Development

Y.V. KRISHNA RAO

1. Introduction

Presently Indian agriculture faces an acute, unprecedented and multi-dimensional crisis. The manifestations of this crisis are not restricted to a single region or sub-sector but are visible throughout the country affecting the entire farm sector with varying degrees of severity. The most tragic indicator of the deep and growing agrarian crisis is the alarming increase in the numbers of farmers committing suicides. More than 4,000 farmers have ended their lives in the last four years. More than three-fourths of the reported suicide deaths by farmers in the country are in Andhra Pradesh while Punjab, Karnataka and Rajasthan are the other states where farmers have ended their lives in large numbers. In several cases in Andhra Pradesh, entire families consumed the poisonous pesticides to end their lives along with the head of the household. These acts of tragic desperation show the utter hopelessness in the farmers' lives and the zero-option situation faced by the farmer with recurring crop loss, mounting indebtedness, unstable agricultural commodity prices, no other source of livelihood and the collapse of all support structures around him. Death seemed to be the only way out and death has been stalking the countryside with relentless cruelty over the past five years or more.

The worst sufferers of this crisis are the small and marginal farmers as well as tenants, who have no rights what so ever, as their tenancy is not recorded.

Our paper makes a modest attempt to analyse the root causes of the present agrarian distress and also the importance of small farmer economy in the agrarian sector and offers some policy prescriptions in the end.

2. Structural Composition of Country's Landholdings

India's 127 million cultivators and over 267 million agricultural and other workers in the rural sector—about 400 million persons—have to find their livelihoods. The country's net sown area of 142.6 million hectares covers 36 agro-climatic zones and more than 30 crops are grown in both the *Kharif* and *Rabi* seasons. But, more than 60 per cent of the cultivated area is without assured irrigation and hence is rainfall-dependent. This has major implications for small and marginal farmers who are resource-poor and have a low asset-base.

The number of small and marginal holdings is about 83.42 per cent of the total ownership holdings of about 112 millions with about 35.53 per cent area of the total ownership holdings, in 1991-92, according to the report on land and livestock holdings, 48th round 1992, N.S.S. Report No. 398.

But according to operational holdings, the number of small and marginal holdings forms 80.0 per cent of the total operational holdings, with about 34.30 per cent of the total operational areas. This brings out beyond any doubt, the important place the small and marginal farms occupy in the agrarian economy of our country. The percentage share of these small and marginal farms and the percentage share of area under them is even greater in some states like Kerala, West Bengal, Tamil Nadu, Bihar, Orissa and Uttar Pradesh than the All India average and these farms play a major role in the agricultural economy of these states.

Many of the problems of the resource-poor Indian farmer begin at this point as he has a very weak asset-base in a socio-economic context where land ownership or cultivation is the primary means of livelihood in the rural sector in the absence of viable employment opportunities. Changing agrarian relations in different parts of the country have made tenancy highly insecure and unviable. The rents charged by landowners are often as high as half of the produce (as in coastal Andhra, for example).

The failure of the second phase of post-independence land reforms to alter the structural constraints determining the distribution of land-holdings in India has been well documented and needs no repetition. Asset-concentration in large farms at the top end and unviable holdings in the lower size classes is a picture that has remained unchanged in most of the states across the country where implementation of land reforms and tenancy legislation has been unsuccessful. The average size of operational holding is as low as 0.39 hectare for marginal farmers and 1.43 hectare for small farmers. For the resource-poor farmer, cultivating this small tract of land (with limited access to water and unaffordable prices of vital inputs) is the only source of livelihood. Declining employment opportunities in the rural sector have trapped millions of farmers into low-income subsistence farming.

3. Importance of Small Farm Economy

It is very necessary as well as important to realise that India will continue to be a small farm dominated economy and the planners and the rulers have to plan for viability and sustainability of these small farms. A development model for agriculture, giving a central place for allround development of small farms, is very much needed.

With a broad base and diversified high growth rate, together with technological upgradation, it is possible to achieve 4.5 per cent or even a higher growth rate, which alone will meet the growing needs of our people and industry and also leave reasonable level of surpluses for exports.

So this is the institutional and social setting in which we have to discuss about the prospects for small and marginal farms. The experience of the East and Far-East countries like Japan, South Korea, Taiwan, Indonesia, and China, show that they have achieved high agricultural growth rates for quite a long period, with small farms predominating. West Bengal with more than 90.0 per cent of small and marginal farms has achieved higher per cent growth rates in the eighties and nineties in foodgrains production when compared to other states of the country.

Therefore, the economic liberalisation and trade liberalisation under GATT and its effect on small and marginal farmers would have to be studied very carefully with a view to counteracting any negative impact of liberalisation of the agricultural sector on the small and marginal farmers. The entry of corporate sector including MNCs into agriculture by acquiring land for large-scale farming would initiate a process of depeasantisation. It would also entrench the corporations in the control of technology including biotechnology and the markets, for not only technology-based products like hybrid seeds, tissue culture based plant varieties, micro-organism induced plant nutrients but also the agro-based processing. There are instances of systematic dispossession of small and marginal farmers.

The rate of growth of employment has declined for the economy as a whole from 2.7 per cent per annum in the period of 1983-94 to 1.07 per cent per annum in the period of 1994-2000. This has happened despite higher growth rates in the GDP indicating a declining employment elasticity of growth. Sectoral data show that the drop in employment growth in agriculture has been very sharp during the same two periods having declined from 2.23 per cent per annum during 1983-94 to 0.02 per cent per annum at the end of 2000. The seasonal nature of the agricultural cycle, the structure of rural labour markets with upward rigidity of wages, the lack of adequate non-farm opportunities in the rural sector—all point to an alarming picture for the rural population in terms of finding a secure and viable source of income. The only available options are either to cultivate own or leased land under conditions of high risk and insecure income or work as agricultural labourers for the limited duration of time when work is available. In the absence of either of these options, the only recourse is migration to other more prosperous regions or cities. Millions of rural people—often-entire villages—are forced by economic circumstances to choose this route in their search for livelihoods. It is estimated that more than 10 million people are on the move. Despite choosing such desperate survival strategies, the number of unemployed persons in the rural sector is growing rapidly and was as high a figure as 20 million in 1999-2000 alone. Given the virtual stagnation of employment opportunities in the rural sector and the severe drought in different parts of the country over the last four years, the numbers are likely to soar in the medium-term in the absence of a coherent national or state-level strategy to tackle the problems of unemployment on such a massive scale.

Persisting Poverty

The implications of inadequate access to land and other means of livelihood on poverty and per capita consumption levels can be easily inferred. Though, it is claimed by official estimates that poverty ratio in India has been on the decline, in absolute terms, the number of those living in poverty is still as high as 260 million persons (1999-2000) and 75 per cent of those are the rural poor. The Tenth Plan has targeted a reduction to 220 million by 2007. The actual number of persons living in poverty in the country would, in reality, be much higher than the official figures. Several economists and other experts have pointed out, based on nutritional norms, the inaccuracies in the official calculations of poverty estimates, which tend to overestimate the decline in poverty ratios and arrive at very low figures to show the number of poor persons at the all India level. As pointed out by Utsa Patnaik[46]:

---

46. Please see Utsa Patnaik, Frontline.

"...The Planning Commission estimate of rural poverty ... is based on the inappropriate procedure used by all official and most academic estimates, which value the quantities consumed by people 30 years ago (quantities required to give 2,400 calories at that time) and apply a price index to update that old poverty line. Quite apart from the problem of a base year for amounts consumed, which is far back in time, the very method of applying a price index to an old 'poverty line' is bound to give perverse results in recent years, when falling employment and falling output prices have been the major causes of distress. The more prices fall, actual agrarian poverty rises and distress intensifies, the lower is the rise in the price index and the lower the official 'poverty line'; hence the greater 'poverty reduction' as per the faulty official method."

If one looks at the figures for per capita net availability of food over the last five years, there has been a sharp drop from 465.7 gms. in 1999 to 438.2 gms. in 2003. For cereals, the drop has been from 429.2 gms. to 409.9 gms. over the same period. For pulses, this decline in per capita availability was from 36.5 gms. in 1999 to 28.2 gms. in 2003. This is the sharpest decline in food availability per capita since the droughts and food crisis of the mid-1960s. While the population increased by 18 million in 2003, foodgrain dropped by 32 million tonnes in that year. Declining agricultural production, declining food availability and increasing poverty and chronic hunger in real terms characterise the agricultural scenario today.

Development Model

In an agrarian country like India, with more than a billion people, 60 per cent of whom are dependent on agriculture, agriculture and rural development should claim utmost attention of all sectors of economy and receive high priority in any programme of national reconstruction and development. Western models of socio-economic and cultural development are not suitable to our country. In western countries, agriculture is based on large and corporate farms. Where as our agriculture is peasants based one with small farms and small farmers predominating. Our model of development should be based on the specifics of our country. Since India is a country of diverse cultures with different languages, religions, castes, customs and traditions, no achievement can be said to have occurred, if the basics of development in terms of the socio-cultural aspects are ignored. The real development is human development and all development initiatives are to be guided with human dimensions of development.

The neo-liberal approach to economic development was based on freeing market forces to operate without restriction and reducing the role of the state in the economy to one of facilitation rather than direct intervention. The most serious implications of this approach were clearly evident in the deteriorating state of agriculture in terms of key economic indicators during the 1990s.

By the eighties, the model of capitalist development based on state capitalism and state regulation to promote the interest of the bourgeoisie-landlord classes had exhausted its possibilities and reached a dead-end. By 1991, the balance of payments crisis had reached unmanageable proportions. Financing the capitalist development had led to huge borrowings. The external debt stood at Rs. 1,63,000 crore ($ 83.8 Billion) at the end of March 1991. India had emerged as the third largest debtor in the world.

An appropriate development model for agricultural development, basing on the specificities of our country is very much needed at this particular context. Imitating western models of development have been proved un-suitable for our country with more than 100 crore population, of which nearly 70.0 per cent depend directly or indirectly on agriculture and allied sectors for their livelihood. For such a highly populated, agrarian society with small peasant economy, a different model of development that can utilise the abundant land and manpower, is very much needed.

After liberalisation and opening up of the agriculture to the entry of corporate sector, including the MNCs and globalisation of agricultural trade, a new situation has arisen. It is also being argued that for higher agricultural growth rates and for export promotion of agricultural products, bigger sized farms are needed. The experience of East and South-East Asian countries, where small farms predominate negates the above argument. Japan's rice yields exceed 7 tonnes per hectare.

The only thing, which the country needs, is primacy of agricultural development and to make the small and marginal farmers economy the centre stage of our agricultural development. The number of marginal and small farmers was ever swelling due to various reasons. Their percentage share in the total operational holdings in the country was 60.1, with 16.2 per cent of the total area under cultivation in 1950-51.

By 1990-91, the number of these holdings as well as the area under them has increased, with sharp differences from state to state. The percentage share of the marginal and small operational holdings stood at

78.0 of the total of 105 millions or so in 1990-91 with 32.2 per cent of the total area under cultivation. The social composition of these sections is overwhelmingly backward classes, Scheduled Castes and Scheduled Tribes. They are the most disadvantaged sections, exploited by the landlords and moneylenders and also often subjected to social oppression and physical attacks by the upper sections of the rural society.

In addition, these sections are also exploited in the exchange market both as producers as well as purchasers by the monopolies and middleman. Under the various Five Year Plans, much is said about the betterment of these poorer sections of the rural society, but nothing much was achieved so far. The various schemes launched by the Government, have not yielded the desired results because of faulty planning and wrong implementation.

Today these are the sections, which are mostly under the poverty line. For this distressing and sorry state of affairs after half a century of our independence, the major factor is utter lack of commitment and political will on the part of the ruling classes. Recently New Economic Policy was initiated, with liberalisation of all aspects of the economic life of this country. All these policies are affecting the Indian agriculture and related sectors. But the pity is that the urgent problem of all round development of small and marginal farmers has not so far received the attention of the policymakers and the government. So much so these problems have not yet occupied the centre stage of overall developmental plans.

4. Root Causes for the Present Agrarian Distress

The present crisis in the agricultural sector is the result of several factors that have been operating for the last two to three decades. In the absence of policy interventions to address these factors, the outcome is a grim scenario for millions of farmers in the country. India has one of the largest agricultural sectors in the world with the task of ensuring food security to more than one billion people. The sector generates around 23 per cent of the country's GDP, which declined from almost 29 per cent in 1993-94. But, despite the sector's contribution to GDP falling, the slow— almost stagnant—absorption of the rural workforce into other sectors has kept 650 million people dependent on the fortunes of agriculture for their livelihood. Why is Indian agriculture unable to develop and transform the socio-economic status of rural households? Despite high rates of growth achieved in specific crops restricted to specific regions of the country, the performance of the sector has been inadequate and output growth has slowed down in the 1990s. By the late 1990s, the looming agricultural crisis recognised to be substantially the consequence of inadequate agricultural services, including extension, reliable seed supply, quality pesticides, machinery, proper soil testing, soil conservation, market information and market intelligence. The impressive growth in foodgrain production from 50 million tonnes in 1950-51 to over 212 million tonnes in 2001-02, which has brought the country to self-sufficiency in terms of zero foodgrain imports, has led to complacency and diverted attention from the underlying structural weaknesses of Indian agriculture and the overwhelming constraints now facing the Indian farmer.

The causes of this wide spread crisis are complex and manifold, reflecting technological and weather-related factors, changes in relative prices and reduced levels of public involvement. It is true that climatic shifts have played a negative role, especially in terms of generally lower rainfall, more uneven and untimely rain and growing regional variation in the rainfall. However, the main causes are dominantly related to public policy, and in particular to an economic strategy at both central government and state government levels, which systematically reduced the protection afforded to farmers and exposed them to market volatility and private profiteering without adequate regulation, reduced critical forms of public expenditure, destroyed important public institutions and did not adequately generate other non-agricultural economic activities.

The crisis in agriculture in turn has affected other sectors also. Rural and agricultural development have received a severe setback and employment opportunities have declined in the rural economy. Unemployment has increased very sharply. Poverty has increased. So also rural indebtedness has increased by leaps and bounds. The closure of many small-scale industries worsened the problems of people living in surrounding villages, as they lost their employment and chances for self-employment received a setback.

The increase in the number of farmers' suicides was the most distressing sign of extreme despair and hopelessness, and where as the starvation deaths are the most blatant indicators of the extent of rural devastation. The proximate cause of such suicide is usually the inability to cope with the burden of debt, which the farmers find them unable to repay.

This entire process is sometimes presented as a situation in which rural people have been 'left out' of the process of globalisation, and have been 'marginalised' or 'excluded.' But the problem is not only that all cultivators and workers in this state have been 'left out.' Rather they have been incorporated and integrated into market systems that are intrinsically loaded against them, in which their lack of assets, poor protection through regulation and low bargaining power have operated to make their material conditions more adverse and living conditions more miserable.

The technological breakthrough in high-yielding varieties of wheat and later in rice combined with input-intensive farm practices led to the green revolution. The resulting record levels in output were spatially restricted to the well-irrigated regions of a small number of states—mainly Punjab, Haryana, Western Uttar Pradesh and Andhra Pradesh. But, the environmental costs of the high-yielding technology became evident only in the 1980s with depletion in soil nutrients through over-application of chemical fertilisers. Declining growth rates in productivity set in over a period of time in most of the regions that led the technology-driven growth of agricultural crops. All-India data on yield growth rates for major crops show a significant decline in the 1990s compared with the 1980s. For rice, the decline was from 3.19 per cent in the first period to 1.27 per cent in the second period; for wheat from 3.11 per cent to 2.11 per cent; for pulses, from 1.61 per cent to 0.96 per cent and for oilseeds, from 2.43 per cent to 1.25 per cent. The sharpest fall was recorded for cotton with the yield growth rate declining from 4.1 per cent in the 1980s to 0.61 per cent by 1999-2000. For total foodgrains as a whole, there was a drop in yield growth rates from 2.74 per cent in the 1980s to 1.52 per cent in the 1990s. Non-foodgrains recorded a decline in yields from 2.31 per cent to 1.04 per cent over the same period.

With limits to output growth through area expansion, high yields combined with high sustainability have to be achieved to expand output. But, this objective is becoming more and more difficult to achieve in the present policy climate, where the necessary thrust to bring about a second technological revolution and reverse the trend of declining total factor productivity in agriculture is lacking. As stated by Mellor several years ago[47]: "The rate of growth of foodgrain production is determined by the basic structural forces of investment in irrigation systems, biological research, the diffusion of technical innovations to farmers, and their education for using new inputs intensively. The strength of each of these forces is the product of public policy. ...

---

47. Please see Mellor John W. (1976). *The New Economics of Growth.*

Achieving high levels of production will require assigning top priority to each of these functions and engaging in vigorous action" (Mellor, 1976: p.65).

This brings us to the key factor responsible for the present agrarian crisis that threatens to engulf every vulnerable region and farmer in the country. The multifarious problems faced by the Indian farmer can be traced to the neo-liberal economic policies being pursued in the country with emphasis on a substantial withdrawal or retreat of the state from proactive interventions in the economy. The paradigm shift in economic policy since the 1980s towards 'free markets' and relaxation of controls on key sectors and areas of the economy, have been largely responsible for the present situation, which the farmer confronts at every stage of his day-to-day existence. Whether it is the high cost of inputs like chemical fertilisers and pesticides, or the non-availability of quality, certified seed, or lack of access to timely and adequate water, or low-priced power to run his pumps, or non-availability of efficient extension services, marketing facilities, and remunerative prices—in all these areas, the farmer today is deprived of each and every facility that is essential for efficient and profitable cultivation. Volumes have been written on these deprivations— most notably, the total failure of institutional credit—forcing the farmer to resort to borrowing from informal sources at exorbitant rates of interest. The virtual collapse of adequate credit delivery mechanisms for the small and marginal farmer is at the root of the sad saga of growing indebtedness and ultimate suicide.

An analysis of the current agrarian crisis in the country has to begin with the developments prior to 1980, which brought about a paradigm shift at the policy level in both industrialised and developing countries worldwide. Without going into the details of the theoretical debate of 'state *versus* market,' which dominated approaches to economic policy, the present agrarian crisis can not be analysed properly. It can be said that by 1980 the intellectual hegemony of neo-liberal theories based on market-driven economics ('getting the prices right') was clearly established. Free markets operating with a minimum of government intervention were put forward as the most efficient resource-allocaters with the potential of bringing about the best possible economic outcomes. The aim of policy intervention by the government, therefore, is to be limited in this approach to removing market-distortions and allowing market forces to operate without restrictions. This view became dominant in countries across the world despite their diverse economic systems and different stages of capitalist development. Globalisation facilitated this process with disastrous results in several economies where unregulated markets wreaked havoc—most notably in the financial sector. The hazards of free market-based theories have been critiqued by several experts.

The structural adjustment policies and what has come to be known as the 'Washington Consensus' have legitimised this approach to economic policy. The key thrust areas of this approach are: the withdrawal of the state from direct intervention in the economy; full play of market forces; privatisation of state-owned enterprises; liberalisation of trade through lowering of tariff barriers and other trade-distorting measures; and fiscal restructuring through reallocation of budgetary priorities.

The whole package of neo-liberal policies as outlined above (with minor variants adapted to suit each country) constituted 'economic reforms' that were implemented in country after country during the 1980s and 1990s.

Warnings Ignored

Not that there were no prior warnings of this calamitous situation. Eminent economic experts cautioned the government long back that if the government continues its step-motherly attitude towards agriculture and its development, the country will face a serious situation in the agricultural sector. The most regrettable and shameful thing is the state and central governments continues their callous and criminal attitude. Now it is more than clear that the present agrarian distress is not, nature made but man-made *viz.*, by government.

Gross Capital Formation in Agriculture

Resources allocated to agriculture are important tools in the state's control, which can accelerate the pace of growth in the agricultural sector. However, this vital instrument has been wasted by abysmal levels of public investment in agriculture. The share of this indicator in GDP declined from 1.6 per cent in 1993-94 to 1.3 per cent in 2000-01. The share of the public sector in gross capital formation in agriculture has dropped from 17.1 per cent in 1980-81 to 4.9 per cent in 2000-01 (Table 14.1). This decline over the last two decades has been a cause for growing concern about sustainable growth and the future of the agricultural sector. The creation of productive assets is no longer possible in a sector that contributes about a quarter of the country's GDP. Starving the sector of investment resources is occurring at a time

Table 14.1

Share of Agricultural and Allied Sectors in Gross Capital Formation

(at 1993-94 prices in percentage)

Year	Public Sector	Private Sector	Total
1980-81	17.10	13.60	15.40
1981-82	14.10	09.20	11.20
1982-83	13.10	12.30	12.70
1983-84	13.50	14.40	13.90
1984-85	11.80	11.50	11.70
1985-86	10.20	09.50	09.80
1986-87	08.90	10.10	09.60
1987-88	10.10	13.20	11.70
1988-89	08.80	09.70	09.30
1989-90	07.50	09.10	08.40
1990-91	07.10	11.90	09,90
1991-92	06.60	09.90	08.70
1992-93	06.70	10.50	09.10
1993-94	06.90	09.40	08.40
1994-95	06.70	07.70	07.30
1995-96	07.10	05.90	06.20
1996-97	07.00	07.50	07.40
1997-98	06.20	07.50	07.10
1998-99	05.70	07.80	07.20
1999-2000	05.10	08.20	07.20
2000-01	04.90	08.20	07.10

Source: Central Statistical Organisation, New Delhi.

when the sector faces enormous challenges from several fronts and the vulnerability of small farmers and landless agricultural labourers has increased to alarming levels.

In this connection the RBI Annual Report 2003-04 in Para 2.14 observes as follows:

"Slowdown of investment in agriculture has impacted the pace and pattern of technological change. During the ten-year period spanning from 1993-94 to 2002-03, the ratio of gross capital formation in agriculture to real GDP originating in agriculture increased only by one percentage point from 6.1 per cent to 7.1 per cent. This was mainly on account of the share of the public sector in gross capital formation in agriculture, which declined from 33 per cent in 1993-94 to 24.2 per cent in 2000-01. Decelerating public sector investment in agriculture, which goes primarily towards major irrigation projects, has also impeded adequate private sector investment in critical areas. The Committee on Capital Formation in Agriculture (2003) (Chairman: Prof. B.B. Bhattacharya) had noted that the lagging share of agriculture in aggregate capital formation relative to its share in real GDP raises a strong case for increasing the capital formation in agriculture commensurate with its share in GDP."

The declining policy priority to agriculture is further reflected in the declining plan allocations to agriculture and the development programmes directed towards the sector (Table 14.2). The share of total plan outlay allocated to this sector declined from 37 per cent in the First Plan to about 20.1 per cent in the Tenth Plan.

Table 14.2

Declining Plan Allocations to Agriculture and Allied Activities and Development Programmes

Particulars	Agriculture & Allied	Rural Development	Special Area Programme	Irrigation & Flood Control	Total (in percentage)
First Plan (1951-56)					37.0
Second Plan (1956-61)					20.9
Third Plan (1961-66)					20.5
Fourth Plan (1969-74)	19.7			8.6	28.3
Fifth Plan (1974-79)	12.4			9.8	22.2
Sixth Plan (1980-85)	6.1	6.4	1.4	10.0	23.9
Seventh Plan (1985-90)	5.8	7.0	1.6	7.6	22.0
Eighth Plan (1992-97)	5.2	7.9	1.6	7.5	22.2
Ninth Plan (1997-2002)	4.4	8.5	0.4	6.5	19.8
Tenth Plan (2002-07)	3.9	8.0	1.4	6.8	20.1

Source: Rangarao,[48] 2004.

The Supply of Inputs for Agriculture

Given the vast size of cultivated area in the country and the regional diversities across agro-climatic regions, the State has a major role to play

---

48. Rangarao Ganamanani (2004).

in ensuring an adequate supply of quality of inputs. This role gains greater importance in a context where the majority of cultivators are resource-poor farmers. Seed, water, power, chemical fertilisers and pesticides are the key inputs whose assured supply at low cost and timely availability is vital for agriculture. The weight of fertilisers, pesticides and diesel, which accounted for barely 15 per cent of total inputs in 1970-71, rose to 55 per cent in 1995-96.

The price-support mechanism in the form of MSP extends to 24 crops and is an essential instrument to protect farm incomes. However, the procurement is mainly from farmers with large surpluses and, therefore, it is large farmers, who benefit most from this policy. The issue of un-remunerative prices for small and marginal farmers who are unprotected from market fluctuations remains.

Social Sector Development

The neglect of rural population by successive governments over the last fifty years is the most clearly evident in the state of physical and social infrastructure. The impact of neo-liberal policies on the development of the social sector has been immense. The combined expenditure of the centre and the states on social services (education, health, women and child development, rural development, etc.) has remained relatively stagnant since the late 1980s. Expenditure under this head accounted for 18.9 per cent of total expenditure in 1986-87 and, apart from a slight increase at the end of the 1990s; it remained at about 19.8 per cent in 2003-04.[49]

In terms of the UNDP's Human Development Index (HDI), India ranks 127 among 175 countries, down from 124 in 2000. The HDI measures over all achievements in terms of three basic dimensions—health and longevity, education and standard of living. A disturbing trend is that the total plan and non-plan expenditures on the social sector by both the Centre and the States show a continuous decline in the share of social sector in total expenditures since 2000-01.

However, rural distress and the material problems of farmers also have social counterparts, in that many farmers have become indebted because of the increased expenditure on health and education, as well as other spending due to social pressures such as dowry demands. This has added to farmers' problems because given the precarious economic situation,

---

49. GoI. (2004), *Economic Survey*, Ministry of Finance, Government of India, New Delhi.

even small debts contracted to pay the health expenses for a member of a family can push a farmer, especially small farmer, into a downward spiral of greater indebtedness

The debt trap has emerged in the agricultural sector due to a number of reasons that have been traced earlier. Rising input costs, shrinking operational holdings, increasing instability of output, low access to institutional credit, dominance of private dealers in inputs in rural areas, increased threat of crop loss through natural calamities as climate change globally disturbs the weather and monsoon cycle, lack of crop insurance and unending risk faced by small and marginal farmers, are the main reasons leading the farmer into the debt trap where he is at the mercy of non-institutional, private money-lenders. On taking loans at the exorbitant rates charged by informal credit sources, the farmer's fate is sealed even before the harvest season.

Loans from institutional secures need to be made available to farmers before the agricultural operations commence. So, the government should direct all credit delivery institutions to begin the procedures well in time for the coming season. Banks need to inform potential and actual borrowers of all the various loans schemes available, the terms and conditions attached to loans, and particularly, the terms of rescheduling etc. Special attention should be taken to ensure that illiterate borrowers and potential borrowers are aware of the terms and conditions of loans. The attitude of bank staff towards farmers needs to be reoriented and monitored, with orientation to ensure that bank workers have a farmer-friendly attitude and avoid delays in sanctioning small loans.

5. UPA Government

As stated above the policy failures in agriculture since the 1980s have been monumental. The task of revitalising the agricultural sector now rests with the new UPA coalition government. This is a long neglected stupendous and many-sided problem. This requires utmost attention, concentration and priority in the activities of the governments.

The present UPA government should rise to the occasion and take drastic steps on a war footing to redress the situation and revitalise the agriculture sector. Nothing short of a complete reversal of the policies followed up to now by the NDA Government is urgently needed. A new development model-environmental friendly and sustainable-of planning and its implementation is very much needed. The new agricultural policy prepared by the NDA Government has to be scraped and a new rapid agricultural development policy should be announced and speedily implemented.

As a first step the UPA Government should strictly and urgently implement the National Common Minimum Programme, enlisting the cooperation of the people, particularly the oppressed and down-trodden.

6. Policy Prescriptions

- Public investment in agriculture and allied sectors should be stepped-up at least to the level of 10.0 per cent of the GDP from agriculture, so that this can attract more private sector investments.

- While doubling the flow of rural credit, steps should be taken to see that 50 per cent of the credit in the public sector should go to the small and marginal farmers. Restructuring and democratisation of cooperative sector should be done without delay.

- Employment guarantee for 100 days in rural areas should be made a legally enforceable right and the scheme should be oriented to create permanent assets in agricultural and rural development sectors.

- Restructuring of agrarian relations by strictly implementing the land reform acts and also by unearthing *benami* transactions. Distribution of all cultivable government waste lands as well as the reclaimed waste lands should be taken up without further loss of time.

- A different model of development taking into consideration of our country's specifics should be worked out and implemented by mobilising our abundant land and labour resources.

- States and Central Governments should encourage and establish small-scale agro-based and skill-based rural industries on a big scale to provide employment to all the unemployed in the rural side.

- To find financial resources for all such developmental schemes, the present low Tax-GDP ratio should be raised.

- Fiscal Responsibility and Budget Management Act, adapted at the Centre and States level should be scraped, so that it gives government elbowroom to take some monetary measures to raise funds for productive purposes.

- In addition government should take steps to unearth the black money and end corruption. Strict measures should be taken to end tax avoidance. All tax arrears should be collected speedily.

These steps energise the latent productive forces and make our agricultural sector a healthy and a resilient sector achieving 4.0 or even 4.5 per cent annual growth Rate.

Mass mobilisation and vigilance is the only guarantee for the strict and speedy implementation of above detailed policy options.

References

Ganamanani, Rangarao (2004). "Performance of Agricultural Sector in India since 1990s" (Paper presented at the *National Seminar on Institutional Policy Options for Sustainable Agricultural Development*, organised by the Department of Economics, Osmania University, Hyderabad during 10-11, April 2004).

Mellor, John W. (1976). *The New Economics of Growth*, Cornell University Press, Ithaca, New York, p. 65.

Patnaik, Utsa (2004). "The Immediate Way Out," *Frontline*, Vol. 21, Issue 13, June 19-July 2, http://www.flonet.com/fl2113/fl211300.htm.

15

Changes in Agrarian Structure and Agricultural Technology: Is Peasant Farming Sustainable under Institutional Retrogression

D. NARASIMHA REDDY

1. Introduction

The main objective of this paper is to bring out the hiatus between the peasantry's growing need and willingness to switch to high productivity agriculture on the one hand, and the failure of the support systems, including public investment in infrastructure, research, extension, insurance, institutional credit, marketing and regulatory systems on the other. The paper is divided into four sections. The first section provides an overview of the changes in the agrarian structure in India, which brings out those land reforms, in spite of inadequacies, along with demographic change effected a change in the landholding structure predominantly towards small-marginal holdings. The second section briefly refers to the emerging challenges by way of technological changes in the farming systems, pressures on resources and ecological sustainability, the needed innovations and growing risks. The third section draws attention to the specificities of certain structural changes and institutional failures. These include some micro-experiences from Andhra Pradesh, during the last decade, which tend to exasperate sustainability of peasant agriculture. The last part argues for revival of source as well as creation of more appropriate support and regulatory institutional systems with specific attention to small peasants.

2. Agrarian Reforms and Changes in Agrarian Structure

The diversity and complexity of the Indian agrarian conditions are proverbial, either in their existence form as inherited in the middle of the century or in terms of the changes over the last half a century. Yet, certain broad trends are discernible. The post-independent India has experienced considerable institutional and technological changes, which have contributed substantially to the evolving production conditions and production relations of the Indian agriculture. Though, several political struggles in the pre-independence period were aimed against the feudal dominance of agrarian relations, land reforms in the post-independent India, not withstanding all its limitations, marked a beginning towards abolishing feudal exploitation in agriculture. Whatever the other flaws that went with the implementation of the abolition of intermediaries, the absentee landlordism came to an end by the middle of 1950s. The consolidation of holdings as a measure of reform had a relatively less scope for changing land relations. Though it might have improved productivity by bringing small fragments of holdings together, its implementation was confined to only a few States. The two major distributive land reforms, *viz.* ceilings on holdings and tenancy reforms, which were introduced through State Legislative Acts in the 1950s and 1960s, came for severe criticism on their implementation failures attributed to lack of political will or the willing administrative collusion to dilute their impact. Such a capacity of the bureaucracy to act in tandem with the political interests was attributed to the common interest of upper caste rich peasantry from which both the political leadership and the administrative cadres are drawn. In some States, where political parties had peasant and working class support, had a different experience. The ceilings and tenancy legislations have acquired varying degrees of deformation in their implementation in different parts of the country. For the present purpose of the paper, it would be worthwhile to confine to Rao's excellent stylised typology to capture the divergence in the land reforms experience of India (Rao, 1992). He observes four broad patterns in the implementation of land reforms in India.

First, the semi-feudal areas like Bihar, where, according to scholars like Pradhan Prasad, the barriers to reforms inherent in the prevailing structure of society are too strong to be overcome by the scale and intensity of efforts for land reforms made so far.

Second, areas (e.g. Karnataka) with less formidable barriers to land reforms and stronger thrust for reforms as compared to 'semi-feudal' areas but having mixed and, on the whole, modest results of reforms.

Third, areas (e.g. West Bengal and Kerala) with strong political mobilisation and effective land reforms but where the growth performance has been too weak to complement reforms to bring about enduring structural change.

Fourth, the 'Green Revolution' areas (e.g. Punjab) where capitalist farming is firmly entrenched and where reforms are needed mainly to improve wages, work environment and economic conditions of labourers. (Rao, 1992).

On the basis of detailed analysis of the land reforms experience in these four divergent areas, Rao draws the following conclusions, which are again worth quoting at length.

i) In none of the four situations did the land reforms help the rural poor in obtaining secure and equitable access to land in the context of growing population pressure on land and keen competition for its control among the different rural strata.

ii) The dominant rural groups, e.g. *zamindars* in Bihar, large cultivators in Karnataka and capitalist farmers in Punjab—exert decisive influence on the processes of formulation and implementation of land reforms to divert the benefits of the reforms from the rural poor to themselves.

iii) Even where they are politically well organised, as in Kerala and West Bengal, the rural poor get only the direct and proximate benefits of land reforms but do not succeed in bringing about an enduring improvement in their economic status.

iv) The policymakers usually spend considerable time and energy in improving the legislative and implementation aspects of land reforms. While these are important aspects, the crucial criterion for successful land reforms is the extent to which they form part of a cohesive development strategy capable of integrating the objective growth with those of equity and poverty eradication. Without the support of such a strategy, no amount of tinkering with legislation and implementation would be of much help in getting effective land reforms (Rao, 1992).

As the experience reveals, one cannot 'lump together highly capitalist developed agriculture of Punjab with the pre-feudal communal land cultivation in the North-East; the semi-feudalism of Bihar, dominated by the caste-based private armies of the rich, and the dominant peasant self-cultivation of the Southern part of the country. There cannot be a single recipe for all their agricultural ills. Different parts of India are at different levels of agricultural development, requiring diverse ownership-tenancy arrangements' (Dasgupta, 1999).

Table 15.1

Changes in the Distribution of Operational Holdings in India
(Per cent share of each size group)

Years	Marginal Farms (< 1 Hect.)		Small Farms (1-2 Hects.)		Semi-Medium (2-4 Hects.)		Medium Farms (4-10 Hects.)		Large Farms (Above 10 Hects.)		Average Size (Hects.)	Gini Ratio
	No.	Area	No.	Area	No.	Area	No.	Area	No.	Area		
1950-51	38.4	6.0	21.7	10.2	19.2	18.2	15.3	31.6	5.4	34.0	N.A	N.A
1960-61	40.7	6.7	22.3	12.2	18.9	20.0	13.4	30.4	4.7	30.7	2.69	0.58
1970-71	50.6	9.0	19.1	11.9	15.2	18.5	11.2	29.7	3.9	30.9	2.30	0.59
1976-77	54.6	10.7	18.0	12.8	14.3	19.9	10.1	30.4	3.0	26.2	2.00	—
1980-81	56.4	12.1	18.1	14.1	14.0	21.2	19.1	29.6	2.4	23.0	1.84	0.63
1985-86	57.8	13.4	18.4	15.6	13.6	22.3	8.2	28.6	2.0	20.1	1.69	—
1990-91	59.0	14.9	19.0	17.3	13.2	23.2	7.2	27.2	1.6	17.4	1.57	0.64
1995-96	61.6	17.2	19.0	18.8	12.3	23.8	6.1	25.3	1.2	14.8	1.41	0.64

Source: Various Reports of Agricultural Census of India.

The impact of land reforms on the agrarian structure has been a subject of extensive research by several scholars (Haque, 1986, 1994; Sharma, 1994, 1999; Nancharaiah, 1999 - to mention a few). But, here a brief reference is made to the structural changes in terms of emerging differentiation, of which size of holdings and landlessness are important aspects. Table 15.1 is far too familiar to those studying land reforms in India. It reveals that there has been a general tendency of increase in the share of households and the area cultivated by small-marginal farmers; that there has been a reduction in the share of holdings as well as the area cultivated by the large farmers, and that the average size of holdings in all size-classes is on the decline. There has been a marginal increase, nonetheless, in the concentration ratios. The asset concentration would be much high if non-land assets like farm machinery, buildings are included. But the worst part is the phenomenal increase in the 'near landless households.' Although, rural landless households increased only marginally from about 10 per cent in 1970-71 to 11 per cent in 1991-92, if we take those households with less than about half an acre of land, which are referred to as 'near landless' along with the landless, their proportion has increased from about 30 per cent in 1970-71 to about 48 per cent—nearly half of the rural households—by 1990-91 (Sharma 1999). These are the households, which constitute the vast and growing rural underclass.

If we take all those households with about 10 acres (about 4 hectares) or more (medium and large holdings) as constituting the rich peasantry, it is this class, which has emerged as the 'masters of the countryside.' Table 15.1 shows that in the case of this rich peasantry class, until 1970-71, there had been no substantive change either in the share of households or in the share of land operated. They still constituted 15 to 20 per cent of the households and held 60 to 65 per cent of the operational holdings. But in 1970-71, this group of rich peasantry had already emerged as the class for itself and wielded power, not only in the countryside but also acquired capability to influence public policy, apparently to appease the masses; and at the same time, to manipulate the implementation of these policies to their own advantage. It is well-known that land reform legislation, particularly relating to land ceilings, hardly had any effect on the landholdings of the rich peasantry till the end of 1960s. By 1970s, when considerable political pressure called for effective legislation and implementation, the rich peasant class was already strategically well entrenched. Wherever land was emerging as an increasingly productive asset, both because of public investment and because of new technology, the land reforms were subverted with impunity. The ceiling surpluses were kept to the minimum, and the surplus land surrendered often was of very poor quality. Even with surrenders of substandard surplus land, the total ceiling surplus land redistributed to the poorer peasantry hardly constitutes about two per cent of the total cultivated land in India, in comparison to about 25 to 40 per cent in the case of East Asian countries. What is retained by the rich peasantry is not only better quality of land but also the land which became better productive asset because of benefits of State investments in providing infrastructure like irrigation and power facilities. This was also the land of the rich peasantry that was ready to receive the improved technology along with the heavy doses of State subsidies.

Thus, when we refer to the top 15 per cent of the rural households operating about 50 per cent of the land, at the end of 1960s substantive proportion of this land was more productive land, while the small-marginal farmers who constituted about 80 per cent of the households operating only about 30 per cent of the land, substantive part of which was of near poor quality, with the exception of command areas. The gini ratios or worsening nature of land concentration in some of the States need to be read along with the qualitative differences in the land operated by the rich and the poor. It was not until the 1970s, when the revised land ceiling legislative measures acquired a certain cutting edge, there appeared a tendency towards a shift in the proportion of households as well as area held under the large peasant category.

The tenancy legislation, which apparently had the objective of transferring land to the cultivator (with the exception of tenants under the *zamindars* and other intermediaries who were abolished in 1950s), has never been nearer the objective of 'land to the tiller.' On the contrary, it has driven the tenancy underground in most of the States including Andhra Pradesh. There has been faster growth of unrecorded tenancy in the relatively better-endowed parts of Andhra Pradesh with hardly any protection but with intensification of growing exploitation. The most acclaimed tenancy reform of West Bengal, the 'Operation Barger,' only helped in formalising the share-cropper-owner relations; and in Kerala, it made the owners to keep their land fallow, lest they should loose it to tenants, if leased out. What is emerging as 'reverse tenancy' in States like Punjab and Haryana is only making the rich peasantry to improve their command over rural resources, while reducing the small peasantry to the brink of threatened dispossession! The class character of the entire gamut of agrarian reforms in all its variations are best summed-up when V.M. Rao draws attention to J.P. Singh's study of land reforms in Punjab. It is a classic instance of how the capitalist farmers were the net beneficiaries of both the ill-implemented and the well-implemented agrarian reform programmes (Rao, 1992).

Many of the peasant movements for better prices and subsidies often turn out to be at the behest of the rich peasantry. That none of these so-called farmers' movements have ever demanded streamlining the process of transfer of ownership rights to cultivating tenants or effective implementation of ceilings legislation, are reasons adequate to reveal their class character. A large proportion of the small peasantry, because of the caste loyalties or hopes of benefits from the State, has become part of the rich peasant mobilisations and often makes common cause against agricultural labourers whose interests are actually much closer to the small peasantry.

2.1 Technology and Equity

By 1980s, it was apparent that small-marginal farmers come to numerically dominate the Indian agriculture but yet end up in a precarious position because of technological changes as much as policy and other prominent changes over which they could not assert their power. The introduction of 'Green Revolution Technology' in its first phase during 1960s and 1970s eluded the small-marginal farmers not only because of its limited spread, but also because of their inability to access resources. There have been a number of studies on Green Revolution's implications to growth of output, employment and equity or distributional aspects. Its contribution to the growth of output has not been contested much. Questions are, nonetheless, raised on its sustainability in terms of productivity growth, soil fertility and environmental impact. In the first phase (1967-68–1980-81) of Green Revolution, agricultural output in India increased by 2.38 per cent per annum, and during the second phase (1980-81–1991-92), there was a wider spread and a faster growth rate of 3.21 per cent. However, its employment implications have been ambiguous. The distributional effects, both in terms of inter-regional and inter-class terms, have come for close scrutiny (Byres, 1981; Rao, 1971; Dasgupta, 1977; Bhalla, 1977). In the spread of the technology till the end of 1970s, it was largely confined to wheat crop and the irrigated belt of Punjab, Haryana and Western Uttar Pradesh to begin with, and later to HYV paddy too in these parts. The spread from these limited regions extended to pockets of assured irrigation in the Western and Southern parts. The induction in terms of new crops came with the entry of hybrid cotton, *Jowar* and *Bajra* in the 1970s. Still, the technology growth was skewed towards Northwest, West and Southern regions till 1983-84 (Bhalla and Tyagi, 1989). It was not until the early 1980s that HYV paddy spread to substantial areas in the Eastern States of Orissa, West Bengal, Bihar and parts of Assam. The 1980s witnessed not only the spread of HYV technology, but also diversification of agriculture led by faster growth of non-food crops (Sawant and Achutan, 1995).

While land reforms failed to bring about any radical redistribution of land, the introduction of new technology has brought about sharper differentiation among peasantry by opening up more profitable opportunities in agriculture to the rich peasantry. The impression created is that the 'HYV technology,' unlike the heavy farm machinery-based technology, does not impose any size barriers of entry for small-marginal farmers. But in actual practice, the '... new technology' has been biased in favour of those who have better command over resources. Even those studies, which found that the new technology benefited all, had come out with an emphatic observation that, "the gains of larger farmers ... were disproportionately large' (Rao, 1975). The rich peasants with better resources, access to information, risk bearing capacity, input buying capacity, access to cheap credit and better reach to scarce inputs through cooperatives or the government agencies have become adept in adopting the new technology (Byres, 1981). Some of the middle peasantry who could access all the resources seem to have become rich themselves by adopting the new technology. But the small peasantries are caught in this milieu and suffer the worst deprivation, though their knowledge is adequate for new technology, (but) their economic capacity to mobilise resources and bear the risks are very inadequate.

3. Challenges Before Small Peasantry

By 1980s, just at a time when the small-marginal peasantry needed to find its feet in high productivity agriculture, there have emerged a number of technological, resource related and institutional changes. First, farming systems have been undergoing shift from crops based on traditional variety to high-yielding varieties to hybrids to Genetically Modified (GM) crops. The shift to high value but high-risk GM crops is also accompanied by increasing exposure to market dependence for seeds, which may also carry *sui generis* kind of intellectual property rights for which farmers end up paying exorbitant prices. These changing cropping systems necessitate knowledge-based practices, timely and comprehensive extension systems and services. The cropping-pattern is also bound to change from the cereal bias to more diversified and high value crops, because of the demand driven factors like fast changing composition of the food consumption basket.

Secondly, there has been growing pressure on the agricultural resource base, requiring measures to mitigate the adverse impact. Land degradation due to excessive use of chemical fertilisers and soil-erosion due to extension of cultivation to marginal lands are problems that are more familiar. The answers, in the form of shift towards organic farming and crop rotation, are not easy options particularly to small farmers, unless accompanied by appropriate institutional support systems. More challenging is the pressure on water resources. While the problems of water-logging, salinity and reduction of wastage are some of the problems often addressed in the context of command areas, the serious crisis is as a consequence of over-exploitation and resulting irreversible depletion of groundwater resources, especially in dry and drought-prone areas. Apart from resource depletion and un-sustainability of groundwater exploitation, the major problem thrown up by dependence on groundwater as a source of irrigation arises out of the fact that it involves farmer-based private investment, which is obtained even by small farmers at very high interest rates from non-institutional sources. The risks are high and the failure or depletion of water table has often been the trigger for many suicides in these regions.

Third, the institutional sources of credit, and other inputs supplies like fertilisers, pesticides and seeds, have been on the decline over the years. Most of the small-marginal farmers are driven to depend on unregulated and unscrupulous sources. While the emerging system of agriculture necessitate more sophisticated knowledge based information systems, extension systems are almost defunct or in disarray.

Fourth, while it is well recognised that a reasonable livelihood for a small-marginal farm could only be ensured, if part or even half of the income sources are in non-farm activities, there is very little evidence of this fact forming the basis of rural development strategy. There is considerable experience of other countries in this regard, but without much impact on the strategy in India.

Fifth, the challenge of the shift towards free trade driven agriculture even under the AoA of World Trade Organisation (WTO) does not demand indiscriminate abandoning of State support systems. There has been focused strategy of cost reduction based on State supported research and extension investments even in North America and Europe. A small farmer-based agriculture, if it should not only face the challenges of the competition but also rise to the possibility of export orientation, needs strong research and extension support in the whole range of areas from developing appropriate plant varieties to sustainable resource use to market facilitation.

4. Neo-Liberal Reforms and Institutional Retrogression

The roots of the present all pervading crisis in the Indian agriculture could be traced back to the complacency and benign neglect of mid-1980s. Agriculture had fallen from policy priority under the euphoria that the country had left behind the days of shortages and achieved sustainable self-sufficiency in foodgrain production that agriculture reached a level of development where it could respond to the domestic market as well as global prices, if only the market restrictions are revised and that preferential and institutional interventions are anachronisms. But the worse deal had to wait till the 1990s when the reforms influenced every measure of public policy including agriculture at the behest of the Central Government and was carried on with different degrees of zeal at the State level. The unfinished distributive reforms were seen as obstacles to incentives, and liberal markets are expected to bring about technological break through. The result is rapid decline of institutional support to agriculture based on well-deliberated principles of growth and equity. The evidence compiled here, both at macro and micro-level, suggests the rapid retrogression in the agricultural support systems, which have been at the root of the present crisis in the agricultural sector in general, and the vast majority of the poor peasantry in particular.

Table 15.2

Gross Capital Formation (GCF) in Agriculture in India

Years	GCF in Agriculture as a Percentage of Total CGF	Public Sector GCF in Agriculture as a Percentage of Total Public Sector CGF
1980-81	19.1	16.08
1981-82	18.0	15.93
1982-83	13.9	11.17
1983-84	14.1	N.A
1984-85	12.8	N.A
1985-86	13.7	N.A
1986-87	11.2	5.37
1987-88	10.4	9.44
1988-89	11.7	8.17
1989-90	9.7	6.89
1990-91	9.8	6.53
1991-92	9.2	5.91
1992-93	10.1	5.72
1993-94	10.3	6.95
1994-95	9.8	6.83
1995-96	8.8	7.21
1996-97	9.1	6.90
1997-98	9.4	5.92
1998-99	9.0	5.56
1999-00	8.8	5.40

Note: N.A. – Not Available.

Source: National Account Statistics, Central Statistical Organisation (various issues).

A clear indication of the neglect of agriculture could be seen from a steep decline in the share of public investment in agriculture as could be seen from Table 15.2. The Table also shows that there has been decline in the overall investment in agriculture, because the rise in private investment is far too small to compensate for the declining share of public investment.

Table 15.3

Trends in Public Expenditure on Agriculture and Allied Activities in Andhra Pradesh (As Percentage of GSDP)

Years	Plan Expenditure	Non-Plan Expenditure	Revenue Expenditure	Capital Expenditure	Total Expenditure
1990-91	0.21	0.63	0.82	0.02	0.84
1991-92	0.28	0.70	0.96	0.02	0.98
1992-93	0.47	0.63	1.07	0.03	1.10
1993-94	0.23	0.52	0.73	0.03	0.76
1994-95	0.24	0.44	0.66	0.01	0.67
1995-96	0.19	0.41	0.58	0.01	0.59
1996-97	0.27	0.37	0.62	0.01	0.64
1997-98	0.26	0.38	0.62	0.02	0.64
1998-99	0.25	0.37	0.59	0.03	0.62
1999-00	0.16	0.38	0.53	0.01	0.54
2000-01	0.23	0.39	0.60	0.01	0.61
2001-02	0.16	0.36	0.50	0.01	0.51
2002-03	0.17	0.38	0.54	0.01	0.55

Source: Handbook of Statistics on State Government Finances, RBI, 2004.

For instance, in States like Andhra Pradesh (Table 15.3) there has been a systematic decline in the budgetary expenditure on agriculture and allied activities. Extension suffered a worst set back as a matter of deliberate policy. In a policy document on agriculture (Government of Andhra Pradesh, 1999), referring to the declining staff in the agriculture service, the State Government declared that it did not have resources to employ any more extension workers. It was proposed that the entire cadre of agricultural extension officers be wound up. It stated, 'without any additional financial funds to the state', the extension services would be encouraged to become part of the licensed dealers of fertilisers, pesticides and seeds. It proposed to reduce the burden on the Andhra Pradesh Seed Corporation by making private sector more accountable by appropriate Memorandum of Understandings (MoUs) and went on to suggest that soil survey, soil conservation, collection of market information 'can be encouraged to be developed in private sector with appropriate policy incentives' (GoAP, 1999). The failure of extension services, the mushrooming of spurious seed and pesticide companies, the absence of regulatory mechanisms to control their activities and the relegation of the agricultural university and Andhra Pradesh Seeds Corporation to an

Table 15.4

Source-Wise Net Area Irrigated in Andhra Pradesh (Area in '000 hectares)

Years	Sources of Irrigation					Total Net Area Irrigated	Per cent of Net Area Irrigated to Net Area Sown	Area Irrigated More than Once	Gross Area Irrigated	Per cent of Gross Area Irrigated to Gross Area Sown
	Canals	Tanks	Tubewells	Other-Wells	Other Sources					
1990-91	1868	969	283	1021	165	4306	39.07	1169	5454	40.7
1991-92	1826	964	336	1066	177	4351	39.41	1064	5370	40.76
1992-93	1727	728	284	1027	163	4029	38.5	1027	5378	39.9
1993-94	1659	633	526	916	156	3890	37.5	1056	5085	39.6
1994-95	1606	692	599	881	181	3959	38.2	1130	5020	40.5
1995-96	1539	747	709	947	181	4123	38.8	1181	5304	40.6
1996-97	1629	844	741	988	193	4395	40.6	1387	5782	43.1
1997-98	1537	562	774	903	168	3944	40.1	1214	5158	42.5
1998-99	1634	810	916	981	198	4539	41.3	1553	6092	44.7
1999-00	1634	652	1000	900	198	4384	41.3	1362	5746	44.1
2000-01	1649	727	1066	888	198	4528	40.7	1388	5916	43.7
2001-02	1563	567	1116	812	180	4238	40.7	1311	5549	43.5
2002-03	1209	425	1153	690	137	3614	37.6	922	4536	39.2

Source: Season and Crops Report, Directorate of Economics & Statistics, GoAP, Hyderabad, (Various Years).

insignificant role in the research, development and propagation of seeds of non-food crops, are all the consequences of deliberate policy changes in the State. Even a critical infrastructure like irrigation suffered adversely and resulted in the lopsided development of private groundwater sources engendering as the single largest source with all the attendant ecological adversities (Table 15.4). One of the worst set backs agricultural sector and particularly to the small-marginal farmers, is the diminishing share of institutional credit. It fits into the erosion of agriculture as priority and targeted credit as a measure that should be liberated. Table 15.5 shows the decline of the share of both short-term and long-term loans as share of total commercial bank credit to agriculture.

Table 15.5

Short-Term and Long-Term Loans for Agriculture and Allied Activities by Formal Financial Institutions (Amount in Rs. Crore)

Years	Short-Term		Long-Term		Total Bank
	Amount Out-Standing	*Percentage to the Total Bank Credit*	*Amount Out-Standing*	*Percentage to the Total Bank Credit*	*Credit*
1980-81	3367	13.3	4289	16.9	25371
1981-82	4237	14.3	4862	16.4	29682
1982-83	3685	10.4	5995	16.9	35493
1983-84	4339	10.5	7185	17.4	41294
1984-85	5006	10.2	8670	17.7	48953
1985-86	5858	10.4	10377	18.5	56067
1986-87	6236	9.9	11645	18.4	63308
1987-88	7342	10.4	13742	19.5	70536
1988-89	8561	10.1	15239	18.0	84719
1989-90	9527	9.4	18160	17.9	101453
1990-91	10002	8.6	19313	16.6	116301
1991-92	11126	8.9	20723	16.5	125592
1992-93	13713	9.0	22512	14.8	151982
1993-94	12952	7.9	24037	14.6	164418
1994-95	14360	6.8	24691	11.7	211560
1995-96	17793	7.0	28226	11.1	254015
1996-97	20009	7.2	30911	11.1	278401
1997-98	21469	6.6	32949	10.2	324079
1998-99	23521	6.4	33885	9.2	368837
1999-00	26387	6.1	36220	8.3	435958

Source: RBI, Handbook of Statistics on Indian Economy, 2001.

Table 15.6

Trends in Number and Amount Outstanding of Small Borrowal Accounts (SBAs) in All the Rural Financial Institutions

Years	Number of Accounts (in lakh)		Share of SBAs (Per cent)	Amount Outstanding (in Rs. Crore)		Share of SBAs (Per cent)
	All	SBAs		All	SBAs	
1984	295	282	99.5	43326	8897	20.5
1985	336	321	95.6	49995	10028	20.1
1986	388	371	95.8	56182	12615	22.5
1987	434	416	95.8	63727	15444	24.2
1988	480	459	95.6	71285	17954	25.2
1989	521	497	95.4	88027	22330	25.4
1990	539	512	95.0	104312	24147	23.1
1991	619	588	94.9	124203	27323	22.0
1992	659	625	95.0	136706	29945	21.9
1993	621	585	94.2	162467	32091	19.8
1994	596	558	93.6	175891	32188	18.3
1995	581	539	92.8	210939	34060	16.2
1996	567	519	91.6	254692	36252	14.2
1997	556	500	90.1	284373	37446	13.2
1998	535	468	87.4	329944	41095	12.5
1999	523	427	81.7	382425	38284	10.0
2000	543	392	72.2	460080	36408	7.9
2001	523	372	71.1	538433	37816	7.0

Source: RBI, Basic Statistical Returns, 1984-2001 as compiled by P.S.M. Rao(2003).

The small borrowers are worse affected (Table 15.6). While cooperatives appear to languish as the lowest providers of institutional credit because of political interaction and abuse, the special institutions like Regional Rural Banks (RRBs) created with a mission to target weaker sections for rural lending have completely been disoriented towards profits without priority under the reforms.

Table 15.7, based on a survey of eight villages spread across different regions of Andhra Pradesh covering about 1152 loans to farming households, holds a mirror to the starvation of institutional credit to agriculture and continued exploitation of the peasantry with usurious interest charges. The institutional loans account only for about 20 per cent of the loans and about the same proportion of the amount borrowed. The modal interest rate on the private credit is 36 per cent, and over 83 per cent of private lending is at 24 per cent or more. Thus, credit that is the basic requirement in the market-linked agriculture comes at an unsustainable high premium that ends as a major drain on peasant farming. And this is not to mention the harassments of recovery, often to the point of suicides, regardless of the hazards of crop husbandry faced by the farming community.

Table 15.7

Source-wise Interest Changes on Agricultural Loans in Select Villages of Andhra Pradesh

SI. No.	Rate of Interest	Institutional Loans		Non-Institutional Loans		Total Loans	
		Numbers	Per cent	Numbers	Per cent	No.	Per cent
1	<12%	4	1.75	0	0	4	0.04
2	12%	112	49.12	14	1.51	126	10.94
3	13 to 23%	73	32.02	3	0.32	71	6.16
4	24%	31	13.59	370	40.04	401	34.81
5	36%	8	3.5	479	51.84	487	42.27
6	48%	0	0	5	0.54	5	0.04
7	60%	0	0	37	4.0	37	3.21
8	>60%	0	0	16	1.73	16	1.39
Total		228 (19.79)	100	924(80.21)	100	1152(100)	100

Sources: N. Shyam Sundar (2003) and R.S. Rao & M. Bharati (2003).

There are other poignant institutional crises that could be seen from the micro-level studies, which often do not appear in any aggregate on official surveys. Table 15.8 relates to the village studies referred to above. It includes two more villages and in all ten villages from across the State of Andhra Pradesh. Attention is drawn here to the tenancy, which is officially reported more or less non-prevalent. For instance, it is official reported as zero in agriculturally well-endowed West Godavari. But the Table 15.9 shows that in first two villages, both belonging to the district tenancy accounts for 50 per cent to about 70 per cent of the net sown area. The tenants are invariably poor peasants or agricultural labourers and annual rents are fixed in kind at an exorbitantly high level of 36 bags (75kg) of paddy per acre. The tenancy is most even recorded, leave above regulated. The tenants are perpetually exploited by the owners, who are often absentee landowners and the tenants' cultivators are hardly left with the wages for their labour. Yet another manifestation of the crisis in

Table 15.8

Land-Holding Structure in Select Villages of Andhra Pradesh

Name of the Region	Name of the Village	Total No. of Households	Total Owned Area (Acres)	Total Leasing Households		Total Leased-in Area		Average Size of Ownership Holdings (Acres)
				Numbers	% of Leased in Household to Total Households	Area (Acres)	% of Leased in Area to Total Owned Area	
I. South Coastal Andhra	Mentipudi	90	119	37	41.11	60	50.00	1.32
	Kothapalli	208	116	78	37.5	80	69.00	0.55
	Seethampet	170	375	28	16.47	64	17.07	2.21
II. South Telangana	Arepalli	339	1016	18	5.31	54	5.31	2.99
	Tadiparti	216	724	15	6.94	68	9.39	3.35
III. North Telangana	Chinnapur	216	297	23	10.65	43	19.91	1.37
	Nagaram	170	379	14	8.24	24	6.33	2.22
IV. North Coastal Andhra	Jonanki	151	271	43	28.48	59	21.77	1.8
	B. Koduru	171	407	6	3.5	28	6.89	2.29
V. Rayalaseema	Cheldiganipalli	101	228	1	0.03	1	Negl	2.25
	Total	1838	3931	263	14.3	641	16.31	2.14

Source: R.S. Rao and M. Bharati (2003).

Table 15.9

Peasant Migration According to Labour Use Classification of Households in 10 Villages of Andhra Pradesh

Sl. No	Classification of Households	Total Households	No. of Households Reporting Migration	Percentage of the Households Reporting Migration
1.	Non-Cultivating Households (7.58)	102	26	25.45
2.	Rich Peasant Households (8.18)	80	2	2.5
3.	Middle Peasant Households (3.20)	352	52	14.77
4.	Poor Peasants (1.75)	759	158	20.81
5.	Agricultural Labourers (0.09)	545	99	18.16
	All Households (2.14)	1838	337	18.33

Note: Figures in parentheses shows class specific average size of holdings in acres.
Source: R.S. Rao and M. Bharati (2003).

agriculture could be seen in the form growing resort to migration across all the classes of peasantry except the small proportion of rich peasants. Table 15.9 shows data from 1838 peasants households in ten villages spread across Andhra Pradesh. Almost 20 per cent of the households migrate, mostly seasonal, to eke out supplementary livelihood. Earning the top ten per cent of the households who migrate to avail better opportunities, most of the poor peasantry migrants for wage labour cope with the distressed agricultural conditions, and often to repay the debts incurred at usurious interest charges from private sources. Often for many of the peasants to have some money in spite of suffering all gravitations at the place of destination of migration, to repay their debt or to meet Pont of the investment in the next crop, is the sole objective of migration. For more than a decade now there have been observations that real input costs have been continuously rising while output prices have been volatile. For instance, prices of fertilisers have been decontrolled and the price of urea has increased from Rs. 2350 per tonne in 1990-91 to Rs. 3660 in 1997-98. During the same period the price of DAP per tonne increased from Rs. 3600 to around Rs. 10,000 (GoI, 2000). Since fertilisers are most important other than irrigation, the rise in prices had significant impact on farm input costs. A similarly upward surge in charges is found in the case of other inputs like power tariffs and water rates. For instance, in the reform from Andhra Pradesh the irrigation charges and power tariffs were steeply raised (Tables 15.10 and 15.11).

Table 15.10

Agricultural Power Tariff in Andhra Pradesh (Rs./H.P)

Particulars		Years			
		1-1-92	*1-8-96*	*2000-2001*	*2002-2003*
I. Drought	Up to 3 H.P	—	100	200	225
Prone Areas	3 H.P. to 5 H.P	—	200	350	375
	5 H.P. to 10 H.P	—	300	450	475
	10 H.P. Above	—	400	550	575
II. Other Areas	Up to 3 H.P	100	150	250	275
	3 H.P. to 5 H.P	100	250	400	425
	5 H.P. to 10 H.P	250	350	500	525
	10 H.P. Above	400	400	600	625

Source: A.P. Rythu Sangham, Hyderabad.

Table 15.11

Water Cess in Andhra Pradesh (Rs. per acre)

Particulars	Category I		Category II	
	Old Rates	*New Rates**	*Old Rates*	*New Rates**
First and Singal Wet Crop	60	200	40	100
Second and Third Wet Crop	60	150	40	100
First Irrigated Dry Crop	40	100	20	60
Second and Third Irrigated Dry Crop	40	100	20	60
Dufussal Crop in Crop Year	120	350	80	350
Aquaculture/Year	—	500	—	500

Source: A.P. Rythu Sangham, Hyderabad.

Note: *(Rates as per Water Tax Act, 1988 as amended on 5-3-1997 and implemented retrospectively from 1-7-1996).

A persistent complaint is that market prices of most of the agricultural commodities fall steeply at harvest time, only to rise steeply when the farmer had already granted his stock. This is yet another form of usury that benefits the trader-dealer who has a tie-up with a moneylender for buying the commodity at the harvest time. Is the peasant farming, which is exposed to perpetuation of such a multiple modes of exploitation, sustainable?

5. Primacies of State and Other Institutions

The historical specifications of changes in the agrarian structure and the development of commodity relations in India suggest that instead of vanishing of peasantry, there has been proliferation and persistence of peasantry. The small-farm family based production is the pervasive phenomenon of the Indian agriculture. With no immediate prospect of any substantial shift of the workforce to other sectors, the prospects of improving the condition of the peasantry is linked to switch towards higher productivity on-farm and off-farm activities requiring improved capabilities of farm households as much as improved infrastructure. These call for higher levels of public investment in education, health and housing facilities as much as improved institutional support systems for the small-farm agriculture. Contrary to these requirements, the reform agenda appears to assume small farm based agriculture is an anachronism of the times. For instance, the policy document of the previous Government of Andhra Pradesh contested the wisdom of an agrarian strategy, which, *inter alia*, believes in equity through redistributitive land reforms, and better productivity of small farms. It declared: 'Theoretically, the small farm may be ideal for knowledge intensive technologies but small farmer suffers from several handicaps like security of ownership, production inputs, credit and remunerative marketing opportunities' (GoAP, 1999). Since small-farm agrarian structure cannot be wished away, there is need to reorient the reforms by bringing the State and the institutions to enable the 'small farmer' economy not only to overcome these handicaps but also be in a position to face competition.

References

Bhalla, G.S. and D.S. Tyagi (1989). *Pattern in Indian Agricultural Development: A District Level Study.* New Delhi: Institute for Studies in Industrial Development.

Byres, T.J. (1981). "The New Technology, Class Formation and Class Action in the Indian Countryside," *Journal of Peasant Studies,* Vol. 8, No. 4, July.

Chand, Ramesh (2000). *Emerging Trends and Regional Variations in Agricultural Investments and their Implications for Growth and Equity,* NCAP, New Delhi.

Dasgupta, Biplab (1999). "Whither Land Reforms?," *National Workshop on Whither Tenancy?,* LBSNAA, 24-25 September, Mussorie.

———. (1977). *The New Agrarian Technology and India,* UNRISD and Macmillan, London.

GoAP (1999). *Working Paper Agriculture (Vision 2020),*Depatment of Agriculture, GoAP, Hyderabad.

Haque, T. *et al.,* (1986). *Agrarian Reforms and Institutional Change in India,* Concept, New Delhi.

Nancharaiah, G. (1999). "Agrarian Reform and Agrarian Change," *National Workshop on Whither Tenancy?,* 24-25 September, LBSNAA, Mussorie.

Rao, R.S. and M. Bharati (2003). "Comprehensive Study on Land Poverty in Andhra Pradesh: A Preliminary Report" (Mimeo) SERP-IHD, New Delhi.

Rao, V.M. (1992). "Land Reform Experiences: Perspective for Strategy and Programmes," *Economic and Political Weekly,* June 27.

———. (1998). "Policies for Rural Labour: From Relief to Structural Change" in, R. Radhakrishna and A.N. Sharma (ed.) *Empowering Rural Labour in India: Market, State and Mobalisation,* Institute of Human Development, New Delhi.

Rao, C.H.H. (1975). *Technological Change and Distribution of Gains in Indian Agriculture,* Macmillan, New Delhi.

———. (2000). "Agricultural Growth, Sustainability and Poverty Alleviation in India: Recent Trends and Major Issues of Reform" (Mimeo).

Rao, P.S.M. (2000). "Regional Rural Banks: Commercial Viability *verses* Equity Goals," Ph.D thesis, BRAOU, Hyderabad.

Rao, V.M. & H.G. Hanumappa (1999). "Marginalisation Process in Agriculture," Paper presented at the Foundation Day Seminar, 4-5 November, NIRD, Hyderabad.

Sawant, S.D. and C.V. Achutan (1995). "Agricultural Growth Across Crops and Regions: Emerging Trends and Patterns." *Economic and Political Weekly* (Review on Agriculture), Vol.XXX No.12.

Sharma, H.R. (1999) "Agrarian Structure and Agricultural Development in Rural India: Emerging Trends and Patterns" (Mimeo)

———. (1994). "Distribution of Landholdings in Rural India 1953-54 to 1981-1982," *Economic and Political Weekly,* March 26.

Syamsunder, N. (2003). "Nature of Credit Markets: An Analysis Based on Select Village Surveys in A.P." Unpublished M.Phil Thesis, Department of Economics, University of Hyderabad, Hyderabad.

Srivatsava, R. (1989). "Interlinked Modes of Exploitation in Indian Agriculture During Transition: A Case Study," *Journal of Peasant Studies,* Vol. 16, No. 3, April, pp. 493-522.

Vamsi, V. (2004). "Immiserising Growth, Globalisation and Agrarian Change in Telangana.....!1985-2000" (Mimeo) Ph.D Dissertation, Department of Economics, University of Massachusetts, Amherst.

16

Insuring Against Bad Weather: Recent Thinking

PETER HAZELL
JERRY SKEES

1. Introduction

Given the objective of protecting rural household incomes, a government typically has a range of policy options, depending on the kinds of risk involved. It is important to begin by assessing the real sources of risk, since some risks can be reduced directly. For example, production variability arising from unreliable fertiliser deliveries can often be resolved by consistent import policies and improved transport, distribution and storage systems. Likewise, some weather-related risk may be diminished through irrigation investments, which also contribute to increased production. Plant breeders might also be able to reduce some yield risks by selecting for lower sensitivity to environmental stress. But many risks cannot be prevented in this way and may require appropriate instruments that provide compensation when severe losses occur. Insurance has an important role to play in this context.

Instability in agricultural production, income, and employment has been a persistent and challenging problem for India and her poor, as analysed in many of the pioneering writings of Professor C.H. Hanumantha Rao (e.g., Rao, 1970; Rao et al., 1988; Rao, 1994). Professor Rao recognised long ago that there are many methods for removing risk in agriculture and that insurance was only one policy tool. For example, some risk can be removed with investments in technology and infrastructure (Rao, 1971), and which may even contribute to increased productivity as well as reduced risk (e.g. irrigation). Where they exist, these options can be superior to investments in crop insurance by either government or individuals. This chapter clearly acknowledges this to be true. However, not all risks can be reduced at reasonable cost in this way, and there are certain correlated risks where the optimal blending of insurance and capital investments may be optimal as well. Thus, this chapter focuses on providing the basic motivation for and innovation in insurance against adverse weather events. Progress has been made in creating new schemes to share natural disaster risk where correlated losses are quite common.

Recently, there has been growing interest amongst researchers, international development agencies (e.g. the World Bank), policymakers and private insurers in investigating and testing innovations in risk sharing for developing countries. India is in the midst of such experimentation with rainfall index insurance (Hess, 2003). And while it is too early to reach definitive conclusions on these experiments, ongoing consideration of innovations in light of their potential and their limitations is useful. This chapter is motivated to that end. Institutional developments must accompany market developments that involve both the broader financial community as well as the global community to effectively supply needed products.

2. What Role Can Insurance Play in Economic Development?

Droughts, floods, and other natural disasters lead to severe income losses for rural people, especially farmers and poor people. Given their limited ability to offset these losses, many rural people suffer extreme hardship, lose assets, and default on their debts in disaster years. The economic development literature increasingly links poverty and shocks (Dercon, 2004). Studies find that a large portion of the poor in developing countries are transitory—moving in and out of poverty—as they encounter shocks to household income. These poverty traps justify some type of public intervention for equity and efficiency enhancement. As Dercon (2004) concludes, "social protection may well be good for growth."

The prevalence of natural disasters is not new, and farmers, rural institutions, and lenders have, over generations, developed ways of reducing and coping with risk (e.g., crop diversification, farm fragmentation, kin support networks, storage, and asset accumulation). Although the virtues of these traditional risk management instruments are widely recognised (Walker and Jodha, 1986; Walker and Ryan, 1990), they also have their limitations. They can be costly in terms of the income opportunities that rural people forego (e.g., crop diversification is typically less profitable than specialisation).[50] They can also discourage investments

---

50. Using econometric methods and panel farm household data from South India, Gautam, Hazell and Alderman (1994) estimated that households paid an implicit risk premium of between 13 and 17 per cent in terms of the average income they forewent to reduce risk. Similar findings have been reported by Binswanger and Sillers (1983) and Antle (1987).

and technological changes that, while risky, enhance long-term productivity growth. Also, risk exposure can reduce access to credit because of greater risk of debt default in bad years. And finally, shocks that accompany extreme events also create the poverty traps described above. Traditional risk management methods have limited capacity to spread covariate risks, like droughts, that affect most people in a region at the same time. In theory, these limitations would not exist if capital and insurance markets were perfect and could pool risks over wider regions and over time, but the reality in many developing countries is quite the opposite: relevant capital and insurance markets are poorly developed and weakly linked across regions and with urban areas.

Seminal works by Arrow (1964) and Debreu (1959) have addressed the value of risk sharing markets for society. Failures in insurance markets provide a rationale for governmental intervention, but only if government can fix the problem at a lower cost than the social benefits derived. Many governments have intervened with a range of risk management programmes for rural people (e.g., crop insurance, livestock feed subsidies, and debt forgiveness). Such programmes have often been an expensive drain on the public purse, and there is little evidence to show that these interventions have generated any sizeable social benefits or that the benefits exceed their costs (Hazell, 1992; Hazell, Pomareda, and Valdes, 1986).

Given these failings, many governments turn to various forms of direct disaster assistance to relieve the problems of stricken areas. Such assistance is costly, and costs may escalate in the future as more people live in vulnerable areas and as global climate change increases the frequency and severity of many natural disasters. Moreover, once disaster assistance has been institutionalised and taken for granted, it can lead to many of the same perverse incentive problems as an insurance subsidy, inadvertently worsening future problems by encouraging people to increase their exposure to potential losses. For example, assured compensation for flood or hurricane damage to homes can lead to the building of more houses in flood and hurricane prone areas than prudent investors would otherwise build.[51] Similarly, assured compensation for crop losses in drought-prone areas may encourage farmers to grow more of the compensated crops even when they are more vulnerable to drought than alternative crops or land uses.

---

51. See Dennis Mileti's 1999 book, *Disasters by Design*, for an excellent assessment of how U.S. public policy on disaster relief has compounded the suffering and loss due to disasters.

More effective risk management instruments are needed to enable rural people to better manage their own catastrophic risks. While some disaster assistance should never be ruled out, new developments in insurance raise the possibility of substantially reducing the financial burden on governments.

3. New Approaches to Insurance

Natural hazard risks are different than many types of risk that are insured. In the traditional insurance literature these types of risk are not insurable. Insurance works best when the losses from risk being insured are independent. For example, not everyone is expected to have an automobile accident at the same time. With natural hazards it is expected that many people will have losses at the same time. Mixing markets and government may be needed at some level to effectively create insurance markets that meet the following requirements:

- Affordable and accessible to all kinds of rural people including the poor.

- Protects consumption and debt repayment capacity through compensation for catastrophic income losses.

- Practical to implement, given the limited kinds of data available in most developing countries.

- A core market-orientation with little or no government subsidies.

- Avoidance of the moral hazard and adverse selection problems that have bedevilled most agricultural insurance programmes.

Area-based index contracts, such as regional rainfall insurance, could meet all these requirements.[52] The essential principle of area-based index insurance is that contracts are written against specific perils or events (e.g., yield loss, drought, or flood) defined and recorded at a regional level (e.g., at a county or district level in the case of yields, or at a local weather station in the case of insured weather events). In its simplest form, insurance is sold based on the value of protection desired. The insured should be able to select any value of insurance. The premium rate can be quoted as dollars per one hundred dollars of protection. Buyers in the same region would pay the same premium rate. Likewise, once an event has triggered a payment, all buyers in the region would

---

52. In point of fact, the idea of area-based insurance is not new. Chakravati wrote about how this approach was the only appropriate approach for India as early as 1920.

receive the same rate of payment. That rate would be multiplied by the value insured.

Besides drought or area-index insurance, similar kinds of index-insurance contracts can be written against other natural disasters, including flood, excess rainfall, wind speed from hurricanes, earthquake events using the Richter scale, mortality rates for animals in Mongolia, etc.

Payouts for index insurance can be structured in a variety of ways:[53] 1) a simple zero/one contract (once the threshold is crossed, the payment rate is 100 per cent); 2) a layered payment schedule (e.g., a 33.3 per cent payment rate as different thresholds are crossed); or 3) a proportional payment schedule. The U.S. area-yield insurance, the Group Risk Plan (GRP), is an example of a proportional payment schedule. The payout function appears below:

$$Indemnity = max \left(0, \frac{Index\ Trigger - Realised\ Index}{Index\ Trigger} \right) \times Liability$$

In the case of area-yield index insurance, the insurance is written against the average yield for a region (e.g., a county or district), and a payment is made whenever the realised (or estimated) yield for the region falls below some pre-defined yield (say, 90 per cent of normal). The pre-defined yield is referred to as the *Index Trigger* in the equation above. Area-yield programmes exist in the United States, India, Brazil and Canadian province of Quebec (Miranda, 1991; Mishra, 1996; Skees, Black, and Barnett, 1997).

Area-based yield insurance requires long and reliable series of area-yield data, and this kind of data is not available in most developing countries. Hence, alternative weather indices may be more attractive, such as area rainfall or temperature, for which there are available time-series data collected on a regular basis. Mexico has made some progress in using weather index insurance to reinsure the book of business on traditional crop insurance. The state agricultural insurance company (Agroasemex) also has experience with offering individual farmers weather index insurance (Skees *et al.*, 2005). India has made significant progress in offering rainfall index insurance (Hess, 2003).

4. Some Attractive Features of Area-Based Index Insurance

Less Adverse Selection

Because all buyers in a region pay the same premium and receive the same indemnity per unit of insurance, it avoids adverse selection problems. Moreover, the insured's management decisions after planting a crop will not be influenced by the index contract, greatly reducing moral hazard. A farmer with rainfall insurance, for example, possesses the same economic incentives to produce a profitable crop as the uninsured farmer.

Less Expensive to Administer

Index insurance contracts should be considerably less expensive to administer than traditional insurance: there are no individual contracts to write; no on-farm inspections; and no individual loss assessments. Index insurance uses only data on a single regional index, and this can be based on data that is available and generally reliable. It is also easy to market; insurance contracts could be sold rather like traveler's checks, and presentation of the certificate would be sufficient to claim a payment when one is due.

Potential for a Secondary Market

As long as the insurance is voluntary and unsubsidised, it will only be purchased when it is a less expensive or more effective alternative to existing risk management strategies. A secondary market for insurance certificates could also emerge enabling people to cash in the tradeable value of an insurance certificate at any time. This type of market would enable a more dynamic pricing of risk as conditions change.

Could be Sold to Non-Farmers (Others are at Risk)

Index insurance can be sold to anyone. Purchasers need not be farmers, nor even have to live or work in the region. The insurance should be attractive to anybody whose income is correlated with the insured event, including agricultural traders and processors, input suppliers, banks, shopkeepers, and labourers. Defining insurance contracts in small denominations would raise their appeal to the poor. Insurance could also be built into credit and into the purchase price of key inputs like fertiliser.

Can be Linked to Microfinance

Recent developments in microfinance also make area-based index insurance an increasingly viable proposition for helping poor people better manage risk (Skees, 2003; Mahul, 2002; Hess, 2003). The same borrowing groups established for microfinance could be used as a conduit for selling index insurance, either to the group as a whole, or to individuals who might wish to insure their loans. Banks and rural finance institutions could purchase such insurance to protect their portfolios against defaults caused by severe weather events. Rural finance entities aggregate and pool risk. With index insurance contracts one can take advantage of such entities to become the means of mitigating basis risk via loans to farmers who have a loss and do not receive a payment from the index insurance. In 2004 the microfinance group, BASIX, purchased rainfall insurance to hedge their portfolio of loans. This idea is also being pursued in Peru with COPEME — a group that represents a number of microfinance entities.[54]

Can Clear the Way for Innovation in Mutual Insurance

Index insurance contracts should be relatively easy for the private sector to run, and might even provide an entry point for private insurers to develop other kinds of insurance products for rural people. For example, once an area-based index removes much of the covariate risk in a region, an insurer can wrap individual coverage around such a policy to handle independent risk (e.g., individual losses not compensated by the area-based index). This would, of course, require special considerations and could most effectively be tried *via* mutual insurance groups such as the FONDOS of Mexico, where members know the farming practices of their neighbours and don't face the same degree of adverse selection and moral hazard as someone from the outside does. Black, Barnett, and Hu (1999) wrote about using agricultural cooperatives in the United States as the aggregator of farmers when purchasing index insurance and then acting as a mutual insurance company for independent risk.

5. Challenges for Index Insurance Contracts

While limited experience to date demonstrates that people will purchase index insurance contracts,[55] a key question is whether index insurance will prove attractive to enough individuals. An index product should be more affordable than individual insurance, particularly if government does not subsidise either. Moreover, by offering an index

---

54. Personal communication between Skees and a BASIX manager in Rome, May 2004. Skees is involved in the work in Peru.

55. Where the U.S. area-yield product was marketed, participation levels have been reasonable. Anecdotal evidence suggests that between 15,000 and 20,000 farmers in India have purchased the new rainfall insurance in 2004. Participation in the rainfall insurance contracts that were introduced in Ontario, Canada, in 2001 has also been strong.

contract that removes most of the systemic, correlated risk that an individual faces, independent risks may more easily be insured through conventional insurance or credit markets. Blending index insurance and credit will likely prove the most effective way to deal with both correlated and independent risk. Index insurance removes the big risk, and credit markets provide savings and loans when more isolated risk events create individual losses.

A problem with index contracts is that an individual can suffer a loss and not be paid because the major event triggering a payment has not occurred. For example, a farmer with rainfall insurance could lose a crop to drought at a micro-location, but not receive an indemnity if the rainfall at the regional weather station remains above the trigger point. With index contracts it is also possible for an individual to be paid when they suffer no losses. In futures markets, this type of risk is referred to as basis risk. Index contracts essentially trade off higher basis risks for lower transaction costs, and the insurance will not be attractive if the basis risk becomes too high.

Additionally, rainfall events impact crop yields quite differently depending on the soil moisture holding capacity. In some cases, a good deal of time has been spent attempting to create more complex rainfall insurance contracts that have various weights associated with different timings during the growing season. Since farmers know their own soils and operations best, it may be critical to allow farmers to determine the optimal rainfall insurance contract.[56]

For a rainfall index, the degree of correlation between net receipts from the index and farm income will play a large role in the effectiveness of the risk protection offered to a farmer. With higher correlation there will be less basis risk. It is possible that offering a set of rainfall indexes may fit better for different farming systems than any one index. For example, farm income risks for certain crops may be most sensitive to rainfall shortfalls at specific times of the growing season (e.g., planting and flowering), and offering insurance contracts against rainfall during those specific periods could help reduce the basis risk. Basis risk is also likely to be much less of a problem if the insurance is written only against catastrophic events (e.g., a severe regional drought) rather than against a wider range of downside risks.

---

56. Skees encountered this when presenting work in Mexico a few years ago. A technical advisory, one of the FONDOS, confronted him in a relatively aggressive fashion asking "What makes you think you know more about the weather events that concern us than do we?"

6. Issues to be Addressed in Creating Sustainable Area-Based Index Insurance

Despite the promise of area-based index insurance, there are significant issues that must be resolved before it could be widely adopted. These include a) the need for secure weather event measurements; b) the actuarial challenges that are present due to oscillations in sea surface temperatures;[57] c) the covariate risk problem for the insurer; and d) the high frequency of some catastrophic events.

Secure Rainfall Measures

The proposed insurance depends on independent and secure methods for obtaining reliable information about weather events. While ground-level stations are at the core of such systems, they are not the only means for achieving this goal. Increasingly, Doppler radar is being installed in developing countries. Also, satellite images can be used as a means of cross-checking information from ground stations. Nonetheless, ground stations will continue to be used in the near term if rainfall index insurance is to be widely adopted.

Ground weather stations are rarely very secure and could easily be tampered with once significant sums of money are dependent upon their readings. Enhanced security is one option, which might require relocating some stations to more secure sites. New hardware systems that eliminate any direct human involvement in the recording process could also help. One company in the United States offers a rain gauge operated by a battery with a five-year life. Tiny buckets trip the measuring device so that rainfall at .01 of an inch can be recorded, but no rain is actually collected and stored. By using a data jack with computer software, a worker simply plugs into the rainfall-measuring device and downloads the data. Since the rain is not collected, there is no need to download the information on a daily basis. Another kind of measuring device uses a laser beam to record rainfall and again no water is captured and stored. The cost of these types of gauges is quite reasonable (just a few hundred dollars each) so there is opportunity to densely populate a region with rain gauges. Such coverage would permit readings from several adjacent gauges to be averaged, for a region. It would also reduce the danger of distorted readings should an individual tamper with a single gauge. Again, the optimal system will likely use a variety of verification systems including

---

57. For example, El Niño Southern Oscillation (ENSO) gives strong and early signals about the coming cropping season in many parts of the world.

remote sensing data taken from satellite images, Doppler radar, or soil moisture readings to verify low rainfall.

Sea Temperature Oscillation

The actuarial soundness of the insurance could be undermined by the ability to use sea surface temperature oscillations to predict the insured events. The most common measures are associated with El Niño-Southern Oscillation (ENSO).[58] It may be necessary to adjust the cost of the insurance when an oscillation event is confirmed, although this would require sufficient lead-time between knowledge of the pending event and the time of selling insurance. The most troublesome aspect of ENSO events in some parts of the world is that they extend across several crop seasons, raising the prospect that the demand for insurance would follow the same cycle and be highest (lowest) in those years when payouts were most (least) likely. Clearly, the insurance could not remain financially viable on this basis. One solution is to sell multi-year insurance contracts a few years into the future before anyone has knowledge of an oscillation anomaly. For some regions of the world, writing an index insurance contract on ENSO measures may be a reasonable alternative.[59]

Finding Efficient and Affordable Mechanisms to Share Covariate Risk

The insurer faces high risk because of the covariate nature of the insured risk. When a payment is due, then all those who have purchased insurance against the same weather station must be paid at the same time. Moreover, if insured risks at different rainfall stations are highly correlated, then the insurer faces the possibility of having to make huge payments in the same year. To hedge against this, the insurer can either diversify regionally by selecting weather stations and risks that are not highly and positively correlated, or sell part of the risk in the reinsurance and financial markets.

The possibility for diversifying risks across regions is feasible within larger and agro-climatically diverse countries, but is unlikely to be sufficient for most developing countries. The dominance of the agricultural

---

58. A variable widely accepted as a measurement of ENSO is Sea Surface Temperature (SST). Sea surface temperatures are recorded in four regions of the pacific basin. Regions 1 and 2 are located off the coast of Peru and Ecuador. Regions 3 and 4 are located at the level of the equator from South Asia to the borders of ENSO regions 1 and 2.

59. While working in Peru, Skees and others find that changes in the ENSO 1 and 2 are good predictors of extreme rainfall events. ENSO 1 and 2 are also strongly correlated with bad crop yields.

sector in many developing countries also limits possibilities for pooling climate risks within the broader national economy. Financial instruments for pooling climate risks across countries would, therefore, be of some importance.

International reinsurance is already available for some kinds of natural disaster risk. The simplest form of reinsurance is a stop loss contract where the primary insurer pays a premium to get protection if their losses exceed certain levels. Other forms of reinsurance are also common. Quota-share arrangements involve simply sharing both premiums and indemnities. Despite significant growth in the international reinsurance markets in recent years, reinsurance markets are still thin with few large international firms and limited capacity. Moreover, reinsurers often display short memories and after a major catastrophe, reinsurance premiums have been known to increase sharply or the insurer simply pulls out of the market.

As an alternative to formal reinsurance, recent developments in global financial markets are making it increasingly feasible to use new financial instruments to spread covariate risks, like regional rainfall, more widely (Skees, 1999; Doherty, 1997). While a good deal of experimentation has occurred with instruments such as catastrophe bonds and by trading state yields on the Chicago Board of Trade, these ideas have not yet proven viable for agricultural risks. The transaction costs associated with these arrangements have likely been a major impediment in their use for developing countries and for agricultural risk. Governments can play a role in aggregating risk within the country to the greatest extent possible before going to the global markets. Special pooling of risks that are reasonably standard and use reliable measures can then be more efficiently priced in the global markets.

Skees and Barnett (1999) and Lewis and Murdock (1996) go further by proposing that governments could offer some very low-level index contracts to reinsurers to assure that adequate capital is forthcoming. Since the insurer will likely load for events that have not yet happened, this may be a highly useful way to make these contracts more affordable while maintaining market principles. One way to facilitate this is for government to offer options on rainfall that is at the lowest level experienced in recent decades. Primary insurers and reinsurers would determine how many and what mix of such contracts to purchase from the government. These contracts could be simply rated at the historical breakeven rate, or they could be auctioned to the highest bidder.

International development banks, such as the World Bank or others in the capital markets, could back up these contracts with a contingency loan so that the government would have sufficient capital to pay all losses if the bad year came before an adequate reserve had been built up. In effect, the capital markets would be offering a stop loss-type contract to the government.

High Frequency Events and the Vulnerable Poor

Another difficulty with area-based index insurance is that some catastrophic weather events occur with such sufficient frequency that insurance may not be affordable (e.g., if one attempted to write a zero/one index-insurance contract against droughts that occur one year in five, it would require a 20 per cent premium just to cover the expected indemnity payments). This is often a problem for many of the poorest regions where insurance is most needed. It is also a problem for many of the poorest and most vulnerable people who simply cannot afford to pay the full cost of insurance even when it is available. These are the kinds of situations where governments (often with donor support) find it most necessary to provide free but targeted relief and safety net programs.

However, even in these situations, area-based index insurance may provide a more cost effective and less distorting way of assisting the vulnerable, but it would have to be sold on a subsidised basis (Goes and Skees, 2003). Unlike public relief, insurance provides an automatic right to compensation when an insured event occurs, and payments need not be delayed while policymakers try to determine if an emergency has arisen, or until relief agencies have launched their field operations. Moreover, if the insurance is routinely sold to the most vulnerable, then, unlike relief programmes, there is no need to target payments in times of crisis when things are most difficult.

Subsidising regional index insurance for poor, high risk regions and households may also distort incentives less than publicly provided relief that is not charged at all. As mentioned earlier, perverse incentive problems can arise once people take relief like food aid or disaster payments for granted. There is reduced incentive for farmers to pursue prudent risk management options and increased incentive to adopt farming practices that while more profitable on average, are also more vulnerable to drought. Such induced behavioural changes can lead to greater losses in drought years and increased dependence on emergency relief for managing losses in the future. If insurance is heavily subsidised then these same incentive problems arise. But incentive problems can be reduced by insisting that the insured pay a reasonable share of the insurance premium out of pocket (a co-insurance requirement) and by targeting subsidies wherever possible to the poorest and most vulnerable groups.

7. Examples and Experience with Index Insurance Contracts

Area-Yield and Revenue Insurance in the United States

The U.S. government has supported crop insurance in some fashion since 1938. Farms in the United States are very different than those in India, both in terms of size and the technologies used for production. Less then two per cent of the U.S. population now live on farms. Average farm size in the United States is over 100 times greater than those farms in India. The United States is also a rich country that has a history of subsidising farmers. The U.S. farmer pays less than 25 per cent of the cost of crop insurance programmes (Skees, 2001).

In the United States, multiple-peril crop insurance (MPCI) is designed to protect against losses from a wide array of natural occurrences, including drought, excess moisture, hail, plant disease, insects, and wind. The intent is to insure only acts of nature and not bad management. Policyholders must follow "generally accepted farming practices." While this provision is in place to reduce the impact of moral hazard, it is difficult to enforce.

Indemnifiable losses include quality adjusted yield shortfalls, prevented planting, and in some cases, replanting costs. Contracts for annual crops must be purchased no later than approximately six weeks prior to planting. Contracts for perennial crops must be purchased in the fall of the year before the crop is harvested. These dates are set to reduce the possibility that farmers will purchase insurance only when the likelihood and/or magnitude of a potential loss is greater than normal—a phenomenon known as intertemporal adverse selection.

Beyond the base MPCI product that insures against individual farm yield losses, the United States now offers a wide array of products. Revenue insurance products for the individual farm yields have been the fastest growing in the set of new products. Interestingly, the United States also has an area based product that pays based on losses at the countyyield level (Skees, Black, and Barnett, 1997). The Group Risk Plan (GRP) is remarkably similar to the Indian crop insurance product, with important differences in the manner in which the expected county yield is determined and premium rates are established. County premium rates are designed to be actuarially sound and the procedures have been approved by both the U.S. government and the international reinsurance community.

The United States also offers a number of revenue insurance products, including a product that is based on county yields and the national average movement in prices. The Gross Revenue Insurance Product (GRIP) is offered only for commodities where a futures exchange market can be used as the base for establishing the expected price. This is important as revenue insurance requires a reliable source for determining the expected price for the current season. Expected county revenue shortfalls with triggers as high as 90 per cent of the expected level and liability up to 150 per cent of the expected county revenue are available under GRIP.

The combined business of GRP and GRIP represent only about 5 per cent of the total acres insured for corn and soybeans in the United States. This is not surprising given that the United States has heavily subsidised individualised insurance programmes that compete with area-yield index insurance products. Nonetheless, for corn and soybeans, these programmes still comprised over US$100 million of gross premium on 5.8 million acres in 2004. The loss experience for the combined GRP and GRIP for corn and soybeans from 1995-2003 is 0.86.[60] Thus, the U.S. area-yield insurance programmes have been actuarially sound.

The Indian Crop Insurance Programme

Indian agriculture accounts for 24 per cent of the gross domestic product and provides work for almost 60 per cent of the population. The performance of current crop insurance programmes can be considered disappointing (Kalavakonda and Mahul, 2003; Mishra, 1996; Parchure, 2002). Over the period from 1985 to 2002 the Indian crop insurance programme experienced an average loss ratio of over 5. This implies that the government contributed over 80 per cent of the total costs of the programme while farmers contributed only 20 per cent. This problem emerged not because of a direct intent to subsidise farmers, but because premium rates charged to farmers were not based upon actuarial principles. There is very little price discrimination among rates to reflect the large differences in relative risk that occur among the different Indian states. These differences and the poor rate-making procedures also mean that the preponderance of payments from the Indian crop insurance programme have been made to only one state—Gujarat.

---

60. The U.S. crop insurance programme performance is calculated using the "Summary of Business" database available from the United States Department of Agriculture (USDA) online.

The basic concept of using area yields to indemnify farmers in India is sound given the small size of farms. However, the fundamental flaw associated with premium rates must be addressed if the Indian programme is to become sustainable. Largely due to rate-making problems, the average annual cost of the crop insurance programme to the Indian government is already in excess of US$0.5 billion and seems destined to grow quite rapidly. This cost is present even though the current participation rate is only about 10 per cent for India.

Another significant problem with the Indian crop insurance programme is timely payment. In many cases, farmers must wait as long as one year after a loss to receive a payment. These long delays are created by the bureaucratic process associated with making the final estimates for area yields. Since the Indian crop insurance programme is delivered *via* Indian banks, long delays in payments add to interest payments for farmers with loans. For the poorest farm households such delays increase the likelihood that they will need to borrow in the expensive informal credit markets when there is a crop failure. A fundamental issue that should also be addressed is to what extent more subsidies on crop insurance will prevent farmers from making needed adjustments in what they grow or how they use their other resources. At some point, crop insurance subsidies will slow adjustments and cause farmers to continue to produce high risk crops that are almost certain to have problems given bad weather. Finally, since crop insurance subsidies are positively associated with the size of the farm, careful consideration is needed to prevent these programmes from benefiting only the larger farms. Many of the rural poor in India have little or no plantings of crops and, thus, will not benefit from subsidising the existing crop insurance programme in India.

The Indian government response to crop insurance challenges might consider using limited government funds to achieve the most impact. Given this constraint, it is likely that the government of India would also do well to consider how this can be done by facilitating emerging markets. There are several things that can be done to facilitate improved crop insurance in India. First, actuarial procedures can be applied to improve rate making for the existing area-yield insurance programme. Second, the Indian government can continue to encourage the development of weather index insurance products that is ongoing in India. One way to facilitate this development would be to allow private insurance companies the right to have farmers assign indemnity payments from the government area-yield programme to the insurance provider in exchange for an improved private product. Rainfall insurance products should be able to make significantly more timely payments than the Indian area-yield insurance product. Combining products in this fashion would basically turn area-yield insurance into a form of reinsurance for private providers. Third, the Indian government could follow the lead of the Mexican insurance programme in the short run to provide some basic reinsurance for large losses from their insurance programme.

Rainfall Index Insurance in India

Monsoons in India can bring damaging cyclones and flooding to the coastal plains. Drought has also been a significant problem in India. Parchure (2002) estimates that about 90 per cent of the variation of crop production in India is due either to inadequate rainfall or to excess rainfall. To address this problem, Parchure recommends what he calls, *Varsha Bonds and Options*. These instruments would pay for extreme rainfall events.

By 2003, significant developments were emerging in India to offer rainfall insurance contracts. ICICI Lombard General Insurance Company began a pilot insurance programme that will pay farmers when there are rain shortfalls in one area, and pay others in case of excess rain. In the first year, ICICI Lombard offered drought policies *via* a small microfinance bank in southern India (BASIX) and the excess rain covers through the ICICI Bank. As discussed above, these contracts also should solve the delayed payment problem associated with the existing crop insurance programme in India.

BASIX used ICICI Lombard and technical assistance from the Commodity Risk Management Group of the World Bank to develop and launch the new rainfall insurance products. BASIX is a microfinance institution offering a wide array of financial services to rural customers. BASIX began operations in March 2001, in the districts of Mahbubnagar in Andhra Pradesh and Raichur and Gulbarga in Karnataka. In 2003, the new rainfall insurance was targeted at individual farmers for three categories of groundnut and castor farmers: small, medium, and large. A weighted and capped rainfall index insurance policy was developed in the first year (Hess, 2003). Since 2003, rainfall insurance is being offered in several states across India with continued expansion from ICICI Lombard, IFCCO-Tokyo of India, and the state insurance programme, Agricultural Insurance Company of India. Unconfirmed reports suggest that around 18,000 policies have been sold in 2004.[61]

---

61. Personal communication between Jerry Skees and Ulrich Hess, November 2004. According to industry sources cited by Ulrich Hess and Joanna Syroka, ICICI Lombard sold 3000 policies to orange farmers in Rajasthan, 600 policies to groundnut/castor farmers in AP. IFCCO Tokyo AIC are reported to have sold respectively 3,000 and 13,000 policies.

In 2004 BASIX insured its crop lending portfolio with a "Weather based loan portfolio insurance." ICICI Lombard would compensate BSFL for deviations in rainfall below the threshold level, which is fixed at a per cent of the average rainfall in the area.[62] ICICI Lombard in turn reinsured this risk with one of the top international reinsurers. The insurance is designed to cover drought induced default costs in drought-prone areas and, therefore, allows BASIX to continue lending in these riskier areas.

Mongolian Pilot Programme to Index Livestock Mortality Rates[63]

The government of Mongolia is on the verge of launching a pilot programme to test index-based livestock insurance in three states in Mongolia. From 2000 to 2002, over 11 million adult animals died in Mongolia due to harsh winter disasters (*dzud*). The total population of animals was reduced from over 33 million to less than 26 million–over 48 per cent of the cattle and yak died. Skees and Enkh-Amgalan (2002) recommended an index insurance product that would indemnify herders based on the death rate of adult animals in a *sum* (the name for local areas in Mongolia). These contracts would be offered by species for cattle and yak, sheep, goats, and horses. In the past year, considerable effort has been undertaken to design a sustainable insurance programme that has both commercial and social dimensions. Mongolia may be the only country in the world that has suffered from widespread deaths of livestock. This likely makes the application of index-based livestock insurance unique to Mongolia. While there may only be a few countries in the world where a similar project on livestock mortality could be tried, there are a number of new aspects of what is being designed that should have wider application to natural hazard risk in developing countries.

Extreme death rates of adult animals in a *sum* are not uncommon. In 2001 a number of areas lost in excess of half of the animals. Still, these are rare events and represent an extreme risk for a commercial insurance provider. Thus, a social programme called a Disaster Response Plan (DRP) was designed to allow the government to pay for losses beyond a certain extreme threshold (25 or 30 per cent of the animal deaths). Herders will automatically qualify for the DRP if they purchase the Base Insurance

---

62. *Economic Times*, July 20, 2004: ICICI Lombard to Design Weather Insurance.

63. Skees and GlobalAgRisk, Inc. had a First Initiative contract and a PHRD grant to assist in designing and making recommendations to the Mongolian government regarding livestock mortality insurance and social programmes. Olivier Mahul of the World Bank has been assisting in this work and his contributions are gratefully acknowledged.

Product (BIP). The BIP pays for losses between 7 per cent mortality up to the DRP threshold. Herders choosing not to purchase the BIP can obtain the DRP by paying a small administrative fee.

The combination of BIP and DRP offers more protection for herders who chose to purchase BIP at a lower price as the commercial insurer does not have to pay for losses in the DRP range. Furthermore, extreme losses are less likely to be in the calculus of herder decisions meaning that they are not likely to create perverse behaviour like a heavy subsidy would for BIP. BIP is priced in a commercial fashion by loading for extreme losses that occur when many herders lose animals at the same time. Still BIP exposure is significant. Unique financial arrangements facilitate sharing these risks with the government of Mongolia only after the insurance providers have pooled all sales into a common pooling arrangement. The government of Mongolia plans to offer a stop loss for the pooled risk at a fair premium for the insurance companies. Reinsurance premiums will allow the government to build a reserve to pay for these losses at some level. However, extreme losses beyond the reserve are quite possible, especially in the early years. Thus, the World Bank is willing to offer contingent loans to pay for these losses should they occur. The unique financing and structure of the contracts could be transferred to rainfall insurance contracts for developing countries.

8. Conclusions

Unlike traditional agricultural insurance, properly designed area-yield or weather-index insurance contracts require less monitoring to control adverse selection and moral hazard. In addition, administrative costs should be low. A variety of rural people could purchase area-index insurance contracts in addition to small-scale farmers. They could also be sold in small units that might appeal to poor people. Finally, creative forces within financial markets should be able to use index insurance contracts to handle covariate risk. Wrap-around products that cover some additional risk are possible. Microfinance entities could use the contracts to handle major risk, hedging their portfolio of loans and offering better terms of credit. Many possibilities exist for using this type of insurance to further develop markets for sharing risk.

Despite the promise of index insurance contracts, some key issues must be addressed. All parties must be confident that the measurement of what triggers payment is secure and accurate. There must also be confidence and transparency in the procedures used to develop premium rates. Great care must be used in designing contracts that match what is at risk for most people, and more active involvement of the contract end-user is needed to assure that this is the case. Marketing plans must be developed that address how, when, and where index contracts are to be sold. Also, the government and other involved institutions must consider whether to facilitate and regulate secondary markets of exchange for the contracts. Finally, reinsurance or effective and efficient use of other financial markets will be critical for sharing the covariate risk represented in index contracts. These risks must be spread around the world to obtain the best pricing.

Once properly constructed index contracts are in place, it should be possible to obtain efficient pricing in the international markets. Governments can build the infrastructure for measuring the index and monitoring the information to add credibility. Governments may also become involved in selling very low options on the index to improve the pricing. These options could be secured by contingency loans with an international bank (e.g., the Inter-American Development Bank or the World Bank). While some government support is needed for infrastructure development and to facilitate better pricing of low-frequency/high-consequence events, it will remain important not to launch insurance on a heavily subsidised basis. Doing so would distort incentives for private insurers, farmers, and other decision-makers. The government role should be targeted at exploiting the many possible market evolutions and uses of an effective index insurance contract. It is critical that governments not engage in attempting to protect individual farmers from independent risk, rather this effort should be left to the market *via* index insurance that removes the big risk and other effective financial markets that can help farmers and others cope with the independent risk.

Given the apparent attractiveness of area-based index insurance, one might expect the private sector would already have initiated its development in many countries. But this has not happened on any widespread scale. One reason for this is that there are several setup problems that might require public intervention to jumpstart activity, particularly in developing countries. Setting up basic infrastructure to get started may be an important role for government. The Mongolian Index-Based Livestock Insurance pilot programme offers an excellent example of how government can help in starting index-based insurance products. Start-up activities for weather index insurance products may include a) funding the research costs of identifying key catastrophic weather events that correlate strongly with agricultural production and income in different types of agricultural regions; b) educating rural people about the value of weather insurance; c) ensuring secure rainfall stations; d) establishing an appropriate legal and regulatory framework for weather insurance; and e) underwriting the insurance in some way (perhaps through contingency loans) until a sufficient volume of business has been established, so that international reinsurers are willing to assume the underwriting role.

A market-based, risk-sharing insurance alternative for natural disasters has many potential advantages. By making insurance available, government may not have to provide free disaster aid except for the poorest and most vulnerable groups. Farmers may be more flexible in taking advantage of the benefits of specialisation, and other efficiency gains should be expected, as well. As market-based insurance can serve the risk management needs of the rural poor, it can also help redress important food security problems. Finally, to the extent that indemnity payments can keep a household from slipping back into the ranks of the poor just when they are making progress, these instruments can also be used to motivate economic growth.

References

Antle, J. (1987). "Econometric Estimation of Producer's Risk Attitudes." *American Journal of Agricultural Economics* 69(3): 509-522.

Arrow, K.J. (1964). "The Role of Securities in the Optimal Allocation of Risk Bearing." *Review of Economic Studies* 31: 91-96.

Binswanger, H.P. and D.A. Sillers (1983). "Risk Aversion and Credit Constraints in Farmers' Decision-Making: A Reinterpretation." *Journal of Development Studies* 21: 5-21.

Black, J.R., B.J. Barnett and Y. Hu. (1999). "Cooperatives and Capital Markets: The Case of Minnesota-Dakota Sugar Cooperatives." *American Journal of Agricultural Economics* 81: 1240-1246.

Chakravati, J.S. (1920). *Agricultural Insurance: A Practical Scheme Suited to Indian Conditions.* Government Press, Bangalore, India.

Debreu, G. (1959). *Theory of Value: An Axiomatic Analysis of Economic Equilibrium.* New York: Wiley.

Dercon, S. (2004). "Growth and Shocks: Evidence from Rural Ethiopia". *Journal of Development Economics.* August Vol. 74 (2): 309-329.

Doherty, N.A. (1997). "Financial Innovation in the Management of Catastrophic Risk." Paper presented at the *ASTIN/AFIR Conference*, Cairns, Queensland, August 1015.

Goes, A. and Skees, J.R. (2003). "Financing Natural Disaster Risk Using Charity Contributions and *ex ante* Index Insurance." Paper presented at the *American Agricultural Economics Meetings*, Montreal, Canada, August.

Guatam, M., P.B.R. Hazell and H. Alderman (1994). "Rural Demand for Drought Insurance." *Policy Research Working Paper* 1383. The World Bank, Washington DC.

Hazell, P.B.R. (1992). "The Appropriate Role of Agricultural Insurance in Developing Countries." *Journal of International Development* 4: 567-581.

Hazell, P.B.R., C. Pomareda and A. Valdes (1986). *Crop Insurance for Agricultural Development: Issues and Experience.* Baltimore: The John Hopkins University Press.

Hess, U. (2003). "Innovative Financial Services for Rural India: Monsoon-Indexed Lending and Insurance for Small Holders." *Agriculture and Rural Development Working Paper* 9, The World Bank, Washington DC. Available online at: *http://www.itf-commrisk.org/documents/weather/India.pdf].*

Kalavakonda, V. and O. Mahul (2003). "Karnataka Crop Insurance Study." *Report to the South Asia Region World Bank*, Washington D.C. September 1.

Lewis, C.M. and K.C. Murdock (1996). "The Role of Government Contracts in Discretionary Reinsurance Markets for Natural Disasters." *Journal of Risk and Insurance* 63: 567-597.

Mahul, O. (1999). "Optimum Area Yield Crop Insurance." *American Journal of Agricultural Economics* 81: 75-82.

————. (2001). "Optimal Insurance Against Climatic Experience." *American Journal of Agricultural Economics* 83(3):593–604.

————. (2002). "Coping with Catastrophic Risk: The Role of (Non) Participating Contracts." Paper presented at the 29th *Seminar of the European Group of Risk Economists*, Nottingham, England. September 16-18.

Martin, S.W., B.J. Barnett and K.H. Coble (2001). "Developing and Pricing Precipitation Insurance." *Journal of Agricultural and Resource Economics* 26(1): 261-274.

Mileti, Dennis (1999). *Disasters by Design: A Reassessment of Natural Hazards in the United States.* Washington DC: Joseph Henry Press.

Miranda, M.J. (1991). "Area-Yield Crop Insurance Reconsidered." *American Journal of Agricultural Economics* 73: 233-42.

Miranda, M.J. and J.W. Glauber (1997). "Systemic Risk, Reinsurance, and the Failure of Crop Insurance Markets." *American Journal of Agricultural Economics.* 79(February): 206-215.

Miranda, M.J. and D. Vedenov (2001) "Innovations in Agricultural and Natural Insurance." *American Journal of Agricultural Economics* 83(3): 650–655.

Mishra, P. (1996). *Agricultural Risk, Insurance and Income: A Study of the Impact and Design of India's Comprehensive Crop Insurance Scheme.* Brookfield: Avebury Press.

Parchure, R. (2002). "Varsha Bonds and Options: Capital Market Solutions for Crop Insurance Problems." *National Insurance Academy Working Paper Balewadi*, India. *http://www.utiicm.com/rajaskparchure.html.*

Rao, C.H.H. (1970). *Prospects for Crop Insurance in India: Some Issues for Consideration.* Expert Paper Prepared for the Government of India.

————. (1980). "Fluctuations in Agricultural Growth: An Analysis of Unstable Increase in Productivity." *Economic and Political Weekly*, Annual Number, January.

————. (1994). *Agricultural Growth, Rural Poverty and Environmental Degradation in India.* Delhi, Oxford University Press.

Rao, C.H.H., S.K. Rao and K. Subbarao (1988). *Unstable Agriculture and Droughts: Implications for Policy.* New Delhi, Vikas Publishing House.

Skees, J.R. (1999). "Opportunities for Improved Efficiency in Risk Sharing Using Capital Markets." *American Journal of Agricultural Economics* 81(5): 1228-1233.

————. (2000). "A Role for Capital Markets in Natural Disasters: A Piece of the Food Security Puzzle". *Food Policy.* 25: 365-378.

————. (2001). "The Bad Harvest." *Regulation: The CATO Review of Business and Government.* 24: 1621.

————. (2003). "Risk Management Challenges in Rural Financial Markets: Blending Risk Management Innovations with Rural Finance." Thematic Paper presented at *Paving the Way Forward for Rural Finance: An International Conference on Best Practices.* June 2–4. Washington, DC.

Skees, J.R. and B.J. Barnett (1999). "Conceptual and Practical Considerations for Sharing Catastrophic/Systemic Risks." *Review of Agricultural Economics* 21(2):42441.

Skees, J.R. and A. Enkh-Amgalan (2002). "Examining the Feasibility of Livestock Insurance in Mongolia." *World Bank Working Paper* 2886, September 17, 2002.

Skees, J.R., J.R. Black, and B.J. Barnett (1997). "Designing and Rating an Area-Yield Crop Insurance Contract." *American Journal Agricultural Economics* 79: 430-438.

Skees, J.R., P.B.R. Hazell, and M.J. Miranda (1999). "New Approaches to Crop-Yield Insurance in Developing Countries." *EPTD Discussion Paper* 55, IFPRI, Washington DC.

Skees. J.R., D. Varangis, D. Larson and P. Siegel (2005) "Can Financial Markets be Tapped to Help Poor People Cope with Weather Risks?" in Dercon, S. (ed.), *Insurance Against Poverty*, Oxford University Press, WIDER Studies in Development Economics.

Stoppa, A. and U. Hess (2003). "Design and Use of Weather Derivatives in Agricultural Policies: The Case of Rainfall Insurance in Morocco." International Conference on *Agricultural Policy Reform and the WTO: Where are We Heading?*, Italy.

Walker, T.S. and N.S. Jodha (1986). "How Small Farms Adapt to Risk" in P. Hazell, C. Pomareda and A. Valdes (eds.), *Crop Insurance for Agricultural Development: Issues and Experience.* Baltimore: The Johns Hopkins University Press.

Walker, T.S. and J.G. Ryan (1990). *Village and Household Economies in India's Semi-Arid Tropics.* Baltimore: The John Hopkins University Press.

Section IV

Poverty and Environment

17

The Elusive Goal of Empowerment: A Review of the Emerging Phase in Poverty Reduction[64]

V.M. RAO

1. Introduction

India has by now over three decades of experience in measuring poverty, identifying the poor and devising a wide range of development programmes for them. The concept of poverty line and related analytical and evaluation frameworks provided the foundation for the formulation of anti-poverty strategy and policies. Judged by the reduction achieved in poverty ratio, the Indian performance has been impressive.

Table 17.1

Estimates of Incidence of Poverty in India

Year	Poverty Ratio (per cent)			Number of Poor (million)		
	Rural	*Urban*	*Combined*	*Rural*	*Urban*	*Combined*
1973-74	56.4	49.0	54.9	261.3	60.0	321.3
1977-78	53.1	45.2	51.3	264.3	64.6	328.9
1983	45.7	40.8	44.5	252.0	70.9	322.9
1987-88	39.1	38.2	38.9	231.9	75.2	307.1
1993-94	37.3	32.4	36.0	244.0	76.3	320.3
1999-00	27.1	23.6	26.1	193.2	67.1	260.3

Source: GoI, 2003: P.213.

---

64. This is a slightly revised version of the author's V.B. Singh Memorial Lecture on Political Economy of Development delivered at Giri Institute of Development Studies (GIDS), Lucknow in March 2003. My thanks are due to GIDS for the invitation to deliver the lecture and to Professor G.P. Mishra, Director, GIDS and his colleagues for the facilities and hospitality received during the visit to Lucknow.

There has been a steady decline in the poverty ratio over the three decades with the 90s registering a sharp reduction from 36.0 per cent to 26.1 per cent. More important, Table 17.1 indicates that the numbers of the poor declined sharply during the 90s in both rural and urban areas while there was no clear trend in this respect in the earlier decades. Indeed, there are fierce controversies on the official estimates contained in Table 17.1. But, we do believe there is a broad consensus among the academics and policymakers about substantial reduction in poverty ratio from the 70s to the 90s.

The 90s witnessed a momentous shift in India's perspective on poverty. The perspective got extended beyond income poverty (that is poverty ratio) to focus on other dimensions of deprivation suffered by the poor. This has brought into prominence measures like Human Development Index (HDI) to assess the poverty status and changes in it. The increasing use of HDI and similar measures, in turn, is likely to bring in its trail major modifications in analytical frameworks used in poverty research and in the norms and criteria guiding policy-making towards the poor. The indications are that the changing perspective on poverty is moving beyond the familiar dimensions like education and health to concerns like alienation and powerlessness of the poor pointing to the roots of poverty embedded in the social structure and relations forming the foundation of the mainstream society and its growth-cum-development dynamics. A little reflection would show that the anti-poverty strategy would eventually find itself facing a difficult dilemma. It is necessary to remember here that the initiative for formulation and implementation of anti-poverty strategy rests with the ruling elites and the organised groups in the society with the poor themselves playing practically no role in these matters. Keeping in mind this context, consider the following sequence:

- Anti-poverty strategy had its origin in a situation of high poverty ratio. Reduction in poverty ratio needs primarily relief measures like provision of subsidised foodgrains and generation of unskilled employment. There is little reason on the part of ruling elites and organised groups to oppose these measures. In fact, given the extreme and widespread poverty prevailing at the beginning stage of anti-poverty strategy, the ruling elites and organised groups may be expected to be quite willing to accept the burden of relief measures as a part of their responsibility towards the poorer sections in the society. It may be recalled here that in traditional societies in the past charity operations on a sizeable scale were quite common during periods of drought and scarcity.

- When poverty ratio reaches low level and the anti-poverty strategy shifts its focus to dimensions beyond income poverty, the anti-poverty strategy comes under pressure to expand its scale and to broaden the range of programmes to deal with the multiple-deprivations highlighted by the changing perspective on poverty. It is unlikely that the ruling elites and organised groups would readily yield to such pressures. This is the beginning of the dilemma faced by the ruling elites and organised groups when they find that the burden of poverty eradication is far heavier than that imposed by the relief measures employed in the beginning phase to bring down poverty ratio. They could neither disown the poor nor decide to carry the full burden of removing their poverty! The dilemma gets reflected in the widening gap between the rhetoric of anti-poverty strategy and its very modest enduring achievements.

- With the ascendance of conceptualisation of poverty in terms of powerlessness of the poor and their alienation from the mainstream society, the anti-poverty strategy enters an intriguing phase. When it seeks to promote empowerment of the poor, it would in effect put the poor on a course leading eventually to confrontation between them and the ruling elites and organised groups implementing the strategy. The prospects of sharing power with the poor would hardly be welcomed by the latter. India is currently on the threshold of this intriguing phase.

Our attempt in this paper is to take a look at the transition of anti-poverty strategy in India from its somewhat simplistic beginning with the poverty ratio to the current phase marked by far more sophisticated conceptualisation of poverty in terms of multiple deprivations including dimensions like power, dignity and justice. The purpose is to point out the weaknesses in the strategy and the blocks impeding its progress. We proceed as follows in developing this theme. If we take empowerment of the poor as the ultimate aim of poverty reduction, the achievement of this aim would depend on two sets of conditions. First, the anti-poverty strategy should lay the foundation for the progress of the poor from an attitude of acceptance of poverty as their fate to a frame of mind and worldview motivating them to actively seek and work for empowerment. Concurrently, there should be improvement in their living conditions and credible prospects of a better future. Second, the mainstream society should have enough space and opportunities to accommodate the poor and to give them access to viable income-yielding activities. The evidence that we have is quite overwhelming that there is continuing and flagrant violation of these conditions right from the beginning of India's war against poverty.

2. Weak Foundations for Empowerment

To demonstrate the weak foundations for empowerment of the poor, we have selected three critical policy areas: Employment, food and land security; human development and access to resources and decision-making power. Without an adequate measure of security in relation to availability of employment (including access to land) and basic needs like food, the poor would not be able to look and plan beyond the day-to-day struggle for subsistence. The next step is to provide them with opportunities to invest in their own health, education, skills and assets to strengthen their capabilities to participate in and benefit from mainstream growth and development processes. There are by now several examples of developing countries achieving dramatic reduction in poverty by promoting human development. In a democratic polity like India, improvement in human development needs to be complemented by building up institutions enabling the poor to play a role in the formulation of development strategies and priorities affecting their lives and welfare.

Security

Employment Security

Employment programmes in India do reach the poor in need of them. However, the system behind them lacks the features essential to make it a provider of employment security. The scale of the programme and its time profile must be such as to make available employment to the poor at the place and time they need employment. The wage rate should be high enough to prevent exploitation of labourer in the labour market. Employment programmes should be part of local level planning to facilitate identification of the needs, targeting the programmes on them and making the programmes productive by linking them up with investments in economic and social infrastructures. The current system of employment programmes relies on line departments and their perceptions on how relief measures can be initiated speedily. There is no desire on their part to become providers of employment security to the poor. Nor is there any collective effort on their part or on the part of the government to move in that direction. Employment programmes remain hastily implemented *ad hoc* schemes with scarcely a thought being given to targeting, provision of employment security and making the programmes productive by linking them up with area development plans. It would be reasonable to regard charity to relieve the pangs of poverty rather than its elimination as the driving motive behind employment programmes. A good indicator to mention is that even in Maharashtra known for its employment guarantee programme, the focus remains on relief during periods of scarcity rather than on growth-oriented use of surplus labour to create economic and social infrastructure. Development economics views such a use of surplus labour as an important policy instrument available to labour- surplus poor economies. India's planning documents fully share this perspective but, interestingly, this has made no difference to the Indian practice of treating employment programme as only a relief measure.

Food Security

From the point of view of providing relief to the poor, the public distribution system (PDS) has been even more important than employment programmes. However, judged by the norm of capacity to provide food security to the poor, PDS has a poor record. It shares with the employment programmes the weak institutional base at the ground level. Fair Price Shops—the contact points of the system with the poor—have hardly the characteristics of a provider of food security. They operate irregularly, receive poor quality grains, are often without stocks and are known to be in league with the traders resulting in diversion to market of the subsidised grains meant for the poor. The surprising feature of the system is that it works reasonably well during periods of widespread scarcity. A paradoxical finding in field studies is that the poor in some areas report better access to foodgrains during years of scarcity than during normal times! As is well known, Independent India has banished famines but is helpless in tackling latent hunger among the poor prevailing in agriculturally normal years.

The reasons for this state of food security system at the ground level need to be sought in the processes shaping the food policy at the top. It is best to begin with the green revolution which enabled India to become self-sufficient in foodgrains. It was in response to a situation of serious food crisis threatening the economic and political stability of the country as a whole. It was this perception rather than concern for the poor which galvanised the Central Government into devising an effective strategy to engineer green revolution. The approach was technocratic, the focus was on relatively better-off farmers and areas and the policy measures relied heavily on input subsidies and price support. Countrywide PDS emerged as an afterthought as input subsidies and price support led to spectacular increases in production threatening fall in prices and deadstocks in godowns. Even over two decades after overcoming food crisis and achieving broadbased agricultural growth in other foodgrains, PDS remains tied up with rice and wheat surpluses procured in a few states and distributed over long distances. The reason is the inability of the government to phase-out input subsidies and price support to green revolution farmers. They are now a powerful lobby and have a strong grip over agricultural and food policy. Remembering that the green revolution farmers were once themselves people with modest economic status—if not poor—they provide a good illustration of how policies and related institutions intended to benefit the poor come under the influence of erstwhile poor harming the interest of very poor and poor. This is even more true of influence wielded by more powerful groups of elites in the polity. Policies and schemes designed to benefit the poor and reckoned as such in records may not reach them at all or benefit only small sections among them.

The weaknesses of the present PDS as a food security system for the poor are listed below.

- The system is inherently cost-ineffective as it relies on two superior cereals procured in a few states, stored for long periods and sent for distribution to distant destinations.

- Price policy often leads to procuring huge stocks much beyond the requirements of PDS. Further, increases in minimum support prices make it necessary to raise issue prices leading to fall in demand for PDS grains by the poor.

- As an unwieldy and overstretched organisation, Food Corporation of India lacks capacity to ensure efficiency and equity in its operations as a provider of food security to the poor.

- The emerging agricultural context and the new paradigm of decentralisation offer scope to building up a food security system based on local grains, local procurement and tighter targeting of the system on the poor. However, there are no signs of any early or quick developments in this direction. All stakeholders, except the poor, seem happy with the present set up!

Secure Access to Land

In the interest of brevity and a focus appropriate to this paper, our discussion of agrarian reforms takes a different route than the conventional one. The usual approach to agrarian reforms is to look at them in terms of huge mass of legislations and their different incarnations over time. Pushing them aside, we begin by presenting in some detail the distinctive features of the prevailing agrarian structure and, then, indicate roughly the contribution of agrarian reforms to changes in agrarian structure. A word of caution about the sources of information on agrarian structure. Official statistics on land holdings, tenancy, etc., have limited credibility among the researchers. Our attempt is to enumerate points on which there would be a fair measure of consensus among researchers.

- Currently, small and marginal holdings account for nearly 90 per cent of total holdings and nearly a half of cultivated area. It would be a reasonable inference that landlessness is rising in agriculture.

- This does not necessarily mean immiserisation of small and marginal farmers and agricultural labourers though there are areas where this might be true. Overall, small and marginal farmers and labourers have gained from growth, technological change, rise in wages in agriculture. However, they remain exposed to numerous risks and face an uncertain future. A serious drought can make them destitutes wiping out gains which took long years to materialise.

- The main contributors to agricultural growth and also its beneficiaries are the middle and upper strata of farmers. They have been able to add to their land under cultivation from both large holders and small by purchases and leasing in. The large farmers are becoming more non-agriculture and urban oriented in their economic activities. The middle and upper strata of farmers are likely to be a dominant entity in the rural economy with some ambiguity about their attitude towards and relationship with the lower rural strata. The former realises the importance of political support of the latter. But, at the same time, they would want to grab more land from them and beat down agricultural wages. The agricultural and rural scenario would be shaped to a large extent by conflicts or truce among these rural strata. Neither is likely to get a walkover on the other.

- There are pockets with different agrarian structures. Two types merit a mention here. First, there are extremely backward areas and communities with stagnant agriculture and high incidence of poverty left untouched by development processes. Their priority need is for a whole range of developmental services and investments. Second, there are naxalite groups and similar protest movement, reminding us that there are still feudal relics in Indian agriculture. There appears to be a stalemate in these pockets with no clear indication of the direction of impending changes in agrarian structure.

A careful reading of the prevailing agrarian structure described above would show that it has little resemblance to the agrarian structure which was the goal of the agrarian reforms. The agrarian structure seems to be shaped more by market and other economic forces and political processes typical of an unequal society. This is not surprising. There is a voluminous literature on agrarian reforms bringing out how strong vested interests frustrate the reforms from the beginning legislative phase to their implementation at the ground level. Often, the policymaker himself is the first link in the chain! Loopholes are cleverly planted in the legislations so that judicial disputes in courts last beyond the lifetime of many intended beneficiaries! The following propositions would be acceptable to most as truisms:

- Very little land has been redistributed to the poor by imposing ceiling on holdings. Where small plots have been distributed to the poor, land was of poor quality and few among the allottees cultivated the plots.

- There are no reliable official data on tenancy. The official data indicate very low extent of tenancy but field studies give clues to wide prevalence of concealed tenancies. Concealed tenancies escape regulation and make it difficult for the tenants to seek enforcement of their rights. It is obvious that the poor are likely to be victims in concealed tenancies.

- Absentee ownership of land, particularly by urban dwellers, has declined but the beneficiaries have been the intermediate and upper strata of farmers and not the poor.

- Access to accurate and updated land records is of vital importance to the poor in their struggle against their exploiters. The situation in this respect is tragic. There is a trend towards computerisation of land records without a thought being given to the lack of accuracy and reliability of the existing land data and land record system!

It must be mentioned that there are exceptions like Operation Barga in West Bengal which benefited the poor substantially. But the broad lesson to be learnt from agrarian reforms is that in the absence of political commitment at the top and mobilisation of the poor at the ground level, it is wishful to hope that radical legislative measures will help in bringing about changes in institutional structure necessary to add thrust to the process of poverty reduction. Curiously, interest in agrarian reforms appears to be diminishing among intellectuals and academics who were once its vocal advocates. In fact, there is an audible murmur among them about the virtues of free land and lease markets and liberal ceiling limits!

Human Development

When the poor have to cope with lack of security and the resulting distress, they would remain deficient in both ability and willingness to utilise opportunities to improve their human development status. To compound their difficulties, the provision of such opportunities through programmes for health, education, nutrition, skill formation etc. hardly receive the attention and priority they deserve from the policymaker. Given the constraints of space, we can only present selected summary indicators of low level of human development prevailing in India and of states which have remained at the bottom over long decades. Table 17.2, based on UNDP Human Development Reports, indicates the relative position of India *vis-à-vis* a few developed, developing and least developed countries.

Table 17.2

UNDP Indices of Human Development

	HDI Rank (2000)	*HDI 2000*	*GDI 2000*	*GEM 2000*
Norway	1	0.942	0.941	0.837
Sri Lanka	89	0.741	0.737	0.274
China	96	0.726	0.724	0.483
India	124	0.577	0.560	0.240
Ethiopia	168	0.327	0.313	—
Niger	172	0.277	0.263	0.119

HDI= Human Development Index GDI= Gender Development Index.
GEM= Gender Empowerment Index.
Source: GoI, 2003: P.211.

Two points need to be noted in Table 17.2. First, India falls in the lowest one-third category by HDI rank. It has a rank much lower than that of Sri Lanka and China, which have comparable economic development. The case of Sri Lanka is often cited as an example of how relevant policies help a country to raise its HDI even at modest income level. The point is the poor performance of India in human development is an outcome of weak policies rather than of slow growth alone. Second, improvement in empowerment is even slower than that in human development as indicated by the wide gap prevailing between GDI and GEM observed in Table 17.2. A simplistic interpretation—but which is helpful in understanding the distinction between human development and empowerment—is that empowerment encounters resistance from the groups who have to share power with the group striving for empowerment. We will presently see how this factor impedes empowerment of vulnerable groups in India.

Table 17.3
States in India with Very Low HDI Values

	1981	1991	2001
Rajasthan	0.256	0.347	0.424
Orissa	0.267	0.345	0.404
Madhya Pradesh	0.245	0.328	0.394
Uttar Pradesh	0.255	0.314	0.388
Bihar	0.237	0.308	0.367
INDIA	0.302	0.381	0.472

Source: GoI, 2001 Note: HDI not comparable between Tables 2 and 3.

The states included in Table 17.3 are known as BIMARU states owing to their chronic backwardness. 1981 to 2001 was a period of relatively high growth in India. BIMARU states show some improvement in human development over this period. But, they continue to remain at the bottom falling below the Indian average by a wide margin. It is possible that states like Rajasthan and Orissa are moving ahead a little faster than, say, Bihar. However, it seems unlikely that in the years ahead the BIMARU states would be able to reduce the gap between themselves and the relatively developed states in India. The BIMARU states account for a significant proportion of India's population. Tables 17.2 and 17.3 bring out well the preparatory ground that needs to be covered to promote human development before India can look forward to making a major advance towards the goal of empowerment of the poor.

Before we move on, we take a quick look at the human development status of village communities. The findigs below come from a recent large-scale survey conducted by NCAER (Shariff, 1999)

- 63 per cent of villages do not have *pucca*/all weather connecting roads. In some states, this is true of over 80 per cent of villages (page 186).

- The survey reports the "startling fact that about one-half of all villages in India do not have any source of protected drinking water" (page 187).

- "Overall, 88 per cent of all villages in rural India have a primary school within the village (but) about a quarter of villages in Uttar Pradesh, Himachal Pradesh and Orissa do not have even primary schools. Given the relatively poor transport network in these states, implementing the goal of universal primary education in these states seems remote" (page 188).

- "Only about 22 per cent of all villages had a (health) sub-centre within the village" (page 189).

- A bare 10 per cent of all villages reported development programmes being implemented by the NGOs (page 190).

Providing infrastructures and facilities to villages faces serious problems owing to the small size of the villages and their dispersed location. But the shocking findings given above are an outcome of other factors too. For example, the policymaker shows little interest and concern in fulfilling the targets laid down by himself in the plan documents. A good illustration is the universalisation of primary education which still remains a distant goal despite getting "highest priority" in every Five Year Plan and in plan appraisals. It is important to note that neither the governments in the country nor the political parties show any anxiety about the tendency in our system to make promises to the poor—backward villages, target groups, disadvantaged communities—without any intention to act on them. In comparison, villages which are relatively large and better off manage to attract attention and monopolise development schemes. As a result, a periphery emerges within the rural areas consisting of villages characterised by multiple handicaps—small size, poor accessibility, weak infrastructure and stagnant economy. Many of such villages are settlements of disadvantaged groups. It would be apt to call such villages the forgotten communities belonging to a periphery not taken much note of by the mainstream—*i.e.* governments, markets, political parties, NGOs and activists.

Access to Resources and Power

A major exercise in progress in India towards empowerment of the rural poor and vulnerable groups is the activation of Panchayati Raj Institutions (PRIs). The objective is to pass on the programmes for rural development and poverty alleviation to PRIs and give them the necessary access to resources and decision-making power. Simultaneously, the active participation of the poor and the vulnerable groups is being promoted through provisions like reservations for these groups in the elected membership of PRIs and in office-bearers heading and managing PRIs. PRIs can be considered as only a small preliminary step towards empowerment of the poor. Full empowerment has to be conceived in terms of fundamental systemic changes in the mainstream society.

Given the attitude of the policymaker towards the poor noted above, it is only to be expected that he would have little enthusiasm to build PRIs and to give them power and resources commensurate with their mandate for rural development and poverty eradication. This is clearly reflected in a recent study (Rao, 2002).

The study notes that whoever holds political power would be reluctant to part with it unless there is sufficiently strong compulsion on the present holders of power. In India, devolution of political power from the centre to the states has made considerable progress owing to the growing political clout of the states. But the further phase of devolution below the state level has not even begun properly. In a formal sense, PRIs came into existence all over rural India in 1993 after the enactment of 73rd Constitutional amendment. But vast areas in rural India are likely to remain without a fully operational institutional framework of PRIs for many years to come.

What are the reasons for the current state of PRIs? The reasons are complex and rooted in the political processes. The basic point to note is that the traditional village *Panchayats* need to be replaced now by new institutional forms which may be called by the old name of *Panchayats* but are totally different from what prevailed in villages in the past. Traditional *Panchayats* belonged to an era marked by caste hierarchy, dominance of rural upper strata, concentration of land in the hands of a few and bondages of various kinds keeping the masses of poor at the bottom of the ladder. The PRIs that we now need assume a radically different social structure based on upliftment and "empowerment" of the lower castes, equitable distribution of land, toning down the advantages of status and privileges enjoyed by the rural elite and democratic polity at all levels from the village upwards. Given the conditions that actually prevail, many powerful influences work against the realisation of such a social structure in rural India. These include: the political clout of the groups which are now wielding power and influence in villages; linkages of these groups commanding "vote banks" with the centres of power at the central and state levels; and weak "political will" at the highest level to implement radical measures like redistribution of land. Thus, many substantive provisions of the constitutional amendment—reservation for weaker categories to enable them to participate actively in the PRIs, devolution of finances and functions on a scale large enough to invest PRIs with adequate power and authority, responsibility for district planning giving PRIs a major role in the planning process—are likely to remain a dead letter in the immediate years to come. This is admitted even by the policymakers at the top. At the meeting of the Consultative Committee attached to the Ministry of Rural Development, Government of India held on October 20, 2001, Shri M Venkaiah Naidu, the then Union Minister for Rural Development observed that "devolution of power upon Panchayati Raj Institutions involved both a process of political awakening and a measure of administrative organisation. It could not be achieved merely by enacting legislation and issuing guidelines. A sustained movement should be organised to ensure that powers and funds were devolved to PRIs at the earliest. Shri Naidu stressed that without adequate funds and financial autonomy, PRIs will not be able to function as institutions of self-government. Most of the states have not transferred funds in respect of the subjects transferred to them..... Members expressed concern over the slow pace of devolution of powers and funds to PRIs in various states...(they) felt that States are clamoring for decentralisation from the Centre but not showing enough interest in devolving the funds and functionaries(sic) to the local bodies" (PIB Release on October 21, 2001 on Centre to Convene Conference of Panchayati Raj Institutions to Discuss Devolution of Funds and Power).

3. Poverty Generation Processes: Two Illustrations

The mainstream economy presents a far more formidable barrier to empowerment of the poor than those noted in the preceding section. These are the poverty generation process operating in the economy. Any explanation of poverty needs to be based on an understanding of these processes. Similarly, policies to counter these processes should be at the core of any strategy seeking to eradicate poverty. It may seem surprising that poverty researchers and policymakers pay little attention to the poverty generation processes. These processes continue to operate unhindered as we shall presently see. The explanation is simple. Indian anti-poverty strategy focuses on the limited objective of providing relief and support to the poor without going to the roots and sources of poverty. Seen from this perspective, the weaknesses in poverty reduction observed in the preceding section would fall in a pattern. They are a necessary part of the soft strategy which the ruling elite pursue towards the problem of poverty.

Poverty generation processes form a vast area. We can only provide here a few glimpses to illustrate their thrust and their impact on the fundamental structures of the mainstream economy and its dynamics. The first illustration we give is the marginalisation process in agriculture. The increase in the proportion of small and marginal farmers in Indian agriculture has now reached a point where these holdings account for over 90 per cent of total holdings. More important, marginal and small farms cultivate increasing proportion of total land which could affect the capacity of agriculture to generate growth and assimilate technological change. If the marginalisation process continues over the coming decades, as it is likely to, growing landlessness and the resulting poverty and distress would be widespread in rural areas. The second illustration we give is in a sense complementary to the first. There are clear indications that even after acquiring education beyond the school level the rural poor are unable to have access to urban growth activities and stagnate in informal sector with wages and working conditions no better than those in agriculture.

The Marginalisation Process in Agriculture[65]

In a land-based economy, like the Indian rural economy, access to land and to economic opportunities linked to land-based activities would be a good indicator of the economic status of a household. In such an economy, it would be reasonable to infer marginalisation of cultivators if the structure of land holding has a strong trend towards proliferation of small and marginal farmers who are usually viewed as the principal target groups, along with landless labourers, for the anti-poverty programmes. This would be particularly true in the case of Indian economy where two-thirds of the rural population derives livelihood in agriculture—a sector accounting for sharply diminishing share of national GDP and marked by much slower per capita income growth than that occurring in the non-agricultural sector. Even so, the inferences given below based on the

---

65. For details see Rao and Hanumappa, 1999.

National Sample Survey data on land holdings from the different rounds are best viewed as indicative rather than definitive. Table 17.4 shows the percentage of rural households which were "landless" (owning less than 0.002 ha) and "near landless" (owning between 0.002 ha and 0.200 ha).

Table 17.4

Rural Landless Households

(per cent of Rural Households)

Year	Landless (Households owning less than 0.002 ha)	Near Landless (Households owning between 0.002 ha and 0.200 ha)	Total
1960-61	11.68	26.22	37.90
1970-71	9.64	27.78	37.42
1981-82	11.33	28.60	39.93
1991-92	11.25	31.15	42.40

Source: NSS 17th, 26th, 37th and 48th rounds.

It is significant to note that the liberalisation-era began in India with over 40 per cent of rural households being landless or near landless. The proportion of the latter category shows a modest but steady increase since the beginning of the green revolution in the early seventies. It would be easy to appreciate the significance of this trend when it is considered along with the trend in the distribution of ownership holdings (Table 17.5).

Table 17.5

Distribution of Owned Holdings

(per cent of Total Holdings and Total Area)

Year	Marginal (< 1 ha)		Small (1 to 2 ha)		Semi-Medium (2 to 4 ha)		Medium (4 to 10 ha)		Large (10 ha & above)	
	Hold-ing	Area	Hold-ing	Area	Hold-ing	Area	Hold-ing	Area	Hold-ing	Area
1960-61	60.06	7.59	15.16	12.40	12.86	20.54	9.07	31.23	2.85	28.24
1970-71	62.62	9.76	15.49	14.68	11.40	21.92	7.83	30.75	2.12	22.91
1981-82	66.64	12.22	14.70	16.49	10.78	23.38	6.45	29.83	1.42	18.07
1991-92	69.38	16.93	21.75	33.97	5.06	17.63	2.84	17.64	0.95	13.83

It is worth noting that by the early nineties, over 96 per cent of owned holdings belonged to the size-groups marginal, small and semi-medium *i.e.*, owners ranging between vulnerable to those likely to have only modest potential for viability. More important, over two-thirds of owned land was with the lower three groups with the medium and large owners accounting for less than a third of total land. Around the mid-fifties Professor Dantwala had drawn attention to the feature of the Indian agriculture that while the small and marginal holdings predominated in numbers, large part of land was in the hands of medium and large owners. Thus, apparently, the marginalisation process has brought about a major change in the production structure in agriculture. Much more than before, the small and marginal owners would have to shoulder in future the responsibility for the tasks necessitated by agricultural growth and modernisation.

Would the small and marginal owners have strong enough shoulders to bear this burden? Table 17.5 offers little room for optimism. A disturbing point to note is that the decade of 1981-82 to 1991-92 seems to have witnessed a marked intensification of the marginalisation process—the percentage of small owners increased from 14.70 per cent to 21.75 per cent. Further, the small owners emerged as the size-group with the largest share in total land. The group accounted in 1991-92 for over a third of total land with its share more than doubling over the decade 1981-82 to 1991-92. In contrast, the medium owners who had the largest share in total land at the three earlier time points covered by Table 17.4 suffered a drastic reduction both in numbers and in the share in total land.

As regards the large owners, they were less than one per cent of the total owners in 1991-92 but owned nearly 14 per cent of total land. An interesting, but frankly speculative, inference would be that the changing position of the large owners represents the other side of the marginalisation process *i.e.*, the presence, and possibly growing strength, of a small but dominant and influential group in agriculture. It must be borne in mind that the diminishing proportion of the large owners and reduction in their land share could in part be due to their moving out of agriculture to more lucrative opportunities in other sectors and, also, preference for investment in non-land capital rather than only further addition to size of holding. It may be recalled that the newer opportunities in agriculture depend critically on investments in modern inputs and technologies and not merely on larger and growing size of holding.

Put together, the clues provided by Tables 17.4 and 17.5 yield the following scenario of the marginalisation process in agriculture since the beginning of the planning-era in India. The era began with substantial landlessness in rural areas. The process instead of being reversed—or even arrested—has continued to operate over the post-Independence decades with landlessness reaching the extent of over 40 per cent in 1991-92. What should cause particular concern is the apparent intensification of the process during the eighties with a noticeable impact on the production structure in which small and marginal owners now account for a half of the total land. At the same time, there is also an indication of the large owners diminishing in proportion but, possibly, gaining in status and dominance through modernising their farming activities. The features of the prevailing policy-cum-market environment create a strong presumption that the marginalisation process could gather further momentum in the years ahead to become an explosive source of economic and political turbulence. Our political system is already under a severe strain owing to its inability to accommodate the rising expectations of the lower strata in the society, particularly those in the rural areas. Unchecked marginalisation of the poor in agriculture could prove to be the last straw on the back of the camel.

Access to Urban Growth

This illustration is drawn from a field study done in a few villages in close vicinity of Bangalore in mid-nineties. Bangalore is among the fastest growing urban agglomerations in India. The rural poor covered in the study belong to villages adjoining Bangalore. They would be free from the difficulties which a migrant would face in finding economic opportunities in Bangalore. And, yet, the study findings clearly show that Bangalore has little to offer to the poor at its door steps!

There are diverse ways in which rural households could get access to growth processes. Increased demand and prices for the items they produce could bring them gains without their having to leave their village/ occupation. This would also be true of benefits they derive from improvements in inputs, technology, credit and marketing. Higher employment and wages available within the village or its neighbourhood to agricultural and other labourers would also fall in this category. Alternatively, rural households may migrate out of their village and/or change their occupation in their search to find new and better economic opportunities. In the case of our sample villages, which are practically being swallowed-up by the expanding limits of the city and its outgrowth, the target groups are likely to benefit chiefly from the new job opportunities made available by the upsurge in economic activities. The data collected for the households have not been designed to analyse the full range of benefits accruing to them through growth. A readily available indicator in our data is the current occupations of young workers who entered the labour market during the last two decades of active phase of the city's growth (Table 17.6). It would be reasonable to assume that the young workers chose the best among the available occupations and that the characteristics of these occupations could provide a pointer to the extent and quality of the access of target group households to opportunities arising in the wake of growth.

Table 17.6
Occupations of Young Males (15 to 35)

Target Groups	No. of YM	Lit.	Lab.	Agri.	UI	RJ	St.	Un
Cultivators	57	53	—	28	14	2	8	5
Landless labourers	66	37	37	—	16	1	7	5
Artisans	27	24	2	1	15	—	5	4
Scheduled Castes	103	73	34	11	30	3	13	12
Villages								
Begur	53	45	11	7	15	3	10	7
Jigani	75	67	13	9	37	1	8	7
Giddenahalli	40	19	16	12	7	—	4	1

Notes: YM : Young Males St. : Students
Lit. : Literates Un : Unemployed
Lab. : Casual Labour in Villages RJ : Regular Job
Agri. : Agriculture UI : Urban Informal

The telling clue in Table 17.6 is the negligible number reporting regular job as their occupation in different target groups and villages. It is tempting to interpret the relatively large numbers reporting themselves as students and unemployed (20 per cent to 30 per cent) as aspirants waiting for regular jobs. This interpretation seems all the more plausible when we consider the extent of literacy which is quite high (over 70 per cent among SC young workers and 56 per cent among young workers belonging to landless labour households). It is clear from the table that the only avenue of "new" employment—other than the traditional avenues of agriculture and wage labour in the village—is the urban informal sector. An interesting point to note is that the young workers in cultivator households, apparently, prefer the urban informal sector jobs to casual labour in the village; and not a single worker among them reported casual labour in village as their occupation, while 14 out of 57 worked in the urban informal sector. In fact, these workers who could have chosen to work on their own farms but instead entered the urban informal sector show by implication that they also prefer the latter to the former. As regards the young males from the artisans households, excluding students and unemployed, the rest almost wholly work in the urban informal sector.

Did the young workers fare better during the Reforms-era? Table 17.7 indicates the occupations of young males in the age group 15 to 20. A happy feature shown by the table is that out of 51 young males appearing in the table only three are illiterate and one who dropped out before completing the primary stage. Out of 47 who have crossed the primary stage, 19 still continue to be the students. It is even more heartening to see that these two features hold for young males belonging to the scheduled caste landless labourer households which could reasonably be assumed to belong to the lowest strata in the villages. However, this could also be a warning signal. Would these students on completion of their studies be able to build up good careers? Among the young males belonging to the Scheduled Castes' landless labourers, 20 per cent are unemployed and those who have taken up jobs are either labourers or factory workers (urban informal sector). The position is almost the same in the case of non-scheduled caste households—mostly cultivators—*viz.* 20 per cent unemployed and those working belonging to either agriculture or urban informal sector. It is clear that those among the young males in Table 17.6 who work have the same pattern of occupations as the larger set of young workers figuring in Table 17.5. The warning signal is that if the young males either unemployed or still continuing as students are finally driven to accept low-status avenues of employment they could become a source of political and social unrest. This may eventually lead to political mobilisation and organisation of target groups but it is also possible that the unrest merely results in pressures and disruptions without any positive impact on the larger society.

Table 17.7

Occupations of Young Males (Age 15 to 20)

Type of Households	Literacy Status			
	Illit.	*Upto Primary*	*Upto Secondary*	*Secondary and above*
Scheduled Castes Landless Labourers	2 Labour-2	Nil	11 Labour-3 Factory worker-3 Student-3 Unemployed-2	8 Electrician-1 Factory worker-1 Student-4 Unemployed-2
Scheduled Castes Other Occupations	Nil	Nil	3 Agril.-2 Factory worker-1	6 Factory worker-1 Student-4 Unemployed-1
Non-Scheduled Castes	1 Factory worker-1	1 Agril.-1	5 Business-1 Agril.-1 Student-3	14 Agril.-1 Driver-1 Factory worker-3 Student-5 Unemployed-4

Note: "Factory Workers" are employed mostly in small factories located near the village of residence.

A critical variable casting a shadow on the future is the capacity of the urban informal sector to provide adequate income earning opportunities. The experience so far in this respect has been disappointing. We quote below from two recent assessments. A study of villages close to Hyderabad finds that those working in Hyderabad earn a little more but not enough to improve their status. "Males can earn about Rs. 5 more per day and females Rs. 3 more per day. But they spend more on housing and transport than in the village and this may leave them not in any better condition really... There is no evidence of the surpluses generated being invested for productive purposes" (Krishnaiah, 1996). Even more revealing are the findings of Papola which though somewhat dated still seem to retain validity. "The evidence thrown up in this study suggests that degree of exploitation of workers is certainly higher in this sector than in the formal sector. Hours of work are not regulated effectively and a sizeable proportion of workers have to work for over 10 hours a day. Wages in the manufacturing establishments in the informal sector are around one-half of those in the organised sector though labour productivity does not differ between them significantly" (Papola, 1981). Papola also finds that the urban informal sector is not an independent contributor to growth but remains an appendage and a poor cousin of the organised sector. The recent literature on growth of informal and small scale sector in centres like Bhivandi in Maharashtra and Surat in Gujarat suggests that it would be appropriate to view the urban informal sector as an arrangement which enables the organised sector to use the labour and skills of the poor without giving them the earnings, status and security available to workers in the organised sector. In this sense, it can be considered as a mechanism, which the organised groups use to bring the poor within their production and economic activities but exclude them from the privileges, which they themselves enjoy. Given such exclusion mechanisms, it would be idle to expect the benefits of growth-promoting reforms to reach the poor unless the political mobilisation referred to above help the poor to build up a credible confrontation against the organised groups. This would indeed be a formidable task as the urban informal sector is likely to have powerful godfathers nurturing and protecting it.

The two illustrations given above should leave little room for any doubt about the precarious position of the poor in the Indian society. They should also warn us about interpreting the reduction in poverty ratio achieved in recent years as anything more than an indicator of relief provided to the poor. The emerging situation must indeed cause anxiety when we consider that the poor have continued to remain vulnerable to poverty generation processes throughout the period when India claimed—and international observers applauded—the country's achievements in its campaign against poverty!

4. Concluding Remarks

It may appear at first sight that we have sketched a very pessimistic scenario for the future of the poor. This is indeed true, as we have confined ourselves to policy impacts and poverty generation processes. A fuller picture of poverty in the context of total social system is likely to show up forces and processes helping the poor. Any attempt to construct the full picture would face the problems of poor visibility ahead and difficulties in projecting the future from a past belonging to a different phase. What is practicable is to describe the motivations and moves of the principal actors in the poverty scenario. It is hoped that the brief comments given below would be of help to poverty researchers to identify lines of investigation which it would be worthwhile to pursue in getting a fuller picture of the emerging poverty scenario.

The poor of today are very different from those on the eve of the planning-era. They have witnessed improvement in their conditions kindling their aspirations. They are acquiring capacity to put pressure on the government and other development agencies to do more for the poor. More important, the poor are far more mobile now and have a wider range of activities to choose from compared to the past. Casualisation of rural labour, which makes the life of the labourer more precarious has also the effect of leaving him free to search across space and other occupations.

The traditional closed village community is opening up to the wider world. We have already seen this in the case of rural labourers. Cultivators are becoming more market-oriented and also modern-input-oriented developing strong linkages with urban centres, networks and institutions. Rural elites shift their attention from rural activities to urban and from agriculture to secondary and tertiary activities. The overall impact is to strengthen the integration of the village with the mainstream economy and society.

It is only to be expected that these changes will have an impact on the polity. It is likely that the political mobilisation of the poor gains momentum. The middle and upper strata in rural society are already getting drawn into party-cum-electoral politics. The politicisation of village communities is likely to bring about profound changes in inter-strata relationships within village communities as also in their relationships with those located outside. Equally important is the wider politicisation of rural people at the state and national levels. Laloo Prasad and Mayavati herald the beginning of a process having the potential to shake the very foundations of the polity and reshape its structure.

What do these changes signify for the future of the poor? We will not attempt an answer except suggesting that the question could lead us towards poverty issues and themes helping to make poverty researches more relevant and meaningful. We have spent far too much time in measuring poverty and in settling the statistical quarrels. The need is to move towards understanding the poor and investigating how developing societies generate and mitigate poverty.

References

GoI (2003). *Economic Survey 2002-2003*, Government of India, New Delhi.

————.(2001). *National Human Development Report, 2001*, Planning Commission, Government of India, New Delhi.

Krishaniah (1996). *Rural Migrant Labour Systems in Semi-Arid Areas*, Centre for Economic and Social Studies, Hyderabad, 1996, Unpublished study.

Papola, T.S. (1981). *Urban Informal Sector in a Developing Economy*, Delhi: Vikas.

Rao, V.M. (2002). "Growth, Modernisation and Poverty: The Emerging Institutional Issues in Indian Agriculture," in (eds.) S.S. Acharya *et al.*, *Sustainable Agriculture, Poverty and Food Security*, Jaipur: Rawat Publications.

Rao, V.M. and H.G. Hanumappa (1999). "Marginalisation Process in Agriculture," *Economic and Political Weekly*, Vol. 34, No. 52, December 25.

Shariff, Abusaleh, (1999). *India Human Development Report*, National Council of Applied Economic Research, New Delhi: Oxford University Press.

18

Environment, Employment and Sustainable Development: Understanding the Linkages in India

A Capital-Theoretic Approach[66]

INDIRA HIRWAY
PIET TERHAL

1. Introduction

This paper reflects on the concept of sustainable development. It aims at integrating various dimensions of sustainability in a capital- theoretic context. It uses the concepts of virtuous and vicious circles of causation introduced by G. Myrdal (1968) for characterising development and discusses the conditions for sustainable development in the context of these concepts. Finally, it discusses the prospects of and conditions for sustainable development with reference to empirical studies in three Indian states.

The paper is divided in to four sections: section two presents the capital–theoretic approach, while section three discusses the empirical study and the final section concludes.

2. Sustainable Development—A Capital-Theoretic Approach

The concept of sustainable development, which is a goal as well as a development paradigm, is frequently criticised as a 'development truism' or as an 'umbrella concept' that encompasses all good ideas on development. The term can be useful only if it is defined precisely in the context of a sound paradigm.

---

66. This paper is based on the larger study by the authors entitled Environment, Employment and Sustainable Development: A study in three Indian States, Final Report to Indo-Dutch Programme on Alternatives in Development (IDPAD), June 2002.

To start with, development is not economic growth and, therefore, it cannot be equated with GDP. Development essentially refers to total human well-being, which is determined by the capabilities of human beings to lead the life they value. That is, development needs to be seen as a process that expands opportunities or increases choices for people through their improved capabilities. The capabilities, however, depend not only on their individual abilities, but also on the macro environment. An enabling macro environment will provide opportunities to people to use their individual abilities. The term development, thus, also refers to a paradigm, which creates an enabling environment that expands choices in life for people leading to their improved well-being.

The term sustainability refers to environmental sustainability as well as to economic and socio-political sustainability. Environmental sustainability refers to the way 'natural resources' are affected by development. A starting definition of sustainability, therefore, could be the three simple rules given by Daly (1990) for development to be sustainable: (a) those resources which are renewable are not used at a rate which surpasses the rate of their regeneration, (b) those resources which are not renewable are not used at a rate which surpasses the rate at which a substituting resource becomes available, and (c) the rate at which polluting materials are disposed off does not surpass the carrying capacity of the environment, *i.e.* the rate at which the material can either be turned in to something useful or be made harmless and be absorbed by the environment. The boundaries implied by "sustainability" in this operational definition of Daly are not to be understood as static. They are dynamic and subject to technological progress in the long-term context.

The Brundtland Report, the report of the World Commission on Environment and Development (1987), is an important contribution to the concept of sustainable development. The report observed that humanity has the ability to make development sustainable—to ensure that it meets the needs of the present without compromising the ability of future generations to meet their own needs. The report for the first time included the specific environmental problems of poverty into its analysis and showed that the concept of sustainable development is relevant to developing countries. It brought home the insight that reduction in poverty and reduction in environmental vulnerability are intimately linked with each other.

Circular Causation and Vicious/Virtuous Circles

The linkages between environment and poverty can be understood better with the help of G. Mydal's concept of circular causation, which implies that a variable impacts on another variable, which in turn has a feed back on the first variable and so on. Depending on the signs (positive or negative), an accumulative or an equilibrating process is set in, and depending on the qualitative direction of the motion, one can call the circular causation 'virtuous' or 'vicious.' Sustainable development can be then, described as a systematic and sustained increase in the human welfare through virtuous circles of causation between the variables positively affecting the welfare. One aspect of sustainable development is that vicious circles between poverty and environmental degradation are turned into virtuous circles between poverty reduction and reduction of environmental vulnerability. This can be considered as an important message of the Brundtland Report.

Concept of Capital: What are the key variables in the virtuous circles? An important variable is clearly 'capital,' which can be defined as a set of goods that enables a flow of useful goods and services. This flow can be measured in terms of income. However, income derives its ultimate value from real use made of it, *i.e.* from its contribution to human welfare. Therefore, the capacity of financial capital to generate a continuous stream of incomes is only a reflection of the capacity of the real capital, *i.e.* man-made capital as well as natural capital, to generate flows of goods and services.

Man-made capital is a stock of material goods designed and constructed primarily for enhancing productivity. Its role is crucial and strategic in sustainable development. Since it was assumed by growth theories that natural capital is unlimited and can be taken for granted, high productivity was supposed to demand large amounts of sophisticated man-made capital, and steady accumulation and renewal of man-made capital was identified as an important source of economic growth. However, this implied a serious neglect of "nature" particularly living nature, as natural resources are neither unlimited nor can be taken for granted.

Nature forms a huge integral system of living and non-living creatures, which are interconnected through numerous processes of energy transformation, and physical and chemical interactions of incredible complexity, supporting subtle balances of living and dead materials. Though, they operate independently of human control, human activities do have an impact on them. Nature can function as 'natural capital' as long as the integrity of ecosystems is maintained adequately. This demands a careful process of adaptations of humans to the laws governing the eco-system. Nature can continue to provide services only when this is observed.

In developing countries, particularly in rural areas, the majority of the population, including the poor, directly depends on natural resources, as they are engaged in activities of agriculture, forestry, animal husbandry, fishery etc. It has been estimated that a significant proportion of the total time of the population is spent on cultivation, collection of fuel wood and other forest products, fodder collection, animal grazing and animal care, fishery etc. In such a situation, the overwhelming importance of natural capital for productivity of labour is beyond dispute.

What is the relationship between the services from nature and the services that man-made capital provides, and how does the relationship change during a process of sustainable development? Conceptually speaking there are four types of possible relationships between natural and man-made capital:

- Natural and man-made capital can complement each other in providing streams of benefits (for example, a water harvesting structure).

- Man-made capital can substitute for natural capital and take over the role of providing streams of benefits (for example, substitution of fuel wood by electricity).

- Natural capital is destroyed without any substitute (for example, loss of bio-diversity).

- Investment can upgrade natural capital (for example, afforestation).

According to the rules of Herman Daly, development can be sustainable even when a non-renewable resource is exhausted, provided that another substituting resource becomes available in sufficient quantity. In such a case, the relationship 2 from the above would apply and 3 would be excluded. However, the concept of sustainable development is richer than that. It is more than exclusion of unsustainability, because it may imply a self-enforcing process of enhancement of natural and man-made capital together, according to relationship 1 and 4. A prime example of this is agriculture, where the fertility of life supporting nature can be upgraded through investment and brought in to higher sustained levels of productivity.

Human Agency and Human Capital: A process of simultaneous enrichment and enhancement of natural and man-made capital is crucially dependent on a third dimension, namely, purposeful human action. Human beings play a decisive role in turning the process of circular causation from vicious into virtuous for generating sustainable development.

Three aspects of human agency should be distinguished here. Firstly, through their labour, human-beings, by taking individual or collective decisions, impact on nature and natural processes.

Secondly, human-beings are continuously enriched through expansion of knowledge (education) and technology. This process can be termed as human capital formation, and it plays a pivotal role in shaping the rate and pattern of development. Human capital can be divided in to two parts: individual capital and collective capital. Individual human capital refers to individual skills, capacities and attitudes, while collective capital includes knowledge systems, institutions and cultural traditions in a wider sense.

The third aspect of human agency refers to the goals of development, determined by human-beings. The goals depend on economic, social, political and ethical dimensions of development. If the goals of development are not adequately formulated, development will not be sustainable. Thus, human agency has a normative connotation, as the collective norms of the society determine whether the development will be sustainable. In short, the human agency impacts on the sustainability of development in multiple ways.

Development is an upward process of the total system in terms of the system's capacity to satisfy human needs. As discussed earlier, the capacity includes not only man-made capital, but also natural capital and human capital (*i.e.* capability, Sen, 1985 and Drèze and Sen, 1995). The sustainability of development requires that the increase in the total capital is managed in a sustainable manner. The World Bank also has presented a similar concept, expanding the measure of wealth and the concept of genuine savings, which argues that the total wealth should include man-made capital, natural capital, human capital and social capital. A basic premise under the concept of sustainable development is that the total wealth or the total capital in the economy should increase or at least remain constant. The concept of 'genuine savings' again refers to an increase in the total capital or total wealth of the economy implying sustainable development.

Development not only implies changes in the stocks of capital, but also in the ownership pattern of capital. Ownership of capital directly impacts on the distribution of the benefits generated through the stocks. For development to be sustainable, issues of equality and justice are important. When choices have to be made, the satisfaction of luxury for some needs certainly a low priority than the primary needs of others. As Goulet (1985) has put it, there is no justification for allowing a few wealthy societies to use a disproportionate share of world's resources for the satisfaction of luxury, while the basic needs of the masses are left unmet. Such a skewed distribution has intragenerational as well as intergenerational consequences. If meeting luxury needs of present generations militates against meeting the life sustenance needs of future generations, the latter have normative priority. Sustainable development, therefore, is a process, which first of all favours the poor. Highly unequal distribution of incomes and assets is not sustainable (see Goulet, 1996).

Employment and Sustainable Development: Employment, which can be defined as productive engagement of labour with capital, is at the core of sustainable development. Employment links human agency with capital and ensures benefits of production to human-beings. For sustainable development, it is necessary that the links between man-made capital and natural capital are strengthened through engagement of human capital. That is, environment is linked with sustainable development through a strong medium of employment. Massive employment generation that promotes the integration between natural capital and man-made capital tends to make development participatory and equitable. It also opens up the possibility for virtuous circles.

Disruptive Capital Accumulation and Unsustainable Development

The established model of development tends to exclude natural capital from its purview. It does not, therefore, focus on strengthening the linkages between natural capital and man-made capital. Also, the model neither includes ownership of capital and the consequent distribution of benefits nor gives adequate weight to employment and human agency. As a result, the process of capital accumulation tends to be disruptive and unsustainable. The process can be described as disruptive because it destroys natural capital, without building up substitutive capital, and it feeds on the destruction of the symbiotic structures of nature and people on which traditional livelihood is based.

In a ruthless competitive process of (man-made) capital accumulation under the established model, the stream of benefits generated by capital tends to enhance human welfare for some and not for all. Loss of natural resources generated in the process of economic growth, not only affects directly the level of living of the poor, but it also sets in motion a vicious circle between environmental degradation and impoverishment. The poor remain at the margin and are often the losers, struggling to eke out their living. Also, privatisation of village commons and forest lands can have disastrous distributional impact on the poor.

A relevant question therefore is: what is the scope for sustainable development when the established model is adopted at the global and national levels? At the global level, under the present globalisation model, the system operates on the basis of financial profitability, creating an economic environment to which all countries (have to) adapt. The accumulation process is also set in motion through national, regional and local parameters of ownership and appropriation, supported by transnational power structures and accumulation processes. Natural resources and human capital operate at the service of financial capital, leading to destructive growth and unequal global distribution.

Is it possible to reverse the process at the national level or at the sub-national level to direct policies to sustainable development? That is, is it possible to broaden the reach of the economic process of capital accumulation to benefit all, to meet their basic needs and build their capabilities? It is possible to integrate natural resources fully in to the mainstream processes? One can say that not-withstanding the predominance of disruptive capitalism, given the degree of freedom for policy making at the national and sub-national levels, a gradual transformation of the prevailing global development paradigm in to a sustainable one does not seem to be impossible.

To start with, it will be necessary to turn vicious circles of man-made capital and natural capital into virtuous circles through growth of employment. The underlying premise is that environmental regeneration is labour intensive and it leads to strengthening of natural capital and then of man-made capital. As Ragnar Nurkse (1957) pointed out long ago, surplus labour can be used in generating capital. It is feasible to use human labour for strengthening natural capital and man-made capital, which can in the long run expand the labour absorbing capacity of the main stream economy. Again, improvement in natural resources and reduction in poverty go hand in hand. (Dasgupta and Maeler, 1993). That is, improvement in the status of environment (through massive employment generation) tends to strengthen the sectors where majority of the poor are employed. The employment intensity of the processes ensures equitable distribution of incomes and benefits.

Turning the negative relationship between poverty and environmental degradation into a positive relationship between environmental regeneration and reduction in poverty has been accepted as an important approach to poverty reduction by many. (Ghai and Vivian, 1992, Agrawal and Narain, 1990, Mazzucato and Niemeijer, 2000). The virtuous circles of poverty reduction and environmental regeneration need to start at the local level in a decentralised framework. Participation of people at the local level is accepted as a key to this approach, because of the following reasons:

- As the natural environment is of vital importance to local people, they will be motivated to take care of it.

- Traditional local technologies and rules of social behaviour are very often well adapted to environmental protection.

- Community participation will ensure equitable distribution of benefits.

There is a considerable degree of flexibility of traditional practices and innovative behaviour of local people. Several micro studies of natural resource management present alternative approaches giving opportunities for virtuous circles. From this positive perspective on people's role, one can derive some policy implications for sustainable development. The main points are people's participation, preference for decentralised locally controlled efforts above centralised large-scale modern technologies and coalition between local people and outside groups (NGOs) that bring in scientific knowledge.

To sum up, the disruptive capital accumulation of the established growth model and the prevalence of the present unequal global system can be challenged through initiating virtuous circles, to start with at a local level, that strengthen the links between natural capital and man-made capital based on human agency, *i.e.* massive employment generation. The virtuous circles at the local level can collectively impact on the macro level under an enabling macro environment.

In the next section, we shall examine how such efforts have performed in different environmental situations in three Indian states, and what lessons one can learn from these state level studies.

3. Promoting Virtuous Circles in Three Indian States

The three environmental problems addressed in the study are (1) degradation of coastal regions in Gujarat, (2) depletion and degradation of forests in Orissa, and (3) environmental degradation in dry regions in Andhra Pradesh.

One common feature of all the three regions is that economic growth has put tremendous pressure on environmental resources, and as a result, the environment is severely depleted and degraded in these regions. It seems that the development strategies adopted by the state governments have not viewed natural capital as an important component of the total capital stock. The process of man-made capital accumulation, therefore, has neglected natural capital, leading to its destruction.

Coastal Regions in Gujarat

Gujarat state is one of the prosperous states in India, located in the western part of the country. It has a long seacoast (the longest seacoast among the Indian states) of about 1600 km. Coastal regions, where land and water meet are unique eco-regions, which are rich in coastal and marine eco-systems. These regions are also attractive for a large number of economic activities like trade and ports, shipbuilding and ship breaking, fisheries, tourism, refineries, industries, defence (navy) etc. Though these economic activities appear to promote economic growth, they also cost in terms of loss of coastal and marine resources, which provide livelihood as well as important ecological services to people. Since negligible or no value is attached to these resources, the right signals are not available for taking appropriate decisions about economic activities. A major challenge for policymakers in these regions is how to manage the balance between economic development and ecological health of the coastal region.

The major problems of the coastal region in Gujarat have their roots in the policies of economic growth designed for the region. It appears that the state government has decided to tap the full potential of the coast for promoting economic growth. The series of the industrial policies, particularly after the introduction of the economic reforms has promoted industrial estates and industrial parks on the coast and attracted huge private industrial investments in mineral based and chemical industries, refineries, salt pans and salt manufacturing, ship building and ship breaking etc, without any specific policy for their location. Also, the government (Gujarat Pollution Control Board) has not been able to control pollution generated by these industries in spite of the efforts made. The infrastructure policy of the government has aggressively promoted construction of ports and jetties, roads and bridges etc. on the coast. In addition, agricultural policy has continuously promoted withdrawal of ground water by subsidising investments as well as energy in the withdrawals. This has led to seawater intrusion on a massive scale.

The net result is severe depletion and degradation of coastal environment: (1) depletion and degradation of coastal eco-systems like mangroves, coral reefs, sea weeds, marshy lands etc. (2) large scale salinity ingress in land and water in the region, (3) severe pollution of rivers and the sea near all major industrial centres, and (4) decline in biodiversity in the region. The depletion and degradation have created serious problems in the state, particularly for the poor.

- One major problem faced by people in the coastal region is the shortage of potable water. More than 60 per cent of the villages on the coast suffer from shortage of potable water in the summer months (Hirway, 2004). Coastal salinity of land and water has created severe health problems for the local people. Diseases like fluorosis, skin diseases, water-borne diseases as well as occupational diseases (from industrialisation) are common here (Hirway and Mahadevia, 2004).

- Another major problem is with respect to livelihood, as agriculture, which is still the major occupation of the people here, suffers from poor irrigation facilities (due to salinity ingress in ground water), frequent droughts and low productivity of land.

- Destruction of mangroves and other local vegetation has affected the livelihood of local people in animal husbandry adversely. Over-fishing (encouraged by liberalised policies of fisheries) as well as reduction in fishery due to destruction of mangroves and indiscriminate discharge of pollutants into the sea have affected the livelihood of the fishing population adversely.

- Destruction of mangroves and vegetation has also reduced the protection to the coast from cyclones and sea erosion. The devastating cyclone at Kachchh a few years ago clearly indicated how the destruction of mangroves could intensify a natural calamity.

- As the coast is used for development of industries like dyes and drugs and pharmaceuticals, oil refinery, petro-chemicals, cement, quarries and mines, salt and related industries, the solid and liquid discharge have affected the coastal and marine environment very badly.

It needs to be noted that sustainable development does not rule out promotion of infrastructure like ports and jetties or industries of different types, as there are certain advantages of setting up economic activities on the coast, and these must be exploited. What is important, however, is to consider the ecological aspects while deciding about their location. For example, the number of ports and jetties can be minimised and the location of ports should be decided keeping in mind the ecological conditions of the coast as well as the CRZ rules and regulations. The rules and regulations laid down about the disposal of industrial discharges should be implemented strictly and scientific methods like the GIS should be used in deciding location of industries.

Apart from the regulatory aspects, the coast should also be explored for its positive opportunities. The coast offers many sustainable opportunities for promoting economic growth. Some of these are: (1) mangrove plantation, which can promote animal husbandry, fishery and innumerable processing industries based on the products of mangroves, and eco-tourism, (2) wind energy, solar energy, tidal energy and energy based on biomass for the power deficient state, (3) promotion of alternative land use pattern for more productive use of coastal lands – this can include grass lands, horticulture, mixed farming, and salt pans and even aquaculture in suitable locations, and (4) farming, developing and processing of coastal products like coral reefs, sea weeds and other vegetations in shallow water areas, as there are several industrial and non-industrial uses of these products. It will be useful if these alternatives are examined carefully and implemented systematically. Somehow these alternatives are neither on the agenda of the Government nor on the plans of the projects of NGOs. It is important to go beyond the conventional thinking of protecting environment and try out options that are not only sustainable, but are also leading the economy on the path of high tech development.

In short, there are possibilities that the same coast can contribute to the development and welfare of the state with environmental sustainability if the coastal capital is treated as such, that is as "capital."

As against this, the state government has taken up some programmes to address the local problems that have emerged from the coastal degradation. A number of civil society organisations (NGOs) have also undertaken programmes to create positive virtuous circles for environmental regeneration and poverty reduction. The major programmes are in the following areas:

- Ensuring potable drinking water for people by promoting suitable rainwater harvesting structures.

- Promoting watershed development, check dams and other water harvesting structures for promoting agricultural growth.

- Reclamation of saline land, wasteland and degraded land for productive use.

- Organising workers working in fisheries, saltpans, animal husbandry, agriculture etc. to promote their livelihood.

- Government schemes for promoting plantation of mangroves, afforestation etc. for environmental regeneration.

The study has examined the following three successful cases at the micro level:

1. Aga Khan Rural Support Programme, India (AKRSP-1) : This NGO is working in Junagadh district. Its activities mainly focus on soil and water conservation, water resource development, agricultural extension and drinking water. A village with their intensive activities has been selected for the micro study.

2. Vivekand Research and Training Institute (VRTI) in Kachchh district: This NGO has done considerable work on watershed development. A sub-surface dyke constructed by VRTI for salinity control in Mundha Taluka and its impact on neighbouring villages has been examined in the micro study.

3. Vikas Centre For Development: This NGO is primarily engaged in natural resource management activities in Bharuch district in South Gujarat. Their activities relating to check dam for controlling salinity ingress and follow up activities in Neja village is selected for the micro study.

The major findings of the case studies and the emerging lessons are discussed later on.

Depleted and Degraded Forests in Orissa

Orissa is a major state, located on the eastern coast of India. The state is very rich in environmental resources like forests, mines and minerals, water resources etc., but is almost at the bottom in terms of economic development as well as in all the major sectors of human development, *i.e.* literacy and education, health and nutrition etc.

More than 35 per cent of the geographical area in Orissa is under forests. This is of the order of magnitude of percentage of net sown area in the state. However, one observes a severe depletion and degradation of forests in Orissa during the past few decades. The area under forests has declined from 43.52 per cent of the total geographic area in the state in 1970-71 to 36.00 per cent in the late 1990s.

This is confirmed by satellite imageries (Forest Survey of India Report). The remote sensing data show that the actual cover of forests in Orissa declined from 48383 sq. km. in the early seventies to 46941 sq. km. in the late 1990s, indicating a 3 per cent decline in the area. A careful look at the data indicates that (a) the area under open degraded forests almost doubled, from 10829 sq. km. to 20629 sq. km. during the period, (b) the area under protected forests declined from 37320 sq. km. to 26101 sq. km. (by 30 per cent), and (c) mangrove forests declined from 234 sq. km. to 211 sq. km. during the period. According to the latest forest statistics, dense forests (with 40 per cent and above crown density) cover only 16.76 per cent of the area of the state, while degraded forests and forest wastelands together cover more than 19 per cent of the geographical area of the state. In short, forests have declined not only in terms of area but also qualitatively. In fact, qualitative degradation has been much more than the area decline.

The major factors responsible for the depletion and degradation of forests have been observed to be illicit felling of trees for timber or for raw materials for industries, encroachment of forest lands for cultivation and habitation, mining in forest areas, poaching, tourism as well as uncontrolled grazing, uncontrolled forest fires (frequently induced by people for collection of NTFP – non timber forest produce) and illicit collection of fuel wood. In short, forests have been depleted and degraded largely for promoting economic growth, *i.e.* mineral extraction, timber production, crop cultivation, etc., and to an extent for providing fuel wood, and other forest products by people, mainly poor.

The destruction and depletion of forests have impacted on life and livelihood of people in multiple ways:

- The depletion and degradation has resulted in drastic reduction in the output of NTFPs. Since many people live on the incomes from collection of these products, their livelihood is affected adversely.

- The depletion and degradation also reduces the supply of fodder for animals, fuel wood for households and other forest products for home consumption.

- The depletion and degradation of forests has resulted in massive soil erosion, which has increased the frequency and intensity of floods and cyclones in the state, increasing the sufferings of people.

- The massive soil erosion has affected agriculture adversely, resulting in low production as well as droughts in some parts. The recent starvation deaths in the state are not independent of this.

- The frequent floods, cyclones and droughts have forced the state government to spend thousands of crore of rupees on rescue and rehabilitation of the victims, which has created financial crisis for the state exchequer, and this has reduced government expenditure in other important sectors.

- Degradation of forests has had an adverse impact on the availability of water, as the water retention capacity of forests declines when they are degraded. This results in to shortages of drinking water in the summer months.

- Ecologically speaking, degraded forests tend to become weak in carrying out their ecological functions, such as storage of water, carbon sequestration, protection to bio-diversity etc. This can have serious implications for the ecological health of the state as well as the country, and the world.

- In short, the depletion and degradation have made the poor vulnerable to ecological insecurity and calamities like floods, cyclones, droughts and food insecurity.

It appears that the government of Orissa is strongly oriented towards future growth of the state economy, particularly for the purpose of tapping the new opportunities created in the post-economic reforms period. Focus is on development of modern industries, based on rich mineral and other industries. However, it has not so far looked at forest resources as natural capital that can be integrated with man-made capital for promoting forest-based industrialisation and forest-based economic development in the state. Forests are not considered as a natural capital that can generate a steady flow of income and employment for people. This is because its potential use in the growth process of the economy is not appreciated. Forests are seen as a source of timber and fuel wood or as a raw material in paper and other industries for which they are to be destroyed. They are also encroached upon for agriculture, mining and habitation. That non-timber forest products can promote sound industries—based on processing the variety of NTFPs—is not taken seriously. Not much effort has been made for generating massive employment/income opportunities for people by promoting such industries.

If Orissa uses forest resources in a positive way, *i.e.* as a capital to be accumulated and enhanced for raising the rate of growth, regeneration of forests can reduce the vulnerability of the poor by (a) meeting basic needs like those for fuel wood and fodder, (b) by protecting them from natural calamities, (c) by protecting their livelihoods, and (d) by reducing their vulnerability to ecological and other insecurities. It can also raise the rate of growth of the state economy and lead the state to higher levels of living in a modernised and globalised economy.

Non-timber forest produces include a wide range of forest produces like medicinal plants, gums and resins, vegetables and oil seeds, barks and skins, flowers and seeds, leaves and fruits, wood for craft, a wide range of animals and birds and innumerable insects (including bees) as well as other produces like grasses etc. These products can generate innumerable activities in collection, procurement, sorting and classification, trading, processing, packing and marketing activities. As has been listed by a careful researcher, these products have immense possibilities of promoting modern industries like (a) drugs and pharmaceuticals, (b) cosmetics and related industries, (c) dyes and chemicals (d) food and food products, (e) wines and beverages, and (f) domestic goods like furniture, bamboo products and other crafts. It is, therefore, possible to promote forest-based industrialisation in Orissa. This industrialisation will generate sustainable employment for the masses in the state and it will be employment intensive as well as environmentally sustainable.

Unfortunately the present conditions with respect to NTFP is very poor. To start with, there is no complete information about the availability of the types and uses of NTFPs in Orissa. Also, there are no systematic estimates of the quality and quantity of even the known NTFPs. There is a need to fill in the gaps in the information. Secondly, there are not well-established systems of procurement, storage, sorting, processing and trading of NTFPs. In fact, there is no concept of promoting processing units with modern systems and technologies. Whatever systems are there, they do not pass on any benefits to tribal population. And lastly, there is incomplete knowledge about the medicinal uses of herbs and other produces by tribals. In short, there is a need to collect complete information on NTFPs and plan for their possible uses and processing systematically.

In addition, forests can also generate remunerative modern sector employment in tourism and eco-tourism. Ideal locations can be identified.

It has been estimated that NTFPs and tourism together can provide full employment with remunerative incomes to the tribal population in the state. What is needed is to integrate forests in the mainstream development strategy.

Government of Orissa, donor agencies and NGOs have undertaken forest regeneration activities at the local and with community participation. The objective here is to regenerate forests to turn the vicious circle of poverty and forest degradation into virtuous circles of forest regeneration and poverty reduction. It is expected that these virtuous circles will ultimately lead to broad-based sustainable development in the state.

Environmental scientists have developed two distinct methods of regeneration of forests, namely natural regeneration (creating an environment for forests to get regenerated on its own) and artificial regeneration through plantation. Both the methods need community participation as well as a decentralised framework. For artificial regeneration of forests one may use a "watershed approach" and a "forestry approach." Under the first approach the primary aim is to ensure optimum utilisation of basic natural resources, such as land, water, vegetation etc. for achieving integrated development of a given area. The forestry approach concentrates directly on plantation, joint forest management, protection to forests etc.

The major objectives of these micro level projects by GO and NGO have been (1) to explore various possibilities of income/employment generating projects of forest regeneration, (2) to generate short term and long-term employment for people around forest regeneration in the short run and sustainable employment in the long run, (3) to involve communities in the different activities of forest regeneration and empower community organisations to manage these, and (4) to ensure equitable distribution of gains of forest regeneration and the follow-up activities.

The following successful case studies have been selected for in-depth studies:

1. Watershed development projects in forest areas undertaken by the NGOs Agragamee and Lokdrushti in Raigada and Navapada districts.

2. Joint Forest Management projects undertaken by the state government and an NGO (VSS) in Kalahandi district.

3. Forest Plantation Project taken up by an NGO (LNSRD) in Rayagada district, and,

4. Forest Protection Project taken up in Navapada district by an NGO (Sambhab)

The major findings of the case studies and the emerging lessons are discussed later on.

Dry Regions of Andhra Pradesh

Andhra Pradesh is a major South Indian state of India, located on the eastern coast of the country. The state is neither at the top nor at the bottom in terms of economic development and human development. However, it is known for the progress it has made in the recent decade.

The state can be divided into three regions: Coastal Andhra (9 districts), Rayalseema (4 districts) and Telangana (10 districts) While most of the districts in coastal Andhra have assured irrigation, the other two regions are mostly rain-fed.

Historically speaking, in the nineteenth century the state is reported to be covered by dense forests with a variety of flora and fauna. During the British period, clearing of forests was encouraged on a large scale, which continued after Independence. Destruction of dense forests and vegetation resulted in soil erosion, also affecting the large tanks that were used for irrigation purposes. With the decline in the local systems of natural resource management, the status of the resources became worse. In the past, vast tracts of lands were being irrigated by a large network of tanks, which gradually got silted due to neglect and faulty management. The catchments of these tanks have been eroded and illegal occupations of catchments have taken place. The same is the plight of common property resources. The dependence on CPRs is higher for the poor households rather than the rich. However, the poor households fail to recognise the importance of managing these CPRs and it often does not make any economic sense to them for investing in CPRs, as the returns are long-term in nature. Gradually there has been reduction in grazing lands too.

The pressure on land has continuously increased in the state because of (1) unequal distribution of land, (2) population increase and (3) overgrazing. There has also been an increasing pressure on the water resources in the state due to increasing demand and dwindling supply. Over-withdrawal of ground water (encouraged by capital subsidies and subsidised energy to draw water) on the one hand and the decline in surface water bodies (local) on the other hand created an overall shortage of water supply in many parts of Andhra Pradesh, particularly in Rayalseema and Telangana regions.

About 55 per cent of the total geographic area of Andhra Pradesh is affected by various soil degradation problems. Water erosion seems to be a major problem causing loss of top soil and terrain deformation, and it is prevalent in about 46 per cent of the area. The same survey shows that about 4 per cent of the area in the state is very severely eroded, 19 per cent area is severely eroded and 34 per cent area is moderately eroded. Thus, about 57 per cent area of the state needs immediate soil and water conservation measures. About 34 per cent area has slightly eroded soils and the rest is rock and other miscellaneous land.

To sum up, the overall degradation of natural resources has resulted in expansion of dry areas—arid and semi-arid areas—in Andhra Pradesh. In addition, erosion of land caused by water, salinity ingress in coastal regions and water logging and salinity in canal-irrigated areas have caused severe land degradation in the state. The major factor responsible for this state of affairs is of course a lack of attention and consideration of these natural resources as "capital". This implies a systematic undervaluation of these resources, leading to their over-use and misuse.

Environmental degradation of dry regions in Andhra Pradesh poses serious problems for the people, and particularly the poor whose poverty is closely linked with environmental vulnerability:

- Inadequate livelihood opportunities is one of the most serious problems in the regions. Since there is only one crop, *i.e. Kharif* crop, grown in most of these regions, there are limited employment avenues available after the *Kharif* season is over. Most people remain seasonally unemployed. Often they migrate on a large scale for 6-8 months in a year in search of livelihood. These migrant workers constitute the most vulnerable groups in the state.

- Shortage of potable drinking water is another major problem of the dry regions. Women and children spend long hours on fetching not only water but also fodder and fuel wood, which affects their health and nutrition adversely. It also affects education of children adversely.

- The incidence of income poverty and human poverty is relatively high in these regions. Neither the human agency nor the natural resources are well used or well maintained in these regions.

- The marginalisation of these regions on the one hand and the high vulnerability of the people on the other hand has had some severe political consequences. The emergence of violent movements—

Naxal movement—is a consequence of the marginalization and sufferings.

Using vast tracts of dry lands productively by promoting agricultural growth in these regions appears to be a major solution for poverty reduction in Andhra Pradesh. Watershed development projects have emerged as a major programme for the purpose. This programme was first introduced in 1989 as IWDP, Integrated Watershed Development Programme, and was followed by a National Watershed Development Programme in Rainfed Areas (NWDPRA). In 1994, however, it was decided to merge all WSD programmes under DPAP, DDP, JRY and EAS of the Ministry of Rural Development into one programme as per the recommendation of the Technical Committee headed by C.H. Hanumantha Rao.

Watershed development is now accepted as a major programme for drought-prone areas leading to drought proofing. It is now seen as a strategy for protecting the livelihoods of people inhabiting the fragile ecosystems experiencing soil erosion and moisture stress through increased agricultural production and productivity. Some of the important features of this approach are:

- Simultaneous development of land, water and biomass resources in the light of symbiotic relationship among them.
- Integrated farming system approach.
- Meeting food, fodder, fuel needs of human-beings and livestock.
- Ensuring environmental sustainability along with economic viability by promoting low cost technology.
- Improving land productivity by promoting better agronomic practices and input use.
- Releasing population pressure on land by creating non-farm employment, and
- Development of local institutions for management through participatory approach.

Optimum resource use in dry regions calls for several additional inputs. The involvement of the agricultural sector with a suitable agricultural policy and a long term plan is necessary to carry forward watershed development not only to stabilise agriculture, but also to achieve sustainable agriculture growth. Agriculture department has to create an enabling environment by organising (a) infrastructure for agriculture, (b) R & D, extension and training, (c) access to credit, and (d) GO-NGO (CBO) partnership in the entire process. That is, watershed development programmes need to be carried out with a clear focus on drought proofing at the household level as well as at the regional level. Watershed development also requires support from the agricultural department to create and promote enabling conditions for sustainable agricultural development.

The state government has implemented several programmes for the purpose of promoting better management of land and water resources. Several NGOs also have taken up programmes for better management of natural resources either in collaboration with the government or independently. The major programmes have been watershed development programmes, soil conservation measures, management of common property resources, construction of water harvesting structures etc.

The following case studies have been examined in depth at the field level:

1. Watershed development project at Mallapuram and at Kadiridevalapalli in Anantpur district implemented by Rural Development Trust.

2. Watershed development project implemented under DPAP programme at Kodur in Mahabubnagar district.

3. Watershed development programme in Anantpur district implemented by the state forest department.

4. Watershed development project implemented in Kakanoor in Mehabubnagar district by an NGO (VASORD), and

5. Watershed development project implemented in Anantpur district by the state forest department.

The major findings of these studies are discussed later on.

Successful Case Studies at the Micro Level

Instead of mainstreaming natural capital by integrating it with the development strategy, all the three governments have designed programmes for environmental regeneration at the micro level to address the micro level problems emerging from the environmental degradation. NGOs also have taken up such programmes on their own or under government programmes. The major programmes are watershed development programmes, joint forest management programmes, soil and water conservation programmes, wasteland development programmes, water-harvesting structures etc. These programmes primarily address the sufferings of the local people including the poor. They attempt to meet their basic needs like fuel wood, fodder and water; to protect their livelihood in agriculture, forestry, fishery, animal husbandry etc. and to protect them for natural calamities (caused by environmental depletion and degradation) like droughts, floods, cyclones and even tsunamis. In short, the programmes aim at promoting virtuous circles of poverty reduction and environmental regeneration.

One major observation of the different successful case studies is that strong community organisation, identification of the right technology, equitable ownership of assets, equal distribution of benefits and inclusion of the poor are some of the essential conditions for virtuous circles to operate successfully. More or less all the case studies have these characteristics. Those who do not have these, show a relatively low level of achievements.

How have these programmes fared? Careful examination of the successful case studies in each of the three states lead us to observe the following:

- The successful cases have clearly shown that it has been possible to identify at the micro level the right kind of activities and suitable technologies for environmental regeneration as well as for employment generation and livelihood protection of the poor.

- It has also been possible to involve people in these activities not only in implementation, but also in planning, decision-making and management of assets. The successful case studies do suggest that the poor at the bottom have benefited by these micro interventions.

- There has been good success in terms of generation of short-term employment for people while regenerating environmental resources. Though, the employment generated has not been enough to meet the needs of the poor, the case studies do indicate that it is possible to generate more employment with larger funds and higher scale of activities.

- The achievements in terms of awareness generation, organisation of people, their education etc. have been considerable.

The success in generating long-term employment, however, has been limited—in most cases it has not been achieved. Though, many NGOs involved do talk about the long-term goal of generating sustainable employment and livelihood for the poor, they have not been able to achieve this primarily because (1) it is not planned systematically, (2) the required funds and support are not available, and (3) frequently it is assumed (particularly under government programmes) that the goal of the programme is to complete the programme without bothering about tapping its long term potential. The virtuous circles at the micro level, thus, play a limited role, even in successful cases.

Can these virtuous circles make an impact at the macro level? The answer does not seem to be very positive. At the empirical level, one does not see an improvement in the environmental status of the three selected regions, namely, coastal region in Gujarat, forests in Orissa and dry regions in Andhra Pradesh. It seems that the interventions have not made much impact at the macro level so far. This is not to deny the importance of micro level work, but it must be accepted that a scale of operation is needed for successful cases to make an impact at the macro level. A few successful cases cannot reverse the trends.

Secondly, there are several environmental issues, which cannot be addressed only at the micro level. For example, coastal salinity cannot be controlled by micro interventions alone, as it requires a regional approach of constructing tidal regulators, *bandharas*, long spreading channels etc. which need huge investments and which need to be planned at the regional level. Similarly, the NTFP based industrial development in Orissa needs a regional/state level approach and interventions. In other words successful micro interventions need a macro support.

Thirdly, the degeneration and depletion of environment has occurred in the states because of certain macro policies and the development path chosen by the government. To expect micro processes to be able to reverse the situation will not be very realistic. For example recharge of ground water by micro interventions will not help much if electricity and drilling of wells is subsidised and there are no restrictions on drawing ground water. Or mangroves plantation in some spots will not help if ports and other developments destroy mangroves on a massive scale. That is, a reversal of macro policies will also be needed for supplementing micro level interventions.

And lastly, the micro level interventions should not be treated as separate interventions, independent of macro policies, but should be linked with a long-term strategy of development—for diversifying the regional economy. This will lead to employment intensive development process. The long-term strategy of developing modern agri-business in dry regions or 'watershed plus approach' need to be formulated along with watershed programmes. Similarly NTFP based industrial development need to be designed under JFM plus approach.

4. Concluding Observations

The empirical evidences in the literature seems to suggest that economic growth is usually accompanied by environmental degradation, as consumption of natural resources contribute to economic growth. However, when environmental degradation leads to loss of livelihood, shortage of drinking water and of basic needs like fuel wood, fodder etc, increased intensity and frequency of natural disasters like droughts, floods and cyclones, and to increased vulnerability of the poor, it is clear that it is not the *consumption* of natural resources, but it is the *neglect* of the resources, which is responsible for the problems. As seen earlier, environment and man-made capital accumulation (which is seen as a precondition for economic growth under the established model) have complex relationship with each other and there are possibilities where both can go hand in hand. The established development paradigm ignores this positive relationship and focuses only on man-made capital accumulation. Such an approach leads to disruptive capital accumulation.

The above discussion has shown that all the three states have neither treated their respective natural resources as a part of their capital stock, nor have they chosen a growth path that strengthens this capital and integrates it with the other capital stock, namely, man-made capital and human capital. As a result, there are striking similarities in their growth policies in the post-economic reforms period. These similarities are observed in their respective industrial policies and in subsidies and concessions offered to prospective investors as well as in infrastructure policies and in the broad path that they have chosen for raising the rate of economic growth. All the states are looking at their natural resources to exploit them to promote modern industries. Orissa is looking at forests and mines to exploit them for promoting modern industries; Gujarat is looking at the coast to tap its unique potential for promoting economic growth and Andhra Pradesh also does not look at the resources of its dry regions for linking them with the mainstream development. There is no attempt to develop a strategy that integrates natural resources with the mainstream development. In short, the policymakers have treated natural resources not as an asset or capital to be accumulated and to be developed for expanding its economic base, but as an input for economic growth to be used up in the process of growth.

Efforts to turn the vicious circles between environmental degradation and poverty in to virtuous circles between poverty reduction and environmental regeneration at the micro level are not only welcome, but also essential for reversing the impact of disruptive capital accumulation. The case studies have given enough evidence to indicate that such efforts are feasible and desirable. The virtuous circles at the local level do contribute to poverty reduction and can contribute more in the long run. However, they can collectively impact on the macro level only under an enabling macro environment.

While concluding the paper it can be observed that the prevailing pattern of globalisation reflects disruptive capitalism. However, its consequences at the micro level have generated forces that resist the impact. In fact, there is a wide-spread awareness and concern about the environment. There are several technological breakthroughs, which can help micro level regeneration of natural resources. These technological interventions, accompanied by strong community organisations have shown how to turn the vicious circles of poverty and environmental degradation in to virtuous circles of environmental regeneration and poverty reduction. The Brundtland Report's convincing message is based on such experiences.

This message has important implications for macro level development that can lead to sustainable development. A major message is that natural resources need to be treated as natural capital and human capital/human agency can play an important role in integrating natural capital with man-made capital. Unrestrained (man-made) capital accumulation under the established model of global development will lead to insatiable economic expansion and over-valuation of materialistic consumption, fuelled by greed of some. The alternative seems to be a decentralised regime of participatory command and control over capital accumulation climbing from the local to sub-national to national level. This alternative decentralised regime, however, cannot be realised without macro planning. Only then the present vicious circles between poverty, inequality and environmental decay may turn into virtuous circles supporting sustainable development.

Jan Tinbergen's observation, while discussing the need for world economic planning, is relevant here: "Complicated processes, such as those involved in any world economic policy, require prior preparation in order to avoid at least some of the foreseeable inconsistencies that may arise. Planning is just that" (Tinbergen, 1996). Sustainable development is how to avoid, given the limited carrying capacity of the earth, the foreseeable inconsistencies between the need of all and the greed of some.

References

Agarwal, A. and S. Narain (1990). *Towards Green Villages*, Centre for Science and Environment, New Delhi.

Daly, Herman (1990). "Towards Some Operational Principles of Sustainable Development," *Ecological Economics*, 2, 1-6.

Dasgupta, P. and K-G Maeler (1993). *Poverty, Institutions and the Environmental-Resource Base*, The Development Economics Research Programme, No 48, London School of Economics, September.

Dreze, J. and A. Sen (1995). *India. Economic Development and Social Opportunity*, Delhi: Oxford . University Press.

Ghai, D. and J.M. Vivian (1992). *Grassroot Environmental Action: People's Participation in Sustainable Development*.

Goulet, D. (1985). *The Cruel Choice*, New York: University Press of America.

————. (1996). "Authentic Development: Is it Sustainable?" in Denis C. Pirages (ed) *Building Sustainable Societies*, New York: M.E. Sharpe.

Hirway, Indira (2004). *Drinking Water Supply in Gujarat: Towards a Sustainable Approach*, World Health Organisation, New Delhi.

Hirway, Indira and Darshini Mahadevia (2004). *Gujarat State Human Development Report 2004*, Planning Commission, Government of India, New Delhi and UNDP, New Delhi.

Hirway, Indira and P. Terhal (1994). "Towards Employment Guarantee in India. Indian and International Experiences in Rural Public Works," *Indo-Dutch Studies on Development Alternatives*, No. 14, New Delhi: Sage Publications.

————. (2002). *Environment, Employment and Sustainable Development: A Study in Three Indian States*, Final Report to Indo-Dutch Programme on Alternatives in Development, June.

Mazzucato, V. and D. Niemeijer (2000). *Rethinking Soil and Water Conservation in a Changing Society: A Case Study in Eastern Burkina Faso*, PhD thesis Wageningen University.

Myrdal, G. (1968). *Asian Drama: An Inquiry into the Poverty of Nations*, Pantheon Books.

Nurkse, R. (1957). *Problems of Capital Formation in Underdeveloped Economies*, Oxford University Press.

Sen, A. (1985). *Commodities and Capabilities*, Amsterdam: North Holland.

Tinbergen, J. (1996). "A European Perspective on World Economic Planning," in Denis Munby (ed) *Economic Growth in World Perspective*, New York: Association Press.

World Commission on Environment and Development (1987). *Our Common Future*. Oxford University Press.

19

Climate Change and its Abatement: Towards a Better Project Design

GOPAL K. KADEKODI[66]

1. Introduction

Climate change effects are being talked as a global common problem.[67] Both national economies, multi-lateral agencies such as United Nation Environment Programme (UNEP), IPCC and World Bank and major civil society groups such as CITIES and IUCN are posing one common economic question: How to develop models of climate change impacts and scientific, economic and political strategies to abate their growing adverse effects? Climate change being such a slow process that generation-by-generation one can ignore it or develop short run strategies. But keeping its long-term implications, designing a specific economic strategy on accounting for the costs and benefits of abating and developing adaptation is taken up in this paper. More specifically, the question of appropriate discount rate for an abatement project forms the core of this paper.

Climate change refers to a long-term shift or alteration in the climate of a specific location, a region or the entire planet (Shukla *et al.*, 2003). They are the result of various green house gas emissions and depletion of Ozone layer in the atmosphere. Climate change primarily manifests itself in terms of temperature increase, sea level rise, variability of precipitation pattern, change in the frequency and intensity of extreme events like cyclones, etc. Effects of such *primary changes* are observed on humidity, water availability, flooding and water logging, vegetation growth, geo-morphological structure instability, landslides and land erosion and so on. The *secondary changes* are more visible in the forms of impacts on sectors

---

66. Thanks to Dr. HK Amarnath, Manager, Data Bank Centre at ISEC for arranging all the necessary data for the econometric analysis. Thanks are also to Ms Sandhya and Kavita Babu for assisting me in the computation and compilation of data and information.

67. See Annexure A-19.1 for a glimpse on international perspectives of climate change.

like water, land, forest, landscape, coastal zone and quality of life through visible changes in temperature, rainfall and health.

Water is fundamental to human life, and to many activities such as agriculture, industry, power generation, transportation, and waste management. Hence, apart from availability of clean drinking water, the potential impacts of climate change on hydrology and water resources resulting in possible changes in the water balance and in stream flow cannot be ignored. Land is affected by climate change through soil changes. This includes the accelerated decomposition of organic matter that releases nutrients in the short-run but may reduce fertility in the long-run. Soil temperature changes influence rates of organic matter decomposition, nutrient release and intake, and plant metabolic processes. Furthermore, climate is one of the most important determinants of vegetation pattern, which in turn has shapes societal development (e.g., food habits) over centuries. The spread of diseases due to changes in global temperature is expected to raise the incidences and spread of major diseases in the country. Of the many, re-emergence of malaria is being talked about wide universally.

Various factors and activities that also contribute to climate change over long period of time are volcanic eruptions, changes in the sun's intensity, very slow changes in ocean circulation or land surfaces (occurring over decades, centuries or longer), anthropogenic activities like fossil fuel combustion, industrial activities, agriculture systems, changing land use patterns, and waste decomposition (releasing green house gases into the atmosphere) and so on.

2. Vulnerability of Climate Change: A National Perspective

A recent report by the Ministry of Environment and Forests (MoEF, 2004) on climate change makes several suggestions on scientific methods to abate and develop adaptation strategies. It also cautioned on the economic fronts about the kinds of resources needed to deal with the problem, socially and economically.

Restricting the discussion to the socio-economic problems, it is time to make some serious thinking on the design of economic instruments to arrest the rate of such climate changes. Some of the major scientific findings and projections signal serious warnings, a glimpse of which is presented in Box 19.1 below.

Box 19.1

Extracts on Long-term Climate Change Effects on Indian Sub-Continent

- Using the second generation Hardley Centre Regional Model future scenarios of increased greenhouse gas concentrations, marked increase in seasonal surface air temperature is projected into the 21st century, becoming conspicuous after the 2040s ....Climate projections indicate increases in both maximum as well as minimum temperature and projected to increase by 2-4⁰ –C during the 2050s (MoEF, 2004; p. vi).

- The projected water demand of over 980 billion cubic meters in 2050 will require intensive development of groundwater resources, exploiting both dynamic and in-storage potential.....Even in a relatively short span of about 50 years, most of the forest biomass in India seem to be highly vulnerable to the projected change in climate (MoEF, 2004, p.viii).

- One meter sea level rise is projected to displace approximately 7.1 million people in India and about 5764 square kilometers of land area will be lost, along with 4200 kms of roads,...It is projected that malaria will move to higher latitudes and altitudes in India, with 10 per cent more area offering climate opportunities for the malaria vector to breed throughout the year during the 2080s (MoEF, 2004, p.x).

2.1 Health Effect: A Case of Malaria in India

Climate change is expected to affect human health, both directly through increased mortality due to extreme temperatures and weather events, and also indirectly through effects on morbidity, changes in food production, exacerbated air pollution, demographic displacement and the re-distribution of biological organisms that transmit vector-borne diseases (Mc Michael *et al.*, 1996).

It is useful to take a look at the emergence of malaria in the country as a case of socio-economic impacts. It is expected that the change in the surface temperature in India would increase the occurrence of malaria especially among the poorer section. Projections show that malaria transmission would increase the area under malaria by 10 per cent in future (MoEF, 2004). Malaria has already become a most serious and complex health problem in India, and it has become an endemic disease in certain regions of the country. It should be noted that around 75 million cases of malaria with 0.8 million deaths every year had been reported in India prior to launching of National Malaria Control Programme during 1953. Even though it declined significantly during the 60's, malaria has become one of the major health issues in the late 70's and at present, it is considered a major challenge with 2 to 2.5 million cases reported annually (*www. Malaria-Ipca.com*; Figure 19.1 and Annexure A-19.2 for some more data). Though detailed estimates are not available, the available estimates suggest that the economic loss due to malaria in India from 1990-1993 is $506.82 million to $630.82 million (Sharma, 1996c). It is also estimated that around 25 per cent of India's health budget goes to malaria control. However, the total economic costs—both direct and indirect costs—of mortality and morbidity due to malaria in India would be substantial and this has larger implications on the well-being of the population. The malaria related mortality rates also provide a similar kind of scenario. For example, from 1976 onwards, the mortality rate is increasing gradually and this increase is very steep in 1994. In 1994, the increase in the mortality rate is three times greater than that of in 1993. Though, the mortality rate has come down during the next four years till 1998, it is still at the higher level compared to the year 1993 (Figure 19.2).

Figure 19.1

Trend in the Total Malaria Cases and P. Falciparum in India

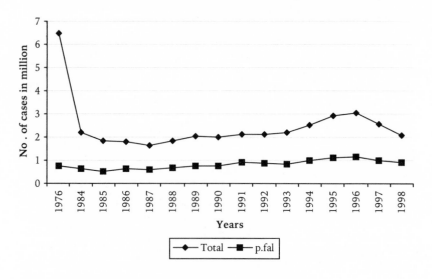

Figure 19.2

Trend in Number of Deaths Due to Malaria in India

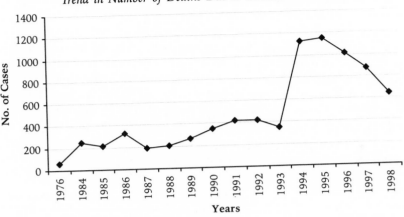

3. A Tour of Climate Change Effects: Case Studies from Karnataka

3.1 Temperature Changes

Karnataka has witnessed an increasing trend in mean, maximum and minimum temperatures over the past 30 years and more (Figure 19.3 to

Figure 19.3

Average Yearly Mean Temperature in Karnataka (Various Districts)

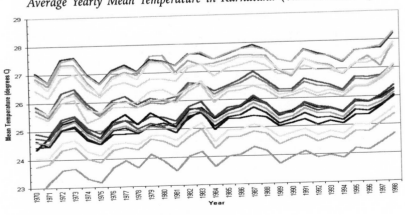

Note: The Chart shows the trend for 18 districts.

Figure 19.4

Highest Temperatures at Select Places of Karnataka

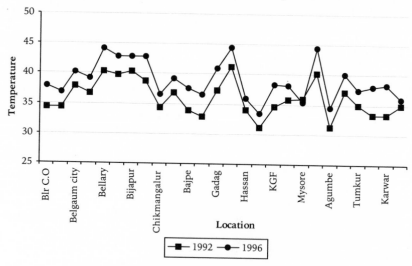

Figure 19.5

Lowest Temperatures at Select Places of Karnataka

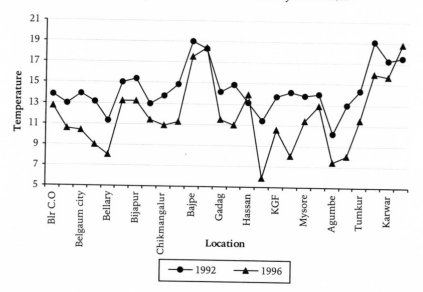

19.5). Effects are felt in terms of continuous droughts in northern Karnataka during the recent years in districts such as Raichur, Bellary, Bidar, Dharwad, Bijapur and Gulbarga (Reid, 2000). An increase in temperature has been observed to be highly significant in the forest regions of Karnataka. Ravindranath *et al.,* (2003, 1998) have forecasted that in the Western Ghat region, even moderate climate sensitivity projections can cause temperature changes any where from 1.05 to 1.40 °C in the region.

3.2 Precipitation Changes

Karnataka is a tropical State. Annual normal rainfall is 1139 mm, received over 55 normal rainy days. However, the distribution of rainfall over space and time is not uniform. For the twenty year period between 1961 and 1981, a comparison of normal rainfall with the percentage deviation of actual year-wise rainfall reveals that though annual rainfall was normal in nine years, it fell below normal in six years and was above normal in five years (CMDR, 2004).

Figure 19.6

Total Yearly Precipitaton in Karnataka (Various Districts)

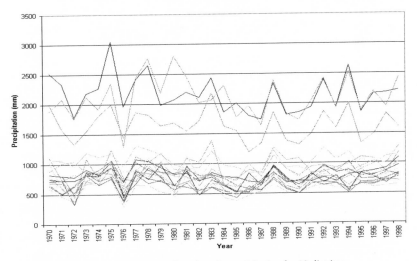

Note: The chart shows the trend of total yearly precipitation for 18 districts.

For the past four years (1999-2003), Karnataka has suffered from the adverse fallout of monsoonal failure as well as deficient post-monsoonal precipitation. Rainfall deficiency during the 2001 monsoon was nearly 20 per cent, as compared to the normal. According to the Drought Monitoring Cell, Karnataka is next only to Rajasthan in terms of total area affected by drought (CMDR 2004).

> While monsoon has been good in most parts of the country, large parts of Karnataka have received below average rainfall—in as many 125 *taluks*; sowing of the *Kharif* crop has been delayed. A total of 159 *taluks* in Karnataka have been declared drought-affected while another 20 are facing acute water shortage. Worried about the farmers who face the impact of drought for a third consecutive year, the State Government has decided to resort to cloud seeding to bring rain to the affected areas, at a cost of Rs. 5.65 crore. This is the first time in the country such an exercise is being planned on such a large scale—an aircraft armed with chemicals will 'seed' rain from clouds, an artificial way of making rain-bearing clouds precipitate in designated regions (*http:// www.ndtv.com*, June 2, 2003).

> The severe drought in Karnataka's Kolar district has forced a large number of people to leave their villages and head towards the cities. For three years now, it has barely rained and villagers say they have no choice but to leave. Eguva Maddalakana village in Kolar bears a deserted look. Of the 60-odd families, less than 30 remain and even in those it's only women, children and the old. The men have all left for the cities in search of jobs. The fields are barren, there is little food and even less water. Nagalakshmi, a villager, said, "There is no food to eat, no water, no fodder for our cattle, people have left for Bangalore to find work. It's the same story in several neighbouring villages that have seen large-scale migration to towns. (*http://www.ndtv.com*, June 9, 2003)

A detailed study of the impact of drought on agriculture carried out in 18 sample *taluks* of Karnataka, taken together as well as for two broad *taluk* categories as Category A and Category B, reveals several interesting findings (CMDR, 2004). Briefly stated, both Category A and Category B *taluks* show negative deviations in annual rainfall from the normal, except the slight positive deviations for Channapatna, Bangarpet, Hospet, Yadgir and Raichur in 2001, all of which belong to Category B *taluks*.

3.3 Water Balance

The impact of local, regional and global changes in climatic patterns is predicted to be highly significant, particularly upon the water resources and water balance. Examples are increased evaporation (a result of higher temperature, combined with regional changes in precipitation characteristics such as total amount, variability, frequency and intensity of floods and droughts), changes in soil moisture and water supplies for irrigation and hydroelectric power generation.

Although, most of the sedimentation rates observed in catchments in Karnataka are predominantly due to deforestation and land degradation, it is possible that increased precipitation will increase sedimentation rates,

Figure 19.7

Percentage Deviation in Annual Rainfall from Normal

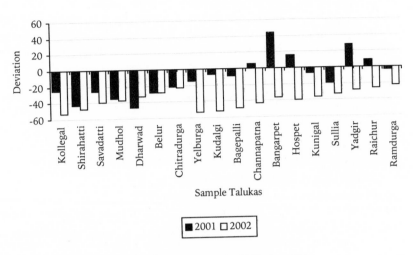

Sample Talukas

■ 2001 □ 2002

Source: Incidence and Effects of Drought-Report by CMDR Jan. 2004.

Note: Category A contains 7 sample *taluks* that recorded deficits in their respective *taluk* level average rainfall during both 2001 and 2002.

Category B includes the remaining 11 sample *taluks* with a recorded rainfall deficit in 2002 only.

particularly if land degradation continues. Hence, increased monsoonal precipitation does not necessarily lead to higher agricultural production. In a study, Gosain and Rao (2003) modelled water balance components expressed as a percentage of rainfall. The model predicts that in the case of the Cauvery basin an increase of 2.7 per cent rainfall will occur. Runoff will fall by two per cent, while actual evapo-transpiration increases by about two per cent. In the Krishna river basin, however, change in rainfall with respect to the control has been predicted as a negative, -5.8 per cent, while runoff will fall by two per cent and the actual evapotranspiration will increase by 2.6 per cent. This may be either due to an increase in temperature and/or changes in rainfall distribution patterns in time.

On the other hand, most of the tanks in Karnataka have been silted up to more than 30 per cent of their capacities reducing their command area by 35 per cent. The rate of silt deposition in irrigated tanks is estimated at 8.51 ha-m/100 Km^2/yr against the assumed siltation of 3.02 ha-m/100 km^2/yr (Karnataka Tank Improvement Project AFC Report, 2000).

3.4 Land Use and Cropping Pattern Changes

Both rainfall and temperature changes have immediate impacts upon land use patterns. Changes in cropping patterns, decline in productivity and movement in pre- and post-prices in Karnataka is predicted with the changing climate scenario (CMDR, 2004). Paddy crops would be vulnerable to an increase in minimum temperature. The adverse impacts of likely water shortage would result in a net decline in paddy yields. One study assesses that the loss in farm-level net revenue will range between nine and 25 per cent for a temperature rise of 2-3.5°C (Kumar and Parikh, 1998). A rise in mean temperature of 2°C and a seven per cent increase in mean precipitation will reduce net revenues by 12.3 per cent for the country as a whole, while agriculture in the coastal regions of Gujarat, Maharashtra and Karnataka is likely to be affected negatively.

According to a study by CMDR (2004), drought impacts were observed in the *kharif* seasons of both 2001 and 2002, as compared to normal years for all *taluks* of the two categories of A and B (mentioned above). While in Category A *taluks* with two consequent years of deficit rainfall, the

Table 19.1

Changes in Cropping Pattern (per cent Net Sown Area (NSA))

Taluk Category	Crop Type	Kharif			Rabi		
		Per cent change in 2001 over 1990s	Per cent change in 2002 over 1990s	Per cent change in 2002 over 2001	Per cent change in 2001 over 1990s	Per cent change in 2002 over 1990s	Per cent change in 2002 over 2001
A	Low	9.0	-9.6	-17.1	-10.1	-5.2	5.4
	Medium	-25.6	-17.5	10.9	17.6	-20.8	-32.6
	High	105.6	96.9	-4.2	-73.1	-33.7	146.3
	Low	-53.7	-17.7	77.5	-19.0	-33.0	-17.3
B	Medium	-17.2	-15.9	1.6	-4.3	-31.9	-28.9
	High	-16.3	1.6	21.4	-40.0	-91.8	-86.3
	Low	-37.4	-15.6	34.8	-16.1	-24.0	-9.4
All *Taluks*	Medium	-21.0	-16.6	5.5	8.0	-25.7	-31.2
	High	-0.7	13.8	14.6	-50.5	-73.3	-46.1

Notes: The classification of crops according to the intensity of water requirement are as follows:

Low: Jowar, Bajra, Ragi, Horsegram, Sajji, Save, Castor Seed, Navane, Cow gram, Linseed, Alasandi, Sesame, Black gram, Tor dal, Bengal gram, Green gram, Onion;

Medium: Sunflower, Wheat, Maize, Cotton, Groundnut, Chilli, Potato, Mango, Turmeric;

High: Paddy, Sugarcane, Banana, Betel nut, Coconut, Silk, Rubber, Geru

Source: Incidence and effects of drought-CMDR, 2004 Report.

situation further deteriorated in 2002, there appears to have occurred a recovery to the extent of nearly 20 per cent on an average in Category B *taluks*, with deficit rainfall only in one year. These studies can be taken as evidences of emerging climate change impacts on crop seasons. One possible impact of such climate changes can be farmers to shift away from the cultivation of high water intensive crops (such as paddy and sugarcane) to less water intensive crops (e.g. *jowar* and maize) (Table 19.1).

Consider the B category *taluks*. In *kharif* 2001, the decline in net sown area as compared to normal is greatest for the Low Water Intensive (LWI) crops (-37 per cent), followed by the Medium Water Intensive (MWI) and High Water Intensive (HWI) categories. During the second year of drought, while the NSA increased by nearly 35 per cent for the LWI category over the previous year (2001), for the HWI crop category there was an improvement to the lesser extent of 21 per cent. The switching to LWI crops comes out more marked in the *Rabi* seasons of the drought years. In *Rabi* 2001, the percentage decline in the NSA of LWI crops is 16 per cent as compared to the 40 per cent decline for HWI crops. In case of HWI crops, in *Rabi* 2002 the difference between these two crop categories is higher (86 per cent) with the LWI category recording a percentage decline of 9 per cent.

Moreover, for all *taluks* taken together, the shortfall in average yield rates in the *Rabi* season is much in excess of 50 per cent from the normal figures in both the drought years, irrespective of the agricultural season.

3.5 Coastal Areas

Karnataka is endowed with a coastline of over 320 km. The average population-density of the coastal districts is 275 persons per square kilometers. The region is rich in agricultural production and fishing.

This coastal zone is also influenced by a wide range of climate related factors impacting with erosion, sea level rise, flooding, subsidence, salinisation and the deterioration of coastal ecosystems. The washing of soil and sediment, which occurs to a marked degree in the Western Ghats, causes a large amount of sediments to pass into the sea along the coasts, and affects the shore features. At the same time, erosion due to cyclonic storms takes place all along the coast. River flooding (the temporary inundation of coastal areas by river water) also occurs in coastal areas, estuaries and deltaic areas. Probable impacts as a result of increase in sea level include—land loss and population displacement; increased loss due to flooding of low lying coastal areas; agricultural and employment losses resulting from inundation, salinisation, and land loss; impacts on coastal aquaculture, and impacts on coastal tourism. A study, carried out by the School of Environmental Sciences, Jawaharlal Nehru University (1993), predicts that 0.15 per cent of the total 19.179 Mha of coastal Karnataka will be inundated by rising seas. Of the 44.81 million people in coastal Karnataka, 0.25 million (0.56 per cent) would be affected for each one-meter increase in sea level.

3.6 Impacting Forests

Climate change is an additional stress factor, contributing to the degradation of the State's forest ecosystems. Karnataka has 20.5 per cent of its geographical area as forests with a host of forest types. These include fragile coastal mangroves systems, tropical wet evergreen forests of the Western Ghats, pockets of *shola* forests interspersed with high altitude grass lands, and the tropical thorn scrub forests of the North-Eastern plains, which have evolved specifically in response to scanty rainfall and high temperatures. These forests are sources of livelihood to many peoples, in addition to their role as carbon sinks.

A study by Ravindranath and Sukumar (1998) indicates that in the absence of proper management, the present day plantations of exotics such as wattles (*Acacia* species) could invade the grasslands. Longer dry spells may cause increase in dry season fires, threatening the moist and dry deciduous forests. A change in precipitation pattern is projected that will weaken the Indian summer monsoon (Ravindranath *et al.*, 2003).

3.7 Health and Climate Change

A study on the occurrence of malaria in Karnataka reveals that the Annual Parasite Index (API) and Slide Positivity Rates (SPR) show similar trends from 1975-1995: high malaria levels in the 1970s decreasing to low levels in 1985 and then increasing in some districts again in the 1990s (Colleen Reid, 2000).

The number of cases of malaria has increased from 1994 to 1995 and then started declining from 1995 onward whereas in Dakshina Kannada district it has increased from 1994 upto 1996 and from 1996 onwards it shows a slow declining trend. More than at the district level, an urban area such as Mangalore city in the coastal region of Karnataka is highly vulnerable for malaria incidence. From 1990 to 1994, number of cases reported has increased drastically and different types of malaria cases

Table 19.2

Incidence of Malaria in Karnataka State and Dakshina Kannada District

	Karnataka State		Dakshina Kannada	
Year	Total	P. falciparum	Total	P. falciparum
1994	266682	37934	4744	21
1995	285883	39700	9221	1694
1996	219198	32639	12481	1749
1997	181447	46517	10057	989
1998	118685	26369	8834	685
Upto June 1999	42731	6235	2392	115

Source: www.malariasite.com/malaria/MalariaInIndia.htm.

show different kind of trends during this period (see Figure 19.8). For example, majority of the cases reported during this period were *P. vivax* type while the *P. falciparum* type constituted only a small part. This is also evident from results coming from a case study conducted during 1995.

Figure 19.8

Trend in Malaria Cases in Dakshina Kannada District

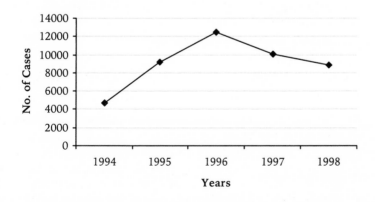

Figure 19.9

Trend in Malaria in Mangalore City

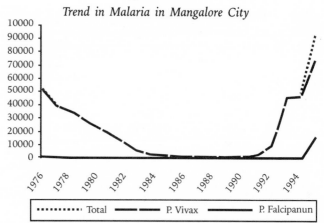

Source: Kakkilaya *et al.* (2000). Effect of a Community Centred, Voluntary Initiative for Malaria Control in Mangalore. In: *http://www.malariasite.com/post.html.*

4. Need for Long-Term Policy Interventions

Climate change effects are visible only slowly, but very remarkably and irreversibly over long periods of time. The net effects are permanent losses of soil, soil fertility, forest cover, changes in water resources and surface hydrology and increasing human health problems. These invariably lead to a cycle of human misery and migration due to threats to food and livelihood security and increased risks. Policy interventions, therefore, need to be woven into other sectoral, social and economic measures.

Policies requiring immediate recognition include:

*   Forest protection and conservation policy (on JFM, compensatory plantation, stoppage of forest lands for non-forest uses).

*   Strict imposition of Coastal Zone Regulation.

*   Watershed and rain water harvesting programmes to increase available water resources.

*   Soil conservation policies .

*   Wetlands conservation and development.

It is not easy to identify the abatement investment policies in one go. Restricting the discussion only to the management of carbon emissions, one can view the long-term investment requirements, some glimpse of which is given in Table 19.3. Forestry offers a good prospect of carbon

Table 19.3

Cost of Various Carbon Dioxide Mitigation Options for India

Technology	Greenhouse Gas Emission Reduction	Investment Cost	Cost Effectiveness (dollar/tonne carbon dioxide)
Transport Sector			
CNG (compressed natural gas) car	0.017 kg/P-km	10,965 dollar/unit	4500
CNG bus	0.41 kg/P-km	31,000 dollar/unit	12
Mass rapid transport system	0	1.4 Billion dollar	0
BOV (battery-operated vehicle)—three wheeler	0	2444 dollar/unit	0
Two-wheeler (four-stroke)	0.0014 kg/P-km	1156 dollar/unit	30,000
Renewable Energy for Power			
Small hydro	1.3 kg/kWh	1950 dollar/KW	88
Wind farms	1.3 kg/kWh	1405 dollar/KW	257
Biomass	1.3 kg/kWh	710 dollar/KW	102
Solar thermal	1.3 kg/kWh	3730 dollar/KW	592
Solar photovoltaic (PV)	1.6 kg/kWh	5952 dollar/KWp	541
Agriculture Sector			
Agro-based gasifier	1.6 kg/kWh	760 dollar/KW	119
Wood-based gasifier	1.6 kg/kWh	694 dollar/KW	115
Wind-based shallow pumping	1.6 kg/kWh	1157 dollar/KW	173
Wind-based deep wells	1.6 kg/kWh	2149 dollar/KW	176
PV pump	1.6 kg/kWh	8598 dollar/KWp	1602
Power Generation			
Co-generation	1.50 kg/kWh	900 dollar/KW	10
Combined cycle	0.96 kg/kWh	818 dollar/KW	54
Inter-cooled steam injected gas turbine	0.76 kg/kWh	947 dollar/KW	77
Pressurised fluidised bed combustion	0.18 kg/kWh	1894 dollar/KW	503
Integrated gasification combined cycle	0.23 kg/kWh	1578 dollar/KW	340
Pulverised coal super-critical boilers	0.18 kg/kWh	1202 dollar/KW	342
Coal washing	0.125 kg/kWh	11 dollar tonnes a year	179
Domestic Lighting			
Compact fluorescent lamps	6.49 teragram/year	8 dollar/unit	0
36 W fluorescent	0.09 teragram/year	0.9 dollar/unit	0

Source: ADB–GEF–UNDP. 1998.

sequestration, but the programme will spill over 30-40 years. But many of the investment policies are on sectors outside of forestry itself. But, most of the climate change management programmes require long-term investments.

There are alternative strategies being talked about in dealing with climate change abatement. There are elements of measuring the costs and benefits of climate change effects, developing adaptive strategies (e.g., adaptation, rehabilitation and sharing the costs and benefits). Some major alternatives are:

- Fiscal measures (e.g., transfer of resources to countries that are affected) to be taken up by the countries that are significantly responsible for global climate changes: Examples are collection of carbon emission taxes and gasoline taxes and payments on trading emission permits etc.

- Promoting and investing on Clean Development Mechanisms (CDM) technologies, investing on alternative sources of energy (e.g., solar and wind energy), changing food habits (e.g., switching to herbal foods) and life styles (e.g., less dependence on automobiles) and so on.

- Promotion of several adaptation and coping strategies: As much as climate change effects and impacts are visible over a long time horizon, many of the economic, scientific and technological changes and improvements also take long periods of time. For instance, even after three decades of oil crisis, societies have not reversed away from the use of fossil fuels. A major thrust on adaptation methods, (e.g., school education on awareness), changing work styles (e.g., working at nights, switching to IT and out-sourcing methods) and many such strategies merit immediate attention.

As against the conventional project planning methods, new economic strategies are required to deal with climate change problems. This is mainly because of the fact that climate change is a slow process. Even the impact of any scientific project strategy is visible only in the long run for any agency (be they governments, civil societies or individuals). While introducing any economic and investment oriented projects and strategies, one has to deal with the long-term costs and benefits from abating and arresting climate change effects and development of adaptive strategies.[68] That begs a major question on discounting the costs and benefits on such activities.

---

68. Being myopic to short-run problems, it is very common for governments and societies to postpone strategies involving hundreds of years.

5. The Issue of Discounting for Climate Change Related Investments

When it comes to project planning for long-term projects of the kinds mentioned above, there are serious issues on the rate of discounting.[69] The starting point here is climate change in the context of natural resources. Here, two separate pointers have been raised in recent literature.

• First, when it comes to sustainability of resources, the concern and regard for inter-generational equity has been voiced differently from pure welfare measures (Howarth and Norgaard, 1990, 1991,1993; Padilla, 2002; Schelling, 1995). In this context, the issue is one of 'valuing the utility of costs by the present generation with their own utility preferences against the benefits for the people of next generation (whose utility preferences are not revealed).' However, when the present generation invests (foregoing present consumption) for the benefits of the future generation there is a matter of transferring the consumption benefits from one generation to the next. This is a matter of redistribution of consumption or wealth. Such redistribution weights are not same as the pure time preference rates. The discount rate may however, reflect the 'altruistic' preferences of the people of the present generation, which of course is very difficult to estimate. But it will be much lower than the pure time preference rate.

• The second reason for re-examining the discount rate issue is in the context of long-term environmental changes such as climate change. The myopic view of the future has to be countered upon differently (Weitzeman, 1998; Howarth, 2003). There is lot more uncertainty about the outcomes of climate change in the future. For instance, one does not know how exactly the sea rise effects will be due to temperature changes, or greenhouse gas effects on health. Moreover, on account of climate changes, whenever resources are to be diverted from currently beneficial development activities to abate or arrest the future climate change effects, the resource costs and benefits are asymmetrically distributed over the period of climate change. For instance, with a view to stabilise green house gas emission or global warming problems, when one talks of fiscal policy interventions with emission taxes now (e.g., carbon tax), the cost burden on the present generation and the benefits to the future

---

69. There are several related issues on the rate of discount. For better understanding of the issues see UNIDO, 1972; Little and Mirrless, 1974; Arrow and Kurz, 1970; Gijsbers and Nijkamp,1987.

generation are not of equal opportunities. Psychologically people may have to learn to weigh the distant future.

Therefore, there is some reason for a declining discount rate over long time period.[70] Since, climate changes as well as inter-generational issues are directly relevant for India as well, some attempts are made here to estimate the declining social discount rates and test the hypothesis on its declining rate itself.

6. Two Alternative Approaches to Declining Discount Rates

In the United Nation Industrial Development Organisation (UNIDO, 1972) framework the discount rate depends upon three parameters, namely the pure time preference rate 'p,' the elasticity of social marginal utility 'v,' and the expected growth rate of consumption 'g.' A time dependent social discount rate can be defined as:

$$r(t) = p(t) + [-v(t). \ g(t)] \tag{1}$$

Alternatively, one can explicitly define and estimate a hyperbolically declining discount rate. Weitzman (1998, 2001) provides a rationale for an exponentially declining discount factor over time D(t) defined as:

$$D(t) = r/[1+t.\sigma^2/r], \tag{2}$$

where r = initial or average discount rate (treated as constant and uniform), t = time, σ^2 is the variance in the average discount rate 'r' over time.[71]

It may be useful to empirically estimate the declining discount rates under these two alternative methods. An estimate based on the UNIDO methodology is made first. This approach requires an estimate of elasticity of social marginal utility 'v' at different point in time. We estimate 'v' for the Indian economy by following Stern (1977) and Murty et al., (1992) based on an approach of designing optimising taxation. To begin with, we assume that the Indian income tax structure is based on the 'principle of equal absolute sacrifice.' Then, the income tax rate structure is so designed that the 'social sacrifice value' attached on the amounts of income tax government collects from the individuals in different income groups to be identical.[72] With the assumption of diminishing marginal

---

70. In a recent paper Winkler (2004) links hyperbolic preference ordering over time to declining discount rate.
71. In Wietzman's 2001 paper, he uses the average of expert opinion as the relevant constant time preference rate, and also estimates its variance.
72. Incidentally this is also the principle used for progressive income taxes.

utility of income, this principle implies that people with higher incomes will pay higher absolute amounts of taxes. Let the utility of income U(Y) defined as:

$$U(Y) = A \, Y^{1+v} / (1+v) \tag{3}$$

where 'v' is elasticity of marginal utility with respect to income, which is constant and negative, and 'A' is a constant.

. If the tax levied on income Y is T(Y), For equal absolute sacrifice of utility we should have, U(Y) – U[Y-T(Y)] = constant absolute sacrifice of utility $\tag{4}$

for all Y where T(Y) > 0. Then, for any change in income Y, the corresponding income tax is such that there is no change in one's sacrifice of utility. Then we should have:

$$U'(Y) - U'[Y-T(Y)] \, [1-T'(Y)] = 0 \tag{5}$$

From (1) to (5) we then have:

$$Ln \, [1- T'(Y) \,] = v \ln Y/[Y- T(Y)] \tag{6}$$

Using regression method with data on income Y and tax T at different income levels, equation (6) can be used to estimate the value of 'v.' Data on All India Annual Income Tax for the years 1990-91 to 1997-98 are used for the estimation purposes. The yearly estimates of 'v' for these years are shown in column 2 of Table 19.4.

How to empirically estimate 'p' ? This requires assigning a meaning to 'p'. It is the extra premium an individual puts on the present consumption due to one's uncertainty of life. Higher the probability of non-survival, higher will be the value attached to the present consumptions, and hence, higher is the time preference rate. But the probability of an individual not surviving one more year differs at different age levels. Therefore, only an average of the probabilities of people not surviving one more year at different age levels can be taken as an average time preference rate. Using the data on the distribution of Indian population in different age-groups and the estimates of probability of a person not surviving a year after as available from the Abridged Life Tables being prepared by the Registrar General of Census of India, an average probability of non-survival as an estimate of pure time preference rate is estimated. Figure 19.10 shows the estimates of p(t) for different years in the last two decades. The estimates of time preference rates are fairly constant during the last twenty years, with an average of 0.0566.

Figure 19.10
Estimates of Time Preference Rate

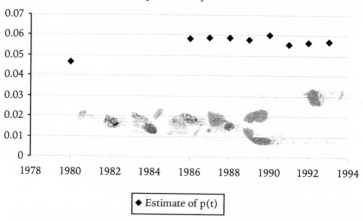

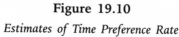

◆ Estimate of p(t)

An estimate for the annual growth of the economy 'g' is made based on National Accounts Statistics. The series on GDP growth rate in 1993-94 prices have been used for this purpose. Using an average annual growth of population between 1991 and 2001 as 1.93, the estimates of 'g(t)' are shown in column 3 in Table 19.4. Subsequently, using formula (1), the estimated discount rates for these years are also shown in the same table.

Table 19.4
Estimates of Discount Rates

Years (1)	Estimates of v(t) (2)	Estimates of g(t) (per cent) (3)	Discount Rate (per cent)* (4)
1990-91	-1.231	3.57	10.05
1991-92	-1.179	-0.83	9.91
1992-93	-1.292	3.17	9.76
1993-94	-1.276	3.97	10.72
1994-95	-0.958	5.27	10.71
1995-96	-1.180	5.57	12.23
1996-97	-1.192	6.27	13.13
1997-98	-1.224	2.97	9.29
Average	-1.192		10.73

*: An average value of 5.66 per cent is used for the 'time preference rate' p, to estimate the discount rate using formula (1).

As can be seen from Table 19.4 the elasticity of social marginal utility 'v' seems to be fairly constant in the recent periods, with an average of (–) 1.192. But the annual growth rates of per capita incomes 'g' increased on a trend basis (except for 1997-98). Therefore, the estimates of discount rate also show a positive trend for those years. The average discount rate based on data from 1990 to 1998 is 0.1073 with a variance of 0.06278. This implied discount rate is not only quite high for long-term resource allocation models, but does not provide much clues for any declining trend in the discount rates.

That makes it necessary to opt for the second approach for identifying the appropriate discount rate for climate change models. The average discount rate in the recent period has been varying around 0.1073 with a variance of 0.06278. Using these estimates of mean and variance, the time dependent declining discount rate D(t) can be derived from formula 2 as:

$$D(t) = 0.1073/[1+ 0.5851*t] \qquad (8)$$

Where t = 0 for 1993-94, 1 for 1994-95 and so on.

A graph of this declining discount rate be viewed in Figure 19.11

Figure 19.11

Time Dependent Climate Discount Rate

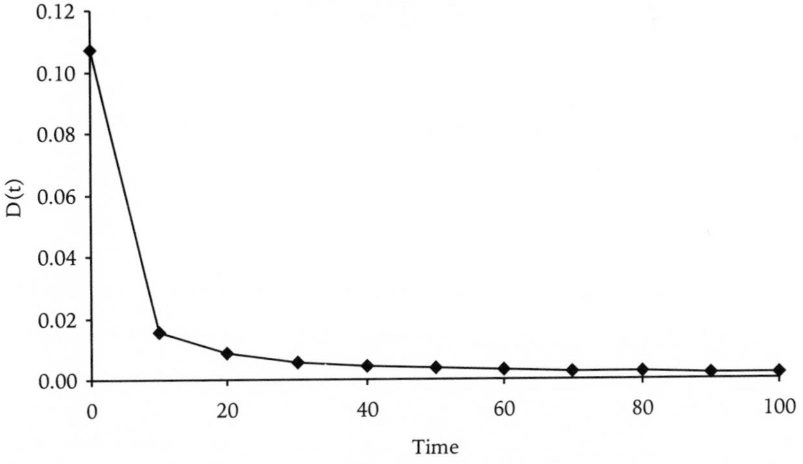

As can be seen from the graph, the discount rate can be put in to three major phases of declining rates. In the first phase of ten years the discount rate be maintained at 10.75 per cent, in the next leg of ten years it can be kept at 6.75 per cent, subsequently, the discount rate be kept a low of 1.5 per cent.

7. Implications for Climate Change Models

The present trends in growth rates, estimates of social valuation of gains from resource allocation and pure time preference rates do not provide sufficient clues for correcting the currently held high and constant discount rate to be replaced by a declining one. But the case of refining this stand remains, whenever the climate change effects start impacting the present and near-present generations as well. Therefore, it is always preferable to start operating on some notionally declining discount rates for climate change related projects even in the medium term and crossing over generations. For instance, in the development of non-conventional or wind energy development programmes, it is time to use very low discount rates and that too declining over the years. Likewise, in the climate change related negotiations on compensations for the effects of ocean rise, temperature rise and shifts in the maximum and minimum temperatures, shifting of rainfall cycles, or green house gas emissions, countries such as India should make a case for compensations and investment strategies against long-run health and other adverse impacts on land, water and forests. This is possible with models of possible impacts in the long-run only. That makes a case of declining discount rates in the relevant economic models.

References

Arrow, K.J. and M. Kurz (1970). *Public Investment, the Rate of Return and Optimal Fiscal Policy*, Baltimore: Johns Hopkins Press.

Azfar, O. (1999). "Rationalising Hyperbolic Discounting," *Journal of Economic Behaviour and Organisation*, 38, pp. 245-52.

CMDR, (2004). *Incidence and Effects of Drought: A Case Study for Karnataka* (Monograph), Pages 84.

Colleen Reid, (2000). *http://envstudies.brown.edu/thesis/2000/undergrad/cried.*

Dasgupta, P.S., S.A. Marglin and A.K. Sen (1972). *Guidelines for Project Analysis*, New York: United Nations.

Frederick, S., G. Loewenstein, and T. O'Donoghue (2002). "Time Discounting and Time Preference: A Critical Review," *Journal of Economic Literature*, 40, pp. 351-401.

Gijsbers, D. and P. Nijkamp (1987). "Non-uniform Social Rates of Discount in a Natural Resource Models: An Overview of Arguments and Consequences," *Research Memorandum*, 1987-73, Amsterdam: Vrije Universiteit.

Gosain, A. K. and Sandhya Rao (2003). "Impacts of Climate Change on Water Sector," ed. by Shukla. P.R, Subodh K. Sharma, Ravindranath. N.H., Amit Garg, Sumana Bhattacharya in *Climate Change and India—Vulnerability Assessment and Adaptation*, Universities Press (India) Private Limited, pp. 171-192.

Government of India (2004). *India's Initial National Communication to the United Nations Framework on Climate Change*, Ministry of Environment and Forests, p. 268.

Howarth, R.B. (2003). "Discounting and Uncertainty in Climate Change Policy Analysis," *Land Economics*, 79 (3), pp. 369-381.

Howarth, R.B. and R.B. Norgaard (1990). "Intergenerational Resource Rights: Efficiency and Social Opportunity," *Land Economics*, Vol. 66, pp. 1-11.

————. (1993). "Intergenerational Transfers and the Social Discount Rate," *Environmental and Resource Economics*, Vol. 3, No. 4, pp. 337-358.

————. (1995). "Inter-generational Choices Under Global Environmental Change," ed. by Bromley in *Handbook of Environmental Economics*, Oxford: Blackwell Publications, pp.111-38.

Kumar, K. and Parikh, J. (1998). "Climate Change Impacts on Indian Agriculture: The Ricardian Approach," ed. by Dinar, A., Mendelsohn, R., Everson, Parika, J., Sanghi, A., Kumar, K., McKinsey, J., and Lonergan, S. in *Measuring the Impact of Climate Change on Indian Agriculture*, World Bank Technical Paper No. 402, Washington, D.C: The World Bank.

Little, I.M.D. and J.A. Mirrlees (1974). *Project Appraisal and Planning for Developing Countries*, London: Heinemann Press.

Ministry of Forests and Environment (2004). *India's Initial National Communication to the United Nationals Framework Convention on Climate Change,*

Norgaard R.B. and R.B. Howarth (1991). "Sustainability and Discounting the Future," in R. Costanza (Ed.): *Economical Economics: The Science and Management of Sustainability*, Colombia University press, p. 525

Murty, M.N., B.N. Goldar, Gopal Kadekodi, and S.N. Mishra (1992). "National Parameters for Investment Project Appraisal in India," Institute of Economic Growth Monograph (unpublished).

Ravindranath N.H., R. Sukumar and P. Deshingkar (1998). "Climate Change and Forests: Impacts and Adaptation- A Regional Assessment for the Western Ghats, India." *Report on Atmospheric Environment Issues in Developing Countries Series – No.4.* Pub. Stockholm Environment Institute.

Ravindranath N.H., N.V. Joshi, R. Sukumar, Indu K. Murthy, and H.S. Suresh (2003). "Vulnerability and Adaptation to Climate Change in the Forest Sector," ed. by P.R Shukla, Subodh K. Sharma, N.H. Ravindranath, Amit Garg, Sumana Bhattacharya in *Climate Change and India-Vulnerability Assessment and Adaptatio*, Universities Press (India) Private Limited. Pp. 227-265.

Shukla, P.R. (2003). "Climate Change Vulnerability Assessment and Adaptation: The Context" ed. by Shukla. P.R., Subodh K. Sharma, Ravindranath. N.H., Amit Garg, Sumana Bhattacharya, in *Climate Change and India–Vulnerability Assessment and Adaptation,* Universities Press (India) Private Limited, pp. 1-28.

Schleeing, T.C. (1995). "Intergenerational Discounting," *Energy Policy*, Vol. 23, No. 4/5, p. 395-401.

Sharma, R.A., M.J. McGregor, and J.F. Blyth (1991). "The Social Discount Rate for Land Use Projects in India," *Journal of Agricultural Economics*, 42(1), pp. 86-92.

Weitzman, M.L. (1998). "Why the Far-Distant Future Should be Discounted at its Lowest Possible Rate," *Journal of Environmental Economics and Management*, 36, pp. 201-208.

————. (2001). "Gamma Discounting," *American Economic Review*, Vol. 91, pp. 260-71.

Winkler, R. (2004). "Inter-Temporal Efficiency and Equity Under Hyperbolic Preferences," paper presented at ISEE conference at Vancouver, June 2004.

Annexure A-19.1

Some Glimpses on the International Climate Change Scene

- The Artic Climate Impact Assessment Report: The Artic will lose 50-60 per cent of its ice distribution by 2100. In fact one model predicts that the **North Pole in summer will be completely ice-free by 2070**
- The most threatened country on Earth is the tiny Pacific Island-nation of Tuvalu, with a population of 10,000, which will be submerged by 2050.
- The planet's temperature has risen by 0.6 degrees centigrade over the past 100 years. In the last 25 years the rate of increase in temperature has become greater than it was in the last one hundred years prior to that.

Annexure A-19.2

Incidence of Malaria in India

Year	Total Cases	P. Falciparum	Deaths
1947	75 million	NA	8,00,000
1961	49151	NA	NA
1965	99667	NA	NA
1976	6.47 million	0.75 million	59
1984	2.18 million	0.65 million	247
1985	1.86 million	0.54 million	213
1986	1.79 million	0.64 million	323
1987	1.66 million	0.62 million	188
1988	1.85 million	0.68 million	209
1989	2.05 million	0.76 million	268
1990	2.02 million	0.75 million	353
1991	2.12 million	0.92 million	421
1992	2.13 million	0.88 million	422
1993	2.21 million	0.85 million	354
1994	2.51 million	0.99 million	1122
1995	2.93 million	1.14 million	1151
1996	3.04 million	1.18 million	1010
1997	2.57 million	0.99 million	874
1998	2.09 million	0.91 million	648

Source: www.malariasite.com/malaria/MalariaInIndia.htm.

Annexure A-19.3

Activities Implemented Jointly (AIJ) Projects Endorsed by the Government of India

Name of the Project	Location	Investing Party	Host Party
Integrated agriculture demand-side management	Andhra Pradesh	World Bank	Andhra Pradesh State Electricity Board
Direct reduced iron	Gujarat	New Energy Development Organisation, Japan	Essar, Gujarat, India
Energy recovery from waste gas and liquid	Gujarat		Indian Petrochemicals Ltd, Plant at Vadodara, Gujarat, India
DESI - Power:biomass gasification	20 sites in India	The Netherlands	DESI Power, Development Alternatives, India
Tamarind orchard agro-forestry for dry land	Karnataka	USA	ADAT, Bagepalli Karnataka, India

Note: DESI – Decentralised Energy Systems India Private Limited.
Source: ADB–GEF–UNDP. 1998.